Studies in Church History

18

RELIGION AND NATIONAL IDENTITY

RELIGION AND NATIONAL IDENTITY

PAPERS READ AT
THE NINETEENTH SUMMER MEETING AND
THE TWENTIETH WINTER MEETING
OF THE
ECCLESIASTICAL HISTORY SOCIETY

EDITED BY

STUART MEWS

PUBLISHED FOR
THE ECCLESIASTICAL HISTORY SOCIETY

BY

BASIL BLACKWELL · OXFORD

1982

ISBN 0 631 18060 5

Printed in Great Britain
by Crampton & Sons Ltd, Sawston, Cambridge

PREFACE

'Religion and national identity' was the theme of two gatherings of the Ecclesiastical History Society which met under the presidency of Professor Keith Robbins. All the papers included in this volume were read either at a summer conference at the University of Nottingham or at a winter meeting at King's College, London. They were selected for inclusion after the usual consultations, by Mr. Derek Baker, then the Society's editor, who asked my assistance in the early stages of preparing the typescript for publication. When he was compelled by the pressures of new duties to relinquish the editorship, the committee of the Society entrusted me with full responsibility for the completion of the volume. Nevertheless I wish to record that even after his resignation, Mr Baker continued to take an interest in the project and made an invaluable contribution at the sub-editing stage.

Generous financial assistance has once again been received from the British Academy, for which the Society wishes to express its gratitude.

Stuart Mews

CONTENTS

CONTENTS

CONTENTS

CONTRIBUTORS

KEITH ROBBINS, *(President)*
Professor of Modern History, University of Glasgow

STELLA ALEXANDER,
formerly Secretary of the East-West Relations Committee of
the Society of Friends

JOHN BOSSY,
Professor of History, University of York.

SEBASTIAN BROCK,
Fellow of Wolfson College, Oxford

ANNE HUDSON,
Fellow of Lady Margaret Hall, Oxford

FRANCES LANNON,
Fellow and Tutor in Modern History, Lady Margaret Hall,
Oxford

PETER LINEHAN,
Fellow of St John's College, Cambridge

BERNARD ASPINWALL,
Lecturer in Modern History, University of Glasgow

NICHOLAS BANTON,
New College, Oxford

D. W. BEBBINGTON,
Lecturer in History, University of Stirling

DOMINIC BELLENGER,
Downside School

CLYDE BINFIELD,
Senior Lecturer in History, University of Sheffield

RICHARD CARWARDINE,
Lecturer in American History, University of Sheffield

ANNE DAWTRY,
Westfield College, University of London

PETER DOYLE,
Senior Lecturer in History, Bedford College of Higher
Education

EAMON DUFFY,
Fellow of Magdalene College and Lecturer in Ecclesiastical
History, University of Cambridge.

ANTHONY FLETCHER,
Senior Lecturer in History, University of Sheffield

W. H. C. FREND
Professor of Ecclesiastical History, University of Glasgow

SHERIDAN GILLEY,
Lecturer in Theology, University of Durham

JOHN R. GUY,
Diocesan Tutor, St David's University College, Lampeter

ELIZABETH M. HALLAM,
Assistant Keeper, Public Records Office

MARGARET HARVEY,
Tutor and Part-Time Lecturer in History, St Aidan's College,
University of Durham

R. F. G. HOLMES,
Professor of Christian History and Doctrine, Union
Theological College, Belfast

DAVID KEEP,
Senior Lecturer, Rolle College, Exeter

LINDA KIRK,
Lecturer in History, University of Sheffield

G. M. LEE,
  Bedford

DAVID LOADES,
  Professor of History, University College of North Wales,
  Bangor

G. A. LOUD,
  Lecturer in Medieval History, University of Leeds

A. K. McHARDY,
  Lecturer in Medieval History, University of Aberdeen

EMMA MASON,
  Senior Lecturer in Medieval History, Birkbeck College,
  University of London

W. B. PATTERSON,
  Professor of History, University of the South, Sewanee, USA

ROSALIND RANSFORD,
  Birkbeck College, University of London

R. K. ROSE,
  University of Edinburgh

HENRY R. SEFTON,
  Lecturer in Church History, University of Aberdeen

JULIA H. M. SMITH,
  Lecturer in History, University of Sheffield.

WILLIAM STAFFORD,
  Lecturer, Huddersfield Polytechnic

D. M. WEBB,
  Lecturer in History, King's College, University of London

GAVIN WHITE,
  Lecturer in Ecclesiastical History, University of Glasgow

INTRODUCTION

To borrow one contributor's title, readers of this volume will be presented with 'A kind of Noah's ark'. This present collection of papers ranges far and wide and, perhaps fortunately, contributors do not linger long on matters of definition. National identity is a complex concept and contributors have felt free to interpret it loosely. Dr Brock points out that only when European concepts of nationalism reached the middle east in the nineteenth century did members of the Church of the East contemplate a national identity that was not solely based on the idea of membership of a religious community. Just what those European concepts of nationalism were has proved controversial. Likewise, there is little agreement on when they first appeared in history. Although not unaware of these issues, the contributors normally only approach them obliquely. We are fortunate in being able to publish groups of papers with an obviously close relationship to each other. The papers on English history in the two hundred years up to 1150, for example, bring out well the tensions – regional, 'national', linguistic and cultural – inevitable in welding together a kingdom of such mixed ingredients. The church was of vital significance in this process but it is also evident that it too experienced these conflicts. That fact becomes evident in almost every century or area considered in this volume. As Dr. Linehan points out, there were special reasons why this should be so in the case of medieval Spain but other essays on England, France and Italy draw attention to similar sentiments in these countries and the conflict of loyalties they disclosed, at least potentially. These matters erupted with the advent of the Reformation and several papers explore the origins and development of English protestant nationalism while Professor Bossy considers the question of catholicity and nationality in the north European counter-reformation.

The legacy of these disputes is still present in the modern world. Reformed and Lutheran churches (though, unfortunately, there is no coverage of the latter) have become entangled with the life of their communities or nations in a particularly complicated fashion and a group of contributions trace these connexions in some detail in the modern history of the British Isles. Here, variously, the churches can be seen as representing either an expression of national identity or providing a substitute for it. The political ramifications of these connexions are obvious and require no further elaboration. Yet, despite the strength of these British contributions with their use, in some cases, of literary and architectural illustration, it is right to conclude the volume by emphasizing that the tensions engendered by sometimes conflicting and sometimes competing ecclesiastical and national loyalties are not merely insular. Dr Lannon discusses the 'project of a national catholicism' in Spain in the twentieth century in a fashion which immediately turns the reader's mind back to the medieval papers. Finally, Mrs Alexander manages to provide a feast of examples of almost every conceivable religious and ethnic alignment in her paper on Yugoslavia. The reader will be hard put to it to draw together from this volume a 'normative' picture of the relationship between religion and national identity but the theme has been opened up on a scale not previously attempted.

CHRISTIANS IN THE SASANIAN EMPIRE: A CASE OF DIVIDED LOYALTIES

by S. P. BROCK

IN THAT much discussed panegyric, the *Life of Constantine*, Eusebius tells how the emperor, having heard that there were 'many churches of God in Persia and that large numbers were gathered into the fold of Christ, resolved to extend his concern for the general welfare to that country also, as one whose aim it was to care for all alike in every nation.'[1] He goes on to give what purports to be a letter from Constantine to the Sasanid shah, Shapur II; in this, not only does the emperor neatly explain away his predecessor Valerian's humiliating capture by the Persians in 260 as divine punishment for his persecution of Christians[2] but he presumes to draw a lesson from this for Shapur as well: by protecting his own Christian population Shapur will experience the beneficence of Constantine's Deity.[3]

Eusebius provides us with a useful starting point from two quite different points of view. In the first place, by his general identification of the Roman empire as an *eikon* of the kingdom of God,[4]

---

[1] *Vita Constantini*, *GCS*, Eusebius I.12, IV.8. Grégoire's thesis that the *Life* is a late fourth-century forgery has not found general favour: see for example H. Chadwick's preface to the second edition of N. H. Baynes, *Constantine the Great and the Christian Church* (London 1972) pp iv–vii; Baynes discusses the Letter to Shapur on pp 26–9.

[2] *Vita Constantini*, IV.11. On the Letter see especially H. Dörries, *AAWG* III.34 (1954) pp 125–7. The argument that persecution brings political disaster (which has its roots in the literature of Hellenistic Judaism) is found applied to the Sasanids in the *Acts of Jacob* (martyred *c* 422), A[cta] M[artyrum et] S[anctorum], ed P. Bedjan, 4 (Paris/Leipzig 1894) p 196: Jacob tells Bahram II, 'your father Yazdgard ruled the kingdom in peace and well-being for twenty one years and all his enemies everywhere were subjected and friendly to him. This was because he honoured the Christians, he built churches and granted them peace. At the end of his reign, when he turned away from this beneficial policy and became a persecutor of the Christians, spilling the innocent blood of a God-fearing people, you know very well yourself of the extraordinary death he died . . .'.

[3] *Vita Constantini*, IV.13.

[4] On this see R. Farina, *L'impero e l'imperatore cristiano in Eusebio di Cesarea* (Zürich 1966) pp 107–23, 154–65, and F. Dvornik, *Early Christian and Byzantine Political Philosophy*, 2 (Washington, DC., 1966) pp 614–22.

Eusebius has provided a model for the writing of ecclesiastical history which ignores the presence of a large Christian community outside the confines of the Roman empire, and subject to the Sasanid. Secondly, the emperor's role, portrayed by Eusebius in the passage quoted, as advocate for the Christian minority living under the Zoroastrian Sasanids, was to have an important bearing on relationships between these Christians and their overlords in the ensuing centuries.

Eusebius's picture of the history of the Christian church as being inextricably interwoven with the history of the Roman empire has proved to have had a pernicious influence on the writing of almost all subsequent ecclesiastical history down to our present day:[5] one has only to glance at the contents of the standard handbooks in every European language to observe the insidious effect that the father of church history has had; the very existence of this by no means insignificant Christian church in Sasanid Iran is only given token recognition at the very most. Interestingly enough, the English translation of volume 3 of Fliche-Martin's *Histoire de l'Église* tacitly draws attention to this inbalance by renaming this volume *The Church in the Christian Roman Empire*.

The practical result of this lack of perspective which goes back to the fountain-head of ecclesiastical history is that very poor coverage is given to the church in the Sasanid empire with the result that the interested reader has to resort directly to specialised works on the subject, among which J. Labourt's *Le christianisme dans l'empire perse sous la dynastie sassanide* still takes pride of place.[6]

The neglect by church historians of this Persian church has also led to a general inattention to a model of church-state relations which, while irrelevant to European Christianity, has always been applicable to several of the oriental churches and which in fact still exists to-day for Christian communities living under Islamic governments. Whereas a great deal has been written on two other patterns of relationship, the state that is openly opposed to and

---

[5] As far as German works are concerned this was well pointed by P. Kawerau in his inaugural lecture as professor of Ostkirchengeschichte at Marburg, 'Allgemeine Kirchengeschichte und Ostkirchengeschichte', *ZRGG* 14 (1962) pp 305–15.
[6] Paris 1904. Labourt's work is brought up to date in certain respects by J. M. Fiey's useful sketch of the same period, *Jalons pour une histoire de l'église en Iraq*, *CSCO* 310(1970). In English the best works available are [W. A.]Wigram, *An Introduction [to the History of the Assyrian Church]* (London 1910) and W. G. Young, *Patriarch Shah and Caliph* (Rawalpindi 1974), although neither of these is sufficiently critical.

persecutes Christianity, and the state that proclaims itself as being Christian, there has been remarkably little study of cases where the state, having an official religion of its own, nevertheless recognises the existence of a Christian minority within its midst.[7]

Eusebius speaks of 'large numbers of Christians' in Persia in the first half of the fourth century, and there are no good grounds for doubting the general correctness of this statement. Certainly by 410, when the synod of Seleucia met under the auspices of the Roman envoy, bishop Marutha of Martyropolis, there were already six metropolitan sees and over thirty bishoprics; by the time of the collapse of the Sasanid dynasty before the Arab armies in the mid seventh century there were ten metropolitan sees (including the patriarchate) and ninety-six bishoprics.[8] In the course of the sixth and seventh centuries several members of the royal family were Christians, as were a number of high officials, such as Chosroes II's doctor, Gabriel of Sinjar, and his chief tax collector Yazdin. When the Arabs took over north Mesopotamia it is likely that the majority of the population were Christian, while in many other areas they would have constituted a sizeable minority.[9]

Although later tradition traces back the origins of the Christianity in Persia to apostolic times, it is not until the fourth century that we have reliable sources in any quantity. A factor of considerable importance for the history of the Persian church at this time was the presence in Sasanid territory of large communities deported from Roman territory in the wars of Shapur I's reign (240–71); amongst these were many Christians who retained their separate identity and hierarchy, alongside that of the native Christians, well into the fifth century when several synods condemn the practice current in several towns of having two bishops, one Greek speaking and the other Syriac. It is possible that even the Zoroastrian authorities gave different names to these two bodies of Christians, calling the native Christians *naṣrāyē* (subsequently taken over into Arabic) and those of western origin *krestyānē*[10] In any case it is certain that the

---

[7] This provides the starting point for Young's book (p iii).

[8] The detailed information is to be found in *S[ynodicon] O[rientale*, ed J. B. Chabot] (Paris 1902).

[9] In what is to-day north Iraq conversions to Christianity from Zoroastrianism and paganism continued into the early Islamic period; see M. Morony, 'The effects of the Muslim conquest on the Persian population of Iraq', *Iran* 14 (London 1976) p 54.

[10] See note 21 below.

'captivity', as the deported Christians called themselves, played an important part in the spreading of Christianity within the Sasanid empire. The author of the *Acts of Pusai*, a prominent martyr from the 'captivity' in the mid fourth century, perceptively put it as follows:

> Shapur (II) built the city of Karka d–Ladan, brought captives from various places and settled them there. He also had the idea of bringing about thirty families apiece from each of the ethnic groups living in the cities belonging to his realm, and settling them among the deported captives, so that through intermarriage the latter should become tied down by the bonds of family and affection, thus making it less easy for them to slip away gradually in flight and return to the areas from which they had been deported. Such was Shapur's crafty plan, but God in his mercy turned it to good use, for thanks to intermarriage between the deported population and the native pagans, the latter were brought to knowledge of the faith.[11]

The very fact that it was at the shah's winter residence, Seleucia-Ctesiphon, that one particular metropolitan see merged in the early fourth century as possessing some sort of primacy indicates that both church and state were already finding it convenient to communicate through a single spokesman:[12] thus it was to the bishop of Seleucia-Ctesiphon, Simeon, that Shapur II addressed his demand for a double tax contribution from Christians to help his war effort against Constantius.[13] In the early fifth century it is with Yazdgard I's authorisation that the synod of Seleucia convened (410), and many later synods specifically refer to the shah's initiative in such matters.[14] In the last century of Sasanid rule we

---

[11] *AMS* 2 p 209. It should also be recalled that when Jovian ceded Nisibis to the Persians in 363, together with five eastern provinces, this territory would have included many Christians, even though the Christian population of Nisibis itself (among them Ephrem) was compelled to leave, according to Ammianus Marcellinus, *Res gestae* XXV.9.

[12] Later, at the Synod of Seleucia (410), Yazdgard himself specifically ordered the subordination of the other bishops to the Catholicos: *SO* p 26. For the emergence of the see and its authority see W. Macomber, 'The authority of the Catholicos Patriarch of Seleucia-Ctesiphon', *Orientalia Christiana Analecta* 181 (Rome 1968) pp 179–200, and the literature cited on p 179.

[13] *Acts of Simeon*, ed M. Kmosko, *Patrologia Syriaca* 2 (Paris 1907), B 4. The *Acts* survive in two recensions, to which I refer as A and B, employing Kmosko's section numbers.

[14] Zamasp (498–501), for example, summoned a synod to discuss the matter of

find Chosroes I imposing his own nominee in 552, while in 609 Chosroes II, angered because an earlier synod had passed over his own candidate for patriarch, forbade the election of any further patriarch once the bishops' own choice had died; the ensuing vacancy lasted until Chosroes's own death in 628.

But although Christians constituted a recognized minority religion, there was a darker side, manifested by outbreaks of persecution and martyrdom. Persecution on a large scale was confined to times of war and took place notably under Shapur II (drawn out over some forty years, down to Shapur's death in 379), under Yazdgard I (right at the end of his reign) and Bahram V (c420–2), and under Yazdgard II (c446–8).[15] As we shall see, the widespread nature of these persecutions was due to the suspicion that Christians favoured the enemy.

Other martyrs under the Sasanids were individuals, most of whom were converts of high-born Zoroastrian origin, whose prominence in society led to their denunciation by the Magian clergy and subsequent sentencing to death. Martyrs in this category continue to be found right up to the end of Sasanid rule.[16] What is surprising is, not so much the number of converts from Zoroastrianism who met their end in this way, but the fact that many others appear to have held high office unmolested. It is also interesting to learn that in several cases – most notably in that of the patriarch Aba (†552)—the shah does his best to protect the victim from the zeal of the Zoroastrian clergy; indeed on more than one occasion a shah issued specific orders that Christians were not to be

---

marriages (*SO* p 63), over which complications had arisen owing to the fact that converts from Zoroastrianism carried over with them Zoroastrian marriage customs. The prominence of this topic in the sixth-century synods indicates how central a problem it was at that time; the earliest treatise of canon law, by the Catholicos Aba, is also devoted to this subject.

[15] It is only for these three periods that we have groups of martyrdoms. The most convenient survey of the Persian martyr literature is P. Devos, 'Les martyrs persans à travers leurs actes syriaques', *Atti del Convegno sul Tema: La Persia e il Mondo Greco-Romano*, Accademia Nazionale dei Lincei, 363 (Rome 1966) pp 213–25; for the martyrs under Shapur II see G. Wiessner, *Untersuchungen zur syrischen Literaturgeschichte I: Zur Märtyrerüberlieferung aus der Christenverfolgung Schapurs II, AAWG* III.67 (1967), with my review in *JTS*, ns 19 (1968) pp 300–9.

[16] Particularly informative are the lives of Aba, Grigor, Yazidpaneh and Giwargis, in [P.] Bedjan, *Histoire [de Mar-Jabalaha, de trois autres patriarches, d'un prêtre et de deux laiques, nestoriens]* (Paris/Leipzig 1895).

molested by Magians.[17] A consequence of this tension between the shah and the Zoroastrian authorities was that martyrdoms were much more apt to occur when a shah had to rely on Magian support for his position.[18] In other cases we hear of death sentences being imposed against the express orders of the shah.[19] A splendid illustration of this religious zeal shown by the Magian clergy is to be found in a nineteen-line inscription[20] put up in the reign of Bahram II (276–93) by Kartir; having listed all the titles accorded to him by Shapur I, Hormizd I and Bahram II, this high-ranking Zoroastrian official proudly records how the Mazdean religion and the Magian caste were now held in great honour throughout the empire, and how the doctrines of Ahriman and the demons had been eliminated: Jews, shamans, Brahmins, *nazarai, kristidan,* zandiks (Manicheans) and others had all become dejected.[21]

Yet other martyrs met their fate through vandalism of Zoroastrian fire shrines,[22] or through making too many converts (especially if they were of good family),[23] or indeed through palace intrigue—as happened to one of the earliest known martyrs, Candida,[24] a prisoner from Roman territory whose beauty had won her

[17] For an edict of toleration probably under Shapur III see M. L. Chaumont, 'A propos d'un édit de paix religieuse d'époque sassanide', *Mélanges d'histoire des religions offerts à H–C. Puech* (Paris 1974) pp 71–80. The *Acts of Grigor* (in Bedjan, *Histoire* pp 347–8) states that in the early sixth century Christians were given letters patent ordering that no Magian or pagan should harm them, while the Life of Sabrisho (*ibid* p 306) says that on his election as patriarch (595) Sabrisho persuaded Chosroes II to allow Christians complete freedom of worship, as a result of which many courtiers converted.

[18] Socrates, *HE* VII.18 mentions this specifically in the case of Bahram V; see also J. P. Asmussen, 'Das Christentum in Iran und sein Verhältnis zum Zoroastrismus', *Studia Theologica* 16 (Aarhus 1962) p 10.

[19] There is a good example (under Shapur II) in *AMS* 2 pp 244–6.

[20] A French translation of the Middle Iranian text is given in M. L. Chaumont, 'L'inscription de Kartir à la Ka'abah de Zoroastre', *Journal asiatique* 248 (Paris 1960) pp 339–80.

[21] The precise identity of the *nazarai* and *kristidan* is disputed; I have suggested elsewhere that the former represent the native Christians and the latter the deported Christians of Greek origin: see my 'Some aspects of Greek words in Syriac', *AAWG* III.96 (1975) pp 91–5.

[22] This applies to several martyrs under Yazdgard I and Bahram V; Theodoret, *HE* V.39, relates the story of one of these and comments 'I confess that the destruction of this fire shrine was quite mis-timed'.

[23] The Syrian Orthodox martyr Ahudemmeh (†575) was first arrested after it had been revealed that he had baptised a son of Chosroes I: *PO* 3 pp 33–6. See also n 41.

[24] See S. P. Brock, 'A martyr at the Sasanid court under Vahran II: Candida', *An Bol* 96 (1978) pp 167–81.

a place in Bahram II's harem; it was only the jealousy of her fellow royal wives that led to her denunciation and presentation with the choice of apostasy or death.

Even before the conversation of Constantine the attitude of the Sasanid authorities to their Christian subjects had to some extent been governed by the course of international politics:[25] Valerian's persecution of Christians in the eastern provinces had led Shapur I to treat the large numbers of Christians included among the populace he deported from Syria in 260 with considerable favour, to such an extent indeed that one chronicler states that they were better off in their captivity than they had been beforehand.[26] The advent of a Christian emperor on the throne of the 'kingdom of the west', however, was to reverse the situation, to the permanent disadvantage of Persian Christians.[27] In particular for the next century and a half the fate of the Christian population in Persia was intimately linked with the course of political relationships between the 'two shoulders of the world' (as the synod of 420 put it):[28] times of war were times when persecution was apt to break out, while political peace meant peace for the church.[29]

Constantine's intervention at the end of his life in newly Christianised Armenia led to the outbreak of hostilities between the two empires. That the war for Constantine had religious overtones seems entirely likely;[30] in any case, it is clear from the words of one of the earliest extant Syriac authors, Aphrahat, writing in or shortly before 337, that at least some Christians living under Sasanid rule were caught up in disloyal expectations and hopes engendered by the appearance of a Christian emperor in the west:

---

[25] This point is well brought out by [F.] Decret, ['Les conséquences sur le christianisme en Perse de l'affrontement des empires romain et sassanide. De Shapur Ie à Yazdgard Ie'], *Recherches Augustiniennes* 14 (Paris 1979) pp 91–152.

[26] *Chronicle of Seert, PO* 4 pp 222–3. The *Acts of Simeon* (B 98) state that it was out of special favour towards the 'captivity' that Shapur II exempted the inhabitants of Karka d-Ladan from persecution (though of course several martyrs from other places were brought thither to be put to death).

[27] See especially W. Hage, 'Die oströmische Staatskirche und die Christenheit des Perserreiches', *ZKG* 84 (1973) 174–87.

[28] *SO* p 37.

[29] See for example, *Acts of Pethion* in *AMS* 2 pp 559–60.

[30] See Decret, p 139.

The people of God have received prosperity, and success awaits the man who has been the instrument of that prosperity (Constantine); but disaster threatens the army which has been gathered together by the efforts of a wicked and proud man puffed up with vanity (Shapur) . . . The (Roman) empire will not be conquered, for the hero whose name is Jesus is coming with his power, and his armour will uphold the whole army of the empire.[31]

In the war which ensued Shapur's humiliating loss of his harem to Constantius and his failure to take the border city of Nisibis in 338 would both, no doubt, have encouraged him to find a scapegoat, and Aphrahat's unashamed words suggest that there may well have been an inkling of truth behind the accusations brought by Jews and Manicheans that Shapur's Christian subjects were disloyal or even rebellious.[32] Thus, on being told of Simeon's refusal to levy double taxes from his flock, Shapur exclaims 'Simeon wants to make his followers and his people rebel against my kingdom and convert them into servants of Caesar, their coreligionist'.[33]

This is a theme taken up again by the Zoroastrian authorities at the trial of Peroz, martyred in 422. This man was a wealthy Christian who apostatised and became Zoroastrian under torture, but then repented of his apostasy; Mihrshabur, the Magian official in charge of the case, hoping to get the shah Bahram V to condemn Peroz to death, tells the shah:

From this moment on, my lord, all the Christians (naṣrāyē) have rebelled against you: they no longer do your will, they despise your orders, they refuse to worship your gods. If the shah would hear me, let him give orders that the Christians convert from their religion, for they hold the same faith as the Romans, and they are in entire agreement together: should a war interpose between the two empires these Christians will turn out to be defectors from our side in any fighting, and through their playing false they will bring down your power.[34]

---

[31] *Demonstration* 5.1,24 ed J. Parisot, *Patrologia Syriaca* I (Paris 1894).
[32] Typical are the denunciations of a bishop Abdisho (made by his renegade nephew) to be found in the *Acts of Forty Martyrs, AMS2*, p 333: Abdisho and another priest are alleged to harbour Roman spies and write letters to Caesar about affairs in the orient.
[33] *Acts of Simeon B 11*.
[34] *AMS* 4 pp 258–9. Even in the mid sixth century the catholicos Aba is suspected by

Accusations of this sort were clearly commonplace in times of political tension between the two empires, and, if we may believe a hostile source, it was precisely in order to avoid this kind of suspicion that Barsauma, metropolitan of Nisibis, decided to adopt at the synod of Beth Lapat in 484 a christological profession at variance with that then current in the Roman empire: 'unless', he told the shah Peroz, 'the confession of Christians in your territory is made different from that in Greek territory, their affection and loyalty towards you will not be firmly fixed'.[35]

The fact that a foreign power was apt to express interest in a minority, and send gifts to its leaders,[36] was not unnaturally a further source of irritation and dislike, all the more so in that this minority had already made itself abhorrent to all good Zoroastrians by its food, marriage and burial customs.[37] In the *Acts of Simeon* some Jews are represented as pointing out to Shapur II that if he, the king of kings, sends resplendent missives to Caesar, they are received coldly, whereas a puny letter from Simeon is welcomed with both hands and its contents quickly seen to.[38]

Envoys from the west were particularly apt to show concern for the well-being of the Christian community in Persia. The extended visit of Marutha, bishop of Martyropolis, which culminated in the

---

Chosroes I of having given support to a rebellion by the shah's son (who was a Christian convert): see Bedjan, *Histoire* pp 264-7.

[35] Barhebraeus, *Chronicon Ecclesiasticum* 3, ed J. B. Abbeloos and T. Lamy (Louvain 1877) col 65.

[36] According to the *Acts of Peroz, AMS* 4, p 256, the Christian community at Seleucia were presented with splendid fittings for their church in 410. Sabrisho, on becoming catholicos in 595, was sent a gold cross containing a relic of the true cross by Maurice (Bedjan, *Histoire* pp 302–3).

[37] Refusal to eat 'blood' (that is, meat ritually slaughtered) is frequently found in the Shapur II martyrdoms. That one's religion could be deduced from eating habits is clear from several later texts: Anahid, a convert martyred under Yazdgard II, 'refused to eat in the presence of her parents in case they saw she was now a Christian' (*AMS* 2 p 569). Celibacy was abhorrent to Zoroastrians, and the synod of 486, by allowing marriage to all ranks of clergy, was certainly making a concession to this feeling; even so the conflict between Zoroastrian and Christian 'tables of affinity' still remained and brought much trouble, especially in the sixth century as can be seen from the *Life of Aba* (Bedjan, *Histoire* p 235); see also note 14 above. Burial was of course also abhorrent to Zoroastrian sensibilities; Bahram V even had Christians disinterred (AMS 4 p 254). As the nobles and Magians complained to Yazdgard I, Christians 'mock fire and water' and 'they despise our customs in no small way' (*AMS* 4 p 250).

[38] *Acts of Simeon* A 13.

famous synod of 410 at which the church of the East officially recognised the Council of Nicaea and its canons, is only one of many such embassies. The sort of hopes raised by these western visitors in the minds of the shah's aggrieved subjects can well be seen from the wishful thinking to be found in the embellished story of the converted general, Ma'in, martyr under Shapur II: the Roman envoy arrives to find the convert in the middle of being tortured; alighting from his horse, he kisses the martyr's feet and gives peremptory orders that the man be set free, whereupon he hands over to the shah a letter from Constantine demanding the release of all Christian prisoners; if this is not carried out, all Persian hostages at Constantinople will be put to death.[39] Although this melodramatic scenario might fit reality in the twentieth century, it hardly does in the fourth. Closer to the truth, no doubt, are the activities of western envoys described in two sixth-century martyrdoms of aristocratic lady converts. In the *Acts of Shirin* we are told that the proximity of a Byzantine embassy obliged the Zoroastrian authorities to transfer Shirin hastily from one prison to another in order to avoid their prying eyes.[40] The other heroine, Golinducht (martyred in 591), was a relative of Chosroes I and had been married to a Magian general; she had been converted, significantly enough, by some Christian prisoners of war who had been introduced into her household. On her refusal to revert to Zoroastrianism she is sent to the fortress of 'Oblivion', where she is eventually visited by Aristoboulos, a legate from the emperor Maurice on a peace mission. Aristoboulos had asked for special permission to visit this dreaded fortress so that he might petition the shah for the release of any Christian prisoners there. Discovering Golinducht incarcerated inside, he assures her that he will ask the shah to have her released. 'I will condemn you before the throne of Christ if you do this', retorted the indignant woman. He does not leave totally unrewarded, however, for, besides receiving a prediction of war, he was able to depart with a souvenir of one of her fetters.[41]

---

[39] MS Add 12174 fol 392[r/v]; on these Acts see J. M. Fiey, 'Ma'in, général de Sapor II, confesseur et évêque', *Le Muséon* 84 (Louvain 1971) pp 437–53.

[40] *Acts of Shirin* 17, ed P. Devos, *An Bol* 64 (1946) pp 87–131, with Devos's remarks on pp 101–2.

[41] *Acts of Golinducht* 7, ed G. Garitte, *An Bol* 74 (1956) pp 405–40. According to the Armenian *Life of Abda* (*Vark' ew vkayabanutiwnk' srboc'* I (Venice 1894) p 3) already in the early fifth century Theodosius's ambassadors request Yazdgard

While there is no doubt that the loyalty of some Christians towards the Sasanids really was suspect, especially in the fourth and fifth centuries,[42] at the same time it should be noted that the martyrs are quite often specifically represented as assuring the shah that their political loyalty is genuine. A touching case concerns Gushtazad, a Christian courtier who apostatised in the persecution and then repented: he insists on sending a last message to Shapur II as he is led off: 'I have always been loyal to you and your father; grant me one request: let a herald proclaim that Gushtazad is being put to death, not for treason, but because he was a Christian who refused to renounce God'.[43]

That this loyalty must often have been entirely genuine can be seen from the fact that many Christians served in the army. In the early sixth century we even hear of a case of a known convert from Zoroastrianism, Grigor, who was appointed general by Cawad during war against to west.[44]

An indication of the extent to which the church in Persia viewed itself, by the mid sixth century, as an integral part of Sasanian society is to be found in some of the epithets accorded to the shah in the *Synodicon*. Thus Chosroes I (who at one point is called 'the second Cyrus')[45] is referred to several times as being 'preserved by divine grace,'[46] while at the synod of 576 the following instructions were issued:

> It is right that in all the churches of this exalted and glorious kingdom that our lord the victorious Chosroes, king of kings, be named in the litanies during the liturgy. No metropolitan or bishop has any authority to waive this canon in any of the churches of his diocese and jurisdiction.[47]

---

to release the deacon Benjamin from prison: 'Give me assurance in his own handwriting that he will not convert to his faith any more Magians in Persia', the shah replied; 'if so, at your request I will free him from chains'. This was an undertaking that of course proved unacceptable—even though it was actually written into the terms of Justinian's peace treaty of 561, see A. Guillaumont, 'Justinien et l'église de Perse', *DOP* 23/4 (1969/70) pp 49–50.

[42] Shapur's exemption of the Christians of the 'captivity' at Karka d-Ladan from persecution (see note 26 above) might suggest that he feared their defection.

[43] *Acts of Simeon* A 32.

[44] *Acts of Grigor*, in Bedjan, *Histoire* pp 359–61.

[45] *SO* p 69.

[46] *SO* pp 68, 94, 544 (likewise of Hormizd IV, pp 130–1).

[47] *SO* p 121 (canon 14).

When Arab succeeded Sasanid rule in the mid seventh century it is clear that a reasonably satisfactory *modus vivendi* had been achieved for the church: vandalism of fire shrines, which features predominantly in the fifth century, seems to have become a thing of the past, and it is chiefly conversions among high caste Magians that upset the balance and induce the authorities to act, almost invariably at the instigation of the Zoroastrian clergy. It would appear that most of the rights of, and restrictions laid upon, the 'peoples of the book' under the new Arab rulers were simply formulations of what had already been general practice under the later Sasanids.[48] Indeed, in embryo, all the main elements of the Ottoman *millet* system were already present, as far as the Christian community was concerned, in pre-Islamic times.

So far nothing has been said about national identity, and the reason for this is a simple one: such a concept (at least as we now understand it) never existed in Sasanid Iran, any more than it did in the Ottoman empire before the rise of nationalism. Across the border in the Roman empire, it is true, one can occasionally find a non-Chalcedonian writer like Jacob of Serugh (†521) speaking of 'us Rhomaioi',[49] but this is only possible because the state is a Christian one. For Christians in Persia, on the other hand, their 'nation' was that of their religious community. As Wigram put it, 'religion is the determinant of nationality'.[50] The situation is indeed very similar to that of the Jewish religious community, another *ethnos* which spanned two political empires, though of course in their case they suffered the same sort of disabilities in both empires. These two religious communities consisted of individuals of very diverse racial and geographic origins, the Christian even more so than the Jewish; both communities nevertheless called themselves a 'People' or 'Nation' (Syriac *'amma*, corresponding to both *ethnos* (singular) and *laos*).

A very prominent theme among all early Syriac writers, borrowing here from the Jewish conceptual model, is that of the new

---

[48] See E. Sachau, 'Von den rechtlichen Verhältnissen der Christen im Sasanidenreich', *Mitteilungen des Seminars für orientalische Sprachen* X.2 (Berlin 1907) pp 69–95.
[49] *Epistulae*, ed G. Olinder, CSCO 110 (1937) p 92.
[50] Wigram, *An Introduction* p 66; similarly M. Morony, 'Religious communities in late Sasanian and early Muslim Iraq', *Journal of the Economic and Social History of the Orient* 17 (Leiden 1974) pp 113–35. Morony sees this as a development of the late Sasanian period in particular.

'People' (or 'Nation') who emerge from the (gentile) 'Peoples' (or, from the Jewish 'People' and the gentile 'Peoples').[51] The theme is furthermore developed by the introduction of bridal imagery: the betrothed bride was originally the Jewish People, but when she eventually rejected the Bridegroom at his appearance, her place was taken by a new bride, the church, a new People drawn from both Jews and gentiles. As we shall see shortly, this bridal imagery is given some interesting extensions in the Persian context.

Now in both the acts of the earliest synod (410) and in a variety of other texts produced by Christians in Sasanid Iran it is significant that one of the standard forms of self-identification is precisely the biblical term 'People of God': Aphrahat already uses the terminology in the mid fourth century,[52] while in the synod of 410 it is laid down that anyone who disregards its canons is to be anathematised by the 'People of God'.[53] Several hagiographers also employ the phrase; one, for example, complains 'how can we sufficiently tell of all that the shah caused the People of God to endure?'.[54] Related terms are likewise found, such as 'People and Church of God',[55] while later variations on this are 'People of the Christians',[56] 'People of the believers'[57] or 'People of Christendom'.[58] The world is divided, not between *Rhomāyē* and *Persāyē*, but between the 'People of God' and those outside, *barrāyē* (or, less frequently, 'pagans' *ḥanpē*).[59]

Just as Syriac monastic literature speaks of two co-existant modes of being and experience, that of the spiritual world (*rūḥānōtā*) and that of the physical (*pagrānōtā*), both at tension with each other but of which the former alone is of true significance, so

---

[51] See R. Murray, *Symbols of Church and Kingdom: a Study in Early Syriac Tradition* (Cambridge 1975) pp 41–68; this is the topic of Aphrahat's *Demonstration* 16 (English translation in J. Neusner, *Aphrahat and Judaism (Leiden 1971) pp 60–7)*.

[52] *Demonstration* 5.1 and 25; 14.1.

[53] SO p 21; the term occurs elsewhere too in the *acta* of this synod. The Greek equivalent, *laos tou theou* is found several times in Eusebius, *Vita Constantini* (II.63; IV.62.3; IV.71.2); for the use of the term within the Roman empire see E. von Ivanka, *Rhomäerreich und Gottesvolk* (Freiburg/München 1968) pp 49–61. Similarly of Jewish origin is the word *knushātā* (lit. 'synagogues') employed for Christian communities (*SO* pp 26, 37).

[54] *AMS* 4 p 257; for some other references see my note in *An Bol* 96 (1978) p 180.

[55] SO p 22.

[56] SO pp 50, 131; *Acts of Simeon* B 11.

[57] SO p 65.

[58] *ibid* p 544.

[59] *ibid* pp 49, 56, 77, 96, 98–9 and often; 'pagans': *Ibid* pp 117, 127 etc.

in the Persian church (and above all in the martyr acts) we can observe a similar tension expressed between two modes of allegiance: the Persian Christian was servant of two different shahanshahs, Christ and the temporal shah. Under normal conditions there was not necessarily any clash of loyalties since member ship of the 'People of God' and of the Persian state belonged to separate modes of existence and so were not exclusive of each other. Trouble arose only when matters became polarised and one side or other asserted that loyalty to the one conflicted with, and was detrimental to, loyalty to the other, a situation illustrated by the following dialogue between Pusai, the shah's chief craftsman, and Shapur II:

> Pusai: Far be it from a servant of the living God to consider you to be despicable and contemptible, o mighty king. Rather, he hold you to be a mighty king, a renowned king, the king of kings.
>
> Shapur: How can you consider me to be so, as you claim to, seeing that you have the audacity to swear in my presence by God, and not by the gods?
>
> Pusai: I swore by God because I am a Christian; I did not swear by the gods because I am not a pagan.
>
> Shapur: How can you consider me to be king of kings, mighty and powerful, when you have had the effrontery to say in my presence that you are a Christian?[60]

At times a hagiographer will deliberately play on the ambiguity of the term 'king of kings'. Thus the Magian official gives Simeon and his companions a last chance as they are being led off to execution:[61] 'will you worship the sun as a deity and do the will of Shapur, king of kings and lord of all the earth? If so, you will be spared'. 'Indeed we will perform the will of the King of kings and Lord of all the earth', they reply. The official is taken in and the confessors have a good laugh as they point out that the title belongs properly to God and not to Shapur.

Similar deliberate irony is frequently employed in another particularly sensitive area, the Christian ideal of virginity, utterly abhorrent to Zoroastrian religious sensibility. Martha, the daughter of Pusai and another martyr under Shapur II, is told by the interrogating judge: 'you are a young girl, and a very pretty one at

[60] *AMS* 2 p 214.
[61] *Acts of Simeon* B 83.

that; go and find a husband, get married and have children; do not hold on to the disgusting pretext of the 'covenant' (that is, vow of virginity)'. Martha objects: does the law tell a betrothed girl to marry someone other than her fiancé? When pressed to say where this fiancé is, she replies 'he has gone on a long journey on business, but he will soon be back'. She even goes on to give his name, Jesus, but it is only when the Zoroastrian official has asked what city he was visiting and received the reply 'Jerusalem on high' that he realises and bursts out in exasperation, 'did I not say at the outset that this was a stubborn people, not open to persuasion?'.[62]

The logical consequences of the use of bridal imagery are here applied to the individual, rather than to the collective 'People of God', in a way that is entirely typical of early Syriac Christianity as a whole.[63] How deeply ingrained this whole way of thinking was to Christians in Persia can be seen from its extension in the synodical literature to the relationship between bishops and their flocks. In the synod of 554 the transfer of bishops from one see to another is forbidden on the grounds that this is a form of adultery; each bishop's see being 'a pure spiritual wife who has been given to him'.[64]

In Sasanid Iran, then, as far as Christians themselves were concerned, religion and 'national' identity can be said to have coincided, in that the nation concerned was the 'Nation, or People, of God'. This identity successfully cut across – since it transcended—all the various other factors which might have gone to consitute a national identity of the kind that would be recognisable as such to-day—the sense of belonging to the Sasanid state, to a particular region, town, racial or linguistic group. This is not to deny the relevance of these other factors in Sasanian society, and there is certainly some evidence that they did play a role,[65] but it was never an important one as long as religion was considered the ultimate determining factor of allegiance in the structure of the

---

[62] *AMS* 2 pp 236–7. The virgin martyr betrothed to Christ is a theme found in almost all the martyrdoms of women.

[63] It is a recurrent theme in liturgical texts: see H. Engberding, 'Die Kirche als Braut in der ostsyrischen Liturgie', *OCP* 3 (1937) pp 5–44.

[64] Canon 5 (*SO* p 100); compare also canon 3 (*SO* p 99).

[65] It was no doubt among converts from Zoroastrianism that Zoroaster came to be accredited with a prophecy about the birth of Christ and that certain legends were developed around the Magi of the Gospels—see U. Monneret de Villard, *Le leggende orientali sui Magi evangelici*, Studi e Testi, 163 (Rome 1952).

society, and as long as none of these other groupings—political, geographical, ethnic or linguistic—came to be seen as being co-terminous with that of the religious community.

As far as oriental Christianity is concerned, it is only with the Armenian church that we can witness, possibly already in the pre-Islamic period, the beginnings of a convergence of these two modes of self-identity, in their case of the religious community with the ethnic and linguistic group, both of which cut across the two empires. A hint of this development can perhaps be seen in the extensive use made of the Books of Maccabees by early Armenian historical writers.[66] It is not until the eighth century, however, with the rise of the Bagratid dynasty, that we really find ourselves presented with a recognisable image of Armenian national identity, in Moses Khorenatsi's influential *History of the Armenians*.

In Syriac sources of the Sasanian period 'Armenian' is simply a term to denote a person's geographical provenance, just as 'Aramean' denotes a man from Beth Aramāyē (the area around Seleucia-Ctesiphon),[67] or 'Median' someone from Media. There is, nevertheless, perhaps one area where there was a significant sub-current of local self-identity among Christians (but by no means confined to them): this is to be found in the ecclesiastical provinces of Adiabene (Hadyab) and Beth Garmai, whose metropolitan sees were Arbela and Karka d-Beth Slokh (modern Erbil and Kirkuk in north Iraq).[68] Here there was evidently some continuing awareness of the past Assyrian empire, and the terms *Athor, Athorāyē* (Assyria, Assyrians) are sometimes used (in a purely geographical sense)[69] in preference to the names of current administrative usage, whether ecclesiastical or secular. The semi-legendary fourth-century martyr Kardah, for example, is said to be 'of the stock of the kingdom of the Assyrians', his mother's side going back to Sennacherib; later in the *Acts* we find him made 'prefect of Athor', and Arbela is

---

[66] See R. W. Thomson, 'The Maccabees in early Armenian historiography', *JTS* ns 26 (1975) pp 329–41. Only passing use of Maccabees is found in Syriac writers (for example *Acts of Simeon* A 2–3,7–8).

[67] So, for example, in Simeon of Beth Arsham's famous letter concerning the spread of Nestorian doctrines in Persia: ed J. S. Assemani, *Bibliotheca Orientalis Clementino-Vaticana* I (Rome 1719) pp 351, 353 (the Latin translation is very misleading). The meaning 'pagan', found in Syriac texts of more westerly provenance, is extremely rare in works written in the Persian empire.

[68] For the contrast between north and south in this respect see P. Crone and M. Cook, *Hagarism* (Cambridge 1977) pp 56–60.

[69] In strong contrast to modern usage, for which see below.

described as 'the capital of the Athorāyē'.[70] This sort of usage indeed occasionally finds its way into official church documents: at the synod of 585 the archdeacon Aba from Arbela signs 'on behalf of Henana, metropolitan of the Athoraye' (the usual terminology is 'of Arbela and the whole region of Adiabene').[71]

A little further south, in Beth Garmai, the local history of Karka d-Beth Slokh starts with Sennacherib's son Sardana and ends with the martyrdoms under Yazdgard II. As a matter of fact there was a liturgical rationale for this, hinted at by the chronicler himself when he goes on to say that it was during Sardana's reign that Jonah preached to the Ninevites:[72] it was a metropolitan of Karka, Sabrisho, who in the late sixth century introduced the pre-Lenten 'Fast of Nineveh' into the calendar of the Church of the East.[73]

In contrast, the Babylonian heritage of further south elicited no such sense of continuity among the Christian community living in south Mesopotamia: indeed one can observe an active dissociation in that the term 'Chaldean' normally designates a pagan astrologer.[74]

Just as membership of the 'People of God' had nothing to do with modern concepts of nationhood, so also it was totally unconnected with any idea of belonging to a particular linguistic group. Christians in the Sasanid empire employed a whole number of different languages for ecclesiastical use.[75] Although we tend today to think of Syriac as the cultural language of the Church of the East, during the Sasanian period it was by no means the only one in

---

[70] *Acts of Kardagh* 3, 5, 6, ed J. B. Abbeloos, *An Bol* 9 (1890) pp 5–106. Nevertheless it is the Iranian element which is uppermost in these acts: see G. Wiessner, 'Christlicher Heiligenkult im Umkreis eines sassanidischen Grosskönigs', in *Festgabe deutscher Iranisten zur 2500 Jahrfeier Irans*, ed W. Eilers (Stuttgart 1971) pp 149–55.

[71] *SO* p 165.

[72] *AMS* 2 p 507.

[73] See J. M. Fiey, *Assyrie chretienne* 3 (Beirut 1968) pp 20–2. Fiey's hesitations about the date of Sabrisho are unnecessary in the light of the 'Nestorian' edition of the *Hudra* I (Trichur 1960) p 259, where Sabrisho is located in the Persian period—his name is omitted in the uniate *Breviarium Chaldaicum* I (Rome 1938) p 161.

[74] In this connection it is significant that almost all the shrines connected with biblical history, such as the monastery of the Ark on mount Kardu and the tomb of Nahum at Alkosh, are situated in the north.

[75] This not unnaturally gave rise to occasional local conflict: according to the *Life of John of Dailam* (Harvard Ms syr. 38 fol 185[r/v]) this seventh-century saint, having founded one monastery, had to build a second one alongside it in order to resolve the quarrel between the Persian and Syriac speaking monks over which language to use in church services.

17

currency: Greek continued to be the liturgical language of the 'captivity' for a considerable time, while in Persian Armenia Armenian will have replaced Syriac in the fifth century. From the late fifth century onwards Persian became an increasingly important literary vehicle for Christians: of the once extensive Christian literature in this language only a few fragments of biblical and liturgical texts happen to survive to-day,[76] but quite a number of extant Syriac hagiographical, legal and literary texts are in fact translations from lost Middle Persian originals.[77] As the church expanded eastwards, yet other languages were adopted for ecclesiastical use.[78]

One further, and final, point needs to be mentioned in passing: in the sixth and early seventh centuries, as a result of the christological controversies surrounding the council of Chalcedon, the 'People of God' in Persia found themselves torn by internal divisions. Ever since the late fifth century the church in Persia had opted for a distinctive Antiochene theological position,[79] whereas in the sixth century the rest of the Christian world to the west—including supporters of Chalcedon as well as its opponents, the so-called Monophysites—were taking an increasingly Alexandrine stance on christology. One result of this was that, towards the end of the sixth century, the Monophysites began to make considerable inroads into north Mesopotamia, especially in monastic circles. Since, however, each side in effect saw itself as the true 'People of God' and the other as 'heretics',[80] no need was ever felt to alter the basic conceptual model of self identity.

In conclusion, then, one can see how, within the Sasanid empire, the self-identification of Christians as the 'People of God', which had originally been engendered through religious enthusiasm and

---

[76] See B. M. Metzger, *The Early Versions of the New Testament* (Oxford 1977) pp 274–7 and *Theologische Realenzyklopädie* 6 (Berlin 1980) under 'Bibelübersetzungen'.

[77] These include the Acts of Aba and of Grigor in Bedjan, *Histoire*: see K. Czeglédy, *Acta Orientalia* 4 (Budapest 1954) p 66.

[78] See W. Hage, 'Einheimische Volkssprachen und syrische Kirchensprache in der nestorianischen Asienmission', in *Erkenntnisse und Meinungen* 2, ed G. Wiessner, *Göttinger Orientforschungen* I.17 (Wiesbaden 1978) pp 131–60.

[79] See W. Macomber, 'The christology of the synod of Seleucia-Ctesiphon AD 486', *OCP* 24 (1958) pp 142–54.

[80] In the *Synodicon orientale* the term is first found in the synod of 486 (*SO* p 54); 'orthodox' now becomes the standard term for one's own side (the first occurrence of 'orthodoxy' is in the synod of 544, *SO* p 69).

which had no doubt been further strengthened under the stimulus of persecution, in due course came to be formalised as a result of the way in which church-state relations developed in the Sasanian empire. The situation eventually became fossilised, as it were, under Islam, where membership of a particular religious group served as the overriding means of self-identification. Only when European concepts of nationalism reached the middle east in the late nineteenth century did members of the Church of the East begin to feel the need to discover a national identity that was not solely based on the idea of membership of a religious community. For them a suitable focus was found in the term 'Assyrian',[81] and the resultant Assyrian nationalist movement has to-day even been extended to include members of other churches of Syriac liturgical tradition such as the Syrian Orthodox.[82] Such developments would of course have been unthinkable in Sasanian Iran.

The French Old Testament scholar Antonin Causse once wrote an important study of ancient Israel entitled *Du groupe ethnique à la communauté religieuse* (1937). It would, in my opinion, be sad indeed if a future historian of the Church of the East found himself having to reverse this title.

University of Oxford

---

[81] For the adoption of this name see J. M. Fiey, "Assyriens" ou "Araméens", *L'Orient Syrien* 10 (Paris 1965) pp 141–60.
[82] See G. Yonan, *Assyrer heute* (Hamburg Vienna 1978); the nationalist-minded among the Syrian Orthodox migrant workers from Turkey, now in western Europe, put out a periodical entitled *Egarto* ('Letter').

NATIONALISM AS A FACTOR IN ANTI-CHALCEDONIAN FEELING IN EGYPT

by W. H. C. FREND

THE WRITER of the *History of the Patriarchs* preserves an interesting tradition concerning the attitude of the monks of the monastery of Metras towards the Monophysite patriarch Benjamin (619–661/5)[1] during the reign of the emperor Heraclius. 'The inmates,' we are told, 'were especially powerful.' They were Egyptians (*Miswrani*) by race, all natives, and there was no stranger among them. Therefore, Heraclius could not make their hearts pliant, and therefore they received Apa Benjamin when he returned from Upper Egypt, because they kept the orthodox (that is, Monophysite) faith and did not deviate from it'.[2] Other monasteries might bow to 'Heraclius the heretic', but not they.

The account shows the extent to which in the mid-seventh century, race had become identified with religion in Egypt. No credit was given to Heraclius for his efforts through Monoenergism to find common ground between Constantinople and Alexandria. The Copts represented orthodoxy: the emperor's creed was heretical, and because he had attempted to foist heresy on his dominions his armies were defeated by the Moslems. In this belief, the writer of the *History of the Patriarchs* did not stand alone. Seventh century chroniclers in Egypt gave the same explanation for the defeat of the Byzantine armies. Thus, John of Nikiou c680 stated: 'And everyone said, "This expulsion [of the Romans] and the victory of the Moslems is due to the wickedness of Heraclius and the persecution of the orthodox through the Patriarch Cyrus. This was the cause of the ruin of the Romans and the subjugation of Egypt by the Moslems" '[3]. Another writer, Theophilus of Alexandria also c680, even welcomed the arrival of the Arabs as 'the

---

[1] The year of Benjamin's death is usually given as 661. For the alternative of 665, see, C. Detlef G. Müller, *Le Muséon*, 69 (Munich 1956) pp 313 *seq*.
[2] Severus of Ashmounein, *History of the Patriarchs*, ed B. Evetts, *PO* 1, 2 (Paris 1907) cap 14, p 498.
[3] John of Nikiou, *Chronicle*, ed R. H. Charles (London 1916) cap 121, 1.

coming of a powerful nation who would have care for the welfare of the Churches of Christ'.[4] And so it seemed nearly half a century after the fall of Alexandria.

These statements demonstrate the breakdown of confidence that had occurred between the authorities and the great mass of Egyptian Christians in this decisive period in Egypt's history. Even so, the issue was confined to religion. It had been impossible, despite constant efforts extending for nearly two centuries to find a formula which would satisfy the Egyptian view that the Two-Nature Christology proclaimed at Chalcedon was incompatible with the theology of Cyril, and on the other hand, the emperor's need to maintain the canonical status of Chalcedon in order to safeguard the legal rights of the patriarchate of Constantinople and to maintain communion with the papacy. There had, however, been no national rising of the Copts against Byzantine institutions and Byzantine landowners, like the insurrections of the Donatist Circumcellions in North Africa in the fourth and early-fifth centuries.[5] Instead, Egypt was gripped by sullen discontent, and relief finally that the age of Heraclius and his patriarch Cyrus 'the Caucasian' had been ended.

In this brief paper we shall look closer at some of the factors that brought about this situation. It resulted in outright rejection of the religious hegemony of Constantinople, but was not accompanied by any attempt to overthrow the various social structures and institutions connected with Byzantium, a fact that contributed to the maintenance of a basically Byzantine administration of Egypt though politically independent of Constantinople for another fifty years.

The first point is that the Monophysite creed was not separatist in the same way as Donatism had tended to become in North Africa: far from it. Looking back indeed from the time of the third Crusade, but drawing on much earlier material, Michael the Syrian castigated the emperor Marcian for approving the definition of Chalcedon, because he thereby broke the unity of the empire as well as dividing the faith.[6] 'Barbarian power increased from that

---

[4] Theophilus of Alexandria, ed H. Fleisch, 'Une Homélie de Théophile d'Alexandrie,' *Revue de l'Orient chrétien*, 30 (Paris 1935–6) pp 374–5.
[5] See H. J. Diesner, *Der Untergang der römischen Herrschaft in Nordafrika*, (Weimar 1964) pp 107–10.
[6] Michael the Syrian, *Chronicle*, ed J. Chabot (Paris 1901) 8, 14, p 122.

time on,'[7] commented Michael. For many One Nature theologians, Chalcedon pointed the way to secular as well as ecclesiastical schism, whereas the One Nature doctrine represented the sacred unity between Christ and the Imperial realm. James of Serug for instance, in a letter to the monks of Mar Bassus in c520, pointed out the incongruity of the emperor wearing the cross on his crown if he did not believe that Christ was truly God. The cross of a man would have no significance.[8] Even after ten years of persecution through Justin and Justinian the Monophysite leaders were almost pathetic in their expression of loyalty towards the emperor when in 531 they were summoned to confer with Chalcedonians at Constantinople.[9] The issues that divided them from Justinian lay wholly in the sphere of religious belief. In intention at least Monophysitism was not 'a national and social movement in disguise'.[10]

Moreover, the Coptic Christians never imagined themselves in the guise of nationalists harking back to the glories of Egypt before the imposition of Roman rule. This characteristic of later nationalist movements was left to pagan antiquarians.[11] Among the Christians radical assertion of self-identity rejected the Egyptian as well as the Hellenistic heritage. Thus already in c310 the Egyptian confessors from the Thebaid who had been sentenced to exile in Palestine defied the judge at Caesarea before whom they had been brought. Asked their names they renounced their Egyptian theophoric birth-names 'as those belonging to idols', and claiming instead names of Hebrew prophets, such as Jeremiah, Isaiah and Elijah and that they

[7] *Ibid* 8, 12, pp 87–8.
[8] James of Serug, 'Letter of James of Serug to the monks of the Monastery of Mar Bassus', cited from A. Vasiliev, *Justin the First* (Dumbarton Oaks 1950) p 234, who translates the relevant passage James was loyal to Justin, telling the Monophysite Christians of southern Arabia that 'we Romans live quietly under Christian kings' and was full of praise for their sacrifices under hostile rulers.
[9] The text of their letter to Justinian is given in Zacharias Rhetor, *HE*, ed E. W. Brooks, *CSCO, SS* 3, 6, ix, 15, pp 79–84;
[10] The title of A. H. M. Jones' fine study, 'Were ancient heresies national or social movements in disguise', *JTS*, ns10 (1959) pp 281–98. For the opposite view see E. L. Woodward, *Christianity and Nationalism in the Later Roman Empire* (London, 1916) and more moderately by J. Maspero, *Histoire des patriarches d'Alexandrie depuis la mort de l'empereur Anastase jusqu'à la reconciliation des églises jacobites* (Paris 1923) pp 518–616.
[11] Such as Horappolon, the fifth-century authority on hieroglyphs and Alexandrian antiquities. See H. I. Bell, *Egypt from Alexander the Great to the Arab Conquest* (Oxford 1948) p 148.

were themselves from Jerusalem, the city of the Christians. The judge believed he was confronted by conspirators from across Rome's eastern frontier.[12] Egypt with its tombs infested with representations of idols and its tradition of animal worship was a veritable land of sin. The contrast in the mind of Egyptian Christians even in the sixth century was still between Egypt and Jerusalem. The monk Isaiah was described by his biographer Zacharias Scholasticus as 'being in body an Egyptian, but in nobility of soul an inhabitant of Jerusalem'.[13]

Christianity, however, gave the Copts a sense of identity and purpose that they had lacked for centuries. It liberated them from the thraldom of age-old fears and superstitions, and for the first time gave them a conviction that their Christian wisdom was superior to all the philosophy and arguments of their Greek masters. No one, said Antony, was ever converted to philosophy by the philosophers, or inspired by them to suffer martyrdom for his beliefs. Unlike the Christians they had no answers to the questions they posed.[14] This feeling could only be enhanced by the emergence by the end of the third century of Bibles translated in Sahidic,[15] a proof that in adopting Christianity they were no longer dependent on the language of the cities and above all, of that symbol of Egypt's slavery, Alexandria.

Another factor reinforced this attitude, namely the continued adherence to paganism of many of the Greek-speaking obligarchies in the towns.[16] These individuals were landowners as well, and in case of dispute between them and their tenants economic animosities were combined with differences of religion. Thus in Besa's *Life of Shenute*, we find Shenute consigning the vineyards of pagan landowners near Panopolis suspected of extorting too high rents from their tenants, to the floodwaters of the Nile.[17] Shenute himself had a smattering of Greek, just enough to pour scorn on the

[12] Eusebius, *Martyrs of Palestine*, ed and trans H. Lawlor and H. Oulton (London, 1954) 8.1. Antony had no use for the legacy of the religious past of Egypt, see V[ita]A[ntonii] 79, PG 26 (1854) col 952c.
[13] Zacharias Scholasticus, *Vita Isaiah*, ed E. W. Brooks, CSCO 3, 25 (1907) p 3.
[14] VA, 69–78, PG 26, cols 949–52.
[15] For the early date of the appearance of Coptic Scriptures, see G. Steindorff, 'Bemerkungen über die Anfänge der koptischen Sprache', in *Coptic Studies in honour of W. E. Crum* (Boston 1950) p 211.
[16] Antinous, near Thebes is an example, see Theodoret, HE 4, 18—'The greater part of the inhabitants were pagans'—in Valens' reign.
[17] Besa, *Vie de Schenoudi*, ed H. Wiesman, CSCO, SC 16 (1951) cap 85.

works of Aristophanes and Plato. His monasteries also, provided welfare services for the surrounding districts and more effective security for the inhabitants against the raids of the Blemmyes than the 'Greek generals', as Shenute contemptuously calls them, were able to do.[18]

The sense of religious superiority coupled with continued economic servitude might be expected to have resulted in a nationalist movement directed against the representatives of the empire. That this did not take place was due to two main factors. First, Constantine was extraordinarily successful in transferring the odium felt towards the 'era of Diocletian' exclusively onto the shoulders of the persecuting emperors. Not only did he welcome ostentatiously the confessor bishop Paphnutius at the Council of Nicaea,[19] but both he and his son Constantius II maintained a lively correspondence with Antony.[20] Instructively, they accepted that the monks were 'men of God', whose views therefore were sanctified by the higher powers with whom they were in contact, while the monk themselves never wavered in their loyalty either to the Alexandrian patriarchate or the empire. Thus the emperors enabled the Coptic monks to bring influence to bear on the councils of the empire in a way impossible to conceive by previous generations of Egyptian peasants; and when their prophecies of doom against emperors, such as Valens who attempted to control them, proved correct, their power increased accordingly.[21] The price, however, was acceptance of a role, albeit a privileged one, within the framework of the Christian Byzantine empire and resultant abandonment of any ideas of radical reform of their surroundings. The second factor was the genius of Athanasius. Though he was an Alexandrian Greek without a trace of Egyptian national sentiment, he took the trouble to make himself known and communicate with the Egyptian Christians. That he sometimes preached in Coptic seems undeniable,[22] and through his friendship with Antony and Pachomius he was able to steer Egyptian monasticism from

---

[18] *Sermo* 21, pp 37–8, ed H. Wiesman *CSCO, SC* 2, 4 (1931); for welfare services see *ibid Sermo* 22.
[19] Socrates, *HE*, 1, 11.
[20] Sozomen, *HE*, 1, 13, 1, ed J. Bidez-Hansen, p 27. Compare *VA* 81.
[21] Sozomen, *HE*, 6, 40.
[22] See Th. Lefort, 'S. Athanase écrivain copte', *Le Muséon* 46 (1929) pp 197–224, and compare J. B. Bernardin, *JTS* 37 (1937) pp 113–129.

incipient separatism represented by the Meletians into a firm alliance with the patriarchate of Alexandria. Thanks to this alliance the Nile valley was henceforth to form a religious unity, under an all-powerful pharaoh, the patriarch of Alexandria. Cyril and Dioscorus were heirs to the position created by Athanasius in the previous century.

The alliance however, could never quite be taken for granted. Theophilus could rely on the support of monks to break up the Serapeum in 391, but the Tall Brethren, monks of Nitria, took their complaints against his condemnation of Origen and high-handed behaviour towards them to John Chrysostom in Constantinople in 399. In 429 Cyril had to write a long and exceedingly able letter to the monks, explaining in detail why *Theotokos* was an orthodox expression despite apparent absence of biblical warrant, before he could be sure of their support against Nestorius.[23] By this time, however, instinctive loyalty to the patriarch outweighed any theological doubts. It would have needed subtler minds than those of Shenute and his companions to realise that the literal, bible-inspired theology of the monks which accepted even the explicitly Antiochene *Acts of Archelaus*[24] could not be blended with the *logos-sarx* Christology of their patriarch. No such questions, however, ever seem to have crossed Shenute's mind. Nestorius was a heretic condemned by Cyril, and that was enough for him.

On the eve of Chalcedon Egypt appeared to be united under the banner of Dioscorus. At Ephesus II in August 449 the latter gained all the objectives for which his predecessors had striven.[25] As the emperor Theodosius II's plenipotentiary he had sat in judgement and deposed the patriarchs of Antioch and Constantinople. He had reduced the representatives of pope Leo to impotence. Amid cries of 'Long live Alexandria, city of the orthodox', he had witnessed Cyril's extreme doctrinal propositions expounded in the *Twelve Anathemas* declared canonical and himself hailed as 'Ecumenical Patriarch' and 'supreme Guardian of the faith'.[26] For all this he had

---

[23] Cyril, *Ep* 1, *PG* 77 (1854) cols 3–40.

[24] See J. Leipoldt, 'Schenute von Atripe,' *Texte und Untersuchungen* xxv Leipzig 1904, p 86, and compare Leipoldt's assessment, *ibid* p 74, 'Nirgends habe ich auch eine Anspielung gefunden an den Grundgedanken griecischer Frommigheit, der Mensch werde durch den Logos vergothet.'

[25] For the transcript report of the proceedings of the second council of Ephesus, see [J.] Flemming, *AKGWG*, NF 15 (1914–17) Ph-H Kl pp 1–159.

[26] Michael the Syrian. [*Chronicle*], 8, 7, ed. J. Chabot, 2, p 31. For a contemporary

received the emperor's personal thanks,[27] and on his return to Alexandria had not hesitated to demonstrate whose writ ran in that city, by open disobedience to imperial instructions concerning the relief of famine in Cyrenaica which formed part of his diocese.[28] He deserved fully the half-fearful, half-envious title of pharaoh given to him by his opponents.

There was, however, a flaw in Dioscorus's position which his enemies were able to exploit. However devoted he was to Cyril's theology, this devotion did not extend to Cyril's ecclesiastical relatives. His treatment of the presbyter Athanasius, Cyril's nephew, raised a party against him in Alexandria and at a vital moment when he stood at bay at the first session of the council of Chalcedon turned a significant part of the Egyptian episcopate against him. This opposition was supported, moreover, by some of the Pachomian monasteries situated around Alexandria, particularly the monastery of Canopus where Athanasius had found refuge. Put to the test, whatever local patriotism had sustained Dioscorus two years before, evaporated in face of the emperor's will. The imperial idea that this represented was not challenged, and was indeed unchallengeable at the time.

The ensuing division within the Alexandrian patriarchate had a significant effect on the alignment of social and cultural forces for and against Chalcedon after the deposition of Dioscorus. It is true that on the whole, as Liberatus states a century later, the nobility and officials, those whose connections with Constantinople were closest, supported the Chalcedonian nominee, Proterius[29] On the other side, as Zacharias Rhetor's vivid description of events makes clear, Proterius was bitterly opposed by the magistrates, members of the artisan guilds and people of Alexandria who fought a desperate battle with the *Romani* (that is, the soldiers, usually Gothic *foederati*) who attempted to assert his position.[30] These

---

western view of Dioscorus' ambitions, see Prosper Tiro, *Chronicon ad annum 449* —'In quo concilio Dioscorus episcopus primatum sibi vindicans . . .' *PL* 51 (1854) col 601C.

[27] Flemming pp 151–5.

[28] See Athanasius' letter which was read at the third session of the council of Chalcedon. Dioscorus was alleged to have refused to send corn to Cyrenaica and to have sold it instead at a large profit for his own benefit. *ACO* 2, 1, 2, p 17 (Mansi 6, cols 1021 *seq*).

[29] Liberatus, *Breviarium* (ed E. Schwartz *ACO* 2, 5) xiv 98.

[30] Zacharias Rhetor, *HE*, 3, 2, compare Evagrius, *HE* 2, 5, quoting an eyewitness account by Priscus of Paniou.

events in the winter of 451/52 need not however be interpreted as a national rising against the empire. The Pachomian monks supporting Proterius were just as Coptic as their opponents. The Alexandrian Greeks were divided. The divisions went across families as much as classes.[31] In the towns, as Peter the Iberian records, it was sometimes touch-and-go whether the Christian congregation rallied to Proterius or continued loyal to Dioscorus.[32] When the emperor's wishes became indubitably known open resistance ceased.[33] Whatever the majority thought of Chalcedon the emperor's will was law.

In the event, Proterius and his good-natured successor Timothy Salofaciolus ('Wobble-cap?') failed to outbid their rival, Timothy the Cat (died 477), because in the eyes of the great majority of the Egyptian Christians both Copt and Alexandrine, the latter represented more truly the theology of Cyril. This was the crucial point, and for nearly the whole period between Chalcedon and the Arab invasions the objective of successive Monophysite patriarchs of Alexandria was to secure the emperor's acceptance of their theological position and the status of their see. They wanted to put the clock back to the second council of Ephesus. This ambition was shown clearly by Timothy the Cat in his dealings with the usurper Basiliscus in 475–6.[34] The latter's policy was designed, as Michael the Syrian comments, 'to please the Alexandrians',[35] and to that end the Encyclical of early 475 accepted both councils of Ephesus as confirming 'the bulwark of the faith', Nicaea, and condemned the 'so-called Tome of Leo' as well as 'all things said and done at Chalcedon in innovation of the holy symbol of Nicaea' (that is, just stopping short of denouncing Chalcedon itself).[36] Timothy's new Council of Ephesus (autumn 475) not only denounced Chalcedon in toto but conferred on Ephesus the patriarchal status it had long claimed.[37] Timothy's ambitions failed however, when Zeno was

---

[31] So, John Rufus writing C 500, Plerophoria 38 and 39, ed F. Nau, PO3 (1912).
[32] John Rufus, Vita Petri Iberii, ed R. Raabe (Leipzig 1895) pp 59–62.
[33] Zacharias Rhetor, HE, 3, 11—Marciani regis minas timuerunt'.
[34] Ibid 5, 1–2. Compare, Evagrius, HE, 3, 3–8, and Theodore Lector, HE, 1. 30.
[35] Michael the Syrian, 9, 5, p 144.
[36] Zacharias Rhetor, HE, 5, 2. Evagrius' text, HE, 3, 4, omits any reference to 'the two Councils at Ephesus'.
[37] Zacharias Rhetor HE, 5, 3, Evagrius HE, 3, 5 and 6.

restored to the throne in August 476. His successor Peter Mongus (died 490) regarded the *Henotikon* of July 482 as sufficiently elastic as to allow him to maintain communion with Acacius and at the same time to denounce the *Tome* of Leo and Chalcedon. The Alexandrian patriarchs through the reign of Anastasius thought likewise.[38]

The reigns of Zeno and Anastasius tell us much about the cross-currents of Egyptian regional and religious sentiment. On the one hand, the interplay of internal and external considerations kept the successive patriarchs of Alexandria loyal to Constantinople but strictly on their own terms. Thus, no sooner had Peter Mongus accepted the *Henotikon* than he found himself threatened by a tide of public opinion which demanded from him an unequivocal denunciation of Leo's *Tome* and the council of Chalcedon. Two of his priests and two deacons sided with the mob against him, and in the countryside, Theodore, Bishop of Antinoë, and ever increasing numbers of monks threatened secession.[39] These *Acephaloi* as they came to be called, as their leadership was anonymous, represented an uncompromising element among the Egyptian Christians, especially the monks, that could perhaps be termed nationalist. But they failed to become a majority movement, and in the sixth century had degenerated into one of the twenty or so sects and offshoots from the main Monophysite church in Egypt.[40] Peter Mongus was able to ride out the storm, but the insecurity of his position served as a warning to his three successors, Athanasius II (died 496), John Hemula (died 505) and John of Nikiou (died 516) that support from Constantinople could not safely be dispensed with. The price demanded by the monks involving acceptance of Eutychism as orthodox and the consequent forfeiture of any claims to enforce Cyril's doctrines as the religion of the empire, was too high. John Hemula and John of Nikiou both denounced the *Tome* and Chalcedon, but while attempting in vain to get the patriarchs of Constantinope to do likewise, also exchanged synodical letters

---

[38] Zacharias Rhetor *HE*, 5, 10. Compare Evagrius, *HE*, 3, 17 (Peter Mongus): Zacharias *HE*, 7, 1. Athanasius 2,(490–6) 'freely and openly cursed the Tome and synod', yet remained in communion with Constantinople.

[39] Liberatus, ed E. Schwartz, *ACO*, 2, 5, [*Breviarium*], 17, 122. Compare Zacharias Rhetor *HE* 6, 1–2, and Michael the Syrian, 9, 6, p 153.

[40] On the survival of the Meletians and Acephaloi in late sixth century Egypt, the latter in much straitened circumstances, see *History of the Patriarchs*, 1, cap 14, ed B. Evetts, *PO* 1 (1907) p 473.

with them.[41] Their attitude was reflected in the support provided by
wealthy families, such as that of the patrician Apion as well as by
the people as a whole.[42]

All this time, however, Alexandria maintained what outsiders
regarded as a quite inordinate civic pride. Severus of Antioch
writing to Hippocrates the lawyer in 516–17 while he was still
patriarch of Antioch, commented that 'it was the habit of the
Alexandrians to think that the sun rises for them only, and towards
them only its lamp burns, so that they even jestingly term outside
cities "lampless" '.[43] Others found the jest excessive. There was
always an undercurrent of trouble between the Alexandrians and
the imperial troops, and in 509 the patriarchal palace had been burnt
down by the soldiers.[44] How this could turn into an anti-Byzantine
riot was demonstrated seven years later. In May 516 John of Nikiou
died. At this period the emperor Anastasius was making no secret
of his Monophysite sympathies and appointed Dioscorus II as
patriarch. The latter was to be on good terms with Severus and his
Monophysite background was impeccable. The populace, however, would have none of it. They rioted, insisted that clergy who
had accepted Dioscorus's appointment should go through a form of
election again, and on the following day murdered the augustal
prefect in angry protest against his praise of the emperor.[45] Malalas
indicates that a food shortage had aggravated tempers,[46] but such
scenes would hardly have been possible in any other city of the
empire. Alexandria was a special case. The Alexandrians were
determined to have a patriarch of their own choice.

Eighteen years later almost exactly the same sequence of events
was repeated. In February 535, while the empress Theodora
favoured the election of the deacon Theodosius, the population,

---

[41] Zacharias Rhetor, *HE*, 6, 1 and 7, 1, and compare Liberatus, 18, 128. Probably no
bishop in office between 484 and 518 rejected the *Henotikon* of Zeno.

[42] On Apion's Monophysitism, see the statement of his son, the *Comes* Strategius to
the Severan bishops convoked to the capital by Justinian for theological confer-
ences in 532–3. Letter of Innocentius of Maronia in Schwartz *ACO*, 4, 2. p 170.
Apion's descendants were also anti-Chalcedonian.

[43] Severus, *Letter* 46 to Hippocrates in 516, *A Collection of Letters* ed E. W. Brooks,
PO, 12, 2 (1854) p 318.

[44] Theophanes, *Chronicon A. M. 6001*.

[45] See the full account of the affair given in E. Stein, *Histoire du Bas-Empire*
(Paris/Bruxelles/Amsterdam 1949) 2, p 164, based on the accounts of Theodore
Lector, Theophanes and Malalas.

[46] Malalas, *Chronicon*, Bonn ed p 401.

supported by what Zacharias of Mitylene calls 'the rich', preferred a certain Gaianus, a monk who was known to favour the views of Julian of Halicarnassus. Julian was opposed by Severus of Antioch and other members of the Monophysite 'establishment' who regarded him as a Eutychist,[47] but it made no difference to his popularity. Liberatus, the well-informed archdeacon of Carthage, states that 'some of the clergy, the landowners, the guilds, the soldiers and the nobles and the whole province' rallied to him.[48] Once again, however, the effort was short-lived. Gaianus was arrested after a three month rule: Theodosius survived to become, in exile, like Timothy the Cat, one of the legendary figures of Egyptian Monophysitism.

The emperor Justin I, for all his enthusiasm for Chalcedonian orthodoxy, had been wise enough to leave the Alexandrian patriarchate in Monophysite hands. Timothy IV reigned unmolested nearly eighteen years until his death in February 535. The Egyptians whom in the autumn of 518 Severus of Antioch describes as 'stripping themselves for battle for their faith',[49] found themselves with no fight on their hands. Without any hindrance from Constantinople, Alexandria offered a refuge to Severus of Antioch, Julian of Halicarnassus, Isidore of Q'enneserim (Chalcis) and other Syrian leaders whom Justin had sent into exile. Though Severus established a sort of Monophysite 'Home Synod' in Alexandria his influence on Egyptian religious life seems to have been minimal, and was not directed towards fostering anti-imperial feeling in Egypt. He might distrust Justin and Justinian personally,[50] but the last question he would have asked would have been Donatus of Carthage's 'What has the emperor to do with the Church?'[51] He and his friends demanded the renunciation of the *Tome* of Leo and Chalcedon, but by imperial order. Imperial disinterest in religious matters was not a possibility that entered into their reckoning. In

---

[47] The vast controversial correspondence between Severus and Julian while both were in exile in Alexandria is now published by R. Hespel, in *CSCO* 104–5, 124–7 and 136 (1964, 1968 and 1971).

[48] Liberatus 20, 143.

[49] Severus, *The Sixth Book, Select Letters*, ed E. W. Brooks 5, 11, p 328.

[50] Note Severus' reported comment on Justinian's religious policy before he left for Constantinople in 534/5, 'Don't be deceived. In the lifetime of these emperors no means of peace will be found, but so that I do not hinder or oppose it, I will go, though with heartsearchings. I will return without anything accomplished'. From John of Ephesus, *Lives of Five Patriarchs*, ed E. W. Brooks, PO18 (1854) p 687.

[51] Optatus of Milevis, *De Schismate Donatistarum* ed C. Ziwsa, *CSEL*, 26 (1923) 3, 3.

Alexandria, too, so long as the pro-Monophysite Anthimus remained patriarch of Constantinople (535–6) Theodosius remained in communion with him. Harmony between the patriarchates and especially between Constantinople and Alexandria was in the natural order of affairs.[52]

For Egypt the decisive move towards an independent religious self-identity was the restoration of a Chalcedonian patriarchal succession by Justinian in 537/8 in the person of Paul the Tabennesiot. By the end of 537 the papal legate at Constantinople, Pelagius, had won the ear of the emperor with the result that Justinian committed himself to an even more strongly Rome-oriented religious policy than previously. This included an attempt to put the clock back half a century in Egypt and restore a Chalcedonian patriarch to Alexandria. The choice of a Pachomian monk belonging to the traditional opposition to Dioscorus I underlined this aspect of his policy. Perhaps to emphasise also the superiority of Constantinople over Alexandria, Paul was consecrated in the capital by the patriarch Menas. Justinian's policy, however, received a setback in 540 through the actions of Paul himself. He was unworthy of his high office, was implicated in the murder of his archdeacon, and was deposed. From now on, the emperors seem invariably to have chosen a non-Egyptian as patriarch of Alexandria. This need not of itself have proved fatal to a policy directed towards winning Egyptian loyalty to Chalcedon. In 587 the Monophysites were to consecrate a Syrian, Damian, as their patriarch. Coupled, however, with the civil authority often entrusted to the patriarch and the military or official background of a high proportion of the imperial nominees, it became easy for Chalceondianism to be identified with the dominance of the capital in Egyptian ecclesiastical affairs, sustained by a narrow range of official and Greek-speaking society centred in Alexandria. Differences between Alexandria and the remainder of Egypt, always latent, were brought into the open once more and associated with a wider issue of the ecclesiastical dominance of the emperor's creed in Egypt.

In the event, Chalcedon enjoyed a good deal more support than is generally recognised. The emperors appointed a succession of able and energetic men as patriarchs, and two of these, Apollinaris

[52] Note the friendly tone of the synodical letters exchanged between Anthimus and Theodosius in 535/6. Reproduced in Michael the Syrian, 9, 25.

(551–70) and John the Almsgiver (611–19) were outstanding. While making the most of possessing the main churches in Alexandria they built up congregations in some of the larger mainly Greek-speaking centres of population such as Antinoë and Rhinoclura near the Palestinian border,[53] and also in some rural areas in the Delta.[54] In Cyrenaica too, they may have had success, for the sixth century churches there that have been excavated give no hint of Coptic Monophysite influence.[55] Their plan and the motifs used in their mosaics are no different from those of orthodox churches in other parts of the Mediterranean and notably in those of the Greek islands. At the same time, the organised opposition to Chalcedon was weak. From his place of exile outside Constantinople, the patriarch Theodosius recognised that the situation in Egypt was one of 'difficulties and persecutions', and he 'sighed and wept' because the Alexandrians had the reputation of always acquiescing in the orders of the emperor.[56] Commenting of the same period, Michael the Syrian affirms that Alexandria 'had been cast into the heresy of the Diphysites' (that is, Chalcedonian orthodoxy).[57] This was 'because they loved pomp and honour'. Their chauvinism and vanity therefore, could favour either closer ties with Byzantium or separatism according to circumstances. At the end of Justinian's reign there were only four or five non-Chalcedonian bishops in Egypt of whom only the redoubtable Theodore of Philae (consecrated c524 and died 577) was a man of any stature.

Despite this discouraging situation there were other factors working in their favour. These were steadily drawing the mass of the inhabitants of Egypt into a Coptic church which began to find itself separated irrevocably from that of the emperor. First, there was the creation of a separate Monophysite hierarchy in the 530s. This had come about as a direct result of Justin I's abrogation of the *Henotikon* and persecution of clergy who would not accept the ending of the Acacian Schism in 519. Very gradually the dissenting

---

[53] On the distribution of Chalcedonian strength in Egypt at the end of the sixth century see [E. R.] Hardy, [*Christian Egypt: Church and people* (New York/Oxford 1952)] p 163.

[54] For Chalcedonian communities in the Delta in the seventh century see *History of the Patriarchs*, 1, cap 15, ed B. Evetts, *PO* 5 (1910) pp 18–19.

[55] See R. G. Goodchild's assessment of the situation in Cyrenaica in 'Byzantines, Berbers and Arabs in 7th century Libya, *Antiquity* 41 (1967) pp 119–122.

[56] *History of the Patriarchs*, 1, cap 13 p 467.

[57] Michael the Syrian, 9, 29, pp 243–4.

leaders, with the exiled Severus of Antioch at their head, concluded
that they would have to establish their own 'orthodox' hierarchy if
their adherents were to receive a truly valid Eucharist.[58] By 530 the
first Monophysite priests had been ordained, followed in 536 by the
ordination of the first bishops, and then from 542 onwards by the
great missionary journeys of John Bar'adai resulting in the establishment of a Jacobite church with its own hierarchy in Syria and
elsewhere in the east Roman empire. Egypt did not stand outside
this movement although the patriarch Theodosius was as reluctant
to establish an opposition hierarchy as were the other Monophysite
leaders. The establishment, however, of a Chalcedonian episcopate
after 538 only emphasised the need for the creation of an episcopate
devoted to Cyrilline orthodoxy and untainted by acceptance of
Chalcedon. By the end of Justinian's reign, Theodosius had
consecrated twelve bishops for Egypt. Though these never took up
their appointments the pattern had been set for the establishment of
a Monophysite hierarchy by the patriarch Peter in 576. In his single
year as a patriarch, Peter consecrated no less than seventy bishops[59]
thus creating a hierarchy that was both Coptic and Monophysite.
The identity of the two may be said to date from this time. In
addition the custom in Egypt for centuries had been for the
suffragan bishops to render complete obedience to the bishop of
Alexandria, Peter's action made the separation between two organised churches in Egypt final.

A second factor that consolidated religious opinion in Egypt in
favour of a separate Coptic Monophysite church was the steady
increase in the power and wealth of the monasteries and their
growing influence in every aspect of the life of the people. From the
middle of the fourth century onwards the monasteries had indeed
been a powerful factor in Egyptian rural life. In the fifth century
Shenute's White Monastery served a wide area as a centre for a
variety of social and charitable services, and above all, as a refuge
from the invading Blemmyes from the south.[60] In the sixth century
one finds evidence that in addition, many monasteries and churches
had become great landowners and the farmers on their lands had

[58] For Severus' motives in permitting ordinations for a separate 'orthodox' (Monophysite) hierarchy, see John of Ephesus, *Lives of the Eastern Saints* (Life of John of
Tella), ed E. W. Brooks, *Patrologia Orientalis, PO* 18 (1923) pp. 516-18.
[59] John of Epherus *HE* ed E. W. Brooks, 3, 4.12. Peter died in January 578.
[60] Shenute, *Sermo* 22, 3, ed H. Wiesmann (Paris 1931) *CSCO, SC*, 2, 4, p 39.

fallen into a relation of dependence upon them. For instance, in 528 agents of the church of Oxyrhynchus record the issue of machinery to their tenants in the same form as secular proprietors used. The 'most reverend Philo, presbyter and catholic steward' issued an axle to the registered labourer Pseeis through the agency of the monk Luke.[61] The *history of the Patriarchs* recounting the situation at the end of the sixth century, says that near Alexandria 'there were six hundred flourishing monasteries, all of them inhabited by the orthodox (that is, the Monophysites) and their cultivators who "all held the true faith." '[62] The situation in Egypt seems reminiscent of that which had developed at this time in northern Syria in which dependence on the monastery was a powerful factor in influencing the religious allegiance of the people. In addition, from 576 onwards the Egyptians also had an episcopate consecrated by the Monophysite patriarch of Alexandria, independent of the Chalcedonians. Its presence added to the already self-conscious religious identity of the Copts. It is interesting that at this period Coptic bishops, such as John of Hermopolis (Smin) c600, were praising Egypt as the home of monasticism and criticising the appearance of non-Egyptian saints on the calendar.[63] This is one of the rare pieces of evidence for Coptic Monophysites thinking of themselves in national terms, during the period of Byzantine rule. It is not difficult to imagine that when the Chalcedonian patriarch was living in Alexandria with all the trapping of state power, and rivals as influential as Peter IV (576–8) and Damian (579–604) had to be content with dwelling in the semi-obscurity of a monastery outside the city[64], the adherents of the two communities should regard themselves in terms of belonging to Melkite and 'imperial' or Coptic and 'national' churches.

Until the misconceived effort of Heraclius to find in Monoenergism a universally acceptable religious compromise, there is little to show that the sense of religious identity among the Copts coincided with hostility to the empire. Rather, the contrary seems to have been the case. Where any evidence exists, as from the late sixth

---

[61] *Oxyrhynchus Papyrus* 1900. See Hardy, p 165.
[62] *History of the Patriarchs*, I, cap 14, p 472.
[63] See [C. Detlef G.] Müller, ['Die Koptische Kirche zwischen Chalkedon und dem Arabereinmarsch'], *ZKG*, 4 series, 13 (1964) pp 271–308, at p 295.
[64] *History of the Patriarchs*, I, cap 14, p 472. The patriarch Peter IV (576–8) resided at the Enaton monastery.

century records from the village of Aphrodite in Upper Egypt in the reign of Justin II, the local people were always ready to make the arrival of the imperial images an occasion for rejoicing and even celebration in execrable Greek verse.[65] The embittered disputes between the Monophysite hierarchies in Egypt and Syria which led to schism lasting from 587/616 shows also that the Monophysite church in Egypt had other objects of hostility than the emperor and his officials. The latter, indeed, were more tactful than usually credited, sometimes silently accepting the Monophysite bishops as orthodox, such as Apa Abraham the monk of Phoibammon and bishop of Hermouthis in Upper Egypt, c600.[66]

It took a rare combination of events for the Copts to prefer Arab to Byzantine rule. One effect of the chaotic conditions produced by the usurpation of Phocas in 602 had been to draw the Copts and Chalcedonians together. John the Faster, the Chalcedonian patriarch from 611–19, achieved a lasting reputation for shrewd but open-handed charity and on his death became a saint in the Coptic calendar. Niketas, Heraclius' representative in Egypt from 609 who led the campaign against Phocas's partisans, was also trusted by the Copts, and was largely instrumental in healing the schism between them and the Syrian Monophysites in 616.[67] Though the swift success of the Persians may have undermined Egyptian confidence in the Byzantines, the invaders received no help from the Copts. The treachery that resulted in the fall of Alexandria in 620/1 was the work of a Persian merchant resident in the city and not that of a disgruntled Egyptian.[68] Indeed, the Copts seem to have regarded the Persians with horror, as forerunners of anti-Christ and the like, but significantly their presence was also accepted as the will of God.[69] There was all the more reason to accept the Arabs likewise.

The events which led the downfall of the Byzantine power in Egypt are well known. The stupendous character of Heraclius's victory over the Persians in 628–9 gave him a final opportunity of solving the religious issues that had plagued the empire since Chalcedon. Monoenergism provided just a chance of success, but the

[65] See H. I. Bell, 'An Egyptian Village in the Age of Justinian', *Journal of Hellenic Studies*, 64 (London 1944) pp 21–36.
[66] See Müller, p 284.
[67] Michael the Syrian, 10, 26, pp 385–6.
[68] *Chronicon Edessenum*, ed I. Guidi (Paris 1903) CSCO 3, 4, p 22.
[69] Pisentios, cited from E. Amélineau, *Vie d'un évêque de Keft au VIIe siècle*, 'Etude sur le christianisme en Egypte au Vii, siècle' (Paris 1887) p 30.

emperor's doctrine required the utmost skill and tact in explaining it to the Monophysite populations of Syria and Egypt. In Syria he very nearly succeeded, but in Egypt his choice of patriarch to combine the chief civil and religious power, Cyrus, former metropolitan of Lazica, could hardly have been less fortunate. Cyrus, though possessing great energy, was also ruthless, and a foreigner who was rightly suspected of concealed Chalcedonian leanings.[70] Distrust between him and the Coptic patriarch, Benjamin (623–61/3) soon became complete and the result was a disaster for the empire. But even though the Copts in retrospect looked back to deliverance from the Byzantines at the hands of the Arab armies, it would be misleading to see in the events of 640–2 anything in the nature of a Coptic rising against Byzantium. Indeed, some Copts fought for the Byzantines, some remained neutral, while some aided the Arabs.[71] The text of a liturgical prayer dating probably from these times, has survived in a curious half-Greek form. 'We pray', it reads, 'for our benefit in order to wage war against them, [the Arabs] to subdue all that belongs to the enemy host. We pray on behalf of our citizens living among them, for our city, and all the cities, and our land and the villages and the common faith.'[72] The curious modernity of the petition found at Tebtunis hardly suggests enthusiasm for the invading host, but its author is unknown. It might even have been Cyrus himself!

To return to the monks of the monastery of Metras who sheltered patriarch Benjamin during the troubles of Cyrus's rule. It is clear that the persistent, nagging persecution associated with Cyrus had alienated finally the Monophysites from the Chalcedonians in Egypt. The attempt by this 'foreigner'—a 'Caucasian'—to impose Chalcedon 'by force or guile' had awoken the latent xenophobia among the Copts which others in the previous two centuries had found characteristic.[73] This was now directed against

[70] On the Coptic memories of Cyrus 'the Caucasian', see *History of the Patriarchs*, 1, cap 14, pp 491–2, and on his pro-Chalcedonian leanings despite his acceptance of the emperor's Monoenergist compromise, see his first letter to the patriarch Sergius of Constantinople, Mansi 11, col 561.

[71] For a graphic description of the utter confusion occasioned by the Arab invasions see the *Chronicle* of John of Nikiou, ed and Eng tr R. Charles, caps 118–119, written *c* 680. John regards the Arab invasion as a calamity, a judgment of God on Heraclius for perverting orthodoxy.

[72] See P. J. Photiades, 'A semi-Greek, semi-Coptic Parchment', *Klio* 4 (Athens 1963) pp 234–5.

[73] *History of the Patriarchs*, 1, Cap 14, pp 491–2.

both the religion of the emperor and his representative in Egypt. For the first time the emperor himself had become associated with Chalcedonian persecution, and this was perhaps a decisive factor in rendering permanent the rejection of Byzantium. What had nearly taken place in the last bitter stages of the Great Persecution now occurred. The great majority of the Egyptian people were totally alienated from the empire, and sufficient numbers of educated Greeks and Copts were prepared to maintain the administrative machine for the benefit of their new Arab masters. Given the choice they came to prefer the 'sons of Ishmael'. As the Nestorians in Persia or Monophysites in Syria, the Copts found it was easier to maintain an orthodox faith under a pagan ruler than under the emperor and the inquisitorial survey of Byzantium. By the seventh century loyalty to the doctrines of Cyril, whether understood or not, had become the hall-mark of Coptic national feeling. To this Byzantium, attempting always to conciliate Rome and maintain the fiction of universal rule, had no answer. Cyril and Leo did not '*teach alike*', and for the Copt the truth lay with Cyril of Alexandria.

University of Glasgow

COPTIC CHRISTIANITY IN A CHANGING
WORLD

by G. M. LEE

IN the year 619 the forces of Sassanid Persia crossed the Eyptian
border, and a long-lasting conquest, like that of the
Achaemenids of old, was to be feared. The bishop of Keft,
Pisentios, though an ascetic detached from worldly interests, did
not fail to take note of this critical development. He put the affairs
of his diocese in order and set out with a faithful disciple, John, to
the mountain of Gimi to pray. Although Keft (better known
perhaps as Coptos) had not yet been captured, we may wonder
why he did not stay with his flock at such an anxious moment and
pray with them.

In the life of Pisentios—edited by the Abbé E. Amélineau,[2] there
now follows a remarkable passage which reads almost as a farewell
to the ancient world. I know of nothing else quite like it in Coptic
literature.[3] The narrator is John:

> It happened one day that while my father [John always
> describes him so] was still with me on the mountain of Gimi
> he said to me, 'John, my son, rise and follow me; I will show
> you the place where I shall make my retreat, that you may visit
> me every Saturday and bring a little food and water to sustain
> me' . . . . . When we had walked some three miles, according
> to my reckoning, we came on a passage that had the appear-

---

[1] 'Probably in the spring of 619' according to N. H. Baynes, *CMH* 2 p 291.
[2] In *Étude sur le Christianisme en Égypte au Septième Siècle*. Paris 1887. For an account
of the Abbé Amélineau as the incompetent excavator of Abydo but a good copticist
see my paper in *SCH* 17. By a strange coincidence, on the day of completing this
paper I read in a book review that he 'deliberately destroyed some of his finds,
enhancing the value of what he preserved for his backers' (*The Times*, 30 May
1980). I reserve my opinion; so authoritative an Egyptologist as Sir Alan Gardiner
makes no such serious charge.
[3] Though the element of the macabre can be abundantly paralleled and might pass as
an Egyptian national trait. My translation of this extract is independent of the one
by Battiscombe Gunn in *Land of Enchanters*, ed Bernard Lewis (London 1948) pp 89
seq.

ance of a door wide open,[4] and, entering the precinct, we found it was like a sculptured rock, with six columns rising on top; it was 52 cubits wide, square in shape and of height to match, and in it were a great number of mummies . . . We took the coffins and piled them on one another. They were very broad, and the cases containing the bodies were richly ornamented. The fabric in which the first mummy, which lay near the door, had been buried was of silk fit for a king . . .

My father asked me 'How many years have these people been dead? And from what districts did they come?' I answered 'God knows'. He said to me 'Go, my son, and remain in your monastery. Watch out for yourself. This world is vanity. Every hour is an hour of parting . . .' I was about to go. I looked at one of the columns, and noticed a little roll of parchment. My father unfolded it and read it. He found inscribed there the names of all who had been embalmed in that place . . . 'You see these mummies' [he said]; 'such must we all be. Some of these folk, whose sins were many, are now in Amenti, others are in outer darkness, others in wells and pits filled with fire . . . others in the fiery river, having as yet been granted no rest. But some are in the place of rest owing to their good deeds. When man goes from this world, all that is past is past.'[5]

Amélineau sees here conclusive proof that the hieroglyphics, contrary to general opinion, could still be read at this late date. But we are not told that the writing was in hieroglyphics, and since there were evidently Christians among the dead—no pagan could possibly have been saved by 'good deeds'—we may be sure that it was in Coptic. The Copts, so far as I know, were without any fellow-feeling for their pagan forebears.

Later Pisentios talks with one of the mummies, a pagan woman who had never heard the name of Christ. She gives a harrowing account of her unmerited sufferings in the life beyond.

As we all know, the Persian threat amazingly evaporated thanks to Heraclius; but the same emperor lived to see another reversal of fortune as a deadlier enemy swallowed up his eastern provinces. When he died in 641, discredited with the church because of his

---

[4] I have translated literally, and Amélineau gives an equivalent sense, but the Coptic is uncommonly clumsy at this point.
[5] There is no doctrine of Purgatory.

uncanonical marriage to his niece Martina, the history of Egypt as an Arab country had begun.

Coptic writings that bear on life under the Crescent are few. A curious document purporting to be a contemporary account of the invasion of Egypt by Cambyses was probably aimed at fomenting a revolt against Arab rule. H. Ludin Jansen, however, in his edition,[6] argues that it is a pre-Christian historical romance revised in the interests of pro-Jewish propaganda. He lays stress on the lack of Christian influence. It would be impertinence for me to venture an opinion,[7] but at first sight I should have thought this was a concession to verisimilitude in a supposed monument of the fifth century BC. The beginning and end are missing and there are lacunae in what remains. It is a work of literary pretensions, and might be read with more pleasure if it were more intelligible.

More interesting though somewhat devoid of incident, is the life of Abba John Khame,[8] a gentle ascetic of a type that alternated in Egypt with such martinets (or worse) as Shenute and his successor Besa. (Even Pisentios, though relatively subdued, had an unkind way of calling a disciple *Gehazi* without much provocation.) The story of how John Khame persuaded his young bride to join with him in renouncing marriage for a life of celibacy—a favourite early Christian theme—is told with considerable grace.

But I want to devote the rest of this paper to the life of Isaac, patriarch of Alexandria from 686–9, which seems to me a jewel of Coptic literature. Less dramatic than the life of Pisentios and without its bizarre features, it is far more attractive, and its gracious hero seems, in spite of all differences of time and circumstance, a man curiously similar to cardinal Hume. This too has been edited by Amélineau.[9] There is a later edition by E. Porcher in the *Patrologia Orientalis*.[10] I will translate and paraphrase by turn:

'This saint, my brethren, was an Egyptian by race, of the district known as Pisho. His parents were very devout people, with great possessions and many serving men and women. When they had

[6] *The Coptic Story of Cambyses' Invasion of Egypt* (Oslo 1950).
[7] I should be afraid to differ from W. E. Crum 'Coptic Documents in Greek Script', *PBA* 25 (939) pp 249–71, who is decisive for a date under the Arabs.
[8] Edited by M. H. Davis, *PO* (1919).
[9] *Publications de l'École des Lettres d'Alger Bulletin de Correspondance Africaine* (Paris 1890).
[10] Paris 1914.

brought this holy child into the world, they called his name Isaac, the meaning of which is "joy."

At his baptism the bishop saw a cross of light over the infant's head . . . and he said to the parents "Take this child: he is a gift from God, for he will be a great high priest in the house of God, and will be entrusted with the care of many peoples." On hearing that, his parents lifted up their voices and said "May the name of the Lord be blest, from now on and for ever!"'

In due course the child was sent to school, where he made such progress that he was the wonder of all and his fellow-pupils deferred to him. He was then put under Meneson, a relative, who was chartularius to George, eparch in the land of Egypt, that he might become his notary, or secretary. [It will be observed that the Greek and Latin administrative titles, preserved in Coptic, were continued under Arab rule].

While he was in this place he exhibited the life of a monk. First of all he said the Psalms by heart. . .

Let us go back to Pisentios for a moment and see how that grim personage memorised the Psalms. 'It is said of him that, from the time he first became a monk, he set about learning the Psalter by heart . . . When the mountains were blazing in the sun, he went out in the heat of the day and stood upright in a part of the desert where no one could see him, and hung a big stone round his neck; he did not let it fall to the ground until he had recited the whole Psalter from memory . . . . His eyes were filled with blood as if they would burst from their sockets.'From the psalms he went on to the Minor Prophets, learning one a day—the day given to the twenty-one verses of Obadiah must have been almost a holiday—and the Minor Prophets themselves each came to hear the recital of his own portion and embraced Pisentios when he had done. We may assume that Isaac studied the Scriptures in a more normal way. He did, however, wear a hair shirt under a splendid robe.

'One day the governor' (presumably George the eparch) 'called for Meneson, who was the chief of his notaries. He had an important letter for him to write, but, as he could not be found, George immediately flew into a great rage. He called the boy Isaac. "Where is your master?" he asked. "I do not know," he answered. Then, seeing that his face was sad, he spoke to him as David spoke before the King of Israel: "Why is my lord's face sad? Say the word, and I will write the letter in the way you wish." The governor was astonished at his reply, and to test him said, "Go into one of these rooms: write this and bring it for me to see." He wrote it, and brought it for him to see. The governor looked at the letter that the boy had written and was amazed. "You are so gifted," he said, "and I did not know it until today . . ." and from that time forward he made him his chief notary . . .'¹¹

Soon after this George the eparch died, and Isaac resolved to abandon a wordly career. We now have one of those pathetic episodes in which the aspirant after sanctity is determined to leave his fond parents for ever in spite of their tears and entreaties. I remember, as a boy, reading Lecky's *European Morals* on this subject, so frequent in the literature of the early church, and being deeply affected. It almost seems as if the relationship between parents and children in antiquity had a tenderness often missing in modern times, when families drift apart and their members lose touch with one another.

'Now his parents looked on him as it were on a mirror, and hoped that he would become master of all their possessions. They wanted to find him a wife, hoping to see children born of him.' Isaac had other ambitions, but they arranged his betrothal by compulsion.

Isaac took refuge on the mountain of Scete, memorable in monastic history, and attached himself to the kindly priest and abbot Zacharias, who was to become bishop of Sais. Among those who joined him in the course of time was that same Meneson whose absence at a crucial moment had had such unexpected results. Isaac performed there many miracles of healing which his biographer has the restraint to leave undescribed.¹² There was great astonishment when a viper settled on his hand and he merely shook it off (like St Paul on the island of Malta) without suffering any harm. It is interesting to compare the more sensational life of Pisentios, who was himself stung by a scorpion and 'continued his meditations although the pain had penetrated to his heart'—until he was healed by divine intervention.

---

¹¹ This is difficult to explain. We cannot suppose that he allowed himself to be promoted over Meneson's head.
¹² There are some descriptions of healings at a later stage, after Isaac has become patriarch. One, the headling of the son of Athanasius, a court official who was working against him, is notable for the Christian spirit of forgiveness which it breathes and for the touching repentance of the grateful father.

One pleasing little miracle is worthy of mention. He went to keep his lenten retreat, and his brother monks forgot to bring him his pittance of bread. Days went by. It was the fifth day of his fast, when he saw before him a great slab of bread as if hot from the oven. He ate a small piece of this God-sent gift, and took the rest back to the monastery the next day, and gave it to the brethren, apparently without a word of reproach for their criminal forgetfulness.

Here is a picture of Isaac's dietary habits. 'Once Abba Abraham and Abba George, the great ascetics, paid him a visit, and exchanged ideas with him to their great profit. Now, on looking inside his cell, they saw nothing but a few loaves and a little salt, and they marvelled at his abstinence. They asked him "What do you eat these days, father?" "What the brethren eat," he replied. "But we see nothing except bread and salt." "That is what the brethren eat." They protested to him, saying "Should we bring you a few olives?" But he would not allow it and said" What I need is to suffer a little more hardship than the brethren" '[13]

Some time earlier he had been summoned to Alexandria by the patriarch, who wanted a clever man for his syncellus and notary and had heard of Isaac's accomplishments. He set him to write a letter, which Isaac deliberately did amiss, hoping to be left in his monastic seclusion. (It is clear that calligraphy, a favourite art of the Copts, was his special skill.) But the patriarch was not deceived. He pretended to be pleased with Isaac's effort, and warned him that there was no escape. Nevertheless, after many entreaties, Isaac secured permission to work only one month a year for the patriarch, drawing up the list of festivals, and to pass the rest of his time in the desert which he loved.

The years went by and Isaac himself was elected patriarch of the Egyptian capital. There was a rival candidate, another George, a squalid intriguer who turned out to be a married man with evil-living children. To these disadvantages he added the sin of simony, so that he was ignominiously rejected.

As patriarch, he was in high favour with the Arab ruler Abd-el-Aziz. The saint's biography is full of biblical echoes, and this part is clearly influenced by the lovely old story of Joseph. Once or twice,

[13] I am not sure that Amélineau's comment, 'On peut voir par cela que les grandes abstinences du temps passé avaient cessé avec la ferveur' is altogether justified. There were doubtless at all times varying degrees of asceticism.

through the intrigues of mischief-makers, he came near to losing his life, but each time he was able to recover the potentate's respect and affection.

The Abbé Amélineau deserves our gratitude for making this Coptic masterpiece available to the world. I have been able to convey only a very imperfect view of it, but I hope at least that its thoroughly Egyptian spirit stands clearly revealed: not the fierce, fanatical Egyptian spirit so often apparent in the history of the Christological controversies, but the spirit of those desert fathers whose humility and whose charity Helen Waddell fragrantly portrayed. And if I had to find a suitable motto for the hero of our tale I think I would choose the one which P. S. Allen provided for a very different man, the German humanist Beatus Rhenanus, when he compared him, in the words of the psalmist, to 'a tree planted by the waterside that will bring forth his fruit in due season.'

Bedford

CULTURAL CONFLICTS IN THE MISSIONS
OF SAINT BONIFACE

by DAVID KEEP

A PASSING comment from a visitor from Fulda to the thirteen hundredth anniversary celebrations for the birth of Boniface at Crediton on 5 June 1980 aptly sums up the purpose of this paper. He observed that without the work of Boniface there could have been no Bismarck. Thus in a sense the Wessex missionary who was so much more a papal legate than an evengelist laid the foundation for the third as well as the second Reich when he consecrated Pepin III king of the Franks in 751. Whether like John Foxe 'we find of him in stories, that he was a great setter-up and upholder of such blind superstition, and of all popery' or like his latest biographer we consider that 'a devotion and a perseverence equal to that which he so nobly exhibited will be needed if our fragmented Church is to become that one true family which the Saviour himself desired it to be',[1] there is no doubt that he worked for a supranational rather than an intertribal ideal. He has as much claim as Benedict to be the patron saint of a united Europe since it was his work which inspired the imperial decrees of 743, 754 and 757 which made the Rule obligatory.[2] Christopher Dawson's judgement that he was 'the greatest Englishman' is based more on his subtle blending of Frankish with papal influence over the Saxons and his diplomatic regularisation of the Frankish church. As a missionary he is one of a noble line of Celts, Angles and Saxons who converted the heathen. This tradition inspired his original visit to Radbod of Frisia in 716 and his work with Willibrord 719–21. It underlay all his work in Germany and led to his final journey north and his death at Dokkum on 5 June in 754 or

---

[1] [*The Acts and Monuments of John Foxe*], ed Josiah Pratt, 8 vols (London) 1, p 368; [John Cyril] Sladden [*Boniface of Devon Apostle of Germany*] (Exeter 1980) p 217.

[2] David Hugh Farmer, *The Oxford Dictionary of Saints* (Oxford 1978) p 36. The relationship between Boniface and the Rule of St Benedict is discussed by Christopher Holdsworth in 'Saint Boniface the Monk,' in *The Greatest Englishman* [*Essays on St Boniface and the Church at Credition*], ed Timothy Reuter] (Exeter 1980) pp 55–7, 60–64.

755. Reuter argues that it would be false to distinguish the papal reformer from the missionary:

> Boniface's work was done in lands either controlled by or under the influence of Christian rulers. The existence of pagans in those lands was one of many offences against the right order of things, a serious one it is true, but not qualitatively different from other breaches of order. What Boniface was concerned to do was not simply to bring Christianity to those who had never heard of it, but by example, by legislation, and by enlisting the support of those who held power, to see that the Christianity practised by all was brought nearer to the *canonica rectitudo,* canonical rightness.[3]

In his struggle for that canonical rightness Boniface faced problems which arose from the national customs of the conglomeration of tribes which came under or bordered on the Franks. These were of three kinds. Two of these were closely linked so far as the theme of these papers is concerned. A strong sense of tribal identity helped to preserve pagan practices and continue to revive them among that vast majority who lived outside cities. This same sense of local loyalty focussed on the itinerant celtic evangelist and on the localised form of christianity which some of these produced. Boniface stood for orthodoxy. His third problem was to identify exactly what this was. The conflicting interpretations of the implications of canon law themselves depended on distinct national traditions. The relationship between paganism and national identity may be clearly seen in the description by Willibald, Boniface's earliest biographer, of the English monk's first visit to the Netherlands.

> But a fierce quarrel which broke out between prince Charles, the noble duke of the Franks, and Radbod, the king of the Frisians, as a result of a hostile incursion by the pagans, caused great disturbances among the population of both sides, and through the dispersion of the priests and the persecution of Radbod the greater part of the Christian churches, which had previously been subject to the Frankish empire, were laid waste and brought to ruin. Moreover, the pagan shrines were rebuilt and, what is worse, the worship of idols was restored.[4]

---

[3] Timothy Reuter, 'Saint Boniface and Europe', *The Greatest Englishman* p 80.
[4] C. H. Talbot, *The Anglo-Saxon Missionaries in Germany* (London 1954) p 35.

It is quite clear from this that churches were the agencies of Frankish imperialism. Although Winfrith and his companions failed to draw Radbod from the faith of his fathers, the party of Wessex monks were allowed to travel round the country unharmed. Willibrord was able to resume his mission from Utrecht, from 719–21 with the help of Boniface. By 754 when Boniface returned to his mission field paganism only survived in the watery north. Even then his murderers seem to have been moved by greed rather than loyalty to the old religion—as indeed was the force who so quickly and violently took revenge in the name of Christianity. This is clear even in Willibald's pious account of a reign of terror:

> So the Christians, after taking as their spoil the wives and children, men and maidservants of the pagan worshippers, returned to their homes. As a result the pagans round about, dismayed at their recent misfortune and seeking to avoid everlasting punishment, opened their minds and hearts to the glory of the faith. Struck with terror at the visitation of God's vengeance, they embraced after Boniface's death the teaching they had rejected whilst he still lived.[5]

It is impossible to investigate the nature of this kind of conflict, but not unrealistic to compare it with conflicts between the clans in the eighteenth century Highlands and between tribes in the new nations of Africa today.

Boniface's second great conflict with pure paganism was in his missionary work among the Saxons. His function here was 'to make a report on the savage peoples of Germany'.[6] From Willibald's account it is clear that he visited churches already established in Thuringia and in Frisia and helped to spread the gospel. He put his experience in Frisia to good use when he converted the twins Dettic and Deurrulf and built his first church at Amöneburg. On his return to Rome in 722 he was given a roving episcopate. He returned to Hesse and cut down the famous oak at Geismar. Willibald's description confirms Tacitus's account of Saxon sacrifice and divination. Boniface succeeded because he had desecrated the sacred grove unharmed. As so often happened, a Christian church was built on the pagan shrine. Sturm may well have been

---

[5] *Ibid* p 58.
[6] *Ibid* p 39.

'guided' by some similar tradition when he identified the site for the new monastery at Fulda in 'the frightful wilderness'. The high-place had been fortified by the Merovingians, even if it was not a sacred spot in its own right.[7] German monasticism flourished in the countryside in contrast to the more latinised urban christianity of Gaul.

It would be wrong to suggest that paganism was strong only on the rural marches of the Roman empire. The instinctive puritanism of the Germans which Tacitus praised was both shocked and attracted by the new-year revels which persisted in Rome. Boniface wrote to pope Zacharias on his accession in 742 on the reports of 'ignorant common people':

> They say that on the first day of January year after year, in the city of Rome and in the neighbourhood of St. Peter's church by day or by night, they have seen bands of singers parading the streets in pagan fashion, shouting and chanting sacrilegious songs and loading tables with food by day and night, while no one in his own house is willing to lend his neighbour fire or tools or any other convenience. They say also that they have seen women with amulets and bracelets of heathen fashion on their arms and legs, offering them for sale to willing buyers.

In the same year the Frankish synod condemned 'sacrifices to the dead, casting of lots, divinations, amulets and auguries.[8]' The later legend which arose round the cult of Boniface that the first christmas tree sprang from the roots of Thor's oak suggests the survival of a midwinter custom. Many of our modern christmas customs have their origin in local pre-christian midwinter fes-tivities. The church was unable to suppress them, so found it more expedient to blend them subtly into its cult. The second and more serious cultural conflict faced by Boniface was the variety of Christian belief and discipline in the lax Merovingian churches. He had seen this as a boy in the survival of the Celtic community at Exeter. Bishops were already effectively the secular rulers of cities and episcopal office was regarded as a right by the ruling families. Their duties were sometimes carried out by chorepiscopi, and at

---

[7] *Ibid* pp 186–7; Sladden pp 158–9.
[8] Letters 50 and 56, [*The Letters of Saint Boniface* trans Ephraim] Emerton (New York 1940) pp 81–2, 92. Reuter in a footnote commented 'feasts in honour of the dead helped to strengthen the solidarity of kin-groups' as evidence for the co-existence of paganism with Christianity, *The Greatest Englishman* pp 90, 76.

other times neglected altogether. There was in any case no universal code of canon Law. When Boniface was consecrated as bishop for Germany on St Andrew's day 722 he was given a law book. This may have been the *corpus* of the sixth century monk Dionysius Exiguus. Apart from this, he had letters from the popes and from fellow-bishops advising him about proper custom. After his elevation to archbishop in 732, with these tools and by the authority of the Frankish rulers he set up ideal episcopal systems for Bavaria and Hesse-Thuringia and tried to do the same for Gaul.[9] As in the north of England, the papal plans were never carried out and Rouen remained supreme while Boniface had to make do with Mainz rather than the ancient centre of Cologne. He only obtained this after a series of pastoral conflicts which culminated in the deposition of Gewlib of Mainz for killing his father's murderer. The church fought long and unsuccessfully against priests bearing arms. In this case Boniface had the help of Carloman in enforcing the papal decrees of 743. His two synods established papal discipline over Austrasia, while a further meeting, probably at Soissons in 744, did the same for Neustria and paved the way for ecclesiastical and political union under Pepin. Full order was never achieved, and Zacharias in his last letter commiserated over the difficulties caused by Milo the bishop of Trier and Rheims.[10]

Some hint of the extent of heterodox belief and practice may be gained from the two well-documented cases which Boniface transferred to Rome in 745. As Boniface could not attend in person he wrote at length. His request that the two should be imprisoned for life was sent by the hand of the priest Denehard. The two dissident priests Adalbert, or Aldebert, and Clemens were quite different. Aldebert was a prophet who claimed to have had a vision of an angel. This experience he shared with Gideon, Joseph, Peter, Mahomet and Joseph Smith, to say nothing of the monk of Wenlock who was transported to paradise.[11] Aldebert had bribed his way to ordination and then set up his own church and a cult in his own name. Boniface wrote:

[9] Ideal since he incorporated honorary new sees at Büraburg and Erfurt into Mainz. *The Greatest Englishman* p 79, 90 n 51.
[10] Letters 51, 56 and 87. Emerton pp 84, 92, 162. Sladden deals in detail with the events of the Frankish synods and provides valuable suggestions about the Anglo-Saxon synod of 746 and the Frankish synod of 747 in his appendices pp 223–9.
[11] Letter 10, Emerton pp 25–31.

He set crosses and small oratories in the fields or at springs or wherever he pleased and ordered public prayers to be said there until multitudes of people, scorning other bishops and deserting the established churches held their celebrations in such places saying: 'The merits of St. Aldebert will help us.' He distributed his own fingernails and hairs from his head to be honoured (as sacred objects) and carried about with the relics of St. Peter, prince of the Apostles.

Aldebert had obvious charisma and was extremely popular. There have been countless similar personality cults, especially since the proclamation of religious toleration in the United States. With the Scot Clemens nonconformists who developed their doctrine through the Age of Reason will have even more sympathy. This is how Boniface presented his errors:

The other heretic, whose name is Clemens, argues against the Catholic Church, denies and contradicts the canons of the churches of Christ, and rejects the writings and teachings of the holy fathers, Jerome, Augustine, and Gregory. Despising the decrees of the councils, he declares according to his own interpretation that he has a right to be a bishop under Christian law even though he had two children born in adultery after he had been called by that title. Reviving the Jewish law, he maintains that it is right for a Christian, if he so please, to marry his brother's widow. Contrary to the teaching of the holy fathers he contends that Christ, descending to the lower world, set free all who were imprisoned there, believers and unbelievers, those who praised God and the worshippers of idols. And many other horrible things concerning God's predestination he sets forth contrary to the catholic faith. Wherefore I beg you to send your written order to duke Karlmann that this heretic also may be put in custody, so that he may no longer spread abroad the seed of Satan, lest perchance the whole flock be contaminated by one unsound sheep.[12]

This is the logical position of any body which demands orthodoxy in doctrine. In the end, heresy must be stopped. Clemens was condemned for teaching the authority of scripture and a form of universalism, but it does not matter what the form of the local

[12] Letter 59, *ibid* pp 101–2.

difference was. The church was fighting for universal order. After three days of hearings both were condemned by the pope. Aldebert for praying to angels, whom Zacharias on rather esoteric grounds declared to be demons, and Clemens for rejecting the fathers and the decrees of councils. Their writings were burned. The imprisonment of the unfrocked priests was left to the secular ruler. Excommunication has never proved effective enough to suppress schism on its own, but the church had not achieved that degree of authority which enabled it to run its own prisons. Aldebert and Clemens were the most prominent problems in the lax Merovingian church. The pope, like Boniface and his companions, was a monk. As in the orthodox churches today, celibacy was not required of parish priests until Gregory VII in the eleventh century. Although the synod of 742 had forbidden priests to live in the same house as a woman, celibacy for secular clergy was not achieved until the Council of Trent. The instructions which Gregory II had given to Boniface on 1 December 722 were more realistic:

> He shall not admit to the sacred office one who has married a second time, or who had married a woman not a virgin, or who is illiterate, or is defective in any part of his body, or is under penance or court order, or is known to be subject to any liability. If he shall find any such persons already in office he shall not advance them. Africans who dare to apply for admission to ecclesiastical orders he may not accept upon any terms whatsoever; some of these are Manichaeans and others have often been shown to be rebaptized.[13]

These African refugees from Islam are an intriguing minor cultural conflict. We do not know how many had fled to Thuringia: probably they were more of a problem in Italy. They seem to have been regarded as responsible for the failure of the church to resist the Arabs. The pope showed a more realistic approach when he wrote to Boniface four years later that he was not to abstain from eating with vicious clergy and chieftains: 'It often happens that those who are slow in coming to a perception of the truth under strict discipline may be led into the paths of righteousness by the influence of their table companions and by gentle admonition.'[14] The situation in the Frankish empire was very confusing. When

[13] Letter 18, *ibid* p 43.
[14] Letter 26, *ibid* p 55.

Gregory III sent the pallium to Boniface in 732 he ordered rebaptism for those who had not been baptised in the name of the Trinity. He did not advise how Boniface was to discover the form used by the quasi-gnostics and semi-pagans who seem to have staffed the Frankish parishes. He was allowed to accept those who had made grammatical, rather than theological, errors in their Latin!

The papal discipline which the newly consecrated rulers of the Franks enforced was in complete contrast to the spontaneity of the celtic churches which had flourished on the mainland of Europe. The new Empire which the church was instrumental in founding in the west by the strength of the Frankish army was more extensive than the old had been, and was to embrace some of the Slav tribes as well as the Saxons and Vikings. This control was achieved by the extension of the common form of church order through the use of the chrism and the metropolitan pallium being made customary. The pope was attempting to forge an intertribal identity in Europe. He appeared to be most successful in Britain and Germany, the two mission fields which were developed by bishops under his direct care, but these were the very areas where protestantism was able to build on ancient loyalties and secede from Rome. The French church, or perhaps more accurately the French kings, usually steered an independent line and kept firmly in mind that it was French arms which protected the pope for over a thousand years. Loyalty to Rome was strongest in the lands threatened by Islam or orthodoxy. Thus the attempt of Willibrord and Boniface to enforce an international form of religion was successful within the short and medium term. The third conflict of culture faced by Boniface was in the understanding of the Christian discipline itself. There was the persistent question already referred to of whether celibacy was to be required of secular priests. There were the problems of ceremonies carried out wrongly or by improper clerics. In these Boniface had to balance the theoretical ideal with the realities of vast understaffed parishes. He had no difficulty in rebuking king Ethelbald of Mercia for his infamous practice of seducing nuns and refraining from marriage.[16] On one issue he himself came into conflict with a papal ruling. Three letters taken to England by the

[15] Letters 91, 80, 56, 78, *ibid* pp 168, 144–5, 93, 140–1.
[16] Letter 73, *ibid* pp 124–30.

priest Eoban in 735 describe Boniface's problems in detail. He had followed the rules laid down in the replies of Gregory I to Augustine which are quoted by Bede.[17] These he must have learned of while he was a monk at Nursling. They permit a marriage between Christians related in the third degree, Gregory III had instructed Boniface to keep believers from marrying to the seventh degree in his letter which accompanied the pallium in 732. To guide his judgement, Boniface wrote to archbishop Nothelm of Canterbury for a copy of the replies to Augustine as no record of these could be traced at Rome. In the same letter and in those sent to Pethelm bishop of Whithorn and to a former pupil, otherwise unknown, the abbot Duddo, he sought advice on an even more subtle sin of which he had been accused.

> The priests throughout Gaul and Frankland maintain that for them a man who takes a widow, to whose child he has acted as godfather, is guilty of a very serious crime. As to the nature of this sin, if it is a sin, I was entirely ignorant, not have I ever seen it mentioned by the fathers, in the ancient canons, nor in the decrees of popes, nor by the Apostles in their catalogue of sins.[18]

This was a case where the Code of Justinian was in conflict with Germanic and indeed the law of Moses where marriage to a brother's widow was obligatory.[19] This is a very crucial issue within sexual ethics where a line had to be drawn between behaviour which was taboo and virtuous Christian marriage. Boniface observed that all baptised Christians are brothers and sisters, and were hence to some extent related. We do not know whether he carried out the papal ruling that divorce was essential in the case of the man married to his godson's mother. It is clear that he was not in sympathy with Rome's instructions.

On another issue in which Boniface as a good Englishman must have sympathised with the pope, he had been totally unsuccessful. In the same letter of 732 Gregory had commented:

> You say, among other things, that some have the habit of eating wild horses and very many eat tame horses. This, holy brother, you are in no wise to permit in future but are to

---

[17] Bede, *A History of the English Church and People*, trans Leo Shirley-Price (London 1955) pp 71–83.
[18] Letters 32–4, Emerton pp 61–4.
[19] Gen. 38: 8–10; Deut. 25:5–10.

suppress it in every possible way, with the help of Christ, and impose suitable penance upon the offenders. It is a filthy and abominable practice.[20]

Zacharias repeated the prohibitions based on Leviticus 11 in 751, but this part of the Jewish law was treated as ceremonial and so superceded long before Luther!

If the church was unable to change diet, it was equally able to do little in the economics of slavery. Modern selections overlook the sad letter from Berthwald the archbishop of Canterbury asking for there the bishop of Sherborne to try to release a Kentish slave girl from the abbot of Glastonbury for the very large ransom of three hundred shillings.[22] Some christians had sold slaves for human sacrifice. Zacharias tried to ban the sale of any Christian slaves to pagans. No slave could be ordained. The church of the eighth century was struggling to reintroduce the morality of the first so far as the institution of slavery was concerned. Indeed the sad thing about legislation on slavery is that there is a remarkable unanimity of custom among the European tribes. I came to the study of the eighth century as a relative stranger and find there the roots of the national consciousness which reasserted itself at the reformation and in the nineteenth-century nation-state. The quarrels within protestantism were as much due to local loyalties as to doctrinal differences while the rivalry between Austrasia and Neustria underlies two hundred years of wars across the Rhine. Even today a spurious sense of local independence can win quite considerable support for nationalist parties in western democracies. In the same vein, the eight-century popes and Frankish major-domos might be accused of a neo-imperialism as they tried to re-establish the provinces and dioceses of Rome. Boniface and his companions did not see their work in this light. They fought against paganism and against evil and corruption inside the church. Much of their effort went into quelling the venial sins of the clergy[24] and in trying to discern the divine purpose for the Christian society. They sought a universal brotherhood in the *una sancta catholica et apostolica ecclesia.*

[20] Letter 57, Emerton p 58.
[21] Letter 87, *ibid* p 161.
[22] Letter 7. G. F. Browne *Boniface of Crediton and his companions* (London 1910) pp 294–5.
[23] Letters 83, Emerton p 154.
[24] Letters 50, 73, 80, 91, *ibid* pp 80, 128, 144–5 168.

Their pursuit of goodness coincided with the Frankish rulers' pursuit of power. The liberal finds their work offensive because they would allow neither doctrinal nor ethical individualism. As Paul had taught, Christ was to break down the barriers between nations. In the work of St Boniface it almost succeeded but its very success left unresolved conflicts for the two thrones in Europe.

Rolle College, Exmouth.

THE 'ARCHBISHOPRIC' OF DOL AND THE ECCLESIASTICAL POLITICS OF NINTH-CENTURY BRITTANY

JULIA M. H. SMITH

IN THE history of the invasions which marked the end of the Roman empire in the west, the Armorican peninsula of north-western Gaul holds a distinctive place. It witnessed the only substantial settlements by people whose homeland lay within the Roman empire, and who had been subject to Roman civil government for several centuries. These settlers crossed the English Channel probably between the late fourth and early seventh centuries. Establishing new communities in the sparsely populated areas of western Armorica, they brought with them their own language, social patterns and Christian organisation, and a strong sense of affinity with the Celts of Wales and Cornwall from whom they derived.[1] Whilst the Britons were establishing themselves as Bretons, the Franks were asserting their hold over the remainder of northern Gaul. A few of them settled in the eastern approaches to the peninsula, in the Roman *civitates* of Rennes and Nantes. Culturally and politically, only this part of Armorica was attached to Merovingian Gaul, having as its kings the descendants of Clovis, and as its bishops members of the Gallo-Roman aristocracy.[2]

The distinction between Celtic west and Gallo-Frankish east is a

---

[1] The controversies and uncertainties surrounding the Breton migrations are conveniently summarised by L. Musset, *The Germanic Invasions* (London 1975) pp 112–15, 236–7. The linguistic and place-name evidence for which areas of Armorica were settled by the Bretons is set out by K. H. Jackson, *A Historical Phonology of Breton* (Dublin 1967) pp 21–33.

[2] W. C. McDermott, 'Felix of Nantes: a Merovingian bishop' *Traditio* 31 (New York 1975) pp 1–24. Merovingian political interest in eastern Armorica is clear from Gregory of Tours, *Historia Francorum* IV.4, 20, V.16, 26, 29, 31, IX.18, X.9 (*MGH SRM* 1 pp 143–4, 157–8, 207, 221, 223, 224, 372, 416–18).The archaeological evidence for Frankish presence in the eastern fringes of Brittany is discussed by S. Reinach, 'Les Francs et la Bretagne armoricaine' *Revue archéologique* 27 (Paris 1928) pp 246–53 and G. Souillet, 'La Guerche. Le Problème de la marche franco-bretonne' *M[émoires de la] S[ociété d'] H[istoire et d'] A[rchéologie de] B[retagne]* 24 (Rennes 1944) pp 25–46.

59

major theme in the history of early medieval Brittany.[3] But from the ninth century onwards, the emphasis is rather on the gradual coalescence of these two distinct peoples into a single Breton political unity in which both Celtic and Frankish elements were combined. Over the same centuries as the Breton duchy emerged, the Bretons' eastern neighbours were also active, coveting this strategic peninsula, and encouraging the spread of Frankish culture. The first attempt to take direct control of Brittany was that of Charlemagne: the struggle was to continue throughout the middle ages, and only reached its conclusion in the proclamation of unity made by Francis I in 1532. For much of the twelfth century, opposition to the French was bolstered by the active interest in and control of Brittany by the Angevins Henry II, his son Geoffrey and grandson Arthur. It was under their rule that Brittany finally ceased to be a group of petty warring principalities, and came permanently to accept the rule of one family at a time.[4]

One of the weapons in the Angevin armoury for use against the Capetians was the archbishopric of Dol. Though not new in the eleventh century, the archbishopric had first received papal recognition in 1076, when Gregory VII decided that a Breton archbishop would assist his own political schemes.[5] From then on, the status of the see was a matter for contention. Sometimes with Capetian backing, the archbishops of Tours asserted their traditional jurisdiction over the Breton peninsula, whilst opposed to them were the archbishops of Dol, satellites of the Plantagenets: and the papacy intervened from time to time on one side or the other.[6] After many appeals and counterappeals to Rome, the longstanding controversy was finally brought to an end by Innocent III when he ruled in favour of Tours in 1199.[7]

[3] See the cautions against using the term 'Brittany' for the period before the ninth century of B-A. Pocquet du Haut-Jussé, 'Nominoé et la naissance de Bretagne', *MSHAB* 25 (1945) pp 5–6.
[4] The fullest account of the history of Brittany in the middle ages, although unreliable, remains that of [A. de] La Borderie, *Histoire [de la Bretagne]* 4 vols (Paris 1896–1906). More up to date is [*Histoire de la Bretagne*, ed J.] Delumeau (Toulouse 1969).
[5] *Epp* IV 4, 5 (*MGH Epp Sel* 2 pt 1pp 300–3) [F.] Duine, [*La*] *Métropole [de Bretagne]* (Paris 1916). B-A. Pocquet du Haut-Jussé, 'La Bretagne a-t-elle été vassale du Saint-Siège?' *SGre* 1 (1947) pp 189–196 discusses the evidence that Gregory VII wished to make Brittany a papal vassal state.
[6] B-A. Pocquet de Haut-Jussé, 'Les Plantagenets et la Bretagne' *Ann[ales de] Bret[agne]* 53 (Rennes 1946) pp 1–27; W. L. Warren, *Henry II* (London 1973) p 561.
[7] *Epp* II.82, 83, *PL* 214 (1854) cols 625–35.

Throughout the dispute, both sides, Tours and Dol, based their arguments firmly on past events, and in particular on their own interpretation of the surviving records of the ninth century.[8] The later stages of the dispute are clear, but recent historians have favoured either the French or the Breton version of the origins of the quarrel, according to their own particular sympathies. The questions as to why, when and by whom the attempt to alter the status of the bishop of Dol was first made, have never been satisfactorily answered. In exploring the ninth century, some light can perhaps be shed on the reasons why the twelfth-century clerics were unable to agree on whether the bishops of the Breton sees were suffragans of Dol, or whether they all, Dol included, owed their obedience to Tours. I shall argue that these archiepiscopal ambiguities had their origins in the schemes of Salomon, a particularly ambitious and capable ninth-century Breton leader, who tried to manipulate the established ecclesiastical hierarchy not so much in order to arrest the gradual absorption of Brittany into the Frankish kingdom, as to carve out a niche for himself which asserted his own vital role in west Frankish politics and preserved the regional identity of the peninsula. In so doing, he created a focus for Breton loyalties, and raised the issue which was to preoccupy the Welsh some two centuries later, of the extent to which ecclesiastical organisation should respect national identities.[9] To discuss the problem of the archbishopric is one way to accost the question of whether there was in the ninth century any sense of Breton 'national identity' in the face of Frankish domination. It is also a method of exploring the way in which the ecclesiastical structure of Brittany reflected simultaneously the two themes of the emergence of a united Brittany and of the Frankish political interest in the area.

[8] Most of the records pertaining to the litigation were preserved in the Tours archives throughout the middle ages. They are conveniently ressembled as a group by Martène and Durand, *Thesaurus* 3 cols 849–956.

[9] The equation between Celtic nation and ecclesiastical province underlay the unsuccessful attempts to have Saint David's elevated into an archbishopric after the Normans had begun to penetrate Wales. Here, as in ninth-century Brittany, the stimulus for the attempt was political and ecclesiastical intervention by a powerful non-Celtic neighbour coupled with a demand for recognition of his metropolitan archbishop. [J. E.] Lloyd, *A History of Wales* [*from the earliest times to the Edwardian conquest*] (3 ed London 1939) 2 p 486; C. N. L. Brooke, 'The Archbishops of St. David's, Llandaff and Caerleon-on-Usk', *Studes in the early British Church*, ed N. K. Chadwick (Cambridge 1958) pp 201–42, and more recently, M. Richter, 'Professions of Obedience and the metropolitan claims of St. David's', *The National Library of Wales Journal* 15 (Aberystwyth 1967–8) pp 197–214.

Through this discussion, I hope to show that there was no simple equation between a national church and an independent kingdom in the case of ninth-century Brittany. In the rejection of Frankish ecclesiastical supremacy, however, the extent to which the Breton church had been penetrated by Frankish ideas becomes evident.

After several expeditions, Brittany was conquered by Charlemagne in 799. A series of punitive campaigns by Louis the Pious to put down revolts confirmed that the region was part of the Frankish empire. But its position within the Carolingian realm was always ill-defined, and is best summed up as one of 'loose dependency'.[10] In about 830, Louis the Pious appointed Nominoë, a powerful local figure from southern Brittany, to rule the entire peninsula on his behalf, as *missus imperatoris in Brittannia*.[11] He remained loyal to Louis for the rest of the emperor's lifetime, but from 840 until Nominoë's death in 851 Brittany became restive under the continuing overlordship of the young Charles the Bald. Despite a lack of information there is reason to think that the first half of the ninth century witnessed the opening of the Celtic regions of western Brittany to some degree of Frankish influence, particularly in matters of religious organisation and discipline. Charlemagne may perhaps have reorganised the bishoprics here so that they were brought more into line with the Carolingian conception of what the Roman network of bishoprics had been. In this connection he doubtless asserted the jurisdiction of Tours as the metropolitan see with authority over Brittany, since the Armorican *civitates* had all formed part of the late Roman province of *Lugdunensis III*. He may also have introduced a tithing system, or perhaps modified a pre-existing one.[12] Both Charlemagne and Louis the Pious are known to have issued diplomas for Celtic monasteries in Brittany: in one of his, Louis ordered the monks of Landevennec to adopt the Roman tonsure and the Rule of Saint

[10] The phrase is that of W. Schlesinger, who likened Brittany to Gascony in this respect. 'Die Auflösung des Karlsreiches', *Karl der Grosse* 1, *Persönlichkeit und Geschichte*, ed H. Beumann (Düsseldorf 1965) p. 812.

[11] Though the date of Nominoë's appointment is not given by any contemporary writer, it represents an important step in the assertion of Frankish control over Brittany. A. de la Borderie, 'La Chronologie du Cartulaire de Redon', *Ann Bret* 5 (1890) pp 552–6; J. Dhondt, *Études sur la naissance des principautés territoriales en France, IXe au Xe siècle* (Bruges 1948) pp 82–106.

[12] [E.] Lesne, *La Hiérarchie épiscopale*. [*Provinces, métropolitains, primats en Gaule et Germanie 742–882*] (Lille/Paris 1905) pp 57–86; [R.] Merlet, 'L'Émancipation [de l'église de Bretagne et le concile de Tours (848–51)']', *Moyen Age* 11 (1898) pp 1–30.

Benedict.[13] These developing contacts are reflected in the presence of Breton bishops at Carolingian church councils for the first time in the mid ninth century.[14]

To what extent Nominoë favoured and promoted these exchanges is unclear. His uncanonical deposition of four bishops on trumped-up charges of simony in 848 or 849 aroused the fury of Frankish prelates, and has led to accusations that he was expelling Frankish appointees whose influence he had come to regard as excessive. Several historians have seen in Nominoë's high-handed treatment of the church a growing hostility to Frankish interference, furthering his increasingly frequent revolts against Frankish overlordship. The expulsion of the bishops was, it is usually argued, the prelude to the creation by Nominoë of a Breton archbishopric at Dol, having authority over all the other bishops of the peninsula and fully independent of the Frankish church. The establishment of the archbishopric at Dol is thus seen as Nominoë's crowning achievement, completing his creation of a united Breton kingdom, free from Frankish control.[15]

These assertions are made on the basis of the Chronicle of Nantes, which claims that Nominoë wrote to Leo IV, *de regno Brittanniae renovando et de episcoporum depositione*. This chronicle then narrates how Nominoë, having ignored the pope's instructions and deposed the bishops by force, cut the Breton church off from the authority of Tours, raised the monasteries of Dol, Saint-Brieuc and Tréguier into bishoprics, with that of Dol as metropolitan for all Brittany;

[13] [H.] Morice, [*Mémoires pour servir de*] preuves [*à l'histoire ecclésiastique et civile de Bretagne*] I (Paris 1742) cols 225–6; *Cartulaire de l'abbaye de Landevennec*, ed A. de la Borderie (Rennes 1888) I pp 75–6.

[14] The bishops of Nantes and Rennes were frequent attenders at Merovingian church councils. J. Champagne and R. Szramkiewicz, 'Recherches sur les conciles de temps mérovingiens', *RHDFE* 49 (1971) pp 5–49. However, no bishops from any part of Brittany are recorded at Carolingian councils until 835. *MGH Conc* 2 p 703. The only Breton bishop with a Celtic rather than a Frankish name to attend Frankish councils was Uurnarius (Gernobrius) of Rennes; Mansi 14 pp 796, 919.

[15] This is the view advocated by La Borderie, *Histoire* 2 pp 52–9 in particular, and following him by Merlet, 'L'Émancipation', and recently, but more cautiously, by P. Riché, in his contribution to Delumeau, pp 131–2. Attempts to unravel the scanty and conflicting information about what Nominoë was doing are made by L. Levillain, 'Les Réformes ecclésiastiques de Noménoé (847–8), étude sur les sources narratives', *Moyen Age* 15 (1902) pp 201–57; F. Lot, 'Le schisme breton du IXe siècle' in his *Mélanges [d'histoire bretonne]* (Paris 1907) pp 58–96, and in an article published anonymously by F. Duine, 'Le Schisme breton', *Ann Bret* 30 (1914–15) pp 424–472.

lastly, gathering all his newly created bishops together at Dol, he had himself anointed king.[16] Too much credence has been given to this account. This chronicle was written during the 1050s, two centuries after the alleged events, as a piece of polemic directed against lay intervention in affairs of the church and against the irregular archbishopric. It is almost certainly the product of the household of Airard, bishop of Nantes, who was an Italian reforming prelate, abbot of a Roman monastery and friend of Hildebrand's. During his episcopate, the county of Nantes was in the hands of Hoël, son of the count of Cornouaille, and thus representative of the Celtic aristocracy, and hardly likely to favour the reforming zeal of this foreign bishop whose energies were directed towards freeing the churches of his diocese from lay control and in particular towards rooting out simony.[17] The value of the account in the Chronicle of Nantes of Nominoë's domination of the Breton church in the ninth century is thus questionable, and has been much overrated.

It is preferable to turn instead to the contemporary sources, sparse though they are. Immediately striking is the absence of any reference to a Breton archbishopric in the letter sent by a Frankish synod to Nominoë in July or August 850.[18] This letter accuses him of many crimes against the church, including the expulsion of legitimate bishops and their replacement by *mercenarii*. He is also charged with despoiling the church of Tours, but this general comment more probably refers to Nominoë's raids up the Loire valley than to an attack on the ecclesiastical authority of Tours itself.

It is clear that from about 848 onwards, co-operation between the Breton and the Frankish clergy did cease. In 866 it was alleged that the Bretons had not been sending their bishops to participate in Frankish synods, or allowing them to go to Tours for their episcopal consecrations for about the past twenty years, that is, from the later years of Nominoë's term of office onwards.[19] These

---

[16] [*La*] *Chronique de Nantes*, [ed R. Merlet], *Collection de textes pour servir à l'étude et à l'enseignement de l'histoire* (Paris 1896) cap 11 pp 32–9.

[17] *ibid* pp xxv–xi. On Airard's reforms see G. Constable, *Monastic Tithes from their origin to the twelfth century* (Cambridge 1964) pp 85–7.

[18] Loup de Ferrières, *Correspondance*, ed L. Levillain (2 ed Parish 1964) *Ep* 81 2 pp 56–64; L. Levillain 'Étude sur les lettres de Loup de Ferrières', *BEC* 63 (1902) pp 303–12.

[19] *Chronique de Nantes* cap 16 pp 51–7 (=Mansi 15 pp 732–4).

charges are confirmed by a letter from the council of Savonnières to four Breton bishops in 859. This letter again has no hint that the Bretons had set up their own archbishop.[20] That the Bretons were consecrating their own bishops need not mean that they had already created their own metropolitan: it is possible that they had simply reverted to the practice of the early Celtic church in Wales, which was presumably also that of the Breton church itself before Charlemagne asserted the jurisdiction of Tours over it. If so, episcopal consecrations would merely have been performed by three bishops.[21] Nominoë, then, led the Breton church into isolation, but not into separation.[22]

By 859 when the council of Savonnières met, both Nominoë and his son and successor, Erispoë, were dead. This latter had been murdered in 857 by his cousin Salomon, whose rule in Brittany lasted until 874. His lifetime forms a far more convincing period for the attempt to wrench Brittany away from the authority of Tours than does that of his predecessor Nominoë. In place of ill-directed unrest and revolt, accompanied by ecclesiastical non-cooperation with the Franks, Salomon substituted a far more vigorous policy, designed to ensure himself a share in the government of western Neustria, in addition to his rule in Brittany. He was prepared to support Frankish rebels against Charles the Bald one year, be a loyal vassal the next, to ally with the Vikings against the Franks, or to help the Franks beat off the Northmen, as suited his purpose. His aim appears to have been to prevent the establishment of any very powerful Frankish magnate in Neustria who might threaten his own control of the eastern marches of Brittany. Hence he supported both Louis the Stammerer and Robert the Strong in their revolts, but attacked them in turn whilst they were invested with authority in the lower Loire area.[23]

---

[20] Mansi 15 pp 532–3.

[21] R. Fawtier, La Vie de Saint Samson. Essai de critique hagiographique, BEHE 197 (1912) I.43–44 pp 138–40. On the correct interpretation of this passage, O. Chadwick, 'The evidence of dedications in the early history of the Welsh church', Studies in Early British History, ed N. K. Chadwick (Cambridge 1954) pp 173–4.

[22] Certainly in the twelfth century Tours did not possess any evidence to suggest that the dispute had been originated by Nominoë. All the stages of the controversy were reviewed by Innocent III in the ruling which brought the affair to a close. See n7 above.

[23] The best narrative of Salomon's relations with the Franks is that of Prudentius and Hincmar, Annales de Saint-Bertin, ed F. Grat, J. Viellard, S. Clémencet, Société de l'histoire de France (Paris 1964) a 857–74 passim.

Salomon's rebelliousness against Charles the Bald, to whom he had taken an oath of loyalty on at least one occasion, reached a climax in 865–6, following the appointment first of Louis the Stammerer and then of Robert the Strong to a position of overall responsibility within Neustria. It is at this time that the first contemporary references to the archbishopric of Dol occur. There survive four letters of Nicholas I which deal with a request by Salomon that the pallium be sent to Festinian, bishop of Dol.[24] Though none of the Breton letters to the pope is extant, it is evident from these replies that the Bretons did not couch their request in a correct form, and repeatedly failed to submit evidence to back up their assertions that Dol had always been an archbishopric whose incumbent was entitled to receive the pallium. When Festinian finally did send a statement of the grounds on which he based his claims, Nicholas I could find nothing in the papal archives which substantiated them. Not surprisingly: the Breton case rested at least in part on a misreading of the *Liber Pontificalis*.[25] Neither Festinian nor Salomon ever sent any of the official documents which Nicholas I wanted to see, and indeed, there can have been none.

After 866 the question as to whether Festinian should be given the pallium appears to have been dropped. No further references to the dispute occur during the lifetimes of either Nicholas I or Salomon. Nor is there any mention of it in the one letter which survives from Salomon to Hadrian II, written in 871.[26] In it, he apologised for his inability to fulfil his intention of travelling to

---

[24] *MGH Epp* 6 pp 639–40, 646–7, 648–9, 619–22. A date of 866 for this last is preferable to 862 (as suggested by E. Perels) for the reasons given by Merlet, *Chronique de Nantes* p 62 n2. The identity and career of Festinian (or Festinianus, Festgen) are discussed by F. Lot, 'Festien "archevêque" de Dol', *Mélanges* pp 14–32.

[25] L. Duchesne, *Fastes épiscopaux de l'ancienne Gaule* 2 (Paris 1899) p 268. Duchesne was the first to notice that Festinian's claim (*MGH Epp* VI pp 648–9) that pope Severinus had bestowed the pallium on a Breton Restoaldus was most probably a misreading of the notice of Sergius sending the pallium to Bertoaldus of Canterbury in 693. In the *Liber Pontificalis* the phrase *Bertoaldum Britanniae archiepiscopum* will have caused this error.

[26] *Cartulaire de Redon*, ed A. de Courson, *Collection de documents inédits sur l'histoire de France*, (Paris 1863) no 89 p 67. Allegations that this letter is a forgery have been made on no good grounds, B-A. Pocquet du Haut-Jussé, *Les Papes et les ducs de Bretagne*, BEFAR 133 (1928) I p 17. It does however survive in a version interpolated in the eleventh century, Duine, *Métropole* pp 61–4. I am grateful to Dr Chaplais for his opinion that the version preserved in the Redon cartulary has every appearance of authenticity.

Rome that year, owing to the gravity of the Viking menace. Instead he sent lavish gifts to the pope: a lifesize gold statue of himself, a donkey with saddle and harness, a gold crown set with precious stones, thirty tunics, thirty dyed woollen cloths of varying colours, thirty deerskins and forty pairs of socks *ad opus domesticorum vestri fidelium*, and three hundred *solidi*. Perhaps Salomon was only too glad to be able to avoid meeting the pope face to face and having to explain himself to him.

There are however to be found some claims that the pallium was indeed bestowed on Festinian, but these are demonstrably eleventh-century forgeries, or propaganda put forward on behalf of Dol at that time.[27] Though it is certain that metropolitan status was never conferred on any Breton bishop in the ninth century, it would seem that the church of Dol abandoned the attempt to win papal approval, but nevertheless persisted, at least at times, in regarding its prelate as an archbishop throughout the rest of the ninth century and on until Gregory VII made this status legitimate. There is no explicit mention of the archbishopric in a letter from John VIII reprimanding the Breton bishops for their failure to obey Tours in all matters, and for consecrating each other on the sole authority of their duke.[28] Although it is possible that after Salomon's death earlier Celtic practices were resumed, the scant tenth-century evidence does however suggest that at least some of the tenth-century bishops of Dol were regarded as *archiepiscopi*.[29]

The long and bitter controversy between Tours and Dol thus first arose while Brittany was under the control of Salomon, almost certainly in 865, and not, as is commonly believed, during Nominoë's term of office. Though the desire to create a Breton ecclesiastical province independent of the Frankish hierarchy may

---

[27] Duine, *Métropole* pp 33–4. The Chronicle of Dol was written between 1076 and 1080 to set out the case that the archbishopric had existed since the time of Samson onwards. It also narrated the alleged grant of the pallium to Festinian. The text is printed by Duine, *ibid* pp 38–54.

[28] *MGH Epp* 7 pp 87–8.

[29] Letter of Radbod, prior of Dol, to Athelstan in William of Malmesbury, *De Gestis Pontificum Anglorum*, ed N. E. S. A. Hamilton, *RS* (1870) pp 399–400, and letter of John XIII to the Breton bishops, *PL* 126 (1854) col 959 (where it is misattributed to John VIII). Perhaps the title was used in the tenth century as an honorific one only, without indicating that the archbishop enjoyed metropolitan rights. For the use of *archiepiscopus* in this sense in Wales at about the same time see Lloyd, *A History of Wales* 2 p 486 and T. M. Charles-Edwards, 'The Seven Bishop-Houses of Dyfed', *Bulletin of the Board of Celtic Studies* 24 (Cardiff 1971) p 257.

perhaps have been Salomon's in the first place, the idea evidently attracted more general support within Brittany, for the scheme did not founder with Salomon's death. Rather, as has been seen, the idea of the archiepiscopal dignity of Dol was kept alive by the Breton episcopate during the political strife and fragmentation which Brittany underwent in the late ninth and tenth centuries.

Yet there can be little doubt that the dispute was in origin one strand in Salomon's secular political ambitions. As I have suggested, he first pressed the case during that revolt against Charles the Bald which culminated in the battle of Brissarthe, and the death there of many Neustrian magnates at the hands of a mixed band of Bretons and Vikings. When Salomon made peace with the Frankish king the following year, the terms were very different from those of the treaty between them in 863. On that occasion, Hincmar of Rheims recorded that in addition to Salomon being granted the lay abbacy of Saint-Aubin d'Angers, and part of western Anjou, he and his followers had commended themselves to Charles, sworn loyalty and undertaken to pay the traditional tribute.[30] In 867, by contrast, there is no mention of commendation, or of tribute. Rather, Hincmar notes that Charles the Bald was required to hand over hostages to the Breton envoys. As well as confirming Salomon's possession of Rennes, Nantes, the pays de Retz and Entre-Deux-Eaux, Charles gave to the Breton *princeps* the county of Coûtances, and all royal perquisites there.[31]

From 867 onwards Salomon remained loyal to Charles the Bald, and fulfilled his promise to send troops to help the Franks fight off the Danes on at least two occasions. This change in his behaviour is marked, and furthermore, it coincides with the first appearance of Breton charters describing Salomon as *rex*, a title never previously applied in them to a ninth-century Breton *princeps*. The phrase *Salomon rex (totius) Britanniae* occurs both in charters issued by Salomon himself, and those of private individuals, and though not every Breton charter from 868 to 874 does use this style, it forms a noteworthy development in the diplomatic of late ninth-century Brittany.[32]

It is perhaps thus possible that Salomon's revolt of 865–6 was

[30] *Annales de Saint-Bertin* pp 6–7.
[31] *Ibid* pp 136–7.
[32] *Cartulaire de Redon* nos 21, 225, 240, 243, 247, 257, pp 18–9, 173–4, 187–9, 194–5, 198–9, 207–8 and Morice, *Preuves* 1 col 308.

directed towards forcing the Frankish king to recognise that the Breton leader was not merely a royal official, a *missus*, as Nominoë had been, but that his power was more extensive, both in geographical range and in authority. He may even have been aiming to equate his status more closely with that of Charles himself, and that once this was achieved, he was content to remain a loyal ally where previously he had been a rebellious vassal. The imitation of royal Carolingian diploma forms shows just how self-consciously Salomon was modelling his rule on that of his Frankish neighbour.[33]

If this interpretation of Salomon's aims and ambitions is correct, then the letters he wrote to the pope requesting the pallium for Festinian find a ready context and explanation. To have an archbishop in his retinue would increase Salomon's political standing in the eyes of those at home and elsewhere. For his rulership to reflect Carolingian practices, the Breton church would have to be organised along the same lines, subject, that is, to a defined ecclesiastical hierarchy, with an episcopacy dependent on their secular leader, buttressing his authority. Perhaps Salomon also wanted an archbishop in order to imitate Carolingian kingship in a further respect, and be a consecrated ruler.[34]

If Salomon was indeed striving to adopt the style and manner of ruling of his Frankish neighbours, then his aims were twofold. Firstly, as he has been shown, to raise himself to a position more nearly of equality with Charles, but secondly, and as important, Salomon must have been concerned with the impact of his policies upon his own subjects. There are several clear hints that although Brittany was nominally under the rule of one man from c830 onwards, the region was torn by civil strife and faction, and that in this respect, Salomon's position was no more secure than had been

---

[33] Especially *Cartulaire de Redon* nos 240 and 241, pp 187–92.

[34] There is nothing whatever to substantiate the claim of the Chronicle of Nantes that Nominoë was anointed at Dol in 848 or 849. However, the link made in this chronicle between the creation of the archbishopric and the introduction into Brittany of some form of royal consecration ceremony may perhaps hold some truth. There is good evidence that one of Salomon's successors, Alan the Great, received anointing at the hands of a bishop in 878. Since his reign is not otherwise noteworthy for any innovations in Breton governance, the suggestion that it was rather Salomon who was the first ecclesiastically consecrated ruler is perhaps worth bearing in mind. He would need an archbishop in order to receive consecration. Lesne, *La Hiérarchie épiscopale* pp 289–90.

that of either Nominoë or Erispoë.[35] To establish an archbishop was to encourage ecclesiastical unity as a prop to fragile political unity.[36] To create a Frankish style metropolitan archbishopric at a see whose patron was Samson, the most famous of all Celtic Breton saints, was thus an excellent compromise. In manipulating the ecclesiastical hierarchy, Salomon was showing a similar outlook to that employed nearly a century earlier by Offa of Mercia. Salomon was thus seeking to find a delicate balance between imitation of the Carolingians and freedom from their close oversight. His restructuring of the church was crucial to these political ambitions, and it is perhaps not too much to suggest that Salomon wished to set up an archbishopric at Dol in order to foster feelings of Breton unity and national identity.

Yet Salomon failed to establish a united Brittany, and the factions he struggled to suppress finally erupted and led directly to his own death. Thereafter, Brittany was rent with feuding which lasted, with brief intermissions of tranquillity under a single ruler, until the Angevins established themselves in the peninsula. But the idea of a single archbishop, uniting the Breton dioceses and independent of the Frankish church, lived on, and continued until 1199 to act as a focus for French grievances against the Bretons, and for Breton resistance to French ecclesiastical domination.[37]

University of Sheffield

---

[35] See for instance the account of Salomon's murder in *Annales de Saint-Bertin*, a 874, p 196.

[36] It is impossible to tell how far the ninth-century 'archbishopric' of Dol had the support of the rest of the Breton episcopate. The ordination of Electramnus as bishop of Rennes in 866 was performed at Tours; this may suggest that Salomon never succeeded in detaching the bishops of the largely Frankish east of Brittany from their allegiance to Tours. *Ordinatio Electramni, GalC* 14 *Instrumenta* col 163.

[37] I should like to thank Peregrine Horden for his helpful comments on this paper.

MONASTIC REFORM AND THE UNIFICATION OF TENTH-CENTURY ENGLAND

by NICHOLAS BANTON

A SINGLE kingdom of England was created in the tenth century. While the military successes of king Alfred and his son king Edward the Elder had established some authority over all the English kingdoms for the West Saxon kings, their claims could be only tentative. Both kings had governed Wessex during the lifetimes of Aethelred and Aethelflaed, the rulers of Mercia, and Athelstan was probably the first West Saxon king to be crowned king of Mercia at his accession. He had been separately acclaimed king of Mercia and of Wessex, and in a contemporary text he is recorded as *Rex Angulsaxonum et Mercianorum*.[1] The coronation rite used by the early tenth century kings appears to have endowed them with the government of three peoples, the Saxons, the Mercians, and the Northumbrians.[2] A charter of King Eadred at his accession in 946 describes his kingship as a fourfold office representing the Anglo-Saxons, the Northumbrians, the Danes and the Britons.[3] Eadwig was separately chosen king in Mercia and in Wessex in 955, and during his reign his brother Edgar ruled Mercia, firstly as *regulus*, and then as full king.[4] At Eadwig's death in 959 the Anglo-Saxon Chronicle reports that 'Edgar succeeded to the kingdom both in Wessex and in Mercia and

---

[1] [J. A.] Robinson, [*The Times of Saint*] *Dunstan* (Oxford 1923) pp 28–36; [D. A.] Bullough, 'The Continental Background [of the Reform',] *T [enth] C[entury] S [tudies,* ed D. Parsons] (London 1975) p 34.

[2] [C. E.] Hohler, ['Some Service Books of the Later Saxon Church'], *TCS*, pp 67–9.

[3] [P. H.] S[awyer, *Anglo-Saxon Charters: An Annotated List and Bibliography*] (London 1968) no 520.

[4] *Memorials [of Saint Dunstan, archbishop of Canterbury,* ed W. Stubbs], RS, (1874) [p 32; *S* no 633; [*Two of the Saxon*] *Chronicles [Parallel,* ed J. Earle and C. Plummer] 2 vols (Oxford 1892–9) I p 113. The Worcester charter and the 'D' Chronicle suggest that Worcester documents (virtually the only midland source at this time) gave Edgar some royal status in Mercia from 955.

in Northumbria'.⁵ The traditions of the individual kingdoms of England had not yet ended.

The limitations on the authority of the West Saxon dynasty in the first half of the tenth century can be seen through their intinerary, their royal estates, and the distribution of royal charters, all of which were, as far as can be judged, still concentrated in Wessex.⁶ This was to have important consequences for the progress of monastic reforms, for all the houses reformed or refounded before late in the reign of king Edgar lay in Wessex. Abbots of monastic houses, whether reformed or not, appear to have attended the royal court only seldomly, for they were not usually included as witnesses to royal diplomas between 900 and 955. There are, however, some important groups of diplomas in which abbots are listed as signatories and these charters reveal an interesting link between the new monks and the political aspirations of the West Saxon kings. Abbots were included in a number of charters issued by king Athelstan from 931 to 934.⁷ These form part of a series of diplomas, distinctive in so many features, including their language, formulas, and witness lists, to suggest that they may have been drafted by a different cleric, possibly in a separate scriptorium, than that responsible for most royal diplomas from 935 to 955.⁸ This series of charters began after Athelstan's conquest of Northumbria in 927, and Athelstan's lordship over Mercia and Northumbria was emphasised by the inclusion in the witness lists of Northumbrian and Welsh lords, who do not witness Athelstan's later grants. Athelstan is also given an emphatic royal style, for instance *rex Anglorum per omnipatrantis dexteram totius Britanniae regni solio sublimatus*, rather than the simple *rex Anglorum*, or the *totius Britanniae orbis curagulus*, of the other diplomas of Athelstan.⁹

⁵ *Chronicles* I p 113; trans D. Whitelock, *EHD* I (2 ed 1979) p 225.
⁶ [F. M.] Stenton, [*Anglo-Saxon England*] (3 ed Oxford 1970) pp 349–51; [S.] Keynes. [*The Diplomas of King Aethlred 'the Unready' 978–1016*] (Cambridge 1908) pp 269–73.
⁷ S nos 409, 412, 423, 416, 417, 418, 422, 425, 379, 1604, 393, 410, 423, 453.
⁸ Compare [R.] Drögereit, 'Gab es ein angelsächsische Königskanzlei?', *Archiv für Urkundenforschung* 13 (Berlin 1935) pp 361–9, 418–22; Bullough, 'The Educational Tradition [in England from Alfred to Aelfric: Teaching *Utriusque Linguae*]', *SSSpoleto*, 19 (1972) pp 466–77; P. Chaplais, 'The Origin and Authenticity of the Royal Anglo-Saxon Diploma', *JSArch*, 3 (1965) pp 59–60; N. P. Brooks, 'Anglo-Saxon Charters: the work of the last twenty years', *A[nglo-] S[axon] E[ngland]*. 3 (Cambridge 1974) p 218; Keynes pp 21–26, 43–4.
⁹ S nos 412, 413, 416, 417, 418, 419, 422, 407, 425, 426, 458.

Abbots did not witness any of the royal diplomas of Athelstan that were issued after 935, nor any of those for his successors, Edmund and Eadred, that are thought to have been composed at Winchester.[10] They were, in contrast, often included in the charters drafted by bishop Cenwald of Worcester for these kings.[11] These charters were all for Mercian estates or for Mercian noblemen. The Worcester diplomas are distinctive for their rhyming, metrical phrases, for some unusual formulas, and for the number and arrangement of the witnesses. They included the signature of Northumbrian and Welsh lords who did not usually appear in charters from Winchester. In addition the Worcester diplomas stressed the overlordship of the West Saxon kings by giving them such titles as *rex Aengulsaexna ond Northhymbra imperator paganorum gubernator Brittonumque propugnator*, while the Winchester texts were usually content to call these kings the vague *rex Anglorum ceterarumque gentium in circuitu persistentium gubernator et rector*.[12]

Another group of charters that contain some abbots in their witness lists are a few diplomas written by Dunstan of Glastonbury.[13] One of these charters reveals similarities both in its language and in its witness list (for it includes a Northumbrian *dux*) with the Worcester charters, and with the earlier flamboyant charters of Athelstan.[14] Both Dunstan and Cenwald were monks, in touch with new trends from the continent, and it is quite possible that the diplomas of about 928 to 934 were also drafted by someone close to the European reforms, for these charters, along with the later Worcester and Glastonbury charters, display a style of language, the so-called hermeneutic latin popular among continental reformers such as Abbo of Fleury or Odo of Cluny.[15] The diplomas that appear to have been drafted by the new monks or in centres of

---

[10] There are two apparent exceptions, S nos 518 and 539.

[11] S nos 520, 544, 550, 556, 557, and see also no 633. These charters were first associated with Worcester in [R.] Drögereit, 'Kaiseridee [und Kaisertitel bei den Angelsachsen]' *ZRG Gabt Abt*, 69 (1952) pp 63, 67. See also Whitelock, *EHD*, 1, pp 372–3; Sawyer, *Charters of Burton Abbey* (Oxford 1979) pp xlvii–slix.

[12] S nos 392, 520, 549, 550, 544, 548, 569, 572, and also no 566.

[13] S nos 509, 546, 553, 555.

[14] S no 546 (on this and other Glastonbury charters P. Chaplais 'The Anglo-Saxon Chancery: from the Diploma to the Writ', *JSArch*, 3 (1966) pp 163–5); Drögereit, 'Kaiseridee', pp 62, 65; Keynes, pp 46–8, 82.

[15] Bullough, 'The Educational Tradition', pp 467–9; M. Lapidge 'The Hermeneutic Style in Tenth Century Anglo-Latin Literature', *ASE*, 4 (1975) pp 67–111. On Conwald, see Robinson, *Dunstan* p 39.

reform in early tenth century England were the same charters that emphasised West Saxon control over Mercia and Northumbria and the presence of abbots in the entourage of the kings.

The number of abbots who regularly appear in royal diplomas after 955 was to increase slowly. Aethelwold was the only abbot to witness charters at all regularly until 964, although he was occasionally joined by some other abbots, probably from Glastonbury, Bath, and saint Augustine's Canterbury.[16] After the reforms of 964 at Winchester, Chertsey, and Milton the number of abbots increased, but reform had scarcely taken off for in the next six years they were to be joined by only one other abbot from a reformed house, Sideman of Exeter.[17] In 970 this was to change: while in 969 royal charters had been witnessed by only nine abbots, the number in the following year almost doubled to seventeen.[18] This increase in the number of abbots at the royal court was sudden and stopped soon after 970, for only one new house was to be represented in the later charters of Edgar, Winchcombe, for which Germanus signs in 972. All the other names that first appear in charters later this decade replace old names.[19] Because of this marked change in the number of abbots at the royal court, one may conclude that the great Easter meeting, described in the earliest life of saint Oswald, at which king Edgar ordered the foundation of more than forty new monasteries took place in 970.[20]

The year 970 was a turning point in the history of monastic reform in Edgar's reign. It was not just a matter of abbots now beginning to attend the king's court, for all the new abbots came

---

[16] The other abbots are included only in 959 (S nos 586, 658, 660, 673), and once in 963 (S no 708). The Ealdred of S no/675 may be a mistake by duplication for Aethelwold. Dunstan had witnessed some charters of Eadwig in 956 (S nos 582, 597, 633, 663).

[17] HRH pp 38, 48, 56, 80–1. The tradition that Chertsey had monks from Abingdon before 964 is unjustified. The confusion stems from a later cartulary, summarised in VCH Surrey, 2, p 56.

[18] To this number may be added Sideman who witnesses in 969 and then again in 972.

[19] S nos 786, 788. Leofric replaces Sideman at Exeter. Sigegar follows Aelfstan at Glastonbury, and Aelfnoth (not Aethelnoth see S no 795) probably takes over from Aelfric at Saint Augustine's Canterbury, HRH pp 35, 48, 50.

[20] H[istorians of the] C[hurch of] Y[ork, ed J. Raine], 3 vols RS (1879) 1 pp 425–7. The Easter meeting could perhaps have taken place in 969 as many new abbots witness one charter (S/no/779) from an Easter gemot in 970, but is possible that these abbots were in fact appointed at the very assembly that set up the new houses.

from newly reformed houses. Aelfric's life of bishop Aethelwold records his foundations of Ely, Peterborough, and Thorney as if they were almost contemporary.[21] Ely was founded in 970.[22] Peterborough was founded by 971 and as one charter, even though a forgery, is dated 970 in one copy, it may like Ely have been founded in that year.[23] Thorney was also founded about the same time: its spurious charter of liberties, although dated 973, was fabricated from the Peterborough charters.[24] The date of these diplomas is often no certain guide as foundation charters were often not drafted until some years after the actual event.[25] The houses of bishop Aethelwold in the east Midlands may thus date from 970 or soon afterwards.

The same seems to be true of the foundations in the west Midlands and other houses reformed by bishop Oswald. The abbots of Deerhurst, Evesham, and Pershore all first witness royal diplomas in 970.[26] The foundation of Ramsey Abbey is difficult to establish as later Ramsey sources record 969, 970, 972, and 974 as all important dates.[27] All these accounts are ultimately based on the *Vita Oswaldi* by Byrhtferth of Ramsey which, while leaving the reform undated, places it between the Easter meeting and the coronation of Edgar in 973.[28] The *Vita* puts the agreement for the foundation of a house soon after an Easter *gemot*, probably the same meeting that instituted the other monasteries, as in fact concluded

---

[21] *Three Lives of English Saints*, ed M. Winterbottom (Toronto 1972) pp 24–5.

[22] S nos/779, 780, 781; *Liber Eliensis*, [ed E. O. Blake], *CSer* 3 ser 92 (1962) pp 74–8; *HRH* p 44.

[23] S nos 782, 787 (see *CS* no 1258). The date 966 which is often given is simply a later confusion.

[24] S no 792. The date of Crowland Abbey is impossible to establish as all the early charters are forgeries, but see *HRH* p 44.

[25] See S nos 370, 745, 786 for Winchester and Pershore, and V. H. Galbraith, 'Monastic Foundation Charters of the Eleventh and Twelfth Centuries', *CHJ*, 4 (1934) pp 205–22, 296–8.

[26] *HRH* pp 46, 58, 102. Aelfheah who witnesses from 970 was from Deerhurst and not Bath (as given in *HRH* pp 27–8). He must have been at Deerhurst when he was called to the deathbed of Foldbriht at the nearby abbey of Pershore, and he is called abbot then in the life of Oswald, *HCY*, 1 p 439.

[27] S no 798; *C[hronicon Abbatiae] R[amesiensis*, ed W. D. Macray], *RS* (1886) pp 40, 43–4. See Robinson, *Saint Oswald [and the Church of Worcester]*, British Academy, Supplemental Papers, (London 1919) pp 36–37. The date 969 is added in the margin of only a fourteenth-century manuscript of the Ramsey Chronicle, which is in other respects less reliable than the main early copy, *CR* pp ix, 40.

[28] *HCY* pp 427–34.

by the Ramsey Chronicle.[29] The *Vita* adds that the building of the abbey took place at the same time as other monasteries were being founded by Oswald and Aethelwold.[30] The reform of Ramsey therefore occurred between 970 and 973, perhaps 970 itself.

The reform of the community at Oswald's own cathedral at Worcester may have been almost contemporary. There is a break in the survival of full witness lists of episcopal leases in the years between 969 and 977, but it is in these years that the greatest changes took place in the community, and only after this time was the title *monachus* used of any witnesses in reliable charters.[31] The reforms at the cathedral may well have been planned along with those elsewhere, because in 971 at Oswald's promotion to the archbishopric of York he simultaneously appointed new heads at Ramsey, Winchcombe, and at Worcester itself.[32] A community of monks had also probably existed therefore at Winchcombe shortly before the appointment of Germanus in 971. Oswald had of course been interested in monastic reform for some years, and his biographer records that he set up a priory at Westbury for the churchmen who had followed him to Worcester. This community was started just over four years before the Easter assembly, after which these monks were moved to Ramsey. Therefore if the Easter meeting is to be dated 970, the beginning of the house at Westbury took place about 965.[33] Westbury was staffed from Oswald's household at Worcester, and a comparison of Worcester leases from 963 and 966 has shown marked differences in the community that can be best explained as the departure of some of these Worcester churchmen for the priory at Westbury.[34]

There were other houses founded in or soon after 970, for instance Westminster which receives a charter from king Edgar where the date 951 is likely to be a mistake for 971, as the witnesses

[29] *CR* pp 29–30.
[30] *HCY* p 434.
[31] Robinson, *Saint Oswald* pp 18–20, 35–6; Sawyer, '[Charters of the Reform Movement, the] Worcester [Archive]', *TCS* p 89. For a different approach to this and many other matters discussed here, see [E.] John, *O[rbis] B[ritanniae]* (Leicester, 1966).
[32] *HCY* 1 p 435; Robinson, *Saint Oswald*, p 37.
[33] *HCY* 1 pp 423–5. This fact makes Eric John's date for the Easter assembly (964) almost impossible, as Oswald does not sign charters as a bishop until 961. John, *OB* pp 249–64.
[34] For other interpretations, John, *OB* pp 234–48; Sawyer, 'Worcester', p 89.

(only preserved in a forgery expanded from this charter) probably date from between 970 and 972.[35] Other unknown abbots who witness charters in 970 presumably represent other houses in the process of foundation or reform, for instance Saint Alban's.[36] When Aethelwold can be seen acquiring other old religious sites such as Barrow or Breedon in these years, he was presumably attempting to fulfil Edgar's intention of founding forty monasteries.[37] This was, it must be remembered, a reform that had only just begun when it was checked by the death of Edgar in 975.

The new foundations of 970 and the following thus appear to have been the result of a synod such as that described in the life of saint Oswald. The later histories of Evesham, Ramsey, and Ely all connect the refoundation or reform of these houses with a large council in Edgar's reign, led by Dunstan and Aethelwold, similar to that Easter assembly.[38] At this meeting Edgar ordered the foundation of more than forty monasteries. The geography of the new houses is important, for all the new monastic communities begun in the years following 970 lay in Mercia: Ely, Ramsey, Peterborough, Thorney, Crowland, Westminster, Worcester. Winchcombe, Pershore, Deerhurst, Evesham, and Saint Alban's. While Edgar had encouraged reforms in the religious houses of Wessex during the opening decade of his reign, only from 970 were such reforms to spread into Mercia.[39] Florence of Worcester reports for the year 969 that Edgar ordered Dunstan, Oswald, and

[35] *S* nos 670, 1450; *The Crawford Collection of Early Charters and Documents*, ed A. S. Napier and W. H. Stevenson (Oxford 1895) p 90. Some late, related sources attempt to connect Dunstan's involvement in the reform of Westminster with his short tenure of the see of London in 959, but there is no contemporary support for this; for the alternative view see D. Whitelock, *Some Anglo-Saxon Bishops of London* (London 1975) p 22. All the contemporary evidence that connects Dunstan and Westminster relates to the period after his appointment to Canterbury, for instance *S* nos 670, 1447, 1451. Other bishops were involved in monasteries outside their dioceses, and the links between Christchurch, Canterbury, and Westminster Abbey in the late tenth century were very close involving the possible transfer of charters, calendars, psalters and pontificals, P. M. Korhammer, 'The Origin of the Bosworth Psalter', *ASE*, 2 (1973) pp 173–87.

[36] For the charter signature of Martin, Godwine, and Brihtheah, *HRH* pp 226–7.

[37] *S* nos 782, 749 (possibly dated 972, see Sawyer, *Charters of Burton Abbey*, p 36); Stenton pp 451–2.

[38] *Chronica Abbatiae de Evesham ad annum 1418*, ed W. D. Macray, *RS*, (1863) pp 77–8; *CR* pp 29–30; *Liber Eliensis*, p 118.

[39] The only midland abbot to witness charters in the 960s was Thurcytel head of the apparently unreformed house of Bedford, *HRH* p 30.

Aethelwold to expel the clerks and found new monasteries in Mercia.[40] Bishop Aethelwold himself maintained the distinction between the reform in the two kingdoms, when he said of Edgar that 'he cleansed holy places from all men's foulnesses, not only in the kingdom of the West Saxons but in the land of the Mercians also'.[41]

Reformed monasticism may have spread to Northumbria as well after 970. The biography of Oswald relates how the archbishop founded a monastery at Wilfrid's old cathedral, although by this he may have intended York rather than Ripon.[42] There may also have been a scriptorium at York in Oswald's time if the one York document written for him has more affinities with the language of later York texts than with contemporary Worcester leases.[43]

The reforms within the church are not the only developments that reveal an altered relationship between Wessex, Mercia and Northumbria after 970. The pattern of attendance of the leading noblemen, the *duces*, at Edgar's court was to change. The ealdormen of Wessex are no longer included as witnesses in reliable charters after 970: when they died they were not replaced, possibly not even until after Edgar's death. The only *duces* to witness diplomas regularly betwen 970 and 975 were Aethelwine, Aelfhere, Byrhtnoth, and Oslac. The last name is the most interesting, for no previous earl of Northumbria had ever been regularly included as a witness to royal charters, not even Oslac himself in the first years of his appointment, yet he was to witness almost every royal diploma between 970 and 975. Edgar's assertion of his kingship in Mercia

[40] Florence of Worcester, *Chronicon ex Chronicis*, ed B. Thorpe, 2 vols (London 1848) I p 141. As this is dated 969, it appears to prove that the Easter meeting took place in 969, but the date may be simply based on the Worcester tradition of the reform of the community subsequently mentioned in the annal. The tradition that Worcester was reformed in 969 is very unreliable, see Robinson, *Saint Oswald* pp 35–6.

[41] *EHD* I p 921.

[42] *HCY* I p 462; D. Whitelock, 'The Dealings of the Kings of England with Northumbria in the Tenth and Eleventh Centuries', *The Anglo-Saxons: Studies in some Aspects of their History and Culture presented to Bruce Dickins*, ed P. Clemoes (London 1959) p 76. This reform cannot refer to Worcester because the *eius* looks back to Wilfrid, and as Worcester has not been mentioned for many pages of the text, it can hardly be assumed as by John, *OB* pp 244, 258–9.

[43] *Sermo Lupi ad Anglos*, ed D. Whitelock 3 ed London 1963) pp 41–2.

after 970 appears to have meant that Northumbrian officials were now expected to attend royal assemblies.[44]

Because of this development in the lists of *duces* given in the charters, it has been possible to date one of Edgar's law-codes to the years 970 to 975, for this code makes Aelfhere, Aethelwine, and Oslac responsible for its dissemination.[45] Within the broad limits of these years it is even possible that the code derives from the years 970 to 971, because the clause that talks of 'I and the archbishop' would more naturally fit these years when there was probably a short vacancy at the archbishopric of York.[46] Most other law-codes of the tenth and early eleventh centuries that refer to archbishops mention them in the plural, and both archbishops of Canterbury and York would be likely to have been present at the great assemblies from which such legislation stemmed, especially as this code was intended to cover provinces under the spiritual care of the archbishop of York.[47] In any case this legislation should not be connected only with the coronation of Edgar in 973, but reflects the developments within the church after 970, for it is the first code of the tenth century kings to survive that definitely deals with Mercia and Northumbria as well as Wessex. The earlier codes were mostly West Saxon laws: the assemblies from which they derive were, when recorded almost all in Wessex, and when one law gives a list of minting-places, they are all in Wessex.[48] The legislation of Edgar

---

[44] Eadulf of Bernicia and Malcolm of Strathclyde witness a diploma of Easter 970, *S* no 779. In August 970 bishop Aelfsige of Chester-le-Street was in Dorset, presumably waiting on the king although he does not witness any surviving charters from that year, *The Durham Ritual*, ed T. J. Brown (Copenhagen 1969) p 24.

[45] [F. Liebermann, *Die*] *Gesetze* [*der Angelsachsen*] 3 vols (Halle 1903–16) 1 pp 206–215; C. R. Hart, 'Athelstan "Half-King" and his family', *ASE*, 2 (1973) p 133.

[46] *Gesetze* 1/ pp 206–7. For the dates of Oscytel's death and Oswald's appointment, see Symeon of Durham, *Opera Omnia*, ed T. Arnold, 2 vols, *RS* (1882–5) 1 p 226. The Anglo-Saxon Chronicle gives Oscytel's death as All Saints' Eve 971, but the Chronicle may have been using a year beginning in autumn as in other tenth century obits, see *Chronicles* 1 p 119; *EHD* 1 p 125; and D. Whitelock, 'The Appointment of Dunstan in Archbishop of Canterbury', *Otium et Negotium: Studies in Onomatology and Library Science presented to Olof von Feilitzen*ed F. Sandgren (Stockholm 1973) pp 238, 245.

[47] Compare *Gesetze* 1 pp 184–5, 273, 276.

[48] *Gesetze* 1 pp 140–1, 166–7, 170–1, 173, 181–2, 184–5, 190, 208–9; 158–9. An assembly at Whittlebury mentioned in one code may be an exception, although only a few commands from there survive, *Gesetze* 1 pp 182–3. The position of London is anomalous: while considered Mercian still, it was already under the close control of the West Saxon kings. It has been pointed out that the references to

may itself have been another product of the reforming impetus in the church for its homiletic style and ecclesiastical concerns suggest that it was drafted by a leading churchman of this movement, possibly Dunstan.[49]

Developments in Mercia affected Northumbria as well. The beginning of monastic reform in Northumbria coincided with that in Mercia. Bishop Oswald of Worcester, called by his biographer the leading bishop of Mercia, was appointed in 971 to the archbishopric of York.[50] The first lawcode that clearly applied to the Midlands concerned Northumbria as well. The attendance of Northumbrian earls at the royal court followed the assertion of Edgar's rule in Mercia. Equally significantly it was the Mercian and not the West Saxon charters of Edmund and Eadred that had included the names of the Northumbrian and Welsh princes. In almost all the major divisions of tenth and early eleventh century England the allegiance of Northumbria belonged to the lords of Mercia, and therefore after his assertion of power in the Midlands, Edgar commanded the submission of the Northern and Welsh rulers.[51]

The year 970 marked also a high-point in the royal titles assumed by the West Saxon kings. Tenth century diplomas had always granted these kings some vague superiority over all the English. Some Worcester charters had even called these kings *imperator*, but this does not mean that these kings ever claimed the status of emperor, for otherwise they were content to be known as king, in charters, laws, coins, the coronation order, and in the narrative chronicles.[52] *Imperator* is used as no more than a grand synonym for *rex, basileus*, or *gubernator*. Edmund and Eadred were 'emperor of

---

Edgar's broad dominions are unparalleled in earlier laws, [J. L.] Nelson, ['Inauguration Rituals', *Early Medieval Kingship*, ed P. H. Sawyer and I. N. Wood] (Leeds 1977) p 69. This code is only known from Worcester sources, not being included in the southern compilation *Quadripartitus*.

[49] Whitelock, *EHD* p 434.

[50] *HCY* 1 p 435.

[51] See *S* no 779 for the lords (kings ?) of Bernicia and Strathclyde at Edgar's court in 970, and, for the submission of 973, Stenton pp 369–70.

[52] On the problem of the imperial title of the English kings, [C.] Erdmann, [*Forschungen zur Politischen Ideenwalt des Fruhmittelalters*] (Berlin 1951) pp 37–43: Drögereit, 'Kaiseridee', pp 57–73; H. R. Loyn, 'The Imperial Style of the Tenth Century Anglo-Saxon Kings', *History*, 40 (London 1955) pp 111–15; [E. E.] Stengel, ['Imperator und Imperium bei den Angelsachsen'] *DA* 16 (1960) pp 54–66; John, *OB* pp 52–6. The Worcester charters are *S* nos 392, 549, 550, 548,

Northumbria', or of the Danes, just as they might be styled *rector* or *gubernator* or these peoples in the same charters. Emperor is used as only a territorial title, one familiar to the reformers from their continental contacts and their interest in elaborate language, but when speaking of these kings as emperor of the pagans, they have taken it a long way from its usual continental context. In the reign of Edgar, however, one authentic charter does survive to give the king a genuinely imperial title, a grant from 970 that entitles him *imperator augustus*.[53] This year also saw other unusual titles that attempted to express Edgar's lordship over the peoples of Britain that are not found in reliable charters either beforehand or afterwards.[54]

The royal styles on the English coins show some other interesting developments at this time. Although some early coins had claimed the title *rex Angl(orum)*, it was only after Eadgar's reform of the coinage in 973 that the legend *Rex Anglorum* was to become the unchanged style of the English kings. On some coins Athelstan could be called king of all Britain, Edmund could be called king of York, and Edgar king of Britain until the reform of 973.[55] As this coinage reform, which saw Edgar rejecting the varied royal titles from the uniform title king of the English, took place in the same year as Edgar's famous coronation at Bath, it provides an important perspective on his intentions at that event.

While the early tenth century coronation order had granted the kings at their accession the government of two or three nations, by

---

569, 572. Although it has been claimed that the early life of Oswald proves that *Imperator* was a contemporary title, this work always calls the English kings *rex* and instead calls the east Frankish ruler *Imperator* without any qualification. *Imperator* is used of the English king only in its sense of commander, not necessarily implying a higher status than *rex*. The life also uses the allied terms *imperiosus* or *imperium*, the latter to describe the power of the nobleman Athelstan, see *HCY* I pp 425, 426, 428, 434, 435, 436.

[53] *S* no 775, on the authenticity of this charter see Drögereit, 'Kaiseridee', p 70; Stengel p 57.

[54] *S* nos 777, 778, 779, 781. Of these two use a regnal style of Athelstan's diplomas between 931 and 934, and one repeats a title found only otherwise in a charter of Edgar for Northumbria in 963, *S* no 712. One may compare also the title in Aethelwold's charter of 971, *S* no 782. The titles in *S* nos 731, 741, 751, 787, 796, 797, 798, 799 come from spurious and suspicious charters.

[55] R. H. M. Dolley and D. M. Metcalf, 'The Reform of the English Coinage under Eadgar', *Anglo-Saxon Coins: Studies presented to F. M. Stanton*, ed R. H. M. Dolley (London 1961) pp 136–68. Recent work on the royal styles in the coins has been

Edgar's coronation in 973 the king's office was simply that of *Rex*.[56] The site of this spectacle, Bath, was also that of one of the new reformed monasteries, and both the Anglo-Saxon Chronicle and the life of Oswald emphasise the participation of the religious orders in the ceremony.[57] But perhaps it was equally important that Bath lay on the borders of Wessex and Mercia, and the coronation of the king at such a site visibly stressed the position of Edgar as king of both peoples.[58] Edgar had always claimed an authority over Mercia, but in the decade in which he asserted his lordship he was crowned again, just as in ninth century West Francia, Charles the Bald, who had always claimed Aquitaine was crowned king at Orleans when he asserted his power there in 848.[59]

The English reformers, like their continental counterparts, stressed the unity of both church and kingdom. In Aethelwold's account of the reform king Eadwig is criticised because he had 'dispersed his kingdom and divided its unity', while Edgar by contrast 'obtained by God's grace the whole dominion of England and brought back to unity the divisions of the kingdom'.[60] Byrhtferth of Ramsey overreacted to a succession dispute, not in itself an unusual occurrence, that followed the death of Edgar, and complained at length how sedition set kings against kings, nobles against nobles, *gentes* against *gentes*, and bishops and priests against their flocks.[61] While in eastern Francia the great Ottonian royal monasteries encouraged the tradition of shared rule among the royal family, in England this found no favour in the new monasteries.[62] Aethelwold's pupil Aelfric viewed the idea of shared rule with such distaste that he omitted all mention in his translations of joint rule among the ancient Romans.[63]

---

summarised by Whitelock in *Asser's Life of King Alfred*, ed W. H. Stevenson rev ed (Oxford 1959) p cxxxvii. See also I. Stewart, *Spink's Numismatic Circular* 75 (London 1967) p 271.

[56] Hohler pp 67–9.

[57] *Chronicles* 1 pp 118–9; *HCY* 1 pp 436–8.

[58] C. S. Taylor, 'Bath, Mercian and West Saxon', *Transactions of the Bristol and Gloucestershire Archaeological Society*, 23 (Gloucester 1900) pp 129–61; Nelson pp 63–70.

[59] Nelson pp 60–62.

[60] *EHD* 1 p 920. A similar refrain is found in *Memorials* p 36.

[61] *HCY* 1 pp 448–9.

[62] [K. J.] Leyser, *Rule and Conflict* [*in an Early Medieval Society: Ottonian Saxony*] (London 1979) pp 16–17.

[63] Whitelock, *EHD* 1 p 60.

Monastic reform in Tenth-Century England

Such a concern is not surprising for the hallmark of the reform was its insistence on uniformity of obedience to the Benedictine Rule. This is shown from the early charters of the reform, and the introduction to the *Regularis Concordia*, the rule agreed upon for England, attaches a great importance to unity in monastic life.[64] The *Concordia* itself may have been drafted about the time of the Easter meeting for the biography of saint Oswald associates the mention of saint Benedict at the assembly with the institution of new houses, and the rule is also mentioned in the diploma that survives from Easter 970.[65] The charters show that an agreed rule was needed for the foundation of new houses, not only afterwards. The accent on uniformity was felt elsewhere. The works of Aelfric were especially concerned about theological correctness, and the language and grammar of the writings of this school also reveal an emphasis on regularity that has been called the origin of standard Old English.[66]

It has long been recognised that the main document of the reform movement, the *Regularis Concordia*, was indebted to the reforms of Benedict of Aniane and the emperor Louis the Pious in the early ninth century, but the parallels in the progress of the reforms are even more revealing.[67] During the reign of Charlemagne the reformed monasticism of Benedict was largely confined to Aquitaine, the kingdom of his son Louis, but after his accession to the whole empire these reforms were to be decreed for all of the Frankish empire at councils in 816 and 817.[68] It was to be at one of

---

[64] *S* nos 605, 607, 779, and the suspect nos 658, 786, 788, 792, 798, 812. Aethwold's refoundation charter for the New Minster, Winchester, was cast in the form of a rule, *S* no 745, and many other charters include a reference to living *regulariter, S* nos 670, 688, 689, 690, 701, 786, 788. For the English rule, *Regularis Concordia*, ed T. Symons (London 1953) pp 2–4.

[65] *HCY* 1 p 426; *S* no 779. This was first suggested in Knowles, *MO* p 42. The date 973 is proposed by T. Symons, '*Regularis Concordia*: History and Derivation', *TCS* pp 39–42. Similarities between the Easter meeting and the synod at Winchester mentioned in the rule include the special importance of bishop Aethwold, author of the *Concordia*, and the great vilification of the clerks, *HCY* 1 pp 425, 426–7.

[66] M. Mc. Grath, *Preaching and Theology in Anglo-Saxon England: Ælfric and Wulfstan* (Toronto 1977); H. Gneuss, 'The Origin of Standard old English and Aethelwold's Schol at Winchester', *ASE* 1 (1972) pp 63–83; P. Clemoes, 'Late Old English Literature', *TCS* p 110.

[67] Knowles, *MO* p 42.

[68] J. Semmler, 'Karl der Grosse und das Fränkische Monchtum', *Karl der Grosse: Das Geistige Leben*, ed B. Bischoff (Düsseldorf 1965) pp 255–89.

these meetings in 817 that Louis, under the influence of the church reformers, declared the indivisibility of the empire in the *Ordinatio Imperii*.[69] In Francia as in England the progress of reforms was at first limited by, but later helped to break down, the boundaries of the kingdoms. The events of these years were clearly in the minds of the English churchmen one hundred and fifty years later, and it may be this that explains the use of the title taken by Louis, *imperator augustus*, in the charter of 970.[70]

The effects of the English developments in Edgar's reign were felt in the mechanics of royal government. The reform of the coinage in 973 increased royal control of the mints throughout the kingdom by the multiplication of mints, the regular demonetisations, and the uniform issues. More charters were now issued for midland estates, and the royal itinerary now took in more sites north of the Thames, and some of Edgar's later charters reveal a recognisably midland entourage.[71] Midland churches were now the object of royal generosity gaining land, money, books, ornaments, and perhaps above all saints, or their relics. The interest in relics of the late tenth century centred on insular saints, unlike the foreign relics with their imperial overtones that were gained by Athelstan.[72] The new monasteries were to subsume the spiritual traditions of the early kingdoms, being for the most part founded on sites of acknowledged holiness such as Ely or Saint Alban's.

This is not to say that England was governed by a uniform system of administration after AD 1000. In many important ways

[69] J. Semmler, 'Reichsidee und Kirchliche Gesetzegebung bei Ludwig dem Frommen', *KRG* 71 (1960) pp 37–65; F. L. Ganshof 'Some Observations on the Ordinatio Imperii of 817', *The Carolingians and the Frankish Monarchy* (London 1971) pp 273–88.

[70] For English manuscripts of the decrees of 817, M. Bateson, 'Rules for Monks and Secular Canons After the Revival under King Edgar', *EHR* 9 (1894) pp 690–708, esp pp 694–5.

[71] See *S* nos 779, 781, 782, and the doubtful 787 and 792 for thegns often recognisable from Ely and Peterborough records.

[72] The evidence for late tenth century translations is mostly contained in the list analysed in D. W. Rollason, 'Lists of Saints' Resting-Places in Anglo-Saxon England', *ASE* 7 (1978) pp 61–93. This list was itself a product of the new interest in the saints of Mercia and Northumbria. On Athelstan's relics, Robinson, *Dunstan* pp 72–8; Leyser, 'The Tenth Century in Byzantine-Western Relationships', *Relations between East and West in the Middle Ages*, ed D. Baker (Edinburgh 1973); Leyser, *Rule and Conflict* p 88.

government was becoming more diverse, not less so.[73] Nor can it be said that the church reformers glorified kingship for the contemporary saints' lives, especially those of Dunstan and Oswald, contain discussions of kingship and obedience that could easily include sharp criticism. But England after the tenth century was seen as one kingdom. The word *Englaland* has appeared by the turn of the century.[74] This development can be attributed to the efforts of the monastic reformers who were at this critical juncture the advisers of the kings. The reforms in the church had concentrated on a uniform monastic custom. This was a reform programme that was less concerned about the position of the church in society than with the internal organisation of the church. The emphasis of later reformers such as Wulfstan was to be quite the reverse. While it was not perhaps unusual for churchmen at any time to value unity, the history of tenth century England vividly illustrates how this could in one respect influence political developments.[75]

Oxford

---

[73] J. Campbell, 'Observations on English Government from the ninth to the twelfth century', *TRHS* 5 ser 25 (1975) pp 39–54.

[74] *Gesetze* I pp 222–3; E. A. Freeman, *The Norman Conquest* 5 vols (2 ed Oxford 1867–79) I p 605. Both Byrhtferth of Ramsey and the ealdorman Aethelweard were so enthusiastic in their use of the term *Angli* that they could both even describe the West Saxons as the West Angles, a title that was never to catch on. The term East Angles can be used by Byrhtferth to mean the eastern Mercians, and by Aethelweard to mean the East Saxons. Aethelweard may also have been the first to use the term *Anglia* for England, see *HCY* I pp 428, 428, 444, 446; *The Chronicle of Aethelweard*, ed A. Campbell (London 1962) pp li, 9. When Aethelweard says *Britannia nunc Anglia appellatur*, he may be speaking of a more recent development than his context at first suggests.

[75] I am grateful to Mr J. Campbell and Mr K. J. Leyser for helpful comments on this paper.

THE BENEDICTINE REVIVAL IN THE NORTH: THE LAST BULWARK OF ANGLO-SAXON MONASTICISM?

by ANNE DAWTRY

THE MIDLAND houses of Winchcombe and Evesham restored monasticism to the north in a fervent and wholly English form. No one can read the history of this migration and the subsequent history of Durham without feeling that here, at least, English monastic life was sound.[1]

In these words, Knowles summed up his view of the type of monastic observance which was instituted in the houses of the northern *renovatio* after the Norman Conquest.[2] Certainly there were important Anglo-Saxon elements present in the revival of Benedictine monasticism in the north of England; Durham, Whitby and St Mary's, York, owed much to the Anglo-Saxon monastic life as retained at Worcester and Evesham after the Norman Conquest.

Since the Scandinavian invasions which had destroyed the great Northumbrian monasteries, there had been no Benedictine houses in the north of England.[3] The attempts of bishop Aethelric of Durham in the mid-eleventh century to reintroduce the monastic life at Durham had been treated with hostility by the secular community there.[4] Those in charge of the tomb of Cuthbert in 1066 were described by Symeon of Durham as following a way of life which conformed neither to monastic customs nor to those of

[1] D. Knowles, 'The Norman Plantation', *D Rev* 49 (1931) pp 441–56, pp 455–6
[2] Other works on the revival of monasticism in the north include Knowles, *MO* pp 159–71; L. G. D. Baker, 'The Desert in the North', *NH* 5 (1970) pp 1–11; B. Meehan, 'Outsiders, insiders, and property in Durham around 1100', *SCH* 12 (1975) pp 45–58; D. Bethell, 'The Foundation of Fountains Abbey and the State of St. Mary's, York in 1132', *JEH* 17 (1966) pp 11–27. Derek Baker, '*The Narratio de Fundationis* of Fountains Abbey', 1 and 2, *Asoc*. The most recent work on the subject is J. Burton, 'The Origin and Development of the Religious Orders in Yorkshire', unpublished University of York PhD thesis (1977)
[3] Knowles, *MO* p 165.
[4] J. M. Cooper, 'The Last Four Anglo-Saxon Archbishops of York', *Borthwick Paper* 38 (York 1970) p 1.

the regular canons.[5] Jarrow was so desolate that traces of its ancient renown were scarcely visible,[6] whilst at Whitby we are told that the monastic cells were ruinous and roofless.[7]

At Worcester, Wulfstan II, the last Anglo-Saxon bishop gave new life to his cathedral priory. Between his appointment to the see of Worcester in 1062 and his death in 1095 he increased the number of monks there from twelve to fifty.[8] It was also men of Anglo-Saxon origin, this time from Winchcombe and Evesham,[9] the latter under the direction of Aethelwig, the last of the great Anglo-Saxon abbots, until 1077,[10] who revived Benedictine monasticism in the north. Two of those who undertook the first *peregrinatio* northwards in 1073–4, Aeldwin prior of Winchcombe, who eventually settled at Wearmouth,[11] and Aelfwig a deacon and monk of Evesham who remained at their early settlement of Jarrow,[12] were Anglo-Saxon by birth. The third, Reinfrid, although formerly a knight in the service of king William, had probably been influenced by surviving Anglo-Saxon monastic ideas at Evesham where he had served his novitiate and it is likely that he put some of these into practice when he reestablished the monastic life at Whitby.[13] Since St. Mary's, York was founded from Whitby[14] and the cathedral priory at Durham was initially staffed with monks from Jarrow and Wearmouth[15] these two houses may also be regarded as somewhat Anglo-Saxon in their sympathies.

It was probably also from Worcester and Evesham that Durham inherited its attitude towards the Anglo-Saxon saints. It is true that a few Anglo-Norman saints were retained in the liturgy of the

---

[5] Symeon [of Durham] *Historia [Ecclesiae] Dunelm[ensis]*, ed T. Arnold *RS* (1882) p 120. Although it is unlikely that Symeon was amongst the original community who were transferred from Jarrow and Wearmouth to Durham, his name does appear thirty-seventh on the list of those who had taken monastic vows at Durham before 1104.

[6] Vix aliquod antiquae nobilitatis servaverat signum', Symeon, *Historia Dunelm* p 109.

[7] 'altaria vacua et discooperata remanserunt', *Memorial [of the Foundation of Whitby]*, *Cart[ularium Abbathiae de] Whit[eby]*, ed J. C. Atkinson *SS* 69 (1879) p 2.

[8] Knowles, *MO* p 160.

[9] Symeon, *Historia Dunelm*, pp 108–9.

[10] *HRH* p 47.

[11] Symeon, *Historia Dunelm* p 112.

[12] *ibid.* p 111.

[13] *Memorial, Cart Whit* p 1.

[14] Symeon, *Historia Dunelm* p 111.

[15] *ibid* p 122.

Anglo-Norman church. Alphege, after a brief wrangle with the new Norman clergy continued to be venerated at Christ Church, Canterbury under Lanfranc's régime,[16] the feast of Cuthbert was kept at Gloucester[17] and the relics of Aetheldrida and Withburga were translated from the old to the new minster at Ely by abbot Richard, a Norman formerly from Bec.[18] An interest was also taken in Anglo-Saxon saints' cults by professional hagiographers from the continent such as Folcard, abbot of Thorney (1067–83), who composed a *vita* of John of Beverley[19] and Goscelin who wrote many English saints lives,[20] both of whom had come from St.Bertin.[21] Many of the Norman clergy, however, were ill at ease with the English custom of venerating local saints. In Normandy and on the continent as a whole at this time local and national saints received little attention in comparison to more universally accepted figures such as the Holy Trinity and the saints Stephen and Peter,[22] and this had its effect in post-conquest England. Many Anglo-Saxon saints were never again to receive the veneration which had been theirs in the pre-conquest period.[23]

At Worcester and Durham, on the other hand, the cult of many of the Anglo-Saxon saints was maintained with considerable enthusiasm. Thus Worcester celebrated the feasts of fifteen Anglo-Saxon saints, only the feasts of Aelgifu and Egwin being removed from the calendar in the post-conquest period.[24] Durham, too,

[16] *The Monastic Constitutions of Lanfranc*, ed D. Knowles (London 1951) p 59.
[17] *English Benedictine Kalendars after 1100*, ed [F. Wormald] 2 vols, *HBS* 77 81 (1939/1946) s p 46.
[18] *Liber Eliensis* ed E. O. Blake *Cser*, 3 ser, 92 (1962) pp 228–39.
[19] Folcard compiled this life for archbishop Ealdred of York (died 1069). Printed in *Historians of the Church of York*, ed J. Raine, 3 vols, *RS* (1879) I, pp 239–91.
[20] A. Gransden *Historical Writing in England c.550–1307* (London 1974) p 107.
[21] A further example of the continuing popularity of Anglo-Saxon saints can be seen from the fact that lists of their burying places continued to be copied until the thirteenth century; see D. W. Rollason, 'Lists of saints resting places in Anglo-Saxon England', *Anglo Saxon England* 7 (Cambridge 1978) pp 61–93 p 69.
[22] One example of this is the policy of dedicating churches on the continent to the Holy Trinity, (Matilda's foundation at Caen – 1066) Stephen, (William's foundation at Caen – 1065) and Peter (Jumièges – 1067.) Evreux, consecrated in 1060 was dedicated to the Saviour.
[23] At Christ Church, Canterbury the feasts of Ermenhilda and Edward the martyr were removed from the calendar whilst at St. Augustine's the feasts of Werburga, Ermenhilda, Aldhelm, Aelgifu, Swithun Eadburga, Withburga and Ceolfrith were no longer celebrated.
[24] Ermenhilda, Edward the martyr, Cuthbert, Guthlac, Alphege, Erkenwold,

maintained many of the feasts of the Anglo-Saxon saints which were eradicated from the liturgy elsewhere. The cult of Cuthbert, for example, was not only maintained but also further developed so that by the beginning of the twelfth century the feast of the saint was widely accepted in the Anglo-Norman church as a whole.[25] Those who attended the translation of Cuthbert in 1104 included not only local abbots such as Hugh of Selby and Stephen of York but also William of Corbeil, the Norman chaplain of the bishop of Durham and the archbishop of Seez.[26] Nor was Cuthbert the only Anglo-Saxon saint to be venerated at Durham. The feasts of Benedict Biscop, Aelphege, Wilfrid, Dunstan, Aetheldrith, Aidan, Aenswith and Edmund, king and martyr, are also to be found in the twelfth century calendar of the house.[27]

The revived Benedictine houses in the north of England after the Norman Conquest were Anglo-Saxon, therefore both in their original inspiration and initial leadership. Durham also appeared to be influenced by the surviving elements of Anglo-Saxon monasticism at Worcester through its veneration of the Anglo-Saxon saints.

Unlike Evesham and Worcester, however, the houses of the northern *renovatio* were also inextricably linked with the Norman régime. The cathedral priory at Durham, for example, owed its very existence to the work of two Norman appointees. Walcher, although a Lotharingian in origin was a protégé of king William I.[28] He encouraged the nascent communities at Jarrow and Wearmouth and wished to become a monk himself, with the intention of establishing a community of monks at Durham to tend the shrine of Cuthbert; in 1080, however, he met a violent death before he could accomplish this project.[29] This task was left to his successor William of St. Carilef (1080–1099) formerly abbot of St. Vincent, Le Mans,[30] who on 26 May 1083, having obtained royal and papal

Dunstan, Aethelbert, Germanus, Alban, Aetheldrith, Swithun, Sexburge, Oswald and Edmund, king and martyr, *English Benedictine Kalendars before 1100*, ed F. Wormald *HBS* 72 (1934) pp 212–23.

[25] B. Colgrave, 'The Post Bedan Miracles and Translations of St. Cuthbert', *The Early Cultures of North-West Europe, H. M. Chadwick Memorial Studies*, ed C. Fox, B. Dickins (Cambridge 1950) pp 305–32.

[26] C. F. Battiscombe, *The Relics of St. Cuthbert* (Oxford 1956) p 55 note 3.

[27] *English Benedictine Kalendars after 1100*, I, pp 167–79.

[28] Le Neve 2 [*Monastic Cathedrals*] p 29.

[29] Symeon *Historia Dunelm* p 113.

[30] Le Neve 2, p 29.

permission for his foundation, transferred the communities from Jarrow and Wearmouth to Durham.[31] The same bishop had previously endowed Wearmouth with Southwick, county Durham.[32] The next bishop, Ranulf Flambard (1099–1128),[33] whom William of Malmesbury describes as: 'The plunderer of the rich, the destroyer of the poor . . . . . unsurpassed as a mercenary advocate,'[34] proved a useful mentor to the cathedral priory. Although he usurped the offerings of the altar, the profits from burial in the cemetery and several pieces of land from the monks' endowment, these were only worth about ten pounds and were in any case utilized in the building of the cathedral.[35] Later Ranulf restored these properties and added gifts of his own including land adjacent to the monks property of Hunsley at Walkington[37] and the tithes of the churches of Welton and Howden,[38] as well as a considerable donation of palls, copes, caskets, dalmatics and tunics for the use of the monks.[39] Whitby, too, received episcopal patronage from Thurstan of York who gave to the abbey the privilege already enjoyed by the churches of Ripon and Beverley,[40] as well as obtaining a papal privilege of protection in favour of the house.[41]

The links between the northern houses are also to be seen in the political sphere. At Worcester, although bishop Wulfstan II was at one time custodian of Worcester castle,[42] the cathedral priory there was markedly Anglo-Saxon in its sympathies,[43] and this provided an excuse for the Norman baronage to encroach upon the monks

---

[31] Symeon *Historia Dunelm* p 122.
[32] H. S. Offler, *Durham Episcopal Charters 1071–1152*, SS 179 (1968) p 63.
[33] Ranulf had formerly been a clerk in the royal chancery and he made considerable use of his chancery experience in the administration of his see. For further details see R. W. Southern, 'Ranulf Flambard and early Anglo-Norman administration, *TRHS, 4 Ser* 16 (1933) pp 95–128, 26.
[34] William of Malmesbury, *Gesta Pontificum Anglorum*, ed N. E. S. A. Hamilton, *RS* (1870) p 274.
[35] R. W. Southern, 'Ranulf Flambard', *Medieval Humanism and other Studies* (Oxford 1970) pp 183–205, 202.
[36] *EYC* 2, 934, pp 273–4, Durham, D[ean and] C[hapter MS] 2 ^{ea}1^{mae} Pont.1.
[37] *ibid* 966, p 297, Durham DC Cartulary 1 fol 49^r.
[38] *ibid* 977, p 306 Durham, DC 2 ^{da}1^{mae} Pont. 3.
[39] Symeon *Historia Dunelm* p 140.
[40] *EYC* 2,876, pp 223–4.
[41] *Whitby Cart* p 116; Jaffé 7230 p 827; D. Nicholl, *Thurstan, Archbishop of York 1114–1140* (York 1964) p 98.
[42] *ASC*, ed D. Whitelock (London 1965) p 166.
[43] Heming, a monk of Worcester during the time of Wulfstan's episcopate shows considerable hostility to the Normans in his cartulary.

endowment. Urse d'Abetôt, for example, encroached upon the monks' cemetery while building the castle there for the king,[44] and further encroachments were made on the monastic property by Robert, his brother,[45] and William fitz Osbern.[46]

In the north the situation was very different. At Durham the bishop was not merely a custodian of the castle but held it in his own right.[47] Since the bishop was also abbot of the cathedral priory, the monks acquired many donations and privileges as a result of the influential position of their abbot. King William I probably granted Hemingborough,[48] William II gave Billingham[49] and Matilda, the wife of Henry I, the church of Carham[50] to the priory, whilst the baronial patrons of the house included Nigel de Aubigny[51] and Robert de Stutteville.[52] The prior also had the power to hold a court separate to that of the bishop and to appoint officers without episcopal interference.[53]

The abbot of York also held a position of political importance in the north of England at this time since he held sole judicial authority in his own lands under the king. The abbey's men were free from attendance at the shire, riding and hundred courts and anyone who wished to bring a case against them was forced to do

[44] J. W. Lamb, *St. Wulfstan, Prelate and Patriot, a Study of his Life and Times* (London 1933) pp 83–4.

[45] Heming, [*Cartulary*, ed T. Hearne], 2 vols (Oxford 1723) 1 pp 253, 268–9. This included land at Lawern, Elmley and Charlton.

[46] Heming p 263. This involved land at Headsoffe. Further encroachments were made by Ralph de Bernay sheriff of Hereford who took Alfinton, Astley and Whitley. Heming pp 255–6.

[47] [*The*] *Letters of Lanfranc* [*Archbishop of Canterbury*] ed H. Clover and M. Gibson (Oxford 1979) pp 126–7. When writing to bishop Walcher Lanfranc refers to *castrum vestrum* a term which seems to imply more than mere custodianship. It is probable that both William of St. Carilef and Ranulf Flambard held similar positions of military responsibility.

[48] *EYC* 2,990, p 315. In its present form this charter is spurious although it is probably based on a genuine writ which no longer survives.

[49] Durham, DC 1^ma^1^mae^Reg 7 (1089–94); *EYC* 929, p 268.

[50] Durham, DC 1^ma^2^dae^Spec 23 (1107–16); *RR* 2,1143, p 135.

[51] Durham, DC 2^da^1^mae^Reg 9 (1116–21); *EYC* 2,933, p 273. Confirmation of the gift of Barmpton. Although the younger son of a Norman baron Nigel de Aubigny was raised to the highest nobility after the battle of Tinchebrai in 1106 inheriting most of the lands in Yorkshire and Lincolnshire forfeited by Hugh fitz Baldric for his support of duke Robert.

[52] Durham, DC 2^da^1^mae^Reg 17; *EYC* 3, 1894, pp 499–500. Confirmation of a gift of land in Hunsley par Rowley (1100–9)

[53] *RR* 2,1574 p 223 (1129)

so in the abbot's court.[54] The political importance of the abbot of St Mary's, York was further strengthened by a royal grant to the abbot of complete jurisdiction over the forest in his own lands.[55] As in the case of Durham the abbot of York's influential position in the political sphere encouraged generous donations to the house. Henry I donated Ousefleet and the royal property at Haldenby to the abbey [56] and it was also generously patronized by Osbern of Arches,[57] William Peverel,[58] Robert de Brus,[59] Alan II of Brittany, Berengar de Todeni and Ilbert de Lacy.[60] In contrast to the majority of religious houses at this date whose privileges were limited to grants of *sac, soc,* and *infangentheof,*[61] freedom from tolls and customs of all that pertained *ad victum monasterii*[62] and permission to collect undergrowth and timber in the forests for fuel and building,[63] St Mary's, York possessed the privileges of *grithbryce, foresteall, hamsocn, ebberethef,* and *fihtwite* normally reserved to the crown,[64] as well as the complete jurisdiction over its own forests already mentioned above.

Politically, therefore, the northern houses were firmly linked to the Norman régime. This is hardly surprising. Since several of the Anglo-Saxon abbots such as Leofric of Peterborough had proved their allegiance to Harold by fighting personally at Hastings,[65] the Norman kings had looked for every opportunity to depose those

---

[54] BM Additional MS 38816 fols 22ᵛ–3ʳ.

[55] *EYC* 1,351, p 268 (1100–15) The forest of Pickering Lithe, Ryedale and part of the forest of Galtres.

[56] *LYC* 1,470, p 361.

[57] *EYC* 1,527, p 408 (1100–16) Land in Nether Poppleton, Appleton, Hessay and St. Saviour's Gate, York.

[58] Manchester, John Rylands Library Latin MS 220 fol 358ᵛ (1100–22) Land in Rudston.

[59] BM Harley MS 236 fol 21ʳ (1125–35); *EYC* 2,648, p 1. The manor of Appleton Wiske and the church of Burton Agnes.

[68] Harley MS 236 fol 2ᵛ; *EYC* 1,350, p 264. Confirmation by William II (1088–93)

[61] For example the grant to abbot Aelsi of Ramsey (died 1087) in *Cartularium Monasterii de Rameseia,* ed W. H. Hart and P. A. Loyons *RS* (1884) p 233; RR 1,295, p 77. For a similar grant to St Albans (*c*1102) see *RR* 2,595, p 23.

[62] Such privileges were enjoyed by Thorney *RR* 2,585, p 211; Battle, *RR* 2, 1075, p 121; and Glastonbury *RR* 2,1525, p 213.

[63] J. C. Cox, *The Royal Forests of England* (London 1905) p 213.

[64] These were the fines payable for a breach of special peace, obstruction, forcible entry, theft and neglect of military service respectively; see N. D. Hurnard, 'The Anglo-Norman Franchises' *EHR* (1949) pp 289–327 and pp 433–60, especially pp 299–300 and F. E. Harmer, *Anglo-Saxon Writs* (Manchester 1952) pp 74–82.

[65] ASC E (1066) p 142.

who showed Anglo-Saxon partisanship and an unwillingness to work with the new regime.[66] Wulfstan of Worcester and Aethelwig of Evesham were only tolerated by William I because they proved useful to the maintenance of royal power in Mercia.[67] Although William of Malmesbury's statement that William would allow no Anglo-Saxon to be preferred to ecclesiastical office must be considered an exaggeration,[68] it is extremely unlikely that the Norman kings would have allowed Durham, Whitby and St Mary's, York to become exclusively Anglo-Saxon in their sympathies, especially as they were situated in a region which had always been politically unstable. Little more than a hundred years before the Norman Conquest, there had been an autonomous kingdom in the north centred at York, which had possessed stronger links with Ireland and Scandinavia than with the rest of England.[69]

The fact that William I dare not risk even the political separation of the north from the rest of England, can be seen in his policy of limiting the power of the archbishop of York, by removing from his jurisdiction the sees of Worcester and Dorchester. This meant that the power of the archbishop was now limited to control over Durham and the Scottish sees.[70] Archbishop Lanfranc, too, when claiming the superiority of Canterbury over York warned that if the north was allowed to become separated, even ecclesiastically, from the rest of the country, political separation might also ensue and an independent kingdom be established in the north under the sway of the Scots or Norwegians[71]

The northern houses were thus politically in accord with the Norman régime however much their personal sympathies tended towards the last surviving remnants of Anglo-Saxon monasticism as retained at Worcester and Evesham. The houses of the northern

[66] Both Godric of Winchcombe and Aethelnoth of Glastonbury were imprisoned by the Conqueror. Knowles, *MO* p 104.

[67] J. H. Round *Feudal England* (London 1895) pp 304–5.

[68] [William of Malmesbury], *Gesta Regum* [*Anglorum*, ed W. Stubbs] *RS* (1889) p 313.

[69] J. Le Patourel, 'The Norman Conquest of Yorkshire', *NH* 6 (1971) pp 1–21 especially p 3.

[70] *Letters of Lanfranc* p 86. Wulfstan II of Worcester was told by Lanfranc that if he assisted the archbishop of York in the consecration of a bishop of the Orkneys this would in no way be allowed to become a precedent for the archbishop of York to exercise jurisdiction over Worcester.

[71] Hugh the Chantor, *History of Four Archbishops of York, Historians of the Church of York*, 2, *RS* (1886) p 100

renovatio, however, possessed links not only with Normandy, but also with the continent as a whole in the spritual and cultural spheres.

In this respect it may advance the argument to examine the development of the cult of the Virgin Mary. In the Anglo-Saxon liturgy the Virgin had been held in great veneration. The *Regularis Concordia* prescribed the singing of the anthem of the Virgin twice a day whilst the principal mass on a Saturday was also to be dedicated to her honour.[72] At Winchester and Canterbury the feast of the Immaculate Conception was observed in the pre-conquest period.[73] In the years immediately following the Norman Conquest the cult of the Virgin was regarded with suspicion. By the middle of the twelfth century however, chiefly through the work of Dominic, prior of Evesham, Anselm, abbot of Bury St. Edmunds, Eadmer and Osbert of Clare, the feast of the Immaculate Conception had been widely accepted into the liturgy of Anglo-Norman England.[74] Durham, on the other hand, clung tenaciously to the practice of the early Anglo-Norman church and the feast was never inserted into the calendar of the house during the twelfth century.[75]

The links with the continent are also clearly demonstrated by an examination of the houses with which Durham made agreements of confraternity during the twelfth century.[76] Whereas Worcester only made agreements with local houses such as Evesham, Bath, Pershore, Winchcombe and Gloucester,[77] Durham counted amongst its *confratres* not only St Mary's, York, Lastingham and Hackness and other English houses such as Christ Church and St. Augustine's, Canterbury, Winchester and Gloucester but also the continental houses of St. Carilef, St. Stephen's, Caen, and Fécamp.[78]

The cultural links which joined the northern houses to the continent as a whole can perhaps best be seen by a comparison

---

[72] *The Regularis Concordia*, ed T. Symons (London 1953) p 20.

[73] R. W. Southern, 'English Origins of the Miracles of the Virgin', *Medieval and Renaissance Studies* 4 (London 1958) pp 176–216, p 196.

[74] *ibid* p 182.

[75] *English Benedictine Kalendars after 1100*, I, p 179.

[76] Confraternity was an agreement made between otherwise independent abbeys that they would be united in prayer for one another's dead.

[77] B. Thorpe, *Diplomatarium Anglicum Aevi Saxonici* (London1863) pp 615–17.

[78] *Liber Vitae Ecclesiae Dunelmensis*, ed A. H. Thompson, SS 136 (1923) fols 33^v,48^v,33^v,48^r,33^v,48^v,48^r.

between the contents of the libraries of the northern houses of Durham and Whitby in the twelfth century and the books possessed by other houses during the same period.[79] According to William of Malmesbury, Anglo-Saxon literary culture had declined to such an extent by 1066, that anyone who understood grammar was regarded as a marvel, while the clergy were scarcely able to stammer out the words of the sacraments.[80] Even Wulfstan II of Worcester was accused of being like an *homo idiota* and *sine litteris*.[81] Late Anglo-Saxon taste concentrated rather on texts relating to the divine office and to private devotions rather than to learning in its strictest sense.[82] Where classical and patristic works were copied it was usually those of Isidore and Boethius's *De Consolatione Philosophiae* rather than the works of Augustine, Gregory and Jerome.[83] with the advent of the Normans into England, however, there was a more conscientious acquisition of the more important classical and patristic texts. Herbert de Losinga, for example, whilst abbot of Ramsey,[84] wrote abroad for copies of Suetonius[85] and Josephus and the letters of Augustine and Jerome.[86] The paucity of classical and patristic texts which was a common feature of the

---

[79] For Durham two booklists survive, one listing the donations of William of St. Carilef and the other being a composite catalogue of c1170. Both are printed in *Catalogi [Veteres Librorum Ecclesiae Cathedralis Dunelmensis]*, SS 7 (1838) pp 117–18 and pp 1–10 respectively. For Whitby we have a catalogue of the late twelfth century printed in *Cart Whit* p 341, whilst the *T[extus] R[offensis]* 2 vols, ed P. H. Sawyer (Copenhagen 1957–62) contains an inventory of the books of the cathedral priory at Rochester. For Canterbury there is a fragmentary list, dealing mainly with classical texts, printed in [M. R. James, *The*] *Ancient Libraries [of Canterbury and Dover]* (Cambridge 1903) pp 7–12. A detailed study of Worcester manuscripts has recently been made by E. A. MacIntyre, 'Early Twelfth Century. Worcester Cathedral Priory with Special Reference to the Manuscripts written there', unpublished Oxford DPhil thesis (1972). For the library of Evesham as well as for the patristic works possessed by Christ Church, Canterbury, we are forced to rely on the evidence of surviving books listed by N. R. Ker in *Medieval Libraries of Great Britain* (2 ed London 1964).

[80] *Gesta Regum* p 304. 'vix sacramentorum verba balbutiebant'.

[81] R. R. Darlington ed., *Vita Wulfstani C ser*, 3 Ser 40 (1928) p 77.

[82] [R.M.] Thomson, 'The Library of Bury St Edmunds Abbey [in the Eleventh and Twelfth Centuries'] *Speculum* 47 (1972) pp 617–45 p 626.

[83] N. R. Ker, *English Manuscripts in the Century after the Norman Conquest* (Oxford 1960) pp 7–8.

[84] 1087–91. In 1091 he became bishop of Thetford from which place he transferred the see to Norwich where he died in 1119.

[85] *Epistolae Herberti de Losinga* ed R. Anstruther, (Brussels 1846) p 7.

[86] *ibid* p 16.

libraries of Anglo-Saxon England,[87] was also to be found at Worcester and Evesham in the twelfth century. Evesham, as far as can be ascertained, acquired no works of Ambrose and Jerome during the twelfth century and only the *Commentary on the Psalms* of Augustine.[88] Worcester, whilst possessing Ambrose's *Epistolae*, the biblical commentaries of Jerome and Gregory's *Dialogues* and *Pastoral Care*,[89] possessed none of the major works of Augustine and was sadly deficient in the classics. Instead Anglo-Saxon texts were still popular there and the cathedral priory possessed three sets of sermons, a compilation of prayers, Bede's *Ecclesiastical History*, the *Vision of Leofric*, a copy of the *Dialogues* and Aelfric's *Grammar* all in Anglo-Saxon and written between the Norman Conquest and the beginning of the thirteenth century.[90] The handwriting and spelling adopted by the *scriptorium* at Worcester in the post-conquest period also owed much to Anglo-Saxon influence whilst the works chosen for correction and annotation suggest a continuance of traditional interests there.[91]

At Durham, although some works continued to be copies in Anglo-Saxon during the course of the twelfth century, such as a *vita* of Cuthbert, a bilingual *Rule of Saint Benedict* and Bede's *Death Song*,[92] the catalogue of the library there shows that there were strong links between Durham and the reform movement which was taking place on the continent. Its library rivals even that of Canterbury and Rochester. From William of St. Carilef Durham received copies of Augustine's *De Civitate Dei, Letters, Confessions, Enchiridion* and his commentaries on the evangelist John and on the psalter, Gregory's *Pastoral Care, Moralia, Register,* and *Homilies* and

---

[87] Thomson, 'The Library of Bury St. Edmunds', p 626.

[88] Oxford, Jesus College MS 93.

[89] BM Royal MS 6Axvi, BM Royal MS 4Cii, BM Cotton MS Otto CI part ii and Cambridge, C[orpus] C[hristi] C[ollege] MS 12 respectively.

[90] [N. R.] Ker, [*Catalogue of Manuscripts containing*] *Anglo-Saxon*, (Oxford 1957) pp 81, 113–115, 412–18, 108–110, 36–7 and 466–7. The references are as follows:- Cambridge, CCC MS 198 fols 321–7 and 367–77; Oxford Bodleian Library MS Junius 121, Cambridge CCC MS 391, C[ambridge,] U[niversity] L[ibrary] MS Kk III. 18, Cambridge, CCC MS 367 part II fols 3–6 and 11–29 and Worcester, Cathedral Library MS F174.

[91] *Early Worcester Cathedral Priory* pp 24, 67 and 82. Thomson, 'The Library of Bury St. Edmund's Abbey', p 625, shows that pre-conquest interests were also retained at Bury until the twelfth century.

[92] Ker, *Anglo Saxon*, pp 148, 298. Durham DC MS B IV 24 fols 74–127, BM MS Cotton Vitellius D xx Burnt Cotton Fragment Bundle 1(16)

Ambrose's *De Poenitentia*.[93] Other important gifts were added during the course of the twelfth century including Jerome's *Commentaries* and several important classical works such as Cicero's *De Amicitia* and *De Senecute*, Virgil's *Bucolics* and Plato's *Timaeus*[94] Whitby, too, although few patristic works are listed in its twelfth century catalogue was in the forefront of intellectual development by virtue of the number of humanistic classical texts which it possessed, including the works of Plato, Virgil and Cicero already mentioned above.[95]

The revived Benedictine houses in the north of England, therefore, cannot be seen as the last bulwark of Anglo-Saxon monasticism. That place is already filled by Worcester and Evesham which, although their leaders worked with the king for the preservation of law and order in Mercia, for a long time maintained Anglo-Saxon ideas in their monastic observance and cultural interests. The northern houses, although they were Anglo-Saxon in their original inspiration and leadership, and in the case of Durham retaining Anglo-Saxon customs in the observance of the feasts of many Anglo-Saxon saints, were also linked politically and culturally with the Norman régime and with the continent as a whole. At Canterbury and St. Albans, Norman elements at first almost totally superseded Anglo-Saxon traditions whilst at Worcester and Evesham Anglo-Saxon monastic life was retained with an enthusiastic fervour. In the north, however, there was a fusion of elements both Anglo-Saxon and Norman in their origin and this produced a monasticism which was truly Anglo-Norman in its outlook.

University of London
Westfield College

---

[93] Durham, *Catalogi*, pp 117–18. TR fols 224^{r/v},227^v. It is likely that Canterbury possessed a similar collection although only copies of Augustine's *Letters*, Gregory's *Register* and *Homilies* and Ambrose's *De Poenitentia* survive, Cambridge, T[rinity] C[ollege,]MS 140, CUL MS Ii III.33 fols 35–195, CUL Ff III.9 and CUL KkI.23 fols 65–80.

[94] Durham, *Catalogi*, pp 1, 4, 5; two copies of Jerome's *Commentaries* survive from Canterbury in Cambridge, TC MSS 142 and 168 whilst Rochester also possessed a copy *TR* fol 225^r. Cicero, Virgil and Plato are listed in the Canterbury Catalogue, *Ancient Libraries* pp 8–10.

[95] *Cart Whit* p 341.

PRO STATU ET INCOLUMNITATE REGNI MEI: ROYAL MONASTIC PATRONAGE 1066–1154

by EMMA MASON

D ANGERS to the cohesion of the Anglo-Norman *regnum* correlate to a marked extent with the fluctuating patronage extended by the Anglo-Norman kings towards Westminster Abbey, and other religious houses, in their search for one which would symbolize and enhance the stability of their dynasty.

Westminster itself had royal connections from the outset. The original church of St Peter, on Thorney Island in the Thames, to the west of London, was founded by Saebert, king of the East Saxons, and his wife Ethelgoda.[1] The couple were allegedly buried there early in the seventh century, but it was some four hundred and fifty years before further royal burials took place in St Peter's[2] The church was restored by Offa of Essex in the early years of the eighth century,[3] and c959 king Edgar sold it to Dunstan, who founded a monastery on the site.[4] Edgar gave several manors to this abbey, and Aethelred II gave or confirmed others.[5] Less exalted donors followed suit, and the house was already fairly prosperous[6] when Harold I Harefoot was buried there in 1040. His successor and half-brother Harthacnut, is said to have had his body thrown out.[7] Edward the Confessor, successor of Harthacnut, regarded Harold Harefoot as a usurper, so that Harold's burial at Westminster did not, it seems, inspire Edward's decision to be buried there

---

[1] [Barbara] Harvey, [*Westminster Abbey and its estates in the middle ages*] (Oxford 1977) p 20.

[2] *Ibid* p 372.

[3] *Ibid* p 21. It has been suggested that Offa the Great took an interest in the church, perhaps with the idea of asserting Mercian supremacy in the neighbourhood of London [C. N. L.] Brooke and [Gillian] Keir, [*London 800–1216: the shaping of a city*] (London 1975) p 295 and n. See also Harvey pp 345–6.

[4] Harvey pp 22–3.

[5] *Ibid* pp 341–2, 345–6, 352–4, 358–9.

[6] *ibid* pp 23–4.

[7] *Ibid* p 372; [F.] Barlow, [*Edward the Confessor*] (London 1970) p 48.

himself.[8] Its dedication was significant, however, since Edward felt obliged to St Peter for his restoration to his kingdom.[9] A late eleventh century Westminster tradition maintained that Edward intended to make a pilgrimage to Rome, but abandoned the project in case the realm was endangered in his absence. He decided instead to honour St Peter by restoring the church which was dedicated to him at Westminster.[10]

Edward was a generous benefactor, giving the abbey twice as much land as it already possessed.[11] He perhaps intended Westminster to be an English counterpart to the abbey of St. Denis, outside Paris.[12] Already the cult of Saint Denis was associated with the wellbeing of the French kings.[13] Edward gave land to St. Denis, and probably realized the importance which an equivalent church could have for the English monarchy,[14] which had experienced frequent upheavals in recent decades. In his last years, Edward had the church of St Peter's rebuilt on a grand scale as his mausoleum.[15] His choice of Westminster for this purpose was, it seems, a deliberate political decision, since most members of the rival dynasty (apart from Harold Harefoot), had been buried at Winchester.[16] In the early eleventh century, several large churches had been built in the western empire. These were intended to reflect the weight of the emperor's rule, and Edward's grandiose plans for the rebuilding of Westminster may have been in conscious imitation of these imperial projects. The rebuilt St Peter's was consecrated just over a week before Edward's death on 6 January 1066.[17]

The reign of Harold II Godwinsson was too brief, and ended too abruptly, for a coherent policy of religious patronage to emerge. While still an earl, Harold had founded the secular collegiate church of Waltham, and, as King, he may have intended it to assume

[8] Barlow, p 230.
[9] v[ita] A[edwardi] R[egis], [ed and transl F. Barlow] (London 1962) pp 9, 44; Brooke and Keir p 296.
[10] Harvey p 24.
[11] Ibid p 27.
[12] Brooke and Keir pp 296–8.
[13] Gabrielle M. Spiegel, 'The cult of St Denis and Capetian kingship', JMedH 1 (1975) pp 43, 53.
[14] Brooke and Keir pp 296–7.
[15] VAR pp 44–6.
[16] Barlow pp 229–30.
[17] Ibid pp 233, 253. I am grateful to Dr Richard Gem for an informal discussion on Edward's possible 'imperial' intentions.

Westminster's role.[18] Westminster, however, was recognized as the coronation church, since it was conveniently at hand on Edward's death, following which Harold was crowned in great haste.[19]

For William the Conqueror, later in 1066, Edward the Confessor was a less than idea symbol of legitimacy. In 1051, he had promised that Duke William should succeed him, and in Norman opinion, this promise was irrevocable. Edward subsequently changed his mind twice, however. First he recalled his kinsman Edward Aetheling from exile, but his untimely death left his young son Edgar as heir. This child's succession would have endangered political stability, and consequently Edward the Confessor, on his deathbed, commended the kingdom to Harold Godwinsson. According to English custom, his words overruled his earlier promise to Duke William, but Norman custom denied that this was so. The battle fought at Hastings was therefore seen by contemporaries as a judicial ordeal in which William vindicated the superiority of his claim to the English throne,[20] but it was no thanks to Edward that he had done so.

William's next priorities were to secure the submission of London and the leading magnates, and be annointed as King. Westminster was conveniently close for the latter purpose, and further reinforcement was given to existing precedents that the Abbey should be the coronation church. The surviving English magnates and *populus* formally acknowledged William as king *de jure*; the ceremony was designed to stress the continuity of English rule, and he was established as the legitimate successor of Edward the Confessor.[21] There is only tenuous evidence for miracles occurring at the Confessor's tomb in the immediate aftermath of his death,[22] and William himself was probably unaware of them when deciding to be crowned in the Abbey. In view of developments since the promise of 1051, he probably regarded Edward as someone distinctly less than a saint.

---

[18] *The legend [of the miraculous cross] of Waltham*, [transl F. S. Baker and K. N. Bascombe, ed Dinah Dean] (2 ed Waltham 1975) pp 3–6; Harvey p 25.

[19] [N. P.] Brooks and [the late H. E.] Walker, ['The authority and interpretation of the Bayeux Tapestry'], P[*roceedings of the*] B[*attle*] C[*onference on Anglo-Norman Studies*] *I. 1978* ed R. Allen Brown (Ipswich 1979) p 21; Barlow, pp 254–5.

[20] Ann Williams, 'Some notes and considerations on problems connected with the English royal succession, 860–1066', *PBC 1* pp 164–7.

[21] [D. C.] Douglas, [*William the Conqueror*] (London 1964) pp 205–7.

[22] Barlow p 261.

William made his first thank-offerings for the Conquest to his own foundations at Caen; to various other Norman houses, and to St. Valery of Picardy for the favourable breeze which blew the Norman fleet to England.[23] If he was conscious of any obligation towards the abbey in which he was transformed into a king, or of a link between his own fortunes and those of this house, we might expect to find a reflection in the wording of his genuine charters for Westminster, whether those issued in the first crucial years of the Norman settlement, down to 1071, or during the crises of the later 1070s and earlier 1080s. There are problems in assigning a precise date to many of William's charters, but of those which relate to new grants of property to the Abbey, three date from the early period of his reign, 1066×75;[24] three can be assigned to the middle years, 1070×82,[25] and one dates from 1087.[26] Almost all the estates which he gave had been Harold Godwinsson's personal property.[27] William established a prudent tradition of granting the monks land which had only recently come into the king's possession, although this cannot be taken to imply that he and his successors held Westminster in low esteem, since Edward himself had done likewise.[28]

In addition to his grants, William issued numerous confirmations of Westminster's existing lands and liberties. From the early years of his reign, there survive four confirmations of estates and customs enjoyed in Edward's time;[29] the middle years of William's reign produced five further confirmations;[30] two were issued at indeterminate dates,[31] while three can be dated to the last few years

---

[23] [D.] Matthew, [*The Norman monasteries and their English possessions*] (Oxford 1962) pp 30–31.

[24] *RR* 1 nos 45, 86–7. To achieve brevity in these footnotes, *RR* calendar numbers of royal charters are given throughout. Reference to the location of published texts of those not printed *in extenso* in *RR* 1 and 2 are given by the editors. In the preparation of this paper, the full texts have been consulted and the printed texts checked against the manuscripts.

[25] *RR* 1 nos 162–3, 166.

[26] *Ibid* no 236.

[27] *Ibid* nos 45, 86, 162–3.

[28] Harvey p 28. Baronial patrons adopted a similar attitude when endowing their own religious houses. (See my 'Timeo barones et dona ferentes', *SCH* 15 (1978) pp 61–2, 71–2).

[29] *RR* 1 nos 17–18, 32, 53.

[30] *Ibid* nos 166, 202, 212–14.

[31] *Ibid* nos 209, 250.

of the reign.[32] In a spurious confirmation supposedly dating from the beginning of William's reign, Edward the Confessor is referred to as the king's kinsman,[33] but in none of William's genuine grants or confirmations is there any attempt to associate the fortunes of the new king with the prestige of his predecessor in this way. Two further grants,[34] and two more confirmations,[35] may have been issued either by William I or William II, but in these, too, there is no association of the new dynasty with Edward or the abbey. On the contrary, William I withheld from Westminster bequests which should have taken effect on the death of Edward's widow, queen Edith,[36] and of William's new gifts, several were actually made in exchange for land appropriated when Windsor was afforested.[37] Overall, he treated Westminster respectfully but not favourably.

Since the king himself did not associate the interests of his dynasty with Westminster, his barons and *curiales* had no incentive to make gifts associated with his. Only one major baron, Geoffrey de Mandeville I, granted a substantial manor,[38] and one *curialis*, William the chamberlain, grudgingly parted with property in which he had succeeded one of Edward's officials, who had intended the land for the abbey.[39]

When queen Edith died in 1075, William I caused her to be buried at Westminster next to her husband,[40] but a few years later the monks themselves were in some doubt as to which of the tombs was his.[41] Gerald of Wales, writing more than a century after the event, described a miracle worked at the Confessor's tomb for Wulfstan of Worcester, thus prompting William I to retain that

---

[32] *Ibid* nos 143, 235, 278.
[33] *Ibid* no 89.
[34] *Ibid* nos 381–2.
[35] *Ibid* nos 417,436.
[36] Harvey p 27.
[37] *Ibid* p 27; *RR* I nos 45, 86–7, 236.
[38] Westminster abbey muniment book 2 fol 100; Harvey p 38.
[39] *Ibid* p 349 and n 6. The donor was probably William Mauduit I (See my 'Magnates, [curiales and the wheel of Fortune'] *PBC* 2 (1979), pp 131–2). His great-grandson, Robert Mauduit II, was a benefactor of the abbey in the early thirteenth century—see my 'The Mauduits and their chamberlainship of the Exchequer', *BIHR* 49 (1976) pp 9, 20–3—but intervening generations seem not to have been benefactors of the abbey.
[40] Barlow p 267.
[41] *Ibid* p 264.

formidable English bishop in office when he was in danger of being removed.[42] It is unlikely, however, that William was actually aware of any evidence that miracles were taking place at Edward's tomb, since he did not associate the new dynasty with the Abbey in any significant way.

In his reign, Battle Abbey was to some extent associated with the welfare of the monarchy. William founded this Benedictine house shortly after 1070, probably in expiation of the killing and plunder caused by the Norman Conquest. Its location and associations also made it popular with those magnates on whom the king relied so strongly in the early years of his reign.[43] William the Conqueror and his immediate successors took seriously their patronal relationship towards this house. Even so, the exceptional royal favour claimed in the Battle Chronicle was, although based on oral tradition, greatly enhanced by twelfth century writers of that house.[44]

The foundation and continuing centre of William's *regnum* lay in Normandy, and consequently he and his wife were buried in their respective foundations in Caen.[45] Here he bequeathed to his monastery of St. Stephen's the crown which he wore on the greater festivals.[46] Although William ruled in England itself as Edward's legitimate successor, his *regnum* comprised not only England and Normandy, but also various adjacent Continental lands. This composite state was welded together solely by military force. It was threatened with disintegration both on William's death in 1087 and at various times in the ensuing decades.[47] The *regnum* was as stable as such an 'empire' could hope to be, considering that it was held together by the members of a dynasty, rather than by other means, and its centre necessarily fluctuated. Both of William's younger sons reassembled this enlarged *regnum* in the course of their reigns,[48] but the fluctuating political conditions which they experi-

---

[42] See my 'Magnates' pp 136–7; Barlow pp 262–3.

[43] [*The*] C[*hronicle of*] B[*attle*] A[*bbey*], ed and transl Eleanor Searle (Oxford 1980) p 20.

[44] *Ibid* pp 15–23.

[45] [*The Ecclesiastical History of*] O[*rderic*] V[*italis*], ed and transl Marjorie Chibnall, 4 (1973) pp 44, 110.

[46] [J.] Le Patourel, [*The Norman*] *Empire* (Oxford 1976) p 241.

[47] [J.] Le Patourel, ['The Norman] Conquest, [1066, 1106, 1154?'], *PBC* 1 p 105.

[48] *Ibid* pp 105–6. I am grateful to Professor John Le Patourel for a helpful discussion on the Norman 'empire'.

enced influenced their successive choices of a church which would provide a focus for the well-being of their dynasty.

Westminster Abbey received no new donations from William Rufus, unless we include the grants of dubious date mentioned above. His genuine charters include, however, six confirmations of Westminster properties. One of these was issued in his first regnal year,[49] but although the dating of the others is problematic,[50] there seems to be no correlation between any of them and any particular political crisis later in the reign. At the outset, he stabilized his position against his elder brother Robert Curthose by promising to uphold the laws of the Confessor,[51] but this was of purely political significance. Neither his contemporary, abbot Gilbert Crispin of Westminster (1085–1117/8), nor the previous abbot, Vitalis (1076–85)[52] encouraged the existence of a tomb cult at Westminster.[53]

Other religious houses, however, gained from their own varied contributions to the safety of the *regnum* in this reign. Safe delivery from the revolt at the outset perhaps prompted William II to cooperate with the Londoner Aldwin Cild in the establishment of the Cluniac house at Bermondsey.[54] This priory was undoubtedly envisaged as being associated to some extent with the fortunes of the royal house. William's sister Adela, countess of Blois; his younger brother Henry I and the latter's wife Edith Matilda all maintained close relations with this monastery.[55] Its value to the monarchy was symbolized by a dream experienced by Henry I in 1118 (a year of crisis in his continental lands): he saw himself being attacked by lions, but saved by the intervention of Petreus, prior of Bermondsey.[56]

Rochester cathedral also gained by the contribution of bishop Gundulf towards the safety of the *regnum*. He negotiated a conclusion to the hostilities when Odo, bishop of Bayeux and earl of

[49] *RR* 1, no 306.
[50] *Ibid* nos 370, 402, 420, 454–5.
[51] 'Winchcombe Annals, 1049–1181', ed R. R. Darlington, [*A medieval*] *miscellany* [*for Doris Mary Stenton*], *PRS* ns 36 (1960) p 119; Barlow p 266n.
[52] *HRH* pp 76–7.
[53] Barlow p 266.
[54] Brooke and Keir pp 312–3; *MRHEW* p 98.
[55] [F.] Barlow, [*The English*] *Church* [*1066–1154*] (London 1979) p 185.
[56] *Ibid* p 91n.

Kent, was besieged in the city. In the course of events, the cathedral had been damaged, and in recompense the king confirmed land granted by Lanfranc, and he himself granted the manor of Lambeth.[57]

Battle Abbey was a third house which received royal donations in this reign, and in this instance their association with the wellbeing of the monarchy was unquestionable. Rufus carried out his father's bequest for Battle by donating a rich manor from the royal demesne; together with the Conqueror's royal cloak; three hundred amulets and a feretory containing many relics, and on which it was the custom of William I to have Mass celebrated when he was on campaign. These objects had all been in the possession of the Old English kings, and had been acquired by the Conqueror together with his kingdom.[58] William II supervised the completion and consecration of Battle; made further donations of his own, and continued to visit it and uphold its dignities.[59] From their account of all this, the Battle writers certainly expect us to infer that it was this English abbey which was particularly associated with the fortunes of the royal house by the Conqueror and his successor.

In the north of England, the Scottish kings considered themselves the political heirs of the old kings of Northumbria,[60] and for much of the eleventh century dominated both Northumbria and Cumbria. The cult of St Cuthbert was very potent in the north, and king Malcolm Canmore (d 1093) and his sons Edgar (1095–1107) and Alexander (1107–24) were all duly deferential to the saint.[61] Nevertheless, the region was firmly reabsorbed into the Anglo-Norman *regnum*, thanks to the campaigns of William I, and more especially to those of William II.[62] The political significance of the attentions paid to St Cuthbert by their Scottish rivals did not escape them, and on appropriate occasions they asserted their own claims to be the protectors of the see of Durham.[63] York was the

---

[57] *The life of the venerable man, Gundulf, bishop of Rochester*, transl by the nuns of Malling abbey (Malling 1968) pp 40–1.

[58] *CBA* pp 90–1.

[59] *Ibid* pp 97–9.

[60] *The life of Ailred of Rievaulx by Walter Daniel*, ed and transl F. M. Powicke (Oxford 1950) p xlii.

[61] [D.] Baker, ['"A nursery of saints":] St Margaret of Scotland [reconsidered'], *Medieval Women, SCH* Subsidia 1 (Oxford 1978) pp 119–120n, 139.

[62] See my 'William Rufus: [myth and reality'] *JMedH* 3 (1977) pp 6–7.

[63] B. Meehan, 'Outsiders, insiders and property at Durham around 1100', *Church, Society and Politics, SCH* 12 (Oxford 1975) pp 53, 55; *RR* 2 pp 400–1.

administrative capital of the north, and here William Rufus established the rich hospital of St Peter's,[64] a social provision which had political, as well as religious, overtones, in view of York's earlier status as the capital of an independant Danelaw. Even in William's own boyhood, that threat had briefly resurfaced,[65] and it was prudent to remind the population of where their political allegiance lay. Threats of a new Scandinavian invasion had, after all, occurred as recently as 1085.[66]

Winchester came to be William's burial place entirely due to his sudden death. It is doubtful whether he would have chosen to be buried in England at all. From 1096, when he was in full control of Normandy, the duchy was apparently regarded as the centre of his *regnum*,[67] and it is likely that he intended his father's resting place to continue to serve as the royal mausoleum. This may be deduced from the way in which he depleted Waltham to further the embellishment of his parents' foundations.[68] The Waltham treasures which he appropriated for this purpose included a gold-embroidered cope donated by Harold Godwinsson[69] and it no doubt seemed fitting that the new dynasty, which had quite literally assumed Harold's mantle, should have its own burial church enriched at the expense of the usurper's foundation.

In the reign of Henry I, the potential of Old English political traditions was exploited much more than before. A union between a representative of the native English house and a member of the new Norman dynasty was first envisaged by William Rufus,[70] but was actually achieved by Henry I, through his marriage to (Edith) Matilda, daughter of king Malcolm Canmore and queen Margaret. The new queen of England evidently shared with her mother a strong awareness of her kinship with the house of Wessex,[71] but in the one gift which she made to Westminster in her later years, there

---

[64] This was possibly a revival of an earlier foundation by Athelstan (*MRHEW* p 407); compare [Elizabeth M.] Hallam, ['Henry II as a founder of monasteries'], *JEH* 28 (1977) p 129.

[65] Douglas p 219.

[66] *Ibid* p 347.

[67] Le Patourel, *Empire* p 330.

[68] *Ibid* p 331.

[69] In return, the town of Waltham was restored to the canons (*The legend of Waltham* p 6; compare p 4 for the value of Harold's royal cloak).

[70] See my 'William Rufus' p 7.

[71] Baker, 'St Margaret of Scotland' p 140.

is no reference to any particular bond between the royal family and the Abbey.[72]

Queen Matilda's particular interest was in the Augustinian priory of Holy Trinity, Aldgate, which she founded about 1108 with the consent of her husband.[73] A leper hospital and a wharf were attached to the priory, thus adding to the amenities of the City of London, and prompting loyalty towards the monarchy.[74] Norman, prior of Aldgate (1107/8–1147),[75] acted as the queen's confessor, and a tradition of the house maintained that she wanted to be buried there, but that her wishes were thwarted by the machinations of the monks of Westminster.[76] The circumstances of her dying at Westminster probably account for her burial there, on the other side of Edward the Confessor's tomb from that of his own wife.[77] Queen (Edith) Matilda's brother, earl (later king) David, made a grant to Westminster shortly after her death, and two more c1141.[78] In view of the influence which his sister is believed to have had on his political views,[79] it is significant that in none of these did he mention any special link between the royal house and the abbey.

Henry I himself issued seven charters granting new donations to Westminster. One of these dates from the early years of his reign;[80] two from the middle years,[81] but issued before the White Ship disaster, in which his only legitimate son was drowned, and four from the immediate aftermath of this tragedy, which had great political implications. One of the new grants in this last group provided for a light before the tomb of queen Matilda,[82] but none of the donations were remarkably generous. Several are simply

[72] *RR* 2 no 1180.

[73] *Ibid* no 897.

[74] Brooke and Keir pp 315, 318.

[75] *HRH* 173.

[76] [J. C.] Dickinson, [*The origins of the Austin Canons and their introduction into England*] (London 1950) pp 110–11. After the queen's death, Henry I did not give to Holy Trinity all the land she had wished the canons to have—*The cartulary of Holy Trinity Aldgate*, cal G. A. J. Hodgett, *London Record Society* 7 (1971) p xv. Perhaps her promised donation had been made in anticipation of burial there.

[77] Harvey pp 373, 388; Barlow p 270.

[78] *The Acts of Malcolm IV king of Scots 1153–1165*, ed G. W. S. Barrow (Edinburgh 1960) nos 6, 13–14, confirmed by his son Earl Henry (*ibid* no 36).

[79] Baker, 'St Margaret of Scotland' p 140.

[80] *RR* 2 no 867.

[81] *Ibid* nos 1053, 1175.

[82] *Ibid* no 1377. The others are nos 1239, 1884–5.

concerned with judicial or financial exemptions, and in none is there any specific association between the fortunes of the royal house and the abbey.

The welfare of his dynasty was, however, stressed in some of Henry I's confirmations to Westminster. The earliest of these, dating from the very beginning of his reign, carries such an implication in the well-known writ in which he ordered that a *liberacio* should be given to the convent, and an ounce of gold to the cantors, when he wore his crown at Westminster (and Winchester, and Gloucester).[83] From 1120 there survives a confirmation made for the soul of queen Matilda,[84] and, from the immediate aftermath of the White Ship disaster, three which are more specific. Two were made for the souls of king Henry himself, king Edward his kinsman, and those of his *antecessores* and successors,[85] while the third was made not only for the souls of Henry and Edward, but also for those of William I and his wife; William II; the late queen Matilda and William Aetheling, the king's dead heir.[86] A larger group of Westminster confirmations, however, makes no reference to the spiritual welfare of the royal family. Five date from the years 1100–8;[87] four date from the middle years of the reign, but before the White Ship disaster;[88] five date from its immediate aftermath, 1121–3;[89] five more may have been issued at any time over a long stretch of the middle years of the reign;[90] while six date from Henry's last years.[91]

England itself was in no military danger after 1102, although Henry's continental lands were seriously threatened in 1117–19, and to some extent also in 1123–4.[92] Following the death of William Aetheling, and the failure of the king's new wife to produce an heir, it seemed for several years as though Henry's nephew William Clito, son of his imprisoned elder brother Robert Curthose, might

[83] *Ibid* no 490.
[84] *Ibid* no 1240.
[85] *Ibid* nos 1247–8.
[86] *Ibid* no 1249. There was no competition between Caen and Westminster to offer burial to William Aetheling, since his body was not among those recovered from the wreck—*OV* 6 (1978) p 307.
[87] *RR* 2 nos 667, 769, 818, 851, 903.
[88] *Ibid* nos 1123, 1173, 1178–9.
[89] *Ibid* nos 1250–2, 1383, 1416.
[90] *Ibid* nos 1538–9, 1878, 1880, 1987.
[91] *Ibid* nos 1758, 1838, 1879, 1882–3, 1988.
[92] C. W. Hollister, 'Henry I and the Anglo-Norman magnates', *PBA* 2 p 93.

emerge as the eventual ruler of the continental lands, at least.[93]

It is now questioned whether Henry did, in fact, suffer an intense spiritual crisis immediately after the death of his heir.[94] The quasi-Cluniac abbey of Reading, which he founded in 1121,[95] may well have owed its existence primarily, in fact, to the uncertain future of Henry's continental lands. From the outset, Reading was envisaged as playing a major part in ensuring the safety of the realm. In 1125, the widowed empress Matilda, returning to her father from the imperial court, thoughtfully appropriated from her late husband's treasures a most potent relic, the hand of St James, and 'thus did irreparable damage to the *regnum Francorum*', according to the annals of Disibodenberg.[96] The hand was bestowed on Reading, a strong indication that Henry envisaged this abbey as the new religious focus for the monarchy.[97] Further appropriate relics were supplied (willingly in their case) by the Byzantine emperors Alexius and John Comnenus.[98]

Henry is now thought to have experienced a more pronounced religious crisis about 1129,[99] by which time tensions had arisen in his daughter's Angevin marriage, which had been designed to safeguard his continental lands.[100] The king associated himself with the foundation of various religious houses, but claimed as his several which had essentially been established by others.[101] The Augustinian priory of Porchester (Hants), for instance, had been founded by the *curialis* William de Pont de L'Arche in the early 1120s, but in 1133 Henry claimed it as his own foundation, established on behalf of the souls of his parents, his brother William, and those of his *antecessores, pro statu et incolumitate regni mei*.[102]

Battle continued to receive from Henry the support which his

---

[93] S B. Hicks, 'The impact of William Clito upon the Continental policies of Henry I of England', *Viator* 10 (1979) pp 9, 11–12.

[94] [M.] Brett, [*The English Church under Henry I*] (Oxford 1975) p 112 and n 4.

[95] *MRHEW* p 74.

[96] [K.] Leyser, ['Frederick Barbarossa, Henry II and the hand of St James], *EHR* 90 (1975) p 491.

[97] *Ibid* p 492; Hallam p 130.

[98] Leyser p 499.

[99] Brett p 112 and n 4.

[100] Le Patourel, *Empire* pp 87, 90, 189.

[101] Hallam p 130.

[102] See my 'The king, the chamberlain and Southwick priory' *BIHR* 53 (1980) pp 1–2, 8.

predecessors had given. According to the abbey's chronicle he defended this house 'as the ensign of his crown'.[103] Unperturbed by a sense of inconsistency, the chronicler subsequently noted that Henry 'was buried in the monastery so splendidly founded by him at Reading.'[104] The significance of his choosing to be buried in England is considerable. It has been maintained that he regarded his *regnum* as comprising Normandy and its peripheral dependencies, as well as England,[105] and that when he died in 1135, even though his daughter and son-in-law were in revolt, there was no general supposition that this composite realm was about to dissolve.[106] It is arguable that Henry himself had suspected otherwise since he founded Reading. His decision to be buried there may, on the other hand, have been influenced by social, rather than political consider-ations, since from the mid 1120s, members of leading baronial families had increasingly chosen to be buried in English, rather than Norman, religious houses.[107] Perhaps the king, like his subjects, was coming to think of England as the natural focus of his lands.[108]

King Stephen's *regnum* comprised initially both England and Normandy, with peripheral lands on both sides of the Channel.[109] Soon, however, many of these components were whittled away. For much of 1141 he governed no kingdom at all, although after his release from captivity towards the end of that year, he gradually recovered a good deal of England itself.[110] Yet he never formally abandoned the idea that some day he or his successor would recover the whole of Henry I's realm,[111] and until coronation was formally refused to Eustace, his heir, in 1151,[112] he maintained that he could transmit those lands which he actually held.[113] The

---

[103] *CBA* p 109.
[104] *Ibid* p 140. Henry insisted on burial at Reading when struck down by his last illness at Lyons-la-Forêt (Eure) in Normandy—*OV* 6, p 448.
[105] [J.] Le Patourel, ['What did not happen in] Stephen's reign', *History* 58 (1973) p 2.
[106] Le Patourel, *Empire* pp 189–90.
[107] See my 'English tithe income of Norman religious houses' *BIHR* 48 (1975) p 91. The burials of Athelaise and Geoffrey de Mandeville in Westminster Abbey, a generation or more earlier, are exceptional—Harvey pp 372–3.
[108] Matthew p 28. However, Le Patourel, in an informal discussion of this point doubted whether Henry can be regarded as any more 'English' than his predecessors.
[109] Le Patourel, 'Stephen's reign' pp 2, 4.
[110] *Ibid* pp 8, 13.
[111] *Ibid* p 14.
[112] [H. A.] Cronne, [*The Reign of Stephen 1135–1154*] (London 1970) p 63.
[113] Le Patourel, 'Stephen's reign' p 8.

increasing uncertainty about the extent and durability of the *regnum* seems to have caused changes in his ideas about an appropriate church as a focus for the well-being of his dynasty.

Stephen's attitude towards Westminster abbey is problematic on two counts. The first is that since he had his illegitimate son Gervase appointed abbot in 1138,[114] instances where he was simply doing his best for his son cannot always be distinguished from those where he was paying due respect to the Abbey itself. Moreover, by the early years of this reign, prior Osbert de Clare was already masterminding the production of numerous forged charters designed to further the interests of Edward the Confessor's foundation.[115] The Westminster forgeries are largely disregarded in this essay, since they reflect the prior's views of what the royal attitude towards Westminster ought to have been, rather than what it was, whether in Stephen's reign, or in those of his three predecessors. However, the proposals for the canonization of Edward the Confessor were approved by Stephen. Osbert de Clare, the prime mover in this enterprise, drafted an enthusiastic letter of support for his mission to the papal court in 1139–42, when he attempted to have Edward canonized. Stephen ratified this letter,[116] and it has been argued that he did so chiefly in the expectation that Gervase would benefit if the project succeeded, and only marginally in the hope of enhancing the status of the English monarchy.[117] This is borne out by the evidence of Stephen's genuine charters for Westminster. These suggest that he placed no reliance on the cult of the Confessor, although he increasingly turned to the Abbey itself, as the reign progressed and his troubles increased. To a considerable extent, this is matched by a decline in his enthusiasm for Reading abbey.

One grant of Stephen's to Westminster dating from the beginning of his reign,[118] and another of uncertain date,[119] have no dynastic connotations whatever, but there is a change in the case of

[114] *HRH* p 77.

[115] [P.] Chaplais, ['The original charters of Herbert and Gervase abbots of Westminster (1121–1157)'], *Miscellany* pp 89–110; Brooke and Keir pp 306, 308–9; C. N. L. Brooke, 'Approaches to medieval forgery', *Medieval Church and Society* (London 1971) pp 106–8, 110, 115–16.

[116] Chaplais p 91; Barlow p 275.

[117] *Ibid* pp 275–6.

[118] *RR* 3 no 927.

[119] *Ibid* no 931.

two grants made when the stability of the realm was endangered. One of these, made no earlier than 1141, the year of Stephen's captivity, was made for the souls of himself and his wife; that of king Henry his uncle, and those of Eustace and his other children.[120] The other grant, dating from 1149×52 (when the young Henry of Anjou had taken up the challenge against him) was made for the souls of Stephen and his wife; and those of king Henry and his other predecessors as kings of England.[121] Stephen's confirmations of Westminster's existing rights bear no dynastic connotations whatever. This is equally true of the two early ones,[122] and the five of later and less certain date.[123] His rival for the throne, the empress Matilda, issued only one charter for Westminster, merely confirming a tenancy agreement.[124]

Stephen issued numerous charters in favour of his predecessor's foundation at Reading. His grants include two from the early years of his reign. One of these, dated 1137, was made for the souls of Stephen, his wife; his children and brothers, *et pro statu et incolumitate regni mei*.[125] Eight more charters date from the middle or later years of his reign.[126] One of these, of uncertain date, was granted for the souls of Stephen and of king Henry, and another, dated 1146–7, was made for the souls of Stephen himself and his wife; Eustace and their other children, and king Henry.[127] Stephen's confirmations for Reading include five which are clearly from the early years of his reign. One of these, dating from 1139–40, was made for the souls of Stephen and Henry, *et pro incolumitate totius regni mei*.[128] He also issued for Reading six further confirmations of uncertain date and mainly from his middle and later years. One of this group, however, may be as early as 1136. This confirmation was made for the souls of Stephen and his wife; William I his grandfather; and William and Henry his uncles.[129] It seems likely,

---

[120] *Ibid* no 932.
[121] *Ibid* no 938.
[122] *Ibid* nos 925–6.
[123] *Ibid* nos 930, 933–6.
[124] *Ibid* no 259.
[125] *Ibid* no 681. The other early charter is *RR* 3 no 684.
[126] *Ibid* nos 676–7, 682, 687, 691–4.
[127] *Ibid* nos 691, 694. Eustace issued a confirmation of the latter (*ibid* no 694a).
[128] *Ibid* no 690. The others are nos 678, 685–6, 688.
[129] *Ibid* no 675. The others are nos 680, 683, 689, 695–6. There is also one forgery purporting to be a confirmation of his (*ibid* no 679).

therefore, that at the outset of his reign Stephen regarded Reading as upholding the monarchy, but that once open warfare erupted, he perhaps increasingly suspected this abbey of favouring the cause of its founder's descendants. At that juncture, Westminster was briefly assigned Reading's role, before he made new, and more exclusive arrangements, for the welfare of the monarchy.

The goodwill of Henry I's annointed successor was naturally welcome to Reading, but once Stephen was challenged, the abbey was equally happy to receive charters from the empress Matilda. She issued two grants and two confirmations for Reading in 1141,[130] and two more grants a few years later.[131] The wording of some of these charters shows that in 1140–1 she associated Reading with the wellbeing of the *regnum* which she claimed. One confirmation was made for the soul of king Henry her father, and the safety of the whole kingdom of England,[132] and one grant for her parents, all her *antecessores* . . . and for the stability and peace of the kingdom of England.[133]

Henry of Anjou, her heir, issued seven charters and writs for Reading between 1147 and 1154. One confirmation, dating from 1147 or 1149, was made for the souls of his grandparents, Henry I and his wife, and for his other *antecessores*, while another confirmation, of 1150–1, was made for his own soul, and those of Henry I and his own parents and brothers.[134] During the years of Henry's struggle against Stephen, therefore, it seems that he too regarded Reading as upholding his claim to the English throne. Shortly after his accession, he had William, his infant first-born son, buried in the abbey,[135] although the far greater extent of his own *regnum* led him in time to look elsewhere for a mausoleum for his own dynasty.

Two of Stephen's children, Baldwin and Matilda, were buried in Holy Trinity, Aldgate.[136] Stephen made a grant to the priory for their souls in 1139×46, and a confirmation for them in 1147×8[137]

---

[130] *Ibid* nos 697–8, 700–1.
[131] *Ibid* nos 702–3
[132] *Ibid* no 698.
[133] *Ibid* no 702. Compare the wording of a Reading forgery purporting to be a confirmation of hers *(ibid* no 699).
[134] *Ibid* nos 704, 706. His other charters are nos 705, 707–10.
[135] Leyser p 497.
[136] Dickinson p 144.
[137] *MRHEW* p 119; *RR 3* no 337.

when his wife also made a confirmation for them.[138] The queen made another confirmation to the priory in 1139×46,[139] and two grants, one in 1147×48, for the souls of Stephen and herself,[140] and the other in 1147×52 for their own souls; those of their sons Eustace and William, and their other offspring.[141] In addition, the second prior, Ralph (1147–67), was her confessor.[142]

Stephen restored land to Holy Trinity in 1140×6 for the souls of king Henry; for those of himself and his own wife, and for those of Eustace and his other children,[143] but two grants, one from the latter part of his reign, and the other of indeterminate date, have no such associations.[144] Of his confirmations, however, one of indeterminate date was made for the souls of king Henry and his other *antecessores*; another for the souls of his parents, friends, kinsfolk and predecessors,[145] and a third, from the beginning of the reign, was made for the soul of queen (Edith) Matilda.[146] Eight further confirmations, made at various times throughout the reign, have no particular associations.[147] Holy Trinity, therefore, was perhaps considered as upholding the status of the dynasty to some limited extent.

Stephen promised the abbot of Battle, according to the abbey's chronicler, that 'he . . . would . . . defend the abbey . . . as he would his own private chapel and royal crown',[148] but his own foundations can more accurately be considered in this light. Stephen had founded Furness abbey (of the order of Savigny) while he was still count of Boulogne and Mortain, in 1124. In 1136, he confirmed its property for the soul of king Henry his lord and uncle; and for those of his kinsmen and *antecessores* . . . *et pro stabilitate regni mei*.[149] In 1147–8, however, it was forcibly absorbed into the Cistercian order, whose spokesmen were so hostile to

---

[138] *RR* 3 nos 508, 511.
[139] *Ibid* no 512.
[140] *Ibid* no 509.
[141] *Ibid* no 513.
[142] *Ibid* no 503.
[143] *HRH* p 173; Dickinson p 144.
[144] *RR* 3 no 507.
[145] *Ibid* nos 514, 516.
[146] *Ibid* nos 517, 520.
[147] *Ibid* no 500. The empress issued one grant to Holy Trinity *c*1141, for the souls of her parents and herself (*ibid* no 518).
[148] *Ibid* nos 499, 501–2, 504–5, 510, 515, 519.
[149] *CBA* p 152.

Stephen and his kindred. Furness, therefore, could no longer be relied on to uphold the interests of his dynasty. Probably in direct consequence of this, Stephen founded the quasi Cluniac abbey of Faversham in 1148, when it was colonized from the explicitly Cluniac Bermondsey favoured by his predecessors.[150] Although Reading, Westminster, and Holy Trinity Aldgate were to some extent still regarded as upholding the welfare of the royal family, they had all enjoyed close associations with the Empress's forebears, and by 1148 the political situation perhaps prompted Stephen to found another monastery exclusively devoted to the interests of his own line. Geoffrey of Anjou was by now well entrenched in Normandy,[151] and already there had been ominous signs that there would be difficulties in obtaining papal recognition of Eustace as the rightful heir to the throne.[152] The ambivalent affiliation both of Faversham and of Reading underline the fact that whereas the splendid Cluniac liturgy was evidently seen as being appropriate for a monastery specifically intended to uphold the monarchy, neither Stephen nor his predecessor was willing that such an abbey should owe formal obedience to a mother house outside his *regnum*. Stephen's initial grant of the site of Faversham was made for the souls of himself and his wife; those of Eustace and his other children, and his *antecessores* the kings of England.[153] However, a subsequent grant by his wife, and a later confirmation of his own, were simply made for the souls of the queen and all the faithful.[154] This may indicate tacit admission of political failure. All hope for Stephen's line ended with the death of Eustace in August 1153,[155] and the young man was buried at Faversham, where his mother's body already lay, and Stephen's was to follow shortly.[156]

The composite Anglo-Norman *regnum* always faced the possibil-

[150] *MRHEW* p 65.
[151] Le Patourel, *Empire* p 95.
[152] Cronne pp 60, 101.
[153] *RR* 3 no 300.
[154] *Ibid* nos 301–2.
[155] *Gesta Stephani*, ed and transl K. R. Potter, introd R. H. C. Davis (Oxford 1976) p 238.
[156] *The Chronicle of Battle Abbey* p 152; Barlow, *Church* p 193.

ity of disintegration,[157] and perhaps it was this very impermanence which led to the continued search by its rulers for an effective monastic focus *pro statu et incolumitate regni mei.*

University of London
Birkbeck College

[157] Le Patourel, 'Conquest' p 105.

CUMBRIAN SOCIETY AND THE ANGLO-NORMAN CHURCH

by R. K. ROSE

THE TWELFTH century was a period of both political and ecclesiastical settlement in the north-west of England, when the conquerors were seeking to establish Anglo-Norman institutions in an area as much Celtic and Norse as Anglo-Saxon. The church was re-vitalised, monasticism re-established, and parish churches were built and re-built to an extent previously unknown. The response of Cumbrian[1] society was favourable, but a 'national' flavour of the diverse elements making up that society was retained. When in 1092 William Rufus marched into the north-west, seized Carlisle, and drove out the 'ruler', Dolfin son of earl Gospatric of Dunbar, he was enacting the final phase of the Norman conquest of England.[2] The border between England and Scotland was established, and this only deviated when David I brought the district back under Scottish control during the reign of Stephen. At one time part of the kingdom of Northumbria and then of the kingdom of Strathclyde, by the eleventh century the north-west had become a political no-man's-land, the kings of England and Scotland each regarding it as belonging to his respective realm. Church life had been greatly eroded, and monastic communities, as in the rest of northern England, had totally disappeared, due as much to the unstable political situation over the previous two centuries as to the lack of any strong spiritual control. The region itself was in a depressed condition, depopulated and devastated by the invasions of king Edmund in 945, Ethelred in 1000, and most recently by early Gospatric in 1070.[3] Carlisle

---

[1] For the sake of convenience, the term 'Cumbrian' is used throughout in the modern sense and not as synonymous with the people of the ancient kingdom of Strathclyde. See P. A. Wilson, 'The Use of the Terms "Strathclyde" and "Cumbria"', Trans[actions of the] C[umberland and] W[estmorland] A[ntiquarian and] A[rchaeological] S[ociety], ns 66 (Kendal 1966) pp 57–92.

[2] ASC, sa 1092.

[3] Ibid, sa 945, 1000; Symeon [is Monachi Opera Omnia, ed T. Arnold], 2 vols, RS 75 (1882–5) 2, p 191.

required at least some re-building, and a castle was erected to act as the western counterpart of Newcastle. After his departure Rufus also had groups of peasants and livestock from the south placed there, motivated probably as much by a desire to establish an English population in an area where the Celtic and Norse presence was strong as by a means *ad populandum*.[4]

The ecclesiastical affairs of the area previous to the Norman annexation were directly affected by its political history and the varying cultural influences brought to bear on it. It was nevertheless in the unique position of being the object of attack and take-over only after the respective invaders had been converted from paganism to Christianity. Indeed, if one accepts this region as the birthplace of Patrick[5] and some basis of truth to the legend of Ninian,[6] a case can be made for the continuity of Christian practice from the time of Roman withdrawal to the Norman conquest. The large amount of Christian objects dating from the fourth century which have been found along the western end of Hadrian's Wall testifies to this fact.[7] And the ancient poem *Gododdin*, which relates the story of the resistance of the northern British princes to Anglian expansion in the late sixth century, contrasts strongly the paganism of the invaders with the Christianity of the Britons.[8]

We have nevertheless little idea of the state of the church in the district at this time. Bede, with his characteristic contempt for the Britons and their form of Christianity, does not include in his *Historia Ecclesiastica* any discussion of the church in Rheged, the British kingdom which had been formed round the Solway, until its incorporation into the kingdom of Northumbria about the mid-seventh century. Jocelin of Furness, writing in the late twelfth century, recounted the story of a visit to Carlisle made by the late sixth-century Kentigern, the traditional founder of the see of

---

[4] *ASC, sa* 1092.
[5] J. B. Bury, *The Life of St Patrick and His Place in History* (London 1905) pp 322–5.
[6] [A. C.] Thomas, ['The Evidence from North Britain', *Christianity in Britain, 300–700*, ed M. W. Barley and R. P. C. Hanson] (Leicester 1968) pp 93–121, especially 97–100. Many of the activities, as well as the very existence, of Ninian have been brought into doubt in recent years. See N. K. Chadwick, 'St Ninian: A Preliminary Study of the Sources', *Transactions of the Dumfriesshire and Galloway Antiquarian Society*, 3 ser 28 (Dumfries 1950) pp 9–53; D. Fahy, 'The Historical Reality of St Ninian', *IR*, 15 (1964) pp 35–46; A. Boyle, 'St Ninian: Some Outstanding Problems', *IR*, 19 (1968) pp 57–70.
[7] Thomas, pp 97–100.
[8] K. H. Jackson, *The Gododdin: The Oldest Scottish Poem* (Edinburgh 1969) p 37.

Glasgow, and of his evangelising work in the mountains, but it is doubtful that the saint ever ventured as far south as this.[9] It is only with the Northumbrian acquisition of the lands west of the Pennines that the sources become reliable. From 685 until his death in 687, Cuthbert acted as bishop in the area, and for this period insights into the ecclesiastical establishment of the district are gained. An anonymous monk of Lindisfarne, writing within twenty years of Cuthbert's death, and Bede, writing about 721, have left full and moving accounts of the saint and his activities as bishop.[10] He made two recorded visits to Carlisle and can be seen ordaining clergy and consecrating churches.[11] There were also in existence at least two monasteries, one at Carlisle and another at Dacre,[12] and it is probable that other such establishments could be found elsewhere in the area, until Northumbrian rule was disrupted.

Although the north-west had been free of Viking attack throughout the ninth century, in the early tenth century the migration of groups of Hiberno-Norse, who had been Christianised in Ireland, began. At this time Northumbria, in a weakened condition from over a century of Viking inroads and political in-fighting, relinquished control of the region, and the still independent kingdom of Strathclyde, which lay round the Firth of Clyde, re-asserted British control and influence, probably as far as Stainmore and north and west of the river Derwent.[13]

The ascendant kings of Wessex in their successful bid for supremacy in England did not forget that the district of Carlisle had

---

[9] [Jocelin of Furness]., *Vita Kentegerni*, [*Lives of St Ninian and St Kentigern*], ed [and trans A. P.] Forbes (Edinburgh 1874) pp 73–5, 199–201. K. H. Jackson, 'The Sources for the Life of St Kentigern', *Studies in the Early British Church*, ed N. K. Chadwick (Cambridge 1958) pp 273–357, especially pp 313 *seq*. After a meticulous examination of the surviving sources, Jackson rejected Kentigern's missionary activities in Cumberland and Westmorland and his visit to Wales as later traditions.

[10] Anonymous, [*Vita Sancti Cuthberti*], and Bede, *V[ita] S[ancti] C[uthberti]*, [*Two Lives of St Cuthbert*, ed and trans B. Colgrave] (Cambridge 1940).

[11] Anonymous, bk 4, cap 8, 9; Bede, *VSC*, cap 27, 28; Bede, *HE*, bk 4, cap 29 (27).

[12] *Ibid*; Bede, *HE*, bk 4, cap 32 (30). The twelfth-century *Historia de Sancto Cuthberto* attributed to Symeon of Durham states that Cuthbert founded a monastery and schools at Carlisle, but it seems clear from the works of Bede and the anonymous monk of Lindisfarne that the house was a pre-existing one. *Symeon*, 1, p 199.

[13] [K. H.] Jackson, 'Angles and Britons [in Northumbria and Cumbria', *Angles and Britons*] (Cardiff 1963) p 72; G. W. S. Barrow, 'The Anglo-Scottish Border', *NH*, 1 (1966) pp 24–5.

once been in English hands. In 926 Athelstan annexed the kingdom of Northumbria, and the old Northumbrian claims to the region may have been one of the motives behind the invasion and plunder of Cumbria in 945 by his brother, king Edmund.[14] In return for his homage and alliance 'by land and sea', Edmund then ceded Strathclyde to Malcolm I, and it remained a client kingdom of the Scottish king until its complete absorption into Scotland in the early eleventh century.[15] A thirteenth-century Scottish chronicler stated that the land ceded extended as far as the Rey Cross in Stainmore, that is, most, if not all, of Cumberland and Westmorland, but that Edmund's 'donation was often conquered since then and released in making ofttimes peace'.[16] In other words, from the tenth century the north-west became and remained for some time a bone of contention between the kings of England and Scotland.

A surviving eleventh-century writ of Gospatric, who held Allerdale and Dalston in Cumberland, has given us an indication of the state of affairs in the north-west before 1092.[17] Scottish influence south of the Solway appears to have dwindled. Gospatric seems to have been acting with some degree of independence, referring to his lands as formerly belonging to the kingdom of Strathclyde, and he cites earl Siward of Northumbria as a guarantor of privileges, indicative of a Northumbrian influence once again building up west of the Pennines. Malcolm III of Scotland later succeeded in establishing his authority over the region around 1070, but after becoming a vassal of the Conqueror in 1072, and confirming his vassalage to William II in 1091, he did nothing to prevent the English seizure of the district.[18]

---

[14] *ASC, sa* 926, 945.

[15] *Ibid sa* 945; [A.A.M.] Duncan, [*Scotland: The Making of the Kingdom*] (Edinburgh 1975) pp 98–9.

[16] *Chronicles of the Picts, Chronicles of the Scots, and Other Early Memorials of Scottish History*, ed W. F. Skene (Edinburgh 1867) p 204. The chronicler mistakenly identified the grantee as Donald, king of Scots.

[17] F. E. Harmer, *Anglo-Saxon Writs* (Manchester 1952) pp 419–24, and see p 531 for a bibliography of writings on this writ. There has been some controversy over the identification of the issuer of this writ; see especially H. W. C. Davis, 'Cumberland before the Norman Conquest', *EHR*, 20 (1905) pp 61–5. Davis argued inconclusively against the identification as issuer of Gospatric son of Maldred, the future earl of Northumbria and father of the Dolfin who was expelled from Carlisle by William Rufus. I tend to agree with Duncan that the presence in the district of the sons of Gospatric at the time of the Norman annexation indicates that Maldred and his son held lands there; Duncan, pp 98–9.

[18] *Symeon*, 2, p 191; *ASC, sa* 1072, 1091.

Cumbrian society and the Anglo-Norman Church

To what extent the north-west could be regarded as Celtic, English, or Norse, or a mixture of the three, is not possible to ascertain fully. It is safe to assume, however, that the local aristocracy were at any rate intermarrying and were therefore a blend of these three elements. In a study of village names of British origin in north-west England and south-west Scotland, K. H. Jackson has argued for the endurance of Cumbric, the Brythonic language of the region, as late as the late eleventh and early twelfth centuries.[19] If it may be assumed that Cumbric ceased to be a language of widespread use during the three centuries of Northumbrian rule, then the time of that area's consolidation into the kingdom of Strathclyde might be viewed as a period of the re-strengthening of its use. And place-names in such late forms as 'Castle Hewin' and especially 'Cumwhinton', both found in Cumberland, help to make this view attractive.[20]

Equal attention should be given to the Norse element in Cumbrian society. According to the chronicler Henry of Huntingdon, Ethelred's invasion of Cumbria in 1000 was largely because the area had become a Scandanavian stronghold.[21] The large number of place-names of Norse origin found in the region, particularly in the Lake District proper south of the river Derwent and generally elsewhere, are indicative of steady Scandinavian colonisation from Ireland.[22] As late as the late eleventh century Norse-speaking groups were migrating from the district into Yorkshire, depopulated by the ravages of William the Conqueror.[23] These facts point to the view that the Hiberno-Norse were in the late eleventh century a large, important, and identifiable group, whose language survived for some time.[24]

However, it is not our present purpose merely to affirm the

---

[19] Jackson, 'Angles and Britons', pp 74–84.

[20] *Ibid* p 81. The place-name 'Cumwhinton' combines the British element *cum*, meaning 'glen' or 'valley', with the Norman personal name Quintin, and it is doubtful that such a name would have been attributed long, if at all, before 1092.

[21] *Henrici Archidiaconi Huntendunensis Historia Anglorum*, ed T. Arnold, RS 74 (1879) p 170.

[22] *The Place-Names of Cumberland*, [ed A. M. Armstrong, A. Mawer, F. M. Stenton, and B. Dickins], 3 pts, E[nglish] P[lace-Name] S[ociety] 20–2 (Cambridge 1950–2) pt 3, pp xxii–xxvii; *The Place-Names of Westmorland*, ed A. H. Smith, 2 pts, EPS 42–3 (Cambridge 1967) pt 1, pp xxxix–xlv.

[23] A. E. Smailes, *North England* (London 1960) p 90.

[24] N. J. Higham, 'Continuity Studies in the First Mellennium A.D. in North Cumbria', *NH*, 14 (1978) pp 1–18, particularly 11–18.

existence of the diverse elements of Celtic, English, and Norse in Cumbrian society but to attempt to assess that society's response to the Norman ecclesiastical settlement of the area in the century following 1092. The re-vitalisation of the church was an important part of Norman policy, culminating in the erection of an episcopal see at Carlisle in 1133. In the late eleventh and early twelfth centuries the issue of ecclesiastical allegiance in the district was confused by the claims of various bishops. Spiritual jurisdiction was at first given to Ranulf Flambard, bishop of Durham, a recognition of the fact that his predecessors the bishops of Lindisfarne had exercised authority over the area during the period of Northumbrian over-lordship.[25] However, Flambard's fall from royal favour in 1100 was occasioned by the assignment of Carlisle and Hexham to the archbishopric of York.[26] Matters were complicated by the re-foundation in the early twelfth century of the diocese of Glasgow, whose bishops claimed the area by virtue of its having been part of the kingdom of Strathclyde, and this assertion was being made as late as 1258.[27]

It was precisely this confusion and the question of ecclesiastical relationships that precipitated the events which led up to the foundation of the diocese of Carlisle. While the archbishops of York steadily refused to profess obedience to the archbishops of Canterbury, the Scottish bishops were likewise refusing to profess obedience to the archbishop of York.[28] Because of the dispute between Canterbury and York, archbishop Thurstan had for seven years remained unconsecrated, and with only Durham as an obedientiary, York's need for suffragans in the face of the 'rebellious' Scottish bishops was obvious. In 1125 Whithorn was revived, the only Scottish see to recognise continually the metropolitan authority of York, and later Thurstan was also involved in the foundation of a bishopric for Man and the Isles.[29]

The later Scottish account of Henry I's horror at seeing bishop John of Glasgow performing episcopal functions in Cumberland during his visit there in 1122 is apocryphal, as John was at that time

[25] H. H. E. Craster, 'A Contemporary Record of the Pontificate of Ranulf Flambard', *Archaeologia Aeliana*, 4 ser, 7 (Newcastle 1930) p 38.

[26] *Symeon*, 1, p 139.

[27] *Chronicon de Lanercost*, ed J. Stevenson (Edinburgh 1839) p 65.

[28] [D.] Nicholl, [*Thurstan, Archbishop of York (1114–1140)*] (York 1964) pp 41–110.

[29] *Ibid* pp 137–40.

in Rome, but there may be a grain of truth to the story.[30] Archbishop Thomas II of York had seemingly been content to allow a certain bishop Michael of Glasgow to carry out pontifical duties there, but Michael himself probably had not been accepted in Scotland and had been in any case acting as a suffragan of York.[31] Bishop John's consistent refusal to recognise any English metropolitan authority was a different matter altogether. Thurstan may have approached the king with the problem at the time of his visit to the north, and the idea of a new diocese firmly within the structure of the English church, making political and ecclesiastical boundaries coterminous in the north-west, could not have been anything but attractive to Henry. By 1133 the pope had given the archbishop the right to create new dioceses within his province, and Athelwold, prior of Nostell and the king's confessor, was appointed first bishop of Carlisle, with the Augustinian priory of St Mary as his cathedral church.[32] This measure was of the utmost importance to the future ecclesiastical settlement and development of north-western England.

The Viking invasions and the subsequent instability had caused the disappearance of many of the monastic foundations in England, and by the tenth century no trace was to be found of the once vibrant monasticism of the days of Bede in the north. The monastic revival begun in the south by Dunstan passed by northern England, and only after the conquest were religious houses there re-established.[33] Of the two monasteries in Cumberland mentioned by Bede, that at Carlisle was last noted as still in existence in 883, and nothing more is known of the house at Dacre.[34] At the time of William II's seizure of Carlisle, there seem to have been only a handful of churches serving the needs of the population, small as that population probably was. Of the medieval churches still standing, only those of Long Marton, Morland, and Ormside, all in Westmorland, have any architectural features dating from before

---

[30] *Johannis de Fordun Scotichronicon* ed W. Goodall, 2 vols (Edinburgh 1775), 1, pp 449–50; [M.] Brett, [*The English Church under Henry I*] (Oxford 1975) pp 18–28; Nicholl, pp 140–50.
[31] N. F. Shead, 'The Origins of the Medieval Diocese of Glasgow', *ScHR*, 48 (1969) pp 220–5.
[32] Brett, pp 25–6.
[33] Knowles, *MO* pp 31–56.
[34] *Symeon* 1, p 203.

the twelfth century.[35] Most of the other churches were probably
built of wood or wattle, as was the chapel at Triarmain.[36] Nevertheless, just over thirty churchyards contain carved stone monumental
crosses and fragments, dating in the main from the tenth century,
and these are sure indicators of the location of at least most of the
pre-conquest churches.[37]

In keeping with the spirit of revivalism currently in the air, the
Norman lords who had been implanted in the area began to found
monasteries and stepped up the building of parish churches. Not all
of those granted land after 1092, however, were of Norman
extraction, and some attempt seems to have been made to accommodate at least some of the older local aristocracy. Henry I granted
the entire area to Ranulf le Meschin de Bricquessart, the nephew of
Hugh d'Avranches, earl of Chester, and he began the process of
creating baronies.[38] Waltheof, son of earl Gospatric of Dunbar and
brother of Dolfin, who had been displaced in Carlisle, was granted
the barony of Allerdale, of which he had most likely already been in
possession. Likewise, the claims of the Norse Forne son of Sigulf
were probably recognised by his receiving the barony of Greystoke, and Gille son of Bued, a man with a Gaelic name, held
Gilsland under Henry I. Aside from these cases, the new baronies,

[35] An Inventory of the Historical Monuments in Westmorland, Royal Commission on
Historical Monuments (England) (London 1936) pp 167–9, 175–7, 185–7.
[36] ['A Breviate of the] Cartulary of [the Priory Church of St Mary Magdalene,]
Lanercost', [ed M. E. C. Walcott, Transactions of the Royal Society of Literature of the
United Kingdom,] 2 ser, 8 (London 1866) pp 509–10.
[37] W. G. Collingwood, Northumbrian Crosses of the Pre-Norman Age (London 1927)
passim; R. M. T. Hill, 'Christianity and Geography in Early Northumbria', SCH,
3 (1966) pp 126–39. Place-names having the elements kirk or cros(s) are not
assumed to be the sites of early churches without the evidence of monuments, as
these elements are not necessarily linked to pre-Norman name-giving. For
example, the present Kirkcambeck, Kirklinton, and Kirkbampton only began to
be known as such in the late thirteenth century, having been called before this
simply 'Cambok', 'Levington', and 'Bampton'; The Place-Names of Cumberland,
EPS, pt 1, pp 56, 101–2, 142.
[38] For the creation of baronies in Cumberland and Westmorland, see I. J. Sanders,
English Baronies: A Study of Their Origin and Descent, 1086–1327 (Oxford 1960)
pp 23–4, 50, 56–7, 58–9, 103–4, 115, 124, 129, 134–5. Ranulf succeeded to the
earldom of Chester in 1120, after which his fief was retained by the crown, and
Henry I continued the creation of baronies. The extent of Ranulf's fief was that
area actually seized by William II and was coterminous with the later diocese of
Carlisle, that is, all of Cumberland except Alston and Allerdale above Derwent or
Coupland, and except the barony of Kendal in Westmorland.

Burgh by Sands, Liddell, Coupland, and Westmorland were placed in Norman hands.

About twenty years before the annexation of the district of Carlisle, Aldwin, the prior of Winchcombe, who had read and been inspired by Bede, and two monks of Evesham, Reinfrid and Aelfwig, set out for the north, and their unintentional refoundation of Jarrow set in motion the revival of northern monasticism. From Jarrow the Rule of Saint Benedict was taken to Wearmouth, Whitby, the final resting-place of Cuthbert at Durham, and York in the years before 1090.[39] It was to St Mary's, York that two Norman lords in Cumberland turned in the early twelfth century for the provision of monks for two priories which were to be cells of that abbey. Ranulf le Meschin's foundation between 1106 and 1112 of the Benedictine house at Wetheral, near Carlisle, who was the first view of monasticism in the north-west since its general decline in the tenth century.[40] This foundation was followed around 1120 by the endowment of a cell at St Bees, on the west coast of Cumberland in the barony of Coupland, which had been given to Ranulf's brother William.[41] William's choice of St Bees as the site of the priory was no doubt inspired by the local devotion to and tradition surrounding Bega, a legendary Irish nun who sought an eremitical life on the coast of Cumberland, and whom a twelfth-century hagiographer confused with the Begu who appears in Bede's *Historia Ecclesiastica*.[42]

The lateness of the monastic revival in Cumberland and Westmorland ensured that no more Benedictine houses would be established in the district, and, as in the rest of northern England, the new orders were favoured. Soon after 1122 Augustinian canons were introduced into the church of St Mary, Carlisle, which became the cathedral church in 1133.[43] In the second half of the

[39] Knowles, *MO*, pp 159–71; L. G. D. Baker, 'The Desert in the North', *NH*, 5 (1970) pp 1–11.

[40] *The Register of the Priory of Wetheral*, ed J. E. Prescott C[umberland and] W[estmorland] A[ntiquarian and] A[rchaeological] S[ociety] Rec[ord] Ser[ies] 1 (London 1897) pp 1–19.

[41] [*The Register of the Priory of*] St Bees, [ed J. Wilson] SS 126 (1915) pp 27–36.

[42] *Ibid*, pp iv–v; Bede, *HE*, bk 4, cap 23; *The Life and Miracles of Sancta Bega*, ed G. C. Tomlinson (Carlisle 1842).

[43] The history of the foundation of Carlisle priory has been best dealt with by J. C. Dickinson, 'Walter the Priest and St Mary's, Carlisle', *Trans CWAAS* ns 69 (Kendal 1969) pp 102–14.

twelfth century three additional Augustinian priories were founded at Lanercost by Robert de Vaux, lord of Gilsland,[44] at Conishead by Gamel de Pennington,[45] and at Cartmel by William Marshal, later earl of Pembroke.[46] Towards the end of the century the more austere Premonstratensian canons were provided with lands for an abbey at Shap by Thomas son of Gospatric son of Orm, the only monastic house to be founded in Westmorland.[47] The inhospitable geography of much of the area attracted the equally austere Cistercians, which order had houses at Furness, the first Savigniac plantation in England, founded by Stephen, the future king,[48] at Calder, a daughter house of Furness, founded by Ranulf son of William le Meschin,[49] and at Holmcultram, a daughter of Melrose abbey, founded reputedly by earl Henry, the son of king David I of Scotland.[50]

The immediate favour shown the religious houses by Cumbrian society is evident. Even though most of the ten communities were founded by the Anglo-Norman aristocracy, the older Cumbrian families lost no time in displaying their enthusiasm by granting lands and churches to the new abbeys and priories. In the foundation charter of St Bees, William le Meschin invited 'his knights' to join in the endowment of the priory from their own lands.[51] The response of those who witnessed the charter came quickly. Ketel son of Eldred, who besides large tracts of land in Westmorland, held of William in Coupland, granted Preston near Whitehaven to the priory, and later he donated the churches of Morland and Workington. Waltheof, lord of Allerdale, who held five vills of William, gave the monks Stainburn and the church of Bromfield. Godard de Boivill, lord of Millom, made them a gift of the churches of Whicham and Bootle, and Rainer, a Fleming, granted two bovates of land.[52]

[44] 'Cartulary of Lanercost'; MA, 6, pp 236–8; VCH, Cumberland, 2 vols (1901–5) 2, pp 152–61.
[45] MA, 6, pp 55–8; VCH, Lancaster, 8 vols (1906–14) 2, pp 140–3.
[46] MA, 6, pp 454–5; VCH, Lancaster, 2, pp 143–8.
[47] MA, 6, pp 868–70.
[48] The Coucher Book of Furness Abbey, ed J. C. Atkinson, 6 pts, Chetham Society ns 9, 11, 14, 74, 76, 78 (Manchester 1886–1919) pt 1, pp 122–5.
[49] Knowles, MO, pp 227–8, 249–51; VCH, Cumberland, 2, pp 174–8.
[50] [The Register and Records of] Holm Cultram, [ed F. Grainger and W. G. Collingwood,] CWAAS Rec Ser 7 (Kendal 1929) pp 91–2, 117–20.
[51] St Bees, p 28.
[52] Ibid, pp 29, 106–7, 233–4.

Waltheof, lord of Allerdale, deserves special notice due to the extent of his patronage of the religious houses. He was undoubtedly the most important 'native' lord to be left in possession of his lands. As son of earl Gospatric, his family connections were wide-ranging. His paternal grandmother was a daughter of earl Uhtred of Northumbria and Elgifu, a sister of Edward the Confessor, and his paternal grandfather, Maldred, was the younger brother of Duncan I of Scotland. At the time of the conquest his father had purchased the earldom of Northumbria from William I, but having become involved in plots against the king, he was deprived of the earldom in 1072, and he fled to Scotland, where he was granted the earldom of Dunbar, which eventually passed to Waltheof's brother.[53] Such connections of course gave Waltheof friends in high places, heavenly as well as earthly, for, given his relationship to the Confessor, he was the second cousin of Margaret of Scotland and through his Northumbrian ancestry more distantly related to Waldef de Senlis, the future saintly abbot of Melrose and stepson of Margaret's son David I.

The piety of Waltheof and his son and heir Alan cannot be doubted. Waltheof clearly felt well disposed towards the regular canons and was one of the earliest patrons of Carlisle priory. He granted to that house the churches of Aspatria and Crosscanonby along with two carucates of land, as well as some land in Carlisle near the church of St Cuthbert, and Alan later added the church of Ireby among other grants. Alan's son Waltheof, continuing the family tradition, donated more land in Crosscanonby.[54] To the Augustinian house at Jedburgh Waltheof granted the church of Bassenthwaite,[55] and he and his son Alan together gave to Hexham priory four bovates of land and a fishery.[56] Alan was also closely involved in the foundation of the Cistercian abbey of Holmcultram in 1150, within the time that David I had re-established Scottish control of the district. Ostensibly a foundation of David's son earl Henry, Alan, in whose lordship the lands for the abbey were granted, appears to have been the true originator of the project.[57]

53 *VCH, Cumberland*, 2, pp 235–6.
54 *MA*, 6, p 144.
55 [J.] Nicolson and [R.] Burn, [*The History and Antiquities of Westmorland and Cumberland,*] 2 vols (London 1777) 2, p 93.
56 [*The Priory of*] Hexham, [ed J. Raine,] 2 vols, SS 44, 46 (1864–5) 1, p 59.
57 *Holm Cultram*, pp 117–20.

According to tradition, Waltheof and his son had a hand in stocking the relic collection of Carlisle priory. Upon his son's death, Alan was said to have given the canons, along with the body of his son, bones of Saints Paul and John the Baptist, two fragments of the Holy Sepulchre, and a piece of the true Cross, which his father had brought back from Jerusalem.[58]

The only monastic foundation in north-west England that was able to identify with a pre-conquest saint in the same manner that the Benedictine re-foundations at Durham and Whitby had been able to adopt Cuthbert and Hilda was the priory of St Bees. There had perhaps been a view of 're-foundation' at Carlisle inspired by Bede, but the great historian had identified no member of the old monastery as a saint. As already noted, the author of the *Life of Saint Bega*, probably a monk of St Bees, confused the patron saint of the priory with the Begu of Hilda's monastery. Nevertheless, the composition of such *Lives*, whether factual or not, played an important part in the life of the twelfth-century English church. The story as told by Eadmer of the discussion between Lanfranc and Anselm concerning the former's doubts as to the sanctity of Elphege and other saints venerated by the Anglo-Saxon church is a familiar one.[59] The scepticism of the Norman churchmen regarding the place in heaven of many of the English saints encouraged a spate of hagiographers to take up their pens in defence of the offended holy men.[60] The result of the scholarly hagiography produced in the twelfth century, along with the historical works undertaken by such men as William of Malmesbury, Florence of Worcester, and Symeon of Durham, was to sell to the Norman conquerors the value of pre-conquest history and ultimately to give them a sense of continuity with the English past.[61]

In the north, Durham and York were the important centres of historical writing, and these places and the other monastic houses produced an admirable quantity of Northumbrian saints' *Lives*, such as Ailred of Rievaulx's *De Sanctis Ecclesiae Haugustaldensis*.[62]

---

[58] *VCH, Cumberland*, 2, p 139.

[59] *The Life of St Anselm of Canterbury by Eadmer*, ed and trans R. W. Southern (London 1962) pp 50–4.

[60] Antonia Gransden, *Historical Writing in England, c 550 to c 1307* (London 1974) pp 105–35.

[61] *Ibid* pp 136–85; R. R. Darlington, *Anglo-Norman Historians* (London 1947) 19 pp.

[62] *Hexham*, 1, pp 173–203.

However, on the western side of the Pennines, it was the 'rehabilitation' of Celtic, not Northumbrian, saints that concerned the monastic hagiographers. Ailred himself wrote a *Life of Saint Ninian*.[63] Jocelin, a monk of Furness, chose Kentigern, Patrick, and Saint Helen, mother of Constantine and believed to have been a Briton, as the subjects of his writings, and he is thought to have written a book of the *Lives of British Bishops*.[64] And finally Everard, the first abbot of Holmcultram, was the author of a *Life of Saint Adamnan* and a *Life of Saint Cumin*, both of which are unfortunately lost.[65] The motive behind the composition of such *Lives* was simply a defensive one: to establish beyond doubt the reputed sanctity of the subjects and to make the saints palatable to a twelfth-century audience. Both Ailred and Jocelin decried the barbarous style of their sources when writing about Ninian and Kentigern and clearly felt that this alone was enough to obscure and discourage devotion to the two saints.[66] Jocelin was further horrified to read in the *Life* used by the church of Glasgow that Kentigern was believed to have been born of a virgin, a superstition he denounced as *sane doctrine et catholice fidei adversum*,[67] and it is significant that Everard's two Irish subjects were advocates of Roman observances.

Carlisle was the only medieval English diocese unable to boast the burial-place of a local saint. There was therefore no counterpart to Durham's Cuthbert around whom strong links of local identity and attachment were formed, and Carlisle was forced to import its

[63] [Ailred of Rievaulx,] *Vita Niniani*, ed Forbes, pp 1–26, 137–57. Ailred spent his early years at the court of king David of Scotland; *The Life of Ailred of Rievaulx by Walter Daniel*, ed and trans F. M. Powicke (London 1950) pp 2–5.

[64] *Vita Kentegerni*, ed Forbes, pp 29–119, 159–242; *Vita Sancti Patricii*, in *ASB*, March 2 (1865) pp 536–89; his *Life of Saint Helen* has not been published. Jocelin was also the author of a *Life of Saint Waldef; Vita Sancti Waldeni* in *ASB*, August 1 (1867) pp 249–78. Little is known about Jocelin himself; see G. McFadden, 'The *Life of Waldef* and its Author, Jocelin of Furness', *IR*, 6 (1955) pp 5–13.

[65] T. D. Hardy, *Descriptive Catalogue of Materials relating to the History of Great Britain and Ireland*, 3 vols, *RS* 26 (1862–71) 2, pp 225–6. Like Jocelin, he was the author of a *Life of Saint Waldef*, which is also lost. Everard began his life in religion at the Augustinian priory of Kirkham, where he met and was befriended by Waldef, then prior of that house. He left Kirkham with Waldef to enter the Cistercian abbey of Rievaulx, from which he later went to the abbey of Melrose, where Waldef was abbot, and thence he was sent to become the first abbot of Holmcultram; *Vita Sancti Waldeni*, pp 256, 262.

[66] *Vita Niniani*, ed Forbes, pp 3–5, 137–9; *Vita Kentegerni*, ed Forbes, pp 29–32, 159–61.

[67] *Vita Kentegerni*, ed Forbes, pp 30, 160.

cults from outside. Cuthbert's friend, the hermit Herebehrt, who lived on Derwentwater, had been forgotten by the twelfth century and was only re-discovered by bishop Appleby in the late fourteenth.[68]

The high rate of survival of Celtic saints' cults in the north-west is remarkable. With the multiplication of churches and chapels in the twelfth century,[69] the pattern of dedications reflect fully the various cultural influences existing in Cumbrian society. One need but glance at a list of the church and chapel dedications of Cumberland and Westmorland to perceive the importance of Celtic saints in the district,[70] and when compared with the dedications of neighbouring Northumberland and Durham, where Northumbrian saints naturally predominate, the contrast is evident.[71] Although it is impossible to be certain of who was responsible for the dedication of any particular church, whether the builder or the bishop who actually consecrated the building for sacred use, the fact remains that nothing expresses more clearly the mixture of Briton, Angle and Hiberno-Norse in Cumbrian society than the saints chosen as patrons. Even though a universal saint, Michael was especially popular in Celtic lands,[72] and in the north-west he

[68] Nicolson and Burn, 2, pp 529–30.
[69] C. M. L. Bouch, *Prelates and People of the Lake Counties: A history of the Diocese of Carlisle, 1133–1933* (Kendal 1948) p 9.
[70] The dedications of the churches and chapels of Cumberland and Westmorland have been listed by [T. H. B. Graham and W. G. Collingwood,] 'Patron Saints [of the Diocese of Carlise',] *Trans CWAAS* ns 25 (Kendal 1925) pp 1–27. Of all the known dedications listed, sixty percent are verified by medieval sources, and the others are taken from eighteenth-century compilations. Of those taken from medieval sources, just over half date from the twelfth and thirteenth centuries; the rest date mainly from the fourteenth century. One must approach church-dedication evidence cautiously, as dedications were sometimes changed, as in the case of the church of Farlam, dedicated to Saint Thomas of Canterbury but certainly existing before 1169. However, the sample of certain twelfth- and thirteenth-century dedications is large enough to support the statements made here, and it is unlikely that so large a proportion of the dedications taken from later medieval and eighteenth-century sources would have been changed that the opinions expressed would be radically altered.
[71] J. V. Gregory, 'Dedication Names of Ancient Churches in the Counties of Durham and Northumberland', *The Archaeological Journal*, 42 (London 1885) pp 370–83.
[72] J. M. Mackinlay, *Ancient Church Dedications in Scotland*, 2 vols (Edinburgh 1910–14) I, pp 337–56, 399–401; Owen Chadwick, 'The Evidence of Dedications in the Early History of the Welsh Church', *Studies in Early British History*, ed N. K. Chadwick (Cambridge 1954) pp 173–88, especially 182–4.

easily had more churches under his protection than even the Virgin, whose cult was seemingly all but introduced by the Normans. Of greater interest, however, are those saints of Scottish, Northumbrian, and Irish provenance who were clearly being chosen as patrons of churches and chapels throughout the twelfth century.

The fixation of a political border at the Solway-Tweed line did not of course presage an end to contacts between northern England and Scotland. The facility with which David I was unable to re-absorb the area into his realm and establish himself to Carlisle is exemplary of this, and in the course of the twelfth century the Anglo-Norman aristocracy had little trouble finding lands and positions of influence north of the border.[73] The ecclesiastical reforms and revival of episcopal sees in Scotland carried out by the sons of Saint Margaret encouraged familiar interchange between the northern churchmen. Many of the new Scottish monastic houses were founded from English communities,[74] and, as previously noted, Holmcultram abbey was a daughter house of Melrose. Likewise, contact was maintained between the north-west and Ireland. Furness had daughter houses at Inniscourcy and Abington there, while Holmcultram was the mother house of Grey abbey. Nendrum priory was a cell of St Bees, itself a cell of St Mary's, York, and Augustinian Toberglory belonged to Carlisle priory.[75] It should not therefore be surprising that the cults of Kentigern, Ninian, Bridget, Patrick, and Columba continued to have and to gain importance in Cumberland and Westmorland.

Devotion to Kentigern was probably revived and strengthened by David's re-foundation of the see of Glasgow and the dedication to the traditional founder of the new cathedral church there in the early twelfth century. And it is surely not without significance that his cult was virtually represented in England only in that area which had once been under the domination of the kingdom of Strathclyde, that is, Cumberland and Westmorland.[76] By the time

---

[73] For the most recent work on this subject, see G. W. S. Barrow, *The Anglo-Norman Era in Scottish History* (Oxford 1980).

[74] G. W. S. Barrow, 'Scottish Rulers and the Religious Orders, 1070–1153', *TRHS*, 5 ser 3 (1953) pp 77–100.

[75] *MRHI*, pp 107, 126,, 132, 134, 170; W. T. McIntire, 'A Note on Grey Abbey and Other Religious Foundations on Strangford Lough affiliated to the Abbeys of Cumberland', *Trans CWAAS* ns 41 (Kendal 1941) pp 161–73.

[76] Frances Arnold-Forster, *Studies in Church Dedications*, 3 vols (London 1899) 3, pp 36, 67, 75, 79, 100, 135, 164, 206, 256, 388. According to this work, the only

that Jocelin was composing his *Life of Saint Kentigern*, the bishop had been popularly associated enough with the district that a certain stone cross was believed to have been erected by him and a church was built on the spot in his honour.[77] The widely publicised discovery of the relics of Patrick, Bridget, and Columba at Downpatrick by Malachy in 1186 likewise probably helped to revive the cults of these saints along the west coast of Britain.[78]

The Northumbrian saints who were given the patronage of churches in the north-west were largely re-introduced by the Anglo-Normans after 1092, and it is obvious that the influence of Bede, as in the initial revival of northern monasticism, was at work. The reputations of these Anglian saints had remained relatively unscathed, and especially the cult of saint Cuthbert, re-vitalised by the advertisement of the opening of his tomb in 1104, when his body was found to be uncorrupted by death,[79] became of greater importance in the north. Indeed, after the Virgin, Cuthbert's was the single most important cult in Cumberland and Westmorland throughout the middle ages. To him were dedicated about fifteen churches and chapels, and by synodal statute the celebration of his feast-day was enjoined throughout the diocese of Carlisle.[80] After Cuthbert, the other Northumbrian saints are more modestly represented in church dedications, but the presence of Oswald, whose head was found buried in Cuthbert's tomb,[81] Hilda, and Wilfrid as patrons is nonetheless indicative of the trend.

Cumbrian society in the twelfth century was in the midst of stabilisation, carried out by the new Anglo-Norman aristocracy, and the policies enacted in the north-west affected the religious as much as the political way of life. Before its integration into England, the region's ecclesiastical affairs for the most part marched with those of Scotland. The church from the tenth century, when Northumbrian rule was disrupted, was in decline, and the vibrancy of northern monasticism was lost. The restoration

---

church outside of Cumberland and Westmorland to be dedicated to Kentigern was at Simonburn in Northumberland.

[77] *Vita Kentegerni*, ed Forbes, pp 74, 200.
[78] *AS*, February 1 (1863) pp 111–12.
[79] *Symeon*, 2, pp 236–7.
[80] *Councils and Synods*, ed F. M. Powicke and C. R. Cheney, 2 vols (Oxford 1964) 1, p 628.
[81] *Symeon*, 1, pp 379–81.

of monasticism under the Normans was welcomed by Cumbrian society, but that society remained keenly aware of the diverse influences in its own make-up. The natural orientation of Cumberland and Westmorland was to the north and west through the Stainmore gap and Tyne corridor. Although one would therefore expect Celtic saints to be represented in the area, it is significant that they are so well represented as patrons of churches built after 1092, and it seems clear that a sense of identity was at work. The fact that the Anglo-Norman church accepted these saints helped to integrate the area into the Anglo-Norman kingdom by transforming a 'national' identity into a 'local' identity,[82] and the creation of a new diocese to accommodate the spiritual needs of the population practically helped to enforce the idea of a new 'border' and to orientate the district towards the south and east.

University of Edinburgh

[82] Aside from the parish church dedications of the twelfth century, the foundation of the Benedictine priory of St Bees and its dedication to Saint Mary and Saint Bega, and the dedication of Wetheral priory to Saint Mary and Saint Constantine, who was commonly associated with Kentigern, and the dedication of a chapel there to Saint Serf, Kentigern's teacher, are clear indicators of the acceptance by the Anglo-Norman conquerors of the already existing local cults; 'Patron Saints', pp 9–11, 17, 27.

A KIND OF NOAH'S ARK:
AELRED OF RIEVAULX AND NATIONAL IDENTITY

by ROSALIND RANSFORD

ELRED of Rievaulx was born of English parents at Hexham in about 1110, that is only thirty years after the final Norman punitive harrying of the north and thirty-four years after the execution of earl Waltheof, grandfather of Aelred's lifelong friend, Waldef. Aelred's father was the last of a long line of English 'hereditary' priests of Hexham, a foundation of Saint Wilfred which lay within the patrimony of Saint Cuthbert; Cuthbert and Wilfred were kept alive in Northumbria by the writings of Bede whose bones Aelred's great-grandfather had stolen in a dawn raid on Jarrow and brought to Durham, where Aelred's father ended his days as one of Cuthbert's monks. Such a background could be expected to have given Aelred a strong sense of the difference between Norman and Englishman and of his own Englishness. But national identity in Northumbria in the first half of the twelfth century was a complex affair.

Aelred's adolescent years were spent at the court of the Scots king David who, half-Scottish by birth, had been educated by Henry I in England as a Norman and was, as Aelred well knew, like a foreigner in his own land. When Aelred chose to take up the religious life, he did not follow his father's example and enter the ancient English Benedictine community at Durham but chose the barely two year old Cistercian house at Rievaulx, colonised by French monks from Clairvaux itself.

Conquering Normans and conquered English, a Normanised Scottish king trying in turn to unify and Normanise his disparate subjects, Northumbria whose past was second to none in the history of Christian devotion, learning and art but whose present reality was the often ravaged battleground over which English and Scots fought, and life among French monks at Rievaulx where it was worthy of note that Aelred could speak English:[1] this confu-

[1] [Walter Daniel, *Vita Ailredi*, ed F. M.] Powicke (Edinburgh 1950) p 60.

sion of national identities is the background of Aelred's life and it may be interesting to keep them in mind when reading his historical works.

By Aelred's historical works I mean the *Genealogy of the English Kings* written in 1153 or 1154, the *Report on the Battle of the Standard*, a battle which was fought some fourteen miles from Rievaulx in 1138 when Aelred was already a monk there and which he wrote about in 1155 to 57, and his *Life of Edward the Confessor* written in 1163 to celebrate Edward's canonisation.[2] Each of these is closely concerned with national identity and indeed in the *Report* and the *Genealogy* it is a dominant theme.

The only people concerned in the battle of the standard whose loyalties and national identities were not divided were the men of Galloway. Hardly anyone had a good word for the men of Galloway: they had a national identity and it was bad. In the *Report* Aelred has Walter Espec describe them at length. They murder pregnant women, they delight in spiking babies on their spears, they bash out children's brains, they murder priests, and the only reason why the earth has not swallowed them up hitherto, says the good Walter, is so that Walter's soldiers can kill them and thus 'consecrate their hands in the blood of sinners'.[3] Yet, although they are undoubtedly the villains of the piece, Aelred gives them words of great nobility when they demand of David the right to lead the Scots army—'we need no armour: our bodies are iron, our breasts are bronze, our minds are free from fear'.[4] Later Aelred says they looked like hedgehogs their flesh bristling with enemy spears.[5] Aelred shows Robert de Brus castigating David for allowing his victories to be won by such criminals. 'You say', says Robert to David before the battle, 'that their abominable crimes were committed against your orders, so now show the truth of your words and call them back from further wickedness, for the blood of uncountable innocent men and women is calling out to you from the ground.'[6]

David's difficulties are brought into focus by Robert de Brus, by right the king of England's man, says Aelred, but the king of

---

[2] Texts *PL* [195] (1854) cols 702–790. For the dates of writing, Powicke p xcvii.
[3] *PL* 195 col 706.
[4] *Ibid* col 707.
[5] *Ibid* col 711.
[6] *Ibid* cols 709–710.

Scotland's companion since childhood and bound to him by friendship as well as by fealty. He comes from the English army to treat with David before the battle and his speech is a real pleasure to read. He reminds David that his true and natural allies are the English and Normans and asks where among the Scots has David found such faith. 'Without English advice and Norman arms', he says, 'will Scotsmen be enough to support you against Scotsmen?' and he remembers how often the English, once even Walter Espec himself, have hurried to David's aid. In no uncertain terms Robert reminds David that he owes his throne to English support—'our army'.

Aelred makes interesting use of words here to stress the complexities of David's national identity. At first Robert mentions English and Normans twice in partnership and then English twice alone and at the same time makes seven references to the Scots, always derogatory. Then he switches to 'us' meaning English, Normans and David, repeated fourteen times in contrast to *tu* or *tuus* which is used forty times to emphasise how David is isolating himself amongst enemies and against friends.[7] He almost persuades David to call off the battle, but David's nephew, William FitzDuncan, will have none of that.[8]

In that brief passage Aelred has summarised with great understanding the enormous difficulties which arise when awareness of national identity is allowed to overrule men's more natural feelings. Robert de Brus can formally set aside his fealty when David will not set aside the battle,[9] but the complexities of David's position, personal and political, allowed of no such remedy. By his oath to his brother-in-law Henry I, David was bound to support the claim to the English throne of one of his nieces, the empress Matilda, against Stephen who was married to another of his nieces. David, as earl of Huntingdon, was bound in fealty to the king of England, yet he had to maintain the integrity of his own kingdom against that king. Soon Henry II would be faced with a similar problem over his duchy, his kingdom and the king of France and he too was to find it insoluble.

Also in the *Report* Aelred gives Walter Espec's exhortation to his army before the battle. Walter was the founder of Rievaulx and

[7] *Ibid* cols 708–710.
[8] *Ibid* col 710.
[9] *Ibid* col 710.

may have retired there. He probably died just before Aelred was writing and the *Report* contains a handsome tribute to him. Walter, however, was aware only of Norman identity: 'our army' is a purely Norman army. 'Our forefathers wiped out the very name of Gaul', he says, 'in no time at all we and our fathers conquered this island which Julius Caesar took so long to occupy . . . we have actually seen the king of France . . . and the emperor too . . . turn their backs on us and run away. Who conquered Apulia, Sicily, Calabria if it were not your Norman?' and he then pours scorn on the Scots who wear no armour. He mentions England just once, a reference to *Willelmus victor Anglie*.[10]

In the *Report* Aelred allows great national pride to the men of Galloway and to Walter Espec, but the Galwegians are clearly bad men while Walter is carefully shown as the very epitome of a Christian knight, fighting for the right and generously founding monasteries. The heart of the *Report* and the part over which Aelred seems to have taken most pains is the long speech of Robert de Brus when he urges David to call off the battle. Robert was bound to David by friendship as well as by fealty. When he fails to persuade David he can and does loose the bond of fealty but he goes away *non sine magno dolore* because he cannot loose the bond of friendship.[11]

The *Genealogy of the English Kings* is, in contrast, redolent with pride in Englishness. It is in the form of a letter written by Aelred to duke Henry in the seventeen months between the deaths of David and Stephen. Its purpose was to hold a mirror up to kingship but, whereas a John of Salisbury would have dazzled the young man with the breadth of his classical and scriptural learning, Aelred's theme is more direct and he confines himself to the Christian kings of England whose son—Henry—shines like a new star in whom are gathered the virtues of all his ancestors. Aelred is quite specific in his purpose. 'When you see', he tells duke Henry, 'what goodness there was in your ancestors and how piety shone in them, you will understand how natural it is for you to overflow with riches, to blossom in virtue, to grow famous by your victories and best of all to shine with the Christian life and the prerogative of justice.' These are inborn characteristics but Henry will cultivate

---

[10] *Ibid* col 705. For the date of Walter Espec's death, Powicke p xcix.
[11] *Ibid* 195 col 710.

them too to keep himself from the shame of being the only black sheep of such a family.[12]

Aelred traces Henry's ancestry through the 'most glorious' empress Matilda, her maternal grandmother Saint Margaret of Scotland and then through all the kings of England through Woden back to Adam, the father of all men. There are twenty-three generations from Adam to Woden and twenty-three more from Woden to Alfred to give a dignity to the early English kings. Woden was a sort of founder of the English who commemorate him in the name of the weekday Wednesday, as Aelred carefully tells Henry.[13] All the kings of England from whom Henry is descended were graced by Christian and kingly virtue; even Ethelred 'the Unready' is a good king to Aelred who calls him *virtute potens, strenuissimus* and *gloriosus*. All Ethelred's troubles were due, as Dunstan had foretold, to the treachery of the English at Corfe in murdering the young king Edward who, on account of the holiness of his life, was worthy of the name of saint.[14]

Aelred tells Henry mostly about Alfred—the glory of the English, Edward the Elder, Athelstan, Edgar and David of Scotland. The attributes in them which he picks out for Henry are patronage of the church, mercy, justice, chastity, humility, generosity and reverence for the clergy. Edward the Elder, Edgar and David were all such good men that peoples came willingly to submit to their rule.[15] Edgar and David continually travel around their lands to dispense justice with especial care for the poor and the weak.[16] All work in close cooperation with their bishops and clergy but in particular Edgar summons his clergy and firmly reminds them that, as his jurisdiction is limited to laymen, good order in the church is a debt which the church owes to its patrons who have provided its wealth and, as the greatest of those patrons are kings, so it is a debt owed specifically by the English church to the English kings. Aelred says that the work of Dunstan, Ethelwold and Oswald was in obedience to Edgar's commands and it would be so interesting to know what was in Aelred's mind when he was deliberately recounting the episode to the future king of England.

---

[12] *Ibid* col 716.
[13] *Ibid* col 717.
[14] *Ibid* cols 729–730.
[15] *Ibid* cols 723, 726 and 714 respectively.
[16] *Ibid* cols 727 and 714 respectively.

In the time of Edgar, Aelred continues, just as life in the church began to flourish so also blossomed the devotion of laymen, the moderation of soldiers, the equity of judges and the fertility of the land.[17]

Aelred does not say that these are the virtues of ideal kings or of kings in general; his emphasis always is that they are the virtues of the kings of England. Duke Henry is almost a stranger to England and it appears that in the *Genealogy* Aelred is trying to show him that his true national identity is as Henry the Englishman, Henry the English king.

The *Life of Edward the Confessor* is largely a reworking of Osbert de Clare's attempt to achieve Edward's canonisation in 1138.[18] However, Aelred wrote a prologue addressed to Henry II in which he continues the theme of the *Genealogy* and says that before all the states and kingdoms of the earth, England is glorious for the sanctity of her kings. If nowadays we read of a medieval *rex christianissimus* we would probably think of a French king, but Aelred firmly applies the term to the whole line of English kings and in particular to Alfred who is also called *miles Christi*, to Edward the Elder, Athelstan and Edgar, that *rex sanctissimus* whose birth was heralded by singing angels. The holy lineage continues through Edmund Ironside's exiled children and the descendants of Saint Margaret, a holy family whose heir is duke Henry. Margaret's daughter Maud, wife of Henry I, is twice called *christianissima* and Margaret's son David is another most Christian king.[19]

But Aelred does more than stress the most Christian attributes of English kings. He puts them on a par with emperors and suggests that England has been an empire since the time of Edgar. He likens Edgar to Cyrus, Charlemagne and Romulus; Alfred models himself on the emperor Constantine; Edgar claims to own Constantine's sword; Edmund Ironside rules alone over a land which once had many kings and Aelred says that not even a Virgil or a Homer could adequately describe his greatness.[20] Edgar rules over provinces, having delegated power to his provincial governors. Eight

---

[17] *Ibid* cols 727–29.

[18] *Vita Aedwardi Regis*, ed F. Barlow (London 1962) pp xxxv–vii. The Prologue to Aelfred's *Life* is at *PL* 195 cols 737–740.

[19] *Ibid* cols 719–720 and 740 (Alfred); 726 (Edward the Elder); 724 (Athelstan); 726 (Edgar); 716 and 736 (Maud); 713 (David).

[20] *Ibid* cols 726 and 728 (Edgar); 719 (Alfred); 731 (Edmund Ironside).

kings are subject to him and on his greatest festivity Aelred describes how the eight kings board a boat and take up their oars before Edgar seats himself in the stern of the boat and performs the function of a helmsman—*gubernatoris officio fungebatur*[21]—a perfect twelfth-century definition of an emperor. The very elements, says Aelred, were subject to Edgar's nod and England enjoyed a golden age under his rule when the sun seemed brighter, the sea calmer and the earth more fertile.

As well as the beauty of the land and the goodness of her kings, Aelred seems anxious that Henry should learn to honour the English saints. It was Cuthbert whose visit to Athelney—a long way from home—brought about the turning point in Alfred's struggle with the Danes. It was John of Beverley who promised Athelstan to be an enemy to his enemies and helped him to conquer the Scots. It was probably Edmund who caused the death of Swein Forkbeard.[23] Most recently Edward the Confessor, whom Aelred calls Henry's father, made a dying prophecy about his true heir which the English believe has been fulfilled in Henry. Henry has assumed his father's kingdom by the double right of his own merits and his inherited blood. He is like a cornerstone in whom the two walls of the English and Norman races have come together. But Edward the Confessor is more than a father, he is Henry's patron saint too. Henry must pray to him, must commit himself to Edward's protection and must imitate his holiness.[24]

These three works were all written with Henry II in mind, a king who was to rule directly over more different peoples than any other ruler since the Roman emperors. In the *Genealogy* the theme is straightforward: duke Henry's inheritance is the unrivalled good-ness and sanctity of the kings of England. England is not just for the English but already contains many different peoples, even Welshmen and Danes. Henry is already proclaimed the glory of the Angevins, the protector of the Normans, the splendour of the men of Aquitaine and now he is the hope of the English.[25] The *Report* was written two or three years later when Aelred has had more time to consider the difficulties which national identity can pose to

[21] *Ibid* cols 727 and 729.
[22] *Ibid* col 726; also col 729.
[23] *Ibid* cols 720 (Cuthbert); 724–725 (John); 730 (Edmund).
[24] *Ibid* cols 738–740.
[25] *Ibid* col 713.

a king whose loyalties are due to so many peoples. His condemnation of the men of Galloway is uncharacteristically harsh and must exist here as a criticism of David for giving them free rein, but Aelred's vivid description of Galwegian atrocities also spells out the difficulties of David's position: David must be king of all the men of Scotland, however barbaric, and must listen to the advice they give, but at the same time he is involved in English politics and, first of all the English barons, has sworn to support the empress Matilda. Aelred wrote the *Report* after the deaths of David and his son prince Henry to whom Aelred had been particularly devoted 'since the cradle'[26] as he says. Although both men are continually referred to in the *Report*, it is always as 'the king' or 'the prince' and never once by name. I think what Aelred is saying is that king David and prince Henry would never have led such an army into such a battle but that the king of Scotland and his eldest son at that particular time had no choice but to fight that battle with whatever resources their country could provide. The battle itself is of no significance to Aelred, his purpose is to illustrate the difficulties which beset king David and which will continue to beset future kings of Scotland. To analyse the difficulties of the king is to understand the difficulties of the man and to understand all is to forgive all. 'When a man learns to love and forgive, he becomes a friend to his fellow men.' This last statement is from Aelred's *Speculum Caritatis*.[27]

In the *Speculum Caritatis*, which he wrote in the early 1140s,[28] he says that every creature from the most radiant angel to the tiniest worm contains signs of God's goodness,[29] so for the love of God all men must be loved from dearest kinsman to greatest enemy. He recognises that no one can give his friendship in equal measure to all, so he suggests that we imagine our heart to be a kind of spiritual Noah's ark with different compartments on different levels for the different kinds of people we shall meet. As Noah accommodated wild animals, we must find room for our enemies—that is, those who hate us—on the lower deck and round the edges, while we may reserve the inner rooms and the upper decks for those who

[26] *Ibid* cols 736–737.
[27] *Speculum Caritatis*, [translated and arranged by G. Webb and A. Walker] (London 1962) p 88.
[28] Powicke p xcvii.
[29] *Speculum Caritatis* p 22.

love us and who love God. By arranging things in this way, Aelred says we can make room for everyone in our hearts[30] and so restore our likeness to God.[31]

If this teaching is applied to his historical works their purpose becomes clearer. In the *Genealogy* and the *Report* Aelred is stressing that friendship knows no national boundaries or differences. Although victory in battle will always increase a king's power, the example of a king's own goodness and his capacity to love will induce men willingly to submit themselves to his rule. He presents this lesson not as idealistic theory but as an established fact in the history of England and Scotland.

I think that Aelred is telling duke Henry in the *Report* that, even if men as terrible as the Galwegians come again plundering their way across England, Henry, Noah-like, should find some room for them in his heart, though the bilges would seem acceptable in their instance. In the *Report* and the *Genealogy* he is saying that everyone has a national identity but it is the essence of empire that nations come together under the rule of one man. Everyone contains a sign of God's goodness and it is the duty of a Christian king to recognise it. Even the men of Galloway are capable of noble thoughts. I think, too, that he is suggesting to Henry that he should bind himself in friendship to his fellow kings and ensure that his chief subjects are bound to him and to those fellow kings in friendship as well as in fealty and then the result must be peace. National identity can lead men to place formal fealty before God-like friendship; fealty can be undone and battles can then be fought. Friendship can never be undone.

Aelred does not explicitly tell Henry to model his kingship on Noah, but in the *Genealogy* he has shown that Henry is directly descended from Noah and, just as the preservation of all God's creatures was entrusted to Noah in the ark, so both the government and the care of many peoples have been entrusted to Henry in his empire. The message of the *Genealogy* and the Prologue to the *Life* of the Confessor is that Henry should learn how to guide his peoples through the storms of life from the example of his ancestors. This is the value of national identity. Through it a man can learn of the great achievements of his ancestors and then take

---

[30] *Ibid* pp 136–137.
[31] *Ibid* p 88.

pride in being their heir and emulating them for, as Aelred says, if we do not know for certain that a thing has already been accomplished, we may not have the confidence to try and accomplish it ourselves.[32]

University of London
Birkbeck College

[32] *PL* 195 col 737.

ROYAL CONTROL OF THE CHURCH IN THE TWELFTH-CENTURY KINGDOM OF SICILY

by G. A. LOUD

FOR the king, after the fashion of tyrants, had reduced the church in his kingdom to slavery'. So John of Salisbury stigmatized king Roger II of Sicily. He continued that 'instead of allowing any freedom of elections [Roger] named in advance the candidate to be elected, so disposing of all ecclesiastical offices like palace appointments'.[1] This picture has been accepted by modern historians with very few reservations. To quote the standard history of the Norman kingdom of Sicily of Ferdinand Chalandon, still unrivalled after more than seventy years, *ce qui caractérise la situation des évêques a l'époque normande, c'est la dépendance absolue où ils se trouvent vis-à-vis du roi.*[2]

Roger II and his successors were not of course the only twelfth-century monarchs against whom such charges could be, and were, levelled. Neither was this the only, nor the main, criticism which contemporaries levelled against the 'tyrants of Sicily'—indeed compared with the dubious circumstances in which the kingdom had been founded in 1130 it was a comparatively minor one.[3] But the opinion of contemporaries makes clear that, even in an age when *de facto* royal control of national churches was usual, the kings of Sicily held the church in their dominions in a singularly harsh straitjacket.

A particularly contentious issue, both at the time and among later historians, was the so-called apostolic legation, or more accurately the power to act *legati vice*, conceded by pope Urban II to

---

I should like to thank the late Denis Bethell for his helpful advice on this paper.
[1] [The] *Historia Pontificalis [of John of Salisbury,* ed and trans. M. Chibnall] (London 1956) p 65.
[2] F. Chalandon, [*La Domination Normande en Italie et en Sicile*], 2 vols (Paris 1907) 2 p 595.
[3] See H. Wieruszowski, 'Roger II of Sicily, Rex Tyrannus in twelfth-century Political Thought', *Speculum* 38 (1963) pp 46–78.

count Roger I of Sicily in July 1098. It has long been recognized that the 1098 concession was in practice the acceptance of an existing state of affairs, and of powers over the church which Roger I had already assumed.[4] Some historians have gone so far as to argue that the concession was of no real importance and that Roger II inherited no particularly privileged position from his father.[5] This is to misunderstand the issue. To begin with the text of the 1098 privilege stated unambiguously that the power to act *legati vice* was conceded to Roger I, his eldest son Simon (who died in 1105) and any other legitimate heir.[6] And neither Roger I nor Roger II were very restrained in their interpretation of this power. Not only did Roger I exercise the right of visitation of monasteries, probably granted him by Urban II in 1088, but even before the Salerno concession of July 1098 he actually called himself legate.[7] Roger II summarily deposed the archbishop of Cosenza in 1114, and three years later was reproved by Paschal II who told him that he had no right to refuse legates a latere, and while accomplishing by his secular power what 'ecclesiastical humility' commanded but could not by itself achieve, he was not to judge ecclesiastics himself or to call bishops to synods.[8]

Such abuses (to papal eyes) of lay power were by no means confined to Sicily. Just a year before his rebuke to Roger II Paschal had unleashed battery of very similar, indeed rather more far-reaching, charges against Henry I and the English bishops.[9] Royal interference was just as pronounced in the nomination of higher ecclesiastics in England, as John of Salisbury himself recognized. Henry II too he stigmatised as a tyrant, albeit at the height of the

---

[4] E. Jordan, 'La Politique Ecclésiastique de Roger I et les Origines de la Legation Sicilienne', *Moyen Âge* 33 (1922) p 260. [L. T.] White, *Latin Monasticism [in Norman Sicily]* (Cambridge, Mass., 1938) pp 39–40.

[5] L. R. Ménager, 'L'Institution Monarchique dans les États Normands de l'Italie', *Cahiers de Civilisation Mediévale* 2 (Poitiers 1959) p 318. D. C. Douglas, *The Norman Fate 1100–1154* (London 1976) p 133.

[6] Geoffrey Malaterra, *De Rebus Gestis Rogerii Calabriae et Siciliae Comitis,* ed E. Pontieri (Muratori 2 ed, Bologna 1927) bk 4 cap 29 p 108.

[7] E. Caspar, *Roger II (1101–1154) und die Gründung der Normannisch-Sicilischen Monarchie* (Innsbruck 1904) pp 632–4.

[8] *Chronica Casinenses,* ed W. Wattenbach, bk 4 cap 49, *MGH SS* 7 (1846) p 786. *Le Liber Censuum de l'Eglise Romaine,* ed P. Fabre and L. Duchesne, 3 vols (Paris 1889–1952) 2 pp 125–6.

[9] M. Brett, *The English Church under Henry I* (Oxford 1975) pp 36–7.

Becket dispute.[10] Becket's successor, Richard of Dover, was the victim of 'a stinging rebuke from pope Alexander III for confirming episcopal elections in the king's chamber'.[11] And yet contemporaries seemed to recognise the character of royal control over the church in Sicily as something special. If we turn once again to John of Salisbury, in 1167 he wrote to Alexander III denouncing the justification of Henry II's claims over the church by citing 'the example of the Sicilians and Hungarians'.[12] Richard of Dover, in a letter written by Peter of Blois about 1179, excused the activities of English bishops as royal officials by comparing their performance of their ecclesiastical duties with the abuses which abounded in Sicily, where curialist bishops neglected their churches while for as long as seven or ten years they frequented the royal court.[13] In his tract *De Institutione Episcopo* Peter of Blois harked back to the chains of secular office which, he claimed, bound the Sicilian episcopate.[14] The apostolic legation fuelled extravagant stories by hostile critics of papal concessions of ecclesiastical regalia such as the mitre and dalmatic to the king of Sicily.[15] Chroniclers recorded the physical detention of prelates who sought to appeal to the pope in the troubled decade of the 1140s.[16]

Some of the abuse which was hurled at the Sicilian rulers was based on extravagant fantasy compounded by partisan feeling. Such critics as the cardinals who elected the anti-pope Victor IV in 1159 and who blamed the papal schism primarily on the machinations of William I of Sicily can hardly be taken as unbiased witnesses in their assertion that the king *omnia iura aecclesiae tam*

[10] [*The*] *Letters* [*of John of Salisbury*, ed H. E. Butler, W. J. Millor & C. N. L. Brooke] 2 vols, (London/Oxford 1955–79) 2 pp 614–17 no 281.

[11] C. R. Cheney, *From Becket to Langton* (Manchester 1956) p 23.

[12] *Letters* 2 pp 376–7 no 219.

[13] *PL* 200 (1854) cols 1459–62 no 96; see also *PL* 207 (1854) col 259 no 84.

[14] *Ibid* col 1110.

[15] [*Ottonis et Rahewini*] *G*[*esta*] *F*[*riderici I Imperatoris*, ed G. Waitz and B. de Simson], *MGH SRG* (1912) Bk I cap 29 pp 46–7. Radulfus Niger, *Chronica Universali*, *MGH SS* 27 (1885) p 335. The story probably misinterpreted the concession of the mitre to the abbot of the court monastery of St. John of the Hermits, for which see below n 31.

[16] [*Ignoti Monachi Cisterciensis S. Mariae de*] *Ferraria Chron*[*ica*, ed A. Gaudenzi] (Naples 1888) p 27. This account dates from the early thirteenth century, but is derived from the lost concluding section of the contemporary chronicle of Falco of Benevento. See E. Gervasio, 'Falcone Beneventano e la sua cronaca', *BISIMEAM* 54 (1939) pp 70–7. Later report exaggerated the incident, see *Ex Fragmentis ex Vita Sancti Thomi auctore Herberto de Boseham*, *MGH SS* 27 p 33.

spiritualia quam temporalia violenter abstulerat.[17] But both John of
Salisbury and Peter of Blois were well-acquainted with Sicily. The
former was the close friend both of pope Adrian IV and of Roger
II's chancellor, another Englishman, Robert of Selby.[18] Peter spent
two years in Sicily as tutor to the young king William II, as one of
the retinue attached to Stephen of Perche, chancellor 1166–8 and
archbishop of Palermo 1167–8. Peter's brother William was for a
time abbot of Matina in Calabria.[19] Neither were the criticisms
which he in particular voiced made at random without application
ad hominem. The letter written for archbishop Richard of Canterbury made covert reference to the scandalous case of Richard
Palmer, bishop of Syracuse, the erstwhile correspondent of both
Peter himself and Thomas Becket, whom John of Salisbury
considered had been working against Becket at the Sicilian court.
Richard had deferred his consecration for some twelve years after
his original appointment as bishop in 1157.[20]

Certain qualifications must however be made. Although he
considered the south Italian bishops ready to perjure themselves in
a body to please the king in the divorce case of count Hugh II of
Molise, John of Salisbury was forced to admit that Roger II avoided
simony and generally appointed bishops of good character. Indeed
in the *Policraticus* he recounted an anecdote about his friend Robert
of Selby refusing to be influenced by bribes while supervising an
election to the see of Avellino, and instead installing a monk
untainted by simony.[21]

More importantly, though the papacy disliked the claims of
quasi-legantine powers it was prepared to admit their validity. The
outstanding political and ecclesiastical difficulties between pope and
king were settled in the Treaty of Benevento of June 1156. In this a
specific distinction was drawn between the king's mainland dominions, to which legates were to be admitted, and the island of Sicily,

[17] *GF* bk 4 cap 62 p 304.
[18] *Letters* I pp 57–8 no 33. John also records a visit to Apulia in his *Policraticus,* [ed
C. C. J. Webb], 2 vols (Oxford 1909) 2 pp 270–1.
[19] See his epp nos 46, 90 and 93, *PL* 207 cols 133–7 (to bishop Richard of Syracuse),
281–5, 291–3 (to his brother, for whose career see L. T. White, 'For the Biography
of William of Blois', *EHR* 50 (1935) pp 487–490.
[20] For his career, [N.] Kamp, [*Kirche und Monarchie im Staufischen Königreich Sizilien* I
Prosopographische Grundlegung], 3 vols (Munich 1973–5) 3.1013–1018, and for
John's opinion, *Letters* 2 pp 660–1 no 290.
[21] *Historia Pontificalis* pp 67–8. *Policraticus* 2 pp 173–4.

to which they were not to be unless specifically requested, and from which appeals to Rome were only to be allowed with royal sanction. (Urban II's original concession had applied only to the island). And while technically protecting the freedom of episcopal elections, the treaty allowed the king the right of veto.[22] The special ecclesiastical rights of the Sicilian king were recognized, if not with good grace, by the greatest of late twelfth-century canon lawyers, Huguccio of Pisa. On the power of assenting to the choice of bishops and investing them with the temporalities of their churches, he commented,

> hoc autem fuit speciale privilegium in persona eius (the emperor) et quorumdam aliorum, sicut hodie est in persona regis Apuli, et male', and also, 'prohibetur recipi investituram ecclesie . . . a laico . . . nisi laicus habeat privilegium a papa, ut talem investituram possit dare, ut Apulus.[23]

Furthermore, after the treaty of Benevento the king provided aid and comfort to the papacy during the long war with Frederick Barbarossa. The kingdom of Sicily gave Alexander III refuge when the imperial army took Rome in 1167, Sicilian troops helped to defend the southern Campania against the forces of Christian of Mainz, and Sicilian money, both the regular census specified in the treaty and extraordinary donations as the 60,000 tari given on his deathbed by William I, subsidised the papal cause. Not surprisingly such political aid made the stock of the king of Sicily stand high at the curia. The *Liber Pontificalis* lamented William I as *fidelis et devotus ecclesie Romane filius Willielmus, illustris et gloriosus rex Sicilie*.[24] Hence papal objections to such matters as royal appointments of bishops was not very probable.

Certainly the popes of the last decade of the century tried to

---

[22] *MGH Const* I pp 588–590 no 413, clauses 8 and 11.

[23] R. L. Benson, *The Bishop Elect* (Princeton 8) p 329 n 40. The passages quoted are commentaries on Gratian, *Decretum* D 63 c 23 'Quod si clero et populo quis eligatur episcopus, nisi a supradicto rege laudatur et investiatur, non consecretur', and C 16 qu 7 c 12 'De manu laici episcopatus vel abbatia suscipi non debet', *Corpus Iuris Canonici*, ed E. Friedberg, 2 vols (Leipzig 1879–81) I cols 241, 804.

[24] Romauld [of Salerno, *Chronicon*, ed C. A. Garufi] (Muratori 2 ed, Citta di Castello 1935) p 256. *Annales Ceccanenses* ad annos 1165, 1167, 1176, *MGH SS* 19 (1866) pp 285–6. John of Salisbury, *Letters* 2 pp 116–117 no 168. *Liber Pontificalis*, ed L. Duchesne, 3 vols (Paris 1886–1957) 2 p 414. For the importance of Sicily to papal finances, V. Pfaff, 'Die Einnahmen des Romischen Kurie am Ende des 12 Jahrhunderts', *Vierteljahrsschrift für Sozial und Wirtschaftsgeschichte* 40 (Wiesbaden 1953) p 114.

diminish royal control over the church, taking advantage of the troubled state of the kingdom after the death of William II in 1189, but this involved renegotiation of the terms of the treaty of Benevento, and not simply unilateral papal claims. There was still a recognition of shared interests. Even though Innocent III reproved the empress Constance for her continued interference in episcopal elections, he was prepared to admit that the kings of Sicily had been devoted supporters of the apostolic see both in prosperity and in adversity.[25]

Even before 1156, though political relations between the two were often stormy, the papacy was prepared to exercise a certain restraint in dealing with the king of Sicily. John of Salisbury recorded that because of royal control of episcopal elections, and as a penalty for the capture of Innocent II (at Gallucio in 1139), episcopal consecrations had been forbidden in the *regno* and 'men who had been elected years before but never consecrated resided in almost every cathedral church'.[26] We should be careful not to take this exaggerated account wholly at face value. Though the circumstances of Innocent's recognition of Roger's kingship rankled with some at the curia, notably with Innocent's successor, Celestine II, it was not apparently until 1142 that elections became an issue.[27] There was undoubtedly some sort of ban on consecrations, and the sources for the 1140s show an unusually large number of bishops-elect.[28] But there may never have been a complete prohibition, for Innocent II personally consecrated archbishop John of Amalfi in 1142, and Lucius II archbishop Lupus of Brindisi in 1144, and neither of these seems to have been unacceptable to the king.[29] Neither did papal privileges cease to be given to south Italian churches. There were times admittedly, as the early years of Eugenius III, when very few bulls were given, but there were other periods, most notably towards the end of the pontificate of Lucius

---

[25] P. F. Kehr, 'Das Briefbuch des Thomas von Gaeta', *QFIAB* 8 (1905) pp 59–61 no 14.

[26] *Historia Pontificalis* pp 65–6.

[27] *Ferraria Chron* p 27.

[28] Among the sees with unconsecrated prelates were the archbishoprics of Palermo, Messina, Trani and Sorrento, and the bishoprics of Catania, Cefalu, Troia, Teano, Trivento, Chieti and Valva.

[29] (P. F. Kehr,] I[talia] P[ontificia], 10 vols (Berlin 1905–74) 8 p 391 no 15. *Codice Diplomatico Brindisiano* I [(492–1299) ed G. M. Monti] (Bari 1940) pp 29–31 no 16. Both archbishops remained in office for more than twenty years.

II when relations were comparatively normal (which backs up the chronicler Romuald of Salerno, who said that Roger II considered Lucius to be friendly towards him). Although oppostion from within the college of cardinals prevented a complete settlement, a truce to border warfare was at least arranged towards the end of 1144.[30] And it is clear that well before Roger and Eugenius III met to resolve their differences at Ceprano in 1150, relations were improving, since the pope gave generous ecclesiastical privileges to the abbot of the newly-founded court monastery of St John of the Hermits before July 1148.[31] In spite of all the difficulties in Siculo-papal relations in this period, some churches at least hardly suffered from a deprivation of papal aid and protection. The monastery of Montecassino received nine bulls in its favour in the decade 1139–49, and abbot Rainald II was made a cardinal.[32] The overall level of papal business with regard to the south Italian church was undoubtedly less in the 1140s than in other decades, but, to use a modern analogy, there was a work to rule rather than an all-out strike.

The papacy exercised similar caution after 1156 in the exercise of the powers to which it was entitled under the treaty of Benevento. Although the curia's right to send legates to the mainland provinces had been guaranteed by the treaty, it was one which was seldom exercised. In the thirty-three years between the treaty and the death of William II only four legations were despatched to Apulia, Capua and Calabria; one by Adrian IV, and three by Alexander III. None of them were very active. Three are known from their involvement in one dispute between rival churchmen apiece, the fourth by reference in a decretal collection to two marriage cases, both from the same diocese (Bisceglie, in Apulia).[33] One reason for this

---

[30] Romuald p 228. *Ferraria Chron* p 28. Lucius issued five bulls to south Italian churches, only three of which have exact dates, the earliest being to Montecassino issued on 10 October 1144, *IP* 8 p 179 no 252.

[31] These are recorded in Roger's diploma of that month, R. Pirro, *Sicilia Sacra*, 2 vols (Palermo 1733) 2 pp 1109–1112. A papal peace move in 1148 is reported in a letter to the exiled Prince Robert II of Capua, *Monumenta Corbeiensia*, ed P. Jaffé, *Bibliotheca Rerum Germanicarum*, (Berlin 1864) p 229.

[32] *IP* 8 pp 178–180 nos 248–254, 256–7. Rainald was appointed cardinal by March 1142, L. Fabiani, *La Terra di S. Benedetto*, 2 vols, *Miscellanea Cassinese 33–4* (Montecassino 1968) I pp 424–5 no 3.

[33] The legations were (1) that of Hubald of St. Praxedis and John of SS. Sergius and Bacchus 1154–8 (2) that of Bernard of Porto and Manfred of St. George ad Velum Aureum 1166 (3) Manfred of Praeneste, Peter of St. Susanna and Hyacinth

absence of activity was the lack of real need for it. The assizes of the Norman kings show a lively interest in the defence of ecclesiastical interests,[34] and the royal government gave effective aid to the solution of church problems. For example, in 1175 Alexander III gave a judgement in a case between the bishop of Aquino (province of Capua) and the abbey of St Paul of Rome on the basis of a preliminary investigation by royal justiciars, the results of which had been sent to him by William II.[35] It is symptomatic of the absence of ecclesiastical tension in the *regno* that whereas in England the criminous clerks issue played a mjaor part in causing the six-year agony of the Becket affair, William II of Sicily was prepared to surrender his jurisdiction without protest.[36] Indeed the occasional criticisms of William II by Alexander III were rather complaints that the king did not do enough to supervise the church, rather than that he did too much; he should, for example, prevent laymen alienating churches in the diocese of Nola (province of Naples).[37]

We should therefore conclude by asking how far the king was concerned actually to exercise his control over the church. In particular, let us examine the key issue of the appointment of bishops. Procedural evidence is scarce but consistent. Royal licence was mandatory before an election could be made either to an episcopal see or in one of the major abbeys. The usual process was for a group of envoys from the chapter to go to the royal court for confirmation of the man they had chosen, or, if he was unaccept-able, to make a new election in the king's presence. Sometimes the chapter might be asked to name several possible candidates, and so would have some choice even if their primary nominee proved unsuitable. William II (or more properly the government ruling during his minority) threatened to appoint directly to the see of

of St. Maria in Cosmedin 1177 (4) John of St. Maria in Porticu, at some uncertain date after 1163, *IP* 8 pp 257 nos 9–11; 9 p 148 no 12; p 225 no 2; p 296 nos 25–6.

[34] Edited F. Brandileone, *Il Diretto romano nelle legge normanne e sueve del regno di Sicilia* (Turin 1884) pp 94–138. Note especially assize 2 of the Vatican MS 'De privilegio sanctarum ecclesiarum', p 96.

[35] J. Knöpfer, 'Papsturkunden des 12, 13 und 14 Jahrhunderts aus dem Germanischen Nationalmuseum in Nürnburg', *HJch* 24 (1903) pp 766–7 no 2.

[36] *Liber Augustalis* I.45, *Die Konstitution Friedrichs II von Hohenstaufen für sein Königreich Sizilien*, ed H. Conrad, T. von der Lieck Buyken and W. Wagner (Cologne 1973) p 70. See also D. R. Clementi, 'The Italian Register of Henry VI', *QFIAB* 35 (1955) pp 133–5 no 41 (1195).

[37] W. Holtzmann, 'Kanonistische Ergänzungen zur Italia Pontificia', *QFIAB* 38 (1958) pp 122–3 no 158.

Valva in the Abruzzi in 1168, but, it seems likely, only as a spur to encourage the rival chapters of St Pelinus of Valva and St Panfilius of Sulmona to stop quarrelling and make a decision.[38] The similarities with contemporary English procedure are overwhelming,[39] and can hardly be seen as a mark of particular 'tyranny' on the part of the king. In the Valva election the government accepted the choice made by the two chapters of Oderisius, provost of St Pelinus. In 1181 William II made the envoys of the monastery of St Bartholomew of Carpineto choose another candidate as abbot, but only because the monks had been unable to agree on a first choice, and he took the precaution of getting two local bishops to check that the candidate elected at the royal court was acceptable to the whole congregation of the monastery.[40]

More extensive information on the scope of royal interference can be obtained from study of the type of men elected. And here one discerns a very distinct limitation in the exercise of royal power. In most episcopal sees, at least on the mainland, the bishops were local men, often but not invariably drawn from the knightly class, occasionally scions or protegés of local nobles, with a tendency, though this is very badly documented, to have been canons of the cathedral; in other words, what one might expect if the election was left to capitular discretion.[41] In only a few sees can monastic bishops be found: surprisingly few, even given the abysmal evidence for many of the smaller and poorer dioceses in

---

[38] Kamp I pp 61–2. Licentiae eligendi also survive for the abbeys of Montecassino and Carpineto, Chalandon 2 pp 591–2 n 2, [W.] Holtzmann, 'The Norman Royal] Charters [of S. Bartolomeo di Carpineto', *Papers of the British School of Rome* 24] (London 1956) p 99 no 3. For the continuation of this practice in the Staufen period, Richard of S. Germano, *Chronicon*, ed C. A. Garufi (Muratori 2 ed, Bologna 1938) pp 191–2.

[39] For example, *The Chronicle of Jocelin of Brakelond*, ed and trans H. E. Butler (London 1953) pp 16, 21.

[40] Holtzmann, 'Charters' pp 96 and 99 no 4.

[41] For example, (1) from local knightly families: William I, bishop of Caiazzo (province of Capua) 1152–68, L. Matteo-Cerasoli, 'Di alcuni vescovi poco noti', *Archivio storico per le provincie napoletane* 43 (Naples 1918) pp 372–3; Boniface, bishop of Canne (province of Bari) 1182–8, Kamp 2 p 620 (2) local noble connections: Pandulf, bishop of Sora (exempt see) 1188–1217, related to the lords of Aquino; Peter, bishop of Telese (province of Benevento) 1178–90, a protegé of the counts of Caserta, Kamp I pp 98–9, 291–2 (3) local bourgeois family: Unfridus, bishop of Sarno (province of Salerno) 1181–1202, Kamp I pp 477–8 (4) from the chapter, Lambert, bishop of Aversa (province of Naples) *c* 1192; Peter, archbishop of Brindisi 1183–96, Kamp I pp 339–341, 2 p 664 n 12.

Apulia and Calabria. When William II died only four mainland sees and three on the island of Sicily were certainly held by monks (though with one or two others held by regular canons).[42] A few dioceses, such as Grumentino (province of Salerno), had a monastic tradition,[43] but it is fair to say that compared with the eleventh century when there had been a strong Benedictine element and the thirteenth when there was a massive influx of Cistercians and friars, in the twelfth the monasteries, even such great and hitherto influential houses as Montecassino and La Cava, provided few leaders for the secular church. That there was a strong monastic element in Sicily itself is attributable to the singular presence of three monastic chapters, Monreale, Catania and Lipari-Patti.[44] Indeed had there been more royal or papal interference in elections it seems likely that there might have been a stronger monastic element.

The explanation for the lack of royal involvement is simple, and makes an instructive comparison with the English church. In England and Wales there were twenty-one episcopal sees, and of these Carlisle was in virtual desuetude in the second half of the twelfth century. One or two of the smaller and poorer sees such as Rochester might perhaps be allowed to choose their own pastors, but since the king needed to reward his civil servants and large and wealthy sees had to be provided with efficient diocesan administrators, a large number of episcopal appointments were made from among the ranks of royal *curiales*. By contrast, the kingdom of Sicily contained, in the late twelfth century, 144 dioceses. Even had the king wished to fill all these with his own nominees, a shortage of suitable candidates known to him was likely to have precluded this aim, particularly since a larger proportion of his curialists were layman than was the case in England. And what possible interest could the king have in filling such minuscule and poverty-stricken

---

[42] On the mainland Frigento, Bisceglie, Ugento and the archbishopric of Rossano, in Sicily itself Lipari, Catania and the archbishopric of Monreale. Cefalu was held by an Augustinian canon, and Oderisius of Forcone may also have been a canon regular, Kamp I pp 17, 259; 2 pp 566, 739, 873; 3 pp 1046, 1079, 1186, 1205.

[43] F. Ughelli, *Italia Sacra,* 10 vols, (2 ed Venice 1717–21) 7 cols 497–504 lists three monastic bishops for this see in the twelfth century. Though the first two may be the same man, two other bishops had connections with the abbeys of Carbone and La Cava.

[44] Cefalu had an Augustinian chapter. White, *Latin Monasticism* pp 77–100, 105–117, 132–145, 187–201.

sees as Bitetto in Apulia with its one dependent church, at the other end of the town from the cathedral, or San Leone in Calabria with a thirteenth-century income of twenty tari a year?[45] Whereas England was under-provided with bishops, and the early modern period saw the creation of more sees, southern Italy had far too many bishops with tiny dioceses and inadequate incomes, and by the fifteenth century, in Apulia at least, the unification or outright suppression of dioceses was proceeding apace.[46]

Where the king was interested in placing his own men was in Sicily itself, where clerical courtiers could be suitably rewarded and still be resident at the court without being too far from their dioceses, and in perhaps half a dozen crucial mainland sees, generally metropolitan ones, which were wealthy and strategically important. The archbishopric of Capua, for example, was worth ten times as much as the richest of its suffragan sees,[47] and held a crucial river crossing on the *Via Latina*, the natural invasion route of the *regno*. To such sees archbishops were appointed from families closely connected with the royal administration, often active in it themselves, and even occasionally from outside the *regno*. Thus William, archbishop-elect of Capua 1135–7 and archbishop of Salerno 1137–52, and active as a royal justiciar, was from Ravenna.[48] Archbishop Gerard of Siponto (1170–9) was from Verona.[49] Archbishop Herbert of Conza (1169–81?) and Richard Palmer of Syracuse, later archbishop of Messina (1183–95) were both Englishmen.[50] More usual were members of local administra-

---

[45] R. Brentano, *Two Churches. England and Italy in the Thirteenth Century* (Princeton 1968) pp 219–220. Kamp 2 p 907.

[46] Fiorentino was suppressed *c*1400, Canne in 1425, Volturara and Montecorvino were united in 1433. Lesina was suppressed in 1551, *IP* 9 pp 150–1, 161–2, 289.

[47] In the early fourteenth century, when the first figures of episcopal income appear Capua was worth 1000 unciae a year. Its suffragans varied from Caserta and Teano, worth 100, to Calvi worth only 30. *Rationes Decimarum Italiae. Campania*, ed P. Sella, M. Inguanez & L. Matteo-Cerasoli, *Studi e Testi* 97 (Vatican City 1942) pp 67, 113, 181, and 213.

[48] Alexander of Telese, *Gesta Rogerii Regis Siciliae* bk 3 caps 30–1, G. del Re, *Cronisti e scrittori sincroni napoletani* I (Naples 1845) pp 143–4. C. H. Haskins, 'England and Sicily in the Twelfth Century', *EHR* 26 (1911) p 643.

[49] *Ex Thomae Historia Pontificum Salonitanorum et Spalatinorum*, MGH SS 29 (1892) p 573. Kamp 2 pp 531–2.

[50] Ralph Diceto, *Ymagines Historiarum*, ed W. Stubbs, *RS*, 2 vols (1876) 2 p 37, and see n 20 above. But Walter, archbishop of Palermo 1168–90, and his brother and successor Bartholomew, previously bishop of Agrigento, were not English as was once supposed, L. J. A. Loewenthal, 'For the biography of Walter Ophamil, archbishop of Palermo', *EHR* 87 (1972) 75–82.

tive families such as Samarus, archbishop of Trani 1192–1201, whose father had been a royal chamberlain, and whose relations included two justiciars and another chamberlain.[51] His predecessor, Bertrandus (1157–87), also seems to have had close links with the administration, and went on an embassy to Constantinople in 1167.[52] Archbishop Alfanus of Capua (1153–80) was the uncle of Florius of Camerota, one of the most active and long-lived of royal justiciars.[53]

The three incumbents of the archbishopric of Salerno under the Norman kings provide a classic example of the provision of curialists to an important see. William of Ravenna, the only cleric ever to have been a justiciar, we have already met. His successor, the historian Romuald Guarna (1154–81) was a member of a prominent local family, but played a leading role in the government of the kingdom for two decades, was one of the ten-man regency council set up in 1168, and chief Sicilian negotiator at the Venice peace conference of 1177.[54] Archibishop Nicholas (1182–1222) was a son of the royal vicechancellor and later chancellor, Matthew of Ajello, chief minister of William II in his later years and of Tancred.[55]

It is very difficult to see such as these as other than direct royal appointments. But only a small number of leading sees were so affected. Very few curialists or non-natives were appointed to other than archiepiscopal sees on the mainland, and not all of these were necessarily held by curialists.[56] Even the frontier bishoprics, which would seem to have been obvious candidates for such appointments, escaped unscathed after 1156. Bishop Dionisius of Teramo (1172–4) was admittedly a protegé of the royal minister archbishop

---

[51] Kamp 2 pp 548–9. Another relative was to be a justiciar under Frederick II.

[52] 'De sanctis martyribus Mauro episcopo, Pantaleemone et Sergio. Historia inventionis primae, auctore Amando Episcopo Vigiliensi', *ASB* July 6 (1868) p 368. Kamp 2 pp 545–7.

[53] *PL* 200 col 332. For Florius's career, E. M. Jamison, 'The Norman Administration of Apulia and Capua, more especially under Roger II and William I, 1127–1166', *Papers of the British School at Rome* 6 (1913) pp 365–6, 478–480.

[54] For his career see Garufi's introduction to Romuald pp x–xxiv.

[55] Kamp I pp 425–432.

[56] John, bishop of Catania 1167–9 was a brother of Matthew of Ajello, and Peregrinus, bishop of Umbriatico c1179 had been a royal notary, White, *Latin Monasticism* pp 114–15, Kamp I p 911. But by contrast the archbishoprics of Brindisi and Naples seem to have escaped curialist appointments.

Walter of Palermo, and was translated to the archbishopric of Amalfi; but he appears to have been resident in his diocese and played no part in the royal administration.[57] One purely ecclesiastical peculiarity which could lead to the king intervening was a number of sees with two electing chapters, Valva, Isernia-Venafro, Siponto and Brindisi—it was a dispute between the canons of Brindisi and those of Oria which led to complaints about lay interference in the 1196 election to that see;[58] but as the example already discussed of the Valva election of 1168 shows, the king hardly took advantage of such problems for his own benefit.

We should therefore be careful not to take the denunciations of outside writers about royal control of the Sicilian church too literally. Such men as John of Salisbury and Peter of Blois, though they knew the *regno*, generalised from a few glaring examples. The papacy was indeed wiser and more cautious than they, especially given the desire for a rapprochement with Sicily before 1156, and the need for Sicilian political and financial support thereafter. But the chief reason why neither William I nor William II was at loggerheads with the papacy is clear. Royal control over the Sicilian church was conspicuous for its moderation rather than its severity.

University of Leeds.

---

[57] Kamp I pp 50, 391–3.

[58] Gerard, the archbishop-elect, appears to have been the choice of the canons of Oria, and was opposed by the canons of Brindisi, *Codice Diplomatico Brindisiano* I pp 61–2 no 33; 63–4 no 35.

[59] This paper was written before the publication of H. Enzensberger, 'Der "böse" und der "gute" Wilhelm. Zur Kirchenpolitik der normannischen Könige von Sizilien nach dem Vertrag von Benevent (1156)', *Deutsches Archiv* 36 (1980) pp 385–432. Enzensberger treats the procedure in episcopal elections at some length, without differing very much from my own conclusions.

RELIGION, NATIONALISM AND
NATIONAL IDENTITY IN MEDIEVAL SPAIN
AND PORTUGAL

by PETER LINEHAN

'A NO SER por el Clero, y en especial por el Episcopado
español', declared Vicente de Lafuente a century ago,
'España sería un pais sin historia, pues la historia sin
escribir no es historia'.[1] Lafuente himself was a layman—though it
did not always show—with conventional views regarding the
'democratic tyranny' of his age which a spell as rector of Madrid
university during the student and other troubles of the mid-1870s
served only to reinforce. He found it odd that he rather than an
ecclesiastic should have written the first ecclesiastical history of
Spain.[2] A committee of churchmen had been formed in Rome for
the purpose in 1747, but it is too soon to report on the outcome of
that venture.[3] Lafuente's history, though more than a century old,
is still the only full-scale work of its kind by a Spaniard—'and since
that time there is not a single chronicle that I can discover; though
(like John of Salisbury in his day) I have found in church archives
notes of memorable events which could be of help to any future
writers who may appear'.[4] In presenting some of these notes here,
in the context of the theme of this conference, I find myself
altogether less daunted by the notion of nationalism, which a self-
respecting medievalist is expected fastidiously to eschew,[5] than
by the problem of how to evaluate the testimony of so many
witnesses, clerical and lay, medieval and modern. The difficulty
consists not in locating in the sources evidence of nationalism—or
rather of one of the competing, coexisting nationalisms—but in

[1] [Vicente de] Lafuente, [*Historia Eclesiástica de España*] 6 vols (2 ed Madrid 1873–5)
4, p 307.
[2] *Ibid* 1, p 1; 6, p 268; V. Cacho Viu, *La Institución Libre de Enseñanza* 1 (Madrid
1962) pp 214, 302–17.
[3] Lafuente 1, pp 285–92. Compare the general introduction by [R.] García Villoslada
to the projected five-volume [*Historia de la Iglesia en España*]—of which vols 1 (to
711) and 5 (since 1810) have so far appeared: 1 (Madrid 1979) pp xxiii–xxiv.
[4] *Historia Pontificalis*, ed and trans M. Chibnall (London/Edinburgh 1956) p 2.
[5] Compare K. F. Werner, 'Les nations et le sentiment national dans l'Europe
médiévale', *RH* 244 (1970) pp 285–304, esp pp 285–9.

evaluating sources which derive from a tradition wherein national myth-making has been accompanied by invention and forgery in the service of other loyalties both local and ecumenical, and in handling writers for whom faith and religion can serve as synonymous terms for Christianity in general and Spanish catholicism in particular.[6] Scratch any piece of evidence for our subject before about 1130, it sometimes seems to me, and out sheepishly will come that prince of falsifiers, bishop Pelayo of Oviedo, the ink still wet on his fingers. But at least historians are alert to Pelayo and aware of his loyalties.[7] It is the testimony and the actions of the rest, the mass of bishops and clerics, that are so perplexing. Were they what they were because, being to some degree literate, they reflected common opinions—or even formed them—or because, as the successors in title to the churchmen of Visigothic Spain, they were the servile accomplices of royal authority and licensed mouthpieces of the official line? I wish it were possible to treat history written by bishops as J. C. Russell does, as 'marked by a freedom from servility which might not have been expected in a court-patronised literature', but the all too evident continuity of conduct between the vast majority of Visigothic churchmen and the vast majority of their medieval successors makes this a difficult distinction to sustain.[8] The subject has resisted my attempt to treat it with conceptual sharpness at least in part because it can only be approached through a series of distorting mirrors, darkly. And, to add to this, I have been constrained by the limitations of this paper to provide a manifestly patchy and eclectic account of a subject which in some places would have an entire Institute devoted to its study.

[6] Compare the two English translations of the work of [Américo] Castro: 'Life was grounded in religion, and religion was the station from which, directly or indirectly, every activity emerged' [The] Structure of Spanish History, [transl E. L. King] (Princeton 1954) p 189); 'Life was grounded in faith, and faith was the origin, directly or indirectly, of every activity' The Spaniards[. An Introduction to their History, trans W. F. King and S. Margaretten] (Berkeley/Los Angeles/London 1971) p 456.
[7] [F. J. Fernández Conde, El Libro de los Testamentos de la Catedral de Oviedo (Rome 1971) pp 50–67, 367–72; idem, 'La obra del obispo ovetense D. Pelayo en la historiografía española, Boletín del Instituto de Estudios Asturianos 25 (Oviedo 1971) pp 249–91.
[8] 'Chroniclers of medieval Spain', Hispanic Review 6 (Philadelphia 1938) p 230. Compare C. Sánchez Albornoz, 'El Aula Regia y las asambleas políticas de los godos', CHE 5 (1946) p 86; [A.] Barbero and [M.] Vigil, La formación [del feudalismo en la Península Ibérica] (Barcelona 1978) p 290.

Religion and national identity in medieval Spain

The assertion of Lafuente that but for her churchmen Spain would have had no history, or that but for her Christian writers and tradition her history would have been a poor, sad and wretched affair, has always flowed easily from the pens of Spanish writers —and does so still.[9] Quevedo in the seventeenth century pressed the claim of a very particular churchman, Saint James himself, to be regarded and honoured as Spain's patron, as the man given by God 'when Spain was not' so that Spain might be. At the time Santiago was threatened.[10] (And I mention Santiago now because I will not be returning to him later). Periods of stress and national peril have never failed to elicit such exalted claims. Lecturing in 1935, Zacarius García Villada (whose murder in the following year truncated another ecclesiastical history) delivered himself of the view that he and his audience would have been 'Muslims and real Africans' had it not been for the intransigence of the voluntary martyrs of Córdoba in the mid-ninth century.[11] Echoes of Gibbon apart, past history was being pressed into the service of present politics. The sentiments were those of the street-corner, or the pulpit, rather than of (say) the Ecclesiastical History Society. So was the language: the Jews are described as moving by stealth to encompass the ruin of Visigothic Spain.[12] The victory four years later of the Nationalist cause—of *la cruzada nacional*—released a pent-up flood of invective disguised as history. In a volume in the series *Colección pro Ecclesia et Patria* published in 1942, Dom Justo Pérez de Urbel celebrated the Córdoba martyrs as having given their lives *por la fe y por la patria*, and Saint Isidore as a hero of Spanish nationalism—not, he insisted, a regionalist *de ideas estrechas y mente encanijada*; Isidore's special affection for Baetica notwithstanding, *su patria es la península entera*—and this without detriment

---

[9] '¡Qué pobre, triste y desolada se nos quedaría España!': García Villoslada, pp xlv-xlvi.

[10] 'Hízole Dios patron de España que ya no era, para cuando por su intercesion, por su dotrina y por su espada volviese á ser. Hízole patron de la fe que aun no teniamos, para que la tuviésmos': F. de Quevedo, *Su espada por Santiago* (1628), *Obras*, ed A. Fernández-Guerra y Orbe, B[iblioteca de] A[utores] E[spañoles] 48, 2 (Madrid 1859) p 445. For the context see T. D. Kendrick, *Saint James in Spain* (London 1960) pp 64–7.

[11] [Z] García Villada, [*El destino de España en la historia universal*] (2 ed Madrid 1940) p 111.

[12] Ibid pp 82–3.

to his devotion to Rome.[13] On the strength of the etymological identity of 'Gotalandia, Cathalaunia, Cataluña' meaning the land of the Goths, Mons. José Rius Serra suggested in 1940 that *la restauración del ímperio de la Gocia podría ser una de las flechas de la nueva misión de España en el mundo*,[14] while Jewish pollution of the 'clean' Spanish people was the theme of Manuel Gaibrois Ballesteros—a layman whose interests subsequently shifted to Latin-American anthropology—but who in 1941 was at pains to establish the racial purity of archbishop Rodrigo of Toledo.[15]

The reason for mentioning the galvanised state of these four historians in the aftermath of Franco's victory is that three of them were held in the very highest regard within their profession; it is not that they were priests, though they were that too. Spanish churchmen enjoy no monopoly of the triumphalist interpretation of the medieval Spanish Church: it was Lafuente who in 1880 recommended the *imprimatur* for the book which, as Lannon has mentioned, more than any other has served as the arsenal of such material, Menéndez Pelayo's *Historia de los Heterodoxos Españoles*. Both were laymen, and it is in the latter's epilogue that one finds, stated in Mosaic language, the view that it was neither the sword nor learning that forged Spanish unity and kept it intact throughout the Middle Ages, but the faith, and that it was because of the Church, enshrining that faith, *que fuimos nación, y gran nación, en vez de muchedumbre de gentes colecticias*.[16] The influence of Menéndez Pelayo has been enormous, akin to that of William Cobbett and

[13].[J.] Pérez de Urbel, *El monasterio en la vida española de la Edad Media* (Barcelona 1942) pp 79, 76, and 5–6 on the subject of the debt of 'nuestra patria' to the medieval monks, and their role 'en el desarrollo de nuestra nacionalidad.' In the same year Dom Justo described Saint Isidore as 'el primer español' to have possessed 'una idea clara y fija de la unidad de España, y sin detrimento de la pureza y fervor de un universalismo católico': a revealing protestation: idem and T. Ortega, *San Isidoro (Antologia)* (Madrid 1942) p 34.

[14] J. Rius Serra, 'El derecho visigodo en Cataluña', *S[panischen] F[orschungen der] G[örresgesellschaft]* 8 (Münster 1940) p 67.

[15] References in [P. A.] Linehan, [*The*] *Spanish Church [and the Papacy in the Thirteenth Century]* (Cambridge 1971) p 15. Antisemitic sentiment in these years is described in C. C. Aronsfeld, *The Ghosts of 1492. Jewish aspects of the struggle for religious freedom in Spain 1848–1976* (New York 1979) pp 43–7.

[16] [M.] Menéndez Pelayo, [*Historia de los heterodoxos españoles*,] 1 ed Madrid 1880–82 (ed Biblioteca de Autores Cristianos, Madrid 1956) 2, p 1193. Lafuente's eulogistic appraisal as *censor eclesiástico* is repr. *ibid* 1, pp xiv–xvi. Menendez Pelayo's response in his second edn (1910) was to describe Lafuente's *Historia* as 'demasiado elemental' (*ibid* p 22). See below p 000.

G. M. Trevelyan combined, reaching far beyond scholarly circles, although (or perhaps because) he was himself not a professional medievalist.[17] He has been the mighty battery upon whom many lesser lights have drawn. In his own lifetime he gave respectability to the views of such as M. Hernández Villaescusa, whose own nationalistic zeal was sufficient to make the fourteenth-century cardinal Gil de Albornoz the founder, no less, of the university of Bologna. For Hernández Villaescusa, however, nationalism was a secondary not the primary consideration; the heroes of the Reconquest fought for God, and only incidentally for *la patria*. The Reconquest was the work of the Church.[18] In the present century Menéndez Pidal, the pupil of Menéndez Pelayo and his successor in public esteem, has pronounced a similar judgment, although more modestly phrased and presented: it was *el libre y puro espíritu religioso, salvada en el Norte..que dió aliento y sentido nacional a la Reconquista*; without it Spain would have been *desnacionalizada*, islamicized like the countries across the Straits of Gibraltar.[19] Other explanations are lumped together as *la interpretación laica*, and rejected as *incompatible con el espíritu religioso de la época*.[20]

Consistent with this view of the past, though not essential to it, is the belief that the birth not only of a national church but of Spain itself occurred at the third council of Toledo in 589 when king Reccared announced his conversion to catholicism—providing the beginnings of the nation which the religious spirit preserved from extinction after 711.[21] Here we must touch on a controversy that has blazed for decades, consuming a wealth of energy which might have been more productively harnessed otherwise, between

[17] See V. Palacio Atard, *Menéndez Pelayo y la historia de España* (Valladolid 1956) pp 13, 44.
[18] '¿A quién debe España su gloriosa Reconquista? Al sentimiento religioso. ¿Quién alentó, purificó, dió forma y dirección conveniente y adecuada á este sentimiento? La Iglesia. Todas las proezas de la Reconquista, ya sociales, ya individuales, están marcadas con ese augusto sello. Se luchaba por Dios antes que por la Patria': [M.] Hernández Villaescusa, [*Recaredo y la unidad católica*] (Barcelona 1890) pp 343, 358.
[19] R. Menéndez Pidal, introduction to *Historia de España* (Madrid 1926) 1 p xxvii: quoted approvingly by García Villoslada, p xlv.
[20] Thus [J.] Goñi Gaztambide, [*Historia de la Bula de la Cruzada en España*] (Vitoria 1958) p 39, whose chapter 2 is entitled 'La Reconquista, Guerra Santa': also highly thought of by García Villoslada (pp xl-xli). That the 'finger of providence' guided Spain's destiny during these centuries is asserted by García Villada, p 108.
[21] '¿Cuando nace España? A mi entender, en el momento en que la Iglesia católica la recibe en sus brazos oficialmente y en cierto modo la bautiza en mayo del 589': García Villoslada, p xlii. Cf García Villada, p 104.

Claudio Sánchez-Albornoz and Américo Castro, maintaining respectively the reality of *la contextura vital hispana* before the Arabs came and essentially unaffected by their presence on the one hand, and on the other, the acculturative formation of Spain in the atmosphere of *convivencia* of Moors, Jews and Christians.[22] The wider ramifications of this debate need not concern us here, except to notice that, in the matter of the disputed 'Spanishness' of the Visigoths, (and all that that implies for the national significance of Reccared's conversion), the year 711 is the protagonists' 1066, and that the subject has been debated with all the passionate intensity of the Victorian giants in their pursuit of and repudiation of continuity. Anglo-Saxon historians cannot afford to adopt an attitude of lofty superiority to this aspect of the debate on 'Spanishness', while they themselves continue to play the game of hunting Freeman *redivivus* through other people's footnotes—though the task of drawing parallels between him and Round and Castro and Sánchez-Albornoz would be one for the comparative historian.[23] For all the bitterness of their disagreement, however—and, as P. E. Russell has observed, Sánchez-Albornoz does at times envisage a 'Nazi-like world of Jewish plots against the innocent Christian Spaniards, both in the Middle Ages, and, it is hinted, now'[24]—they do both assume an admixture of religion and nationalism in the reconquest, though they differ as to the proportion and the source of each ingredient.[25] At the very least, *la reconquista del solar nacional*

---

[22] Surveyed by H. Lapeyre, 'Deux interprétations de l'histoire d'Espagne: Américo Castro et Claudio Sánchez-Albornoz', *Annales* 20 (1965) pp 1015–37.

[23] [Roger] Collins has recently spoken of the 'moral or providential explanations' of the events of 711 as 'the kind of interpretations that were used of the closing years of the Anglo-Saxon kingdom and the Battle of Hastings during the last century, and today would rightly be greeted with ridicule': 'Mérida and Toledo [: 550–585]', [*in Visigothic Spain. New Approaches*] ed [E.] James (Oxford 1980) p 189. Compare E. John, 'Edward the Confessor and the Norman succession', *EHR* 94 (1979) p 254 n. 1. John's view that 'to be intelligible the Norman Conquest needs to be understood as the climax of a crisis that had been going on for generations, not as a sudden bolt from the 'blue' (p 267) applies equally to 711, and suggests that a comparative study, both historical and historiographical,. might be of interest. Freeman's remark to Canon Meyrick in 1891 may be noted in passing: 'History of the Church of Spain! That's a large undertaking!' W. R. W. Stephens, *The Life and Letters of E. A. Freeman,* 2 vols (London 1895) 2 p 448.

[24] P. E. Russell, 'The Nessus-shirt of Spanish history', *Bulletin of Hispanic Studies* 36 (Liverpool 1959) p 223.

[25] [C.] Sánchez-Albornoz, *España: un enigma histórico,* 2 vols (Buenos Aires 1956) 1 pp 249 (on 'la naturaleza nacional y "divinal"' of the Reconquest), 283–6 (on

Religion and national identity in medieval Spain

implicaba la guerra contra el enemigo de Cristo y de su Iglesia y ello daba matiz religioso a la contienda;[26] or, more positively put—as Fernando del Pulgar put it to queen Isabella at the end of the affair—the presence of the Moors provided the signal advantage not only of a just war, but of a holy war too, available without stirring from home.[27] So there is no denying that a religious content was present, even if some historians have denied its priority, noting that the movement was one of conquest rather than reconquest, having its origins in an area which had earlier successfully resisted Roman and Visigothic rule, and that Liébana, the epicentre of Christian resistance, had never acquired episcopal status;[28] other questioning its firmity of purpose since booty was preferred to the destruction of the enemy when Al-Andalus lay exposed in the mid-eleventh century;[29] and practitioners of the 'new kind of history' sometimes attaching greater significance to force (Menéndez Pelayo's iron) than to faith,[30] and to human resources, demography and the climate,[31] in their study of the seven and a half centuries after the fatal year 711.

Castro's estimate of the significance of Santiago), 303–11 (denying equivalence of Christian and Moorish zeal in respect of Holy War); Castro, *The Spaniards*, pp 449–56.

[26] Sánchez-Albornoz, *España: un enigma histórico*, 1, p 309.

[27] Compare [J. N.] Hillgarth, *The Spanish Kingdoms [1250–1516,]* 2 vols (Oxford 1976, 1978) 2, pp 372–4.

[28] Barbero and Vigil, *Sobre los orígenes sociales de la Reconquista* (Barcelona 1974) pp 78–9, 96 ('El fenómeno histórico llamado Reconquista no obedeció en sus orígenes a motivos puramente políticos y religiosos, puesto que como tal fenómeno existía ya mucho antes de la llegada de los musulmanes'); idem, *La formación*, pp 234–5, 259–60; G. Menéndez Pidal, 'Mozárabes y asturianos en la cultura de la Alta Edad Media', *B[oletín de la] R[eal] A[cademia de la] H[istoria]* 134 (Madrid, 1954) p 151. Compare the criticisms of Sánchez-Albornoz, 'Observaciones [a unas paginas sobre el inicio de la Reconquista', *CHE* 47–8 (1968)] pp 341–52; [C.–E.] Dufourcq, 'Notes de lecture', *Revue d'histoire et de civilisation du Maghreb* 4 (Rabat 1968) pp 74–8.

[29] I. de las Cagigas, *Minorias etnico-religiosas de la Edad Media española* I: 2 vols (Madrid 1948) 2, p 444.

[30] 'C'est la force des armes qui orienta l'histoire': Dufourcq, 'Berbérie et Ibérie médiévales: un problème de rupture', *RH* 240 (1968) p 323—although in the struggles of the twelfth and thirteenth centuries, he concedes, 'la religion devint un élément caractéristique, essentiel' (p 319). Compare Menéndez Pelayo: 'No elaboraron nuestro unidad el hierro de la conquista ni la sabiduria de los legisladores; la hicieron los dos apóstoles y los siete varones apostólicos.'

[31] [T. F.] Glick, [*Islamic and Christian Spain in the Early Middle Ages. Comparative perspectives on social and cultural formation*] (Princeton 1979) *passim*, esp pp 33–5;

The initial success of the invaders in that year and their over-running of almost the entire peninsula in the two that followed would be regarded as 'completely fabulous', Lafuente observed, if history did not prove it.[32]

The startling claim that history does *not* prove it—that the invasion of 711 is a myth fabricated a century later out of a trivial incident in a civil war between Catholics and Arians which spanned the period 589–800—has been effectively demolished by the results of research into the social structures of al-Andalus.[33] It must be said that the claim would be more difficult to disprove—though it would not be impossible to do so[34]—on the sole strength of purely Christian evidence from the north, for our knowledge of the events of the entire eighth century and most of the ninth derives from accounts which were written up no earlier than the 880s: a circumstance which keeps the beginnings of the Reconquest shrouded in mystery: *La idea central de la Reconquista surgío en la mente de un hombre culto en fecha imprecisa del siglo VIII.*[35] There has been much debate concerning the interrelationship of these chronicles—the so-called *Crónica Albeldense* and the two redactions of the *Crónica de Alfonso III*—and the hypothesis has been advanced of a now lost chronicle which may have been the common source of them all.[36] Amidst the recital of kings poisoned or eaten by bears, no clear view emerges of the rule of particular churchmen. But the

---

T. F. Ruiz, 'Expansion et changement: la conquête de Séville et la société castillane (1248–1350)', *Annales* 34 (1979) pp 548–9.

[32] Lafuente, 3, p 13.

[33] [I.] Olagüe, [*Les Arabes n'ont jamais envahi l'Espagne*] (Bordeaux 1969), *passim*, esp pp 232, 258; [P.] Guichard, *Structures sociales ["orientales" et "occidentales" dans l'Espagne musulmane*] (Paris/The Hague 1977): see my review in *Social History* 2 (London 1978) pp 377–9.

[34] Bitter regret at the fate of 'infelix Spania . . . condam deliciosa et nunc misera effecta' is expressed in the so-called *Cronica Mozárabe de 754* (ed T. Mommsen, *MGH AA*, 11, p 353), but the 'vehemently nationalist' author, though almost certainly a churchman, was evidently a Mozarab writing under Moorish domination. See [B.] Sánchez Alonso, [*Historia de la historiografía española,*] 2 ed (Madrid 1947) 1, pp 101–4; [M. C.] Díaz y Díaz, La historigrafía [hispana desde la invasión árabe hasta el año 1000',] in *De Isidoro al siglo XI* (Barcelona 1976) pp 207–9. The charter evidence of the Christian kingdom is analysed by L. Barrau-Dihigo, 'Étude sur les actes des rois asturiens (718–910)', *Revue hispanique* 46 (Paris 1919) pp 1–192.

[35] Sánchez-Albornoz, 'Observaciones' p 351.

[36] Idem, 'Una crónica asturiana perdida?', *Revista de Filología Hispánica* 7 (Buenos Aires-New York 1945) pp 105–46: reprinted in his *Investigaciones [sobre historio-*

Religion and national identity in medieval Spain

realm of the embattled Christians is defined as just that: *christianorum regnum*, set against Muslim 'Spania', the affairs of which are ignored. The general identity of church and kingdom is tacitly assumed: during the reign of Alfonso III *ecclesia crescit, et regnum ampliatur*.[37] Despite the fact that the circumstances of Pelayo's emergence as leader seem to have been all too human, namely the unwelcome advances to which his sister had been subjected by the Arab governor of Gijón, the origins of *Asturorum regnum* are piously attributed to *divina providencia*.[38]

Because the territorial contest had unavoidable confessional implications it might not be thought remarkable that the clergy should have ensconced themselves as aiders and abettors of the Asturian monarchs during these centuries. But the association of *ecclesia* and *regnum* was not at all inevitable. The clergy received a bad press in the accounts furnished by these very chronicles of the collapse of the Visigothic kingdom; their sins and those of their kings were held to have caused Spain's ruin. Concerning the reign of Wittiza, the *Crónica Rotense*—written *in hac patria Asturiensium* and held to be the earlier version of the *Chronicle of Alfonso III* on account of its inferior Latin, and because of its inferior Latin held to have been the work of a layman[39]—quotes a whole string of scriptural references on the subject of errant priests; and the later version, the *Crónica Ovetense*, although less insistently well-informed on the point, is also sufficiently emphatic: *Quia reges et*

---

grafía hispana medieval (siglos VIII al XII)] (Buenos Aires 1967) pp 111–60. The most revealing recent accounts of this and related matters are Díaz y Díaz, 'La historiografía, *SSSpoleto* 17.i (1970) pp 313–43 (repr. in his *De Isidoro al siglo XI*, pp 205–34), and Barbero and Vigil, 'La historiografía [de la época de Alfonso III]' *La formación*, pp 232–78.

[37] [M.] Gómez-Moreno, ['Las primeras crónicas de la Reconquista: el ciclo de Alfonso III',] *BRAH* 100 (1932) p 604; Barbero and Vigil, *La formación*, p 262. Compare [E.] Benito Ruano, 'La historiografía [en la Alta Edad Media española]', *CHE* 17 (1952) pp 71–4.

[38] Gómez-Moreno, p 601; [L.] Vázquez de Parga, 'La biblia [en el reino astur-leonés',] *SSSpoleto* 10 (1963) pp 278–9. For an anthropological interpretation of another liaison in the Christian camp, also with important political consequences, see Barbero and Vigil, 'La sucesión al trono [en el reino astur]' *La formación*, pp 349–51: here the analysis leads to Frazer's *Golden Bough* rather than to Holy Writ.

[39] Vázquez de Parga, 'La biblia' p 277. Gómez-Moreno (p 586) infers lay authorship—'por sabio que pareciese'—of *Crónica Rotense* from the barbarity of its Latin. Thus too Sánchez-Albornoz, 'La redacción original de la Crónica de Alfonso III', *Investigaciones*, p 25.

169

sacerdotes legem Domini derelinquerunt omnia agmina Gothorum Sar-racenorum gladio perierunt.[40] And their accounts of the very beginnings of the Reconquest at Covadonga are even more damaging to the attempt to identify *ecclesia* and *regnum* in a sense which would accommodate priests and bishops. In both versions a bishop is the villain of the piece: the 'perfidious' Oppa, bishop of Seville (or Toledo) and brother (or son) of king Wittiza who advances from the Moorish ranks bent upon cajoling Pelayo, the Asturians' elected *princeps*, into surrendering. Chided by Oppa about the Christians' prospects of success on that mountaintop when the whole Visi-gothic army had perished on the plain (thanks partly to Oppa's treachery there, as the chronicler observes), Pelayo it is who raises the flag. In a scriptural *tour de force*, he proceeds from Matthew 13 on the *ecclesia domini* as a mustard seed, by way of the ringing declaration that *spes nostra Christus est, quod per istum modicum monticulum, quem conspicis, sit Spanie salus et Gotorum gentis exercitus reparatus*, to the playing of his trump card—a couple of verses of Psalm 89. Whereupon battle commences and the Arabs incur losses of 189,000 (and should the reader be predisposed to scepticism about this, he is advised to remember the story of Moses and the Red Sea).[41]

In the changes wrought upon the primitive *Crónica Rotense* by the compiler of *Crónica Ovetense*, scholars have perceived a deliberate attempt to disguise the earlier failings of the clergy.[42] Yet in neither account of the crucial confrontation of Covadonga does their representative Oppa emerge with any credit. It is a matter which seems until recently not to have intrigued scholars, despite its implications for attempts which would later be made to establish by whatever means the continuity of medieval churchmen with their Visigothic predecessors and with all that they had represented in the Visigothic kingdom. It is possible of course that knowledge of Oppa's perfidy was too widely disseminated for any attempt at rehabilitation even to have been contemplated—or *ever* to have been contemplated. But we do not know when and in what circumstances the attempt was made to make the clergy *but not*

---

[40] *Crónica de Alfonso III*, ed A. Ubieto Arteta (Valencia 1961) pp 18–19.
[41] *Ibid* pp 28–35; Vázquez de Parga, 'La biblia' pp 279–80.
[42] Sánchez-Albornoz, *Investigaciones*, pp 31–7; [P.] David, *Études historiques* [*sur le Galice et le Portugal du VIᵉ au XIIᵉ siècle*] (Lisbon–Paris 1947) p 320. Compare [J. A.] Maravall, *El concepto de España* [*en la Edad Media*] (2 ed Madrid 1964) pp 305–9; Díaz y Díaz, *De Isidoro al siglo XI*, pp 214–15.

Oppa more respectable for the future by tampering with the account of the past—any more than we know for whose edification the whitewash was applied, for whom, that is, these writers thought they were writing. The hypothesis of Sánchez-Albornoz, however, that behind the associated chronicles of Alfonso III's reign lies a now lost common source composed perhaps during the reign of Charlemagne's contemporary, Alfonso II,[43] does provide a suitable context for these alleged happenings, and – though this is to build conjecture upon hypothesis—a context in which the exclusion of bishop Oppa from the retrospective amnesty would be explicable.[44] Alfonso's long reign (791–842) witnessed important developments which reflected and shaped the Christians' perception of their past and future. One was the elaboration of the neogothic myth: the programmatic recreation of 'the Gothic order as it had been at Toledo', the purpose of which was to establish at Oviedo Alfonso's continuity with the Visigothic rulers, as their legitimate heir—just as Leovigild had done at Toledo itself in the sixth century—and thereby to stake his claim to rule over the entire peninsula. The methods employed—or such of them as we know of—were artistic and ceremonial; visual expression was provided in ecclesiastical edifices.[45] Whether this development was indigenous to the Asturias, or had its origins in the initiative of emigré Mozarabic bishops from the south, it cannot be dissociated from either the second issue crucial for a land without a name or a permanent capital: the establishment of the shrine of Saint James at Compostela[46], or from the third: the Adoptionist controversy.

[43] Sánchez-Albornoz, *Investigaciones*, pp 116–18; Díaz y Díaz, *De Isidoro al siglo XI*, pp 215–16.

[44] Barbero and Vigil regard the chronicle's Oppa at Covadonga as 'el prototipo del obispo que ha pactado con los musulmanes', note the development of the historic Oppa (brother of Wittiza and bishop of Seville) into the chronicle's Oppa (son of Wittiza and bishop of Toledo), and suggest that he may have been the literary creation of Mozarabic clergy opposed to the type of alliance with the Muslim which Oppa here was represented as favouring; even that 'con la presencia de Oppas, Asturias se transforma en Toledo': *La formación*, pp 275–6. Compare Díaz y Díaz, *De Isidoro al siglo XI*, p 224.

[45] *Crónica Albeldense*, ed Gómez-Moreno, pp 602–3; [L. de] Valdeavellano, [*Historia de España*], I, 2 vols (4 ed Madrid 1968) 1, pp 435–6; H. Schlunck, 'La iglesia de San Julián de los Prados (Oviedo) y la arquitectura de Alfonso el Casto', *Estudios sobre la monarquía asturiana. Colección de trabajos realizada con motivo del XI centenario de Alfonso II el Casto, celebrado en 1942* (2 ed Oviedo 1971) pp 405–65. On Leovigild's precedent see Collins, 'Mérida and Toledo', pp 212–14.

[46] L. Vázquez de Parga, J. M. Lacarra, J. Uría Ríu, *Las peregrinaciones a Santiago de Compostela*, 3 vols (Madrid 1948) 1 pp 39–46.

Spear-headed by Beatus of Liébana and Etherius, the orthodox revolt of the north provided churchmen there with an eminently respectable opportunity to declare themselves independent of the Mozarabic hierarchy of the south, whose very existence under Muslim rule served to obscure the clear and clean identification of the Asturian monarchy with the Christian cause—quite apart from any question of Adoptionism's alleged Arian content.[47] In a celebrated outburst, Elipand metropolitan of Toledo (who was already suffering harrassment at Roman hands) voiced his indignation at criticism from such a remote quarter: was it not unheard of for Liébana to lay down the law to Toledo?[48] We may ask another question here: what possibility was there in such circumstances of making an honest man of his predecessor at Toledo, Oppa the collaborationist representative of the Visigothic church?

Now how much of this was the work of churchmen *qua* churchmen rather than of churchmen *qua* royal propagandists is a matter for debate—as is the question of whether such a distinction would have had much meaning for contemporaries. Historians further complicate the matter by too confidently inferring clerical authorship of chronicles from their superior latinity, and then too readily claiming to have discovered the cause of any perceptible pro-clerical bias.[49] The difficulty of interpretation is not of course peculiar to ninth-century Asturias, nor until the papacy had developed sufficiently as a tool capable of prising clergy and king apart will there be any prospect of solving it. But if the rehabilitation of bishop Oppa was such a hopeless case in the ninth century, and beyond,[50] and the rewritten history of *Crónica Ovetense* was the best that could be done by those who held the pen while the

---

[47] Valdeavellano, 1 p 444; R. d'Abadal [i de Vinyals], *La batalla del Adopcionismo en la desintegración de la Iglesia visigoda* (Barcelona 1949).

[48] 'Nam nunquam est auditum ut Libanenses Toletanos docuissent': *PL* 96 (1854) col 918C; E. Amann, *L'Époque carolingienne*, FM 6 (Paris 1947) pp 130–34. Compare M. Ríu, 'Revisión del problema adopcionista en la diócesis de Urgel', *AEM* 1 (1964) pp 77–96. The 'anti-Toledanism' of Alfonso II's reign is remarked by Díaz y Díaz, *De Isidoro al siglo XI*, p 221.

[49] Above, n 39. Compare Díaz y Díaz, *De Isidoro al siglo XI*, p 222.

[50] See the version of Oppa's confrontation with Pelayo in the early twelfth-century *Historia Silense*, [ed J. Pérez de Urbel and A. González Ruíz-Zorrilla] (Madrid 1959) pp 132–4. As late as 1216–17 the archbishop of Braga's proctor at the papal curia could seek to damage Toledo's case by recalling 'quod Opa, quondam archiepiscopus Toletanus . . . apostavit cedens in sectam Mohabitarum et per eum amissa fuit tota Hyspania et recuperata per Bracarensem': [P.] Feige [, *Die Anfänge des portugiesischen Königtums und seiner Landeskirche*], *Spanischen Forschungen der*

warriors rested on their spears, then the reinterpretation of the Visigothic past was uphill work indeed. 'It is', E. A. Thompson has remarked, 'scarcely possible to deny that throughout the seventh century, except in Erwig's reign, the bishops of Spain were supine supporters of the king'.[51] True, there were cases of seventh-century bishops who took a tough line with the king, but they were rare,[52] and something of their temporising esprit de corps can be discovered in the way in which they handled the delicate matter of the fate of the rebel Hermenegild at the hands of his Arian father Leovigild five years before Reccared's public conversion. Catholic martyr or thankless rebel? Contemporaries were in no doubt, at least in the record they left for posterity. Hermenegild's action was tyrannical, according to Johannes Biclarensis bishop of Gerona, while the author of the *Vitas SS. Patrum Emeretensium* mentions Hermenegild only incidentally in his description of Reccared's conversion, by removing the reference to martyrdom from the account which he borrowed from Gregory the Great.[53] Gregory's view that Hermenegild had died a martyr's death in the course of a religious war against an unjust and heretical father,[54] might have had some uncomfortable implications for these men. At any event, they did not espouse it. Nor did Isidore,[55] although at a later stage it would triumph and lead eventually to Hermenegild's canonisation at Philip II's insistence in 1586. Hermenegild's changing fortunes reveal something of Spanish churchmen's powers of self-analysis

---

Görresgesellschaft, I. Reihe: *Gesammelte Aufsätze zur Kulturgeschichte Spaniens*, 29 (Münster-in-W 1978) pp 85–436, at p 399.

[51] E. A. Thompson, *The Goths in Spain* (Oxford 1969) pp 316–17. Compare [J. M.] Lacarra, 'La iglesia visigoda [en el siglo VII y sus relaciones con Roma]', *SSSpoleto* 7. i (1960) pp 358–60, 373–5.

[52] Hillgarth, 'Popular religion in Visigothic Spain', James, *Visigothic Spain*, pp 40–41.

[53] *Chronicon Johannis Biclarensis*, ed J. Campos (Madrid 1960) pp 89, 91, 141–3; *Vitas . . .* V.9.4: 'qui [*scil*. Reccaredus] non patrem perfidum sed Christum dominum sequens ab Arianae haereseos pravitate conversus est'—substituting 'Christum dominum' for 'fratrem martyrem' in Gregory, *Dial*. 3. 31—cit. [E. A.] Thompson, '[The] Conversion [of the Visigoths to Catholicism]', *Nottingham Mediaeval Studies* 4 (Nottingham 1960) p 12. Compare J. Fontaine, 'Conversion et culture chez les Wisigoths d'Espagne', *SSSpoleto* 14 (1967) pp 109–12, 117–20, 143–4.

[54] Thompson, 'Conversion' pp 19–22; Hillgarth, 'Coins and Chronicles[: Propaganda in sixth-century Spain and the Byzantine background]', *Historia* 15 (Wiesbaden 1966) pp 491–501.

[55] [*Historia Gothorum*,] ed [T.] Mommsen, *MGH AA*, 11, p 287.

and state of self-confidence over that millennium;[56] as also does the list of other monarchs in whom successive centuries discovered saintly qualities—Pelayo (highly questionable), Fernando III (problematical but possible), and James I of Aragón, Fernando's contemporary and equal in battle, but nevertheless wholly implausible.[57]

'It is ironical', as J. N. Hillgarth has observed, 'that.....Isidore of Seville should have shared in the suppression of the truth (regarding Hermenegild), in the interest of the unity of the Kingdom.'[58] Whether or not this expression of his preconceptions should incline us to describe Isidore as a nationalist spokesman is another question, and one which continues to be much debated. How are we to interpret the fact that his celebrated *Laus Spaniae*, with its glorification of *mater Spania*—'*omnium terrarum, quaequae sunt ab occidu usque ad Indos, pulcherrima es, o sacra semperque felix principum gentiumque mater Spania*—is emblazoned at the beginning of a history which has as its title *Historia Gothorum* rather than *Historia Spaniae*? Is Isidore writing 'national' history or 'royal' history? Are we to understand his pronouncement as the expression of a new *comunidad hispánica*, itself the fruit of the religious unity achieved by Reccared's conversion? If we are—and if we are to view the Visigothic councils as bodies dedicated to furthering the unitary policies of the monarchs—then we must at least note that a consequence, or at least a concomitant of this was that this community's ecclesiastical relationship with Rome was formal at best, and towards the end of the century was distinctly strained. Reccared was in no hurry to inform the pontiff of his conversion, and seventh-century bishops did not hesitate to adopt a patronising tone in their meagre correspondence with successive popes, Braulio of Zaragoza for example advising Honorius I not to concern

---

[56] [J. N.] Garvin, [*The Vitas Sanctorum Patrum Emeretensium*] (Washington 1946) pp 490–91; J. Tamayo Salazar, *Anamnesis sive commemorationis sanctorum Hispanorum . . .*, 1 (Lyons 1652) pp 202–3, 2 p 580; J.-M. del Estal, 'Culto de Felipe II a San Hermenegildo', *La Ciudad de Dios* 174 (El Escorial 1961) pp 550–52; Linehan, *Spanish Church*, p 330. Compare R. de Maio, 'L'ideale eroico nei processi di canonizzazione della controriforma', in *Riforme e miti nella Chiesa del Cinquecento* (Naples 1973) pp 261–2.

[57] Maravall, *El concepto de España* pp 257–8 (Pelayo); Linehan, *Spanish Church* pp 331–3 (Fernando); [J.] Massó Torrents, ['Historiografia de Catalunya en català durant l'epoca nacional'], *Revue hispanique* 15 (1906) pp 546–7.

[58] 'Coins and Chronicles' p 501. If Collins is correct in his suggestion that Hermenegild had not converted to catholicism at the time of his rebellion, then the irony of the situation may be less—but not the interest of the treatment which it received at the hands of later writers: 'Mérida and Toledo' pp 215–18.

himself about the bishops' apparent subservience to the king, and incidentally correcting a faulty biblical reference in the pope's own letter. Certainly there are no signs of that *obediencia castrense* to Rome which Sánchez-Albornoz regards as characteristic of later centuries, and which recent propagandists have strained so hard to detect.[59]

To some degree the debate over these issues must always remain unresolved because the participants cannot agree about defining the terms that they use. What matters more to us, however, is the use which could be made of Isidore, and which *was* made of him in the centuries after the rout of 711—a rout the very occurrence of which casts doubt on the claim that Isidore inspired an intellectual and spiritual renaissance in his lifetime.[60] True, Isidore continued to be read. But those who read him were whistling in the dark themes which only later could be orchestrated for full brass.[61] For nationalism has a geographical dimension as well as a historical one, and Isidore's significance can only be properly appreciated when set in the context of political reality. It is necessary therefore to consider briefly Spain's political developments.

[59] *Laus Spaniae*, ed Mommsen p 268; Hillgarth, 'Historiography in Visigothic Spain', *SSSpoleto* 17 (1969) pp 298–9, and F. Udina Martorell and J. Fontaine in *discussione, ibid* pp 345–50. Compare Lacarra, 'La iglesia visigoda' pp 353–84, and O. Bertolini in *discussione, ibid* p 406; Sánchez-Albornoz, *España: un enigma histórico* I pp 353, 357; Pérez de Urbel, above n 13; Hernández Villaescusa who contents himself with the assumption that the kings nominated bishops 'por una especie de delegación' from Rome (p 352). On Isidore's position see J. M. Wallace-Hadrill, *Early Germanic Kingship in England and on the Continent* (Oxford 1971) pp 53–5; Barbero and Vigil, 'El feudalismo visigodo', *La formación* pp 174–6; and for the view that the events of 589 witnessed 'la aparición de una verdadera Iglesia nacional, al margen no solo del Imperio de Oriente sino de la propria Roma', [J. A.] García de Cortazar, [*La Época medieval: Historia de España Alfaguara*], 2, (5 ed Madrid 1978) p 43.
[60] M. Cruz Hernández, 'San Isidoro y el problema de la "cultura" hispano-visigoda', *AEM* 3 (1966) pp 414, 422–3, commenting on J. Fontaine, *Isidore de Seville et la culture classique dans l'Espagne visigothique* (Paris 1959).
[61] The view that Isidore's writings express a vision of 'una nacionalidad naciente, pero ya inequívocamente diferenciada y autónoma' is found in J. L. Romero, 'San Isidoro de Sevilla. Su pensamiento históricopolítico y sus relaciones con la historia visigoda', *CHE* 8 (1947) pp 57–8; Maravall, *El concepto de España* pp 21–2. Compare L. Vázquez de Parga, 'Notas sobre la obra histórica de S. Isidro', *Isidoriana*, [ed M. C. Díaz y Díaz] (León 1961) p 106: 'No ha hecho, creo yo, historia nacional, sino dar una historia de pueblos no romanos, con independencia, y considerar en la *laus Hispaniae* a España unida al pueblo godo. Pero no hay propiamente concepto de nacionalidad.' For later use of Isidore see Díaz y Díaz, 'Isidoro en la Edad Media hispana', *Isidoriana* pp 345–87 (repr *De Isidoro al siglo XI*, pp 143–201).

The chroniclers of the twelfth century and later deplored those political divisions of Spain which had resulted from the Arab invasion, and the further sub-division of *regna*—the 'principle of fragmentation', as Maravall has called it, which is so marked a feature of Spain's medieval history, and which clerical authors regarded as divine punishment for the sins of men.[62] The Christian kings ruled over places not over peoples. The title *rex Hispanorum* would have implied rule over the Mozarabs of the south. They were kings 'not of a kingdom but of a space'. They lacked any 'corporative or organic concept' of a kingdom'.[63] As the travel posters affirm, 'Spain is different'. All is fluctuation and fragmentation. Squaring the unitary neogothic myth with political reality called for some virtuoso conceptual gymnastics. *Regnum Hispanie* survived only as a latent concept. without a *rex Hispanie* to rule over it. 'King' and 'kingdom' *no son absolutamente correlativos*. Political power was exercised by a number of princes, the plurality of 'kings and princes of Spain' to which both native and foreign writers so often refer, Maravall's *pululación de reyes*, occasional kings promiscuously coming and going, or all together subscribing the remarkable—in our eyes remarkable—document of 1153':

> imperante domno Adefonso imperatore cum domna Rica imperatore uxore sua; domna Sancia infantissa cum fratre suo regnante; Sancius, rex similiter; Fernandus, rex similiter.[64]

One effect of all this was to limit the opportunities open to churchmen to establish a mediating role in the process of king-making. It is striking that the attributes of royalty should have come to enjoy less prominence than elsewhere in Europe in the very land which has provided the earliest recorded evidence of the practice of royal unction.[65]

---

[62] Maravall, *El concepto de España* pp 344, 355: 'Creo que es absolumente indispensable para entender nuestra Edad Media partir de ese principio de fragmentariedad'; Sánchez-Albornoz, 'La sucesión al trono [en los reinos de León y Castilla]', *Boletín de la Academia Argentina de Letras* 14 (Buenos Aires 1945) pp 35–124—repr in his *Estudios [sobre las instituciones medievales españolas]* (Mexico 1965) p 673.

[63] Maravall, *El concepto de España* pp 350, 351, 357, 359.

[64] *Ibid* pp 408–9, 388–99, 366, 380, 384, 369.

[65] [P. E.] Schramm [(trans L. Vázquez de Parga)], *Las insignias[de la realeza en la Edad Media española]* (Madrid 1960) p 63. On unction as 'el factor constitutivo o al menos confirmante de la legitimidad real' in the Visigothic period see J. Orlandis Rovira, 'La iglesia visigoda y los problemas de la sucesión al trono en el siglo VII', *SSSpoleto* 7. i (1960) pp 333–51, esp pp 349–51, and O. Bertolini, G. B. Picotti, L. Prosdocimi, J. M. Lacarra and G. P. Bognetti in *discussione*, *ibid* pp 385–95,

For a century and a half after the death of Alfonso VII in 1157 no king of Castile was crowned.[66] In thirteenth-century Navarre Teobaldo II's attempt to introduce the practice of unction led to popular demand for the retention of the established practice of raising the king on his shield,[67] and in Aragón, despite the later tradition that in order to emphasise the papal role Innocent III in 1204 had intended to impose the crown on Pedro II with his feet—an attempt which the king foiled by providing an unmanoeverable crown of soft bread for the occasion—his son Jaime the Conqueror chose not to be crowned, and though later coronations at Zaragoza may have helped to establish that place as the kingdom's capital, Alfonso III was at pains to emphasise that his own coronation there by the bishop of Huesca in 1286 was not to be taken as implying that he had received his crown *tanquam ab ecclesia romana, nec pro ipsa ecclesia nec contra ecclesiam*, nor that any prejudice was thereby suffered by any other place in his kingdom.[68] The sword not the crown was the king of Aragon's distinctive emblem, and the ceremonial secured no political influence for churchmen whom Peter III could forbid to enforce papal sentences against him *propter naturalitatem quam habetis nobiscum.*[69]

The churchman's role was to be that of acolyte rather than celebrant. This did not mean that their role was entirely passive—in times of crisis, in Castile in 1166 for example, they would move

---

398 404; A. Barbero de Aguilera, 'El pensamiento político visigodo y las primeras unciones regias en la Europa medieval', *Hispania* 30 (Madrid 1970) pp 245–326, esp pp 314–17. For developments after 711 see Barbero and Vigil, 'La sucesión al trono', *La formación*, p 290.

[66] Schramm, *Las insignias*, p 32. Alfonso X in the thirteenth century scoffed at the thaumaturgic pretensions of the kings of France and England: Maravall, ['Del regimen feudal al regimen corporativo en el pensamiento de Alfonso X'], *Estudios* [*de historia del pensamiento español*] (2 ed Madrid 1973) p 117.

[67] Lacarra, *Historia del reino de Navarra en la Edad Media* (Pamplona 1975) p 295 (compare pp 246–7); Schramm, 'Der Königg von Navarra (1035–1512)', *ZRG GAbt* 81 (1951) pp 144–9. I have not seen Lacarra's *El juramento de los reyes de Navarra (1234–1329)* (Madrid 1972).

[68] [B.] Palacios Martín, [*La coronación de los reyes de Aragón 1204–1410. Aportación al estudio de las estructuras medievales*] (Valencia 1975) pp 23, 77–81, 107–8, 308. The importance of the ceremonial of royal unction enacted there in establishing Toledo as the capital of Visigothic Spain is stressed by Collins, 'Julian of Toledo and the royal succession in late seventh-century Spain' in *Early Medieval Kingship*, ed P. H. Sawyer and I. N. Wood (Leeds 1977) pp 45–6.

[69] Palacios Martín pp 83–6; L. González Antón, *Las Uniones aragonesas y las Cortes del reino (1283–1301)* 2 vols (Zaragoza 1975) 1 pp 373–8, 438–40.

into the political vacuum 'to save the nation'.[70] Nor of course were they ever indifferent regarding the political outcome. Strong (but not too strong) central rule was in their best interests—or so archbishop Rodrigo of Toledo implied in his account of the part played by the prelates of the kingdom of León in the negotiations which led to the union of León with Castile in the person of Fernando III in 1230: *regni prelati, quorum interest regnum et sacerdotium contueri*[71] By then the realisation of Visigothic unity may have seemed to be within sight. Three centuries before, while postponing that outcome *sine die*, they busied themselves on a lower plane in the service of the monarch, fabricating false genealogies which connected him with the Visigothic rulers, introducing into charters and diplomas phrases which implied a new judicial theory of the ruler's full hereditary rights; deploying such imperial titles as *Ranimirus, Flavius, princeps magnus, basileus unctus, in regno fultus*, and blessing the king and his army before their campaigns,[72] or bolstering his political power by sanctifying it, bringing to ninth-century Oviedo (as to sixth-century Toledo) quantities of relics from the south, many the remains of venerable martyrs long dead, others of more recent origin. That market was buoyant and the competition international, but this was important work, and the significance of their acquisitions seems to have been crucial.[73]

Of the many puzzling features of the case of the voluntary martyrs of Córdoba in the 850s, none is more surprising than the fact reported of bishop Eulogius of Toledo that he had been partially awakened to the significance of Islam on reading a distorted life of Mohammed in the library of a Navarrese monastery, when, as has been said, 'he could have obtained more accurate information by asking any Muslim in the street'. For Ignacio Olagüe of course here is proof positive that the Arabs had never

[70] Below pp 190–91.

[71] *De Rebus Hispaniae*, 9. 14: ed F. Lorenzana, *PP Toletanorum quotquot extant Opera,* 3 (Madrid 1793, repr Valencia 1968) p 204.

[72] Sánchez-Albornoz, 'La sucesión al trono', *Estudios* p 663 (compare Barbero and Vigil, 'La sucesión al trono', *La formación* pp 279–353); A. Sánchez Candeira, *El "regnum-imperium" leonés hasta 1037* (Madrid 1951) passim, esp pp 11, 65 (Ramiro III *anno* 974); Sánchez-Albornoz, *España: un enigma histórico* 2, pp 373–80; Goñi Gaztambide pp 33–5.

[73] B. de Gaiffier, 'Les notices hispaniques dans le Martyrologe d'Usuard', *An Bol* 55 (1937) pp 268–83; *idem, Recherches d'hagiographie latine* (Brussels 1971) p 8. Compare Collins, 'Mérida and Toledo' p 214.

invaded Spain.[74] The equally remarkable testimony of Paulus Alvarus—'apparently a layman' (but does that matter?)—that the Mozarabic Christians of Córdoba were so enthralled by Arabic culture that they despised or ignored their Christian heritage, is also open to doubt.[75] But it was that version of events that passed to the north, that interpretation of the martyrs' motives that was received together with the remains of Eulogius and Leocadia in 883 (and perhaps, it may be suggested, the conventional wisdom regarding bishop Oppa). We may shrink from the interpretation of García Villada or Pérez de Urbel, for whom Eulogius was chief of *un partido nacional* and endowed with *una generosa tendencia nacionalista*, but it would be difficult to deny all symbolic significance to the translation of their relics, quite apart from the effect of their collective self-sacrifice in establishing the belief that death at Muslim hands automatically counted as martyrdom.[76]

Two hundred years later, in 1063, another relic expedition brought off a further important coup, when the bishops of León and Astorga set off for the south in search of the remains of the third-century martyr Justa. What Ordoño of Astorga returned with from Seville were the remains of Isidore—the complete set apparently.[77] It should cause no surprise that movement between the two zones should have been so easy. It usually was, and thirty years after the collapse of the caliphate of Córdoba, the south was vulnerable as never before to Christian pressure. But the Christian leaders preferred to take booty—*parias*—from the subject Muslim

---

[74] *PL* 115 (1854) col 859; Glick p 176; Olagüe p 268: 'Si nous n'en avions d'autres, ce seul témoignage suffirait à ruiner la légende.' Compare E. P. Colbert, *The Martyrs of Córdoba (850–859): a study of the sources* (Washington 1962).

[75] *Indiculus luminosus: PL* 121 (1854) cols 555–6; [J.] Waltz, ['The significance of the voluntary martyrs of ninth-century Córdoba'], *The Muslim World* 60 (Hartford, Conn., 1970) p 155.

[76] García Villada, above p 163; Pérez de Urbel, *San Eulogio de Córdoba, o la vida andaluza en el siglo IX* (2 ed Madrid 1942) pp 124, 253: 'un gran símbolo. Por ella encomendaba la realización de su más grande anhelo a aquellos montañeses, fuertes e indomables, que habian conservado con toda su pureza la tradición española.' In the south of course 'la tradición española' was tainted: 'estos hombres estaban inficionados hasta la medula por el influjo de la nueva civilización' (p 252), whereas Eulogius and Leocadia were 'los dos campeones del españolismo tradicional' (p 249). Compare Waltz pp 232–5.

[77] *Historia Silense* pp 197–204; A. Vinayo González, 'Cuestiones histórico-críticas en torno a la traslación del cuerpo de San Isidoro', *Isidoriana* pp 285–98. The importance of possessing the complete remains is illustrated by Compostela's reaction when archbishop Mauricio of Braga acquired an extra head of Saint James in the Holy Land: David, *Études historiques* pp 475–7.

kingdom, to the enormous benefit of Cluny incidentally; and if any churchman felt conscientious scruples about this his protest was not recorded. The bringing to León of Isidore's remains in the year after the kingdom of Toledo had for the first time accepted client status vis à vis the king of León, almost amounted to a statement of intent to postpone the prosecution of a decisive policy against Seville and the south.[78] When the struggle was resumed Isidore would be pressed into service both as saint and, improbably enough, as *caudillo*. But the struggle, when resumed, would continue fitfully for a matter of centuries; and part of the reason for that is hinted at in the admission, albeit grudgingly made by the author of the *Historia Silense*, that some trace of virtue was discernible in the Moorish king of Seville.[79] The atmosphere of political tolerance and burgeoning *convivencia* in which these events took place anticipates the non-combative atmosphere which, alongside the military exploits of the thirteenth century, would permit the nuns of Las Huelgas to be tended by mudejar servants who had their own mosque, and enjoy baths and the ministrations of Jewish physicians: the side of the story, in short, which makes it so difficult to regard the history of the Reconquest, whether an exclusively religious phenomenon or not, as a total account of the history of Christian Spain in the Middle Ages.[80]

The unidentified author of *Silense* compiled his account of Isidore's translation some fifty or sixty years after the event, *c*.1118. He marks (for us) some important developments. Regarded as the first writer possessed of 'a complete vision of Spain as the object of the historian's attention', he is notorious for the anti-French bias which he reveals in his account of events from Charlemagne's time

---

[78] Lacarra, 'Aspectos económicos de la sumisión de los reinos de taifas, 1010–1102', *Homenaje a J. Vicens Vives* (Barcelona 1965) pp 255–77; [C. J.] Bishko, 'Fernando I y [los origenes de la alianza castellanoleonesa con] Cluny', *CHE* 47–8 (1968) pp 31–135, 49–50 (1969) pp 50–117, esp pp 47–8, 99–135; P. Segl, *Königtum und Klosterreform in Spanien. Untersuchungen über die Cluniacenserklöster in Kastilien-León vom Beginn des 11. bis zur Mitte des 12. Jahrhunderts* (Kallmünz 1974) pp 73–6; Valdeavellano 2, p 285.

[79] L. López Santos, 'Isidoro en la literatura medioeval castellana', *Isidoriana* pp 402–8; *Historia Silense* p 201: 'Expavit barbarus, et licud infidelis, virtutem tamen Domini admirans . . .' Compare the editors' introduction (p 48) where the significance of this admission seems to be misunderstood.

[80] L. Torres Balbás, *Algunos aspectos del mudejarismo urbano medieval* (Madrid 1954) pp 78–9.

Religion and national identity in medieval Spain

onwards: the *franci* were corruptible and their histories were false.[81] His cry of protest against the all-pervasive French influence of the period has been widely remarked. Whereas the nationalism of Beatus of Liébana and Paulus Alvarus had been apocalyptic and extra-terrestrial, his is firmly rooted in Spanish soil.[82] In him—with whom incidentally Hermenegild re-enters Spanish historiography wearing the martyr's crown[83]—the focus becomes sharper than at any time in the proceeding four centuries. Churchmen formerly have been vague and shadowy figures, their identity and their attitudes largely matters of conjecture. Only rarely can Lafuente's picture of the 'church of Spain' supporting 'the State' during those centuries be substantiated.[84] Through the eyes of the *Silense* author we begin to see matters rather more clearly, just as our field of vision is widened in these years by the inclusion of a new dimension: the papal dimension.

Although Catalonia and Aragón had always been more open to outside influences than had regions farther west, the entire peninsula had tended to be hermetically sealed in spiritual terms and consciously self-sufficient to a marked degree. The air of satisfaction with which modern Spanish writers have regarded the council of Coyanza (1055) faithfully reflects the spirit of the century to which it belongs. Although summoned by king Fernando I, in whose names its decrees were promulgated, and attended by lay magnates—all in true Visigothic style—the council of Coyanza is regarded as demonstrating that the eleventh-century Spanish church had no need of foreigners to reform it, and indeed stood in little need of reform from any quarter. The subject matter of its thirteen canons is taken as showing that there was less cause for remedial action here than elsewhere in Europe; satisfactory performance in all aspects of ecclesiastical practice and discipline is inferred from absence of reference to specific abuses.[85] The argu-

[81] Ed cit pp 129–30; Maravall, *El concepto de España* p 30.
[82] Díaz y Díaz, 'La historiografía' pp 219–21.
[83] Ed cit pp 115–16, reproducing the account of Gregory the Great (above n 53). The *Compilatio Ovetensis* of 883 (cit. Garvin p 488) had not gone so far.
[84] 'La Iglesia de España ha seguido la suerte del Estado en su próspera y adversa fortuna, alentando al combate, exhortando en la pelea, consolando en la derrota, y cortando las rencillas y discordias fraternales: en los escasos momentos de ócio ha manejado la pluma, mientras el guerrero descansaba apoyada en su lanza': Lafuente 3 pp 379–80.
[85] *Ibid* 3 p 290; Menéndez Pelayo 1 p 455; J. López Ortiz (bishop of Túy), 'La restauración de la cristiandad', [*El*] *Concilio de Coyanza* [*(Miscelanea)*] (León 1951)

ment from silence which provides such a favourable impression (and where in Europe would it not produce the same effect before the advent of the Gregorian reformers?) has proved impervious to the results of research into the text of the Coyanza decrees, research which has revealed that what historians have taken to be the authentic legislation of the council is in fact a product of the workshop of Pelayo of Oviedo, a reworking done seventy-odd years later. What is notable about the Pelagian version is that, apart from stressing the king's part in the council's proceedings, the reviser of the text of the decrees seems to have had two purposes in view which did not seem to him to be in any way incompatible: the promotion of Gregorian notions and of the interests of the see of Oviedo.[86] No particular desire to emphasize the nationalist (as against the royalist) content of the original decrees is apparent.[87]

The presence and absence of such preconceptions are relevant to consideration of the impact of the peninsular policies of Gregory VII. It is customary to observe here the confrontation of Spanish catholicism and Spanish nationalism—with the former prevailing as Spanish historians take pride in recalling.[88] Of course, Gregory's

---

pp 5, 11–12. Understanding of this subject began in earnest with A. García Gallo's fundamental monograph ['El Concilio de Coyanza. Contribución al estudio del derecho canónico español en la Alta Edad Media'], *Anuario de Historia del Derecho Español* 20 (Madrid 1950) pp 275–633—although he too assumes the absence of 'situaciones intolerables' (pp 364–6). The same assumption is present throughout the much-quoted work of R. Bidagor, *La "iglesia propria" en España. Estudio histórico-canónico* (Rome 1933) esp pp 82, 98, 115. Indeed, it held to *explain* the slow pace of reform during the twelfth century (p 157). For Bidagor the Visigothic regime is normative (pp 169–70) and its incompatibility with 'Gregorian' notions is not considered. Compare Lacarra, 'La iglesia visigoda' p 384: 'si . . . no se apartó de la Iglesia Universal en sus principios dogmáticos, ni recusó formalmente la autoridad del Romano Pontífice, de hecho vivió encerrada en sí misma'; and E. Magnou-Nortier, *La Société laïque et l'église dans la province ecclésiastique de Narbonne (zone cispyrénéenne) de la fin du VIIIe à la fin du XIe siècle* (Toulouse 1974) pp 447–518, for the experiences during these years of a closed society which was in many ways comparable.

[86] García Gallo pp 321–3; idem, 'Las redacciones de los decretos del Concilio de Coyanza', *Concilio de Coyanza* pp 25–39, esp pp 31–2; G. Martínez Díez, 'El concilio compostelano del reinado de Fernando I', *AEM* I (1964) pp 121–38, esp pp 133–5; O. Engels, 'Papsttum, Reconquista und Spanisches Landeskonzil im Hochmittelalter', *Annuarium Historiae Conciliorum* 1 (Amsterdam 1969) pp 276–87.

[87] García Gallo pp 298–9, 342–3: cc. VII.3; IX (on *Liber iudicum* and *Lex Gothica*). Compare c. XIV of the Pelagian redaction (absent from the earlier *redacción portuguesa*) confirming 'totos illos foros cunctis habitantibus in Legione quos dedit illis rex domnus Adefonsus' (*Ibid* p 302): a royalist interpolation indeed.

[88] 'El sentimiento católico, irresistible en la raza, se sobrepuso a todo instinto de

claim to possession of the *regnum Hyspaniae* was, as has been said, 'grotesquely out of touch with the realities of the Reconquest'. More to the point, however, is the fact that neither in 1073 nor in 1077 did it succeed in eliciting any response from those to whom it was addressed.[89] Spanish churchmen did not need to regard this as a battle of conflicting loyalties. In the matter of the substitution of the Mozarabic rite by the Roman, in which Gregory again acted with characteristic heavy-handedness, there is indeed evidence of popular resistance—but it is evidence from a royal source, and it was the king who settled the matter, albeit to the pope's satisfaction, with his celebrated and decisive aphorism *alla van leyes do quieren reyes*.[90] It is perhaps no exaggeration to describe the response to Gregory's interventions as at best cosmetic. Nowhere in the peninsula do we find churchmen being drawn away from their accustomed allegiance. In Catalonia, indeed, it was precisely at this time, while the papacy was declaring against the practice, that bishops and abbots were entering into vassal relationships with the count of Barcelona and other laymen.[91] In Aragón meanwhile, king Pedro I made clear to Urban II his attitude to trouble-making reforming prelates who sought to introduce new-fangled theories behind his back while he was at the front fighting night and day against the enemies of the Cross. The king's letter contained an unmistakable warning to the pontiff: if Christendom's fight was to be fought in

---

orgullo nacional, por grande y legítimo que·fuese': Menéndez Pelayo 1 p 458; 'No todas las acciones de los Santos son santas, ni tiene el cristiano obligación de aceptar cada una de ellas en particular. ¿Quien hoy proclamará el papa infalible en política y quien podra igualmente defender la conducta de San Gregorio VII con respecto á España?': Lafuente 3 pp 363–4.

[89] H. E. J. Cowdrey, *The Cluniacs and the Gregorian Reform* (Oxford 1970) pp 221–2, 226. Compare David, *Études historiques* pp 377–82; Bishko, 'Fernando I y Cluny', *CHE* 49–50, pp 100–4.

[90] 'De Romano autem ritu quod tua iussione accepimus sciatis nostram terram admodum desolatam esse' (Alfonso VI to Hugh of Cluny, July 1077): David, *Études historiques* pp 402–3, 419–20. See also C. Morris, '*Judicium Dei*: the social and political significance of the ordeal in the eleventh century', *SCH* 12 (1975) pp 98–9; [C.] Servatius, [*Paschalis II. (1099–1118). Studien zu seiner Person und seiner Politik*] (Stuttgart 1979) pp 29–32.

[91] P. Bonnassie, *La Catalogne du milieu du Xe à la fin du XIe siècle* 2 vols (Toulouse 1975–6) 2 pp 701–5, esp p 703: 'Tout révérence gardée envers le successeur de Pierre, l'Eglise catalane n'admet, au temporel, d'autre chef que le comte de Barcelone et elle s'intègre naturellement au nouveau système gouvernemental que celui-ci met en place.'

Spain, then it must be fought on Spain's terms.[92]

The effect of reforms formulated by the papacy—or, as Fletcher has it, of 'what is loosely and unsatisfactorily called "reform"' —failed to disturb the relationship of king and bishop, or to introduce any significant irritant into that relationship, not because the formulation was imperfect but because the parties were deaf to influences outside.[93] The year 1085, then, was significant not for Gregory VII's death, but for Alfonso VI's conquest of Toledo—or 'pseudo-conquest', as it has been described by an historian who sees in it a manoeuvre engineered by the Mozarabic community judging their prospects to be better under Alfonso's rule not because he was Christian but because he was nearer at hand: so the Christians did not reconquer Toledo, just as the Arabs had never invaded Spain![94] Nevertheless, the event—or pseudo-event—certainly created new horizons for the king by his possession of the old Visigothic capital, and new problems in the matter of the treatment of the now subject Muslims. The religious and the political solutions exemplified in Talavera and Cisneros at the end of the fifteenth century had their protagonists four centuries earlier in archbishop Bernard of Toledo (prompted by queen Constance) and the king respectively. Alfonso VI was only deterred from his intention of burning the archbishop and queen for having forcibly converted the Toledo mosque to Christian use by the pleas of the 'prudent' Arabs themselves who, as the story was told by Rodrigo of Toledo in the thirteenth century, were fearful of further reprisals.[95]

The conquest of Toledo gave rise also to a series of problems particularly affecting churchmen, those connected with the issues of ecclesiastical primacy and provincial organisation.[96] To bolster

---

[92] P. Kehr, *Das Papsttum und die Königreiche Navarra und Aragon bis zur Mitte des XII Jahrhunderts, ADAW, PhH Kl* (Berlin 1929) pp 55–7.

[93] [R. A.] Fletcher, [*The Episcopate in the Kingdom of León in the Twelfth Century*] (Oxford 1978) cap 5, esp pp 184, 203.

[94] M. Criado del Val, *Teoría de Castilla la Nueva. La dualidad castellana en los orígenes del español* (Madrid 1960) pp 84–5, 100–101: 'su participación en la Reconquista será de distinto signo religioso que la de Castilla, y en algunos momentos no parecerá tener conciencia de ello' (p 100).

[95] *De Rebus Hispaniae*, 6. 24: ed Lorenzana pp 137–8; J. Orlandis, 'Un problema eclesiástico de la *Reconquista* española: la conversión de mezquitas en iglesias cristianas', *Mélanges offerts à Jean Dauvillier* (Toulouse 1979) pp 597–9. Compare Hillgarth, *The Spanish Kingdoms*, 2 pp 477–8.

[96] D. Mansilla, 'Disputas diocesanas entre Toledo, Braga y Compostela en los siglos XII al XV', *Anthologica Annua* 3 (Rome 1955) pp 89–143, esp pp 91–130; J. F.

the claims of his church each prelate had recourse to the papacy and to forgery, whichever suited him better. Soon the whole issue was bedevilled by the so-called Division of Wamba, bishop Pelayo of Oviedo's re-working in the 1120s of an earlier fabrication which purported to be an authoritative description of the diocesan divisions made, at the bishops' request, by king Wamba in the seventh century.[97] Its influence was to be enormous. In the 1240s it was used by both Toledo and Tarragona in their battle for ecclesiastical control of Valencia, as one of the many evidences both genuine and spurious unearthed by their agents in libraries both within the peninsula and beyond[98] The real interest of the Gothic heritage to these men was here displayed, in an ecclesiastical dispute which was of supreme political and national significance to the kings of Castile and Aragón.[99] Neither monarch was prepared to permit Valencia to be ecclesiastically subject to the province controlled by the other and the other's metropolitan. The dangers and difficulties presented by ecclesiastical boundaries which were not concurrent with political boundaries was a subject on which the kings of Castile-León at least already possessed a century of experience, in their dealings with the count-kings of Portugal.

The first king of Portugal owed no part of his royal title to Portuguese churchmen: between July 1139 and April 1140 Afonso Henriques slipped from describing himself as *princeps* to *rex* parthenogenetically, as a matter of chancery practice merely, without acclamation, enthronement or coronation. Forty years later, at considerable expense, he secured papal recognition from Alexander III.[100] Ecclesiastical complications, however, remained, with the archbishop of Compostela claiming the obedience of all the Portu-

---

Rivera Recio, *La iglesia de Toledo en el siglo XII (1086–1208)* 2 vols (Rome 1966–76) 1 *passim*.

[97] Vázquez de Parga, *La División de Wamba*[. *Contribución al estudio de la historia y geografía eclesiásticas de la Edad Media española*] (Madrid 1943) esp pp 89–93; D. Mansilla, *Iglesia castellano-leonesa y curia romana en los tiempos del rey San Fernando* (Madrid 1945) pp 94–7, esp p 95 n 19.

[98] Vázquez de Parga, *La División de Wamba* p 46; V. Castell Maiques, 'Un elenco de códices de la Hispana del año 1239', *Anthologica Annua* 16 (1968) pp 329–43.

[99] R. I. Burns, 'Canon Law and the Reconquista: convergence and symbiosis in the kingdom of Valencia under Jaume the Conqueror (1213–1276)', *Proceedings of the Fifth International Congress of Medieval Canon Law (Salamanca, 21–25 September 1976)*, ed S. Kuttner and K. Pennington (Vatican City 1980) pp 398–402.

[100] Feige pp 244–5, 300–307.

guese bishops bar Oporto as falling within the ancient province of
Lusitania (of which he, as successor to the authority of the
unreconquered see of Mérida was head), and the archbishop of
Toledo continuing to press for complete peninsular domination.
The evidence submitted in 1198–9 by the archbishops of Braga and
Compostela for control of the church of Zamora aptly illustrated
the political dimension of ecclesiastical divisions. One witness
recalled how Fernando II of León had sought to draw the suffragans
of Braga from obedience to their archbishop because the latter
intended to excommunicate him;[101] another remembered Fernando's pressure on the bishop of Zamora, politically his subject, to
defect from Braga to Compostela *quia magis sibi debebat placere suum
regnum decorare quam alterius*.[102] As to Compostela's claim to control
of the Portuguese sees on the grounds that Braga was not possessed
of metropolitan authority, Braga had 'old histories' to prove the
opposite and no fewer than 144 witnesses—Braga men who would
know the reason why.[103] The adversaries were seasoned litigants,
canonists who knew every trick in the book and employed all
manner of arguments ranging from geography to palaeography,[104]
but the essence of Braga's case was this: by his *strenuitas* and other
virtues Afonso Henriques had made a kingdom for himself which
Rome recognised; Rome had formally excluded all foreign—that is,
Leonese and Castilian—ecclesiastical jurisdiction from Portugal;
the king by his victory over the Saracens had obtained the right to
plant churches where he would; and—incidentally—the archbishop
of Braga, having borne the heat and burden of battle, deserved to
enjoy the fruits of victory.[105]

[101] *Ibid* p 384. At issue was the king's marriage within the forbidden degrees. See
J. González, *Regesta de Fernando II* (Madrid 1943) pp 69–70, 112; Fletcher
pp 195–203.
[102] Feige, pp 384–5.
[103] *Ibid* p 390.
[104] 'Ponit procurator Bracarensis, quod Bracara est in capite provinciarum Hyspanie
habito respectu ad mare Oceanum, cui vicinior est Bracara quam Toleto.
Respondet archiepiscopus Toletanus, quod non est in capite sed in fine'; Braga's
protest that the papal privileges presented by Toledo 'non sint originalia sed
confirmatoria tantum': *ibid* pp 399–400, 409.
[105] 'Accidit ergo quod olim domnus Alfonsus . . . qui antea infans vocabatur,
interim terram illam dilatavit (. . .) regnum latum et spaciosum fecit et ab hac
sacrosancta sede de infante meruit rex vocari, propter cuius strenuitatem et
meritorum dotem concessionem a Romana ecclesia per privilegium obtinuit,
quod nulla ecclesiastica persona (. . .) in regno suo iurisdicionem vel potestatem
aliquam haberet nisi papa vel eius legatus. Obtinuit ius, quod quamcumque

Religion and national identity in medieval Spain

The case for a national church could hardly have been better put—though Aragón and Castile claimed similar privileges for their reconquering monarchs, in the forged bull of Urban II, [106] and Alfonso X's claim to control episcopal elections as *Sennor natural de la tierra ó son fundadas las eglesias.* [107] But it is arresting to find the case being so eloquently put by an archbishop at the court of Innocent III. The king of Portugal controlled the Portuguese church under papal licence, because of not in spite of Portugal's feudal subjection to Rome. [108] National considerations were invoked by the prelate in order to beat off threats to ecclesiastical integrity: the suggestion that Toledo enjoyed primatial authority throughout the whole peninsula was scandalous both politically, because it implied the subjection of the other *reges Hispaniae* to the king of Castile, and also pastorally, because it demeaned the other metropolitans in the estimation of *simplices et laicos.* [109]

For as long as national and ecclesiastical boundaries failed to coincide, prelates would continue to have to endure some uncomfortable consequences. When, additionally, a century further on and with papal influence on the wane, the bishops of Castile and Portugal came to appreciate the distinct disadvantages of the system of royal control which had been advocated by the archbishop of Braga, and braved themselves to petition for relief from royal exactions, it was *two* monarchs that they had to address. But how very restrained they were when they did so, at Salamanca in 1310. They did not aspire to hold anything so formal as a council, because kings did not like councils. And they certainly did not contemplate the use of canonical sanctions in their own

---

terram a Sarracenis occupasset, propter exaltacionem fidei, quam (. . .) christianos (. . .) dilataverat Sarracenos opprimendo et eos per archiepiscopum suum Bracarensem ad fidem convertendo, cuicumque vellet, posset supponere ecclesie'; '(Bracarensis) archiepiscopus (*in captione*) illius terre multas expensas fecerat in expeticione eundo cum rege, sicut mos et consuetudo est terre illius, et ob hoc multas possessiones Bracarensis ecclesie pignerari obligavit, quas pro parte nondum redimere potuit . . .': *ibid* 393–4.

[106] *Ibid* pp 335–7.

[107] Primera Partida, ley 5, tit. 17: *Alfonso X el Sabio. Primera Partida (manuscrito Add. 20.787 del British Museum),* ed J. A. Arias Bonet (Valladolid 1975) p 77; Linehan, *Spanish Church* p 108.

[108] 'Nec videmus causam, quare dominus papa tantam iniuriam nobis vellet facere, cum etiam dampnum romane ecclesie procuraret. Preterea cum regnum Portugalense sit eius et solvat ei annuatim duas marchas auri, quod non facit aliud regnum in Hyspania . . .': Feige p 418.

[109] *Ibid* p 423.

defence.¹¹⁰ As has been observed, religious nationalism and royal interventionism in the affairs of the church prospered in parallel.¹¹¹

Viewed historically in its peninsular setting, the phenomenon under consideration may be said to have its origins in a failure to achieve on a political plane that restoration of the Visigothic system to which churchmen in an ecclesiastical context aspired. The view, widely held, throughout the Middle Ages, of the Moorish occupation, that it was intrusion which left unaffected all rights enjoyed in the year 711 and created no new rights,¹¹² evidently constituted no problem for Afonso Henriques in 1139, nor for the archbishop of Braga in 1199. Yet it was to that very tradition the Portugese churchmen appealed at the siege of Lisbon in 1147, with the bishop of Porto learnedly defining the just war for the benefit of the horny-handed would-be crusaders from Dartmouth, and representing the issue not primarily as a religious struggle (though that aspect was stressed for effect and in order to justify their not proceeding to Jerusalem), but as a venture for the recovery of lost property,¹¹³ and with the archbishop of Braga urging the Moors to return with all their chattels to the place from whence they had come—as if they had been there just a week rather than for the 358 years during which, by his calculations, they had retained *iniuste* the Christians' cities and possessions,¹¹⁴ (If national characteristics were

¹¹⁰ Linehan, '[The] Spanish Church revisited [: the episcopal *gravamina* of 1279]', *Authority and Power: Studies on Medieval Law and Government presented to Walter Ullmann on his seventieth birthday*, ed B. Tierney and P. Linehan (Cambridge 1980) p 127 and references cited there.
¹¹¹ 'En su conjunto *nacionalismo religioso* e intervencionismo regio en la Iglesia crecieron paralelamente': García de Cortazar p 491.
¹¹² 'Cual si ésta hubiera sido un accidente en la vida española, incapaz de crear derechos': Lacarra, 'La reconquista y repoblación del Valle del Ebro' in *La Reconquista española y la repoblación del país* (Zaragoza 1951) p 79. The notion persisted throughout the medieval period; see Fernando del Pulgar, cited Maravall, *El concepto de España* p 274. Compare B. Blanco González, *Del cortesano al discreto*, 1 (Madrid 1962) 374: 'por haber cristalizado prematuramente la unidad espiritual en tres conjuntos, Portugal, Castilla y Aragón, no se logró, ni en la Edad moderna, la unidad definitiva'.
¹¹³ *De Expugnatione* [*Lyxbonensi*, ed C. W. David[(New York 1936) pp 76–80; E.–D. Hehl, *Kirche und Krieg im 12. Jahrhundert. Studien zu kanonischem Recht und politischer Wirklichkeit* (Stuttgart 1980) pp 259–61.
¹¹⁴ '. . . cum omnibus sarcinis vestris, peccuniis, et pecculiis, cum mulieribus et infantibus, patriam Maurorum repeteritis unde venistis, linquentes nobis nostra': *De Expugnatione* pp 114–16. The archbishop's exogamous assumptions deserve consideration in the context of the work of Guichard (above n 33). As to his historical calculations, compare the altogether more sanguinary account of the Muslim occupation which in 1096 Pedro I of Aragón reckoned had already lasted

exhibited on that occasion, and again at the siege of Silves in 1189, it was by the northerners whose sense of fair play was outraged by a Moorish attack on some Bretons out fishing, and who showed such marked interest in the fate of a prize mare in foal).[115]

For foreign consumption, as in 1147, it was politic for a peninsular prelate to stress the international dimension of the national venture—in order to derive benefit from the papally inspired crusading movement.[116] The relationship of the *Reconquista* to the eastern crusades is a large subject into which I cannot enter here—except just to say that Spaniards believed that there were lessons to be learned from the experiences of the Christians of Outremer, and in particular cautionary lessons about the fragility of success and the dangers of false optimism. 'Remember Damietta', warned the versifying Guillelmus Petri de Calciata in the mid-thirteenth century.[117] Thus they were able, kings and bishops alike, to foster pontifical anxiety, summoning up dreadful spectres of imminent disaster to the Christian cause in the west as in the east, unless the pope gave them a 'free hand with the resources of the Spanish church.[118] The papal dimension served to tighten the bonds which bound the national church to the crown.

It is not difficult to produce instances of churchmen in the eleventh, twelfth and thirteenth centuries performing on a national

---

for 460 years: A. Duran Gudiol, *Colección diplomática de la catedral de Huesca* (Zaragoza 1965) p 90. The formation of historical consciousness at this period deserves further study.

[115] *De Expugnatione* pp 140, 176. Forty-two years later, in 1189, the German author's account of the foreign crusaders' participation at the siege of Silves is harshly critical of the Portuguese: 'nec laborabant nec pugnabant, sed tantum insultabant nobis quod in vanum laboremus et quod inexpugnabilis esset munitio': *Narratio [de itinere navali peregrinorum Hierosolymam tendentium et Silviam capientium]*, ed C. W. David, *Proceedings of the American Philosophical Society* 81 (Philadelphia 1939) pp 629–30. J. C. Russell suggests that Glanvill may have been the author of the 1147 account: 'Ranulf de Glanville', *Speculum* 45 (1970) p 74.

[116] 'Nulla ergo itineris incepti vos festinationis seducat occasio, quia non Iherosolimis fuisse sed bene interim invixisse laudabile est', in the words of the bishop of Porto in 1147: *De Expugnatione* p 78. The *Narratio* contains no mention of a similar plea, or the need for one, in 1189.

[117] 'Propter hoc satagite: vigiles estote/Maurorum insidias: o plebs cavetote/Quid egerit Corduba: olim mementote/Damiate insuper: cronicam scitote': 'Guillelmi Petri de Calciata rithmi de Iulia Romula seu Ispalensi urbe', ed D. Catalán and J. Gil, *AEM* 5 (1968) pp 549–57, v 91. See C. J. Bishko, 'The Spanish and Portuguese Reconquest, 1095–1492', *A History of the Crusades*, 3, ed K. M. Setton (Madison-London 1975) pp 396–456.

[118] Linehan, *Spanish Church*, chaps 6–9.

plane the public role of their Visigothic predecessors—both directly, for example promoting the peace movement or the cause of good money,[119] and incidentally by the imposition of more restrictive synodal legislation regarding the permitted number of godparents *pro removenda futura impedimenta matrimonii contrahendi inter liberos patrinorum*,[120] thereby providing conditions more favourable to the production of larger Christian families, as desired by the secular rulers.[121] *La iglesia*, in García de Cortazar's words, *se muestra en estos siglos [XI–XIII], en especial en el XIII, como un instrumento nacionalizante al servicio del poder político.*[122]

In times of crisis or political turmoil the role of churchmen could be decisive.[123] An instance of this is provided by the recently discovered decrees of the synod of Segovia in 1166, at a time when the kingdom of Castile stood in mortal peril. King Sancho III had died eight years before, leaving the crown to the two-year old Alfonso VIII. Competing regents fought for possession of the child while the king of León, Fernando II, threatened from the west and seized control of Toledo, and the Almohads were massing in the

---

[119] Truce of God: synod of Toulouges (1027): 'la primera vegada que apareix en la Història una treva general i periòdica': R. d'Abadal, *L'abat Oliba, bisbe de Vic i la seva època* (3 ed Barcelona 1962) pp 234–7; law and order: council of Palencia (1129): E. S. Procter, *Curia and Cortes in León and Castile 1072–1295* (Cambridge 1980) p 23; prohibition of Christians bearing arms against Christians: council of Vallodolid (1155) c 17: ed C. Erdmann, *Das Papsttum und Portugal im ersten Jahrhundert der portugiesischen Geschichte, ADAW PhH Kl* (Berlin 1928) p 57; good money in Catalonia and Aragon from 1155: T. N. Bisson, *Conservation of Coinage. Monetary exploitation and its restraint in France, Catalonia, and Aragon (c. A.D. 1000–c. 1225)* (Oxford 1979) pp 78–83, 102–4.

[120] I. da Rosa Pereira, 'Les statuts synodaux d'Eudes de Sully au Portugal', *L'Année Canonique* 15 (Paris 1971) p 470 (Lisbon synod 1232x48), permitting a maximum of three godparents. Compare Linehan, 'Pedro de Albalat, arzobispo de Tarragona y su "Summa Septem Sacramentorum"', *Hispania Sacra* 22 (Madrid 1969) p 18 note m (Valencia 1258): limit of two.

[121] Early marriage is recommended in Partida 2, 20, 1, not only for its own sake but also because 'quando los homes casan temprano si fina alguno dellos, el que finca puede casar despues, asi que fará fijos con sazon, lo que non podrien tan bien facer los que tarde casasen': *Las Siete Partidas*, ed Real Academia de la Historia, 3 vols (Madrid 1807) 2 p 190. Inheritance patterns, however, tended to frustrate this effect: H. Dillard, 'Women in Reconquest Castile: the fueros of Sepúlveda and Cuenca', *Women in Medieval Society*, ed S. M. Stuard (Philadelphia 1976) pp 71–94, esp p 87. See also L. C. Kofman de Guarrochena and M. I. Carzolio de Rossi, 'Acerca de la demografía astur-leonesa y castellana en la Alta Edad Media', *CHE* 47–8 (1968) p 155.

[122] García de Cortazar p 344.

[123] For example, in the years after the death of Alfonso VI (1109): Valdeavellano 2, pp 392–423.

south. In these circumstances it was the Castilian bishops—describing themselves as bishops 'of the kingdom of king Alfonso' not as bishops of the province of Toledo—who moved into the political void, employing ecclesiastical sanctions to oblige all holders of honours within the kingdom to swear the Castilian equivalent of the Oath of Salisbury to the king, requiring all Castilians to respond to the royal call to arms 'for the defence of his kingdom', excommunicating all the king's active enemies, and appropriating crusading indulgences to the cause—against the Christians of León as well as against the Almohads.[124] The interest of this testimony consists not least in its context. It is common enough in the thirteenth century, when the tide had turned decisively in favour of the Christians, to find bishops blessing the king's forces as they prepare for battle, or fighting alongside them. Here, however, in March 1166, churchmen seem to be acting as the last line of defence against national disaster.

Sixty years later all had changed. The thirteenth century, which began with the victory of Las Navas de Tolosa and before it had run half its course had seen the recovery of Córdoba, Valencia and Seville, has long been regarded by Spanish historians as 'the great medieval century'.[125] The whole triumphal process was recorded by two mitred contemporaries in Castile—Lucas of Túy and Rodrigo of Toledo. While numbers of nameless churchmen at a lower level provided the human sinews which helped to hold the newly won territories together, colonising Córdoba from Burgos or Jaén from Soria,[126] Lucas proudly proclaimed the more than peninsular significance of the success of the Spanish kings: *Pugnant Hispani reges pro fide et ubique vincunt.*[127] The regrettable fact of a plurality of kings was to a degree compensated for by the unity of faith. The beauty of unity was very apparent to Lucas and his contemporaries, and when the record failed to demonstrate this unity—as in the matter of the survival of Visigothic script—then Lucas adjusted the

---

[124] See Linehan, 'The synod of Segovia (1166)', *Bulletin of Medieval Canon Law* 10 (Berkeley 1980) pp 31–44. Note also the marked Visigothic content of the Burgo de Osma MS from which the text is derived.

[125] 'El siglo XIII es el gran siglo de la Edad Media, superior al siglo VI, equiparable en muchos conceptos al XVI'—and without the 'paganism' of the latter: Lafuente 4 p 6.

[126] Linehan, *La iglesia española [y el papado en el siglo XIII]* (Salamanca 1975) pp 104 n 81, 204–6.

[127] *Chronicon Mundi*, [ed A. Scottus], *Hispania Illustrata* 4 (Frankfurt 1608) p 113.

record.[128] Glossing Innocent III's *Venerabilem*, the canonist Vincentius Hispanus preached a similar message, in response to the claim to universal authority propounded for the Germans by Johannes Teutonicus, asserting that no such claim could encompass the Spaniards who, while the Germans were losing an empire by their folly, had successfully created one *virtute sua*—the equivalent of that quality of *strenuitas* recently attributed to the king of Portugal.[129]

Now was the time to orchestrate Isidore of Seville. Aggressive self-sufficiency is everywhere apparent. No longer was it a case of bargaining for foreign aid, as at Lisbon in 1147, but rather of rejoicing in the fact that those few foreigners who had come for the Las Navas campaign had found the weather too hot and had defected, leaving to Spaniards the salvation 'not only of Spain but of Rome and indeed of the whole of Europe too' in the words of a contemporary chronicler.[130] Appreciation of national characteristics is one of the many remarkable features of *Planeta*, the diatribe which Diego García, cleric and chancellor of the king of Castile, dedicated to archbishop Rodrigo in 1218. Diego ranges far and wide, from the Galicians and Castilians, notable for their loquaciousness and pugnacity respectively, to the *franci* whose *strenuitas* is remarked upon, the Scots and Irish for their studiousness and tall stories, as far afield as the pious Ethiopians and the charitable Indians.[131] Not that amidst all the euphoria there were not some elements of self-doubt. Indeed, Diego García is particularly remarkable for the magnificent and extravagant denunciation which his prologue contains of the Spanish episcopate and clergy— *quod verecunde assero, hispanus de hispanis*. They are idolators, no less, because they look to mammon rather than to God: a condition

---

[128] David, *Études historiques* pp 431–9, esp p 437: 'Luc de Tuy a bien vu que l'unité liturgique exigeait l'accord des écritures.' Compare A. M. Mundó, 'La datación de los códices liturgicos visigóticos toledanos', *Hispania Sacra* 18 (1965) pp 1–25, esp pp 20–21; Servatius pp 26–8. See also Linehan, *Spanish Church*, p 63 n 8, for another aspect of the same attitude.

[129] G. Post, 'Vincentius Hispanus and Spanish nationalism' in *Studies in Medieval Legal Thought* (Princeton 1964) pp 482–93. Compare above p 186.

[130] G. Cirot, ed, 'Chronique latine inédite des Rois de Castile (1236)', *Bulletin Hispanique* 14 (Bordeaux 1912) pp 357–8. (The author was almost certainly Bishop Juan of Osma: [D. W.] Lomax, 'The authorship of the *Chronique Latine des Rois de Castile,*' *Bulletin of Hispanic Studies* 40 (1936) pp 205–11). Compare M. Defourneaux, *Les Français en Espagne aux XIe et XIIe siècles* (Paris 1949) pp 182–93; Lomax, 'Rodrigo Jiménez de Rada [como historiador]', *Actas del Quinto Congreso Internacional de Hispanistas (Bordeaux 1974)* Bordeaux 1977) p 591.

[131] *Planeta*, ed M. Alonso (Madrid 1943) p 178.

which the author attributes to a combination of the proximity of 'the gentiles, long-established custom, and papal connivance.'[132]

Book 7 of *Planeta* is entitled *De Pace*, and there Diego expatiates on the themes of *Deus pacis* and *pax vobis*.[133] What distinguished Spanish churchmen, however—lower clergy as well as bishops —was their *un*peaceful demeanour. A century later Alvarus Pelagius—who was in a position to know, being one himself —reminded them that even peninsular bishops were forbidden by canon law to shed blood. Yet his own writings reveal the inconsistency of his own position.[134] The collective experience went too deep. As Diego García was writing, the rural clergy of the diocese of Segovia were hunting their hapless bishop up hill and down dale because he had tried to discipline them; and only recently Innocent III had had to reprimand the bishop of Sigüenza for lashing out with his pastoral staff in his cathedral church and inflicting fatal wounds on one of his congregation.[135] *Presul probus dapsilis, mauris inhumanus* is the admiring description given of one of them in the mid-thirteenth century—and it was not only Moors to whom they show themselves inhuman or by whom they were themselves inhumanly treated. Lafuente's section entitled *asesinatos de varios obispos* refers to deeds done in the twelfth century by their coreligionists.[136]

In this respect then Spanish churchmen were totally identified with the militaristic aspect of the nationalist cause, despite the unease occasionally voiced. It was natural for them, and traditional of them, to regard the new cathedrals being built in the thirteenth century as physical testimony of Christian Spain's resurgence, as did Lucas of Túy, or Jaime I of Aragón in his expression of regret that the bishop of Huesca's see should be in a converted mosque and not in a proper Christian building.[137] In establishing the pre-

[132] *Ibid* pp 175–6, 183–93, esp p 185.
[133] *Ibid* pp 452–7.
[134] Linehan, *Spanish Church*, pp 239–40.
[135] *Ibid* p 240; idem, 'Segovia: a "frontier" diocese in the thirteenth century', *EHR* 96 (1981) pp 482–6.
[136] Ed Catalán and Gil (above n 117) v 75; Lafuente 4 pp 197–9. For further instances see Hillgarth, *The Spanish Kingdoms*, 1 pp 109–11, 2 p 93.
[137] 'Episcopi, abbates et clerus ecclesias et monasteria construunt, et ruricolae absque formidine agros excolunt, animalia nutriunt, et non est qui exterreat eos': *Chronicon Mundi* p 113; R. I. Burns, 'The parish as frontier institution in thirteenth-century Valencia', *Speculum* 37 (1962) p 250. The attitude was deep-rooted: Benito Ruano, 'La historiografía' pp 78–9.

Gothic historical past of Hispania, Lucas and Rodrigo figure as whole-hearted collaborators in the patriotic programme which is so marked a characteristic of this century.[138] There is, however, one important reservation to be made.

Lucas, Rodrigo and Diego García all wrote in Latin. It was not they, but the royal chancery and Alfonso X in his historical works who led the way in the establishment of the vernacular.[139] Churchmen were of course involved in the king's chancery and in his circle of translators, and churchmen in their historical works do not lag behind in their *expression* of nationalism—the monastic author of the *Gesta Comitum Barchinonensium*, for example, writing in the early 1300s felt it sufficient to describe Martin IV as *gallicus natione* to account for that pontiff's treatment of Pedro III after the Sicilian Vespers.[140] It was their expression of these sentiments in Latin that is at issue. The vernacular was the language of men of action, the language in which Jaime of Aragon's memoirs were written, thus establishing the tradition which was to last until Italian humanism made its impact.[141] When Pere Marsili came to translate king Jaime's work into Latin in 1314 he shamefacedly described the operation as being for the benefit of *clerici et claustrales*.[142] By then in Castile the change had come, with Jofré de Loiasa writing in Spanish too.[143] But half a century earlier the vernacular *Crónica de la población de Ávila* (1255/6) is an aggressively secular production, in which the local bishop appears only to be threatened with having his head broken for attempting to stop a fight between Christians.[144] In this crucial matter churchmen lagged behind.

[138] Maravall, *El concepto de España* pp 335–6; idem, *Estudios* pp 138, 151.
[139] See Lomax, 'La lengua oficial de Castilla', *Actele celui de-al XII-lea Congres Internaţional de Lingvistică şi Filologie Romanică* (Bucarest 1971) pp 411–17.
[140] *Cròniques Catalanes* 2, ed L. Barrau Dihigo and J. Massó Torrents (Barcelona 1925) p 77. Elsewhere he characterizes the *gallici*: 'ad vinum insuper anhelebant, in quo continue consueverant balneari'; attributes the victory of Las Navas de Tolosa to king Pedro II; and chides the *aragoneses* for failing to come to Pedro III's assistance against the *gallicos* (pp 87, 52, 90).
[141] Sánchez Alonso, 1 pp 235–45; R. B. Tate, 'Nebrija the historian', *Bulletin of Hispanic Studies* 34 (1957) p 144.
[142] Massó Torrents pp 517–19. The Latin text of pope Nicholas III's charges against Alfonso X in 1279 were translated into Spanish 'por que sopiessemos meior guardar al Rey e tractar en la corte algunas cosas a su servicio': Linehan, 'Spanish church revisited' p 141.
[143] Only the Latin translation of his chronicle has survived, ed. A. Morel-Fatio, 'Chronique des Rois de Castille (1248–1305)', *BEC* 59 (1898) pp 325–78.
[144] *Crónica de la población de Ávila*, ed A. Hernández Segura (Valencia 1966) p 31.

At the same time it becomes possible to observe, as never before, churchmen gingerly parting company from the king and seeking to distinguish their best interests from those of the nation in so far as these were personified by the king. Whether the reasons for this distancing were primarily conscientious or primarily economic, or in individual cases were related to a shift in the balance of conscientious and economic considerations—as so eloquently (because so ingenuously) expressed by Alvarus Pelagius—it is striking that in the case of Castile these developments should have occurred so soon after all the heady euphoria of the 1230s and 1240s. The forty years after 1243 were critical. In that year Rodrigo of Toledo completed the *Historia Gothica*. Here was enshrined the neo-Gothic myth. An official history—the last such indeed prior to the assumption of the historicising function by the king himself —written at Fernando III's behest, it exclusively identified Fernando's Christian subjects with the Visigoths, the people who had once won and had then re-won Spain, and relegated those others who had had a hand in its history—Romans, Ostrogoths, Huns, Vandals etc and Arabs—to a series of appendices.[145] Yet Rodrigo's 'fundamental loyalty', it has been suggested, was not to the king or his kingdoms, the people or the nations, but to Toledo—*urbs regia* —and above all to the church of Toledo.[146] A generation later, after a number of false starts, Castilian churchmen came out into the open. In 1279 the bishops represented themselves to the pope as helpless victims of an infidel despot. Churches and churchmen had been subjected to wholesale persecution. Their income and property was at the king's mercy. They were forbidden to assemble together or to have contact with Rome. The pilgrimage to Santiago had been seriously disrupted by the king's vendetta against the archbishop of Compostela. Because the king preferred Jews to Christians the latter sought to curry favour with the former and allowed themselves to be corrupted by Jewish rites and traditions. King Alfonso himself was held in thrall by a naturalistic atheistic

---

Compare above n 119. For earlier, minor annalistic writings in Spanish see Sánchez Alonso, 1 pp 145–9; A. D. Deyermond, *A Literary History of Spain. The Middle Ages* (London New York 1971) pp 85–6.
[145] *De Rebus Hispaniae*, praefatio auctoris, ed Lorenzana pp 1–4; Sánchez Alonso, 1, pp 131–7.
[146] Lomax, 'Rodrigo Jiménez de Rada' pp 588–90.

philosophy, and surrounded by astronomers, augurers and sooth-sayers. *Claves ecclesie contempnantur.*[147]

It would be tempting, even it were not altogether too neat, to accept these charges on trust and to treat the episcopal *démarche*, together with episcopal involvement in the rebellion of the Infante Sancho against Alfonso X three years later, as marking the end of an era. But this was not so. Churchmen were soon whipped back into line by Sancho IV, and back into a posture of dutiful acquiescence to the royal will, so that when an era *did* end—when the kings of Aragón and Castile put an end in the next century to that peculiar institution, the practice of dating according to the *era hispanica* which went back to Hidacius—churchmen obediently executed the royal decrees of abolition.[148] But I must now end, by reviewing very summarily the most prominent of the fourteenth- and fifteenth-century themes which have a bearing on the subject and ought properly to receive fullscale treatment.

In 1390 the Cortes of Madrid ritualistically complained that no nation was more put upon by the papacy in the matter of provision of foreign clerics,[149] and in the following year the pogrom at Seville ushered in a period of Spanish history which it would be positively indecent to attempt to analyse in a hurry. How are we to interpret the fact that events there were incited by the archdeacon of Éjica, Ferrán Martínez? As the culmination of anti-Semitic tendencies which had been apparent for at least a century?[150] What fuelled the movement—racial hatred and political considerations, or religious zeal?[151] Should we suspect the existence of nationalistic sentiments? Hillgarth concedes that '1391 was a considerable step towards the

[147] Linehan, *Spanish Church*, cap 8; idem, 'Spanish Church revisited', pp 141–7.

[148] J. Villanueva, *Viage literario a las iglesias de España* 20 vols (Madrid 1803–52) 20 pp 3, 175–6; Lafuente 4 pp 384–5. Compare Benito Ruano, 'La historiografía' p 70.

[149] Sánchez-Albornoz, *España: un enigma histórico* 1 p 356; Hillgarth, *The Spanish Kingdoms* 2 p 92; Linehan, *Spanish Church* p 185.

[150] P. Wolff, 'The 1391 pogrom in Spain. Social crisis or not?', *PP* 50 (1971) pp 4–18, esp pp 8–10, 12, 16. For signs of these tendencies in 1279 and 1313 see Linehan, 'Spanish Church revisited' pp 135–6, 140. Note that in 1278 the standard text of anti-Jewish polemic, Raymundus Martini's *Pugio Fidei*, had been completed —compare I. Willi-Plein and T. Willi, *Glaubensdolch und Messiasbeweis. Die Begegnung von Judentum, Christentum and Islam im 13. Jahrhundert in Spanien* (Neukirchen 1980). For Rodrigo of Toledo's relationship with Jews see H. Grassoti, 'Don Rodrigo Ximénez de Rada, gran señor y hombre de negocios en la Castilla del siglo XIII', *CHE* 57–8 (1973) p 91.

[151] See B. Netanyahu, *The Marranos of Spain from the late XIVth to the early XVIth century according to contemporary sources* (2 ed New York 1973).

spiritual "unification" of Spain', but though he adduces evidence of Catalan patriotism, Portuguese patriotism and Aragonese patriotism, he is no more willing to admit of the reality of Spanish nationalism in the fifteenth century than in the seventh.[152] In the course of making the case for the precedence of the Castilian delegation over the English at the council of Basle in 1434, the bishop of Burgos Alfonso de Cartagena stated that the king of Castile-León was *el principal e primero* of the peninsular monarchs. Because the critical acumen which Alfonso displayed in exploding the myth of the journey of Joseph of Arimathea to England was not applied to the legend of Saint James's to Spain, and despite the awkwardness involved in glossing over the murky passage of his country's Arian past, he succeeded in securing his primary objective on that occasion.[153] But what mattered more at a time when Castile was vying with Portugal for a title to the Canary Islands was his identification of the king of Castile as *rex Hispaniae*—though the objection may be made that this was an expression of a purely factitious nationalism equivalent to the nationalism of the national church for which 'royalism would be a more accurate term'.[154] Even more significant—apart from the threat to royal government in general which conciliarism represented—were the contemporary canonistic debates on the question of the possession of *dominium* by the natives of the Canaries (an enquiry potentially applicable to the case of the peninsular Moors), and—this not least—the failure of the Castilian attempt to nullify by amendment (*salvis remanentibus institutis et legibus regalibus*) the effect of the conciliar decree against clerical concubinage.[155] It would beg altogether too many questions to consider here whether it also mattered that the bishop of Burgos was of *converso* stock and the son of a former rabbi.[156]

---

[152] *The Spanish Kingdoms* 2 pp 141, 197–205.

[153] *Prosistas castellanos del siglo XV*, 1, ed M. Penna *BAE* 116 (Madrid 1959) pp 205–33, esp 210, 225–6, 229. See R. B. Tate, 'The *Anacephaleosis* of Alfonso García de Santa María, bishop of Burgos, 1435–1456', in *Hispanic Studies in honour of I. González Llubera* ed F. Pierce (Oxford 1959) pp 391–3; L. Suárez Fernández, *Castilla, el Cisma y la crisis conciliar (1378–1440)* (Madrid 1960) pp 115–20.

[154] Maravall, *El concepto de España* pp 324–5; Hillgarth, *The Spanish Kingdoms* 2 pp 395–6. Compare T. de Azcona, *La elección y reforma del episcopado español en tiempo de los Reyes Católicos* (Madrid 1960) esp chapter 12.

[155] A. J. Black, *Monarchy and Community: Political Ideas in the Later Conciliar Controversy 1430–1450* (Cambridge 1970) p 88; J. Muldoon, *Popes, Lawyers and Infidels. The Church and the Non-Christian World. 1250–1550* (Liverpool 1979) pp 120–130; Linehan, *Spanish Church* p 326.

[156] L. Serrano, *Los conversos D. Pablo de Santa María y D. Alfonso de Cartagena, obispos*

PETER LINEHAN

It is today still possible to make national catholicism (if not too carefully defined) appear the formative influence in the history of medieval Spain, to represent its society as being permanently affected by the attitudes of the eleventh-century papal reformers: Gregorianism without papalism, indeed, to match patriotism without nationalism.[157] Yet the abiding impression is one of churchmen under the king's control and a church 'enclosed within itself', in Lacarra's phrase.[158] From the seventh century to the twentieth a continuing theme can be perceived which is more enduring than any of the components mythical and real of which it is formed. Historians may debate whether the period can be properly described as 'the age of Reconquest'[159], but there can be no doubt that when Cuba was lost in 1898 the bishop of Segovia called for a crusade against the United States.[160] Only the language was unmistakably twentieth-century when Primo de Rivera in 1926 threatened to send the papal nuncio packing and to proceed to the establishment of a national church if Rome would not cooperate in the removal of a prelate suspected of being a Catalan nationalist; the sentiments were those of Reccared.[161] What was remarkable about cardinal Segura's pastoral letter five years later in May 1931 was not the fond belief that the now fallen monarchy had as a rule respected the rights of the church, nor the accompanying evocation of Toledo's Visigothic councils, but its outspokenness at a time when, as that authentically Gregorian prelate admitted, there could be no question of his being rewarded for his pains.[162] The criteria of most

de Burgos, gobernantes, diplomáticos y escritores (Madrid 1942) esp pp 133–48. Compare Castro, The Spaniards pp 188 n 30, 353, where (n 59) the bishop of Burgos is made the author of España en su historia!
[157] V. Cantarino, Entre monjes y̆ musulmanes. El conflicto que fue España (Madrid 1978) esp pp 121–2, 293–305.
[158] Above n 85.
[159] Barbero and Vigil, La formación p 235, and above p 167. Castro's objection to the term was on different grounds. 'Let us imagine as a fantastic case', he suggested in Structure of Spanish History p 376, 'that after a few centuries the Mexicans should succeed in retaking California—Los Angeles and San Francisco—and let us ask ourselves if this would be a reconquest. The retaking of Toledo, Cordova, Sevilla and Granada must be thought of in the same way.' This passage was suppressed in The Spaniards—wisely perhaps. Compare above n 114.
[160] L. de Granjel, Panorama de la Generación de 98 (Madrid 1959) p 180.
[161] R. Muntanyola, Vidal i Barraquer, El cardenal de la paz (Barcelona 1971) p 146.
[162] J. Requejo San Román, El Cardenal Segura (2 ed Madrid 1932) p 139; R. Garriga[, El Cardenal Segura y el nacional-catolicismo] (Barcelona 1977) pp 157–8.

of his episcopal colleagues—though not his[163]—proved to be different when the civil war came, and, after it, the ecclesiastical historians weighed in with some serviceable history. It is not least for that reason that historians must probe these intricate matters with discretion and delicacy. For they are operating on live tissue.

University of Cambridge
St John's College

[163] Garriga pp 251–348.

PHILIP THE FAIR AND THE CULT OF SAINT LOUIS

by ELIZABETH M. HALLAM

THE BISHOP of Pamiers, Bernard Saisset, said that Philip IV of France was like 'an owl, the most beautiful of birds, but worth absolutely nothing . . . He is the most handsome of beings but he knows only how to stare fixedly at men'.[1] Philip the Fair gave away little about himself to contemporaries, and he remains a controversial and enigmatic figure, whose personal involvement with the events of his reign remains a matter of dispute. For a long time, many scholars followed contemporary critics of the king like Geoffrey of Paris in blaming Philip for allowing himself to be duped and misled by evil councillors. More recently, however, analyses of the copious administrative records of the reign have suggested that Philip, while not often in the forefront of negotiations, retained control over his advisers, and that, while he delegated power, he was not dominated by his councillors. Philip has thus become the moving force behind the events of his reign, if not the director of all the details of policy; but this in its turn makes his character and convictions a matter of great importance.[2]

Philip's reign (1285–1314) was a time of rapid change in French politics, society and government, when the monarchy abandoned

---

[1] [P.] Dupuy, [*Histoire du differend d'entre le pape Boniface VIII et Philippes le Bel*] (Paris 1655) pp 643–4: 'Aves antiquitus fecerunt regem, ut narratur in fabulis, et fecerunt regem de quadam ave vocata Duc, quae est magna et inter aves maior et pulchrior, et absolute nihil valet . . . et talis erat Rex noster Franciae, quod erat pulchrior homo mundi, et quod nihil aliud scit facere nisi respicere homines'.

[2] Bouquet, 21 p 205; 22 pp 97, 119; E. Boutaric, *La France sous Philippe le Bel* (Paris 1861); compare more recently J. Favier, *Philippe le Bel* (Paris 1978); J. Favier, 'Les légistes et le gouvernement de Philippe le Bel', *Journal des Savants* (Paris April/June 1969) pp 92–108; [J. R.] Strayer, *Medieval Statecraft [and the Perspectives of History: Essays by J. R. Strayer]*, ed G. Post (Princeton 1971) pp 195–212; B. Lyon, 'What made a medieval king "constitutional"?' *Essays in Medieval History presented to Bertie Wilkinson*, ed T. A. Sandquist and M. R. Powicke (Toronto 1969) pp 157–75; [R. H.] Bautier, ['Diplomatique et histoire politique: ce que la critique diplomatique nous apprend sur la personnalité de Philippe le Bel'], *RH* (259) (1978) pp 3–27; [J. R.] Strayer, [*The Reign of*] *Philip the Fair* (Princeton 1980) pp 3–35.

the lavish crusading campaigns of the previous half century and concentrated on the subjugation of the French principalities of Flanders and Gascony. This involved a series of costly wars, and to finance them, novel expedients were used: the manipulation of the royal currency and widespread taxation of the French kingdom. These in their turn aroused strong opposition in much of French society. Furthermore the French crown moved away from its support of papal policies and from financing papal wars, and began to use the resources of the French church for its own ends, thus alienating the papacy.[3] These changes took place at a time when there was a growing sense of 'national' identity in France, a strengthening of the idea of the French kingdom as a state, which was drawn in large measure from concepts of Roman law and found regular expression in the writings of royal propagandists.[4] The theoretical powers of the king as the head of this state were also given strong emphasis, and at the same time their real effects became far greater. The novelty of Philip IV's dispute with pope Boniface VIII and of the suppression of the Templars are a clear reflection of these changes, for while the Capetian dynasty had long been recognised as the favoured and obedient sons of the popes, Philip later first became their bitter enemy and then virtually dominated them. At the same time, however, the king demonstrated a strong interest in pious activities. He founded and endowed religious houses, he gave generously to the poor, he promised to go on crusade, and this fitted convincingly with the image of a pious and just monarch, the ruler of a kingdom singled out by God, which his advisers gave him in their writings and speeches justifying his actions.

In the past decade much interest had been shown in these pious activities, and a number of historians have suggested that the king became fanatically and obsessively religious during the last decade of his reign, imbued with a conviction of his own righteousness. It was this which motivated him in the trial and the suppression of the Templars, since he was convinced by the evidence laid before him that they were an evil and heretical sect which menaced the moral fabric of the French kingdom.[5] Such an explanation is a beguiling

[3] [E. M. Hallam,] *Capetian France, [987–1328]* (London 1980) pp 278–83.
[4] Strayer, *Medieval Statecraft* pp 251–65, 300–14.
[5] [E. A. R.] Brown, ['Royal salvation and needs of state in late Capetian France'] *Order and Innovation in the Middle Ages: Essays in honor of J. R. Strayer,* ed W. C.

one, since it exculpates Philip from the charges of greed and cynicism which have so often been levelled against him. However, while the lavishness of Philip's religious patronage is undeniable, for it is well attested by the administrative records of the reign, his personal motives and convictions cannot be known; and although the grants he made may well be an expression of religious faith, there may equally well have been an element of calculated propaganda in them, an intention to build up the image of Philip as a pious and righteous king, a fitting heir of Saint Louis, and to emphasise the glory of the Capetian dynasty and its crown. It is well worth analysing the scope and scale of his pious benefactions in order to see whether they throw any light upon these important questions.

The death of queen Joan of Navarre in 1305 has recently been suggested as a turning-point in the development of Philip's religious faith and patronage. Whereas between about 1298 and 1305 he had made some pious gifts and grants, from 1305 onwards he multiplied his charters of concessions, confirmations and privileges to religious establishments, frequently made in return for prayers for the queen's soul. His third testament, drawn up in 1311, expresses an increased anxiety about the welfare of his own soul.[6] It is certainly true that the number of his administrative *acta* concerning such matters to survive increases from about 1305 onwards, but this may be connected with the fact that a fully organised system for registering or enrolling royal instruments did not emerge until about 1304. We also know that a number of Philip's most important religious projects were begun before this date. It is probable that 1297 marks a more significant turning-point in Philip's pious activities than 1305, for in 1297 Louis IX, Philip's grandfather was canonised. The king's strong desire to imitate or to commemorate Louis, the constant harking-back to his reign, is a striking feature in many of his actions which has often been commented upon,[7] and his religious patronage forms part of this picture.

Jordan, B. McNab and T. F. Ruiz (Princeton 1976) pp 365–83; Bautier; G. Spiegel, review of [M.] Barber, [*The Trial of the*] *Templars* (Cambridge 1978) in *Speculum* 55 (1980) pp 329–32; this builds on R. Fawtier, *The Capetian kings of France, Monarchy and Nation (987–1328)*, trans L. Butler and R. J. Adam (London 1960) pp 35, 38–9.
[6] Bautier pp 20–2; Brown p 371.
[7] For example, recently Bautier and Brown.

Louis IX, king of France (1226–70) had died on crusade in Tunis in 1270, but despite the overwhelming evidence of his sanctity and his suitability for sainthood, it was almost thirty years before he achieved this distinction. The canonisation, performed in 1297 by pope Boniface VIII, seems to have been inspired largely by political expediency, as a conciliatory gesture to Philip IV after their first dispute over the taxation of the French clergy.[8] But it gave the Capetian dynasty something it had long lacked, a tutelary dynastic saint, and Philip, his family and advisers manifested immediate interest and enthusiasm for it. In 1298 a major feast was held at Saint-Denis when Louis's body was translated. His head was granted to the Sainte-Chapelle and his heart went to Philip IV's new monastery at Poissy; and later, fragments of bone were presented to other royal monasteries.

Many of Philip's actions seem to recall those of his grandfather very closely. His testaments, dated 1288, 1297 and 1311, were all modelled on Louis's will of 1270. In the 1297 version Philip increased the donations to the religious orders and especially to the Dominicans.[9] Louis IX had had a lifelong commitment to the ideal of the crusade and had geared all his efforts towards the defence of Outremer. In 1311, when the days of the Templars were numbered, Philip, too, promised to go to the east, although this was probably not a serious undertaking, since he also vowed that if he or his son Louis failed to do so, 100,000 *livres tournois* would be donated to the holy land. Ironically this was eventually to be disregarded in the cause of needs of state.[10] Philip also reissued his grandfather's celebrated ordinances for the reform of the realm on a number of occasions, and he and his councillors often cited the customs of Saint Louis as precedents for their actions. For example, the king claimed in 1303 that he was not abusing his regalian rights as Boniface VIII had claimed, but following the usages of Saint Louis and his other predecessors.[11]

Louis's reputation and achievements were clearly becoming

[8] *Capetian France* pp 312–14.

[9] Brown p 369 and n 28.

[10] *Ibid* pp 372–3 and n 47; *Capetian France* pp 213–14; Strayer, *Philip the Fair* pp 296–7.

[11] Dupuy p 94: 'respondit rex quod nunquam fuit, nec est intentionis, vel voluntatis suae in huiusmodi perceptione Regalium praeiudicialem, vel noxiam facere novitatem, sed intendit eis uti quemadmodum S. Ludovicus, et alii praedecessores sui uti consueverunt . . .'

legendary as his cult grew and flourished. The royal house encouraged *Lives* of the king to be written which emphasised his qualities. William of Saint-Pathus, the queen's confessor, was commissioned to write an account of the saint-king in 1302–3, and John, lord of Joinville, Louis's aged friend and councillor, completed his own *Life* in 1309, and dedicated it to the future Louis X. Both of these, like other biographies or panegyrics of Saint Louis produced at about the same time, laid strong emphasis on his religious patronage as well as on his other virtues. His generosity to the poor and the mendicant orders, his religious foundations for the Franciscans, Dominicans, Cistercians, Carthusians, the major hospitals and royal chapels he had built, are all treated with a great interest and only a minor degree of exaggeration.[12] Here, as in many other ways, Philip the Fair seems to have imitated his grandfather closely.

Philip's first and most important project in his grandfather's memory was the Dominican priory at Poissy, founded in 1297.[13] The royal castle at Poissy had been a favourite place of the French kings and their families during the twelfth and thirteenth centuries. Louis IX had been born here in 1215, and such was his attachment to the area that, according to William of Nangis, he liked to be known as Louis de Poissy.[14] It was thus very suitable that a monastery dedicated to him should be sited here. Boniface VIII actually canonised Louis in August 1297, but Philip had probably already begun work on the house before then in anticipation of the event. In the testament he had drawn up in March 1297 he had asked that the monastery he intended to found in his grandfather's memory should be endowed with lands sufficient to produce 3,000 *livres tournois* each year, and that if necessary his executors should complete the foundation.[15] By November 1297 when the house first appears in the royal accounts, the site had been selected and the

---

[12] *Capetian France* pp 232–5 and notes for Louis's religious patronage. Guillaume de Saint-Pathus, *La Vie et les miracles de Monseigneur Saint Louis, Roi de France*, ed M. C. d'Espagne (Paris 1971) pp 57–70; Jean, sire de Joinville, *Vie de Saint Louis*, ed N. de Wailly (Paris 1874); English translation by [M. R. B.] Shaw [in *Chronicles of the Crusades*] (Penguin 1963) pp 342–4.

[13] [A. Erlande-]Brandenburg, ['La priorale Saint-Louis de Poissy'], *Bulletin Monumental* 129 (Paris 1971) pp 85–112.

[14] *Ibid* p 81; Bouquet 20 p 409.

[15] Brown p 370 and n 33.

works begun,[16] and although the foundation charter was not given until July 1304,[17] by that time the priory was, if not complete, ready for occupation by its community of Dominican nuns.[18] Indeed, it had been accepted by the Dominican general chapter as early as 1298.[19]

The convent of Saint-Louis-de-Poissy was a very substantial foundation on which little expense was spared. So lavish were its endowments and privileges that these occupied almost two quires of the *Liber Rubeus*, a major royal register.[20] Equally splendid was the church itself, with its plan modelled on Louis IX's Cistercian abbey of Royaumont, and with its fine statues and ornaments, many depicting Louis and his family.[21] Although it has now entirely disappeared, enough evidence can be gleaned from archeological evidence and from antiquarian drawings to suggest that it was an excellent example of the court style of architecture, evolved during Louis's own reign.[22] Louis's heart was placed in the church as a focus for the royal cult, and in 1311 Philip, whose interest in the monastery remained undiminished, asked that his own heart should be buried here. In 1314, on his deathbed, he augmented the possessions of the priory still further and again admonished his successors to finish off his work.[23] Here they were somewhat tardy, for the final consecration did not take place until 1331, but once completed, the house was a major monument to late Capetian power.

Among the more celebrated religious foundations attributed to Louis IX were nunneries for the Franciscan and Dominican orders. Joinville, following Geoffrey de Beaulieu, Louis's confessor, recounted that Louis 'founded the abbey of Saint-Mathieu at Rouen, to house sisters of the order of Predicants; and also the abbey of Longchamp, for nuns of the order of Minorists. To each

---

[16] Brandenburg p 91.
[17] *GalC* 8 p 1339 and inst pp 373–4.
[18] Brandenburg p 92.
[19] *Collectio* 6 p 542.
[20] [Ed C. V.] Langlois, [*Registres perdus des archives de la chambre des comptes à Paris*] (Paris 1916) nos 631–50.
[21] In 1297 the Dominicans had modified their statutes to allow large, vaulted churches to be built. Brandenburg pp 95–112.
[22] [R.] Branner, [*Saint Louis and the Court Style in Gothic architecture*] (London 1965) pp 135–7.
[23] Brown pp 371–2 and n 46.

community he assigned an ample revenue for their livelihood.'[24] Philip IV founded a sister-house for Poissy at Moncel for Franciscan nuns. It may have been planned as early as 1298, but problems with the land rights and inheritance of the site held up its creation by about a decade,[25] and its foundation charter was not given until April 1309[26] This long and quite detailed document specified that the sixty Clares were to pray for the souls of the king and his family. The house's possessions were listed and it was given an additional revenue of 1,000 *livres parisis* each year, making it a substantial foundation.

Another house actually dedicated to Louis IX, like Poissy, was founded by Philip the Fair in about 1308. This, Mont-Saint-Louis at Pont L'Evêque near Noyon, was a priory for the Carthusian order,[27] also favoured by Louis IX, who had founded a priory for it in c1259.[28] Not much is known about the early history of Mont-Saint-Louis, but in 1310 Philip gave it letters of safeguard and protection.[29] Another major foundation of the king, Royallieu, also had strong associations with Louis IX. This was begun in about 1303 as a small house based on the royal chapel at Neuville-aux-Bois. It was for the Victorine canons of the Val d'Ecole congregation, whose mother-house's initial establishment was widely, though mistakenly attributed to Louis IX.[30] In 1305 and 1308 Philip augmented the possessions of his new house, and it became an imposing foundation.[31] Its church, like that of Poissy, was evidently modelled on Louis IX's Cistercian abbey church at Royaum-

---

[24] Bouquet 20 p 11; Shaw p 343; [E. M. Hallam, 'Aspects of the] monastic patronage [of the English and French royal houses, *c* 1130–1270]', unpubl university of London PhD thesis (1976) pp 263–4 (Rouen), pp 267–9 (Longchamp, actually founded by Louis's sister, Isabella, but endowed by the king).

[25] *Quelques chartes rélatifs à l'acquisition du Moncel par Philippe le Bel* (Beauvais 1900) pp 10–11 passim.

[26] *GalC* 10 inst pp 270–3 (*vidimus* of Philip VI); [ed. R. Fawtier,] *Registres [du trésor des chartes*, 1, règne de Philippe le Bel] (Paris 1958) no 562.

[27] *GalC* 9 p 1013.

[28] Archives nationales K 182 no 66; 'Monastic patronage' pp 230–1.

[29] *Registres* no 1170.

[30] It was probably founded by a group of royal sergeants who had fought at the battle of Bouvines; Archives nationales L 919; *GalC* 8 p 851; 'Monastic patronage' pp 231–2.

[31] P. Guynemer, *Cartulaire de Royallieu* (Compiègne 1911) introduction and pp 17–18; Bautier p 20; Branner pp 135–7.

ont, described by Joinville as 'pre-eminent for its beauty and grandeur'.[32]

Other lesser grants by Philip also fall into the same pattern, as when in 1310 he gave a new site to the Carmelites of Paris, a house founded by Louis IX himself,[33] or when in the same year he founded an intercessory chapel in the Louvre palace.[34] In 1309 he gave sixty Franciscans and sixty Dominicans annual pittances in return for their celebrating a mass to Saint Louis in the Sainte-Chapelle,[35] while in 1310 he granted all the straw used in royal lodging-places to the nearest hospitals and leper-houses.[36] Moreover he gave material help and privileges to many of the foundations of other patrons which were dedicated to his grandfather. The king's own entourage showed a great zeal for the cult; a royal councillor Chevrier founded the church of Montcabrier and dedicated it to Saint Louis, while Enguerran de Marigny commissioned a fine sculpture of Louis at Mainneville.[37] Other royal servants also founded churches and chapels and the king was ready to help them. In June 1309, for example, he granted amortisation on an annual pension of sixty *livres* given by a royal sergeant, Stephen de Nerestang, to a house he was founding which was to be dedicated to Saint Louis. This royal grant was made in return for an annual mass to be said for Philip and his family.[38] The king gave revenues to many chapels dedicated to Saint Louis, as when in October 1306 he gave forty shillings to one such foundation in the Hôtel-Dieu at Pont-Sainte-Maxence.[39]

In general outline Philip's major grants bear some considerable resemblance to those made by his grandfather, but how much was this a reflection of contemporary interests and trends in monastic patronage? Religious foundations were subject to changes of fashion as much as styles of castle building and the art of warfare, and

---

[32] Shaw p 343. Royaumont was founded by Louis IX and his mother Blanche of Castile in 1228–9 in accordance with the provisions of Louis VIII's testament, which asked for a house of Victorine canons to be created in his memory; but the order was changed to the Cistercians; 'Monastic patronage' pp 240–3.

[33] *Registres* no 1118; 'Monastic patronage' p 270.

[34] Langlois no 511; compare 'Monastic patronage' pp 279–82 on Louis IX's chapels.

[35] *Registres* no 672; compare Shaw pp 342–3.

[36] *Registres* no 1134.

[37] Bautier pp 19–20 n 70.

[38] *Registres* no 654.

[39] *Registres* no 285.

royal houses frequently imitated one another in the orders they favoured. Thus Blanche of Castile brought an enthusiasm for the Cistercians with her from Spain, and greatly influenced Louis IX during the early years of his reign. Henry III of England was anxious to imitate and if possible to emulate Louis IX in his pious activities and in creating friaries, hospitals and magnificent churches.[40] The Franciscans and Dominicans were greatly favoured by the French and English courts in the late thirteenth and early fourteenth centuries; in 1308 Edward II founded a major Dominican house at King's Langley, where Piers Gaveston was to be buried. Edward I had established an important Cistercian monastery at Vale Royal in 1281;[41] Philip III of France had by contrast shown no interest in the religious orders at all. What is remarkable about Philip IV's religious patronage is the relatively large number of houses he founded, the variety of orders he favoured, and their close links with Saint Louis.

Clearly these connections with Louis IX are not the whole picture. Other preoccupations of the king also emerge in his religious patronage, such as the importance he attached to the provision of intercession for himself and his wife. Philip also founded two monasteries for the Celestine hermits, and it seems no coincidence that this was an order created by the saintly and unworldly pope Celestine V, compelled to abdicate in 1295. Boniface VIII who had replaced him had been blamed by his enemies for the imprisonment and death of Celestine. In 1300, following Philip's first victory over Boniface, the French king created a Celestine monastery at Ambert. Another larger house followed in 1308–9, Saint-Pierre-au-Mont-de-Châtres, at a time when pope Clement V was being threatened with the posthumous trial of Boniface VIII.[42] Nevertheless, the importance of Louis's cult has probably been underestimated as a factor in Philip's religious patronage, and it must now be asked why his grandfather was so important to Philip, and what this tells us about his piety and politics.

[40] *Capetian France* pp 205, 232, 262; 'Monastic patronage' pp 307–8, 323–6.
[41] [*The History of the*] *King's Works, 1 and 2,* [*the Middle Ages*], ed R. A. Brown, H. M. Colvin, A. J. Taylor (London 1963), I pp 248–57 (Vale Royal), pp 257–63 (King's Langley).
[42] A. Fongoni, *Celestiana* (Rome 1954) pp 125–45; A. Pommier, 'Essai sur le monastère d'Ambert', *Mémoires de la société archéologique et historique de l'Orléanais*

Was Philip's interest in his grandfather's cult a manifestation of obsessive piety, the sign of a king who believed that he was acting as the extirpator of vice and corruption in his realm? It would be dangerous to dismiss such a possibility, since it is impossible to know from the evidence we have what the king's own convictions were. On the other hand it is equally misleading to take documents like royal testaments and the foundation charters of monasteries at face value. These contain many pious formulae but were based on models established by generations of royal clerks. In its sheer scale, Philip's religious patronage appears unusually generous by contemporary standards, but again, such generosity cannot be taken *a priori* as an index of personal piety. Many of the most able rulers of the middle ages, singled out by contemporary writers and by historians for their political skill rather than their religious convictions, were open-handed patrons of monks or friars. William the Conqueror, Henry I and Henry II of England all showed a realistic grasp of the balance between political power and acts of piety;[43] and much later, Henry VII of England, an outstandingly generous patron of the religious orders, is generally reckoned as a man who, while interested in 'the mechanics of medieval piety', was not personally concerned with religious devotion or spirituality.[44] Even Henry VIII is an interesting illustration of this dichotomy, since he refounded at least three monasteries in 1536–7, in the period between the dissolution of the lesser houses and the attack on the greater ones.[45] Henry III of England by contrast tried to use his religious patronage as a screen for political weakness, and was not very successful in so doing.[46] Here Louis IX was something of an exception, for not only was he a firm master of the French church and an able and effective politician, but he geared his administration towards acts of piety and especially towards crusading, his major obsession.[47] So great was his expenditure on religious patronage

---

34 (Orléans 1915) pp 565–665; *Registres* nos 417, 571, 660; *DHGE* 12 pp 102–3; Archives départementales, Loiret H 230.

[43] E. M. Hallam, 'Henry II as a founder of monasteries', *JEH* 28 (1977) pp 113–32; 'Monastic patronage' pp 49–58.

[44] S. B. Chrimes, *Henry VII* (London 1972) pp 298–304; Knowles *RO* 3 p 3; *King's Works 3 part 1 (1485–1660)*, ed H. M. Colvin, D. R. Ransome, J. Summerson (London 1975) pp 187–222.

[45] E. M. Hallam, 'Henry VIII's monastic refoundations of 1536–7 and the course of the dissolution', *BIHR* 51 (1978) pp 124–31.

[46] *King's Works* 1 pp 131–59; 'Monastic patronage pp 154–5.

[47] *Capetian France* pp 213–23, 268–9.

that, Joinville tells us, he was often criticised for it, and his humble dress and the asceticism of his lifestyle were considered unsuitable in a king.[48] Some rulers managed to gain a reputation for piety on no very solid grounds: Robert II of France (996–1031), for example, was a vigorous but ineffectual ruler who, while occasionally generous to religious houses, also exploited the church as a source of rewards for his followers, burned down a monastery and conducted a long adulterous liaison; yet his biographer, Helgaud of Fleury, wrote of him as a model of pious christian virtue.[49] We should thus treat accounts of Philip IV's piety with some caution, and remember that while Ivo of Saint-Denis and William de Nogaret praised his virtuous life, his holy and exemplary death, other writers take a markedly hostile view. Unlike Louis IX's critics, who found him too pious and dominated by the church, Philip's detractors judged him as indolent, withdrawn, controlled by evil councillors.[50]

It is difficult to believe that there was no element of calculation in Philip's religious patronage. If we accept that he directed the major events of the reign, then his was the responsibility for the dispute with Boniface VIII and the trial of the Templars, the manipulation of the coinage and the taxation of the realm. A major thread links these developments together: the king's desperate need for money to finance his cripplingly expensive wars with England and Flanders.[51] This factor was of fundamental political importance in England, where Edward I's demands for war subsidies to defend Gascony and Flanders aroused major opposition in 1297.[52] In France these continuing demands also produced a growing mistrust of a monarchy which, until that time, had remained one of the most popular in Europe. In the face of this opposition the king's traditional virtues, his piety, his enthusiasm for reform and good government like that of Saint Louis needed emphasis. This was particularly the case since the growing opposition was beginning to

[48] *Ibid* pp 263–4; Shaw p 343.
[49] *Capetian France* pp 69–72.
[50] *Ibid* p 308; H. Bordier, 'Une satire contre Philippe le Bel (vers 1290)', *Bulletin de la société de l'histoire de France,* 2 ser, 1 (Paris 1857–8) pp 198–9.
[51] J. B. Henneman, *Royal taxation in Fourteenth century France: the development of war financing, 1322–1356* (Princeton 1971) pp 27–30.
[52] M. Prestwich, *War, Politics and Finance under Edward I* (London 1972) and *Documents Illustrating the crisis of 1297–8 in England, CSer,* 4 series, 24 (London 1980).

use Louis's cult against the extortion of the royal administration. When in 1303–5 and in 1314 provincial leagues and assemblies complained about royal exactions, demands were made for a return to the good laws and customs of Saint Louis. The king tried to meet this by reissuing his grandfather's reforming ordinances, and Louis X and Philip V were to grant the leagues charters of liberties.[53] The parlement party, standing for the traditions of Louis IX and opposing the financial policies of Enguerran de Marigny, emerged at court during the last years of Philip IV's reign. It exercised a strong control over Louis X, Philip's heir, who was to reverse many of Enguerran's policies during his short reign.[54] It was to Louis that the aged Joinville dedicated his *Vie de Saint Louis*, completed in 1309. The seneschal writes of the joy that greeted Louis's canonisation, and comments:

> It has brought great honour to those of the good king's line who are like him in doing well, and equal dishonour to those descendants of his who will not follow him in good works. Great dishonour, I repeat, to those of his line who choose to do evil; for men will point a finger at them and say that the saintly king, from whom they have sprung, would have shrunk from acting so ill.[55]

In twelfth and thirteenth-century France, official cults like those of Charlemagne and Saint Denis had enhanced Capetian popularity,[56] but now a royal cult was being used as a focus of opposition to royal policy. The phenomenon was a familiar one in England where the cults of Saint Thomas Becket and other opponents of the crown had sanctified opposition to the king and had proved far more popular than official cults like that of Edward the Confessor.[57]

[53] A Artonne, 'Le mouvement de 1314 et les chartes provinciales de 1315,' University of Paris, *Bibliothèque de la Faculté des Lettres*, 19 (1912) p 31; and pp 198–204 for the roll of grievances of the people of the bailliages of Amiens and Vermandois (Archives départementales, Pas-de-Calais A 61): for example, 'VI. Item. Comme selonc les anchienes coustumes du tans le saint roy Loys quant li subgit des seigneurs estoient trait en cause par devant les gens du roy d'aucun cas a la requeste d'autruy fust de trouble ou d'empeechement ou de novelete de quelconques cas que che fust . . .' (etc.)

[54] *Capetian France* pp 298–90.

[55] Shaw p 351.

[56] *Capetian France* pp 174–9, 260–3.

[57] J. C. Russell, 'The canonisation of opposition to the king in Angevin England', *Anniversary Essays in Medieval History by Students of Charles Homer Haskins*, ed C. H. Taylor (Cambridge, Mass., 1929) pp 279–90; *Vita Edwardi Regis*, ed F. Barlow, *NMT* (London 1962) pp 112–33.

It was a new experience for the Capetians; indeed, in part it represents the failure of Philip to exploit Saint Louis for his own ends.

In his imitation of his grandfather Philip was surely trying, whether consciously or unconsciously, to associate himself and his regime with the cult and traditions of Saint Louis, emphasising and glorifying the religious dimensions of the French monarchy, playing up its traditional virtues, perhaps to counterbalance the striking novelty of many of his political and administrative actions. His councillors gave emphasis to these qualities in their writings and speeches, as when Nogaret described Philip as the worthy successor to the kings of his line, who had all been enthusiastic champions of the faith and defenders of the church.

> The king has always been chaste, humble, modest of face and in speech,.... full of grace, charity, piety and mercy, always following truth and justice, never a detraction in his mouth, fervent in the faith, religious in his life, building basilicas and engaging in works of piety . . .[58]

This was truly the stuff of which sacral kingship was made.

There was a further, crucial aspect of the stress laid on the king's power and piety, his worthiness as leader and head of the French church and kingdom. For in the early fourteenth century the idea of France as a 'national' state was becoming of increasing importance, and was buttressed by the concepts of Roman law so strongly emphasised by the king's advisers. The kingdom of France was an entity, separate from and superior to other states. It had a territorial unity and a spiritual wholeness, and the king was the embodiment of its virtue and righteousness.[59] Who could have been a better symbol of such a monarchy than its new tutelary saint, Philip's grandfather? It was thus greatly in Philip's interest to emphasise and to imitate Louis IX, and while it might be a mistake to attribute the scale of his religious patronage and his acts of piety to such considerations alone, it is equally clear that in accepting these actions simply at face value, many historians are in danger of falling victim to the king's own propagandists. After all, Geoffrey of Paris, describing the criticisms of the king made by the leagues in 1314, contrasted the reigns of Philip's predecessors with his own. Louis IX had never demanded unjust taxation from his people, and

[58] Barber, *Templars* pp 29–30 from Dupuy p 518.
[59] Above n 4.

the king should behave as his ancestors had done, and not rely on
his worthless piety.

> Croiserie ne penitence,
> Aumosne, oroison ne jéune
> Ne te vaudra ja une prune.[60]

London
Public Record Office

---

[60] Bouquet 22 pp 152–3, esp lines 6577–80.

LITURGY AND PROPAGANDA IN THE DIOCESE OF LINCOLN DURING THE HUNDRED YEARS WAR

by A. K. McHARDY

8 FEBRUARY 1782. This day being appointed as a Fast on the present Troubles and Wars abroad, I went to Weston church this morning at 11 o'clock and there read Prayers proper on the occasion—but there was no sermon after.
8 March 1789. I read prayers and preached this afternoon at Weston Church. Also read with the greatest pleasure a Prayer composed on the occasion on the restoration of his Majesty's Health, which I received this morning.[1]

In offering special prayers upon occasions of national importance Parson Woodforde was following an old tradition. One earlier phase of this tradition which is worth close scrutiny is the Hundred Years War, which affected all sections of the English population, civilian as well as military, clerical as well as lay.

The involvement of the English church in propaganda on behalf of the war effort during this time has been the subject of comment by several writers in recent years.[2] In particular, H. J. Hewitt, in *The Organisation of War under Edward III*, drew attention to the important role of the church in forming public opinion during the first phase of the war, called for more research on this matter, and suggested lines of enquiry.[3] The purpose of this paper is to examine the evidence for one diocese, Lincoln, evidence which is, at present, entirely in manuscript,[4] to see what light can be thrown on the general problems raised by this subject.

---

[1] James Woodforde, *The Diary of a Country Parson 1758–1802* selected and edited John Beresford (Oxford 1978) pp 179, 344.
[2] C. T. Allmand, 'The War and the Non-combatant', *The Hundred Years War*, ed Kenneth Fowler (London 1971); John Barnie, *War in Medieval Society* (London 1974).
[3] (Manchester 1966) pp 160–5.
[4] All manuscripts cited are housed in the L[incolnshire] A[rchives] O[ffice]. The Memoranda Register of bishop Repingdon is shortly to be published by the Lincoln Record Society.

The period of the Hundred Years War, 1337–1453, covered tenures of Lincoln diocese by eleven bishops. Three episcopates can be set aside at once. Henry Beaufort (1389–1404) was bishop during a period of peace; no evidence survives from the time of Marmaduke Lumley (1450) or of John Chedworth (1452–71). A fourth episcopate can also be set aside for there is no evidence about the liturgical impact of the start of the war in the register of Henry Burghersh (1320–40). This is ironic, for Burghersh played a leading role in negotiations both before and after the outbreak of war. In his absence abroad the diocese was administered by Simon Islip[5] and what steps, if any, he took to inform and exhort his flock, are not known.

In the course of the remaining seven episcopates[6] there were some fifty-one occasions on which special prayers were requested in Lincoln diocese. Not all of them were concerned with the war; in a period which saw repeated visitations of the plague and the scandal of the Great Schism there were other public preoccupations besides the war effort. It is sometimes difficult to distinguish between ceremonies made in connection with the war, and more peaceful prayers. This is not only because causes were sometimes lumped together[7] but also because the line between public and private welfare was not clearly defined; the concerns of individuals could have national or international ramifications. For example, prayers were offered for particular members of the royal family, whether ailing or dead,[8] and these were obviously patriotic gestures. Prayers were also requested for those going abroad on various missions which included negotations in both national and personal disputes.[9]

A total of thirty-four requests for prayers were occasioned solely or mainly by the war.[10] Just under half, fourteen, were intended to

[5] LAO Reg 5 (Burghersh, Memoranda) fol 548ᵛ.
[6] Thomas Bek 1342–7; John Gynewell 1347–62; John Buckingham 1363–98; Philip Repingdon 1405–19; Richard Fleming 1420–31; William Gray 1431–6; William Alnwick 1437–49.
[7] 16 June 1385, peace and the English church, LAO Reg 12 (Buckingham, Memoranda) fol 305ᵛ.
[8] The Prince of Wales's soul and the king's recovery in 1376, *ibid* fol 133.
[9] Mandate to pray for Henry duke of Lancaster going abroad to fight Otto duke of Brunswick, his enemy in 1352, LAO Reg 8 (Gynewell, Memoranda) fol 21ᵛ; undated mandate to pray for Richard, bishop of Lincoln, going abroad as an ambassador of the king, LAO Reg 16 (Fleming) fol 247ᵛ.
[10] See appendix.

promote 'peace' in vague terms. Not all exhortations to pray for peace should be taken at their face value. It is difficult to take too seriously prayers for peace offered in 1369 and 1370 when the war was being re-started after a six-year interval. In general, for 'peace', in these mandates, we should understand 'war'.

In contrast, many other prayers were offered in connection with particular initiatives, both military and diplomatic. If mandates to say prayers were indeed obeyed throughout Lincoln diocese, then a sizeable proportion of England's population ought to have been informed about many of the military expeditions as well as about most peace negotiations. In 1342, in the late summer and autumn, prayers were requested for an expedition which the king was to lead to France—in fact, to Brittany to support the Montfort cause.[11] In December 1355, during a period of some organisational complication, prayers were asked for on behalf of Edward III, the prince of Wales and Henry duke of Lancaster, about to make an expedition.[12] By the time the bishop issued his next instructions on behalf of the war effort the expedition in question had already sailed. Henry duke of Lancaster and his forces sailed across the Channel in two relays between 1 and 18 June 1356, but it was not until 24 June 1356 that bishop Gynewell's mandate was issued. This expedition was part of the great pincers movement to be achieved by the Black Prince campaigning in Aquitaine concurrently with the duke of Lancaster's operations in Normandy, but Gynewell's letter described the purpose of the expedition as the acquisition of peace (*pro pace adquirenda*).[13]

During the second stage of the fourteenth-century part of the war prayers were requested in Lincoln diocese for a series of expeditions led by members of the aristocracy: that of the earl of Cambridge and the duke of Brittany in 1375,[14] the earl of Buckingham's *chevauchée* of 1380,[15] the Norwich crusade,[16] and Gaunt's

---

[11] LAO Reg 7 (Bek, Memoranda) fols 3ᵛ–4; E. Perroy, *The Hundred Years War* (London 1959) p 115.
[12] LAO Reg 8 fol 76; [Kenneth] Fowler, *The King's Lieutenant* (London 1969) pp 148–9.
[13] *Ibid* p 151; LAO Reg 8 fols 65ʳ/ᵛ.
[14] Writ, 8 May, *CalCR 1374–7* p 224; episcopal mandate 25 May, LAO Reg 12 fol 128.
[15] Writ of 24 June, *CalCR 1377–81* p 469; LAO Reg 12B (Buckingham, Royal Writs) fols 30ᵛ–1.
[16] LAO Reg 12 fols 253ᵛ, 259ᵛ–60.

Spanish expedition of 1386.[17] Political realities at home influenced
foreign policy and, hence, patriotic liturgy: prayers were ordered
for the earl of Arundel's expeditions of 1387 and 1388.[18] Less
warlike in tone was an order for prayers to be said for Richard II,
the dukes of Lancaster and Gloucester, and for the king's safe return
to England. Bishop Buckingham's mandate for these prayers was
issued on 10 August 1396 so its occasion was probably Richard II's
forthcoming visit to Calais to marry Isabella of France.[19]

Of all the expeditions during the fourteenth-century phase of the
war, that which was accorded most space in the Lincoln registers
was the Norwich crusade. The diplomatic and economic background to this expedition, its failure and subsequent political
repercussions, need not concern us here,[20] but the arrangements
made to gain support of all kinds for this crusade show very clearly
the intertwining of religion and propaganda. By August 1382
Henry Despenser, bishop of Norwich, had obtained from Urban
VI three bulls committing him to proceed against schismatics, and
on 17 September he sent copies to all the English bishops.
Collectors were then sent out to grant indulgences and to raise
funds.[21] Since this expedition was a holy war, it was to be financed
not only by taxes but also by alms. On 15 December 1382 bishop
Buckingham issued a letter explaining this and pointing out that
Urban's letters gave privileges, indulgences, and full remission of
sins to those who contributed to the expenses of the crusade. His
letter asked that people should be urged to contribute according to
their means, and that those bringing contributions should be
allowed to come to their churches.[22] This seems to indicate that
parish churches were to be used as collection centres for alms. On 5
April 1383 archbishop Courtenay issued a mandate to his suffran-
gans ordering exposition of the reasons for the crusade to be made
in all churches, prayers to be said by clergy and laity alike, masses
to be celebrated and processions held.[23] This was forwarded to the

[17] 23 July 1386, *ibid* fol 330.
[18] Writ, 20 March 1387, *CalCR 1385–9* p 309; episcopal mandate 2 April, LAO Reg
12B fol 50. 20 June 1388, *ibid* fol 53[v].
[19] LAO Reg 12 fol 437[v]. The visit to France took place in October–November, C.
Oman, *The Political History of England 1377–1485* (London 1906) p 130.
[20] See M. E. Aston, 'The Impeachment of Bishop Despenser', *BIHR* 38 (1965) pp
127–48 for a full account with references.
[21] *Ibid* p 134 and n 2.
[22] LAO Reg 12 fol 253[v].
[23] *Ibid* fol 259[v].

218

bishops of the southern province by Robert Braybrooke, bishop of London, on 16 April 1383. It was not until 14 May 1383, two days before bishop Despenser's departure from England, that Buckingham put this into execution. He ordered the archbishop's command to be carried out in all churches and chapels of the diocese, as well as in the cathedral; he offered forty days' indulgence as a reward to those who were present, and he was at paints to stress that the expositions of the reasons for the crusade were to be made in English. The financially successful outcome of the exercise, and Henry Knighton's sour comments thereon are well known.[24]

The second, the fifteenth-century, part of the war began in 1415, but, as had been the case in 1337, this commencement left no mark in the register of the reigning bishop of Lincoln. This was Philip Repingdon, in his student days a leading follower of John Wycliffe, but by now a long-time member of the ecclesiastical establishment. But by the time that Henry V returned to France in July 1417 to begin the systematic conquest of Normandy, Repingdon had issued a mandate for prayers to be said for the king's success. This was dated 14 June 1417.[25] Henry V remained abroad from late-July 1417 until the beginning of February 1421[26] and during this time Repingdon issued three more mandates to pray for the king, his brothers and the army in France, two in 1418, and one the next year.[27] Repingdon's successor, Richard Fleming, issued another mandate for prayers, for the king and his army going abroad, on 12 October 1420.[28] Thereafter there is silence until 1432 when mandates of the archbishop of Canterbury and the bishop of London dated 20 and 28 June were executed on an unknown date by William Gray, bishop of Lincoln. The cause, 'for John, duke of Bedford and the other lords and magnates going to France to recover, defend and conserve English rights', probably referred to Bedford's offensive in Brie and the Ile de France during the early summer of 1432.[29] The last specific cause to be prayed for was diplomatic, not military. The ambassadors to the Council of Basle as well as those going to treat with France—'the cardinal of

[24] *Ibid* fol 260; *Chronicon Henrici Knighton*, ed J. R. Lumby RS 92 (1895) 2 p 198.
[25] LAO Reg 15 (Repingdon, Memoranda) fol 172^v.
[26] *Handbook of British Chronology*, ed F. M. Powicke and E. B. Fryde (2 ed London 1961) p 37.
[27] LAO Reg 15 fols 189$^{r/v}$, 200^v, 207$^{r/v}$.
[28] LAO Reg 16 fols 211$^{r/v}$.
[29] LAO Reg 17 (Gray) fols 106$^{r/v}$; *DNB* (compact edition) I p 1084.

England' (Henry Beaufort) was especially mentioned—were the object of an archiepiscopal letter of 4 July 1435. It was relayed by the bishop of London on 11 July, but, once again, Gray's letter of execution is undated in his register. The delegation going to France was bound for the congress of Arras which saw the ending of the Anglo-Burgundian alliance.[30]

Probably all thirty-four mandates were intended, by the bishops of Lincoln, to be obeyed throughout the diocese. Most of the letters entered in the registers were directed, as was usual with matters of diocesan importance, to the archdeacon of Lincoln or his official, though a few were addressed to the dean and chapter of the cathedral. Despite the almost total absence of those reassuring notes which tell us that all the other archdeacons were written to in similar fashion, there is no reason to believe that execution was intended to apply only to selected parts of the diocese. Each was certainly intended to apply to all the places of worship within a given area, for letters entered in the registers in unusual detail speak of special services in conventual churches and in chapels as well as in parish churches.[31]

The mandates almost always give some instructions about the time and nature of the special ceremonies and prayers they ordered, though the amount of detail they contain varies greatly. Probably well-established tradition made it unneccessary for the bishops of Lincoln to descend to particulars when issuing orders about patriotic liturgical practices. It is known, for example, that the Scottish War of Independence had given rise to similar commands to pray for the national cause.[32]

Two characteristics were constant features of the instructions issued throughout the whole period. One was the inducement to obey: an indulgence of forty days was offered to all present on these occasions, whether clerics or laymen. The other was that the special ceremonies were to take place on Wednesdays and Fridays—*quartis et sextis feriis*. These were not, perhaps, the days on which the greatest numbers of people would have been present in church, but they were the days on which it was permitted to substitute a votive mass for the mass of the day.[33]

[30] LAO Reg 17 fols 180$^{r/v}$; E. Perroy, *The Hundred Years War*, pp 290–6.
[31] LAO Reg 8 fols 65$^{r/v}$; Reg 12 fol 96^v; Reg 16 fols 211$^{r/v}$.
[32] LAO Reg 5 fol 503.
[33] *ODCC* p 500.

Liturgy and propaganda during the hundred years war

The ceremonies themselves were to consist of prayers, processions, and masses. Litanies[34] were sometimes mentioned, also psalms,[35] and occasionally, bell-ringing.[36] Probably chance, rather than the desire for a particularly solemn ritual, has left in John Buckingham's memoranda register the detailed account of the ceremonies to be performed in the summer of 1370. Processions, made with great devotion, were to take place in all conventual and parochial churches on Wednesdays and Fridays; they were to consist of both clergy and laity, bare footed. First, the seven penitential psalms were to be sung in the church and the fifteen gradual psalms, devotedly, on bended knees; then the litany was to be sung, and in every mass celebrated for the peace and tranquility of the king and realm special prayers, imploring divine clemency, were to be said in a fervent manner.[37]

Special prayers were the essential element of patriotic liturgy, but their exact form is usually not known. Even their language is in doubt, for Dr. Hewitt suggested that prayers offered in connection with the French war were perhaps made in English.[38] Most mandates offer no details about the form of prayers to be used during these patriotic church services. They speak only of 'prayers' (*oraciones*), 'special prayers', 'pious prayers'. But others talk of a special collect (*collectam specialem*) or even of a special collect with its secret and postcommunion. There are two possible explanations for such reticence. One is that prayers, commissioned for a particular occasion, were distributed throughout the diocese, or even province, with not so much as their cues being entered in the bishops' registers. The other, much more likely, we may suggest, is that the prayers to be used were so much a matter of standard form that anyone receiving so general an instruction would know where to turn for the precise wording of the prayers to be used. This latter alternative is supported by those pieces of evidence which enable us to discover exactly which prayers were to be used on particular occasions.

Such pieces of evidence are four in number. On 30 May 1382 archbishop Courtenay issued, to the bishops of his province, a

---

[34] LAO Reg 15 fols 189$^{r/v}$; Reg 16 fols 211$^{r/v}$.
[35] LAO Reg 12 fol 96^v.
[36] LAO Reg 16 fols 211$^{r/v}$.
[37] Reg 12 fol 96^v.
[38] H. J. Hewitt, *The Organisation of War*, p 163.

mandate to pray for peace. This letter included the special collect, secret, and postcommunion of the Mass for the Mortality of Man, from the Sarum Missal, written out in full.[39] On 14 June 1417 bishop Repingdon, apparently on his own initiative, ordered prayers for the king and his army going overseas, and specified the three prayers from the Sarum votive mass *Pro salubri statu vivorum*[40] In the following year archbishop Chichele, exhorting his province to pray for the king who was in foreign parts, prescribed the prayer beginning *Quesumus omnipotens deus ut famulus tuus rex noster*, with its secret and postcommunion. This is the Sarum votive Mass for the King.[41] It was also the one used in October 1420 when bishop Fleming ordered prayers to be said throughout the diocese.[42] It is interesting to note that this votive mass, on behalf of the king, was preferred even in time of war, to one of the masses for help against enemies. This evidence, for the use of votive masses in well-known forms, accords well with similar information derived from special prayers not connected with the war effort. The recipients in these cases were directed to votive masses in the Sarum Missal for such causes as The Infirm, or for the Serenity of the Air.[43]

How, if not by English prayers specially-written, was patriotic fervour whipped up? Almost certainly it was roused by exposition, in the vulgar tongue, made in church, usually before or during the special ceremonies, but sometimes on Sundays. This was certainly true of ceremonies in support of the Norwich crusade in 1383.[44] Two fifteenth-century bishops of Lincoln also ordered explanations to be made in English as well as the performance of particular liturgical forms. In 1417 Philip Repingdon ordered particular prayers to be accompanied by *sermonibus publicis in vulgari*[45] while in October 1420 Richard Fleming not only ordered special ceremonies on ferias but prescribed expositions in English to be made when the greatest numbers of people were present, probably on Sundays. Fleming's mandate on this occasion, was a lengthy one, and may well have been intended to form, in translation, the basis of the

---

[39] LAO Reg 12 fols 240ᵛ–1; *The Sarum Missal*, ed J. Wickham Legg (Oxford 1916) pp 404–5.

[40] *Ibid* pp 410–1; LAO Reg 15 fol 172ᵛ.

[41] *Ibid* fols 189ʳ/ᵛ; *Sarum Missal* p 397.

[42] LAO Reg 16 fol 211ᵛ.

[43] LAO Reg 12 fol 133; *Sarum Missal* pp 409, 410 nn 1, 5. *Ibid* p 404; LAO Reg 15 fols 124ʳ/ᵛ.

[44] LAO Reg 12 fol 260.

[45] LAO Reg 15 fols 173ᵛ–174.

patriotic talk. He ordered a copy of his letter to be posted in every church.[46]

Fleming, it could be argued, was an enthusiast for this cause. It is reasonable to ask whether his enthusiasm made him unusual among bishops of Lincoln. It is also fair to ask whether, if individual bishops could organise prayers on their own initiative, there could be such a thing as a typical diocese in matters of propagandist liturgy. Many mandates to pray had their origins outside the diocese, the order coming either directly from the crown,[47] or from the archbishop of Canterbury sent via the bishop of London.[48] Thus, in theory, a similar pattern would obtain throughout the southern province. But, not every archiepiscopal mandate to pray appears in the contemporary Lincoln register; contrariwise, some archiepiscopal mandates entered in the Lincoln registers cannot be found in the archbishop's own register.[49] Moreover, many entries in the Lincoln registers give no indication as to the source of the bishop's instructions to pray; there is no means of knowing whether these were the result of episcopal patriotism or whether their form is due to scribal laziness.

Some of the bishops with whom we have been dealing had private enthusiasms which caused them to order prayers for the sake of individuals. Thus John Gynewell, a former servant of Henry of Grosmont duke of Lancaster, issued instructions for prayers to be said for Grosmont who was pursuing a private quarrel with the duke of Brunswick.[50] John Buckingham ordered prayers to be said for the soul of his late master the earl of Warwick.[51] Richard Fleming, about to set off on an overseas mission on behalf of the crown, ordered prayers to be said for

[46] LAO Reg 16 fols 211[r/v].

[47] For example, 20 August 1374, *CalCR 1374–7* p 96; 8 May 1375, *ibid* p 224.

[48] Mandate of archbishop Courtenay to pray for peace, 30 May 1382; mandate of Robert Braybrooke, bishop of London, ordering execution, 5 June 1382, LAO Reg 12 fols 240[v]–1; mandate of archbishop John Stafford to pray for peace, 3 January 1447; mandate of Robert Gilbert, bishop of London, ordering execution, 4 February 1447, LAO Reg 18 (Alnwick) fols 71[v]–2.

[49] Compare mandates to pray in *The Register of Henry Chichele*, ed E. F. Jacob, 3 CYS 46 (1945) with those in LAO Registers 15–18.

[50] LAO Reg 8 fols 21[v], 28[r/v] (1352); for Lancaster's quarrel with Otto duke of Brunswick see Fowler, *The King's Lieutenant*, pp 106–9: Gynewell had served Lancaster as steward (1343–5) and treasurer (1344–6), *ibid* pp 177, 185.

[51] LAO Reg 12 fol 82[v]; for Buckingham's connection with Warwick see *Nottingham Mediaeval Studies* 19 (1975).

himself.[52] It seems likely then, that some prayers on behalf of the war effort were initiated by individual bishops, though this cannot be conclusively proved.

It can, however, be shown that not all their subjects were willing to obey. During the early part of the fifteenth-century phase of the war, in 1418, both archbishop Chichele and bishop Repingdon complained of the negligence, torpor and inaction with which their mandates to make patriotic prayers had been treated.[53] Such unwillingness to contribute, even without cost, to the war effort, is particularly noteworthy on the morrow of Agincourt when, we are led to believe, enthusiasm for Henry V and his war was very strong among his people.

To sum up: we have seen that, throughout the diocese, during almost the whole of the war, non-combatants, even including members of religious orders, were regularly asked to make or to support with their presence, religious ceremonies in support of the English war effort. To do this they used liturgical forms already available in the votive masses of the Sarum use, but sometimes supplemented them with patriotic speeches designed to be intelligible to all. Zeal in promoting such measures may be suspected of particular bishops though cannot be proved, while, long before the military defeats of the late-1420s or the diplomatic disasters of the 1430s, the people of England were beginning to indicate, if not their hostility, at least their boredom, towards a war which, in their opinion, had gone on too long.

University of Aberdeen

[52] LAO Reg 16 fol 247ᵛ (undated).
[53] LAO Reg 15 fols 189ʳ/ᵛ, 200ᵛ.

Appendix

List of prayers offered in connection with the Hundred Years War in Lincoln diocese.

Date(s)	Reason	Reference
3 October 1342	King's expedition to France	Reg 7 fols 3^v–4
19 December 1355	Expedition of king, prince of Wales and duke of Lancaster	Reg 8 fol 76
24 June 1356	King and duke of Lancaster going overseas 'for peace'	*ibid* fols 65$^{r/v}$
August/September 1366	General: war, plague	Reg 12 fol 34^v
24 April 1367	War: king and prince of Wales	*ibid* fol 41
15 May 1369	Peace and plague	*ibid* fol 71
23 August 1370	Peace	*ibid* fol 96^v
5 May 1372	Peace	*ibid* fol 107
20 August 1374	Peace	*CalCR 1374–7* p 96
4 September 1374		Reg 12 fol 125
8 May 1375	Earl of Cambridge's expedition	*CalCR 1374–7* p 224
25 May 1375		Reg 12 fol 128
1 July 1377	Against the French	*CalCR 1377–81* p 82
4 September 1377	Against the French	*ibid* p 92
24 June 1380	Earl of Buckingham's expedition	*ibid* p 469 Reg 12B fols 30^v–1
12 July 1382	Peace	Reg 12 fol 240^v
14 December 1382	Peace and plague	*ibid* fols 253–3^v
15 December 1382	Norwich crusade	*ibid* 12 fol 253^3

14 May 1382		*ibid* fols 259ᵛ–60
20 October 1384	Peace	*CalCR 1381–5* p 590
20 October 1384		Reg 12B fols 42 ʳ/ᵛ
2 November 1384		Reg 12 fols 291 ʳ/ᵛ
16 June 1385	Peace and English church	*ibid* 12 fol 305ᵛ
23 July 1386	Duke of Lancaster's Spanish expedition	*ibid* fol 330
28 August 1386	Peace	*ibid* fols 330ᵛ–1
20 March 1387	Earl of Arundel's expedition	*CalCR 1385–9* p 309
2 April 1387		Reg 12B fol 50
December 1387– January 1388	Peace	Reg 12 fol 346
12 June 1388 25 June 1388	Earl of Arundel's expedition	Reg 12B fol 53ᵛ
28 August 1391	Peace and English church	*ibid* 12B fol 58
		CalCR 1389–92 p 491
10 August 1396	King, dukes of Lancaster and Gloucester; king's return to England	Reg 12 fol 437ᵛ
September (?) 1397	Peace	*ibid* fol 453
14 June 1417	King's expedition	Reg 15 fol 172
6 May 1418	King, his brothers and army overseas	*ibid* fols 189 ʳ/ᵛ
	army overseas	
after 26 October 1418	King going to Normandy to treat for peace	*ibid* fol 200ᵛ

after 5 October 1419	King's expedition	*ibid* fol 207 ^{r/v}
12 October 1420	King and army going abroad	Reg 16 fols 211 ^{r/v}
after 28 June 1432	Duke of Bedford and other magnates going to France	Reg 17 fols 106 ^{r/v}
after 11 July 1435	Ambassadors to council of Basle and cardinal of England and those going to treat between England and France	*ibid* fols 180 ^{r/v}
after 4 February 147	Dissensions, war, kingdom of England	Reg 18 fol 71^v

ECCLESIA ANGLICANA, CUI ECCLESIASTES NOSTER CHRISTUS VOS PREFECIT: THE POWER OF THE CROWN IN THE ENGLISH CHURCH DURING THE GREAT SCHISM

by MARGARET HARVEY

WHY, AT the Reformation in England, did the king rather than the archbishop of Canterbury become head of the church? Why, with so little distress, did the English accept an autonomous national church? To a medievalist such a development seems startling. Though late medieval kings might manipulate the appointment of bishops or regulate provisions they did not dictate to their subjects what constitutes christian faith or practice. Late medieval churchmen did not believe in autonomous national churches but in a body whose visible institutional unity is linked with obedience to the pope, and in theory it was scandalous when in the Great Schism individual rulers decided for their subjects which pope was to be obeyed or became neutral. In late fourteenth century England only a tiny minority of lollards would have dispensed with the papacy and all other solutions to the schism intended to restore the system, not to abandon it.[1]

On the other hand in the unprecedented crisis we certainly find not only a great deal of emphasis on the nationalistic and political aspects of religious allegiance but also as time went on an increasing tendency to turn to the king to produce both a political and a religious solution. Reactions to a crisis often bring to the fore tendencies hitherto unnoticed and so it was in the schism. My heading is a quotation from a work of Richard Ullerston, writing in 1408 to ask Henry IV for help to reform the church, after the king had already decided that Englishmen would attend the council of Pisa, called by cardinals in defiance of the accepted pope and

[1] This paper summarises material I hope to publish in a book. I would like to thank Professor D. M. Loades and Dr A. W. Orde for a great deal of help.

destined to depose him.[2] By 1408 evidently it was the king (presumably with the parliament) and not the archbishop nor a general council who had the real power to ensure reform in England.

In this paper I wish to discuss first of all the question of allegiance in 1378 and then two most important crises: the period 1394 when attempts were made to heal the schism by persuading both popes to resign and to force them to comply by withdrawing obedience; and the decision in 1408 to support the council of Pisa. I shall not discuss the council of Constance because Professor Crowder's work in emphasising the firm control of the king over the English delegation has sufficiently made my point for me.[3]

Let us begin with the question of allegiance. The early stages of the schism helped to emphasise national religious identity over against schismatics, many of whom were also political enemies. In November 1378 at the parliament of Gloucester the English government reaffirmed allegiance to Urban VI, in reply to a request for support from the rebellious cardinals.[4] From then until 1408 England supported the Roman line of popes and Europe soon divided into two obediences roughly based on its existing political divisions.

At the time not a few observers explained allegiance quite simply in terms of politics. Froissart is typical: 'Ye know well how all England was obeissant to Urban, as well the church as the people, because the French king was Clementine and all France.'[5] The truth however was more complex.

One must distinguish between initial allegiance and the

[2] From the covering letter to the king in Ullerston's *Petitiones* [*quoad reformationem ecclesie militantis*], in Oxford, Magdalen College, MS 89 fols 31$^{r/v}$. The *Petitiones,* without the covering letter, are printed in H. Von der Hardt, *Magnum Oecumenicum Constantientie Concilium,* 4 vols, (Frankfurt/Leipzig 1700) 1 cols 1126–71.

[3] C. M. D. Crowder, 'Henry V, Sigismund and the Council of Constance, a re-examination', *Hist St* 4 (1963) pp 93–110.

[4] *Rotuli Parliamentorum* (London 1783) 3 p 48; *Statutes of the Realm,* (London 1816) 2 p 11. I have discussed the question of the case for Urban in ['The case for Urban VI in England to 1390'], *Genèse et Débuts* [*du Grand Schisme D'Occident, 1362–1394, Colloques Internationaux du Centre National de la Récherche Scientifique,* No 586 (Paris 1980)] pp 541–60.

[5] *The Chronicles of Froissart,* trans John Bourchier, Lord Berners, (Globe edition 1913) p 295 (chapter 428). The chapters are not identical with the original divisions. *Chroniques de J. Froissart,* ed G. Raynaud, (Paris 1899) 2, bk 2 cap 359 p 86.

continued schism. Space forbids too much detail here about the parliament of Gloucester but a few points need to be emphasised. Government in 1378, of course, is difficult to define because the king was a child and at the Parliament the question of allegiance to the pope was left for discussion to archbishop Sudbury of Canterbury and the clergy.[6] The archbishop then came before the parliament and made the case for Urban, which was adopted. Afterwards the secular arm enforced allegiance. The archbishop used as evidence bulls from the dissident cardinals which requested support against the pope,[7] and perhaps at that stage the whole matter looked like a domestic quarrel in the curia. Urban's reputation won the day for him.[8] From the start he had seemed a reformer and the rebellion by the cardinals was viewed as typical behaviour from a group who were already much disliked in England for political reasons and who now seemed to be merely resisting the reforming zeal of the pope.[9] Sudbury evidently distrusted the cardinals as witnesses[10] and at first even so bitter a critic of the papacy as John Wycliffe took this view of the quarrel[11]

Since the English were well-informed it seems likely that by the time of the parliament they knew that the largely French group of rebel cardinals had elected as antipope a relative of the king of France, but that was not what dictated the English decision.[12] At first it was not certain that the French king would support Clement VII and as far as can be ascertained the English choice was made in ignorance of French allegiance.[13] The English were in fact opting for the status quo.

[6] *Eulogium Historiarum*, [ed F. S. Haydon], 3 vols, *RS* 9 (London 1863) 3 pp 346–7.
[7] [T. Walsingham,] *Historia Anglicana*, [ed H. T. Riley], 2 Vols *RS* 28 (London 1863) I p 381. The cardinals' bull was probably *Exigit Sancte*, printed from Sudbury's register, Wilkins 3 pp 128–9.
[8] See *Historia Anglicana* I pp 381–2 for a typical view. For views of leading Englishmen in Rome see [L.] Macfarlane ['An English account of the election of Urban VI, 1378,'] *BIHR* 26 (1953) p 80.
[9] For English attitudes to the cardinals see Easton's view, Macfarlane p 84.
[10] Summary of Sudbury's sermon at the parliament, *The Anonimalle Chronicle 1333–81*, ed V. H. Galbraith (Manchester 1927) p 119.
[11] There are many examples of Wycliffe's initial enthusiasm for Urban. See for instance *Letter to Pope Urban*, J. Wycliffe, *Opera Minora* ed J. Loserth, *Wyclif Society* (London 1913) pp 1–2.
[12] See *Genèse et Débuts* for argument that the English were very well informed.
[13] Roger Foucault, the cardinals' envoy, said in 1386 that his *processus*, seized by the English government, made no mention of the election of Clement VII: A[rchivo] S[egreto] V[aticano] Arm 54 Vol 16 fol 144ᵛ.

There is no question of the decision being forced on an unwilling parliament. The schism was only a minor matter at Gloucester: much more to the fore was the question of liberties of the church, felt to have been threatened by a recent violation by government servants of the sanctuary of Westminster Abbey.[14] This was the perfect atmosphere for an opponent of the government to complain that allegiance to an unlawful pope (Urban) was being foisted on the people. No such thing was said.

Thus it might seem that the question of allegiance was treated in England as a religious matter to be settled by the religious authorities. In fact this is far from the case. First of all politics entered the schism from the start. It is important to realise that contemporaries took it for granted that allegiance in the schism would be by nation. The dissident cardinals and the rival popes addressed themselves to governments as well as to church leaders and all over Europe the role of governments was as important in determining allegiance as the role of ecclesiastics. In England the decision may look more like Sudbury's than it really was because of the minority of the king, but even then it was taken for granted from the start that the whole nation would adopt one loyalty. Politically and religiously this was the only acceptable course. Wycliffe might believe that the question who was pope was essentially indifference: any individual might be *prescitus*.[15] Other churchmen, who believed the papacy essential, spoke as if those adhering to the antipope were in danger of damnation. The government certainly acted, most of the time, at least in public, as if to support the antipope was *ipso facto* to be guilty of the sin of schism[16] Proselytising for the other side was not allowed.[17] England

---

[14] E. Perroy, 'Gras profits et rançons pendant la guerre de cent ans: l'affaire du comte du Denia', *Mélanges d'Histoire du Moyen Age, dédiés à la memoire de Louis Halphen* (Paris 1951) pp 573–86.

[15] This is implied by J. Wycliffe, *De potestate Papae*, ed J. Loserth, *Wyclif Society* (London 1907) pp 251–5.

[16] Exceptions were made for political expediencey. See the treatment of the Hospitallers, who acknowledged the anti-pope, C. L. Tipton, 'The English Hospital during the Great Schism', *Studies in Mediaeval and Renaissance History* 4 (Lincoln, Nebraska 1967) pp 91–124, esp p 99. For attitudes to schismatics see letter of Oxford University, 1396, [G.] Ouy, ['Gerson et L'Angleterre', *Humanism in France*, ed A. H. T. Levi] (Manchester 1970) p 62. The Lollards were condemned for suggesting that no pope was needed, but that we could live *more Grecorum*, *Fasiculi* [*Zizaniorum*, ed W. W. Shirley *RS* 5 (London 1858)] p 494.

[17] Foucault was temporarily imprisoned, [E.] Perroy, *L'Angleterre* [*et le Grand*

was fortunate in being sufficiently united politically for no-one to be able to exploit the schism as a source of rebellion but the matter of loyalty could not be left to the individual conscience as much for political as for religious reasons.

Once the schism was established allegiance was reinforced by the fact that Clement VII was related to the French king and rapidly gained his support. This strengthened belief in the righteousness of the cause of 'noster Urbanus' and there is plenty of anti-French polemic to be found in the English chroniclers who write on the schism.[18]

This prejudice was encouraged by the support of church and state for the 'crusades' of the bishop of Norwich and of John of Gaunt.[19] These crusades emphasised for the general public the confusion between schismatics and political enemies. The English were encouraged by the crusade propaganda to see themselves as the supporters of Christ against the unrighteous French or Spaniards. Thus, for instance, in 1386 a carmelite preacher supporting Gaunt's crusade to Castille, defended it against the criticism that we should not fight our fellow Christians, by maintaining that the Spaniards were not such good Christians as the English because they were denying the article of faith 'one holy church'.[20] Furthermore he rebutted a criticism of the crusade which held that it was contrary to charity to fight since we were bound to forgive those who trespassed against us, by alleging that the injuries which the pope and Gaunt were avenging were not their own personal wrongs but injuries to Christ and his church. The sordid political realities of these crusades contrast painfully with all this lofty theory but it may have had its effect: the crusades did not lack recruits.

Positions hardened as the schism continued. Political considera-

---

Schisme] (Paris 1933) pp 56–7; the cardinal of Poitiers was refused entry in December 1378, [N.] Valois, [*La France et le Grand Schisme*], 4 vols (Paris 1896) I pp 154, 243; two other envoys ended in the Tower in 1379, Valois I p 243; William Buxton, OP, was arrested in 1384, Wilkins 3 pp 191–2.

[18] *Historia Anglicana*, I p 382, 393–4 is typical.

[19] For Despenser's crusade see Perroy, *L'Angleterre* pp 166–209; M. Aston, 'The impeachment of Bishop Despenser', *BIHR* 38 (1965) pp 127–48. For Gaunt's crusade see Perroy, *L'Angleterre*, pp 211–68; P. E. Russell, *English intervention in Spain and Portugal in the time of Edward III and Richard II* (Oxford 1955) pp 400–48, esp p 409.

[20] Fragment of a sermon, *Fasciculi* pp 506–11.

tions made the problem of healing more difficult but also ensured that only politically acceptable solutions had any hope of success. No theologically or canonically acceptable answer was politically neutral and realistic ecclesiastics must rapidly have realised that the schism was bound to continue if the rulers of Europe refused to accept the solutions proposed. The situation was in fact very favourable to an increase in royal initiative. The schism had revealed a huge gap in traditional ecclesiology, which could be covered neither by traditional canon law nor theology. The fourteenth century had been caught without an adequate theology of the government of the church and the answers which the canon lawyers could produce did not help in the particular difficulties of a schism of long standing. Though scholars tried very hard to produce acceptable answers from the theories of earlier academics, these theories were only hypotheses and not doctrines of the church.[21] The schism has sometimes been called a quarrel about law, but in fact the problem was primarily theological in that it really concerned the divine plan for the government of the church.[22] The experts were offering to the politicians various competing theories each presented as respectable and at least compatible with tradition: from the same basic raw material of canon law and theology the most diverse theories could be designed. In these circumstances it was easy for a ruler to choose the theory which best suited the national interest, secure in the knowledge that a good case could be made out for almost anything that he wished to do.

In England no-one seems to have considered trying to solve the problem of the schism by peaceful means until about 1395[23] when a debate began among the learned about the relative merits of various methods of ending the schism including a general council or resignation of both popes. In the light of the theme of this paper it is important to be clear where the initiative for this debate began. It certainly preceded a royal order which came late in 1395 to Oxford

---

[21] B. Tierney, *Foundations of the Conciliar Theory* (Cambridge 1955).

[22] The latest supporter of this view is R. N. Swanson, *Universities, Academics and the Great Schism* (Cambridge 1979) p 23. See W. Ullmann, *The origins of the Great Schism* (London 1948) pp v–vi.

[23] This date is disputed by J. J. N. Palmer, 'England and the Great Western Schism', *EHR* 83 (1968) pp 516–18, but for purposes of this paper his argument would strengthen mine, since he contends that it was the English government which took the lead in the moves to end the schism, even from 1389.

to discuss the matter.[24] On the other hand the terms in which Oxford was discussing make it very clear that the ideas were not original but were imported from France.[25] Before 1395 there is no evidence that Oxford itself had been interested in methods of bringing the schism to an end and the academics were not importing the controversial works being written on the continent. Why then did interest begin in 1395? Undoubtedly because the question then became a pressing matter of politics in the peace negotiations between France and England. By the time Oxford began to discuss these matters the king of England was already involved, as was inevitable. Since the chief opponent had been being denounced as an immoral schismatic for years it was essential to find a solution to the ecclesiastical problem at the same time as the political one. Hence there was no need for the scholars to argue whether or not the secular ruler should be involved: his involvement was unavoidable. The argument was about what he could do.

As part of the negotiations over a peace settlement the French offered Richard II a policy of papal resignation (*cessio*) and then, when the popes refused to resign, offered withdrawal of obedience (*subtractio*). In connection with my theme it is important to stress that *cessio* was adopted by the French crown as its sole policy in the schism for political reasons. When defending it in 1394/5 the university of Paris said that it would 'save the honour of both sides', and undoubtedly one of its chief merits was that it avoided any mechanism for pronouncing on the legitimacy of either pope, which would have involved declaring which rulers of Europe were schismatics.[26] Any such idea would have been very difficult to sell to allies. The most traditional way to end a schism was to hold a general council but this of course was very difficult because, in theory, it had to be called by a pope, and again it would involve deciding which pope was legitimate.

By 1395, when these ideas had become of political importance, there were factors at work which were favourable to giving the king a large say in any solution to the religious question. First of all

[24] Perroy, *L'Angleterre*, pp 338–9.

[25] For the earlier discussion in Oxford in 1395 see M. Harvey, 'Two *questiones* on the Great Schism by Nicholas Fakenham, OFM.', *AFH* 70 (1977) pp 102–8.

[26] The key letter from Paris was *Quoniam Fideles*, of 26 August 1395. I have used Paris BN Fonds Lat. 12542 fols 11–16^v, with Lambeth Palace 194 fols 1–13^v and BL Royal MS 6 E III fols 77–80. See Perroy, *L'Angleterre* pp 366–7; Valois 3 p 70 n3; E. F. Jacob, *Essays in the Conciliar Epoch* (Manchester 1953) pp 61–2.

was a general agreement that in certain ecclesiastical crises secular rulers had a duty to help the church. This view was summed up for instance by the words of the letter which the university of Oxford sent to the king in reply to his order to it to discuss *cessio* in 1395.[27] Quoting canon law the university pointed out that where priests were not strong enough to prevail, the secular power must come to the rescue of the church and that kings would have to answer to God for the way they had acted in preserving church peace and discipline.[28] A view like this, of course, was susceptible of many interpretations. What may have convinced some conservatives to allow Richard to take considerable initiative was a local problem which was felt by many to have grown much worse because of the schism. This was the problem of lollardy. By 1395 many churchmen seem to have been convinced that lollardy was spreading and some writers on the schism thought that this was happening because of the weakness which the schism caused.[29] It was true that Wycliffe had survived without severe ecclesiastical penalties because of the weakness of the central ecclesiastical authority[30] and many churchmen were convinced that the Peasants Revolt was the result of heretical preaching. We find several writers in the years 1394–9 saying that schism allows heresy and sedition to become rampant.[31]

No-one who was orthodox believed, of course, that the king could decide on any policy he liked. The Oxford letter of 1396, for example, makes it plain that he must act at the behest of the church; in other words he had at least to respect doctrine and canon law[32] Richard II accepted this in theory and it is clear that when he consulted Oxford in 1395 about the legality of *cessio* he did so ostensibly because as a layman he needed the advice of the experts.

---

[27] Printed Ouy pp 56–73.

[28] Ouy p 57, citing *Decretum* c 23 q 5 c 20.

[29] On lollardy in general see M. Aston, 'Lollardy and sedition', either in *PP* 17 (1960) pp 1–44 or in *Peasants, knights and heretics*, ed R. H. Hilton (Cambridge 1976) pp 273–318. For the connection between lollardy and schism see Bodleian Library, Oxford, Digby MS 188 fols 62–6, a fragment of a *questio* by a canonist referring to lollardy fols 66[r/v]. See also Nicholas Radcliffe, an *opinio* in BL Royal MS 6D X, esp fol 282[v] asking secular rulers to use force to help pope Boniface IX and the church, now oppressed with schism and lollardy.

[30] K. B. McFarlane, *John Wycliffe and the beginnings of English Non-conformity* (London 1952) p 89.

[31] Above note 29.

[32] Ouy p 57.

However, from his point of view the obvious gap in ecclesiology was very useful and we find with interest that he did not simply ask for expert advice and then wait passively for it to be given before he acted. In 1395 probably[33] and in 1399 (when asking about *subtractio*) certainly[34] he summoned by writ suitable scholars not resident in Oxford to be consulted. In 1399 the assembly included the royal chancellor and several bishops who were primarily royal servants.

The documents produced by these procedures can be considered official, in fact political documents, and not, as some scholars have considered them, scholarly products of a group of academics.[35] The latter view has arisen because, whereas the Oxford letter of 1396 thought that *cessio* would not work and favoured a general council, Richard nonetheless adopted *cessio* and agreed late in 1396 to ask Boniface IX to resign.[36] Hence some historians have assumed that he and the university did not agree.[37] This is very unlikely. Richard allowed the letter advocating a general council to be delivered to the French king as part of the peace negotiations.[38] Besides many contemporaries spoke of it not as a letter of Oxford but as a letter of the English, that is representing the views of the English government.[39] Almost certainly this explains why there are so many copies of it in foreign libraries.[40] Richard did not press for a council at this point, it is true, but that is more likely to have been because he found that the French were determined to try *cessio* and therefore he agreed to try it also. Oxford had not condemned *cessio* if it were

---

[33] PRO E 403/554 m.8, writ from Richard II dated 23 October 1395 summoning from different parts of England suitable doctors of law and other clerics of Oxford to appear before him on 30 November.

[34] [M.] Harvey, 'The letter [of Oxford University on the Schism, 5 February 1399', *A[nnuarium] H[istoriae] C[onciliorum]* 6 (Paderborn 1974) p 129.

[35] Swanson pp 112–13.

[36] See discussion of this, Harvey, 'The letters [of the University of Oxford on withdrawal of obedience from pope Boniface IX',] *SCH* 11 (1975) pp 187–98, esp p 188.

[37] For example Jacob, *Essays*, p 64 'Richard was out of sympathy with the line taken by Oxford'.

[38] Perroy, *L'Angleterre*, pp 376–7; Valois 3 p 78; *Chronique du Religieux de S Denys*, ed L. Bellaguet, 6 Vols, *Documents Inédits sur l'histoire de France* 6 (Paris 1840) 2 pp 432–4.

[39] For instance ASV Arm 54 vol 24 fol 248ᵛ, a refutation of the French attack on the *via justitiae*. The French had said that kings would not accept it but 'Rex Anglorum et sui subjecti eciam hoc requirunt, ut apparet ex epistola per eos missa Regi Francorum.'

[40] At least seven continental manuscripts: a large number for an English work on the schism.

uncoerced. The university had simply said that it would not work.[41]

In the event this proved a true prophecy. Neither pope would accept the policy and the French therefore called on Richard to put into effect what they saw as the essential corollary to *cessio*: withdrawal of obedience.[42] Richard did not withdraw obedience at once but called on both universities to pronounce on its acceptability. Both pronounced in favour of a general council, Oxford this time giving considerable detail about what this entailed.[43] Once more historians have claimed that Richard had intended to withdraw obedience but did not, either because he could not get the church to agree (and in this case Oxford's views represent the church) or because, for purely political reasons, he wished to hedge.[44] Again I think these views are mistaken. There seems no question of Richard disagreeing with the university of Oxford, since he went to lengths to pack the meeting which produced the letter. Furthermore there is no evidence that Richard had ever agreed to withdraw obedience except evidence from French sources.[45] Certainly the instructions which Richard gave to his ambassadors to Boniface IX to persuade the pope to resign talk only of free resignation and give no hint of any sanctions.[46] *Cessio* and *subtractio* went together in French eyes, but were not necessarily part of one policy. If I am correct Richard had always thought that a general council was better and would therefore naturally fall back on it when *cessio* failed. It is thus important that the Oxford letter which advocates this scheme in 1399 includes a plan for a very unorthodox council indeed, assembled by order of secular rulers in defiance of the pope.[47] Oxford did not even want the council to consider withdrawal, but such a body would necessarily involve some form of coercion of the pope.

We do not know what Richard intended to do next because he was deposed, but the evidence suggests that the real decisions about

---

[41] Ouy p 66.
[42] Harvey, 'The letters', p 188.
[43] Details Harvey, 'The letters', pp 190–8. For edition see note 34 above.
[44] Harvey, 'The letters', pp 188–9 for details.
[45] Harvey 'The letters', pp 189–90 for some details of the evidence that the English did not agree to withdraw.
[46] The instructions are ASV Arm 54 vol 28 fols 211–12^v.
[47] Details, Harvey, 'The letter', *AHC* pp 130–2.

church policy between 1394 and 1399 were made by him and that the church in England accepted this.

The same can be said even more certainly about the final crisis which I wish to examine: the crucial decision to support the council of Pisa, called by dissident cardinals in defiance of pope Gregory XII in 1408 and determined to depose him. All the important decisions in this affair were taken by the government. First in July 1408, when word came that Gregory had broken his coronation oath by making new cardinals, convocation agreed to withdraw money from the curia and to send a delegation to threaten withdrawal of obedience if the pope did not act to end the schism.[48] This was in fact the king's decision. He went in person to Lambeth to urge this policy on the committee of clergy.[49] In the event the full policy was not carried out and no delegation left, perhaps because the government was caused to hesitate by receiving an invitation from Gregory to attend his own council or because the king then became very ill.[50] Whatever the cause for hesitation however the next decisive step-the decision to send delegates to the council of Pisa—was a government decision.[51] The clergy were present when cardinal Ugguccione addressed the king to ask support for Pisa but all the signs are that the king (that is, the royal council) took the decisions.[52] When the convocations next met it was to choose delegates to send, not to debate whether to attend.[53] This decision was in fact of crucial importance and one would have expected widespread clerical debate but there is little evidence.

Though we do not know as much about the council of Pisa as about the council of Constance there is some evidence that the king influenced the delegates. There were some purely royal representatives at the council but some delegates doubled their capacities as ecclesiastical and royal proctors.[54] One of the Canterbury proctors

---

[48] Harvey, 'England and the Council of Pisa, [some new information'], *AHC* 2 (1970) pp 276–8.

[49] *Eulogium*, 3 p 412.

[50] See the letters of credence for Henry's envoys returning from Gregory, BN Fonds Lat 12542 fol 109^v and Henry's reply B. L. Harley 431 fols 14^v–15^v.

[51] Harvey, 'England and the Council of Pisa', p 280.

[52] The king had sent his *requisicio* before the orders went to the convocations but of course the results of the *requisicio* could not have been known before the clergy met to choose delegates, Harvey, 'England and the Council of Pisa', p 281–2.

[53] For convocations 'England and the Council of Pisa', p 282.

[54] Some details are available in my thesis (DPhil 1964) in the Bodleian Library, Appendix I B.

signed his acceptance of the deposition of the popes as 'one of the proctors by the will of the king for the province of Canterbury'.[55] These Canterbury proctors seem to have taken a special *procuratorium* to cover their position as royal representatives and this specifically forbade them to discuss anything which affected the royal prerogative.[56] Almost certainly papal provisions were included under that heading. Thanks to Robert Hallum, the bishop of Salisbury who was leader of the group, the delegates took with them a list of reforms for the council to consider, drawn up by Richard Ullerston, fellow of the Queen's College, Oxford.[57] It is very noticeable that the list did not contain any suggestions for the alteration of the provision system. More important, perhaps, is that it was in effect a series of requests that the papacy cease to interfere in the internal workings of the local church. Ullerston certainly believed in the papacy, but he wished its activities to be curtailed. Furthermore, though he wished his reforms to have the backing of the council, he presented them to the king, saying, 'I know that many of the reforms cannot be put into effect nor duly executed without the protection and strength of princes, considering the weakness of priests', and asking Henry to consider the weakness of *Ecclesia Anglicana*, using the phrase which I have taken as my heading to remind the king of his duty to effect such reforms as might be needed.[58] When one realises that this council was one which had been called in defiance of the pope and was to depose him, and that the delegates were attending because the king sanctioned it, the picture is far from traditional. It is worth

[55] 'unus de procuratoribus ex voluntate regis Anglie pro provincia Cantuariensis ecclesie', Thomas Chillenden signed thus and included Robert Hallum and Henry Chichele in this category, J. Vincke, *Shriftstücke zum Pisaner Konzil, Beiträge zur Kirchen und Rechtsgeschichte* 3 (Bonn 1942) p 198 no 170. They were the delegates chosen by the Canterbury province.

[56] Included in the account of convocation was a *procuratorium* to dissent 'hiis que inibi, quod absit, in corone regni Anglie, sive regalie domini nostri regis prejudicium fuerint tractata . . .' with orders to work for the revocation of any prejudicial measures, Wilkins 3 p 312. What seems to be the purely ecclesiastical *procuratorium* follows in Arundel's register headed *Aliud procuratorium ad interessendum in Concilio Pisano*, Wilkins 3 pp 313–14; Arundel's register (Lambeth Palace Library, London) fol 9. This latter is the *procuratorium* which appears in foreign sources.

[57] *Petitiones* as note 2 above. For Ullerston see Emden (P 3 pp 1928–9, and my thesis, with also A. Hudson, 'The debate on bible translation, Oxford 1401', *EHR* 90 (1975) pp 1–18.

[58] From the covering letter to the king as note 2 above.

remembering also that the pope who might be expected to put these reforms into operation for the whole church, Alexander V, was only accepted by the church in England after the king announced that he would accept him.[59] In fact by 1409 the king decided the question of allegiance.

I conclude that by 1408 the English church and king took it for granted that the ecclesiastical crisis was so acute that the king had the right and duty to take a leading part in rectifying matters. The cardinals of course had called the council but the English church participated by the will of the king. All the vital decisions over Pisa were taken by the crown even to the final crucial acceptance of Alexander V. The election of a pope was intended to be a return to the *status quo* and the Lancastrian kings were in fact champions of ecclesiastical authority and privilege, but suppose they had decided to attack these? Or suppose there was another crisis.[60] It was indicative of the future that Richard Ullerston acknowledged that no reform could be carried out in England 'without the protection and strength of princes, considering the weakness of priests'.

University of Durham

[59] News of Alexander V's election was sent to Henry on 26 June, BL Harley MS 431 fols 32ᵛ–33ᵛ. On 18 August Henry allowed money to be collected for the curia, C[alendar of] P[atent] R[olls (London 1901) 1408–13 p 101, C[alendar of] C[lose] R[olls (London 1902)] 1405–9 p 516; W. E. Lunt, *Financial Relations of the Papacy with England*, 2 vols (Cambridge, Mass., 1962) 2 pp 413–14. The announcement to Arundel that Alexander V was going to be recognised is dated 17 October, CCR 1409–13 pp 2–3. On 22 October all sheriffs were ordered to recognise Alexander, CCR 1409–13 p 67. After this Arundel ordered the bishops to proclaim Alexander, Wilkins 3 pp 321–2.

[60] The comments of R. L. Storey, *Diocesan Administration in fifteenth Century England*, *Borthwick Papers*, 16 (2 ed York 1972) pp 19–31 are illuminating.

ITALIANS AND OTHERS: SOME QUATTROCENTO VIEWS OF NATIONALITY AND THE CHURCH

by DIANA M. WEBB

IN HIS excellent study of medieval Italian society, Hyde makes a thought-provoking comparison of 'the Italians of the age of Dante' with the humanists of a later generation. The former he sees as distinguished by 'a sense of continuity with the past and with other parts of the Catholic world' from the humanists who 'concentrated on what was close at hand, digging deep rather than spreading wide, so that their world revolved around central Italy.'[1] It is not my intention here to dispute this assertion, but to use it to stimulate reflection on the nature of Italian self-awareness in the early renaissance period, in the light of a further contrast between Hyde's two ages which he does not himself emphasise.

In the age of Dante and for much of the fourteenth century, the Italians did not rule the church of Rome, and their attempt, in and after 1378, to regain control of it resulted in a crisis of unparalleled proportions for the whole church. The Avignonese residence of the papacy came to be seen as an insult to the providential status of Rome, while Italy in a wider sense was insulted by French popes and legates. This whole long episode was clearly of crucial importance in shaping at least an élite Italian self-consciousness which turned on the idea of Rome and of a presumed continuity between the Roman past, sacred and secular, and the Italian present. Parts of the cumulative legacy of Dante, Petrarch and Salutati to the early humanists were deeply affected by this acute sense of the French challenge to all that Rome represented, or more accurately what they felt Rome should represent, to Italians. In January 1376 Salutati, as the mouthpiece of the Florentine government, informed the Roman people that God had raised up the oppressed against the foul tyranny of the French, and exhorted them to restore liberty by

[1] [J. K.] Hyde, [*Society and Politics in Medieval Italy*] (London 1973) p 197.

expelling the 'abomination' from Italy: 'Our Italy, which your great ancestors with much expense of blood made ruler of the whole world, do not permit it to suffer subjection to barbarians and foreigners.'[2]

After 1417, with the ending of the schism and the election of the Roman Oddo Colonna as pope Martin V, the Italians reclaimed the leadership of the church. The composition of the college of cardinals furnishes one crude measure of the consolidation of this leadership in the fifteenth century.[3] Martin V inevitably inherited a very mixed body of cardinals, and he and his two immediate successors for various reasons made a more ecumenical range of appointments than was to be normal subsequently. Of fifty-three promotions made between 1417 and 1455, twenty-two only were of Italians. The nine creations of the first Borgia pope, Calixtus III (1455–9), numbered four Italians, four Spaniards, and a Frenchman, not perhaps an ecumenical balance. With the next four popes the balance tipped markedly towards the Italians with forty-two appointments out of the sixty-four made between 1459 and 1492. The motivation may frequently have been as much nepotistic as nationalistic, but the effect was clear; and as Hay stresses, supplying the relevant figures, the composition of the conclaves that elected the popes in the fifteenth and early sixteenth century, showing as it does which of the cardinals were within easy reach of the curia, reveals a still more marked Italian preponderance. There were equal numbers of Italian and non-Italian cardinals in the conclaves which elected Eugenius IV in 1431 and Pius II in 1459; there were seven non-Italians to eight Italians at the election of Calixtus III in 1455. Of Pius II's twelve creations, eight were Italians, but in the conclave that elected his successor in 1464 there was a not too scandalous balance of eleven Italians and eight non-Italians. The small conclave of 1471 that elected Sixtus IV showed a larger disproportion of six to two, but it was in 1484, when Innocent VIII was elected by twenty-one Italians and four non-Italians, and in 1492 when the conclave that nonetheless willy-nilly elected the

---

[2] Quoted by R. C. Trexler, 'Rome on the eve of the Great Schism', *Speculum* 42 (1967) p 490.

[3] Lists of cardinals created by popes from Martin V to Alexander VI in K. Eubel, *Hierarchia catholica medii aevi*, 2 (Münster 1901) pp 3–36. I have omitted from my calculations the consolatory creations of the erstwhile popes John XXIII and Felix V as cardinals. See also [D.] Hay, [*The Church in Italy in the Fifteenth Century*] (Cambridge 1977) pp 33–42.

Spanish Alexander VI exhibited the staggering proportions of twenty-two to one, that the trend became blatant. It was then of course temporarily deflected by Alexander's own numerous promotions. 'Italianisation' naturally also took place in the curia generally. To quote Hay: 'The current language of interdepartmental business in the offices of the curia was Italian by the end of the fifteenth century—doubtless a relief for the northerners who had learned a Latin regarded as barbarous at Rome.'[4]

With this significant observation we return to our starting-point. The century of the Italianisation of the church was also the century in which Italian *literati* were pursuing a cultural programme based on a more conscious, systematic and thorough recourse to classical models than had been previously attempted. The models were not exclusively Roman. The growth of Greek studies sharpened for Italian intellectuals the problem of how to reconcile their ideas of Greeks ancient and Greeks modern. If the models and the inspiration were not solely Latin, however, the language of thought and expression was. The curia, the hierarchy and the religious orders meanwhile did not stand aloof from what was happening to Italian letters and education. It becomes then an interesting question whether Italian clerical intellectuals acknowledged an Italian preeminence within the church as such and justified it in terms of a special role assigned to Italy in the divine historical scheme, analogous to her cultural mission; or whether the Italian interest simply fused insensibly with the curial interest, as it seemed was already happening at Constance, so that the *gravamina* of other nations were met with a defence of centralised papal monarchy, the recognition that this was increasingly an Italian monarchy remaining tacit. More generally, we might also ask in what light Italian clerics viewed their fellow-Catholics of other nations when for whatever reason their attention became focused upon them.

In the space available it will be possible only to look at a few scattered testimonies. Predictably the writings of Aeneas Silvius Piccolomini, from 1459 to 1464 pope Pius II, will be much in evidence; so too will the correspondence of his protégé cardinal Jacopo Ammanati, which contains much that is of exceptional interest for this and other topics.[5] Perhaps Pius II, with his wide

---

[4] Hay p 42.
[5] [J.] Ammanati, [*Epistolae*] (Milan 1521). See the article by E. Pásztor, *Dizionario biografico degli italiani*, 2 (Rome 1960) pp 802–3.

travels and European consciousness, bulks too large, but the clever impecunious globetrotter who rose to be pope is a reminder of an important fact. 'No medieval country', says Hyde of Italy, 'lived less exclusively unto itself.'⁶ Early in the fifteenth century that notable vernacular exponent of Florentine patriotism, Gregario Dati, explained how in Florence no man enjoyed any esteem who had not travelled the world in youth.⁷ By way of commerce and diplomacy Italians had been the most travelled of Europeans, and the servants of the church, with its precocious and intense diplomatic activity, scarcely less so than others. The pioneers of humanism travelled, some on the business of the church, others on more purely intellectual business. In a letter written to Jacopo Ammanati in January 1464 the ageing Francesco Filelfo sought to recommend himself to Pius II as a guide on the projected crusade against the Turk, describing at length his travels to Constantinople and in eastern Europe earlier in the century.⁸

It did not of course follow that travel would promote goodwill on the part of the traveller towards his fellow-men of other nations. Jacopo Ammanati received amusingly contrasted, if perhaps equally rhetorical, reactions from humanist friends who accompanied cardinal Francesco Todeschini-Piccolomini on his legation to the diet at Regensburg called in the summer of 1471 in the perennial endeavour to muster action against the Turk. To the Sienese Agostino Patrizi Germany was more magnificent and beautiful than 'our people' (*nostri*) realised, and with its populous cities and splendid building was, he noted (here following in the tracks of an earlier work by Aeneas Silvius), quite unlike what it had been when Strabo, Caesar and Tacitus described it.⁹ To Giovanni Antonio Campana, who noted gloomily how late the roses were to bloom there, Germany was frightful and he was nauseated by the mere mention of it: there was nothing there to delight the eye, the hand or *sensum aliquid humanitatis*. There was no point in complaining to the legate. Cardinal Francesco Piccolomini had been brought up in Germany by his adoptive uncle, Aeneas Silvius, and this was in large part why he had been chosen for this

⁶ Hyde p 2.
⁷ G. Dati, *Istoria di Firenze*, ed L. Pratesi (Norcia 1902) pp 59–60.
⁸ Ammanati pp 12ᵛ–13ᵛ.
⁹ *Ibid*, on the first of four unnumbered leaves between p 208 and p 209. Reference will be made below to Aeneas Silvius's treatise *Germania* or *De moribus Germaniae*.

mission. *Germanus est*, said Campano wryly, *linguam, nasum, ingenia callet.*[10]

More contact, then, would not necessarily create sympathy, but it is the fact of this contact, frequent and sometimes lengthy, that here needs stressing as playing a large part in the lives of at least some prominent Italian clerics. It may also be worth stressing that if as participants in the humanist revival these same men read the ancient historians and geographers their attention and curiosity would not solely be directed towards Greece and Rome. Strabo, Caesar and Tacitus provided Aeneas Silvius and Agostino Patrizi with points of reference for their praises of modern Germany. The Florentine intellectual Donato Acciauioli sent Ammanati a map of France which he thought was fairly correct and which would be of great assistance when, for example, he was reading Caesar's *Gallic Wars.*[11] It was perhaps more particularly due to the influence of his late patron that Ammanati, as he explained to his fellow Lucchese, the bishop of Andria, was composing some historical commentaries on events since the death of pope Pius, *neque italica modo, sed transalpina et graeca.* For this purpose he wanted the bishop to obtain some factual information for him, if possible from the official monk historiographers of France and Burgundy of whom he had heard.[12] There seems in fact in the culture and attitudes of such men something profoundly harmonious with the movement towards an Italian government of the church: an intelligent and sympathetic interest in the wider world which nonetheless remains a world seen from Rome.

It is also a relevant consideration to what extent in this period the religious orders had been nationalised, or whether they managed to preserve an unruptured web of traditions and loyalties spun from different national sources. The Dominican order, thoroughly at home in Italy, looked back to a Spanish saint as its founder. In 1455 the Dominican Pietro da Ranzano, who as a Sicilian lived under the rule of an Aragonese king, wrote the life of the Catalan Dominican Vincent Ferrer in order to promote his canonisation.[13] This same Ranzano we find later sent by his king as ambassador to Matthias Corvinus of Hungary, who in 1476 took Beatrice of Aragon as his

[10] Ammanati pp 200^v^, 204, 209^v^–12.
[11] *Ibid* p 172.
[12] *Ibid* p 203. Ammanati's *Commentarii* are printed with the *Epistolae.*
[13] *ASB* Aprilis 1, pp 477–512.

wife. Ranzano stayed three years in Hungary and wrote a history of the country, enthusiastically praising its royal saints, one of whom, the blessed Margaret (d. 1271) happened to have become a Dominican nun.[14] Various incentives thus aroused in the learned Sicilian that interest in the history of central Europe which we of course find expressed at length by Aeneas Silvius Piccolomini.

One thing we may profitably look for in the writings of such men is not so much overt signs of admiration or disdain, approbation or disapprobation, of what they saw in other lands, as the subtler hints they may let drop of a sense of strangeness or affinity. Could our learned Italians fully accept the oneness of Christendom, not merely in juridical terms but as a human and cultural reality? To Aeneas Silvius the as yet unrepentant conciliarist, Thomas Livingstone of Dundrennan, *abbas quidam scotus* as he calls him, cut an active figure at Basle, arguing (with Aeneas's approval) that Eugenius IV was to be regarded as a lapsed heretic.[15] But his strange native land, where bread was a luxury and there was no wine but what was imported, emerges from the pages of the pope's memoirs as a land on the furthest fringes of that Christian civilization of corn, wine and oil that had grown outwards from the Mediterranean. In the neighbouring far north of England Aeneas was able to obtain, significantly from a monastery, several loaves of white bread and a jug of wine, exciting the liveliest wonder in the barbarians who had never seen such things before.[16] By contrast Hungary as described by Pietro de Ranzano was notably abundant

---

[14] [Petrus] Ranzanus, *Epitome* [*Rerum Ungaricarum per indices descripta*], *Scriptores Rerum Hungaricarum*, ed J. Schwandtner, 3 vols (Tournai 1765) pp 537–694. The fact that Ranzano mentions as bishop of Sirmio one Stephanus Crispus (Index 1, p 544), who was appointed to the see on 26 February 1490, while he seems unaware of the death of Matthias Corvinus in April of the same year, gives the best indication of the date at which the work was completed. Ranzano's life of Margaret is contained in Index 15, pp 613–23, and is printed separately in *ASB* Januarii 2, pp 906–9.

[15] [Pius II,] *De Gestis* [*Concilii Basiliensis Commentariorum libri II*], ed D. Hay and W. K. Smith (Oxford 1967) p 16. It is noteworthy that later (pp 202–3) Aeneas records that there were objections to the nomination of Livingstone as one of the three men to whom the business of naming the electors of a new pope was to be deputed: 'For some people were murmuring that the abbot from Scotland seemed more like a Frenchman than a German, and that in so important a business a man not from an island but from the continent, who knew others, should have been chosen.'

[16] [*The*] *Commentaries* [*of Pius II*], tr F. A. Gragg and ed L. C. Gabel, *Smith College*

in both wine and bread; although to an Italian eye strikingly deficient for its size in artisans and merchants (and most of those there were Germans), it had been beautified by some notable buildings, its bishops exercised great authority and were often men of culture; it had of course been described by Strabo, Ptolemy and Pliny.[17] It was a land which an Italian could at least fit into a comprehensible framework, and there were of course many reasons why Hungary, long since a receptacle of Italian influence,[18] should have received sympathetic attention from Italians in the fifteenth century, especially if they professed a concern for the defence of Christendom against the Turk. It was predictably Aeneas Silvius who in a letter to the archbishop of Gran, written in October 1445, elegantly summarised these reasons:

> If anyone asks me why I, born in Tuscany, presume to speak of the state of the kingdom of Hungary, I shall reply that I am a man and as Terence was wont to say I think nothing that is human is alien to me. I shall say that I as an Italian know that many men of my race have acquired wealth and honours in your kingdom and achieved great glory. I shall say that I have read your histories and have found that the Hungarians are famous for many victories and have raised a name to the heavens, and therefore, as nature commands, I am moved by their virtues. What more? I shall say I am a Christian, and have a concern that the Christian religion may be cultivated in safety, which certainly cannot be unless its rampart, which is Hungary, is intact.

It was therefore desirable for Aeneas to give an ingenious twist to the undoubtedly barbaric past of Hungary: history told him that the Hungarians in the shape of the Lombards had colonised northern Italy.[19] Pietro da Ranzano would tactfully insist that the Hungarians possessed excellent natural abilities, although they were admittedly more inclined to warfare than to the liberal arts.[20]

Studies in History 22, 25, 30, 35, 43 (Northampton, Mass., 1937–57) pp 18–19. See also the one-volume abridgement, *Memoirs [of a Renaissance Pope]* (London 1960) pp 33–5.

[17] Ranzanus, *Epitome*, Index I, pp 537–55.

[18] J. Bialostocki, *The Art of the Renaissance in Eastern Europe*, (London 1976) with full bibliography.

[19] *Der Briefwechsel [des Eneas Silvius Piccolomini]*, ed R. Wolkan, 2 vols, *Fontes rerum Austriacarum* 61–2, 67–8 (Vienna 1909–18) I pt i pp 548, 550.

[20] Ranzanus, *Epitome*, Index I p 554.

The German nation in its relations to the Italians and the centralised church presented another picture, to which we shall return. Different again were what we may term the old nations within the Roman church, the French and the Spanish. The French were frequently, if reluctantly, accorded that honoured place in the hierarchy of the Christian nations that a long tradition going back ultimately to Charlemagne and Clovis had assured them. To the conciliarist Aeneas Silvius, describing the election of the antipope Felix V at Basle in 1439, the French nation 'came second' and had rendered the most valuable services to the church.[21] As pope, urging the abrogation of the Pragmatic Sanction of Bourges and frequently constrained to listen to French envoys praising their nation and its incomparable services, he was to say the least more reserved.[22] Looking back at Basle in a hostile spirit in 1450 he recorded the bitter enmity of the bishop of Tours to the Italians and his determination that the church should be wrested from them, reflecting with satisfaction that the bishop was now dead and the papacy honourably ensconced *apud Italos*.[23] As we shall see shortly he was not above insinuating at the conclave which in 1459 elected him pope that the French challenge for the leadership of the church was by no means dead. The sense of a proud, powerful and dangerous nation with a strong Christian tradition that made it if possible more dangerous hovers over our testimonies. Jacopo Ammanati, writing to cardinal Bessarion on the eve of the latter's departure as legate to France early in 1472, described it as 'a huge nation, populous, militarily distinguished, accustomed to the service of Christ; it possesses the broadest of fields in which you can sow and gather a rich harvest for wretched Italy'. When Bessarion died not long after his return from his abortive legation Ammanati was disposed to put part of the blame on 'hard, hard France, impatient of wise counsel.[24]'

Pius II's entertaining and discreditable account of the 1459 conclave is notable not only for his own alleged manipulation of anti-French sentiment, but for an interesting formulation of the relationship between Italy and the church.[25] The cardinal of Rouen,

[21] *De Gestis* pp 212–13.
[22] For example, *Commentaries* pp 264–8, 510–11; *Memoirs* pp 140–3, 235–6.
[23] *Der Briefwechsel*, 2 p 188. See also A. Black, *Council and Commune*, (London 1979) p 40.
[24] Ammanati pp 219, 248.
[25] *Commentaries* pp 94–100; *Memoirs* pp 80–4.

we are told, first sought to render Aeneas himself suspect to the electors on account of his long connection with Germany. Aeneas reciprocated first by assuring the young Rodrigo Borgia that he had nothing to gain by voting for Rouen. 'You young fool! Will you then put an enemy of your nation in the apostle's chair? . . . . . Will a Frenchman be more friendly to a Frenchman or to a Catalan?'

Warming to his work Aeneas then dissuaded the cardinal of Pavia from voting for Rouen as he had promised, spelling out the consequences of the election of a Frenchman:

> What is our Italy without the Bishop of Rome? We still have the Apostleship though we have lost the Imperium, and in this one light we see light. Shall we be deprived of this with your sympathy, persuasion, help? A French pope will either go to France—and then our dear country is bereft of its splendour; or he will stay among us—and Italy, the queen of nations, will serve a foreign master . . . . You might have taken warning from Calixtus, during whose papacy there was nothing the Catalans did not get. After trying the Catalans are you so eager to try the French? You will be sorry if you do! You will see the college filled with Frenchmen, and the papacy will never again be wrested from them. Are you so dull that you do not realise that this will lay a yoke upon your nation forever?

What matters here is less whether the fears Aeneas depicts himself as trying to arouse had any basis in reality, than whether the ideas on which he based his supposed appeal to Italian sentiment had any currency beyond his rhetorical needs of the moment. It is perhaps worth noting that despite the difference in political organization which to the modern historian for good reasons seems crucial, Aeneas has no difficulty in simply juxtaposing French identity and Italian identity. There is no doubt but that Italy and the Italians exist; but only by keeping hold on all that is left of the Roman legacy, that is the sway of the Roman church, can Italian identity find actual realisation. What Aeneas offers is not a justification of the Italian grip on the church, but an assertion that if the Italians lose it they will have nothing left to call their own.

That the issue was a live one within the curia seems to receive some confirmation from the curious letter which Jacopo Ammanati, made a cardinal by Pius II in 1462, wrote to his fellow cardinals on the death of his patron in 1464. They were called to the great task of electing a pastor for the catholic people:

We must put aside the influence of attachment, and so to speak transalpine prejudices (*ultra montitates*.) Neither let the Italian dread the transalpine, if he is a good one, nor the transalpine disdain the Italian. Our lord was crucified for both; on both he makes the sun and moon to shine, and the rain falls. And sometimes government by an Italian has been best, and also great disasters have been brought by the same.[26]

An outright justification of Italian pre-eminence in the church had been provided, though how convincingly we may question, earlier in the century by the Milanese Augustinian friar Andrea Biglia. His contrived arguments have their interest, not least because they are directed against neither German *gravamina* nor French challenge, real or imagined, but against the vestigial Spanish threat represented by the so-called Clement VIII, elected by a handful of supporters of Benedict XIII on the latter's death in 1423 and, it was feared, backed by Alfonso of Aragon. Alfonso was of course already an Italian power and with his conquest of Naples in 1442 was to become a greater one. In the persons of Calixtus III, at the end of the century his nephew Alexander VI, the Catalans, as we have seen Aeneas Silvius calling them, made a strong presence felt at the curia. In his treatise entitled *Paniscolaria*, which was written probably in 1425 and took its title from the Valencian fortress of Peñiscola where Benedict XIII had ended his days, Biglia used the more classical terminology of nationality in his effort to persuade Alfonso that the Spanish were not qualified to challenge Italian leadership of the church as now personified by Martin V.[27]

In an age when above all things stability was to be sought in the affairs of the church, Biglia argues, the *gens hispana*, but recently come once more to the faith, was peculiarly ill-fitted to set an example. History showed that the faith had come late to Spain and that it had always been prone to sects there. Was this because Spain was remote in the far west from both Greece, where after Palestine and its neighbourhood the faith had found its nearest and safest refuge, and 'the churches of our Italy'? There could be no doubt that Italy had been especially well-equipped by providence to receive the true faith. The special position occupied by Greece and above all Italy was not a matter of desert or merit, but of divine

[26] Ammanati p 22.
[27] [D.] Webb, 'Andrea Biglia [at Bologna, 1424–7: a humanist friar and the troubles of the church]', *BIHR* 49 (1976) pp 41–59, esp pp 49–53.

benevolence. Here anyway were to be found the great councils, the great doctors of the church. Italy had always been distinguished for its energy and constancy in the faith. Anxiously Biglia stresses that this is no vulgar patriotic boasting: 'God is my witness, I am speaking of the common life of the saints in Christ'; but he is asserting a truth that all will surely admit. Would that when 'we' grow sluggish others should flourish, when we are foolish, others should be prudent. It is however a fact that since the word was spread by the apostles, no province of the church has proved more resistant to heresy, schism or other perverse and sinister dogmas; and if any threat has arisen it has not got very far. This is only fitting for the place where the first apostles laid down their lives. From this point an easy transition is made to the universal rights of the Roman church. On the historical plane, Italy and Rome merge.[28]

[28] Milan, Biblioteca Ambrosiana, MS. H. 117 fols 4–5: 'Precipue vero gens illa hispana, que si verum est quod referunt, pene temporibus nostris fidem iterum tanquam rudis et novella suscepit. Illud ferme ex historiis constat serius in Hispania fidem floruisse, semperque eam gentem facile omnium sectarum documenta suscepisse; seu quod tamquam in occidente a primo solis ortu remota, hoc est tum ab ipsius Grecie sedibus in qua post Ierosolimam ac cetera circa Palestinam loca velut in proximo cubili fides tutior atque uberior conquievit, tum ab huius nostris Italie ecclesiis. Nam et ipsi haud dubium suscipiende vere fidei paratam oportunitatem habuimus; neque hoc nostre artis aut virtutis sed prorsus gratie ac misericordie divine. Quid enim nos plus quam ceteri meruimus aut quid Greci preter ceteras gentes meruerant ut primi verbum predicationis audirent? Hic concilia non semel celebrata, hic scripture exposite, hic edite ac vulgate sapientum disputationes et sententie. Atqui si licet divino munere gloriari nescio cui unquam vel puritate fidei vel excellentia doctrine cesserit Italia, sive sacrarum litterarum doctores requiris, sive prestantem martirum constantiam seu peritissimorum hominum prudentiam; semper hec pars Italie quantum ad fidem pertinet solers ac firma exstitit. Neque ego hec dico quod aut ex hac gloria laudes pacisci velim aut gratiam gratie comparari . . . deus anime mee testis est, de communi sanctorum in Christo conversatione loquor; et id nunc satis fidens dico, quod ipsa veritas loquitur atque omnes qui in eam intuentur concessuros et confessuros existimo . . . Utinam quidem etiam si nos torpescamus ceteri floreant, nobis stultis, ceteri sint prudentes . . . Verumtamen dicam quod in mente habeo: posteaquam fides in orbem per apostolos disseminata est atque ita in nos verbum salutis pervenit nullam pene aut provinciam aut gentem fuisse que minus neque heresi neque scismate neque aliis sinistris ac perversis dogmatibus vexata sit. Ac si quid non nunquam vel impium vel male senciendum irrepsit et aliunde evertum est nec usque adeo simplicium mentibus pestis invaluit ut potuerit, veritate obsistente, vulgari. Et quidem sic decuit aream hanc quam primi ipsa apostolorum capita stravere aliquanto solidiorem fieri quo ab ceteris perfugium esset undeque per universum orbem consilia peterentur. Quis vero fidelium nescit sedem romanam summis pontificibus datam que ceteris iure auctoritate dignitate premineat?'

By virtue of Rome, then, Italy retains a special place in the present as in the past, in the church and in the world. In a later historical work entitled *De defectu fidei in oriente* Biglia made it clear that in the course of history Greece and the east had forfeited that early pre-eminence within the church that he had mentioned in the *Paniscolaria*. Strongly, if implicitly, the essentially Roman and therefore Italian character of authentic culture and religion is urged in this work.[29]

Once again we may ask what more general currency such expression had. This apart, it is clear that not all Biglia's thoughts were those of a patriotic Italian. He was a Milanese and an Augustinian. In the *Paniscolaria* it happened that obedience to Martin V could be made to stand for acceptance of Italian religious pre-eminence; it happened also that Martin's Italian policies were broadly acceptable to the Milanese and that he took a benevolent interest in the Augustinians. His successor the Venetian Eugenius IV was hostile to Milan and friendly to Florence; and Biglia in the *De defectu fidei* seems prepared to countenance the threats posed by the council of Basle to this equally Italian pope.[30] Nor did Biglia seem too confident of the powers of resistance of the Italian people, notably the natives of his own province of Lombardy, to religious subversion when that was threatened by the irresponsible preaching of members of the rival religious orders.[31]

This example of one not very important individual merely illustrates a mental situation which was by no means peculiar to Italians in the fifteenth century, but is particularly obvious in the Italian context because of the political fragmentation of the peninsula. Loyalties were not all focused on one point. Italy existed, above all as an entity with a history which made it easy for a clerical intellectual to stress the special relationship that existed between it and the church. Yet the church itself and the subordinate organizations within it represented loyalties that theoretically transcended any such national vision, while loyalties to the various Italian states cut across it. When Biglia criticised the rabble-rousing Dominican preacher Manfredo da Vercelli for adopting Vincent Ferrer as his model, it was Vincent the unruly Dominican rather than Vincent

---

[29] D. Webb, 'The decline and fall of eastern Christianity: a fifteenth-century view', *BIHR* 49 (1976) pp 198–216, esp pp 206–12.
[30] *Ibid* pp 213–15.
[31] Webb, 'Andrea Biglia', pp 53–8.

the unstable Spaniard who aroused his hostility; while Vincent's decision, at the behest of Sigismund, to abandon Benedict XIII and use his influence with the people of Aragon to do likewise proved to Biglia 'the levity of the Dominicans in our age'.[32] If on the one hand he was not unlikely to cross professional swords with fellow-Italians of other orders, Biglia was notionally at least bound by the ties of his own order to men in other lands. We cannot know whether he could have conversed easily and with a complete community of interest with an Augustinian of Prague, Toulouse, Barcelona or Rheims, but the ties of religion in theory made their cause his and brought him news of their grievances and sufferings.[33]

The fact then of belonging to a particular religious network entailed the profession of a particular pattern of interests and loyalties. As the subject of the Aragonese king of Sicily Pietro da Ranzano doubtless had a double incentive to work for the canonisation of Vincent Ferrer. To other Italian Dominicans Vincent would simply be a welcome addition to the ranks of the order's saints. Thus it was that Antonino of Florence included a life of him, derived from Ranzano's, in the section of his chronicle that is devoted to the order.[34] Antonino's secretary Francesco Castiglione, who composed lives of the Dominican saints in turn drawn from Antonino's versions, addressed his life of Vincent to cardinal Ammanati with words which counterbalance Biglia's attack on the religious merits of Spain:

> As you know, most reverend father, Spain has produced remarkable men in different ages; of whom some have been outstanding for literary studies and their great eloquence, others for their forceful fervour in our religion and their notable piety. What does the church possess that is nobler than the martyrdom of Laurence?[35]

A respectable pedigree could of course be composed for any of the nations that made up the Christian world, if one cared to use the right sources. Every land had its saints: Margaret of Hungary could nourish her sanctity on a reading of the lives of her saintly royal predecessors, whom Ranzano enumerates.[36] Although a majority of

[32] *Ibid* pp 57–8; Muratori 19, col 43.
[33] Webb, 'Andrea Biglia', pp 53, 55, 56, 58.
[34] Antoninus, *Chronicorum Opus*, 3 vols (Lyons 1586) 3, pp 657–64.
[35] Ammanati p 52ᵛ. Extracts from Castiglione's life of Vincent are in *ASB* Aprilis 1, pp 512–14.
[36] Ranzanus, *Epitome*, Index 15, p 618.

saints both old and new probably commanded only a geographically limited devotion, some of great celebrity and antiquity were of course universal, while the orders still carried the knowledge of others over long distances and across hardening national boundaries.[37]

It is at least an arguable proposition that in the fifteenth century there were to be found in Italy more cultivated men with a knowledge of other lands and even a sympathy for them than in any country of Europe at the same period. At the same time these men could scarcely fail to be affected by the more localised political loyalties which for the majority of Italians presumably filled the horizon. Any sentiment of Italian identity as such, although some historical, cultural and linguistic basis for it existed, was clearly limited and diluted by other forces. It may be doubted whether there was innately that much more basis for national sentiment in France at this period than in Italy, but for the crucial difference in political organization which meant that the foci of many lesser loyalties had been destroyed and that a ruler existed in whose interest it was, as it had already been in the years around 1300, to present himself as the embodiment of national interests. A distinguished student of late medieval France has said that 'In some sense it was the king alone who was the sole inhabitant of all France.[38]' In Italy there was of course no one to play this role. A pope such as Pius II might claim to be acting in the interests of Italy, as when he argued with Cosimo de' Medici that his support for Ferrante of Naples against the Angevins was an Italian policy, made the more necessary by the French bias of many of the Italian powers.[39] As Vicar of Christ on the one hand, however, and a territorial prince on the other, the pope was bound to be either more or less than the embodiment of Italy. Pius might play intellectually with the idea that the Roman church was itself the supreme expression of Italian identity, but whatever cardinal Piccolomini may or may not have said in the conclave that elected him pope, both before and after his election he took his public stand on the Roman universality and the irrefragible prerogatives of the Holy See.

This is nowhere more notable than in the tractate he composed as

---

[37] In a communication to the Simposio Internazionale Cateriniano-Bernardiniano, Siena 17–20 April 1980, J. Kloczowski discussed the cults of Catherine and Bernardino of Siena in Poland in and after the late fifteenth century.

[38] P. S. Lewis, *Later Medieval France* (London 1968) p 14.

[39] *Commentaries* p 300; *Memoirs* pp 146–7.

cardinal in 1458 in answer to the German *gravamina* that had been reported to him by his friend Martin Meyr, chancellor of the archbishop of Mainz.[40] It is a work remarkable for the adroitness with which the force and direction of a range of hostile arguments are recongised and their flank turned. Where 'Italy' and 'the Italians' are mentioned, it is most often either by way of acknowledging that the German grievances against the Roman curia are in fact grievances against Italians and sidestepping the complaint, or by way of making it plain that Italy and Rome are distinct and that the Italians too are subject to the Roman church.

Coming into the former category is the passage in which Aeneas suggests that all the German complaints come down to money: the Roman curia scrapes together money from Germany by a thousand means. Blithely Aeneas seems to accept the identification of the money-grubbing curialist as an Italian: 'This rumour against the Italians is true. They have always been men greedy for money, insatiable for gold, who as long as they scent profit will more readily spill blood than money.' The fact however is that no one willingly pays money out, while to him who receives it it always seems perfectly just. More specifically:

> You will never find a people who easily permit money to be taken out of their region. It is a common disease and spread equally over all provinces. For just as the Germans hate the Italians for this reason, so the Hungarians hate the Germans. For what is more galling for the folk of Pannonia than that Germans do business in their kingdom and extract all the gold of the region? The Poles have the same grievance, so do the Danes and Swedes. In Germany itself you will find several peoples who accuse one another of extorting their wealth. What is more hateful to the Bavarians and Austrians than the diligence of the Nurembergers in frequenting even the tiny markets?[41]

Aeneas now devotes considerable space to showing that Germany has not, as claimed, been impoverished by Roman exactions. When we hear of Italy in the next few pages it is to be informed that for the splendour of its cities and buildings Germany does not have to fear the comparison. At the end of this section there is a new twist: 'Luxury and ambition, not the Roman curia, exhaust the

[40] Pius II, *Opera Omnia* (Basle 1571) pp 1034–86; several times printed subsequently.
[41] *Ibid* p 1050.

German churches.⁴²' Aeneas now turns to the history of the spread
of the faith, which shows that 'just as neither the French nor the
Spanish nor the English or Italians had any other teacher of the faith
than the prime see, so too the Germans have been taught by her.⁴³'
The point is repeated, but the difficulties of Biglia's attempted
identification of Rome and Italy clearly avoided, a little later: 'Of
the Italian, the French, the Spanish and the German churches there
is none that can lay claim to the primacy, since none of the apostles
came to them, and it is plain that all were instituted by the authority
of the Roman see.'

Having thus established the uniqueness and universality of the
Roman church, Aeneas now quickly points out the unreasonable-
ness of expecting it to live on the uncertain revenues of the
patrimony. Italy might well say 'As the apostolic see is mother of
all, why should we Italians alone support her?' The obvious
objection is at once countered:

> Nor can you say that Italians justly support the Roman church
> because it is in Italy and is ruled solely by Italians. If you look
> at the curialists they are recognisably men of every race,
> Greek, Latin, barbarian. And it is well known that men of
> every nation have held the see itself. He who now presides by
> the gift of God is not Roman or Italian by nation, but Spanish,
> a people from which the Roman republic both ecclesiastical
> and temporal has often received illustrious rulers.

And with a final agile twist, 'It is well known also that when it was
outside Italy the see was not as benign to the Italians as now it is at
Rome it is pleasing to all.⁴⁴'

It would probably be mistaken to suppose that all this was
intended as a mere cloak with which to hide the naked reality of an
Italian church. No one can have known better than an Italian that to
be Italian meant no one thing, or, indeed, that there was nothing
particularly holy about the Italians. Writing to Richard cardinal of
Constance in 1465 Jacopo Ammanati exclaimed

> Most reverend father, I am an Italian, and I have lived for
> fourteen years among the subjects of the church. Believe me,
> our people do not have the same respect for their bishops that
> yours do across the alps. What I remember seeing done before

⁴² *Ibid* p 1061.
⁴³ *Ibid* p 1070.
⁴⁴ *Ibid* p 1075.

the eyes of other legates, I think could happen before yours also.[45]

Ammanati also reports how Paul II in consistory expressed grave doubts about the proposal that the House of Anjou should receive Avignon in exchange for the renunciation of the Angevin claim on Sicily:

> At all costs the Roman see must be prevented from losing its patrimony across the alps. It is a refuge for the pontiffs and a tight rein on the Italians, lest they run wild to vex the church. When we can get no peace here we can obtain safety by threatening to migrate to that city of ours. And fearing lest Italy should lose such an ornament, they do not suffer our lordship and ourselves to be lost.

Ammanati agreed and clearly did not believe that history was going to repeat itself:

> You will scarcely find any transalpine popes who will be so captivated by French climes that they will wish to leave the temporal principality of the Roman see and the see itself to be the prey of robbers. Their standing at Rome is higher, their freedom greater, their power to act as they wish greater. A pope at Avignon is enclosed no less by the power of others than by his own. When he is here, he rules the world. The ignorant know this, how much more will a pope, whether Italian or transalpine, know it . . . .[46]

Two principal threads run from the fifteenth-century testimonies we have been examining down to our own time. The French challenge of the late thirteenth and fourteenth centuries, the uncertainties of the conciliar epoch, were past; despite everything that was to happen to Italy in the next few decades the court, effectively run by Italians, that claimed to rule the Catholic world and has remained a twentieth-century reality, had come into being. The other thread is less easy to discern, because if no one was really trying to establish an Italian nationalism in the fifteenth century, still less were they going to do so in the three centuries that followed. Nonetheless we have seen in the fifteenth-century context some indications of the difficulties that might attend the construction of an Italian identity around the idea of Rome. The

---

[45] Ammanati p 64.
[46] *Ibid* pp 59ᵛ–60.

historian of nineteenth and twentieth century Italy would have rather more to add.

University of London
King's College

LOLLARDY: THE ENGLISH HERESY?

by ANNE HUDSON

SYTHEN witte stondis not in langage but in groundynge of treuthe, for tho same witte is in Laten that is in Grew or Ebrew, and trouthe schuld be openly knowen to alle manere of folke, trowthe moueth mony men to speke sentencis in Yngelysche that thai han gedired in Latyne, and herfore bene men holden heretikis.

Such is the opening sentence of the tract known in the only surviving manuscript as *Tractatus de Regibus*.[1] The text owes much of its material to Wyclif's *De Officio Regis*, though the prologue does not derive from this source, and is undoubtedly of lollard origin; its date cannot be later than the early fifteenth century.[2] The sentiments of the first part of the sentence are typically Wycliffite, though not exclusively so.[3] The interesting part of it is the last clause, and particularly the word *herfore*. I want in this paper to investigate the implications and validity of this word. The meaning of the word is superficially clear: 'for this reason are men considered heretics'—most modern writers would use 'therefore'. But can the anonymous author of this tract really be accurate in seeing a causal connection between the use of English and the detection of heresy? At a time when Chaucer, Gower and the *Gawain* poet were using the vernacular for poetry that is at the least orthodox, in the

[1] The complete tract is edited, with some unfortunate misinterpretations of the medieval English, in *Four English Political Tracts of the Later Middle Ages*, ed J.-P. Genet, *CSer*, 4 series 18 (1977) pp 5–19. The passage here quoted is also printed in [A. Hudson,] *Selections* [*from English Wycliffite Writings*] (Cambridge 1978) no 25/1–5. (In ensuing references to texts, line numbers, where given, follow an oblique stroke; unless the extent of the passage is open to doubt, only the opening line number will be given. In quotations from manuscripts, and from older editions, modern punctuation has been introduced; all abbreviations are expanded without notice.)

[2] See *Selections* pp 200–1; the only contemporary allusions point towards the end of the fourteenth century as the date of composition, though the sole surviving manuscript, Oxford Bodleian MS Douce 273, is paleographically of the early fifteenth century.

[3] For lollard instances see below; for an apparently orthodox statement compare the English version of Robert of Greatham's *Miroir*, Oxford Bodleian MS Holkham Misc. 40 fol 1ᵛ 'and so hit is ful gret foli to speke Latyn to lewd folk, and he entermeteth hym of a fol mister that telleth to hym Latyny. For eche man schal be undurnome and aresound aftur the langage that he hath lered.'

case of Gower declaredly anti-lollard, such a view would seem very unlikely to be right.[4] Admittedly, we may recall the case in the later fifteenth century when a copy of *The Canterbury Tales* was produced for the prosecution in a case of heresy;[5] but the instance is isolated, and is usually dismissed as an instance of neurotic officiousness on the part of the bishop's minions.[6] Yet I think that the quotation needs a little more thought before it is likewise dismissed as an expression of 'persecution mania'. After all, modern scholars have succeeded in demonstrating that almost all the elements of Wyclif's heresy are traceable to earlier thinkers, to Marsilius of Padua, to Bradwardine, to FitzRalph, to Berengar amongst others, and yet none of these aroused the 'witch hunt' that followed the condemnation of Wyclif in 1382.[7] Why did these old ideas suddenly become dangerous? Was it just the combination of so many distasteful notions in the thought of one man? Or was there a new ingredient? One new ingredient was, of course, the fact that these distasteful notions were no longer confined within the precincts of a university debating hall; that, whether with his encouragement or not, Wyclif's followers spread his views not only in writing but also on preaching tours of the countryside.[8]

[4] *The Complete Works of John Gower*, ed G. C. Macaulay, 4 vols (Oxford 1899–1902), *Confessio Amantis*, Prol. 346 *seq*, bk 5. 1803 *seq*; *Carmen super multiplici viciorum pestilencia*, 13 *seq*.

[5] Lincoln register Chedworth fol 62ᵛ, concerning John Baron of Amersham in 1464. The group of lollards in the Chilterns investigated by Chedworth seems to have been well provided with books (see C. Cross, *Church and People 1450–1660* (Edinburgh 1976) pp 32–5 for a brief account of the group), and the authorities particularly undiscriminating in their suspicion. As well as the Chaucer volume, a second containing 'a play of seint Dionise' and a third containing the 'Myrrour of Synners'—for the usual tract that went under this name see C. Horstman, *Yorkshire Writers*, 2 vols (London 1895–6) 2, pp 436–40, manuscripts listed by P. S. Jolliffe, *A Check-List of Middle English Prose Writings of Spiritual Guidance* (Toronto 1974) p 81—the 'Myrrour of Matrimony', the 'lyff of oure Lady, Adam and Eve' and 'other sermones' were confiscated from Baron. The group owned several copies of biblical translations and other religious works.

[6] For instance J. A. F. Thomson, *The Later Lollards 1414–1520* (Oxford 2nd ed 1967) p 243.

[7] See, for example, G. Leff, *Heresy in the Later Middle Ages*, 2 vols (Manchester/ New York 1967) 2, pp 494–558; J. A. Robson, *Wyclif and the Oxford Schools* (Cambridge 1966); M. J. Wilks, 'The *Apostolicus* and the Bishop of Rome', *JTS* ns 14 (1963) pp 338–54. For Wyclif's own references to Berengar see my note appended to 'The Expurgation of a Lollard Sermon-Cycle', *JTS* ns 22 (1971) pp 464–5.

[8] For a reassessment of the evidence that Wyclif initiated the preaching see M. Wilks, '"Reformatio Regni": Wyclif and Hus as leaders of religious protest movements', *SCH* 9 (1972) pp 109–30 especially pp 119–21.

Lollardy: the English Heresy?

This brings me back to my opening quotation: was the crucial new ingredient the use of the vernacular? and the use of that vernacular for the discussion of matters that had hitherto been obscured from the view of most of the populace under the thick veil of Latin? After all, the anonymous author does not assert that the use of English, plain and simple, is the ground of suspicion, but that the trouble is the use of English for the expression of ideas that have been gathered from Latin writings. Was lollardy, then, the *English* heresy?

To attempt to show that the single major heresy known in medieval England arose from a concatenation of peculiarly insular factors would be, I think, a forlorn enterprise. Nor does it seem right to discern nationalism as a major force in the origin of lollardy or in its continuance. Certainly, there were peculiar elements in the heresy of lollardy: almost alone amongst the heresies of the high middle ages, lollardy and its relation Hussitism derive from academic controversies but came to be popular movements. But whilst Hussitism did become identified with the incipient movement towards a recognition of national identity, Lollardy did not.[9] Certainly, Wyclif used arguments that might be described as nationalistic to further his case: one such was his objection to the drain on the resources of the country that resulted from payments to the pope or through religious orders.[10] But this was not a new argument: earlier suppressions of alien priories had partly occurred from the same objection.[11] Equally, as Edith Tatnall has urged, Wyclif did speak often of an *Ecclesia Anglicana*; but frequently this phrase seems merely a useful weapon with which to beat the temporal pretensions of the clergy, and especially the claims of the papacy to jurisdiction in any realm.[12] Whether, as Tatnall

[9] For this aspect of the Hussite movement see especially F. Šmahel, 'Le mouvement des étudiants à Prague dans les années 1408–1412', *Historica* 14 (Prague 1967) pp 33–75, and the same author's 'The Idea of the "Nation" in Hussite Bohemia', *Historica* 16 (1969) pp 143–247 and 17 (1969) pp 93–197; a revised form of these last two was published as *Idea národa v husitských Čechách* (České Budějovice 1971).

[10] All quotations from Wyclif are from the editions of the Wyclif Society (1883–1921). See here, for instance, Wyclif's insistence on the various aspects of the 'dead hand' of clerical possession on property in England, *De Veritate Sacre Scripture*, 3 p 20, *De Ecclesia* p 338, *Dialogus* p 70/23, *De fundatione sectarum, Polemical Works* I p 28/14.

[11] See Knowles, *RO* 2 pp 161–5: more generally compare *Rotuli Parliamentorum* ([London 1767–77]) 46 Edward III item 27, 47 Edward III item 30, 50 Edward III items 95 and 124.

[12] [E. C.] Tatnall, ['John Wyclif and *Ecclesia Anglicana*'], *JEH* 20 (1969) pp 19–43; the

maintains, Wyclif shows himself conscious of a 'distinctly English ecclesiastical tradition' seems to me less than proven. Grosseteste is often quoted with strong approbation, Becket's example is, in contrast to Wyclif's followers, cautiously commended and Pecham once quoted as an example of episcopal good sense; but the references are far from constant, and the nationalistic stress missing.[13] One area which would repay further investigation is that of Wyclif's references to English law: there are a number of occasions when Wyclif sets canon law against civil law, often specifying English law and mentioning Magna Carta as evidence that certain papal claims some of them embodied in canon law, cannot legally be maintained in England.[14] This is a train of thought that was pursued by one of Wyclif's disciples in an unpublished tract in which the assertion that the king and the temporal rulers are entitled to deprive erring clerics is demonstrated by an analysis of the clauses of the king's coronation oath; the date of this tract is likely to be early since the oath used is distinctively that of Richard II.[15] But this is an area where more expertise in law and legal history is needed than I possess.

Two matters relevant to my purpose have been investigated in the recent past and may be summarised first. Wilks incidentally examined the evidence for Wyclif's own views about the use of English, and in particular about the translation of the bible into the vernacular.[16] He concluded that not until the last two years of his

---

earlier discussion in L. J. Daly, *The Political Theory of John Wyclif* (Chicago 1962) pp 132–51 hardly tackles the issue. For cases where 'English' customs or law are merely ancillary references see, for example, *De Civili Dominio* 2 p 134, *De Veritate Sacre Scripture* I p 354 and 3 pp 18, 55.

[13] See Tatnall pp 34–43 where the references to Wyclif's works are given. For lollard views about Becket see J. F. Davis, 'Lollards, Reformers and St. Thomas of Canterbury', *University of Birmingham Historical Journal* 9 (Birmingham 1963) pp 1–15.

[14] Some of these passages are briefly mentioned in Tatnall pp 24–31. See also F. W. Maitland, 'Wyclif on English and Roman Law', *Collected Papers*, ed H. A. L. Fisher (Cambridge 1911) 3 pp 50–3. Despite its title, W. Farr's *John Wyclif as Legal Reformer* (Leiden 1974) does not fully discuss this question.

[15] In Prague University Library MS X.E.9 fols 206–7ᵛ, Vienna Nationalbibliothek MS 3928 fols 189–90 and 3932 fols 155ᵛ–6; for the distinctive character see P. E. Schramm, trans L. G. Wickham Legg, *A History of the English Coronation* (Oxford 1937) p 236.

[16] [M.] Wilks, ['Misleading manuscripts: Wyclif and the non-wycliffite bible'], *SCH* 11 (1975) pp 147–61, especially pp 154–5 and notes. I find it hard to accept the main thesis of Wilks's paper, that there existed a pre- or non-Wycliffite vernacular

life did Wyclif show any interest in the vernacular, or in the need for the laity to be able to study the scriptures in a language that they understood. A couple of incidental references that are probably earlier, one from the *De Veritate Sacre Scripture* and one from the *De Eucharistia*, can be added to Wilks's analysis, but these do not change the basic truth of his assertion.[17] There seems very little evidence that Wyclif himself thought the vernacular important before the last years of his life, or at least explicitly so.[18] But if we are prepared to accept the view, so cogently revived by Wilks himself, that Wyclif did envisage a band of poor preachers touring the country with the message of the *Doctor Evangelicus*, then we are forced to acknowledge that Wyclif must have confronted the vital question of the medium through which that message was to be conveyed.[19] As I shall argue, it was only very slowly that the authorities of the established church came to see that the vernacular lay at the root of the trouble, and that the use of it was more significant than just the substitution of a despised barbaric tongue for the tradition of Latin—that the substitution threw open to all the possibility of discussing the subtleties of the Eucharist, of clerical claims, of civil dominion and so on, and that this possibility was being seized not only by men such as Walter Brut, *laycus litteratus*, or Sir John Oldcastle whom Hoccleve reproached with 'climbing too high' by meddling with scripture,[20] but also by the artisans of Wiltshire or Norfolk. The readiness with which lollards seized upon the vernacular texts produced has been fully demonstrated by Margaret Aston in her paper 'Lollardy and Literacy' in

---

bible which the lollards took over and modified. My main objection is that when the lollards came to justify their demand for such a bible they cited many precedents, but never alluded to the existence of such a complete translation of scripture; since such a pre-existing, orthodox version would have immensely helped their case, it seems inconceivable that they should have omitted to mention it. This disagreement does not, however, affect the point at issue here.

[17] *De Veritate Sacre Scripture* 2 p 243 urges the necessity of preaching in the vernacular, *De Eucharistia* p 90/13, whilst it states that it is preferable to use Latin rather than English for the consecration of the mass because of custom, implicitly acknowledges the possibility of using the vernacular even whilst denying the desirability.

[18] The constant repetition of the need for preaching to the laity means that Wyclif must have envisaged the use of the vernacular, see *Sermones* 2 p 448/16; 3 pp 75/20, 341/13.

[19] See his paper n 8 above; compare also my paper 'A Lollard Compilation and the Dissemination of Wycliffite Thought', *JTS* ns 23 (1972) pp 65–81.

[20] See *Registrum Johannis Trefnant*, ed W. W. Capes, *CYS* (1916) pp 278–365. The

History 1977.[21] As well as collecting together a large number of references to the ownership of books by lollards, she has exemplified the trouble to which lollards would go to obtain the literacy to read English books, or to find someone who would read to them, and to borrow or purchase such volumes. From the end of the fourteenth century to the Reformation there is no shortage of detail to prove the value that lollards set upon literacy and the possibilities that literacy opened up to them.

My own aim here is to fill the gap between the evidence of Wilks and that of Aston. When is it possible to discern a realisation that the matter of language was a crucial one, and not just an incidental detail? When, in fact, did either the heretics or their opponents realise that in many ways the medium was a significant part of the message? It seems to me that the terminal date for the search can be definitely fixed. By 1407 when the terms of Arundel's Constitutions were drafted the authorities had perceived the danger of English.[22] The details of the Constitutions are worth looking at again, for, though their general import is well enough known, their precise implications are much less so, and are indeed much less clear. The first two Constitutions are fairly straightforward reiterations of previous legislation: that no-one should preach in the vernacular or in Latin without a proper licence, such licences should only be given to those whose orthodoxy had been assured by examination, and that anyone admitting an unlicensed preacher should be excommunicated. The third is more significant: the preacher should regulate his observations according to his congregation, specifically that clerical vices should only be castigated to a congregation of

---

learning of Brut is evident from the length of his written replies to the charges made against him; since there is no indication to the contrary, and elsewhere Trefnant's register records in English replies given in that language, the Latin in which these replies are couched must be Brut's own. For the taunt of Hoccleve see *Hoccleve's Works: The Minor Poems*, ed F. J. Furnivall and I. Gollancz, revised J. Mitchell and A. I. Doyle, *EETS* extra series 61 and 73 (1970) no II/194, with which compare II/137–60.

[21] *History* 62 (1977) pp 347–71.

[22] I have used the text in Wilkins 3 pp 314–19; Arundel appears to have drafted the Constitutions in 1407 and issued them in 1409 (see E. F. Jacob, *The Register of Henry Chichele, archbishop of Canterbury 1414–1443*, 4 vols (Oxford 1938–47) I pp cxxx–cxxxi). For lollard references to the Constitutions see *The Lantern of Lizt*, ed L. M. Swinburn, *EETS* 151 (1917) pp 17/17, 100/1; BL MS Egerton 2820 fols 48ᵛ–9, BL MS Cotton Titus D V fols 46, 57.

clergy and not before one in which the laity were present.[23] The fourth forbade the discussion by any preacher of any of the sacraments of the church: the determinations of the church might be set out, but no doubt cast on any part of these. The next went beyond the preacher to forbid anyone teaching others from concerning himself in his instruction with any matter of theology. The sixth and seventh are those that mainly concern the present issue, and I will return to them more fully in a moment. The eighth and ninth dealt in more detail with the discussion or disputation of theological or ecclesiastical questions in the universities; the tenth goes back to the matter of licenses, this time specifying the need for a chaplain to have one before celebrating mass in the province of Canterbury. The eleventh contains the provision for enquiry about the views of every student in an Oxford hall once a month; this was the final defeat in Oxford's longstanding dispute over the right of the metropolitan to interfere in the university's affairs.[24] The two final sections dealt with the penalties for infringing the Constitutions and the method of procedure against such infringements. The central sixth section made the precise target of Arundel's legislation plain: no book or tract by John Wyclif or by any other written at his time or since should be read in the schools or anywhere else unless it had been examined and found orthodox; such an examination must be carried out by a minimum of twelve members of the university who had been approved by the archbishop or his successors, and the judgment of orthodoxy must be by unanimous vote.[25] The seventh went on to forbid the translation of any text of sacred scripture into English, and the ownership of any translation of the bible made in the time of Wyclif or later without the express

---

[23] Wilkins III p 316 'Praedicator . . . in praedicando clero sive populo, secundum materiam subjectam se honeste habeat, spargendo semen secundum convenientiam subjecti auditorii; clero praesertim praedicans de vitiis pullulantibus inter eos, et laicis de peccatis inter eos communiter usitatis, et non e contra'.

[24] For the earlier stages see K. B. McFarlane, *John Wycliffe and the Beginnings of English Nonconformity* (London 1952) pp 108–16, 156–7; also M. Aston, *Thomas Arundel* (Oxford 1967) pp 329–34.

[25] Wilkins 3 p 317 'nisi per universitatem Oxonii aut Cantabrigiae, seu saltem duodecim personas ex eisdem, quas eaedem universitates aut altera earundem, sub nostra, successorumve nostrorum discretione laudabili duxerint eligendas, primitus examinetur, et examinatus unanimiter per eosdem, deinde per nos seu successores nostros expresse approbetur, et universitatis nomine ac auctoritate stationariis tradatur, ut copietur; et facta collatione fideli, petentibus vendatur justo pretio sive detur, originali in cista aliqua universitatis extunc perpetuo remanente'.

permission of the diocesan, and this permission was only to be given after the translation had been inspected. This restriction upon the date of translation led to the alteration of the date 1408 at the end of one manuscript of the Wycliffite bible to 1308, a date that would have escaped the censure.[26]

The wording of this seventh constitution is, to my mind, obscure. The vital section is this:

> statuimus igitur et ordinamus, ut nemo deinceps aliquem textum sacrae scripturae auctoritate sua in linguam Anglicanam, vel aliam transferat, per viam libri, libelli, aut tractatus, nec legatur aliquis hujusmodi liber, libellus, aut tractatus jam noviter tempore dicti Johannis Wycliff, sive citra, compositus, aut in posterum componendus, in parte vel in toto, publice, vel occulte . . .

The obscurity lies in the force of *per viam*, 'by way of': does this imply that the clause applies whether the translation is of the whole bible, or only of a part of that vast book? or does it mean that any work that involves, even as only a part of a larger whole, the rendering of biblical quotations into English falls under the same condemnation as a complete English bible? That this second interpretation is not over fanciful is surely suggested in the Constitution itself by the word *tractatus*, a term that could hardly be applied to any section of the bible straightforwardly rendered. Lyndwood's annotations to this part of the text in his *Provinciale* confirm the suspicion that this second meaning is relevant: the words *aut tractatus* are glossed

> sic videlicet, quod de dictis doctorum, vel propriis, aliquem tractatum componat applicando textum sacræ scripturæ, et illius sensum transferendo in Anglicum, vel aliud idioma. Et eodem modo potest intelligi, quod dicit de libro sive libello, ut scilicet textum sacræ scripturæ in tali libro vel libello applicet, et textum ipsum transferat in aliud idioma.[27]

---

[26] Oxford Bodleian MS Fairfax 2 fol 385; see H. Hargreaves in *CHB* 2 p 394.

[27] I have used the 1968 Gregg reprint of the *Provinciale* (Oxford 1679) p 286; see C. R. Cheney, 'William Lyndwood's *Provinciale*', reprinted in *Medieval Texts and Studies* (Oxford 1973) pp 158–84. I have checked the gloss in the following manuscripts: Oxford Bodleian MSS Bodley 248 fol 278[v], Laud Misc 608 fol 176, Oxford Corpus Christi College MS B.71 fol 240, BL MS Royal 11 C.viii fol 200, BL MS Royal 11 E.i fol 229[v], Cambridge Peterhouse MS 53 quire 28 leaf 8, Cambridge Peterhouse MS 54 fol 166[v], in all of which the gloss appears as printed; the gloss is abridged in Oxford Magdalen College MS 143 fol 217[v] and Cambridge

This gloss, of course, extends the scope of the Constitution vastly. But it does bring the seventh into line with the sixth: any book, in Latin or in English, that deals with matters of theology or church affairs, may only be used after the archbishop or his appointed surrogates have approved it.

A glance at any lollard text makes it plain why such a ruling could have given rise to the view with which I began this paper: that the expression of ideas gained from Latin books and expressed in English was *ipso facto* evidence of heresy. To Wyclif and his followers the bible was the main, if not the only, source of authority; therefore any view is always supported by the citation of biblical justification. This is true of the Latin *Opus Arduum* or *Floretum*, just as it is of the vernacular writings; but, after the first few years, the latter were much more important to the movement.[28] Indeed, if the confiscated copy of *The Canterbury Tales* had included, for instance, the Pardoner's Tale or, even more, the Parson's Tale, it could on a rigorous interpretation of this Constitution rightly have been regarded as indicative of heresy. Ensuing legislation and proceedings did little to allay the fear that use of the vernacular in itself was dangerous. The address by abbot Whethamsted in 1426/7 to suspected heretics, and the confession of one of them that follows, may detail the errors in the books that the lollard possessed, but the ordinance that precedes these baldly states that the cause of heresy is *librorum possessio et lectura, qui scribuntur in vulgari idiomate nostro*. It orders the investigation of all such books and those who own them, only *præcipue qui aut materiam aut occasionem ministrare poterunt erroneæ opinionis et malignæ*.[29]

By 1407 suspicion of lollardy had embraced the fact of the importance of the vernacular. This seems certain. What is rather more difficult is to establish the date at which this notion first becomes perceptible, and to trace the stages by which it achieved

---

Pembroke College MS 309 fol 316, and does not appear at all in the more heavily abridged glosses in BL MS Royal 9 A.v, BL MS Royal 9 A.xiii and Cambridge University Library MS Ee.6.32.

[28] For the first see my paper 'A Neglected Wycliffite Text', *JEH* 29 (1978) pp 257–79, for the second most recently *The Middle English Translation of the 'Rosarium Theologie'*, ed C. von Nolcken, *Middle English Texts* 10 (Heidelberg 1979); for the vernacular texts compare the footnote biblical references to texts nos 20–6 in *Selections*.

[29] *Annales Monasterii S. Albani a Johanne Amundesham*, ed H. T. Riley, 2 vols, *RS* (London 1870–1) I pp 222–8.

sufficient importance to be formalized in legislation. I have argued elsewhere that in Oxford in 1401 it was still possible for men to urge the desirability of vernacular translations of the bible without being suspected as heretics.[30] Richard Ullerston, a man otherwise known as a pillar of orthodoxy and apparently not one who had sown wild-oats of Wycliffism in his youth, and William Butler, a Franciscan friar, both spoke on the matter at length, though on opposite sides of the debate, without mentioning that the lollards notably supported translation. The case is, of course, stronger for Butler: it would have helped his opposition had he been able to cite the danger of the spread of lollardy as one of the undesirable outcomes of vernacular versions. But to think that the switch of views amongst the orthodox came between 1401 and 1407 is unconvincing, and there is evidence that this debate did not reveal the whole picture. I should like now to look further at the evidence for the period between 1382, when Wyclif mentions the use of the vernacular in enthusiastic terms, and 1407 when Arundel's legislation condemned it outright.

The earliest edicts against Wyclif and his followers do not appear to mention books or pamphlets of any kind, Latin or English.[31] The first statement that I have found comes from 1388 when a series of mandates was sent out by the king to various authorities, secular and ecclesiastical, requiring them to search out the books, booklets or quires written by Wyclif, Hereford, Aston or Purvey. Some of these specify that the books might be written in English or in Latin.[32] Earlier than this there is implicit recognition of the use of English, since we find mention as early as 1382 of the preaching of

[30] ['The Debate on Bible Translation, Oxford 1401',] *EHR* 90 (1975) pp 1–18.
[31] For the stages of early legislation see H. G. Richardson, 'Heresy and the Lay Power under Richard II', *EHR* 51 (1936) pp 1–28. The edicts in *Calendar of Patent Rolls 1381–1385* (London 1897) pp 150, 487 do not mention any heretic by name; Courtenay's letter used by various bishops in 1387 (see Wilkins 3 pp 202–3 for the copy in Wakefield's Worcester register) mentions various heretics by name but not books. Compare A. K. McHardy, 'Bishop Buckingham and the Lollards of Lincoln Diocese', *SCH* 9 (1972) pp 131–5.
[32] *Calendar of Patent Rolls 1385–1389* (London 1900) pp 448, 468, 536; *Calendar of Close Rolls 1385–1389* (London 1921) p 519. [Henry] Knighton, [*Chronicon*], ed J. R. Lumby, 2 vols, RS (London 1889–95) 2 pp 260–5 gives an account of new measures taken in 1388, mentioning (p 263) 'librosque eorum Anglicos plenius examinarent', and giving a specimen royal commission which orders the inspection and confiscation of books 'tam in Anglico quam in Latino' (pp 264–5). Compare the later material exemplified in A. Hudson, 'The Examination of Lollards', *BIHR* 46 (1973) p 156.

Wyclif's views to lay people *utriusque sexus*.[33] But it would appear that the language did not merit mention. The references to preaching to the laity are both early and frequent. The chroniclers, even though the dates they assign cannot be regarded as firm, provide a chorus of testimony on this score. Walsingham under 1382 records that Wyclif himself preached *in vulgari plebe*, and connects Wyclif's escape from censure in 1378 to the way in which he had charmed the ears of the Londoners with his perverse doctrines.[34] Knighton, who notes Wyclif's own part in biblical translation, describes in some detail the preaching of Aston, Purvey and another (who, we might suspect, may have been Knighton's fellow canon, Philip Repingdon); the fact that the chronicler twice mentions vernacular phrases in these accounts makes it clear that the sermons were often, if not always, in English.[35] The continuator of the *Eulogium Historiarum* describes under 1381 how Wyclif's *discipuli . . . hanc doctrinam predicabant et divulgabant per totam Angliam multo laicos seducentes etiam nobiles et magnos dominos qui defendebant tales falsos prædicatores*, and again, under the following year, how these disciples taught the heretical view of the Eucharist *non solum in multis popularibus et laicis, sed etiam in nobilibus et literatis.*[36] More specifically, the notarial account of Nicholas Hereford's Ascension day sermon in Oxford in 1382 particularly states that this highly controversial discourse was *in vulgari ydeomate anglicano*; Hereford might have been chosen to give the sermon by the chancellor, Robert Rigg, an action which led many to think that Rigg had Wycliffite leanings, but his congregation was plainly not limited to an academic group.[37]

But I do not want to multiply evidence of lollard preaching. That is easy to do, but it only implicitly advances my investigation—that the Wycliffites saw the need to use the vernacular if the mass of people was to be convinced of the rightness of their views, and that the opposing authorities equally tried to prevent such unorthodox preaching in whatever language it might be delivered. What is

---

[33] Winchester, reg. Wykeham, ed T. F. Kirby, *Hampshire Record Society* (1896–9) 2 pp 337–8.
[34] [Thomas Walsingham,] *Historia Anglicana*, ed H. T. Riley, 2 vols, *RS* (London 1863–4) II p 51 and I p 363; compare *Chronicon Angliæ*, ed E. M. Thompson, *RS* (London 1874) p 335.
[35] Knighton II pp 151–2; p 176 Aston, p 179 Purvey, p 174 unnamed Wycliffite.
[36] *Continuatio Eulogii Historiarum*, ed F. S. Haydon, *RS* (London 1863) pp 351–5.
[37] For the sermon see Oxford Bodleian MS Bodley 240, p 848; for the assumption see *Fasciculi Zizaniorum*, ed W. W. Shirley, *RS* (London 1858) pp 298–9.

more relevant is the evidence that specifies English, and that which
defines more closely the dangers of using the vernacular. Here
material is rather less easy to discover, at least in any direct form.[38]
Much of the evidence comes from tracts or debates that are overtly
on other subjects. It seems clear from a number of sources that
objections to the use of the vernacular had been raised, and that
defenders of English felt it necessary to answer the points made.
The fact that the same arguments are advanced both by those
defending the vernacular and by those opposed to its use points to
the existence of a widespread debate, even though the two sets of
texts do not formally answer each other. It is also noteworthy that
defenders of the vernacular reveal the same points, whether or not
they are otherwise sympathetic to lollard causes. As I shall show,
the orthodox Ullerston uses some of the same contentions as the
writers of lollard sermons. As usual, there is difficulty with many
of the lollard texts in determining precisely their date of composition. In each case I shall endeavour to provide one example from a
dated text, to show that the idea was current before 1407, even if
some of the evidence comes from works that are later in date than
Arundel's Constitutions.

The first group of arguments focus on the matter of language
itself. Wyclif in his *De nova prevaricancia mandatorum*, dated as late
1382 or 1383, already refers to those who argued that vernacular
scriptures were legitimate since Christ and his apostles had used
various languages in their preaching.[39] This idea was taken up by an
additional prologue to Saint John's gospel found in one manuscript
of the Wycliffite bible and in other anonymous lollard texts.[40] The
Opus Arduum, written between Christmas 1389 and Easter 1390
reiterates this, and reinforces the argument by the observation that
Jerome had written many of his letters to women to whom he must
originally have used the vernacular.[41] In the late *De contrarietate
duorum dominorum* Wyclif had argued that language, whether

[38] There is apparently little in the Latin tracts written against Wyclif by men such as
Woodford, Rymington or Netter.
[39] *Polemical Works* I p 116/6; for the date see Wilks p 155. Compare [T.] Arnold,
[*Select English Works of John Wyclif*], 3 vols (Oxford 1869–71) 3 p 100/20; [F. D.]
Matthew, [*The English Works of Wyclif hitherto unprinted*], EETS 74 (1880) p
429/11.
[40] Printed in [*The Holy Bible . . . made from the Latin Vulgate by John Wycliffe and his
Followers*], ed [J.] Forshall and [F.] Madden, 4 vols (Oxford 1850) 4 p 685b.
[41] Brno University Library MS Mk 28 fols 136ᵛ–7; for the text see my paper 'A
Neglected Wycliffite Text', *JEH* 29 (1978) pp 257–79.

Hebrew, Greek, Latin or English was *quasi habitus legis domini*, that the teaching of Christ was not affected by language and that therefore the most familiar should be used.[42] This was taken up by the anonymous Latin sermons found in three Oxford manuscripts:

> Quamuis enim ydiomata sint diuersa, tamen idem articuli fidei et eorum veritates euangelice sunt eedem in numero vtrobique quia quamuis lingue sint diuerse, tamen veritates euangelice non variantur. Ideo idem euangelium potest scribi et pronunciari in Latinis et Grecis, in Gallicis, in Anglicis et in omni lingua articulata. Et euangelium scriptum in Anglicis quia bonitas euangelii non habet attendi penes bonitatem ydiomatis sed penes perfeccionem veritatis credite et Dei approbantis eandem.[43]

Others, however, had doubts about this equivalence of languages. Ullerston in his 1401 paper refers to the view that English is a barbarous language, lacking a grammatical structure and also deficient in a number of the terms that would be necessary for a rendering of scripture. He himself dismisses these difficulties, arguing that English can find the necessary terms, and observing that even the Vulgate made use of some non-Latin terms such as *hosanna, racha, alleluia* from Hebrew to remedy Latin inadequacies.[44] The insufficiency of English was taken up much more fully by Thomas Palmer in a determination which, from its failure to mention recent legislation effecting the prohibition on vernacular scriptures that its author so much desired, must probably be dated from before 1407. Palmer spends a lot of time labouring the point which had been taken in the prologue to the Wycliffite bible, that languages are not symmetrical—that English, for instance, lacks the fully inflected definite article or relative pronoun of Latin. He also produces a number of Latin words for which he urges English has no equivalent; but the examples hardly forward his argument, since they are mostly cases relevant not to biblical

---

[42] *Polemical Works* 2 p 700/27; compare *De Amore, (Opera Minora)* p 9/20, *Speculum Secularium Dominorum (Opera Minora)* p 74/6, *Opus Evangelicum* 2 p 115/4. With Arnold 3 p 98/4 'the treuthe of God stondeth nou3t in one langage more than in another' compare the Waldensian text cited by [J. Gonnet and A. Molnar,] *Les Vaudois [au moyen âge]* (Turin 1974) p 394 note 120 'sacra scriptura eundem effectum habet in vulgari, quem habet in Latino'.

[43] Quoted from Oxford Bodleian MS Laud Misc 200 fol 201; the other two manuscripts do not extend so far. I owe knowledge of this group to Dr Christina von Nolcken, who is investigating the material.

[44] Vienna Nationalbibliothek MS 4133, fols 195ᵛ, 202.

translation but to theological discussion, and some at that reveal only Palmer's ignorance of contemporary vernacular writing.[45]

Related to this linguistic argument is the citation of precedent for translation. Ullerston produced a long list of earlier English versions, from Bede and Alfred to Richard Rolle. These English models are found also in numerous lollard texts, and are referred to by Palmer.[46] A comparable argument is that other nations have the scriptures in their own tongue. Wyclif in *De triplici vinculo amoris* referred to queen Anne's possession of the gospels in three languages, Czech, German and Latin, and this royal example was taken up by the English tract derived from Ullerston's discussion. The same point in more general terms was made in the *Opus Arduum* and is mentioned, though not discussed, by Palmer.[47]

Coming closer to the heart of the matter is the argument that urges the necessity of communicating essential commands in a language intelligible in those who should obey them. If the English king sent out letters patent in Latin or French 'to do crie his lawis, his statutes and his wille to the peple, and it were cried oonly on Latyn or Frensche and not on Englisch, it were no worschip to the kynge ne warnynge to the peple'. Similarly, what good would it be if a watchman warned of impending danger only in an unknown tongue? To teach Christ's law in Latin is an equally, indeed more, dangerous and foolish enterprise.[48]

An argument that could more easily be disposed of was that if it were legitimate to teach the scriptures in the vernacular through sermons, it must be allowed to write it in the vernacular. This is

---

[45] Palmer's determination was printed from the sole manuscript, Trinity College Cambridge MS B.15. 11 fols 42ᵛ–7ᵛ, by [M.] Deanesly in [*The Lollard Bible*] (Cambridge 1920) pp 418–37, but Deanesly's views about the nature and position of the determination need modification; see here pp 421–2, 425–8, 436–7. The form of Palmer's text is, as it stands, a muddle; it would seem that it may be notes taken from a whole series of debates.

[46] Vienna Nationalbibliothek MS 4133 fol 198ʳ/ᵛ; Palmer, ed Deanesly p 435. For other lollard instances see Matthew p 429/22, Forshall and Madden 1 p 59, and the so-called 'Lollard Chronicle of the Papacy', ed E. W. Talbert, *Journal of English and Germanic Philology*⁴¹ (Urbana 1942) pp 163–93, lines 99 *seq*, 136 *seq*.

[47] Polemical Works I p 168/9; the English text printed by Deanesly p 445 (the conjecture about authorship is unwarranted), where the vernacular in which Anne's books were written has become English; *Opus Arduum*, Brno University Library Mk 28 fol 174ᵛ; Palmer, ed Deanesly pp 419–20.

[48] Cambridge University Library MS Ii.6.26 fols 5ᵛ–6; compare fol 11 where the story of the Ethiopian eunuch in Acts 8:26–38 is told in favour of even partial understanding since this will incite the ignorant to search for more.

alleged in the *Opus Arduum* and in various English tracts.[49] But, as opposition to vernacular scriptures grew, it became obvious that this parallel was far from exact. Sermons could select uncontroversial passages of the bible, the passage could then be explained by the preacher, and, furthermore, the preacher himself would have to be licensed by the bishop if he were to operate legally. The naked text in the ploughman's hand was a much more dangerous and much more readily available weapon, as both sides realised right down to the reformation period.[50] The prefatory epistle to Nicholas Love's translation of the pseudo-Bonaventuran *Meditations on the Life and Passion of Christ* is relevant here. This text is presented as an alternative to the Wycliffite scriptures, by the time of the translation banned, and Love observes that the text offers a commentary on the harmony of the gospels, explaining the significance of the stories retold. The preface also records Arundel's authorization of the text.[51]

The issues here, however, lead on to the central point in this debate on translation: the prerogative of the clergy in scriptural, theological and ecclesiastical matters. Both sides in the debate perceived that the availability of vernacular scriptures would make possible the participation of the laity in questions of such a kind. To William Butler in 1401 this was the chief objection to translation. At one point he cited Aristotle's *Rhetoric* to the effect that 'quanto maior est populus, tanto minor vel remotior est intellectum'. Butler had a strictly hierarchical view of society: the lower ranks

---

[49] Brno University Library MS Mk 28, fol 137; compare Oxford Bodleian MS Bodley 288 fol 133ᵛ (one of the lollard versions of Rolle's Psalter commentary), Cambridge University Library MS Ii.6.26 fol 42, Arnold 3 p 98/10.

[50] See for instance More's *Dialogue concerning Tyndale*, ed W. C. Campbell (London/New York 1931) bk I caps 22–3, bk III caps 14–16, and compare the account in *The Confutation of Tyndale's Answer*, ed L. A. Schuster et al., 3 vols (New Haven/London 1973) 3 p 1155, and|the text *Rede me and be nott wrothe* (*STC* 21427, [1528]) sig. c ii, where the anonymous reforming author narrates how Tunstall 'at Poulis crosse ernestly

> Denounced it to be heresy
> That the gospell shuld come to lyght,
> Callynge theym heretikes execerable
> Whiche caused the gospell venerable
> To come vnto laye mens syght!

[51] For the text see *The Mirrour of the Blessed Lyf of Jesu Christ A Translation . . . by Nicholas Love*, ed L. F. Powell (London 1908) pp 7–13, 300–1; but the manuscript that Powell printed, Oxford Brasenose College MS e.9 does not contain the whole Latin preface, for which see E. Salter, 'Nicholas Love's "Mirrour of the Blessed Lyf of Jesu Christ"', *Analecta Cartusiana* 10 (Salzburg 1974) pp 1–2.

are to be entirely dependent upon the higher for their instruction and since, in his opinion, to read the scriptures is an activity suitable only to the higher ranks, nothing should be done that would foster wider consultation of the bible.[52] The lollard texts are, we may think, more realistic about society at this stage of the medieval period. They point out that, between the clergy and illiterate labourer there is a large group of laymen who are relatively well educated, who can read their native language and who have wealth to purchase books. Teaching of a more sophisticated kind is needed for them. And it is surely better that such literate men should 'ocupie hem and othere in redeynge of Goddis lawe and deuocioun than in redeynge of lesyng, rebaudie and vanite'.[53]

However, as the authorities perceived, the reading of scripture would lead inevitably to the teaching of scripture. Though Ullerston might attempt to answer this by asserting the right, indeed the duty, of a parent to instruct his children, of a master to instruct his servants, or even in the case of a mother with her child or an abbess with her nuns for a woman to teach, this did not really answer the charge.[54] The problem is brought out in numerous heresy cases in the fifteenth century. That of John Edward, priest of Brington in the Lincoln diocese in 1405, epitomises all: Edward's writings were in Latin and in English, and two of his opinions were that any layman can preach the gospel of God anywhere, and that any good man, even if he were not lettered, was a priest.[55] Here the dilemma was pushed one stage further: if any good man, by which Edward would have meant any predestined man, teaching the gospel freely, were a priest, then the rights of the clergy were seriously infringed—it is a short step from there to an assertion of the redundancy of the clergy. This danger was one that is continually stressed by the macaronic sermons that have been described by Roy Haines. They date from after Arundel's Constitutions, but their sentiments echo ideas that are traceable much earlier: 'every lewde man is becomen a

---

[52] Butler's determination, found in Oxford Merton College MS 68 fols 202–4ᵛ, was also printed by Deanesly pp 401–18, here pp 405–7. The text is dated 1401, but, whilst it uses some of the same points as Ullerston's of the same year, neither can be taken as a direct answer to the other. Butler was a Franciscan friar.
[53] Cambridge University Library MS Ii.6.26 fol 3; compare also fols 6ᵛ, 7–8ᵛ, 21, and Oxford Bodleian MS Laud misc.200 fols 32, 128, 146ᵛ, 147ᵛ, 198ᵛ, Bodley 288 fol 96, BL MS Additional 41321 fols 14ᵛ, 30, Arnold 3 p 184/22, Matthew p 159/4.
[54] Vienna Nationalbibliothek MS 4133 fols 202ᵛ–3.
[55] The case is printed from the Arundel register in Wilkins 3 pp 282–4.

clerke and talkys in his termys', the layman now *vult smater se de summa diuinitate, mouebit dubia de venerabili sacramento altaris et intromittet se boldliche de eterna sapiencia Dei,* . . . *isti laici nimis vadant in clerimonia scripturis et consuetudinibus ecclesie.*[56] Ullerston in his determination to some extent anticipated this objection, but did not fully answer it. The various replies of the lollards were even more unacceptable. Hardly likely to find favour was the view that 'Crist seyde that stonys schulde cry, and secler lordys schuld, in defawte of prelatys, lerne and preche the law of God in here modyr tonge'. More outspoken was the retort that, in objecting to the use of the native language, the clergy wanted to make the laity as ignorant as themselves. Equally unpopular was the taunt that the chief cause of the friars' dislike of vernacular scriptures was that '3ef the truthe of Goddes lawe were knowen to the peple, thei schulden lacke miche of her worldely worschepe and of her lucre bothe'.[57]

As time went on a more substantial objection to English scriptures was the danger that such would arouse or further heresy. As I have mentioned, neither Ullerston nor Butler associate support for the vernacular with lollardy, but in Palmer's paper this point is made.[58] But the charge was familiar before the turn of the century. The *Opus Arduum*, written between Christmas 1389 and Easter 1390, refers to the persecution of those *qui scripta ewangelica in Anglicis penes se detinent et legunt* . . . *qui ut lolardi deffamantur.*[59] It is clear also that Ullerston knew of the objection that translation would foster heresy, even if he did not specify heresy as lollardly.

---

[56] '"Wilde wittes and wilfulnes": John Swetstock's attack on those "poyswunmongeres" the Lollards', *SCH* 8 (1972) pp 143–53, and 'Church, society and politics in the early fifteenth century as viewed from an English pulpit', *SCH* 12 (1975) pp 143–57; the attribution to Swetstock is unlikely, see the latter n 95. I have worked from the manuscripts, here Oxford Bodleian MS Laud Misc 706 fol 160ᵛ, Bodley 649 fol 14ᵛ, and compare the latter fols 38ᵛ, 70ᵛ, 80, 98, 125ᵛ and the charge repeated in Matthew p 159/1 and in the citation from Cambridge University Library MS Ii.3.8 fol 149 quoted in [G. R.] Owst, *Preaching [in Medieval England]* (Cambridge 1926) p 135.

[57] See respectively Arnold 3 p 114/10, Cambridge University Library MS Ii.6.26 fol 13 and BL MS Additional 41321 fol 38ᵛ; compare Arnold 3 p 393/22, 405/37 and Matthew p 428/14 and the anti-fraternal poem printed by R. H. Robbins, *Historical Poems of the XIVth and XV Centuries* (New York 1959) no 69 especially lines 1–12.

[58] See *EHR* 90 (1975) p 16; Palmer, ed Deanesly p 425 'Quomodo igitur non errarent simplices, idiote circa scripturam, si eam haberent in vulgari idiomate modo, propter malum intellectum Lollardorum et simplicium grammaticam solum intelligentes.'

[59] Brno University Library MS Mk 28 fol 161ᵛ.

He attempted to answer this charge by alleging that a careful study of scripture, in whatever language, is a useful antidote to heresy. Perhaps more cogently, he later added that heresy may be found in Latin as in English—heresy is not the prerogative of one language.[60] An English lollard tract takes up the same point, and urges it more strongly:

> many men wolen seie that ther is moche eresie in Englische bookis, and therfore no man schulde haue Goddis lawe in Englische. And I seie be the same skile ther schulde no man haue Goddis lawe in bookis of Latyn, for ther is moche heresie in bookis of Latyn, more than in Englische bookis.[61]

The argument that English scriptures lead to heresy was extended into the secular field by the contention that they also led to rebellion. The preaching of Wyclif and his followers was seen in retrospect by Walsingham and the compiler of the *Fasciculi Zizaniorum* as instrumental in the Peasants' Revolt.[62] The accuracy of this hindsight is debated amongst modern historians,[63] but it is obvious that the reproach was a familiar one to the lollards, and that their support for English scriptures was seen as tending towards another rebellion. One lollard answered this charge directly: 'ignoraunce of Goddis lawe is cause of alle meuynge and vnstabilite in the comoun pepel . . . redi to rebelle a3ens her souereyns'.[64]

But was the question of the vernacular really as important as these writers seem to suggest? To us, with our more sophisticated views about language and with our familiarity with translations of

---

[60] Vienna Nationalbibliothek MS 4133 fols 195ᵛ, 196, 199 'nam si propterea non permitteretur ewangelium scribi in Anglico, quia sunt multi tractatus Anglicani continentes hereses et errores, a pari siue a fortiori prohiberent scripturam in Latino que per totam Christianitatem posset disseminari', and fol 205 urges care over Latin 'ex vi lingue incomparabiliter lacius diffundi posset quam in nostro Anglico exaratus qui ultra terminos maris Britannici non posset facilius se diffundere'.

[61] Cambridge University Library MS Ii.6.26 fol 4ᵛ; compare Forshall and Madden I pp 57–8 'no doute he shal fynde ful manye biblis in Latyn ful false if he loke manie, nameli newe; and the comune Latyn biblis han more nede to be correctid . . . than hath the English bible late translatid.'

[62] *Historia Anglicana* 2 pp 32–3, *Fasciculus Zizaniorum* pp 273–4; compare also Knighton 2 p 170.

[63] See the discussion by R. B. Dobson, *The Peasants' Revolt of 1381* (London 1970) pp 5, 373, and M. Aston, 'Lollardy and Sedition', *PP* 17 (1960) pp 1–44, expecially pp 3–5; for another view see J. H. Dahmus, *The Prosecution of John Wyclyf* (New Haven/London 1952) pp 82–5.

[64] Cambridge University Library MS Ii.6.26 fol 19ᵛ.

all kinds, the debate seems merely peripheral. There were surely more important matters in lollard teaching, matters that might more reasonably have led to persecution. It is here perhaps worth while looking at the later case of Reginald Pecock. Pecock was, of course, an outspoken opponent of lollardy; yet he too was convicted of heresy. But in one regard he shared the view of his opponents: that the vernacular must be used. If lollardy were to be refuted, then Pecock conceived that it could only be refuted by means of the medium the heretics themselves used, the English language.[65] V. H. H. Green, who in 1944 wrote the only full-length biography of Pecock, claimed 'the fact that [Pecock] wrote in English was probably even more irritating to his accusers than the views which his books contained.[66] If this opinion is tenable, then it would suggest that the question of the vernacular was in the late fourteenth and fifteenth centuries more central than we can readily perceive. Certainly, in the records of the investigations into Pecock there is mention of the fact that Pecock's writings were in English as well as in Latin, that the books Pecock had to consign to the fire were English tomes and Latin, that the subsequent pursuit of his disciples was directed against owners of his books in either language.[67] But the lists of tenets that Pecock was forced to abjure do not contain any mention of the vernacular.[68] Nor, perhaps more surprisingly, is there any allusion to Pecock's contravention of the terms of Arundel's Constitutions by his publication of books that discussed the sacraments and doctrines of the church, and that cast

---

[65] *Repressor [of Overmuch Blaming of the Clergy]*, ed C. Babington, 2 vols *RS* (London 1860) I pp 1–2; *The Folewer to the Donet*, ed E. V. Hitchcock, *EETS* 164 (1924) pp 7/1–8/21; *The Reule of Crysten Religioun*, ed W. C. Greet, *EETS* 171 (1927) pp 21, 93–4; *The Book of Faith*, ed J. L. Morison (Glasgow 1909) p 116.

[66] [V. H. H.] Green, [*Bishop Reginald Pecock*] (Cambridge 1945) p 188. In addition see [E. F.] Jacob, ['Reynold Pecock, bishop of Chichester'], *PBA* 37 (1951) pp 121–53, especially here pp 141–3.

[67] See *Registrum Abbatiæ Johannis Whethamstede*, ed H. T. Riley, 2 vols *RS* (London 1872–3) I p 280; *Calendar of Entries in the Papal Registers relating to Great Britain and Ireland: Papal Letters II 1455–64*, ed J. A. Twemlow (London 1921) pp 77, 529; *An English Chronicle of the Reigns of Richard II, Henry IV, Henry V and Henry VI*, ed J. S. Davies, *CSer* 64 (1856) p 75 states that Pecock 'had labored meny yeres for to translate holy scripture into Englysshe'. The abjuration recorded in Oxford Bodleian MS Ashmole 789 fols 303ᵛ–4 is in English but the list of articles abjured is in Latin; the same manuscript, fol 324, has a copy of a letter objecting to the graduation of J. Harlowe because of his favour for, and ownership of books by, Pecock.

[68] According to Jacob p 138 n4, the most authentic version of the abjuration is that in Oxford Bodleian MS Ashmole 789 fols 303ᵛ–4.

doubt on the accepted teachings. Interestingly, it is Gascoigne who provides the best evidence in support of Green's contention. Gascoigne records his disapproval of Pecock under many headings.[69] His most extended account starts by narrating how in 1467 the realm of England was much disturbed by the English books that Pecock had written. He then explains that all the lords of the temporal realm agreed that Pecock should be expelled from the Council.[70] The reasons he gives probably omit one of the most important, that Pecock had been backed by political lords who by that time had lost power.[71] But the first reason that Gascoigne produces, however incredible politically it may seem to us, is 'because he wrote such profound matters in English, matters more likely to harm those who read or heard them than to benefit them . . . and also he composed a new creed, large and long, in English words'. The same point is repeated later: Pecock 'wrote high matters and profound in English, which lead the layfolk from good rather than to it'.[72]

The Austin friar John Bury, the first part of whose answer to Pecock's *Repressor* entitled *Gladius Salomonis* survives in MS Bodley 108, takes up Pecock's argument that the laity should be grateful for the availability of books such as his own in their vernacular, since this allows them to learn the rudiments of natural and moral philosophy.[73] Bury quotes from Malachi *labia sacerdotis custodiunt scienciam* and other biblical and patristic passages in his outraged polemic against Pecock. Pecock's books, he laments, are worse than those of Mahomet, Sabelius, Arius and Wyclif. The use of the vernacular passes almost unnoticed in Bury's anger that the laity should dare to meddle in such topics. Bury is outspoken, but his view echoes that of many other clerics of the century.[74]

[69] Thomas Gascoigne, *Loci e Libro Veritatum*, ed J. E. Thorold Rogers (Oxford 1881) pp 15, 26–7, 35, 40, 44.

[70] pp 208–18.

[71] See Jacob pp 130–2, Green pp 28–30, 39–40, 46.

[72] p 213 'una fuit, quia scripsit tales profundas materias in Anglicis, quæ magis aptæ erant lædere legentes et audientes quam illis proficere . . . et ideo novum cimbolum magnum et longum in Anglicis verbis composuit'; p 214 'et magnæ causæ movebant clericos et dominos temporales multum contra eum, scilicet quod scripsit altas materias id est profundas in Anglicis, quæ pocius abducerunt laicos a bono quam ex vero simili plures ducerent ad bonum.'

[73] For Bury see Emden (O) I p 323; extracts from the *Gladius Salomonis* are printed at the end of *Repressor* 2 pp 567–613.

[74] *Repressor* 2 pp 600, 602; Oxford Bodleian MS Bodley 108 fols 51, 53ᵛ. The entire section covers fols 53ᵛ–7ᵛ, but the extracts given pp 600–7 give a reasonable idea of

It is interesting to compare the position at the end of the fifteenth century with that in the first half of the thirteenth. In 1238 Grosseteste had set out his ideas for the reform of his clergy: each parish priest should teach the laity concerning the decalogue, the seven deadly sins, the sacraments of the church and those matters necessary to a true confession; these should be taught *in idiomate communi*; the boys of the parish were to be taught the Lord's prayer, the creed and the Ave Maria; since, Grosseteste has heard, many adults are ignorant of these matters, enquiry should be made of all coming to confession and instruction given as necessary.[75] Grosseteste was, of course, taking up the terms of the 1215 Lateran Council, as many others at that time had done.[76] The ninth canon of that Council, it is often forgotten, had allowed the use of different languages, even in the services of the church *pontifices . . . provideant viros idoneos, qui secundum diversitates rituum et linguarum divina officia illis celebrent*; this section was incorporated into the Decretals.[77] In 1281 Pecham in the Lambeth constitutions ordered the preaching of the basic elements of religion *vulgariter*.[78] But by 1485 John Smith of Coventry was dilated for heresy because he stated *quod quilibet tenetur scire dominicam orationem, salutacionem angelicam et simbolum in Anglicis*; his neighbour Richard Gilmyn was similarly apprehended because *habuit orationem dominicam et salutacionem angelicam et simbolum in Anglicis*.[79] Even earlier than this, in the Norwich diocese it was felt significant when John Burell stated that his brother had in 1426 taught him the Pater, Ave and Credo in English.[80] In some instances, certainly, it is possible to see

---

Bury's argument. For a lollard interpretation of the same passage of Malachi see BL MS Egerton 2820, fols 5ʳ/ᵛ.

[75] *Roberti Grosseteste . . . Epistolæ*, ed H. R. Luard *RS* (London 1861) pp 155–7; compare J. H. Srawley, 'Grosseteste's Administration of the Diocese of Lincoln', *Robert Grosseteste Scholar and Bishop*, ed D. A. Callus (Oxford 1955) pp 168–9.

[76] See E. J. Arnould, *Le Manuel des Péchés* (Paris 1940) pp 1–59.

[77] See HL V.ii (1913) p 1339; *Corpus Iuris Canonici*, ed E. Friedberg 2 vols (Leipzig 1879–81) 2 Decretals lib. i tit.xxxi cap.xiv.

[78] Wilkins 2 p 54.

[79] Lichfield reg Hales fol 166ᵛ; compare the much earlier text described in *Selections* pp 185–6, BL MS Egerton 2820 fol 52 'thei grucchen if ony nedi man haue so moche of this breed that he undirstonde his *pater noster* in his modir tunge'.

[80] *Heresy Trials in the Diocese of Norwich, 1428–31*, ed N. P. Tanner *CSer*, 4 series 20 (1977) p 73; compare p 69 where John Baker of Tunstall 'recognovit iudicialiter se habuisse unum librum de Johanne Burge de Beghton dicte diocesis, qui quidem liber continebat in se Pater Noster et Ave Maria et Credo in lingua Anglicana scripta'.

why the bishops were concerned: the 'one suspecte boke of commaundementis' produced before bishop Langton of Salisbury in 1490 may well have been one of the lollard commentaries on the decalogue, where the command against graven images was predictably seized upon by the heretics for a recitation of their views.[81] Even the apparently innocent words of the Lord's prayer could form the starting point for unorthodox opinions, as they do in two lollard commentaries.[82] But in many cases there is no evidence that a commentary was in question. Though the group of heretics investigated by bishop Longland of Lincoln in the Chilterns between 1518 and 1521 owned a wide selection of books, the terms of the investigation suggest that mere knowledge of the elements of the faith in English was evidence of heresy.[83] Marian Morden had been taught these by her brother; William Littlepage had been taught the creed in English by his grandmother, the Pater Noster and Ave Maria by a brother. Most interestingly, James Morden had used the Pater Noster and creed so often in English that he had forgotten many of the words of these in Latin.[84] Here any question of commentary is ruled out. Also here the matter of language is pin-pointed: knowledge in Latin is acceptable, knowledge in English is not.

Enquiries such as these are, obviously, an extreme. Others in the

[81] Salisbury reg Langton 2 fol 35; the version printed in Arnold 3 pp 82–92 is not outspoken, but more distinctively lollard are those found in BL MS Harley 2398, Trinity College Dublin MS 245, York Minster Library MS XVI.L.12 and Harvard University MS Eng.738. Miss Rachel Pyper is at present engaged in sorting out the various versions of the Decalogue commentaries, an enterprise that will correct and enlarge the scope of A. L. Kellogg and E. W. Talbert, 'The Wycliffite *Pater Noster* and *Ten Commandments* . . .', *BJRL* 42 (1960) pp 345–77. Compare Matthew p 429/30 'and herfore freris han tau3t in Englond the paternoster|in Engli3ch tunge, as men seyen in the pley of 3ork, and in many othere cuntreys', though Cambridge University Library MS Ii.6.26 fol 13 notes the efforts of clerks to prevent people knowing this in English.

[82] See Arnold 3 pp 98–110 and its version in *Selections* no 20, also Matthew pp 198–202. Compare the reason assigned to Arundel for his refusal to return Thorpe's psalter in Thorpe's own account of his trial, Oxford Bodleian MS Rawlinson c.208 fol 38 'forthi that thou woldist gadere out thereof and recorde scharpe verses a3ens vs': such, according to this account, 'is the bisinesse and the maner of this losel and siche other, to pike out scharpe sentencis of holy writ and of doctours, for to maynteyne her sect and her loore a3ens the ordenaunce of holi chirche'.

[83] The investigations are summarized by Foxe in his *Actes and Monuments*, ed S. R. Cattley, 8 vols (London 1837–41) 4 pp 221–41; compare the comments of M. Aston, *History* 62 (1977) p 355.

[84] Foxe 4 p 225, 227–8, and for James Morden p 225.

Lollardy: the English Heresy?

fifteenth century were, we may think, more subtle and more enlightened: English sermons are found in that period that show a declared hostility to lollardy, thus revealing that the use of the vernacular was not necessarily a sign of heresy.[85] Nonetheless, the association of the vernacular with clerical suspicion was not new in lollardy. The Waldensians much earlier on the continent had fallen under suspicion for exactly the same matter: an insistence upon the native language, a preoccupation with vernacular scriptures and, the apparently inevitable consequence, lay preaching.[86] Even the anti-lollard sermons indirectly reflect the importance the Wycliffite movement attached to language: the enemy must be confronted on his own ground. There is then a sense in which it may not be unreasonable to claim lollardy as the heresy of the vernacular, the English heresy.

University of Oxford
Lady Margaret Hall

[85] See, for instance, the material cited by Owst, *Preaching* pp 135–40 and in *Literature and Pulpit in Medieval England* (2 ed Oxford 1966) p 374, to which may be added *Mirk's Festial*, ed T. Erbe, *EETS* extra series 96 (1905) p 171/18, *Jacob's Well*, ed A. Brandeis, *EETS* 115 (1900) pp 19/1, 59/26, Durham University Library MS Cosin V.iv.2 fol 130ᵛ, Lincoln Cathedral MS 66 fols 25 ʳ/ᵛ.
[86] See *Les Vaudois* pp 319–404.

CATHOLICITY AND NATIONALITY IN THE NORTHERN COUNTER-REFORMATION

by JOHN BOSSY

W HY choose this subject? First, because I think there is a general historiographical problem about nationality in early-modern Europe, which has been rather abandoned and is perhaps worth another look. Second because, on the Catholic side of the subject, there is a problem of actuality concerning Ireland and a rather different one concerning Holland. Third, because there is a specific and limited issue in the history of English Catholicism. I shall really be concerned with a simple problem raised by Arnold Oskar Meyer in his *England and the Catholic Church under Queen Elizabeth*: how far the internal conflicts among English Catholics, generally known as the Archpriest controversy, are to be explained as an outbreak or resurgence of 'nationalism', a conflict of 'national' and 'Catholic' tendencies. There have been good reasons for objecting to Meyer's view that this was the case: his conceptions of national character, of 'puritanism', were by present standards shaky, and he weakened his personal position by becoming more closely involved with the Third Reich than he perhaps need have been.[1] The recent historiography of the subject has been largely a history of attempts to find an alternative: in the international competition of France and Spain; in the constitutional hostility of gentry and clergy; in the geographical determinism of Braudelian routes; in the ecclesiastical choice between a traditional and a missionary church. Many of them have been made by myself; most recently Christopher Haigh has added another, connected with the continuity or discontinuity of Elizabethan Catholicism with its pre-Reformation predecessor.[2] I

---

[1] A. O. Meyer, [*England and the Catholic Church under Queen Elizabeth* (English translation, London 1916)]: cf. my own introduction to the 1967 reprint.

[2] J. Bossy, 'Henry IV, [the Appellants and the Jesuits', *Recusant History*, viii (1965)], pp 80–122; 'The Character of Elizabethan Catholicism', in T. Aston (ed), *Crisis in Europe, 1560–1660* (London, 1965) pp 223–246; 'Rome and the Elizabethan Catholics: a Question of Geography', *Historical Journal*, vii (1964), pp 135–149; *The English Catholic Community*[, *1570–1850* (London, 1975)] pp 35 ff; Christopher

think it is fair to say that all of these suggestions have their virtue: all the same, looking at them as a whole, they do give a general impression of racking the brains. It has been pointed out that they are sometimes mutually contradictory; in some cases they are open to the charge of evading the obvious and overcomplicating simple issues. So it seems high time to look at Meyer's original problem again, and see how it stands.

I thought it might be helpful to enlarge the dimension, to remind ourselves that the problems of English catholics occurred in a wider geographical context, as but one of a series of situations arising in consequence of the major success and partial unsuccess of the reformation in Europe from the Baltic to the Atlantic. If we take as our starting point the extension of the Protestant cause throughout northern Europe with the accession of Elizabeth and the revolt of the Netherlands, and the sharpening of Roman interest in the region with the accession of pope Gregory XIII in 1572, we have to deal with the following enterprises: an English mission launched from the Netherlands in the 1570s, with Jesuit participation from 1580; the Swedish mission, a Jesuit enterprise launched in conjunction with King John III's search for a liturgical and doctrinal compromise with Rome in 1576, a dramatic and rather extraordinary affair abandoned in the summer of 1580; a Dutch mission dating from the settlement of Sasbout Vosmeer in Delft in 1583, the Jesuits entering as a separate mission in 1592; and an Irish 'mission' not easily dated. It had its sources in the Old English population of the island during the 1580s, and its principal milestones were the first successful Jesuit mission of 1596, the establishment of a working episcopal order during the first twenty years of the seventeenth century, and the revival of the Irish Franciscans from about 1600.

Two comments before I proceed. I use the word 'mission' to indicate the sending of priests to a country with a reformed government, but it is actually a Jesuit word with a technical meaning. Thus in 'Holland' the *missio hollandica* strictly meant only the Jesuits in the territory of the Republic. The word raised important questions about continuity and jurisdiction; it was characteristic of a *missio* that it operated, as in 'Holland', with

---

Haigh, 'The Continuity of Catholicism in the English Reformation', *Past and Present*, no 93 (1981).

contemporary political boundaries, not with traditional ecclesiastical ones, and so required papal authority. The further and more general comment is that in what follows I have tried to separate the question of national allegiance from that of allegiance to the state: this may seem timid or over-finicky, but I think it is, for the moment at least, the only way to get the national issue into proper perspective.

Within the area delimited I can see evidence for three sorts of feeling which one might term nationalist, and no evidence for another. The first I shall call naive nationalism, and illustrate by the feeling which arose between the English and the Welsh at the time of the foundation of the English college in Rome during the late 1570s. Other interpretations of the trouble have been offered—differences in social *mores* more, or less, determined by kinship (David Mathew); differences between missionary activists and ecclesiastical careerists about what such a college might be for (Anthony Kenny)—and both are certainly valid.[3] But when all is said, there is no evading the primitive facts. These were that, due to overcrowding at Douai, the idea was mooted of setting up another college in Rome; that the proposal, as in an earlier case of the Swedish hospice of St. Bridget, was to convert for the purpose the existing English hospice, designed for the reception of pilgrims; and that the conversion was carried out by the north-Welsh canon lawyer, Owen Lewis, who appointed as rector of the college the incumbent head of the hospice, his countryman Morris Clenock. Shortly afterwards, when there were forty or so students in the college, some thirty-five English and seven Welsh, a student rebellion against the rector occurred which, amid charges of favouritism, incompetence and lack of missionary fervour, succeeded in overthrowing his regime and replacing it by a Jesuit one. Lewis naturally took offence and retired to serve San Carlo Borromeo in Milan.

From the letters of William Allen and Robert Parsons which are our chief source of information about the incident, one has the strong sense that they had been thoroughly taken aback by the outbreak of passions they had not bargained for; by, as Allen wrote to Lewis, 'the common inclinations of Adam to like, and whisper

[3] David Mathew, *The Celtic Peoples and Renaissance Europe* (London, 1933) pp 77 f; Anthony Kenny, 'From Hospice to College', in *The English Hospice in Rome: the Venerabile Sexcentenary Issue* (vol. xxi, 1962) pp 218–273.

underhand for, their own against others of other countries'. He continued: 'But God so help me, as I feel no inclination of partiality either towards your part for the great benefits and comforts which I have received of your hands, so neither towards their—' that is, the students'—'—part for conjunction of country or name of English or for blood or such like . . . But I seek only the honour of God, and the necessary atonement of all sick minds, without which whatsoever we go about for our poor country will be lost . . .' Allen then saw himself confronted with two imperatives: on the one hand, the 'honour of God', the over-riding obligation of the missionary enterprise; on the other, the dense network of relationships, friendships and associations which formed the structure of traditional society. The solidarity arising from national identification, what Parsons called 'national partialities', he saw as a prominent element in this traditional network. In its exacerbated form, he seems to say, it was the product was of a 'sick mind'; in principle, he reserved judgement, suggesting to Lewis that it would have been more sensible to appoint an English candidate as rector, since he was a theologian, 'besides the country, which you know many respect [i.e. take account of], how well or wisely I do not say'. Allen also described the difficulty he was having, as head of the college at Douai, in preventing the same trouble from breaking out there. Clearly one must reckon with nationalism, in this simple sense, as a prime element in the ethos of the Elizabethan seminaries: during the 1590s, it seems to have been directed against the Spaniards. Both Allen and Parsons treated the feeling as primitive, antique, and Parsons saw the trouble at Rome in the context of the social history of the mediaeval university: 'You know what passeth in Oxford on like occasions.'[4]

The second form of nationalism one can detect is ecclesiastical patriotism, by which I mean, loyalty to the national church as a historic institution, to its hierarchy, religious houses, and more especially its sees; the instinct to defend their honour and rights against threats from all comers, including those, perhaps especially those, from Rome. The sentiment was evidently as traditional as the first, though it had been exacerbated in the sixteenth century by exterior disaster, competition with rival hierarchies and pressure from Rome. It was visible in England both in the outlook of the

---

[4] [Letters and Memorials of] William Cardinal Allen, [ed. T. F. Knox (London, 1882)] pp 74 f, 78 ff.

secular clergy and in the revival of the English Benedictines, in Sweden over the destiny of the Bridgettine monastery at Vadstena; but perhaps the best case came from the Netherlands, in the posthumous history of the see of Utrecht. Among the episodes in this long-running saga one may note the survival of the Utrecht chapter after the province had joined the republic; the placing in the canon of the Mass of the name of its first archbishop, Willibrord, by the first Dutch vicar-apostolic, Vosmeer; the appointment of his successor, Philip Rovenius, to the see in 1624 in consequence of an agitation in which a prominent part was played by another northerner, the Louvain theologian Cornelius Jansen; and the ensuing defence of the rights of the see by a sort of commission or quasi-chapter, which led to the election of a schismatic archbishop and the emergence of the Old Catholic Church in the eighteenth century.[5] The hostility to Rome and the Jesuits of which the see of Utrecht was a symbol may well have been more jurisdictional than patriotic in character, and there was of course a large question about what exactly patriotism might mean in a divided Netherlands, but in a context of English, Swedish and perhaps Irish cases of similar nature it might be rather hasty to dismiss the patriotic motive altogether.

The third possible form of nationalism is one of which I can detect no unqualified signs among Elizabethan catholics. It may be called religious patriotism, and in a Catholic context would mean the sense of a religious or charitable obligation to fight or die *pro patria*, or in some special way to pray for or procure the salvation of other members of the nation. This was an obligation understood and defended in mediaeval Christianity, and it was to be revived in a rather strong form by Bossuet at the close of the seventeenth century.[6] But you do not seem to find it where you might expect to find it in England, for example in the declarations of allegiance made to Elizabeth and James I by the Appellant priests. They

---

[5] A convenient summary of the work of L. J. Rogier, *Geschiedenis van het Katholicisme in Noord-Nederland in de 16e en de 17e Eeuw* (3 vols., Amsterdam, 1945–46) and others, will be found in P. Brachin and L. J. Rogier, *Histoire du catholicisme hollandais depuis le XVIe siècle* (Paris, 1974): see. pp 28, 45, 61 etc.; [Pieter] Geyl, *The Netherlands [in the Seventeenth Century: i, 1609–1648]* (English translation, London, 1961) p. 80.

[6] E. Kantorowicz, *The King's Two Bodies* (Princeton, N. J., 1957) pp 232 ff; J.-B. Bossuet, *Politique tirée de paroles de l'Ecriture Sainte* (Versailles, 1818 edn) pp 44 f, 58 f (Livre premier, Art. VI and Conclusion).

certainly undertook, in various statements made between 1602 and 1604, to defend king (or queen) and kingdom against all invasions and conspiracies 'even to the shedding of [their] blood'. But they did not hold, or at least did not publicly defend, what would seem to be the central statement of a Catholic religious patriotism, the doctrine that the *patria* was a *corpus mysticum*. Their doctrine, as presented to King James I in 1604, was that the Church was the mystical body of Christ, the kingdom of England a civil and political body which had nothing to do with the salvation of souls.[7] This is a little surprising, and I do not think they would have been affected by a feeling that religious patriotism, for Englishmen, had been pre-empted by Protestants like Foxe.[8] I fancy that they were, in this respect, the heirs of the generation of Erasmus, More and Pole, for whom religious patriotism was incompatible with Christianity.

Finally, and perhaps of most interest, there are numerous signs among northern catholics of the Counter-reformation of what I shall call patriotic antiquarianism. They appear first among the Swedes Johannes Magnus, archbishop-elect of Uppsala, and his brother Olaus, who slipped away from the country in 1526 and worked in Rome thereafter, Olaus living as head of the hospice of St. Bridget. In 1554 he published his brother's *Historia de omnibus gothorum sueonumque regibus*, giving, as Michael Roberts says, 'definitive form to the national myth of the glories of the ancient Goths'; it expounded the direct descent of the Gothic kings from the Flood, their prowess before Rome was heard of, the achievements of Visigoths and Ostrogoths in Europe from Byzantium to Gibraltar. Four years later he produced his own *Historia de gentibus septentrionalibus*, a gazetteer to subarctic Europe intended to supplement his map of the region published to correct Ptolemy in 1539; it had much of interest to communicate on climate, fauna and customs, on marginal peoples like the Lapps and the Finns, and on runic inscriptions which proved, he felt, that the Goths were civilised when the Romans were still living in mud huts. Olaus's motives were evidently to defend the Goths from humanist

---

[7] Formula of allegiance, March 1604: I use the Latin version in Bibliothèque nationale, fonds français 15976, f. 526; there is a slightly incorrect version in R. G. Usher, *The Reconstruction of the English Church* (2 vols., New York/London, 1910) ii, pp 316 f. Cf. Bossy 'Henri IV' pp 96 f.

[8] William Haller, *Foxe's Book of Martyrs and the Elect Nation* (London 1963).

contempt as barbarians, as was to be shown in Vasari's *Lives of the Artists*. He was also, identifying the Swedish reformation with German influences, striking a blow against the Germanic mythology dependent on Tacitus, and at the same time encouraging Rome to take a missionary interest in his homeland. The work certainly had some effect in preparing the *missio suetica*; but in the end it probably made Rome more nervous of John III than it need have been, by raising in its emissary, the Italian Jesuit Antonio Possevino, the spectre of a deviant national catholicism in Sweden and helping to persuade him to close the mission down. The result was that the Megalogothicism of the catholic Magnuses became the ideology of Gustavus Adolphus and of the Swedish protestant empire of the seventeenth century.[9]

This case has some light to shed on the English situation, for the Elizabethan catholics developed a not dissimilar Megaloanglicism. One can see it beginning before the foundation of the seminary at Douai, in the idea mooted in the 1560s—probably not by Allen, and in fact abortive—of an Anglo-Netherlandish college, harking back to the missionary origins of northern Christianity in the age of Willibrord and Boniface, and cultivating their example by a teaching based on ecclesiastical antiquities. In the college as constituted this kind of attention was concentrated on Bede, with the idea of providing a counterblast to English imperialist claims put forward from Thomas Cromwell onwards and emphasising the pre-Augustinian history of Christianity in Britain.[10] This insistence on the English nature of the *Ecclesia Anglicana* was turned into a comprehensive nationalist or racialist view of English history by a lay collaborator of Allen and, particularly, of Parsons, Richard Verstegan. Verstegan, a long-lived man who was born about 1550 and died in 1640, was a Londoner descended from an immigrant grandfather from Gelderland, a printer, engraver, poet and intelligencer, settled in Antwerp from 1587 and writing in both English and Dutch. His book, *A restitution of decayed intelligence in antiquities concerning the most noble and renowned English nation*, was published in 1605 but had evidently been brewing since the 1590s. The natural

---

[9] Michael Roberts, *The Early Vasas* (Cambridge, 1968) pp 24, 64, 282–289; Oscar Garstein, *Rome and the Couner-Reformation in Scandinavia* i (Oslo 1963) pp 15 ff, 191 ff and *passim*; Olaus Magnus, *A Compendious History of the Goths, Swedes and Vandals* (English translation, London, 1658) pp 26, 103.
[10] *William Cardinal Allen* pp 22, 66.

cultivation of one's ancestors, Verstegan argued, had resulted in divers works by people of divers nations, who thus 'showed themselves most kind lovers of their natural friends and country-men'; in England, however, the effort had gone amiss because people, especially Protestants, had confused the British with the English, and so mistaken their ancestors. If the English wanted to find their ancestors they should go to the Cimbric Chersonesus, or Schleswig, the home of what he called the 'English-Saxons', that is the branch of the Saxon people living in that part of the world at the time of the *Völkerwanderung*; it was they who had arrived in Britain via Friesland and the Netherlands in the time of Hengist and Horsa. It looks as if Verstegan, drawing on a corpus of sixteenth-century German learning, was the first to convey to the English the news of their original homeland.

The book explored a variety of possible consequences of this discovery. On the linguistic side it contained an exposition of the English-Saxon tongue, the first available word-list with modern equivalents, and a list of Old English personal names with their meanings intended to reveal the nobility of Anglo-Saxon cultural and social aspirations; it sought to show, for example by compar-ing proverbs, the persisting closeness of English and 'Dutch'. On the historical side it put forward an English—(or Saxon—) centred view of the national past; dismissed later contributions and espe-cially the Norman Conquest as unimportant or distasteful; and showed distress at the recent bastardisation of the language by French and Latin imports. Chaucer, whom Verstegan took to be some kind of a Walloon, came in for criticism on this score; the object of the word-list was to show that there was perfectly good English alternatives to numerous inauthentic coinages in use. Verstegan also put forward a geographical theory intended to maintain the ultimate unity of England and the Netherlands, whose separation he obviously regarded as one of God's mistakes. If you looked at the cliffs at Dover and Boulogne, he said, you could see that Britain and the continent had originally been connected by land; a breakthrough by the sea in this quarter had led, since the sea level in the Channel was lower than that in the North Sea, to the exposure of much land in the Netherlands which, by observing the operations of canal-diggers, you could prove to have been origi-nally covered by the sea. The theory had much merit, though it did not quite work out; Verstegan did his best to keep it going by publishing in 1613 his *Nederlantsche Antiquiteyten*, which repeated much of the English version but ended with an account of the conversion of the Lower Saxons of the Netherlands by Willibrord and other English missionaries.[11]

To us, all this may seem ancient news, but in 1600 I think it was rather a revelation, and one can see it reverberating in various ways. It had, for example, a distinct effect on Robert Parsons, though Parsons did not exactly become a racialist in the way Verstegan did. In his historical writings Parsons adopted Verstegan's descriptive language, writing of the 'English-Saxons'; and he developed its implications into a long-range quasi-sociological account of English history unifying the Norman conquest, the anti-clerical tradition of the English aristocracy, and the reformation. This was an early version of the Norman Yoke theory as it was to appear in the middle of the seventeenth century. In politics both Parsons and Verstegan were known as supporters of the Infanta Isabella as successor to queen Elizabeth, and collaborators in the *Conference about the Next Succession* of 1594. Perhaps we ought to think of this in the light of Verstegan's theory about the fundamental unity of England and the Netherlands: the idea would be to revive the abortive union planned by Charles V, and to give it an ideological foundation. Finally there were the missionary implications. The Greater English aspect of Verstegan's theory perhaps comes out most clearly in a passage of Parsons's *Memorial for the Reformation of England*, where he put down as a main priority for a restored catholic regime in England the foundation of missionary colleges in London to receive students from, and run missions to, 'Denmark, divers parts near to us of Germany, Poland, Gothland, Sweedland, Scotland, Muscovy and the Isles of Zeeland'—a revival of Anglo-Saxon missionary history which would diffuse the influence of a Greater English catholicism along the seaways of the north.[12]

[11] Richard Verstegan, *A restitution of decayed intelligence* (Antwerp, 1605; repr by Scolar Press, 1976), 'Epistle to the English Nation', and *passim; Nederlantsche Antiquiteyten* (Antwerp, 1613). For Verstegan, see *The Letters and Despatches of Richard Verstegan*, ed. Anthony Petti (Catholic Record Society, vol. lii, 1959), and Geyl, *The Netherlands* i, p 240.

[12] Robert Parsons, *A Treatise of Three Conversions* (1603; Scolar Press repr. 1976) i, p 3; Bossy, *The English Catholic Community* pp 23, 33 f; Christopher Hill, 'The Norman Yoke', in *Puritanism and Revolution* (London 1968 edn), pp 54–125 (index under *Verstegan*).

One can only speculate on the negative effect of this Anglo-Saxon propaganda on the catholicism of the Celtic fringe. It is quite a shock to see Scotland on Parsons's list, though there was *something* to be said for the idea that Scotland ought to be considered as falling within the Greater English *Kulturgebiet*: Verstegan dedicated the *Restitution* to James I as the true successor of the English-Saxon kings. Still, there must have been many on the Celtic fringe who would have echoed Owen Lewis's remark to John Leslie, bishop of Ross, at the time of the stirs in the Roman College: 'My lord, let us stick together, for we are the old and true inhabiters of the Isle of Britanny; these others be but usurpers and mere possessors'.[13] I confine myself to some suggestions about the effect of the Greater English theory in Ireland.

I think Ireland was the one place where it had some practical success. It was appropriate to the existing Old English view that Ireland was in need of a transition to civility, and that this was to be identified with the diffusion of English culture, manners and government. Richard Stanihurst, the Dublin-Oxford humanist, translator of Vergil and chief publicist of this view, had been around 1570 the host of Edmund Campion and source of most of the material for *Two Books of the Histories of Ireland*; by the 1590s he was living in the Netherlands and very friendly with Verstegan, to whose *Restitution* he contributed an appreciative poem describing Verstegan as 'restituens patriae patria verba suae'. Parsons had been similarly close to his fellow-Jesuit William Good, who before taking part in the *missio suetica* had spent a lot of time in Ireland during the 1560s, and written an account of it in Stanihurst's spirit which has remained extremely useful to historians.[14] The first permanent Jesuit mission to Ireland was Old English in character and in its early history much dependent on Henry Garnet and the Jesuits in England; there were similar, though less intimate connections with the Irish secular clergy, who in a succession of synods

[13] *Letters and Memorials of William Cardinal Allen* p 82.
[14] D. B. Quinn, *The Elizabethans and the Irish* (Ithaca, N.Y., 1960) pp 28 f, 46 ff, 80, etc.; Nicholas P. Canny, *The Formation of the Old English Elite in Ireland* (Dublin, 1975), pp 26 ff; Edmund Campion, *Two Bokes of the Histories of Ireland*, ed A. F. Vossen (Assen 1963); for Parsons and William Good, see *Letters and Memorials of Robert Parsons, i: 1588* ed L. Hicks (Catholic Record Society, vol. xxxix 1942) pp 5 ff. See now Colin Lennon, *Richard Stanihurst* (Dublin 1981).

during the 1610s and 1620s attempted to put through an Anglo-
Tridentine reformation of the Irish church.[15] It is a moot point to
what degree they were successful, in the short or the long-run; but
one immediate effect was to set off an extremely vigorous revival
of Gaelic-Irish catholicism, with a strong cultural and linguistic
element, centred on the Franciscan house of St. Anthony's at
Louvain. I oversimplify a complicated situation to make the point
that Irish-speaking catholic nationalism, in its self-conscious as
distinct from its instinctual form, looks more directly a response to
Elizabethan Anglophone catholic nationalism than it does to any
action of the Elizabethan or Jacobean governments.

To return, after this tour of the horizon, to Meyer and his view
that the Archpriest Controversy was a 'great conflict between
national ideas and the universal church', a revolt of 'national
Catholics' against universalist Jesuits, a 'tragic conflict between
religion and patriotism'.[16] It is clear that the view is not impossible
or anachronistic; it would I think fairly describe the Swedish case.
But I do not think it really describes the English one. Nationalism
of various kinds was certainly involved, but both parties seem to be
nationalists of a fairly intense kind: at the cruder level, most
participants on both sides had been students at the English seminaries, whose xenophobic ethos we have encountered; at the more
reflective level they seem however to have been different sorts of
nationalists, Little-Englanders on one side, and Greater-Englanders
on the other. The Little-Englanders, the Appellant priests, are not I
feel a problem; at least I have explained my conception of them
elsewhere. They were ecclesiastical patriots of the same general
tendency as those who, a century later, launched the schism of
Utrecht and the Old Catholic Church; they were not religious
patriots in any proper sense, and unlike Meyer I do not think their
feelings were original: which is not to say that they were not
estimable. The Greater Englanders, Parsons and Verstegan, *are*
rather a problem. Their feelings were original, and by the same

---

[15] E. Hogan (ed), *Ibernia Ignatiana* (Dublin 1880) pp 127 f, 182, 185; H. F. Kearney,
'Ecclesiastical Politics and the Counter-Reformation in Ireland, 1618–1648', *JEH*
xi (1960) pp 202–212; J. Bossy, 'The Counter-Reformation and the People of
Catholic Ireland', in T. D. Williams (ed), *Historical Studies* viii (Dublin 1971),
pp 155–169.
[16] Meyer, pp 376, 419, 428.

token somewhat artificial. In both respects they were not totally unlike those of their *bête noire*, John Foxe. Between them they suggest some of the things which might happen, in an age self-conscious both in its learning and in its piety, to those crude national solidarities which, with cardinal Allen, I take to represent 'the common inclinations of Adam'.

University of York

THE ORIGINS OF ENGLISH PROTESTANT NATIONALISM

by DAVID LOADES

IN 1581, in his *Answer to a seditious pamphlet*, William Charke wrote

> He that smiteth our religion woundeth our commonwealth; because our blessed estate of policie standeth in defence of religion, and our most blessed religion laboureth in maintenance of the commonwealth. Religion and policie are, through God's singular blessings, preserved together in life as with one spirit; he that doth take away the life of the one doth procure the death of the other.[1]

This was, of course, a partisan point of view. However, the extent to which it had won general acceptance among Englishmen of all social classes can be demonstrated by reference to the Armada crisis of seven years later. Not only did pamphleteers like Thomas Deloney appeal for patriotic effort,

> That . . . all with one accord
> On Sion hill may sing the praise
> of our most mightly Lord[2]

but recusant apologetic makes it clear that the catholics were fully aware of the prevailing opinion that papists could not be good Englishmen.

Such a situation had not been created overnight by the war with Spain, nor was it simply the product of a well orchestrated propaganda campaign by William Cecil and his friends since 1559. Papal policy had been, and still was, a major contributory factor. *Regnans in Excelsis*, military adventures in Ireland, and ill concealed support for assassination attempts against Elizabeth, played directly into the hands of those who wished to regard the papacy as the foreign enemy *par excellence*. 'That wicked and illfated conspiracy', wrote the Jesuit Robert Southwell of the Babington plot, '. . . did to the catholic cause so great mischief that even our enemies, had

[1] *STC* 5005; sig C 1 r & v.
[2] T[homas] D[eloney] 'Three Ballads on the Armada fight', *Tudor Tracts*, ed A. F. Pollard (London 1903) p 491.

they the choice, could never have chosen ought more mischievous to us . . .'[3] But even Pius V and his successors did not create the situation which Southwell and the later appellants were to find so distressing; they had merely deepened and confirmed prejudices which were already powerful when Elizabeth came to the throne.

The English had a long-standing reputation for xenophobia. 'They have an antipathy to foreigners', an anonymous Italian had written about 1500, 'and imagine that they never come into their island, but to make themselves masters of it, and to usurp their goods. . .'[4] The Flemings and the French had borne the brunt of this unlovable characteristic since the fourteenth century, but the Italians themselves had not escaped, and the papacy was a sitting target in 1533. However little justification there may have been for such an attitude, charges that the pope was removing great quantities of money from England featured prominently in the early parliamentary attacks upon his jurisdiction.[5] However, one of the reasons why the king succeeded in pressing these attacks to a conclusion was that remarkably few Englishmen seem to have regarded the papal authority as important to their religious faith. Consequently the anti-Roman polemic which accompanied and followed the work of the reformation parliament was much less directly helpful to the early protestants than is sometimes supposed. The emphasis was all upon the usurpation of royal authority which had resulted from the unscrupulous use of spiritual sanctions, rather than upon any perversion of the doctrine or practices of the English church. Indeed, most defenders of the royal supremacy were more concerned to mobilize religious allegiance in support of the king than they were to urge the duties of reform upon him:

> . . . howe muche more aught all Christians to obey their princes absolutlie when thei the kinges themselves are nott only members of the self bodie of Christ, but also ministers of the Christian justice . . .[6]

[3] J. H. Pollen, *English Martyrs, 1584–1603*, CRS 5 (1908) p 314.

[4] *A relation of the Island of England*, ed C. A. Sneyd, *CSer* (1847); reprinted in C. H. Williams, *English Historical Documents*, 5 p 196.

[5] For example 'Forasmuch as it is well perceived by long approved experience that great and inestimable sums of money be daily conveyed out of this realm to the impoverishment of the same, and specially such sums of money as the Pope's Holiness, his predecessors, and the Court of Rome by long time have heretofore taken . . .' (23 Henry VIII, c. 20).

[6] William Thomas, 'Pelegrine'. BL Add MS 33383 fol 19.

or, as Stephen Gardiner put it, 'The king our master hath a special case bicause he is an Emperor in himself and hath no superior.' Naturally, protestants such as Tyndale or Barnes welcomed the royal supremacy, but their alliance was unwelcome to, and unacknowledged by, Gardiner and the conservative nobles. Indeed the Bishop of Winchester consistently argued that the royal supremacy would be seriously weakened by association with heresy.[7] After Henry VIII's death, in the course of his rearguard action against the publication of Cranmer's *Homilies*, he described himself as 'a good Englishman', and observed 'It is incredible that a king shuld set forth a boke tending to the subversion of hys owne estate. . .'[8] In taking this attitude, Gardiner probably spoke for the bulk of English opinion, gentle and simple. Popular reactions to the introduction of the prayer book in 1549 suggest no great enthusiasm for either protestantism or the Pope. Even in Devon and Cornwall, where hostility contributed to a major insurrection, there was no demand for a settlement with Rome. *De vera obedientia* had done its work too well for its author's peace of mind. By 1547 to be 'a good Englishman' meant to support the 'king's proceedings', and that loyalty had made the country more willing to accept a legislated reformation than Gardiner had anticipated, or was prepared to acknowledge.

Without the royal supremacy the advance of protestantism, first to a position of influence under Cromwell's protection, and then to power under Somerset and Northumberland, would have been impossible. Nevertheless it must be remembered that to many supporters of the supremacy, heresy was not only anathema in itself, but subversive of the whole political and social order.

> Libertie lept over this lande
> Lusty at its owne will
> Letchery to breake wedlockes bande
> Likewise doth luste fulfyll. . .[9]

Such views were reinforced by the fact that there appeared to be nothing particularly English about protestant doctrine, which was more associated in the popular mind with Germany, or with the

[7] This was the burden of a number of letters written to Somerset during the latter part of 1547. J. A. Muller, *The Letters of Stephen Gardiner* (Cambridge 1933) pp 378–438; D. M. Loades, *Oxford Martyrs* (London 1970) pp 52–6.

[8] Muller, *Letters*, p 416.

[9] *STC* 13559.5. *A newe ABC paraphrasticallye applied* by Miles Huggarde (London March 1557).

foreign congregations which sprang up in London under the protection of Edward VI and his council. By 1553 any advantage which protestantism may have gained from the Edwardian supremacy had been largely neutralised by Northumberland's unpopularity, by his apparent subservience to the French, and by the influx of Swiss and south German reformers after 1549. The warning of Ridley that Mary might well marry a foreigner, and subject the realm to an alien king, as well as to the 'Anti-Christ of Rome' went unheeded even by committed protestants.[10]

The new queen's conservative and catholic supporters did their best to capitalise upon this situation, and were given useful ammunition by the restiveness of some of the more extreme protestants in London. 'O develyshe libertye', wrote Miles Huggarde, 'I wolde to God that Germany had kept thee still.' Nevertheless, Mary's determination to marry Philip of Spain considerably marred her image as 'a good Englishwoman', and initiated a protracted propaganda campaign against her as 'A Spanyarde at heart', and one who despised and distrusted her native born subjects.[11] This campaign was not, initially at any rate, the work of protestants, most of whom professed their loyalty to the queen. Probably the French ambassador, Antoine de Noailles, who had instructions to inhibit the marriage to the best of his ability, was behind a lot of it.[12] However, there also seems to have been a spontaneous popular dislike of Spaniards, particularly in London, which antedated Noailles efforts and was a source of anxiety to Simon Renard from the beginning of the negotiation. Charles V had recognised that all Englishmen hated 'all foreigners' when he had first instructed Renard to proceed,[13] but the ambassador was soon reporting that a Spanish connection presented particular difficulties. Rather surprisingly, in view of past history, the English were professing their willingness to get along with Flemings or Brabanters, but declaring that they could not live with

[10] J. Ridley, *Nicholas Ridley* (London 1957) pp 303–4.
[11] In spite of her Spanish blood, Mary had never previously been accused of being a foreigner; however, commitment to her mother's cause gave some substance to the charges which began to be voiced after her accession. H. F. M. Prescott, *Mary Tudor* (London 1952); [D. M.] Loades, [*Two Tudor Conspiracies*] (Cambridge 1965).
[12] E. H. Harbison, *Rival Ambassadors at the Court of Queen Mary*, (Princeton 1940) pp 57–88.
[13] Emperor to his ambassadors in England, 23 June 1553. Cal[endar of State Papers,] Span[ish], ed Royall Tyler et al (London 1862–1964) 11 pp 60–65.

Spaniards.[14] It is possible that Renard (who was a Franc-Comptois) was simply hearing what he wanted to hear, but equally likely that the unpopularity which Philip and his entourage had earned for themselves in the Low Countries between 1549 and 1551 had communicated itself across the narrow sea. The Spaniards had certainly begun to acquire an evil reputation for themselves in Italy and Germany before 1553, and it was not to be long before '. . . the horrible practices of the Kyng of Spayne in the Kyngedome of Naples and the miseries whereunto that noble realme is brought. . .' were being exploited for propaganda purposes in England.[15] Whatever their 'real' motivation, Wyatt and his followers professed to be acting 'for the avoidance of strangers', and were fully conscious of the dangers of trying to utilise French support.[16] Although the rebellion failed, the xenophobic fires which it had fanned to life smouldered on, and Renard was soon uneasily reporting that the Londoners had crowded to dip their handkerchiefs in Wyatt's blood, and were muttering that noble blood ought not to be shed for the sake of foreigners.

The government's reaction to these events, and indeed to the anti-Spanish agitation as a whole, was to blame them on the protestants, pouring scorn upon the latters' professions of loyalty.

> And to thintent that they may move men more easily to such a mischevouse enterprise, they cloke the matter with a goodly pretence, and tell them that they entend nothynge elles but to deliver the poore commons from oppression . . . They tell them besyde that everye man is bounde to love his countrye, and to seke for the preservation therof . . . As for theyr prince (they saye) they wyll dye and lyve with him . . .[17]

The gist of the official view was that there was no widespread opposition to the marriage, but that the protestant were seeking to create it as a patriotic smokescreen for their nefarious activities. This position also seems to have been partly shared by some Englishmen who did oppose the match. John Bradford, in *The copye of a letter*, written against Philip's coronation in 1556, justified a fresh outburst of invective on the grounds that previous attacks

---

[14] Simon Renard to the bishop of Arras 9 September 1553. *Cal Span* 11 pp 227–8.
[15] For example *STC* 10024.
[16] Loades; M. R. Thorp, 'Religion and the Wyatt rebellion', *Church History* 47, 4 (1978) pp 363–80.
[17] John Christopherson, *An exhortation to all menne to take hede and beware of rebellion* (London 1554) (STC 5207), sig B iv.

had been produced '. . . by the develishe device of certayne heretickes . . . thinking thereby to grounds in the hartes of all people . . . many abominable heresies.[18]' He then went on to profess his own allegiance to the catholic faith, '. . . which the Queenes Majestie moste graciously setteth oute at thys present . . .' By the time this tract was written the animosity between the two nationalities was manifest, and had been demonstrated in violence, bloodshed and mutual recriminations. This hatred knew no religious boundaries, and was in the murky tradition of Jack Straw and the Evil May Day, but two circumstances conspired to ensure that some of the mud which was hurled at the Spaniards also bespattered the catholic church. One was the undoubted importance of Philip's personal initiative in bringing about the reconciliation of the realm to the church at the end of 1554.[19] The other was the unfortunate coincidence (if such it was) that a religious persecution of unprecedented severity was launched while the foreign king and his militantly orthodox entourage were in residence.[20] Robert Parkyn, Henry Machyn, and other humble religious conservatives who had welcomed the restoration of the mass with paens of joy, showed no such enthusiasm for either the pope or the persecution, to say nothing of the Spaniards. When these circumstances are added to the assiduous (if somewhat sparse) efforts of the governments own propaganda, it is not difficult to see how the protestants were given the opportunity to sail for the first time under patriotic colours.

By 1555 some of them, at least, were willing to grasp this opportunity. A strand of patriotic enthusiasm had been woven into English protestantism many years earlier. Rejoicing over the birth of prince Edward in October 1537, Hugh Latimer had written to Cromwell

> . . . verily (God) hath shewed himself God of England or rather an English God, if we consider and ponder well all his proceedings with us from time to time . . .[21]

---

[18] *The copye of a letter sent by John Bradforth to the right honorable lordes the erles of Arundel, Darbie, Shrewsbury and Pembroke* (London (?) 1556) (*STC* 3480) preface.

[19] [D. M.] Loades, [*The reign of*]*Mary* [*Tudor*] (London 1979) pp 219–21.

[20] Philip's possible share in the responsibility for the persecution has been extensively, but inconclusively discussed. Nevertheless the senior ecclesiastic in his household, Alonso à Castro, the bishop of Cuenca, was a well known and energetic advocate of persecution.

[21] *Sermons and Remains of Bishop Latimer PS* (1845) p 385.

The origins of English Protestant Nationalism

Bales *History of King Johan*, drawing on earlier reformers such as Tyndale and Barnes, and showing an adroit mixture of protestantism and anti-papal nationalism, was published in 1538. Bale is, of course, a key figure in the development of this strand of thought. As early as 1536 in his unpublished history of the English carmelites, *Anglorum Heliades*, he had devoted the preface to a lavish display of patriotic sentiment.[22] This was partly in homage to the antiquarian John Leland, for whom he had a great admiration in spite of the latter's determined religious conservatism, but partly also because his *patria* seems to have taken over much of the loyalty which he had devoted before his conversion to the carmelite order. For whatever reason, by the time he came to write the *Image of both churches* in 1545, Bale had come to identify the opening of the sixth seal with the release of the gospel by John Wycliffe

> The second sabbath here, or lyberte of God's truthe, hath had his shewe in England already, yf ye marke it wel . . .[23]

At the same time, in his *Chronycle concernynge . . . syr John Oldcastell*, he characterised the fifteenth-century Lollard as a patriot and an English saint. By 1555 Bale and his friend John Foxe had made considerable progress in constructing a distinctively English historiography of the reformation, in which the persecution then raging featured as a trial of God's Elect, and the English protestants in general as a 'godly remnant' of the true church. However, it would be a mistake to suppose that either Bale or Foxe postulated a unique dispensation of providence for England. In arguing that God had vouchsafed a particular providence to their fellow countrymen, they were not denying the equally authentic vision of their German or Swiss friends. In 1560 Bale was to write that he had '. . . alwaies bene of thys opinion, that St Jhons Apocalips hath as well his fulfilling in the particular nacion as in the universal church';[24] but he did not say, and clearly did not believe, that such a 'fulfilling' could be in one nation alone. Pendleton's *Homily* 'of the nature of the church', published in 1555, observed the same phenomenon from a hostile point of view.

---

[22] BL Harleian MS 3838; J. P. Fairfield, *John Bale* (West Lafayette, Indiana 1976) pp 50–1.

[23] *Image*, II, sig K vii.

[24] *The first two partes of the Actes or unchast examples of the Englyshe votaryes* (London 1560) sig xvii. Fairfield p 87.

. . . in this late tyme . . . some (were) saying in Germany, here
is Christ, here is the churche; some in Helvetia; here is Christ,
here is the churche; other in Boheme; here is Christ, here is the
churche; and we in England . . .[25]

As long as the protestant vision of England retained its eschatologi-
cal priorities, that is well into the seventeenth century, it is proper
to speak of *an* Elect Nation, but not of *the* Elect Nation.

However, in the context of the persecution, and of the problems
presented by Mary's 'ungodly proceedings', that distinction was
not of first rate importance. What was needed was a means of
mobilising English national feeling for the defence of the gospel,
and it was in this connection that anti-papal and anti-Spanish
prejudices were of the greatest value. 'O lord', prayed one pamphleteer in 1554, 'defend thy elect peple of Inglond from the handes
and force of thy enemyes the Papistes.[26]' As the reign progressed
the inhibitions which had hindered the earlier generation of protestant leaders from direct attacks upon the queen were gradually
abandoned. In place of prayers that the queen's heart would be
turned from idolatry we find savage invective, like the *Admonition
to the Town of Callais*, denouncing

. . . Another Athalia, that is an utter distroier of hir owen
kindred, kyngdome & countrie, a hater of her owne subjects, a
lover of strangers & an unnatural stepdame both unto the & to
thy mother England . . .[27]

Mary, it was alleged, was not only a papist and an idolater, but had
reduced the realm to a state of abject defencelessness '. . . so
debilitated and weakened as well in worthy capitaines and valiante
soldiers as in money, municions & victual, that she is scant able to
defend & releve hir selfe . . .' At the same time the protestants were
at pains to display their own patriotic credentials: '. . . next after
God', wrote John Ponet in 1556, 'men be borne to love, honour
and maintene their countrey'[28] To Christopher Goodman two years
later, the removal of Mary was both a patriotic and a religious
duty, and he lamented the folly of Wyatt and his friends in not

[25] Homily 'of the nature of the churche', *A profitable and necessarye doctryne with certayne homelies* . . . (London 1555) (*STC* 3281.5) p 33.
[26] *A praier to be sayd of all trewe christians against the pope and all the enemies of Christ and his gospell* (London May 1554) *Society of Antiquaries* broadsheet 36A.
[27] Robert Pownall, April 1557. *STC* 19078.
[28] John Ponet, *A Shorte Treatise of politike power* (Strasbourg 1556) (*STC* 20178) sig E vi.

having called more explicitly upon the Lord. After 1555 events also conspired to strengthen the arguments of Goodman and those who thought like him. The child which Mary passionately desired, and which she believed herself to be carrying from October 1554, failed to appear. Despite her continued and rather pathetic hopes, the prospect of a catholic succession, and the continental possessions which would have gone with it, steadily withered after July 1555. Harvest failure in that and the following year were followed by famine and the sweating sickness, leading to heavy mortality. Then in June 1557 came war, and after a hopeful start the disastrous and deeply felt loss of Calais.[29] In 1554 John Christopherson, in celebrating Mary's victories over Northumberland and Wyatt, had drawn the conventional conclusion that such triumphs were evidence of Divine favour. By 1558 the corrollary was obvious, and it did not require a committed protestant like Goodman or Traheron to see it.

In fact the military weakness of England in the latter part of Mary's reign was more a myth than a reality, but it was a myth to which the English council subscribed for reasons of its own.[30] The catholic Miles Huggarde accepted it no less than the author of the *Admonition*, making valiant, if not very convincing attempts to blame it upon the heretics rather than the queen. Since England had fallen from the unity of the church, he claimed.

> . . . it hath fallen from the grace of God into all kyndes of wickedness, skarcitie falshode deceyt and other abhominable vices, and from the accustomed valiaunce in feates of arms into effeminate myndes . . .[31]

In fact Mary's accumulated misfortunes drove the catholics onto the defensive at a time when they might legitimately have expected to exploit a position of strength. As a result we find pamphleteers endeavouring to defend the church on quasi-patriotic grounds, and testifying in the process to the success which the protestants were

[29] The council made strenuous efforts to blame the protestants for the fall of Calais, and the lord deputy, Thomas Wentworth, was arraigned for high treason. These charges, however, seem to have done nothing effective to divert responsibility. C. S. L. Davies, 'England and the French War, 1557–9', *The Mid-Tudor Polity, 1540–1560* ed J. Loach and R. Tittler (London 1980) pp 159–85.

[30] Loades, *Mary* pp 378–80. The council was anxious to save money by refraining from aggressive policies on the grounds of military incapacity.

[31] Miles Huggarde, *The displaying of the Protestantes* (London June 1556) (*STC* 13557) p 92.

having with the 'morning star of the reformation'.

'All the olde heresies' (wrote George Marshall) 'that heretofore
Were put in use by John Wykleffe here
Were confuted by William Wylford
He was a famous clerke and an Englishman borne.[32]

Mary's death in November 1558, at the relatively early age of 42, was of course the crowning mercy from the protestant point of view. Not only did it end the persecution by making way for the sympathetic Elizabeth, it also appeared to justify those prophetic voices which had forecast a brief though firey purgation for the Elect.

> . . . we shall finde mercie in time convenient', John Bale had written in 1553, 'and though he scourge us with these uncircumcised soldiers of Satan for a time yet (as David saithe) When he is angrie he will remember mercie; and restore his blessed Gospel to us again with habundance of blessinge/in case we will (like obedient children) take his chastisings in good parte.[33]

Athalia had come, if not to a sticky end at least to a speedy one, and it is not surprising that many saw in this the intervention of an offended Deity. During the troubled period from June 1557 to November 1558, when the newly reconciled England was deeply at odds with the papacy of Paul IV, and when both the realm and its ailing queen were consistently neglected by their alien lord, the deeply rooted xenophobia of the English people took a further, and critically important step towards association with doctrinal protestantism.

However, none of this would have been decisive if Elizabeth had not been a protestant herself. Cautious and enigmatic she may have been, but Mary had not trusted her conformity, and she had been right. The settlement of 1559 could not depend for success upon the support of the protestants alone. Despite their euphoria they were too few, and had too little support among the aristocracy. Consequently it was of the greatest importance that they, and the queen, could call upon the powerful and growing sentiment of patriotism to rally the country behind a church which few really liked but which had the immense advantage of being 'mere English'.

---

[32] *A compendious treatise in metre* (London 1554) (*STC* 17469).
[33] *De vera obedientia* (Rouen 1553) (*STC* 11585); preface by Bale sig A iii.

My swete realme be obedience to gods holy commandment
and my proceedings embrace,
And for that that is abused shalbe better used, and that within
shorte space

says 'Bessy' in William Birch's famous ballad of 1559.[34] As the
more determined catholics departed reluctantly into exile, John
Aylmer was able to rally his fellow countrymen with the conviction that Elizabeth represented decisive proof of God's particular
favour.

Think not that God will suffer you to be soiled at their hands,
for your fall is his dishonour; if you lose the victory, he must
lose the glory.[35]

How well the still precarious triumph which Aylmer celebrated
would have stood up to the kind of misfortunes which overtook
Mary, we cannot know. In the event England was to enjoy a long
period of peace and relative prosperity, and nothing succeeds like
success. By the time of the Armada it was possible to assume
(although not with complete accuracy) that protestantism and
patriotism were the same thing—but that had required in the
meantime a lot of work, and the benign face of fortune—or
providence.

University College of North Wales, Bangor

---

[34] *A songe betwene the Queens majestie and Englande* (London 1559) *Society of Antiquaries*
broadsheet 47 (*STC* 3079).
[35] J. Aylmer, *An Harborowe for Faithfull and Trewe Subiectes* . . . (Strasburg 1559)
(*STC* 1005) p 35.

THE FIRST CENTURY OF ENGLISH PROTESTANTISM AND THE GROWTH OF NATIONAL IDENTITY

by ANTHONY FLETCHER

T HEIR sense of national identity is not something that men have been in the habit of directly recording. Its strength or weakness, in relation to commitment to international causes or to localist sentiment, can often only be inferred by examining political and religious attitudes and personal behaviour. So far as the early modern period is concerned, the subject is hazardous because groups and individuals must have varied enormously in the extent to which national identity meant something to them or influenced their lives. The temptation to generalise must be resisted. It is all too easy to suppose that national identity became well established in England in the Tudor century, when a national culture, based on widespread literacy among gentry, yeomen and townsmen, flowered as it had never done before, when the bible was first generally available in English, when John Foxe produced his celebrated *Acts and Monuments*, better known as the *Book of Martyrs*. Recent work reassessing the significance of Foxe's account of the English reformation and other Elizabethan polemical writings provdes a convenient starting point for this brief investigation of some of the connections between religious zeal and national consciousness between 1558 and 1642.

Haller's notion that Foxe taught his contemporaries to regard England as an elect nation has been shown to be false.[1] Firth has described Foxe's conception of the true church as international and mystical, 'identifying the church as the congregation of the elect'. She argues that he made an important contribution to the apocalyptic tradition in protestant historiography by placing 'his nation, with other European nations, in a historical context bounded by the prophecies of the Revelation'.[2] Another crucial figure in that

---

[1] W. Haller, *Foxe's Book of Martyrs and the Elect Nation* (London 1693).
[2] K. R. Firth, *The Apocalyptic Tradition in Reformation Britain 1530–1645* (Oxford

tradition was John Bale, but his writings equally fail to substantiate Haller's thesis. 'The idea of a unique providential role for the English nation', writes Bauckham, 'runs entirely counter to Bale's repeated statements or belief that the apocalyptic pattern of history was being worked out all over the world, not even in Europe only but in all three continents'[3]

Lake's examination of the religious ideas of William Whitaker is particularly interesting, since Whitaker was a member of the circle of Cambridge puritans which included such men as Laurence Chaderton, William Fulke and Robert Some. Whitaker enjoyed the support of Elizabethan courtiers ranging in outlook from Whitgift and Burghley to Leicester and Essex. His polemical works were informed by a spirit of internationalism. He used them, Lake suggests, 'to consult a general protestant position of which the English church was assumed to be representative'. For Whitaker 'the antichristian nature of popery, summed up in the identification of the pope as antichrist, provided the central organising principle for a whole view of the world'. Antichrist was the most formidable of all adversaries: the protestant's only weapon was the purity of his doctrine, an uncompromising scriptural Calvinism which produced a dynamic tension in the private and public life of the believer.[4]

Anti-popery was the basis of an alliance between certain leading nobles and gentry and the clerical puritan movement represented by such men as Whitaker. It called forth zeal in protecting the interests of true religion both at home and abroad. The thrust of the clerical argument was, in Lake's words, 'toward English involvement in an ideological struggle against Rome that transcended national boundaries and which was based on the essential unity of all protestants'. Nevertheless the assumption that England had a special role to play in this struggle did emerge in the writings of some ministers at moments of crisis such as 1588.[5] This assumption

---

1979) pp. 106–10; see also P. Christianson, *Reformers and Babylon: English Apocalyptic Visions from the Reformation to the Civil War* (Toronto 1978) pp 13–46.

[3] R. Bauckham, *Tudor Apocalypse*, Courtenay Library of Reformation Classics, 8 (1978) pp. 70–3.

[4] [P] Lake, ['The Significance of the Elizabethan Identification of the Pope as Antichrist',] *JEH*, 31 (1980) pp. 161–71.

[5] Lake pp 164, 177–8.

was probably especially appealing to puritan courtiers, who could hardly have avoided imbibing the secular cult of Elizabeth that was so lavishly propagated by some of those around her. No one has explored this cult more perceptively than Yates whose essay on 'Queen Elizabeth as Astraea' uses literature, paintings and engravings to illustrate the equation of Elizabethan imperialism with the royal supremacy over church and state. Her argument that the Queen's sense of isolation left her closest advisers with no choice but to make everything they could of myth and propaganda is persuasive. The political nation needed 'a symbol strong enough to provide a feeling of spiritual security in face of the break with the rest of Christendom'.[6] The intention was to show Englishmen that Elizabeth's destiny was their destiny, that, as Hurstfield has put it, England's survival was seen to 'depend upon a miracle, the miracle of a virgin goddess who would restore unity and greatness'.[7]

Councillors spelt out the connection between the cult of Gloriana and the protestant cause. Lord Chancellor Hatton, for example, at the opening of the 1589 parliament denounced the Spaniards as insatiable tyrants and went on: 'they never bent themselves with such might and resolution against the very Turk or any other infidel as they have done against a virgin queen, a famous lady and a country which embraceth without corruption to doctrine the true and sincere religion of Christ'.[8] We cannot measure the impact of this kind of propaganda, but the general message must surely have got across to those who listened to such speeches at Westminster or heard them retailed in the inns and manor houses of the localities. Various kinds of evidence can be adduced to indicate that the gentry's sense of national identity did increase during the reign of Elizabeth. Long galleries, for instance, came into fashion and it became de rigeur to fill them with royal portraits and a display of kinship links across the highest ranks of national society.[9] There

---

[6] [F. A.] Yates, *Astraea: [The Imperial Theme in the Sixteenth Century]* (London 1975) pp 29–87.

[7] [J.] Hurstfield, ['Queen and State: the Emergence of an Elizabethan Myth' *Britain and the Netherlands 5, Some Political Mythologies* ed. J. S. Bromley and E. H. Kussmann (The Hague 1975) pp 62, 70–2.

[8] J. E. Neale, *Elizabeth I and Her Parliaments* (London 1953–7) 2 p 197. For the development of anti-Spanish sentiment see W. S. Maltby, *The Black Legend in England* (Durham, North Corolina 1968).

[9] M. Girouard, *Life in the English Country House* (London 1978) pp 101–2.

was also a new fascination with the cartographic image of England.[10]

Yet how deeply and how widely was the Elizabethan myth absorbed? Yates cites a conversation between two old men in the prologue to Thomas Dekker's Old Fortunatus, which reflects the courtly worship of the Virgin Queen: 'Are you then travelling to the temple of Eliza? Even to her temple are my feeble limbs travelling. Some call her Pandora, some Gloriana, some Cynthia, some Belphoebe, some Astraea: all by several names to express several loves . . . I am of her own country and we adore her by the name of Eliza'.[11] Here is the affection and patriotism we have been taught to expect emerging in the work of a popular dramatist, but can Dekker's abstruse references have meant much to the groundlings who watched his play? Hurstfield's claim that the Elizabethan propaganda was met 'by a deeply felt emotional response by the people themselves in city and village' will remain debatable.[12]

The ideological legacy of the Elizabethan age was thus twofold. On the one hand there was the secular cult, based on romanticisation of the queen and her court, on the other the concept of an explicitly protestant foreign policy in conjunction with sympathetic nations against catholic Spain. We would expect the parliament of 1621, the first since the outbreak of European war over the Bohemian question, to have contained many men ready to reminisce about past glories and at least some men who held a deeply ingrained but long frustrated commitment to the cause of international protestantism. Sir James Perrott was in the latter category. A member of the earl of Pembroke's anti-Spanish group at court, he 'has as good a claim to be called a puritan', Russell has suggested, as anyone in that house of commons.[13] The parliament had been summoned because the king wished to give force to his threat of war, following the Spanish invasion of the Palatinate, while he continued to make efforts to negotiate a satisfactory peace.[14] It was Perrott who moved on the last day of the session,

---

[10] V. Morgan, 'The Cartographic Image of "the Country" in Early Modern England', TRHS, 29 XXIX (1979) pp 129–54.
[11] Yates, Astraea p 29.
[12] Hurstfield, Britain and the Netherlands 5, p 72.
[13] [C. S. R.] Russell, [Parliaments and English Politics 1621–1629], (Oxford 1979) pp 13–14.
[14] For the background see R. Zaller, The Parliament of 1621 (Berkeley 1971) pp

after MPs had restrained themselves from discussing a war for eighteen weeks, that the commons should draw up a declaration stating that if James I undertook a war for the Palatinate they would be ready to assist him. The protestant cause, he insisted, was 'near to withering and ruin abroad'. His concern was 'that some special care might be taken for true religion, whose circumference is the glory of God, whose centre is the salvation of souls, whose direct lines are piety and truth'.[15]

Perrott's motivation was international and spiritual. The response of his colleagues, by and large, was nostalgic and nationalistic. The declaration was passed, Russell has argued, on a wave of emotion. MPs were disturbed about the prospect of going home with nothing to offer their friends, so Perrott's motion was exactly timed. They were given a comforting sense of purpose but asked to make no precise commitments. Many showed unthinking enthusiasm: John Delbridge vowed he would go to the Palatinate in person, Gabriel Towerson was so overcome that he said he would give twenty or thirty subsidies. Yet there was something ritualistic about this debate. A display of anti-Spanish and anti-catholic rhetoric cost nothing. War was expensive. Russell has described the debate in terms of a 'reflex orthodoxy which would not overide good neighbourhood'.[16] There were a few men who kept their heads and were ready to remind their colleagues of the guiding principles of local representation, principles like shifting the burden of taxation and defence of county interests. Edward Alford warned against 'too great an engagement', Sir William Strode 'did not like the naming of subsidies', Ralph Hopton saw the dangers of the poor being 'drawn dry'.[17]

Alford, Strode and Hopton were acting soberly and thoughtfully when they shied away from identifying themselves with the protestant cause abroad. They recognised that identification meant responsibility and responsibility implied the necessity for consent in the localities. Their response was poles apart from that of men like Sir Edmund Coke, Delbridge and Towerson. Coke was an

---

16–18; S. L. Adams, 'Foreign Policy and the Parliaments of 1621 and 1624' *Faction and Parliament* ed K. Sharpe (Oxford 1978) pp 139–61.

[15] *Commons Debates 1621* ed W. Notestein, F. H. Relf, H. Simpson (New Haven 1935) 2, pp 428–9; 4, pp 415–16; 5, pp 200–1, 396–7.

[16] Russell pp 119–20.

[17] *Commons Debates 1621*, 2, pp 428–9; 4, pp 415–16; 5, pp 200–1, 396–7.

incurable romantic so far as relations with Spain were concerned: in 1624 he claimed that England had never prospered so well as when at war with Spain and announced that the very thought of its renewal made him feel seven years younger.[18] But the fact was that localist pressures cut sharply across national and international identification.[19] Momentarily, on 4 June 1621, the majority of the commons ignored their own nostrum of putting their country first in the seventeenth, not the twentieth, century sense of the term. But in most cases their sense of national, as opposed to local, identity only went skin deep.

If we turn to 1628 we find a markedly different atmosphere in the house of commons. War had been waged against both France and Spain with all its accompanying national humiliations. Arminianism was in the ascendant at court and on the episcopal bench.[20] In his attack on Richard Montague during the 1625 parliament, John Pym had mentioned his 'slighting those famous divines who have been great lights in this church, Calvin, Beza, Perkins, Whitaker.[21]' Pym, in other words, who was now emerging as a leading figure in the commons, stood in the mainstream of the tradition of international solidarity of the godly that went back to the moderate Cambridge puritans. His circle had now identified the Arminians as the fifth column that would let in popery.

In June 1628 the duke of Buckingham was charged with threatening the ruin of religion. 'Why are Arminians that have threatened the ruin of the Low Countries allowed here?', asked Christopher Sherland. 'They run in a string with the papists', he declared, 'and flatter greatness to oppress the subject'. Russell has emphasised that in this speech Sherland made an intellectual link that is of the utmost significance for the history of the subsequent fifteen years: the link between alteration of religion and alteration of government. In the same debate John Hampden spoke of Buckingham's 'subversion of the whole state' and Richard Knightley accused him of committing treason by granting letters of

[18] Russell pp 168–9.
[19] D. Hirst, *The Representative of the People?* (Cambridge 1975) pp 132–88; A. J. Fletcher, *A County Community in Peace and War* (London 1975) pp 127–233.
[20] Russell pp 204–389; N. R. N. Tyacke, 'Puritanism, Arminianism and Counter-Revolution', [The] *Origins of the English Civil War* ed C. S. R. Russell (London 1973) pp 119–43.
[21] Lake p 178.

marque to papists. In June 1621 the commons had engaged in a display of protestant nationalism on the basis of sympathy and accord with the crown. In June 1628 it was apparent that the gentry's nationalist fervour was being turned, by the skilful leadership of a group of determined men, against the crown and its closest advisers. This is a turning point in seventeenth century English history that has not yet received the stress it deserves.[22]

A group of leading figures in the 1628 parliament then believed the foundations of the protestant state were threatened from within. They regarded the Arminians as a Trojan horse, 'ready to open the gates to Romish tyranny and Spanish monarchy'. They were convinced that the papists sought to break parliaments, 'that so they may break in upon our religion and bring in their own errors'. The whole argument had a certain logical coherence: since parliament was irrevocably committed to protestantism it was only by absolutism that the papists could override it and reestablish their religion. All these fears came fully into the open during the short 1629 session. Sherland alleged that catholics, seeking to make divisions in the state, 'creep into the ears of his Majesty and suggest that those that oppose them do oppose his Majesty and so they put him upon designs that stand not with public liberty, that he may command what he listeth and do what he pleaseth with life, goods and religion'. The only way to answer this challenge was by an appeal to colleagues' patriotism and valour in the protestant cause: 'they involve all true hearted Englishmen and Christians under the name of puritans'[33] The continuity with Elizabethan ideological politics is plain, yet the parliamentary politics of 1628 and 1629 were fiercer than previously and the issues at stake were less amenable to settlement.

The basic assumption made by the leaders of the long parliament was that the English gentry shared a protestant identity and destiny. The political crisis of 1641 and 1642, I have argued elsewhere, arose because Pym and his associates believed that this was under immediate threat. The crisis was rooted in their conviction that a popish conspiracy against the English state was ripe and imminent. The grand remonstrance describes the genesis and nature of this conspiracy. His terror made it essential for Pym to

[22] Russell pp 379–80.
[33] *Ibid* pp 404–8; R. Clifton, 'Fear of Popery' in, *Origins of the English Civil War*, ed C. S. R. Russell (1980) p 156.

magnify parliament's role as the nation's only shield against its papist enemies. The spate of county petitions praising parliament's work in the early months of 1642 shows that the provincial gentry were deeply responsive to his propaganda. National political consciousness thus developed abruptly. Once the gentry had grasped that the country as a whole faced a real emergency, many of them were ready to abandon localist assumptions and involve themselves in the contentions dividing king and parliament. Civil war was a forcing house of national identity.[24]

Throughout the crisis that led to civil war Elizabethan nostalgia and the protestant cause abroad remained powerful influences on men's minds. The ancient belligerence against Spain emerged in debates at the end of August 1641, following the news that the king of Spain was hindering English shipping at Calais. Plans for a West India company were briefly revived, with warm backing from Pym, and there was some bold talk about a campaign aimed at taking the plate fleet, Hispaniola and Cuba.[25] Several times Pym reiterated his vision of how the English nation, once their internal troubles were over, could do good in the world. The current parliament, he asserted on 23 June 1641, might 'lay a foundation for such a greatness of the kingdom, both in power at home and in reputation abroad, as never any of his Majesty's ancestors enjoyed.[26]

In brief then the argument is as follows: both the cult of Elizabeth and the international protestant cause were potent factors in the growth of national identity among the gentry between 1558 and 1642 but neither could in itself overcome the strongly held localist prejudices which made government, and particularly the administration of war, so difficult for the first two Stuarts. Charles I's Arminian policies sharpened ideological conflict and encouraged a broader spectrum of the gentry to engage themselves in national controversy with a new seriousness. Arminian assertion roused a more vehement national sentiment than had ever existed in Elizabethan England and prepared the way for civil war, in the sense that the struggle to defend protestant orthodoxy made possible the threefold identification of parliament, true religion and the national interest. What finally of the people of the towns and

[24] A. J. Fletcher, *The Outbreak of the English Civil War*, (London 1981) pp 191–207.
[25] BL Additional MS 11045, fol 141[r], Sloane MS 3317, fols 24–6.
[26] BL Harleian MS 163, fol 330[r]; Bodleian, Rawlinson MS D 1099: 23 June.

countryside, who have received virtually no attention to this paper? There seems to be no good reason to think they felt a significantly greater sense of national identity in the 1640s than they had done in the 1580s. Their world was still essentially a local one and it was surely to remain so for a good many decades. Specialists in the eighteenth and nineteenth centuries are perhaps better placed than early modernists to chart the growth in the population as a whole of an elusive sentiment, which people have always tended, according to their own predilections, to take for granted or to ignore.

University of Sheffield

KING JAMES I AND THE PROTESTANT CAUSE IN THE CRISIS OF 1618–22

by W. B. PATTERSON

IN THE early seventeenth century, when Europe was divided along religious lines and works of polemical theology circulated widely, most Englishmen seem to have been convinced that their nation was part of a protestant community of nations with certain common interests.[1] This attitude had its roots in the recent past, when the government of queen Elizabeth had aided—albeit adroitly—the Dutch and French Calvinists and had maintained close relations with several protestant states, particularly in the Rhineland. When the 'Invincible Armada' from Spain had been thwarted in its intended object, the English were thankful to Providence for the events which had preserved protestantism on the island.[2] The common cause among protestant states thus came to be thought of, by statesmen and ordinary citizens alike, as an effort to safeguard the political autonomy of the protestant states, particularly against the great Hapsburg monarchy in Spain and Austria, and to preserve the protestant faith against the revived Roman catholicism of the counter-reformation. Religion and national identity were so closely linked that English 'papists' had

---

[1] See, for examples of English views: Marvin A. Breslow, *A Mirror of England, English Puritan Views of Foreign Nations, 1618–1640* (Cambridge, Massachusetts, 1970) esp pp 10–99; William S. Maltby, *The Black Legend in England: The Development of Anti-Spanish Sentiment, 1558–1660* (Durham, North Carolina, 1971) esp pp 100–30; and Louis B. Wright, 'Propaganda against James I's "Appeasement" of Spain', *Huntingdon Library Quarterly* 6 (San Marino, California, 1942–3) pp 149–72. For a sustained political analysis, see Simon L. Adams, 'The Protestant Cause: Religious Alliance with the West European Calvinist Communities as a Political Issue in England, 1585–1630', Oxford University DPhil thesis (1972).
[2] Thomas Fuller, *The Church History of Britain* (London 1655) bk 9, pp 192–3. Elizabethan relations with protestant states are treated in R. B. Wernham, *Before the Armada: The Growth of English Foreign Policy* (London 1966) pp 290–405, and Wallace T. MacCaffrey, *The Shaping of the Elizabethan Regime* (Princeton 1968) pp 268–90, 372–92.

constantly to struggle against a suspicion that they were unpatriotic or disloyal.[3]

Yet at the outbreak of the conflict in central Europe which proved to be the beginning of the Thirty Years' War, England failed to play the role which her own people as well as her friends abroad expected of her. Instead of going resolutely to the aid of the Bohemian protestants in their struggle against Hapsburg rule in 1618 and of Frederick, the elector Palatine, the son-in-law of king James I, when that prince was elected king of Bohemia in 1619, the English government seemed to take refuge in lengthy negotiations. King James even chose to renew discussions aimed at a marriage treaty with Spain at a time when Spanish troops were invading the Palatinate. James's actions have been variously accounted for as the product of his timidity, his awe of the Hapsburgs, his political incompetence, and the extraordinary influence exerted over him by count Gondomar, the Spanish ambassador to England. On a more charitable level his actions have been seen as those of an idealist, out of touch with the political realities of European affairs. The consensus seems to be that the king, by endeavouring to pacify the combatants rather than supporting England's traditional allies, did nothing to mitigate or to localise the German conflict; as a result, England's reputation as a European power sharply declined.[4] James's foreign policy during the crucially important first years of war may, however, have been better conceived and executed than most historians have recognised. His vision, so distinct from that of most of his subjects, deserves, in any case, the close attention of those who seek to understand a complex and puzzling era.

[3] For a discussion of this and other aspects of English catholicism in the period, see Caroline M. Hibbard, 'Early Stuart Catholicism: Revisions and Re-Revisions', *JMH* 52 (1980) pp 1–34.

[4] Discussions of James's foreign policy include [Samuel R.] Gardiner, *History of England [from the Accession of James I to the Outbreak of the Civil War, 1603–1642]* 10 vols (London 1884–6) esp vols 3–5; Leopold von Ranke, *A History of England, Principally in the Seventeenth Century*, 6 vols (Oxford 1875) 1, pp 367–536; [D. Harris] Willson, *King James VI and I* (New York 1956) esp pp 271–87, 399–424; Godfrey Davies, *The Early Stuarts, 1603–1660*(2 ed Oxford 1959) pp 47–67; and [Maurice] Lee, *James I and Henri IV: [An Essay in English Foreign Policy, 1603–1610]* (Urbana 1970) *passim*. Fresh lines of investigation are suggested by [Charles H.] Carter, *[The] Secret Diplomacy [of the Habsburgs, 1598–1625]* (New York 1964) *passim*; [Robert] Zaller, '"Interest of State": [James I and the Palatinate'], *Albion* 6 (Boone, North Carolina, 1974) pp 144–75; and J. V. Polišenský, *War and Society in Europe, 1618–1648*, trans Frederick Snider (Cambridge 1978) pp 59–67, 88–94, 109–12, 163–67.

In 1618, the year of the Bohemian revolt which soon led to the intervention of outside powers, a panegyric to peace was published in England, celebrating James I's achievements as a conciliator. *The Peace-Maker*, dedicated by James 'to all our true-louing and peace-embracing subiects', pointed out that peace, which had formerly been a stranger in England, 'is now become a sister, a Deere and Naturall sister.⁵' Changing the metaphor, the text likened peace to a dove sent out from the ark 'to see if the whole world were not yet couered with the perpetuall deluge of Blood and Enmity.' Finding an olive branch in Britain, 'heere now it hath remained full Sixteene yeeres.'⁶ Enlarging upon this theme, the work observed that England and Scotland had been reconciled in 'their louing Vnion'. Ireland, 'that rebellious Outlaw' had quickly recited the text *Beati Pacifici*. Spain, 'that great and long-lasting opposite, betwixt whome and England, the Ocean ranne with blood not many yeares before' had shaken hands 'in friendly amity'. Between Spain and her 'withstanding Prouinces' in the Netherlands 'leagues of friendship' had been established. Other disputes had also been happily resolved: Denmark and Sweden, Sweden and Poland, Cleves and Brandenburg.⁷ Without undue modesty the work claimed that credit for settling all these conflicts belonged to the British sovereign: 'Heere sits Salomon, and hither come the tribes for Judgments: Oh happy Moderator, blessed Father, not father of thy Country alone, but Father of all thy neighbour Countries about thee.⁸' The pamphlet somewhat overstated James's role in making the years 1603–18 an era of peace for the British Isles and for most of Europe, but it pointed accurately enough to the concerns which led English statesmen to try to bring about a negotiated settlement in many European disputes.⁹ James had every reason to think that his record as an impartial and effective arbiter commanded respect. In the light of his experience, it is not surprising that his first reaction to war in central Europe was to attempt negotiation.

---

⁵ James I, *The Peace-Maker; [or, Great Brittaines, Blessing, Fram'd for the Continuance of That Mightie Happinesse Wherein This Kingdomme Excells Manie Empires* (London 1619) [first published 1618], sig A3 verso. According to Willson, *King James VI and I*, the king 'probably wrote small portions' of the book, 'and Lancelot Andrewes the rest'. (p271) It has also been attributed to Thomas Middleton, the playwright.
⁶ James I, *The Peace-Maker* sig A4.
⁷ *Ibid* sig B1–B1 verso.
⁸ *Ibid* sig B1 verso.
⁹ See Lee, *James I and Henri IV* pp 12–13, 17–18, 61–70, 118–42, 175–6.

The Bohemian revolt, which erupted in the spring of 1618 over the religious and political policies of the new king, Ferdinand of Austria, evidently struck James as a problem which posed a threat to the peace of Europe. Since his government's relations with Spain had been close in recent years it was natural that he should have discussed the problems of the Austrians with their politically and militarily powerful Spanish cousins.[10] On 27 September 1618, the English ambassador Francis Cottington wrote to Sir Robert Naunton, secretary of state, that he had recently visited king Philip III at the Escorial. There he had acquainted the Spanish king that James was concerned that 'those people who had taken armes against the King of Bohemia' had done so for the ostensible purpose of preventing 'the execution of a cruell massacre intended against them meerly for their religion', which was 'the same the King my master professeth'. The king could not in honour and conscience 'leave them to be consumed by the sword, if what they pretended and alleadged were true'. Yet, 'such was his respect to the generall peace and quiet of Cristendom and to the perfect friendship and brotherly amitie' between Philip and himself, that 'he was resolved to use his utmost endeavours and impose his best credit and autoritie for compounding the difference' between the two parties.[11] A hint that such a course would be desirable had already been dropped, it seems, by the Spanish king. Letters from Cottington to John Digby and to Sir Thomas Lake, dated 9 August 1618, had signified that Philip was very willing for James to 'interpose himself for the accommodating of the business of Bohemia'.[12] This seems to have been the origin of the ambitious diplomatic initiative launched by James in the following year. Recent research suggests that Spain was not simply trying to neutralise a potential supporter of the Bohemians by this suggestion. Within the Spanish council opinion was divided as to whether it was in the interest of Spain to aid the Austrians in their dispute in far-away Bohemia. By September it had been decided that aid would be granted. But

[10] Willson, *King James VI amd I* pp 271–87; Carter, *Secret Diplomacy* pp 47–9 and 'Gondomar: Ambassador to James I', *HJ* 7 (1964) pp 189–208.

[11] [*Letters and Other Documents Illustrating the Relations between England and Germany at the Commencement of the Thirty Years' War*] ed [Samuel R.] Gardiner *CSer* 90 p 10. (1865) p 10.

[12] Gardiner p 4.

Philip III also felt that Ferdinand would be well advised to make peace by compromise with the Bohemians.[13]

Count Gondomar, who had represented Spain in England since 1613, was away from his post for reasons of health in the late summer of 1618 but he was still in a position to interpret the actions of the English government to his superiors. On 30 September 1618, the marquis of Buckingham wrote to Gondomar, stating his master's commitment 'to do all that he can and that lies in his power' to resolve the Bohemian problem peaceably.[14] A few months later, on 14 January 1619, Gondomar wrote a *consulta* for his government on the plans which had been developed for this negotiation. 'These good offices of the king of England', he wrote, 'were owing to his inclination to peace, and to his expectation of the difficulties into which the Palatine and the Protestants of Germany would bring him', should the issue be joined between catholics and protestants. It was this, said the ambassador, 'which has more to do with his good offices than your Majesty's friendship or than the representations made to him by the Count of Gondomar'.[15] Gondomar's analysis was accurate. James, as the most powerful ruler in the protestant camp, was particularly anxious that the Bohemian conflict should not become a general religious war, which might sweep his nation and many others into a desperate struggle for survival.

Even before an embassy could be sent to Germany, James was under pressure from the Protestant Union of German states to back the Bohemian rebels. In January 1619, Christopher von Dohna, a member of a politically prominent family in the Palatinate, negotiated a renewal of the defensive alliance between the Union and England which had first been agreed to in 1612.[16] Soon the representatives of several European states were in England seeking men and supplies. James made a gesture—it was hardly more than that—aimed at demonstrating his leadership of the protestant bloc without committing military forces. In early March he authorised

---

[13] Peter Brightwell, 'The Spanish Origins of the Thirty Years' War', *European Studies Review* 9 (London 1979) pp 409–31. This account corrects that in Bohdan Chudoba, *Spain and the Empire, 1519–1643* (Chicago 1952) pp 218–21, where Spanish policy is represented as consistently militant.

[14] Gardiner p 13.

[15] *Ibid* p 30.

[16] Gardiner, *History of England* 3, p 285; Claus-Peter Clasen, *The Palatinate in European History, 1555–1618* (Oxford 1966) pp 22–3.

Sir Henry Wotton, who was being recalled from his post as
ambassador to Venice to visit the elector Palatine, the elector of
Brandenburg, the duke of Württemberg, the landgrave of Hesse,
other princes, and several imperial cities. He was to propose that
seminaries be planted to combat errors in the faith and to instruct
those 'who shall desire to come out of that darkness wherein they
live'.[17] Wotton also presented this idea at the assembly of the Union
at Heilbronn in June, where it was considered less relevant than
proposals for large levies of troops.[18] By this time, in fact, the
escalation of military activity in central Europe had brought in
Silesia and Moravia on the side of Bohemia, as well as Spain on the
side of Austria; intensive fighting was going on around Vienna
itself.

With the chances for peace rapidly diminishing, an English
embassy large enough that it was not likely to be ignored was
organised and sent to the continent. Under the leadership of James
Hay, viscount Doncaster, the mission consisted of 150 persons and
required two ships to be transported across the channel.[19] Doncaster's instructions, given him by the king at Royston on 14 April
1619, called for a cessation of hostilities and an eventual settlement
based on the recognition of Ferdinand's authority, the exclusion of
jesuits from political affairs, the restoration of the privileges
formerly enjoyed by the protestants in Bohemia, and the restoration of protestant officials who had been expelled from office.[20]
James had evidently concluded that it would be useless to send such
a mission to Bohemia alone; he thus provided Doncaster with an
itinerary which took him to many of the main centres of power in
the areas threatened by war. In Brussels the archduke Albert gave
the English emissary a polite hearing. In Heidelberg the elector
Frederick spoke of war rather than peace, and persuaded Doncaster
to ask James to send aid. From the Palatinate Doncaster went not
to Saxony, as had originally been planned, but to Bavaria to

[17] Gardiner pp 46–7. For the earlier stages of the proposal, which had apparently
originated with Wotton, see *Letters and Dispatches from Sir Henry Wotton to James the
First and His Ministers, in the Years MDCXVII–XX*, ed George Tomline (London
1850) pp 35–6, 61–3, 98–100.
[18] Gardiner, *History of England* 3, pp 301–2.
[19] [Edward] McCabe, 'England's Foreign Policy [in 1619: Lord Doncaster's
Embassy to the Princes of Germany'], *Mitteilungen des Instituts für Österreichische
Geschichtsforschung* 58 (Vienna 1950), p 473.
[20] Gardiner pp 64–74.

confer with duke Maximilian, evidently on the suggestion of the Palatines, who saw the Bavarian as a possible rival to Ferdinand in the coming imperial election. Finally, on 6 July 1619, Doncaster intercepted Ferdinand and strove for two days to convince him of the necessity for a treaty. On 3 August, the reply finally came back: four electors had been chosen to mediate, making English efforts unnecessary. A secretary, sent by Doncaster to Prague, came back with an equally discouraging message. The Bohemians thought the English had sided with Ferdinand and put little faith in James's efforts.[21] If these developments were daunting, worse ones were to come. At the end of August, Ferdinand was elected Holy Roman Emperor and Frederick of the Palatinate king of a rebellious Bohemia, where that same Ferdinand had been declared deposed. A long struggle seemed almost certain to ensue.

The failure of Doncaster's mission was only partly due to timing and to the personal characteristics of the European heads of state. An anonymous supporter of James in a memorandum written about 1620 put his finger on the difficulty. The two parties in Europe, he wrote, were so great and so equally balanced that 'neither of them will condiscend to the other, in any thing which they shall deeme prejudicial to themselves'.[22] The controversy, he continued, exceeded that of Guelfs and the Ghibellines, 'it being for no lesse than *pro aris et focis*, for heaven and earth, for their soules and for their bodies, for religion & libertie'.[23] This writer did not deduce from his analysis that England would be well advised to stay out for a conflict so 'unapeasable'; rather, he thought it essential to defeat the Antichrist, who had been responsible for so many dissensions. England, he argued, was the great bulwark of the protestant cause, and as long as she remained 'untouched & entyre', a sentinel at sea and a source of manpower on land, the Roman faction 'cannot prevaile in their warres against o^r friends abroad'.[24]

The growth of the two parties abroad was graphically rep-

---

[21] McCabe, 'England's Foreign Policy', pp 473–76; Gardiner, *History of England* 3, pp 300–7.

[22] [Washington,] Folger [Library,] MS V. a. 24: 'In what lamentable estate, and uppon what unapeasable termes all Europe now stands', by a supporter of James I, *c*1620, p 1.

[23] Folger MS V. a. 24, p 1.

[24] *Ibid* p 17.

resented in a German pamphlet translated into French and published in 1620. *L'estat present des gverres de la Boheme & Allemagne* distinguished two great collective forces in Germany, where 'Mars and Bellona are playing out their tragedies'.[25] The emperor, on the one hand, commanded units supplied by the pope, the kings of Spain and Poland, the duke of Bavaria, the ecclesiastical electors of the empire, the catholic cities of Germany, and the grand duke of Tuscany. The elector Palatine, on the other hand, had units of men from the kings of Great Britain and Denmark, the estates of Holland, the elector of Brandenburg, the landgrave of Hesse, and the protestant cities of the empire.[26] Great desolation, the pamphleteer observed, was to be feared from such large armies drawn from so many nations. The pamphlet concluded by asking king Louis XIII to mediate a peaceful settlement and so become 'the Pacifier' of the whole Christian world.[27] The appeal to Louis seemed almost a testimonial to the need for James's diplomatic efforts, though the British king is not mentioned as a conciliator but only as a supplier of a modest number of troops for his son-in-law's army.

Frederick's election as king of Bohemia in August 1619 put James in a position which became steadily more difficult as time went on. In order to maintain credit with the Spanish court, the English government felt it necessary to show that Doncaster had had nothing to do with Frederick's election as king. This was demonstrated to Sir Walter Aston by Doncaster, Digby, and Naunton in mid-January 1620, before Aston left on his embassy to Madrid. Digby undertook to do the same with Spanish envoys in London.[28] In fact, James had done nothing to encourage Frederick in his scheming with the Bohemians and had advised against accepting the crown when it was offered. Even when the new monarch, along with James's daughter Elizabeth, had taken up residence in Prague, James insisted that his son-in-law's throne had been illicitly

[25] *L'estat present des gverres* [*de la Boheme & Allemagne auec le denombrement des troupes qui y sont ariuees tant pour le secours de l'Empereur, que pour le party du Comte Palatin,*] trans from German into French by J. D. C. (Paris 1620) [Chicago, Newberry Library copy], p 4.
[26] *Ibid* pp 4–9.
[27] *Ibid* p 11.
[28] *The Fortescue Papers,* [*Consisting Chiefly of Letters Relating to State Affairs, Collected by John Packer*], ed [Samuel R. Gardiner,] *CSer* ns 1 (1871) p 114.

and unconstitutionally obtained.[29] But the Palatinate was another matter, and James was insistent that this territory, threatened by Spanish troops, should remain in the possession of the elector. On 25 September 1620, however, Elizabeth asserted in a letter to Buckingham from Prague that the Spanish general Spinola 'hath taken three towns of the King's [Frederick's] in the Lower Palatinat: two of them are my jointur: he will, if he can, take all that countree.' She urged Buckingham to 'move his Majestie now to shew himself a loving father to us, and not suffer his children's inheritance to be taken away'. In a postscript, she added: 'tell the King that the enemie will more regard his blowes then his wordes.[30]'

The autumn of 1620 brought such disasters to Frederick and Elizabeth that James was forced to make preparations for more militant actions. Not only did Spanish troops, under imperial ensigns, invade the Palatinate in force, but the army assembled by the elector Palatine was decisively defeated in early November near Prague, sending the now derisively christened 'Winter King' and his queen into exile. James evidently felt that he could do nothing less than call a parliament to advise him and to provide the means to defend the Palatinate against attack.[31] In his opening speech to parliament on 30 January 1621, the king approached this subject with evident regret. In the eighteen years he had been in England, he said, the country had been at peace, and he considered it an honour 'that you should live quiety under yor vines and fig trees reapinge the frutes of yor owne labours.'[32] Now, however, 'the miserable and torne estate of Christendome, wch none that hath an honest heart can looke on wth out a weepinge eye' urgently required attention.[33] He had not been the cause of this state of affairs, but had attempted to forestall it by Lord Doncaster's mission, which had cost him £30,000. Now that the Palatinate itself was in danger of falling, despite his efforts to preserve it, the crown needed a speedy

[29] Gardiner, *History of England* 3 pp 350, 363.

[30] *The Fortescue Papers* p 138.

[31] [Robert] Zaller, *The Parliament of 1621: [A Study in Constitutional Conflict]* (Berkeley 1971) pp 6–36. For events in central Europe, see J. V. Polišenský, *The Thirty Years War* (London 1970) pp 98–132.

[32] Folger MS Z. E. 1 (15): Historical Papers of the Time of James I, fol 2. For a shorter version of this speech, see [John] Rushworth, *Historical Collections*, 7 vols (London 1659–1701) 1, pp 21–3.

[33] Folger MS Z. e. 1 (15), fol 2 verso.

grant of supply. James was determined to save the Palatinate—and would shed his blood and his fortune if necessary in the attempt—not only for the sake of his kin, but 'that the cause of religion is involved in it, for they will alter religion where they conquer.'[34]

James did not, however, give up his search for peace by negotiation. The return of Gondomar to England in March 1620 was an appropriate occasion for resuming talks aimed at a marriage between prince Charles and the infanta Maria, a matter which was being seriously discussed before the ambassador's departure in the summer of 1618.[35] Now, however, the match had a larger political significance than before. If a firm Anglo-Spanish alliance were concluded by this means, then the two nations would be able to work out a just and lasting settlement in the Palatinate, where their interests overlapped. The marriage negotiations were watched carefully by Rome and by papal nuncios in Brussels and Madrid, in the hope that the results would ameliorate conditions for catholics in England. Rome's insistence that papal permission would be required for such a marriage meant that a speedy conclusion was not likely.[36] In the meantime, James had developed another, more direct strategy for dealing with the crisis on the continent.

John baron Digby was a man of long political experience at home and abroad and had played a major part in earlier negotiations for a Spanish marriage.[37] James evidently hoped that with these discussions again under way with the Spanish government, Digby could bring the contenders in Germany at least to a truce, after which a permanent peace could be made with the help of the rulers of Austria and Spain. Once again, then, an English embassy was prepared for a tour of the European capitals. Digby went on a preliminary visit to Brussels, where, in early March 1621, he prevailed upon the archduke Albert to recommend a truce in the Palatinate to Madrid and to general Spinola. With the Twelve Year Truce between Spain and the United Provinces about to expire in April the archduke would be glad, it seems, to have the general nearer at hand for the defence of the Spanish Netherlands. No sooner had Digby's work been successfully accomplished, how-

[34] *Ibid* fol 3.
[35] Gardiner, *History of England* 3, pp 37–71, 338, 377.
[36] Rome, Vatican Secret Archives, Fondo Borghese, Ser II, vol 103: Reports from the nuncio in Flanders (16 May 1620), fols 54[r/v]; Fondo Borghese, Ser I, vol 827 bis: Instructions to the nuncio in Spain (5 April 1621), fols 95–6.
[37] Zaller, '"Interest of State"', p 155.

ever, than Spain suddenly became a less certain ally. Philip III died at the end of March, leaving as his successor a sixteen-year-old son, Philip IV, whose intentions were still little known.[38]

Digby's embassy, a large company with appropriate trappings to signify the importance its sponsors accorded to it, crossed the channel at the end of May.[39] The king's instructions spelled out an ambitious assignment. Digby was to persuade the emperor to restore the Palatinate to its rightful rulers, in return for which James would see that Frederick gave up any further pretentions to Bohemia and that he submitted to the authority of the emperor in a manner appropriate to his own birth and rank. The ambassador was to add expressions of amity towards the house of Austria, with whom a closer bond would soon be forged when the proposed marriage was agreed upon. In the event the emperor turned a deaf ear, he was to be told that the dispossession of the king of England's children was a matter which could only lead to 'an immortal and irreconcilable quarrel' between the king and the emperor, and that other lawful means would have to be found to right this wrong. The same message and the same resolution were to be used in dealing with Spain, if the mission to Austria was not a success.[40] Frederick himself, under the ban of the empire, deserted by the Protestant Union, which by this time had been effectively dissolved, and forced to live on the charity of the Dutch at the Hague, played almost no part in the English negotiations on his behalf. An anecdote from the following year, quoted by McCabe, related that 'while the King of Denmark would reinforce Frederick's non-existent army with a thousand pickled herrings, and the Hollanders would raise ten thousand butter-boxes, the English contingent would be a hundred thousand ambassadors.[41]'

Though the final results hardly reflected the fact, Digby seems to have carried out his diplomatic responsibilities in a vigorous and resourceful way. Having reached Vienna on 4 July, after stops in Brussels and the Palatinate, he presented his proposals on the following day to the emperor Ferdinand.[42] It was soon clear that the

[38] Gardiner, *History of England* 4, pp 186–90; J. H. Elliott, *Imperial Spain, 1469–1716* (London 1963) pp 318–19.
[39] Zaller, '"Interest of State"', p 160.
[40] Gardiner, *History of England* 4, p 201.
[41] McCabe, 'England's Foreign Policy', p 473.
[42] Zaller, '"Interest of State"', pp 161–2; Gardiner, *History of England* 4, pp 204–5.

emperor and his councillors were interested in them. Not only did war threaten to erupt on the northern, eastern, and western borders of Bohemia, giving the emperor every reason to look for a peaceful settlement, but Madrid and Brussels were in favour of a pacification. So, in fact, was the protestant but pro-imperial state of Saxony. For the better part of two months Digby strove to work out with the emperor and other diplomatic envoys a plan whereby the temporary cessation of arms in the Lower Palatinate might be converted into a secure peace. The difficulties were formidable. Not only did Ernest count of Mansfeld, in charge of an army committed to the defence of the Upper Palatinate, show no sign of wanting to give up his military operations, his master Frederick, as aggressive as ever, exhibited a new interest in his former kingdom of Bohemia. On the other side, Maximilian of Bavaria was ambitious to annex the Upper Palatinate to his own dominions and take Frederick's electoral title for himself. By the time Digby left Vienna, on 5 September 1621, a settlement still seemed possible, especially as the emperor had written to Brussels to urge that the truce be maintained as long as practicable.[43] Digby returned to England by way of Munich, Heidelberg, and Brussels, where he sought to give effect to the agreement tentatively reached in Vienna.[44] Before he arrived home, however, Maximilian had invaded the Upper Palatinate and Mansfeld had fled to the Lower Palatinate, where, despite the truce, the Spanish seemed firmly in control of most of the open country.

By the time Digby reached England at the end of October the collapse of the Palatinate seemed so imminent that James called parliament back into session almost at once to vote supplies for its defence. On 21 November, the second day of the session, Digby described the negotiations he had conducted. The emperor, he said, had been 'very inclinable' to a peaceful settlement, though discussions had been slow to reach a conclusion. Ferdinand had been expecting a meeting of the diet and had had many consultations with the German princes. Maximilian, on the other hand, had been peremptory and rude, declaring that the only peace he sought had

---

[43] Gardiner, *History of England* 4, pp 206–16.

[44] James asked that word be sent to Spinola in September that Frederick had had no hand in Mansfeld's movements, a matter on which Digby would soon be able to give assurance; he asked Spinola to continue to work for a settlement. See *The Fortescue Papers*, pp 160–1.

been attained by bribing Mansfeld to stay out of the way. The infanta Isabella at Brussels, the Spanish governor there since the death of the archduke Albert, 'seemed to understand by the Empo[r] l res that he did rather prepare for warre than peace, & would geve noe direct answer untill she heard from the K. of Spayne'. The latter, though he had so far maintained his neutrality, 'hathe at this instant five Armyes in motion'. With an enlargement of the war likely, 'it will not misbecome the wisdome of this state to feare the worst.'[45] In the debates which followed in the house of commons, speakers ranged widely over the subject of foreign policy, many of them returning to the threat posed by Spain and her presumed agents, the English Roman catholics. On the subject of the match with Spain there was a widespread feeling that such a move was unacceptable on religious and political grounds, besides being remarkably untimely.[46] James, aware of the drift of the debate, though he was residing for reasons of health in Newmarket, replied in a letter delivered to the speaker of the house on 3 December. The king accused 'some fiery & turbulent spirites' with having meddled 'wth matters farre above their capacityes w[ch] tends to the infringing of o[r] prerogative royall'. Accordingly, the house was directed not to deal further with 'o[r] governm[t] or misteryes of state namely o[r] Sonnes mariage' nor disparage 'the k. of Spayne, and other of o[r] frends and allyes'.[47]

The house of commons, in failing to heed this advice, showed just how far apart its members were from the king on the fundamental principles to be followed in the present crisis. Where the king wanted money to defend the Palatinate, while pressing on with his diplomatic measures to secure a settlement, the commons —to judge by its debates and the petition of 3 December, to which the king took exception even before it was passed—wanted a war with Spain, a protestant marriage for the prince, and stronger

---

[45] Folger MS V. b. 303: Speeches delivered in Parliament and Other Political Documents, p 233. The speech is given in a different form in Rushworth, *Historical Collections* 1, p 39.

[46] Zaller, *The Parliament of 1621* pp 145–56; [Conrad] Russell, 'The Foreign Policy Debate [in the House of Commons in 1621]', *HJ* 20 (1977), pp 289–309; S. L. Adams, 'Foreign Policy and the Parliaments of 1621 and 1624', in *Faction and Parliament: Essays on Early Stuart History*, ed Kevin Sharpe (Oxford 1978) pp 149, 159–64.

[47] Folger MS V. b. 303, p 233. The letter is to be found with some differences in Rushworth, *Historical Collections* 1, p 43.

enforcement of the laws against recusants.[48] Between the two positions little compromise was possible. Unfortunately for the effective implementation of any policy this session of parliament ended in a vociferous struggle over parliamentary privilege, especially the exercise of free speech.[49] If there is still uncertainty over the question of whether the house had overstepped its constitutional bounds in discussing foreign policy—as the king claimed[50]—it is certainly clear why James reacted strongly to its policy recommendations. By its proceedings the house threatened to undermine James's entire diplomatic program, followed since the beginning of the Bohemian revolt, which was aimed at reaching an understanding with the Hapsburg powers, particularly Spain. This program had many merits; it was not, however, one to which James's subjects were likely to be sympathetic, nor was it one he took the trouble to explain in any detail to parliament.

In the gloomy aftermath of parliament's dissolution in early January 1622, the prospects for preserving the Palatinate or for a general peace looked increasingly dim. James did not have the means to provide for the adequate defence of the Palatinate where, by the end of the year, only the town of Frankenthal remained in the hands of troops committed to Frederick. Nor, for all of Digby's diplomatic skills, did the continuing negotiations for a Spanish marriage produce a contract or a resolution of the Palatine issue.[51] Meanwhile, the long war between Spain and the northern provinces of the Netherlands had begun again in earnest. But James had one more stratagem aimed at damping down the fires of conflict before they became a conflagration. In early July 1622, a congregation of cardinals, assembled by pope Gregory XV, delivered its judgement on the proposed articles of the Anglo-Spanish marriage treaty. George Gage, the English envoy in Rome, was told that in order to be acceptable, these articles would have to provide for the free exercise of the catholic faith in England. The statement went on to suggest that James—whose conversion had long been desired—declare himself a catholic, since his studies must

[48] Gardiner, *History of England* 4, pp 246–8.
[49] Zaller, *The Parliament of 1621* pp 156–87.
[50] Compare Russell, 'The Foreign Policy Debate', pp 292–9, 309 and Zaller, *The Parliament of 1621* pp 156–9.
[51] Gardiner, *History of England* 4 pp 272–411; Zaller, *The Parliament of 1621* pp 188–90.

have convinced him that the Roman faith was that true and ancient one in which men could find salvation.[52]

James chose to answer this message with a letter of his own to pope Gregory. Dated the last of September 1622 at Hampton Court, the letter begins with the traditional papal title, 'Most Holy Father'—a usage most protestants would presumably have deplored.[53] After noting what must have seemed anomalous, 'that one differing from you in point of Religion should now first salute you with o^r Letter', James declared his deep concern over 'these calamitous discords and bloodshedds wch for these late yeares bypast have so miserably rent the Christian world.' It had been his 'care and dayly solicitude to stoppe the course of these growing evils', especially since 'wee all worshipp the same most blessed Trinity, nor hope for salvation by any other meanes then by the blood and meritts of one Lord and Saviour Christ Jesus'.[54] Having stated his desire for peace and the ecumenical creed on which, at least in part, that desire was based, James sought to move the pope 'to putt yor hand to so pious a worke and so wourthy of a Christian Prince'. He went on to express the hope that, once these storms had ceased, 'the harts of those Princes, whom it any way concernes, may bee reunited in a firme and unchangeable friendshippe'. James did not doubt 'but yor Holinesse out of yor singular piety, and for the creditt and authority that you have with the parties, both may and will further this worke in an extraordinary manner.'[55] There was, he declared, no way in which a man could act more deservingly of 'the state of Christendome'.[56] There is something profoundly moving about the spectacle of the leading protestant prince, in a time of sectarian bitterness and turmoil, writing to the pope to establish their common religious and political concerns and to ask that he use his influence to help stop the fighting. The letter, however, seems not to have had any discernible effect.

Some of the reasons for the failure of James's peacemaking at the beginning of the Thirty Years' War are readily apparent. James

---

[52] Gardiner, *History of England* 4 pp 351–2.
[53] [Oxford,] Bodleian [Library,] Tanner MS 73, fol 236. A Latin version is in the same collection Tanner MS 73, fol 235. See also Gardiner, *History of England* 4 p 372.
[54] Bodleian Tanner MS 73, fol 236.
[55] *Ibid* fols 236^r/v.
[56] *Ibid* fol 236^v.

never had anything like firm control over the actions of his son-in-law, the elector Frederick, though the king had to be, inevitably, that impulsive young man's ally. This was, in fact, a common problem among national leaders of the period. However much the great powers, Spain, Austria, or England, wanted a settlement, there were always adventurers, a Mansfeld, a Maximilian, a Christian of Brunswick, who could and would upset their plans. James also lacked the military means to make a threat of hostilities credible, or even to defend his nation's interests. As a result his demonstrations of firmness gradually lost their value in the course of his negotiations. Perhaps most damaging of all, James did not enjoy the confidence and support of his own people or his parliament in the work he undertook, nor did he make a serious effort to win over the nation. However well-intentioned and rational his peace diplomacy was, it always had something of a personal and arcane quality.

But James I was notably broad in his sympathies and free from some of the national and religious prejudices of his age. Just as he identified himself not so much with England as with Great Britain, so he identified himself not so much with the protestant bloc of nations as with Christendom. To change the terms of reference slightly, it might be said that he was, to a much greater extent than most of his contemporaries at home and abroad, a European.

University of the South
Sewanee

THE SIGNIFICANCE OF INDIGENOUS CLERGY IN THE WELSH CHURCH AT THE RESTORATION

by JOHN R. GUY

'UNTIL 1563 the progress of the reformation in Wales was linked with the use of English as a prescribed language . . . Few decisions had more far-reaching consequences than the decision to abandon this principle so far as religion was concerned in Wales'.[1] Walker believes that this change of policy in the early years of Elizabeth's reign was brought about by what he calls 'the deep-seated conservatism of the Welsh Church',[2] and quotes the letter of bishop Nicolas Robinson of Bangor (1566–86) to Cecil, in which Robinson claims that the slow progress of the reformation in the principality was at least partly due to 'the dregs of superstition which did grew chefly upon the blindness of the clergie' and 'the closing up of God's worde from them [that is, the Welsh people in an unknown tongue'.[3] Richard Davies, bishop successively of St Asaph (1560–1) and of St Davids (1561–79) believed that if the Welsh church was to be directed along the path required by Elizabeth's government then the language of the overwhelming majority of the people would have to be employed in both liturgy and pulpit. Only worship in Welsh would make the Anglican church an acceptable institution in Wales, and that necessitated ministers fluent in the vernacular whose teaching was buttressed by the reading of the scriptures and the performance of divine service in the same tongue.

Significantly, Elizabeth's first bishops in Wales were not only all reliable men of firm reforming sympathies, as Glanmor Williams has noted,[4] but also all natives of the principality. The royal commission of 1559 which travelled around the Welsh dioceses to examine the state of the church included the three men who were to

---

[1] *A History of the Church in Wales*, ed David Walker (Penarth 1976) p 65.
[2] *Ibid* p 68.
[3] *Ibid*.
[4] [Glanmor] Williams, [*Welsh Reformation Essays*] (Cardiff 1967) p 142.

be the first consecrated in the reign to those dioceses. Both Rowland Meyrick (Bangor 1559–66) and Richard Davies (St Asaph 1560–1) were products of the north Walian church where they were appointed to serve, and Thomas Young (St Davids 1560–1) came of a Pembrokeshire family. The picture was completed subsequently by the appointment of Hugh Jones to the see of Llandaff, where he was already an incumbent and cathedral prebendary. The re-ordering of the Welsh church was carried through by Welsh clergy, from the bench of bishops downwards, using the language of their own people.

In his recent book on the restoration church,[5] Green has noticed the parallel between the early years of the reign of Elizabeth and the early years of Charles II, in the Welsh church. In 1560 only one bishop remained from earlier times, Anthony Kitchin of Llandaff, consecrated in 1545 and the only Marian bishop prepared to take the oath of supremacy.[6] In 1660 William Roberts of Bangor re-possessed his see, having survived the commonwealth and protectorate. Green comments upon the 'obscurity' of the men appointed to the three vacant dioceses,[7] but goes on to say that 'one . . . feature of the new nominees, and one which may help to explain the promotion of little known figures, is the close relationship which often existed between them and their new dioceses'.[8] It is his opinion that in 1660, faced with the need to restore and re-order the Welsh church, the court made efforts to 'match bishops and dioceses'.[9] Under Elizabeth, archbishop Parker had considered the hallmark of the Welsh bench as 'reverend mediocrity'.[10] The same judgement holds good for the bishops of Wales in the early years of Charles II if they are considered on a national level. It can, however, be argued that because of the particular situation they were called upon to face, they were carefully and correctly chosen. In her study of Anglesey religion and politics Nesta Evans maintained that in this period the diocese of Bangor 'had been blessed

---

[5] [I. M.] Green, [*The Re-Establishment of the Church of England 1660–1663*] (Oxford 1978) p 95.
[6] Williams p 143. J. C. Whitebrook, *The Consecration of Matthew Parker* (London 1945) has much to say on Kitchin.
[7] Green p 95.
[8] *Ibid* p 96.
[9] *Ibid*.
[10] *Ibid* p 95.

with unusually gifted and energetic leaders',[11] and one historian of that diocese has gone so far as to say that 'the generation following the restoration is distinguished . . . by notes indicative of a living church and by clergy deserving of remembrance'.[12]

In the compass of a short paper it is not possible to analyse the significance of indigenous clergy at the restoration in each of the four Welsh dioceses. Attention is therefore concentrated upon that of Llandaff in the south-eastern corner of the principality.

On 2 December 1660 Hugh Lloyd was consecrated bishop of Llandaff in the Henry VII chapel of Westminster abbey.[13] 'A very pious, learned, charitable and primitive good man',[14] he was seventy-four years of age and a product of the pre-commonwealth Laudian church. He was also a native Welshman long beneficed in the diocese over which he was called to preside, as had been his Elizabethan predecessor, Hugh Jones, almost a century before. Although in all respects Lloyd fits Green's picture of a restoration bishop, elderly, not controversial, and without particular influence or prominence,[15] it is his background and experience which is of importance. He had served for thirty years in the rural heartland of Glamorgan, he had held a prebend in the cathedral church under the last bishop, and experience as a schoolmaster under the commonwealth left him with an abiding concern for the Christian education of the young.[16]

A century before, his predecessor had been faced with a church which was desperately poor, desperately short of preachers (five men fit to preach in the diocese) and where protestant ideas and ways of worship had made little headway. The church which Lloyd inherited was equally poor, equally short of educated and articulate clergy, and equally in need of positive re-direction. After the chaos and confusion of the previous decade the re-establishment of the church of England in Wales required both care and caution. The spearhead of the restoration of church life was to be the employment of indigenous clergy at all levels of the diocesan hierarchy.

[11] G. Nesta Evans, *Religion and Politics in mid Eighteenth-Century Anglesey* (Cardiff 1953) p 93.
[12] A. I. Pryce, *The diocese of Bangor during three centuries* (Cardiff 1929) p xxxviii.
[13] [William] Stubbs, [*Registrum Sacrum Anglicanum*] (Oxford 1897) p 122.
[14] E. J. Newell, *Llandaff* (London 1902) p 191.
[15] Green pp 90, 91, 92.
[16] In 1662 he sent a letter to his clergy concerning the support of free schools in the diocese.

Whiteman has noticed the revival of ordered life and worship in the cathedral churches,[17] and that which took place under Lloyd and his two successors at Llandaff has been detailed elsewhere.[18] It is outside of the scope of this study save in the one respect of the reconstitution of the cathedral chapter. The prebends of Llandaff were in the gift of the diocesan bishop and formed the bulk of the patronage directly available to him. Lloyd was called upon to fill five vacancies, the other prebendaries having survived to repossess their stalls. Two went to his sons-in-law, both Glamorgan clergymen upon whose assistance he was to rely during the years of his episcopate. The other three vacancies were filled by clergy who, like Lloyd himself, had roots deep in the Glamorgan soil. All five of his nominees had been beneficed in the county before the commonwealth, and all were men known to him personally over a long period. Their livings were in each case within a few miles of those formerly possessed by the bishop. The analysis of Lloyd's early appointments to the cathedral chapter show clearly his determination to rebuild church life at Llandaff upon a foundation of experienced, like-minded, indigenous clergy. The new archdeacon, Francis Davies (at Llandaff where there was no dean the archdeacon was head of the chapter), was another pre-commonwealth Glamorgan clergyman long resident in the diocese. Lloyd's appointments compare favourably with the survivors of the old chapter. Of these, only two were men either beneficed or habitually resident in the diocese.

It is, however, the deployment of the parochial clergy which most clearly reveals Lloyd's attempt to staff his diocese with men who could best identify with those they were appointed to serve. The parochial structure of the Llandaff diocese, in common with others, had changed little since the middle ages. The poverty of the church was endemic, and the most valuable preferment in the diocese during Lloyd's episcopate had a reputed value of one hundred and fifty pounds. Most livings were worth only twenty or thirty pounds to their incumbents. Many had no parsonage or glebe house—a situation which was to endure throughout the

[17] A. O. Whiteman, 'The Re-establishment of the Church of England, 1660–1663' *TRHS*, 5 ser, 5 (1955) p 113.

[18] William Rees, *Cardiff—A History of the City* (2 rev ed Cardiff 1969) pp 92–3. This is a critical account and has to be read in the light of entries in the Llandaff Chapter Act Book 1573–1722, (National Library of Wales MS. LL/Ch/4).

ensuing century—and there was the continuing problem of language. The researches of Brian James have shown that even a century later large parts of Glamorgan were 'apparently Welsh-speaking and probably largely monoglot'[19] and Bradney revealed a similar picture in the other county in the diocese, Monmouthshire. Although now the most anglicised part of Wales, Bradney showed that 'the decay of the Welsh language here seems to have commenced about the middle of the eighteenth century',[20] and the surviving visitation returns from the latter part of that century clearly reveal the tenacity of the language in the public worship of the church.

At the end of the civil wars, a contemporary neighbouring incumbent of Lloyd's in Glamorgan had written 'an ordinary talent attended by a good life must hereafter recommend to great livings as well as to curacies'.[21] The words were prophetic. In the immediate post-restoration period, the Welsh bishops were forced to acknowledge their truth. 'For long' Whiting wrote, 'the idea that a graduate with a good reputation for scholarship was sufficiently qualified for the priesthood still held'.[22] He was speaking of the latter part of the seventeenth century, but even this idea, far from satisfactory though it might seem to us, could not be realised in Wales. Bishop William Lloyd of St Asaph (1680–92) informed Sancroft that any prohibition against ordaining non-graduates was 'not practicable in our Welsh diocese. We have a great many more cures of souls than we have graduates in this country; and as most of the people understand nothing but Welsh, we cannot supply the cures with other but Welshmen'.[23] William Lloyd had been a prebendary of Llandaff and he was speaking as much for the church in the south of the principality as in the north. Like Hugh Lloyd he was aware of the necessity of heeding the plea of Thomas Basset, vicar of the vast parish of Llantrisant both before and after the

---

[19] Brian Ll. James, 'The Welsh language in the vale of Glamorgan' *Morgannwg*, 16 (Cardiff 1972) p 24.
[20] Joseph Bradney, *A memorandum, being an attempt to give a chronology of the decay of the Welsh language in the eastern part of the county of Monmouth* (Abergavenny 1926) p 2.
[21] Cardiff Library MS. 1.223.
[22] C. E. Whiting, *Nathaniel, Lord Crewe, Bishop of Durham 1674–1721 and his diocese* (London 1940) p 22.
[23] Quoted by A. T. Hart, *William Lloyd* (London 1952) p 64.

commonwealth, that his bishop should 'not stand too rigorously upon the abilities of curates'.[24]

During an episcopate of some six and a half years, Hugh Lloyd ordained one hundred men, mainly between the years 1662 and 1664.[25] So far as can be ascertained only nineteen of the ordinands were graduates, and of these no more than ten seem to have subsequently served in his diocese. Perhaps significantly, two of these were appointed to the cathedral church itself, and a third was the master of the Abergavenny grammar school, where, as at the Glamorgan equivalent at Cowbridge, some rudimentary training and guidance was given to prospective candidates for holy orders. Of the non-graduate ordinands the careers of only thirty-six can be traced with any certainty from the surviving records, but it is here that Lloyd's policy of appointing indigenous clergy who could identify with the people is most clearly illustrated. All thirty-six returned either at ordination or within a few years of ordination to their home parishes or parishes close at hand. Thus John Jenkins of St Mary Hill in Glamorgan, ordained deacon at Lloyd's first ordination on 13 January 1661 and priest on 30 March of the same year, was instituted to the vicarage of his home parish on 9 April.[26] Thomas Watkins, a native of Llanarth in Monmouthshire where his father was vicar, was ordained deacon in 1662, priest in 1663, and instituted to the living in 1664 on his father's death, and on the presentation of his mother, although the living was in the gift of the archdeacon and chapter of the cathedral.[27] Henry Walker, junior, who signed the subscription book as being 'of the town of Chepstow' was admitted on 2 November 1663 to the vicarage of that place, although then only in deacon's orders. The patron was bishop Lloyd himself, by right of lapse.[28] This practice of returning men to their 'home ground' is true also of curacies. Many of these local non-graduate clergy had little if any chance of promotion, and were likely to remain on their curacies for the whole of their ministry. The stabilising and consolidating influence of such men, returned to their home parishes where both they and their families

[24] Cardiff Library MS. 1.223.
[25] *Llandaff Records 2*, ed [J. A.] Bradney (Cardiff 1908) contains Lloyd's episcopal register.
[26] *Ibid* pp 10, 17. Cardiff Library 'Rayer' MS. p 130.
[27] *Ibid* pp 30, 37, 71.
[28] *Ibid* pp 41, 50. J. A. Bradney, *A History of Monmouthshire*, 4 vols (London 1904–33) 4, 1 p 26.

were well known, to serve among people with whom they had grown up, whose language and outlook they shared, and where they had both friends and relatives, should not be underestimated in the close-knit, small, rural Welsh communities. Thus Edward Rogers of Abergavenny, made deacon in 1662, was serving the curacy of his home town when priested in 1669;[29] John Griffith of Coychurch, ordained deacon in March 1663 received his licence as curate of that parish on 20 December the same year;[30] and his successor, Evan Howell, was also a native of the parish.[31] The use of the patronymic in both of the last two examples is indicative to some degree of the social background and language of these men. Lloyd had no different policy towards his own commendam, the rectory of St Nicholas, which he retained until 1663. On 27 September 1661 Robert Thomas of the parish was made deacon, and his successor Jenkin Evans was also a native of St Nicholas.[32] Both were evidently Welshmen; neither were graduates.

A good example of the kind of men Hugh Lloyd entitled in his diocese is Jenkin John of Llantrisant in Glamorgan, though in fact his ordination took place during the episcopate of Lloyd's successor, Francis Davies, who had been his archdeacon and continued the same policy.[33] John was the younger son of John James, who farmed as freeholder the quarter part of Ynis Allan Uchaf known as Dyffryn Uchaf a few miles from Llantrisant town. The use of patronymics makes the definite identification of generations difficult, but it seems likely that John James's family had farmed at Dyffryn Uchaf for at least two generations, and possibly since 1570. There is good reason to suppose that the family was well established in the area. John James was dead by 1669, his will being proved in that year, and three years later his younger son was in holy orders and serving as curate of one of the chapelries in his home parish. In deeds of 1672–7 he is described as 'clerk' and his elder brother as 'yeoman'. Jenkin John received no promotion in the Llandaff diocese. His ministry as far as can be ascertained was spent entirely with the people among whom he had been brought

[29] Bradney, *Llandaff Records*, 2, pp 32, 80.
[30] *Ibid* pp 6, 36.
[31] *Ibid* pp 68, 74.
[32] *Ibid* pp 22, 23, 24.
[33] Much of the information in this paragraph is taken from the *Llantrisant History Newsletter*, no 28, Dyffryn Uchaf, Dyffryn Isaf and Ynis Allan.

up. He came of a family of 'landowners who were accustomed to having mud on their boots'[34] and was closely identified with the people he was to serve. The importance of this policy of returning men to their home parishes can also be seen on the economic level. If the clergy could live at home and perhaps share in the work and income of their home farm or smallholding then two of Lloyd's persistent problems, poverty and lack of suitable accomodation, were to some extent neutralised.

Lloyd's appointment of Henry Walker to Chepstow in 1663 has another significance. It was an important living, a trading centre, port, and a gateway to England. Yet Walker was only a deacon, and instituted when more senior men in priest's orders were available. The living had been vacant since the ejection in 1662 of an influential nonconformist, Richard Blindman.[35] Walker was a man with local roots, a native of the town, and his appointment may have been motivated by Lloyd's desire to return the parish speedily to the orthodox fold, with the hope that a close identification of incumbent with parish would help bring this about.

Hugh Lloyd was a Laudian. He had been imprisoned in 1648 after the battle of St Fagans for his openly avowed royalist sympathies. The only consecration he took part in as a bishop was that of the bishops of St Andrews, Glasgow, Dunblane and Galloway in December 1661 in the ill-fated attempt to restore episcopacy to Scotland.[36] His surviving articles of enquiry for the primary visitation of 1662 are more outspoken on the subject of episcopal ordination and the searching out of prophesyings, conventicles or meetings than many others issued by his brother bishops at that time.[37] There is reason to believe that the practice of returning men to their home parishes was not a makeshift forced upon him by the exigencies of the times, but a deliberate policy of matching priest to people in an endeavour to re-establish the church of England in the affections of the people. The Compton census of

[34] I owe this vivid description to J. Barry Davies.
[35] Thomas Richards, *Religious Developments in Wales 1654–1662*, (London 1923) pp 51, 488, 495.
[36] Stubbs p 123.
[37] *Articles of Visitation and Enquiry concerning Matters Ecclesiastical . . . in the First Episcopal Visitation of the Right Reverend Father in God Hugh by Divine Providence Lord Bishop of Landaffe* (London 1662), particularly Tit. 3, Arts. 1 and 15. See also Green p 136 n 97.

1676,[38] with all its imperfections and shortcomings, shows that Hugh Lloyd met with some success, perhaps as much as his predecessor, Hugh Jones, in respect of similar problems a century before.

Ash near Martock
Somerset

[38] Microfilm of the returns for the Llandaff diocese at the Newport Central Library.

'ENGLISHMEN IN VAINE': ROMAN CATHOLIC ALLEGIANCE TO GEORGE I.

by EAMON DUFFY

OF THE many problems confronting post-reformation English catholics, that of national identity was among the most acute. For the nation at large, to be English was to be protestant, and to be papist was to be an alien.[1] That catholics owed primary allegiance to the pope, to Spain, to France, was an axiom throughout the sixteenth and seventeenth centuries, and the exile of the catholic Stuarts at the revolution of 1688 merely varied the form in which the national tradition expressed itself. In his last public utterance William III equated 'a Popish Prince, and a French Government', judicial proclamations spoke of 'papists and disaffected persons', and George I's first parliament declared that catholics

> take themselves to be obliged by the Principles they profess to be enemies to His Majesty and to the present happy Establishment, and watch for all opportunities of fomenting and stirring up new Rebellions and Disturbances within the Kingdom and of inviting Foreigners to invade it.[2]

The dilemma of catholics after the Revolution was indeed agonising. After a century of obloquy as enemies of the crown they had at last been given a king to whom none could doubt their loyalty, since he too was a papist, only to find after 1688 that this very loyalty plunged them deeper into national disfavour. Most catholics were, of course, Jacobites, but that blanket term covered a wide variety of attitudes, from an almost messianic hope in the 'Lyon from the north' in whose reign catholic 'peace and truth shall rise again',[3] to a dutiful but unenthusiastic acknowledgement of the

---

[1] On this, see my 'Poor protestant flies', *SCH* 15, especially pp 289–90 and references there cited.
[2] *The Parliamentary History of England* 5 (1809) p 1331; [Basil] Williams, *Stanhope* (Oxford 1932) p 137; Rupert C. Jarvis, *Collected Papers on the Jacobite Risings* (Manchester 1972) 2 p 304.
[3] See for the example the 'Prediction', from which the phrases quoted are taken, inscribed in the end papers of a fifteenth-century manuscript at Upholland College

Stuart right, coupled with a determination to bend with whatever political wind was blowing. Scores of catholics had gone into exile in the wake of the revolution, attainted outlaws; by the beginning of the century many were drifting back, making what peace they could with the new regime. Already, at least in the south, Jacobitism was beginning to seem a lost cause.[4] It was perhaps strongest among the clergy and the English religious houses on the continent. Doting nuns sought bulletins on the teething problems of Stuart infants; when James Edward visited Douai in 1708 he was gratified to find himself followed about by the students there 'gazing at and admiring him', testifying to the sound principles of the education at the English College; in 1715 the President of Douai ordered the observance of the Forty Hours devotion for the success of the rising. Yet even fervently loyalist clergy moderated their zeal in practical matters, and were capable of working to undermine Stuart interference in church affairs when it suited them to do so. Nor did they forget 'the imprudences of the late King James' reign', and a total political passivity was the official policy of the Mission.[5]

The gentry, with more to lose, were even more pragmatic. After the assasination plot of 1696 a group of catholics led by Sir Robert Throckmorton took the oath of allegiance, in a vain attempt to avoid the double land-tax, and even attempted to negotiate a new and more acceptable oath to be taken by all catholics. This came to nothing, and was widely disapproved of[6] but after the shambles of the Fifteen an increasing number of papist landowners sought to accommodate themselves to the government in power. A series of attempts were made during the century to improve their standing in the eyes of government, and to establish the Englishness of English catholic hearts.[7] The earliest of these attempts at the

---

(MS 165) by an early eighteenth-century missioner, Thomas Jameson. I owe this reference to Mr Peter Doyle.

[4] J. C. H. Aveling, *The Handle and the Axe* (London 1976) pp 238–52.

[5] A[rchives of the] A[rchbishop of] W[estminster], *Ep[istolae] Var[iorum]*, 8, 15, G. Haydocke, 10 April 1723. (All letters in *Ep Var* are addressed to Laurence Mayes); *Ep Var* 2, 56, Edward Dicconson 22 December 1708; 5, 48, Edward Dicconson 27 March 1714; 4, 43, same 8 September 1711; AAW 'A' series, 36 no 181 (1698). I am grateful to his eminence the cardinal archbishop of Westminster, and to Miss Elizabeth Poyser his archivist, for permission to quote from material at Archbishop's House, Westminster.

[6] *Ep Var* 5, 100, Edward Dicconson 16 August 1715.

[7] Bernard Ward, *The Dawn of the Catholic Revival* (London 1900); E. Duffy, 'Ecclesiastical Democracy Detected', *Recusant History*, 10 and 13.

beginning of the reign of George I, has often been noticed by historians, but invariably misunderstood. Catholic and non-catholic writers have agreed in seeing the failure of this attempt as at least in part the result of the intransigence of the catholics, who 'almost to a man' were rigid Jacobites, or else of 'an ultramontane element', refusing to repudiate papal claims to a dispensing or deposing power.[8] These assessments are gross oversimplifications. The negotiations were far more extensive than has hitherto been realised, and their failure had less to do with jacobite or ultramontane prejudice than with the ill-conceived form of the proposals themselves, and the nature of the agents employed by government to forward them. The incident is worth attention also for the light it throws on the range of attitudes towards crown and government among the adherents of an international religion in an age of increasing national isolation.

The best known catholic response to the accession of George I was the tragic involvement of a handful of northerners, notably the young earl of Derwentwater, in the Fifteen. Their failure, and the anti-catholic backlash which followed, convinced many that 'nothing but a restoration can rescue religion in [our] nation from ruin'.[9] But although most catholics would have welcomed such an event, by no means all were prepared to seek it. In September 1714 a group of gentry, which included the duke of Norfolk and the poet Pope's friend Edward Blount, a Devonshire landowner with a taste for polite literature, set about organising a declaration of allegiance to George I. Though they were convinced that this was an affair which involved 'no matter of Religious Worship or Doctrine . . . but meerly what relates to temporal Policy, and civill government and Submittion', they nevertheless sought the endorsement of the Vicars Apostolic. The senior Vicar, Bonaventure Giffard, was a septuagenarian, 'slow, irresolute and glad to get business off his hands'. Based in London and therefore a fairly regular target for government harrassment, he was terrified by this demand for an explicit ruling on a political issue. Fearing a government trap, he

---

[8] [Wolfgang] Michael, [*The Quadruple Alliance*] (London 1939) pp 57–63: Williams, *Stanhope* pp 395–8; Williams, *The Whig Supremacy* (2 ed Oxford 1962) pp 72–3; [Basil] Hemphill, [*The Early Vicars Apostolic*] (London 1953) pp 105–17.

[9] *Ep Var* 6, 1, reverend John Ingleton Almoner' to queen Mary of Modena, 17 January 1716.

remained silent. The scheme foundered.[10] The fate of the Jacobite rebels, however, those 'unfortunate rash gentlemen . . . and their miserable followers', and even more the introduction of a Bill into parliament requiring the registration of all papist estates, once more galvanised the southern gentry into action. Men hastened to disown 'those mischievous principles . . . commonly imputed to those they call papists'. 'I am' wrote Sir Henry Englefield,

> by the grace of God, an English Catholic, and as such believe that it is my duty to be actively obedient where I can, without offence to God, and passively where I cannot, to whatever Government God permits to come over me, and . . . therefore I would willingly take an oath of fidelity to King George.[11]

A group of gentry, lawyers and clergy hastily assembled in London, under the patronage of the Duke of Norfolk, to 'justify our selfs by all lawfull means', and, by giving King George assurances of 'that allegiance and fidelity which all catholick subjects do . . . under protestant governours', to gain 'the same protection as other dissenters'.[12] Determined on this occasion to act without the Vicars, the group drew up an oath of 'not acting directly or indirectly against the Government', which it was hoped would fend off the Registration Act. They further demonstrated their independence by adding to the oath the words

> I promise neither directly nor indirectly to assist any one that pretends to this crown, and that I detest that abominable notion that the Pope can dispense from oaths solemnly made or that he can dethrone and give power to murder Kings'.[12]

Though these measures did not prevent the Registering Act from becoming law, they 'so pleased the Ministry that they bad (*sic*) the Catholicks be assured if they themselves would be quiet no body should touch them'. This was encouraging, all the more so since, confronted with a fait accompli, Giffard hastily summoned a meeting of secular and religious clergy leaders in London, and they had agreed that it was lawful to 'swear a submission and promiss

[10] *Ep Var* 5, 81, Edward Dicconson 27 December 1714; 5, 100, Dicconson 16 August 1715; Ushaw College, Durham U[shaw] C[ollection of] M[anuscripts] i, no 103, Edward Blount to Nathaniel Piggott September 1714. I am grateful to the president of Ushaw College and to its librarian for permission to quote from material there.

[11] *The English Catholic Nonjurors of 1715*, ed E. E. Estcourt and J. O. Payne (London, nd) p 8; G. Sherburn, *Correspondence of Alexander Pope* I (Oxford 1956) pp 320–1, Edward Blount to Alexander Pope 11 November 1715.

[12] UCM i, no 143, P. Southcote to the Duke of Norfolk 7 April 1716.

not to disturb the present government', and even to disown the papal dispensing power.[13]

The favourable response of the government encouraged Norfolk and his associates to seek a more formal and permanent settlement. It was clear that many catholics would have 'certain delicacies' of conscience, and ecclesiastical backing of some sort was desirable. Yet despite their retroactive endorsement of the gentry's action, it was equally clear that most of the secular clergy leaders were firmly Jacobite and were not therefore reliable allies. In these circumstances, the appearance on the scene of two young, forceful, even brash clerics committed to the settlement of the allegiance question was to be momentous.

John Talbot Stonor, having taken a Sorbonne doctorate in 1714, was appointed bishop of Thespiae and vicar apostolic of the Midland district in 1716, at the exceptionally early age of thirty-seven, and after only a year on the mission. This meteoric rise was less a testimony to his abilities than to his high birth and family connections. The second son of one of the most ancient catholic families, he was the nephew of the duke of Shrewsbury, the apostate catholic who had played a leading role in the revolution. Shrewsbury, who was ambassador in Paris in 1712, had secured a life-income for his nephew in the form of an abbey in Poitiers. In 1715 he had been appointed lord chamberlain; so powerful a protector was an unique advantage for a catholic bishop.[14] Stonor was a squirarch to his roots. As a clerical student he had sought dispensation to make a dynastic marriage—so much a family affair that when he was refused permission his brother married the girl in question. He identified the future of catholicism in England totally with that of the landed interest, believing that

> Catholick familys, and by Consequence Catholick Relligion here in England are in such an eminent danger of being ruin'd..that..we ought to be ready to lay hold of any occasion of trying even a doubtful remedy.[15]

---

[13] *Ep Var* 6, 19, Robert Witham, President of Douai College, 20 July 1716; 6, 21, John Talbot Stonor 9 August 1716.

[14] W. Maziere Brady, *Annals of the Catholic Hierarchy* (Rome 1877) pp 206–9; J. Kirk, *Biographies of English Catholics in the Eighteenth Century* (London 1909) pp 220–1; Godfrey Anstruther, *The Seminary Priests* 3 (Great Wakering 1976) pp 212–13; *Ep Var* 5, 79, J. Ingleton December 1714; 5, 82, Henry Howard 13 January, 1715.

[15] R. J. Stonor, *Stonor* (Newport 1951) pp 282–5; *Ep Var* 6, 31, J. T. Stonor, 25 November 1716.

This preoccupation, coupled with his Whiggish family connections, explain Stonor's ready acquiescence in the activities of Norfolk and his associates. It is a reflection of the political instability of the period and the fluidity of the dynastic question that less than a year before Stonor had been forced into hiding from government pursuivants, since he had been 'engaged in politicks and getting money for our King'.[16]

Thomas Strickland, Stonor's associate, was, like him, a younger son of a distinguished catholic family. Strickland's father had followed James II into exile at St. Germain, and the boy's education was conducted in France. He had trained for the priesthood at Douai, St. Sulpice, and at St. Gregory's, the English house of studies in Paris. Strickland was never to work on the English mission; restless, ambitious, a compulsive talker and weaver of self-aggrandizing fantasies, his whole energies were bent on the furthering of his own career. He was not conspicuously devout, passing months without celebrating mass, rarely communicating. He was reported to 'talk nasty talk' in his cups, and there were to be rumours of immoral propositions to serving wenches. Yet, although overbearing to his inferiors or those he considered so, he could be both genial and eloquent, and had a knack of gaining the friendship and support of influential men, in England, Stanhope, in the Low Countries the papal nuncio, Mgr. Santini.[17]

United by ambition and a shared contempt for the incompetence of their seniors, these two had since 1714 set the English catholic community by the ears. Before ever arriving in England they had almost succeeded in having the president of St. Gregory's removed on a trumped up charge of Jansenism, hoping to have him replaced by one or other of themselves. Appointed by Giffard as his vicar general as soon as he came on the mission, Stonor repaid this confidence by organising a petition of young malcontent clergy to have his bishop declared senile, and himself appointed as acting bishop with right of succession. After Stonor's elevation to the episcopate they had worked for a similar post for Strickland, and with the help of Strickland's friend Santini Stonor had secured a 'Brief of inspection', authorising him to exercise emergency powers in Giffard's London district in the event of the old man's

---

[16] *Ep Var* 5, 106, Ingleton 12 October 1715; 6, 12, Thomas Witham 27 April 1716.
[17] Hemphill pp 50–4; *DNB*; [D.] Scott,[*The Stricklands of Sizergh Castle*] (Kendall 1908) pp 189–95; *Ep Var* 6, 19, R. Witham 20 July 1716.

absence or incapacity.[18] This alliance was purely opportunistic. Stonor certainly had no illusions about his friend;

'He is one of no manner of integrity', he told Lawrence Mayes, the English clergy agent in Rome

and will sacrifice any busyness he is charg'd with to his own interest..he has no good judgement..but yet he would in a great measure make up the defect by his extempore witt and address if he did not again spoil things by his vain and superabundant talk, and if by a worse fault, which is that he can neither keep his own counsel nor anybody's else.[19]

On a number of occasions Stonor quite ruthlessly dissociated himself from Strickland, refusing, for example to employ him in his district when it seemed likely that this would add to his own unpopularity. Yet quite cynically they cooperated in pursuit of their own ends—for Stonor the right of succession to Giffard's district, where he might pursue his love of 'London, business and writing letters and memorials', for Strickland episcopal consecration and involvement in high politics and high society. Their activities terrified and outraged their colleagues, who felt themselves in 'danger from false brethren, that are building themselves upon the Ruine of others'.[20]

Despite their unpopularity with the clergy, the dynamism and influence of these 'two Sorbonne Doctours' made it inevitable that the gentry should see them as potential allies. Norfolk himself approached Stonor in mid–1716 to secure a firm lead from Rome on the question of allegiance, and to bring the other senior clergy round to the scheme. Strickland travelled to Brussels to engage the nuncio.[21] It became clear to a scandalised court at St. Germain that so far as these two were concerned, the project now extended beyond a mere declaration of non-resistance to the government in power, and included the oath of abjuration.[22]

These developments occupied the summer of 1716. In September came a bombshell. The duke of Norfolk arrived in London with a letter from the Brussels nuncio for bishop Giffard. Rome had

[18] *Ep Var* 5, 96, Edward Dicconson June 1715; 5, 97, Robert Carnaby 23 July 1715; Hemphill pp 41–57.
[19] *Ep Var* 6, 38, Stonor 4 February 1717.
[20] *Ep Var* 5, 97, Robert Carnaby 23 July 1715.
[21] UCM i no 44, Stonor to Robert Witham 5 June 1716.
[22] UCM i no 115, Edward Dicconson to William Dicconson at St Germain, undated; *Ep Var* 6, 18 J. Ingleton 6 July 1716; 6, 19 R. Witham 20 July 1716.

spoken; English catholics could and should swear 'fidelity and intire obedience to the present Government'. No mention must be made, the instructions went on, of papal dispensing or deposing power.[23] This totally unexpected development was clearly the result of Strickland's lobbying at Brussels, and Norfolk and his associates determined to push home their advantage. A fund was raised, largely from Norfolk's own purse, to send Strickland to Rome 'to demand some further explanations upon it and also to solicit Abraham [a code name for the pope] to doe his utmost to engage the Catholick Princes in behalf of the Catholicks here'.[24] Strickland himself went to Hanover to secure George I's approval for the scheme, and since the king was known to take his electoral status very seriously Edward Blount was employed to forward through the nuncios at Brussels and Cologne requests for the support of the catholic electors. In London, Nathaniel Piggott, the ablest catholic lawyer of the time, drew up a list of catholic disabilities which was distributed to sympathetic MPs[25] Stonor despatched to Rome a lengthy series of enquiries about the papal brief, intended to draw out its implications. Did the promise envisaged by Rome, he asked, hold in the event that 'a certain other Person' should 'cause his standard to be set up..and summon all Englishmen to be assistant to him'? Did it not require catholics to defend king George 'against any person whatsoever'? Most crucial of all, did it in fact 'authorize the promiser to take another Oath prescribed by our Laws called of Abjuration'? It would, he urged, 'be most convenient of all, if this Oath could be lawfully taken'.[26] Here, for those engaged in the negotiation, were the vital issues. These suggestions clearly involved the abandonment of the Stuart cause, at least in any active form. Yet there seemed to them no alternative; unless the position of catholics in relation to government were regularised they faced financial ruin. 'The best they can hope is to possess a precarious property in the midst of a free

[23] *Ep Var* 6, 27, J. Ingleton 22 September 1716; 6, 31, Stonor 25 November 1716; BL Add Ms 20310 fol 173 J. Ingleton to Monseigneur Nairne, secretary to the Chevalier at Avignon 15 December 1716.

[24] *Ep Var* 6, 31, Stonor 25 November 1716.

[25] UCM i no 128, duke of Norfolk to Edward Blount 3 December 1716. Text of the document sent to the catholic princes, UCM i no 126, 'The State of the Case'.

[26] 'Bishop Stonor's Querys'—manuscript bound up with a collection of late eighteenth-century pastoral letters (Bishop Walmesley) and other miscellanea Ushaw College, Old Library pressmark X.E.27.

Country to see themselves Englishmen in Vaine and their lands and fortunes at the disposall of Arbitrary Commissioners, hungry Informers and witnesses, whose very mercy . . . would be to reduce all the Catholick Families to Poverty and Contempt.'[27] In a significant phrase Stonor dismissed the Catholic opponents of the scheme as 'mostly women, younger brothers, people of desperate fortune': before the realities of property high-flown notions of divine-right kingship evaporated. In a bleakly pragmatic document Edward Blount, the theoretician of the group, justified their activities. Oaths of allegiance, he maintained, held good only so long as the prince to whom they were made was in power. To venture life and fortune in defence of a king in possession was a rational exercise of citizenship, but to do so for a 'Prince once dispossessed' was to disturb the commonwealth and 'to resist the ordinance of God, who removes one King and sets up another'. Nor should the former ruler complain when his subjects protect life and property by an accommodation with the prince in possession:

..Princes know what they themselves expect from subjects where they have power, whatever there (sic) rights be, and therefore can't complain of their subjects, if they pay it to another Prince in whose power they are. This is the practice of the whole world, and Princes know it.[28]

In any case, argued Stonor, even the oath of abjuration need not damage the Stuart cause—

Then as to the Chevalier either some thing is doing or not. If nothing, 'tis fit we should think of ourselves; if something all this will make but a better blind and be a good *pis aller* in case of a new miscarriage . . . what does he lose, should such proposals, which is very uncertain, be accepted of, and the hands of the chiefs of Familys tyd up? The assistance of some few bold and generous ones amongst them, scarce able to do anything but hurt themselves and him too perhaps by the odium of their name; whose fellows in those countrys where Catholicks most abounded, have bin allready ruin'd upon a like attempt, and basely deserted by those who engaged them, the Torys.[29]

---

[27] UCM i no 126, 'The State of Case'.
[28] *Ep Var* 6, 31, Stonor 25 November 1716: UCM i no 106, 'Mr Blounts Mss on Allegiance'.
[29] *Ep Var* 6, 31, Stonor 25 November 1716.

The proponents of Hanoverian allegiance did not however have undisputed possession of the field. Bishops Giffard, Witham and Pritchard, Stonor's elder colleagues, found reasons to postpone publication of the papal brief, and despatched a remonstrance to Rome against it. When Stonor, exercising the emergency powers he had been granted by his 'brief of inspection', summoned a meeting of clergy in London at which he intended to publish the brief on allegiance, not a single secular clergyman turned up, even his own vicar-general absenting himself.[30] The shrewder among them were sceptical about the likely success of the negotiations, which they held were

> useless and unprofitable for the Catholicks of England, for the Oaths now tender'd by the laws are the oaths of Supremacy and allegiance, the oaths of abjuration and the test . . . so that to propose new oaths..is only to throw seeds of dispute.

Here was the nub of the matter; ultimately the scheme would stand or fall by the willingness of parliament to repeal the legislation which made catholics 'Englishmen in vaine'; in the climate of the time this was almost unthinkable. For all that though, the St.Germain party felt betrayed by Rome, which had conceded so much 'injurious to the King'. There were mutterings against 'foreign Divines, who are strangers to the Constitution and Laws of England', and it was not without satisfaction that they noted that Rome's attempt to prevent encroachment on its dispensing and deposing power such as the gentry had made a year before, was the element in the brief most likely to thwart the project. The government would never 'admit of the oath of submission without a clause renouncing the Pope's authority and power of dispensing in oaths'. There was no ultramontanism here.

> 'I cannot but wonder,' John Ingleton told the clergy agent at Rome 'to see how ready your Court is in sacrificing the King's unquestionable right, and yet so tenacious of an authority which at best can only be put in the class of school opinions.'[31]

At Rome itself, where Strickland was vigorously advocating the oath of abjuration, every effort was being made to prevent any further erosion of the Chevalier's interest. The secular clergy agent,

[30] *Ep Var* 6, 37, R. Witham 31 January 1717.
[31] *Ep Var* 6, 33, R. Witham 20 December 1716; 6, 27, J. Ingleton 22 September 1716; 6, 35, Ingleton 26 December 1716; BL Add MS 20310 fol 173, Ingleton to Nairne 15 December 1716.

Laurence Mayes, was inundated with letters of advice and instruction from Douai, London, Paris and from the Stuart court; cardinal Gualterio, James Edward's representative in the curia, discovered that the ruling on the oath of allegiance had been negotiated hugger mugger in the Holy Office, and had taken the cardinals of Propaganda by surprise. Clement XI himself told Gualterio of his surprise and sorrow that 'things had been carried so far aginst our King'.[32] Either the brief had been the result of dubious wire-pulling by Santini, or the pope, anticipating a shift in policy, was keeping his options open. At any rate, he undertook to ask the catholic princes to intercede for clemency towards the English catholics, and made it clear that Strickland would not be the intermediary.[33] This was a tactical victory for the Jacobites, and Strickland left Rome. 'I suppose' the president of Douai jeered 'he's gone to his rich canonicate in Eutopia'.[34]

In England the first panic over the registering act had passed. At the beginning of 1717 parliament extended the period of time allowed for compliance with the act, and the wholesale sequestration of catholic property which had been feared did not materialize.[35] This lull persuaded the Jacobite clergy that the matter of allegiance could now safely be forgotten; proponents of the oath argued, on the contrary, that the respite was the direct consequence of their activities. Though they conceded that the parliamentary climate was for the time being unfavourable to further action by catholics, Stonor and his associates believed that in the long term 'many hardships might be avoided and favours obtain'd' by settling once and for all the question of catholic loyalty.[36] There were other incentives to perseverance. About a dozen leading catholics had taken the oaths at the height of the panic. Some were 'recovered' by bishop Giffard, but the catholic landed interest could not survive many such scares. Giffard might talk of the replacement of the 'fallen ones' by the conversion of 'great numbers of the inferior or middling sort of people', but this cut no ice with the gentry. Moreover, the growing friendliness between England and the emperor from the summer of 1717 was depriving catholics of one

[32] *Ep Var* 6, 41, R. Witham 27 February 1717.
[33] *Ep Var* 6, 43, Ingleton 27 March 1717; 6, 44 Ingleton 19 May 1717.
[34] *Ep Var* 6, 50, R. Witham 15 July 1717.
[35] *Ep Var* 6, 48, bishop Giffard 28 May 1717.
[36] *Ep Var* 5, 47, Stonor 13 May 1717.

of their traditional protections. The imperial and allied ambassadors in London, at the request of government, closed their chapels to English papists, on the grounds that they were 'centres of cabal'. The gentry therefore continued to plan further approaches to government.[37]

The next move, however, was not to come from them. In the spring of 1718 Thomas Strickland arrived in Paris, and was constantly in the company of Lord Stair, the English ambassador there, on such intimate terms with his household that Lady Stair called him her 'Father Confessor'. His attacks on the claims and the character of the Chevalier were now so blatant that it was assumed that he had abandoned any hope of advancement from English catholic influence, and there was even speculation that he was about to leave 'the communion of the Catholic Church to get lawn sleeves'.[38] Events were to prove these conjectures very wide of the mark. In April 1718 Stair wrote to Stanhope, urging the advantages of gaining some pledge of loyalty from the papists. George I and his ministers agreed and ordered that the matter should be given every encouragement. Strickland visited England in July: by September he was back in Paris in company with Stanhope, whom he lionized at St. Gregory's, and with a thousand pound 'in his pocket and . . . a promiss of a Benefice of 20,000 livres per Annum from the Regent'. Strickland had in fact been entrusted with a formal commission from George I to the court of the emperor Charles VI. In January he travelled to Vienna to solicit the emperor's help in securing papal approval for a scheme of catholic allegiance. It was also hoped that Strickland might be able to pull Roman strings to hinder the marriage of James Edward and the princess Sobieski. He was given the full backing of the English ambassador at Vienna, who even asked the emperor to request that a titular archbishopric should be given to Strickland. Charles VI was impressed, and agreed to help; jubilant, Strickland left Vienna in March 1719. By May, his intimate friendship with the emperor and empress was the talk of the Jacobite community in France, who had watched with

---

[37] *Ep Var*, 6, 55, Giffard 5 August 1717; UCM i no 130 duke of Norfolk to Edward Blount 18 January 1718; *Ep Var* 6, 67, Giffard 21 November 1717.
[38] *Ep Var* 6, 83, R. Witham 24 April 1718; 6, 109, Witham 22 February 1719. Strickland had arrived in Paris from Spa, where he had appeared 'in poor condition' having been mugged and robbed en route from Italy.

mounting indignation and anxiety the activities of this 'little conceited, empty, meddling prig'.[39]

In June 1719 the scheme concocted by the 'travelling Abbot' (for the promised benefice had duly materialised) was unveiled. James Craggs, one of the principle secretaries of state and the man who had handled the London end of Strickland's Viennese negotiation escorted Strickland to a meeting at the duke of Norfolk's house. Lord Waldegrave and Charles Howard of Greystoke were also present. Craggs placed before them a set of proposals, drafted in fact by Strickland, and designed 'to put the Roman Catholicks in a way of deserving some share in the mercy and protection of the Government'. The paper stipulated that eight of the 'most considerable' Catholics should depute a 'proper person' to Rome to press four demands. The pope must order the publication of the 1716 brief on allegiance. He must deprive Gualterio of the title and office of protector of England, and replace him with someone 'no waye . . . obnoxious to this government'. He must deprive the pretender of any influence in the ecclesiastical affairs of Ireland or England, and must give the emperor a solemn undertaking to administer 'these missions' without reference to the Stuart court. Finally, the government should be given the right to request the removal from the mission of any cleric 'upon intimation of any offence by him given'. Since the emperor had engaged 'to bring the pope to these terms' it would be necessary to send a delegate to Vienna with a formal request for his help. The document ended with a threat to invoke the full rigour of the penal laws, and in particular that which transferred the right of succession to property to the next protestant heir, in the event of non-compliance. The reward for co-operation, though this was nowhere stated in writing, was to be the waiving of the double land tax.

After several days discussion the catholic negotiators rejected these proposals, and it was clear to Craggs that they disliked and distrusted Strickland. They had, moreover, refused to consult with bishop Stonor's brother, Thomas, one of those named in the document among the eight representatives, and 'the best intentioned of them all'. Strickland was 'so picqued at this usage', that he urged Craggs to arrest bishop Giffard, the earl of Shrewsbury (a

[39] PRO SP 104/219b fol 161. Stanhope to Lord Stair 29 April 1718; *Ep Var* 6, 98, R. Witham 21 September 1718; *Ep Var* 6, 109, R. Witham 22 February 1719; HMC, *Stuart Papers at Windsor*, 7 pp 255, 545; Scott pp 190–1.

Jesuit priest), and 'some other heads of that set of people', *pour encourager les autres*. Waldegrave approached Craggs with an alternative set of proposals, but Craggs told him that 'if he had any thing to say, he must consult Dr. Strickland. This 'made them alter their course'; they called on Strickland and put to him their difficulties of 'fear, conscience, honour &c', but they persisted in their refusal. Despite a series of arrests, from which Giffard escaped literally by minutes, Strickland left England in July without having achieved his aims.[40]

Why did Norfolk and his colleagues turn down the proposals? None of them were Jacobites; both Norfolk and Waldegrave offered to work out alternative proposals with Craggs, while the most vigorous opponent of Strickland's scheme, Charles Howard, was widely known to favour allegiance to the house of Hanover, and was admitted even by Strickland to be 'well intentioned'.[41] Norfolk, whose young Jacobite wife was to separate from him because of his 'trucking to the usurper'[42], justified their refusal on various grounds. They had not had time to consult with those named in the document but out of town; they could not claim to represent the whole catholic body; they preferred to rely on the clemency of government than on any 'Application to foreign powers'.[43] In fact, one of their principal though unspoken motives was their distrust of the architect of the scheme, Strickland himself. As Edward Blount, Norfolk's chief adviser, was later to put it 'We have nothing to say to the wild projects of a Licentious Abbot who seeks nothing but his own private ends without caring whom he sacrifices to it.'[44] The ministry's insistence that 'they are allowed no other conferant but him', therefore, doomed the negotiations from the start. There were, however, other factors. The catholics were well aware of the weakness of Stanhope's ministry in parliament, from the opportunistic alliance of Walpole's whig schism with the Tories. In his brazen attack on the bill to repeal the Test and Corporation Acts earlier that year, moreover, Walpole had made it

---

[40] Michael pp 59–61; PRO SP 43/57 no 83 Craggs to Stanhope 30 June 1719; no 107 same to same 7 July 1719; BL Stowe MS 121.

[41] Charles Howard, *Historical Anecdotes of some of the Howard Family* (London 1969) pp 127–30.

[42] *The Complete Peerage* 9 (ed 1936) p 631.

[43] PRO SP 43/57 no 109 Norfolk to Craggs 1 July 1719.

[44] UCM i no 104, Edward Blount to Norfolk 8 July 1723 (the manuscript has '1718/1719' but internal evidence makes the date 1723 virtually certain).

abundantly clear that moves to favour papists would receive short shrift from the opposition. Indeed, as Craggs was aware, Norfolk had been warned by Walpole's associate William Pulteney that the opposition intended to 'destroy the present Ministry with the King, and so discouraged them from engaging themselves in a falling house'.[45] In the circumstances, catholics required some concrete assurance that government could deliver what it offered, and not the mere verbal promises which they suspected were, as Sam Goldwyn said, not worth the paper they were written on.

Further, Rome had shown little inclination to abandon the Stuart cause. The emperor's advocacy of the scheme was being politely stonewalled, Gualterio had been appointed protector of England, and private assurances had been given to the Chevalier and his clerical supporters that nothing would be done at Rome to damage his interests. It seemed likely, therefore, that Rome would not accede to the four demands. Finally, Norfolk's point about catholic dislike of appeals to 'foreign powers' was perfectly sincere. Catholic applications to Rome for a clarification of the moral principles underlying the question of allegiance was one thing; they had themselves sought guidance in 1716. Strickland's scheme, however, rested the whole concern on the action of papacy, with the emperor as arbiter. The catholic negotiators were advised by counsel, including a former attorney general, that as it stood the scheme was a breach of the statute of Praemunire. Here was too large a handle for parliamentary 'no-popery', lending credence to the traditional picture of papists as aliens, owning a foreign allegiance. 'It has been a Rule constantly prescib'd us from the Revolution to this day', wrote Edward Blount, 'that we never apply ourselves to any foreign Prince or Court whatsoever for the Redress of any Grievance'. Neither Strickland, Stonor, nor the government would take this objection seriously, but it is one the negotiators recurred to time and again, both in justificatory pieces intended for government eyes and in their private correspondence. There can be no doubt that it weighed heavily with them. In any case, they rejected the notion that they *required* the pope's permission to swear allegiance to king George. 'In divine matters much may be said for implicit faith, but in humane affairs wise men never pretend to pin their belief on any man's sleeve'.[46]

[45] Williams, *Stanhope* p 398.
[46] UCM i no 134, Blount to Norfolk 8 August 1719; BL Add MS 28252 fols 96–7.

The government treated all explanations, however, with icy incomprehension, and warned of 'severer courses': at George I's personal insistence, Strickland was to remain the official negotiator for the government. In desperation Norfolk turned to Stonor, newly returned from a business trip to France. To the delight of king George and Stanhope, Stonor threw his full weight behind Strickland's scheme, and even offered to go himself to Rome to further it; he did however secure further time for consideration for Norfolk and his associates.[47] On 6 December a catholic summit meeting was held at Norfolk's London house, at which Waldegrave, Lord Clifford, the duke of Powis, Sir John Webb, Thomas Giffard of Chillington and the lawyer Nathaniel Piggott all attended. Stonor brought with him the proxy votes of his brother and the earl of Shrewsbury, whom he had brought round to his way of thinking. Characteristically, Giffard was absent, having had a sudden attack of the gravel, and the bishop absented himself from London for a month, while the negotiations were in progress, thus, in Stoner's view, abandoning his flock. Everyone at the meeting was agreed that the proposals raised no issue of conscience, and all accepted the urgency of some action to fend off the wrath of government, but Stonor was unable to budge them from their earlier rejection of the scheme. His exasperation knew no bounds.

> . . . it must be', he told Mayes, 'that my mind is made of a quite different mould from that of other people, so that what seems to me.. lawful, prudent, necessary, conformable to the practice of all ages and of all wise and Holy men, unfortunately proves to be quite otherwise.'

Such appeals to conscience and wise and holy men, however, seemed to the gentry quite beside the point, and Stonor's episcopal assurances of the theological and moral rectitude of the scheme irritated them. Rules of conscience, in their view, 'had little to do in this matter', and those who made them 'may possibly have some views beyond our reach and forraign to our interests. Doctours . . . have no pretence to decide matters of law, nor lawyers cases of conscience; but men are often apt to mind what they least understand.[48]

This document incorporates verbatim parts of Sir Henry Englefield's declaration of 1715 (above, note 11).

[47] PRO SP 43/64 Stanhope to Craggs 23 October 1719.

[48] *Ep Var* 6, 133, Stonor 6 December 1719; 6, 134, Giffard 31 December 1719. UCM i no 135, Edward Blount to Norfolk 3 October 1719.

By now the government were thoroughly incensed, and on the day after this meeting gave notice that they now expected the catholics either to take the oath of allegiance 'which their own bishops and priests' had approved, or prepare 'to be treated as obstinate rebells'. Stonor's brother hastily went to Craggs and assured him of his readiness to comply. Indeed the urgency of action now impressed itself on others. As a 'softening expedient' Shrewsbury, Powis, Mr. Stonor and Norfolk agreed to sign letters not to pope and emperor but to Stonor and Strickland, asking them to go to Vienna and Rome and there 'determine the method and measures proper to be used'. They agreed, and asked for purses of £1000 apiece to finance their trips. This scheme, however, failed to win general acceptance, and instead Edward Blount was despatched to Brussels to secure a copy of the brief of 1716, in order to quiet any scruples about a straightforward oath of allegiance, and legal opinions were secured that such oaths would entail no more than an undertaking to live peaceably. The gulf between the 'two abbots' and the lay gentry widened,[49] not least because the threatened 'sterner measures' were now in effect, with the London clergy having to keep on the move to avoid arrest; Powis and Sir John Webb were both summoned to take the oaths, a prelude to recusancy proceedings. Inevitably, Stonor and Strickland were blamed for all this. The two culprits, sharing Stonor's London lodgings, chose this inauspicious moment to engage in further cloak and dagger-work. With the furore over the Peerage Bill still echoing, and while Walpole moved ever closer to a governmental coup, they attempted 'without communicating any more with any of our indiscreet and self-murthering friends', to have a toleration bill introduced into the commons, in return for oaths of allegiance. The project came to nothing, of course, but news of it leaked out to infuriate the catholic community. 'These two projectors the two Abbes' reported Robert Witham, 'are so odious to all that they themselves are not a little mortified and frighted by letters from unknown hands which threaten them, so that they dare scarce stir

---

[49] *Ep Var* 6, 131, R. Witham 8 December 1719; 6, 133, Stonor 6 December 1719; 6, 132, R. Witham 29 December 1719; 7, 1, Ingleton 1 January 1720; 7, 9, Witham 22 February 1720; 7, 13, Witham 11 April 1720; 7, 17 Witham 3 July 1720; UCM ii nos 15 and 16, Powis, Shrewsbury & Thomas Stonor to Stonor and Strickland, 8 December 1719.

abroad'.[50] Stonor genuinely believed that matters had gone too far for government to be willing to leave the catholics alone, 'too much aggriev'd to love them and yet too powerful to be neglected'. His opponents, however, were convinced that as much as Strickland he was motivated by ambition, that Strickland, indeed, was 'but the cat's foot'. Rumours in the press that the negotiator sent to Rome would be made cardinal protector at the emperor's request seemed to confirm this, and Stonor himself provided further evidence. His desire to succeed or replace Giffard at London was well known; he now began to claim that those who opposed his succession did so 'not only to spight and prejudice me, but also the government'.[51]

The political excitements of 1720, and the bursting of the South Sea Bubble brought all further negotiations to a halt, and even the harrassment of the clergy ceased. Jacobite spirits rose and fell wildly as they watched events in England, but it was clear that the clash of ministry and Parliament made the resumption of Strickland's scheme unlikely. What is it to the purpose, Robert Witham asked 'what George or any of his ministers offer us? they can't alter nor take off the laws in force against us without Parliament'.[52] The deaths first of Stanhope and then of Craggs in February 1721 seemed to clinch the matter, and to 'blast the credit' of Strickland and Stonor with government.[53]

There was however to be a painful and spectacular sequel. In April 1722 Walpole uncovered evidence of a planned Jacobite coup while George I was in Hanover; the story leaked out, and created widespread panic. By August enough evidence had been collected to implicate Francis Atterbury, bishop of Rochester. His arrest was followed by others, and at the end of October the duke of Norfolk was placed in close confinement in the Tower. This seems to have been a token gesture against catholics, since there seems to have been no evidence of his involvement. It was followed by the introduction of a punitive bill into parliament, imposing a levy of

---

[50] *Ep Var* 7, 6, Stonor 14 February 1720; 7, 9 and 10, Witham 22 February, 7 March 1720.

[51] *Ep Var* 7, 3, Witham 25 January 1720; 7, 12, Stonor 23 March 1720; 7, 39, R. Witham 7 January 1721; 7, 40, Giffard 28 January 1721; 7, 62 Stonor 9 June 1721.

[52] *Ep Var* 7, 15, Witham 3 May 1720; 7, 22, Witham 23 September 1720; 7, 23, 26 September 1720.

[53] *Ep Var* 7, 49, Ingleton 21 March 1721.

£100,000 on catholic estates. This bill was considered vindictive even by many Whigs, and Edward Blount, on behalf of the gentry, plunged into frantic lobbying to prevent its passing. But Walpole was now in the saddle, and the bill enshrined his two great hatreds, of Jacobitism and of popery. The intervention of France and of the ambassadors of catholic powers in London were of no avail. The official government position was bleakly simple. The papists were 'a set of men who have ever been restless in their projects and attempts against a government of which they have enjoyed the entire benefit'. The legislation, Cartaret informed the ambassadors, was aimed not at religion but at treason and disaffection which past clemency had done nothing to remove. And, he added, with the recent negotiations in mind, if some of the catholics were indeed innocent of treason, 'yet they persist in refusing to recognise the government, which cannot be justified by any principle of religion'.[54] Despite the opposition of a group of MPs led by Sir Joseph Jekyll, the bill was passed, though the speeches of the 'friends' of the catholics in the Commons encouraged hopes that no further action of this sort would follow.

Strickland had long since abandoned England, and had gone to Vienna to seek his fortune in the emperor's service; he was rewarded in 1727 with the bishopric of Namur.[55] In England, the events of 1722–3 were noted by Stonor with a certain dour satisfaction. Early in 1722 Lord Waldegrave's wife had died in childbirth; her husband quietly abandoned his religion, and launched on what was to prove an extremely distinguished diplomatic career in close association with Walpole. Since he had been one of the firmest opponents of Strickland's scheme, Stonor could not resist the impulse to point a moral—

high screwd notions of Loialty are a weak preservative against the violent temptations with which our Gentry are surrounded. Prudent endeavours to reconcile the duties of Relig-

---

[54] G. V. Bennett, *The Tory Crisis in Church and State* (Oxford 1970) pp 223–75; J. A. Williams, *Catholic Recusancy in Wiltshire*, CRS (1968) pp 60–2; J. H. Plumb, *Sir Robert Walpole, the King's Minister* (London 1960) p 46; *Ep Var* 7,138, Giffard 12 November 1722; 7, 140, Ingleton 16 November 1722; 7, 142, Ingleton 30 November 1722; UCM ii 24, Edward Blount (French) to M. Hoffman, Imperial Envoy in London, 2 November 1722; ii no 25, count Gazola (envoy of duke of Parma) to Blount (French) 8 November 1722; HMC *Polworth* 3, pp 190, 199–204.
[55] UCM i no 104, Blount to Norfolk 8 July 1723; ii, no 1 Blount to Sir Joseph Jekyll, 1 July 1723; ii, nos 26, 27, Blount to his wife 20 December 1722. For Strickland's subsequent career, *DNB* and Scott.

ion with those of obedience to civil power, would very likely be much more effectual, and I take them in the mean while to be the much more promising signs of constancy.

It was now, however, too late; government was, he thought, 'naturally.. much more concern'd for our spoils, than submission'. The passing of the 1723 Act confirmed all this. That 'rough instructor, affliction' would now give his opponents more understanding.

How long it may last we know not; perhaps till all the landed men sink under the burthen. But certainly it would never have been laid upon our shoulders (so wonderfully is the nation now changed and so averse is it become to anything that looks like persecution for Religion) if it were not a principle so publicly but as wrongly avowed amongst us to acknowledge no Prince but him of our Religion.[56]

Stonor was not alone in wishing that the negotiations had been carried through with more unanimity and determination,[57] but it is in fact extremely unlikely that any effective measure of toleration for catholics could have been got through parliament. The blame for the failure of the negotiations on the catholic side, however, must be laid not on the gentry who refused the scheme, or even the Jacobite clergy who argued its sinfulness and illegality, but on Strickland, on Stonor, and on the government which insisted on working through them. Blount's plan for a simple oath of allegiance previously authorised by Rome would have been much more likely to gain the support of a majority of catholics. The complexities of Strickland's scheme with its legally suspect appeals to emperor and pope had little to commend it, and would certainly have been ripped to shreds in parliament. Espoused by George I and Stanhope as a useful counter in their foreign diplomacy, it is hard to avoid the impression that it was conceived by Strickland primarily to further his own status with the emperor and the Hanoverian court; in this respect it entirely succeeded.

Stonor's motives are less easy to fathom; certainly his concern to preserve the catholic gentry, and with them the catholic religion, was real, but personal ambition too played a part. His great error was in presenting the issue primarily as one of conscience, a

[56] On Waldegrave, *DNB*; *Ep Var* 7, 97, Stonor 3 March 1722; *Ep Var* 8, 28, Stonor 21 June 1723.
[57] UCM i no 104, Blount to Norfolk 8 July 1723.

religious question to be settled by pope and bishops. The laity rejected this view as both mistaken and politically dangerous. Secular affairs were the concern of the gentry, and had nothing to do with the pope. They wanted not a concordat, but a simple toleration in return for assurances of civil obedience.

The question of allegiance was not to be raised again for two generations, and although the 1723 Act proved impossible to implement effectively, the whole episode left the catholics profoundly discouraged. Romantic Jacobitism persisted among them well into the 1760s; not until the reign of George III would a Hanoverian king be prayed for in the canon of the mass. In 1763 a catholic lawyer could complain of his 'Papalian' co-religionists who 'will drink Healths that not a man but themselves will drink', and who upheld the 'monarchical Power of their Roman Pontiff'.[58] But this attachment was a sentiment rather than a principle. Edward Blount, reviewing the failure of his efforts in a letter to William Pulteney argued that given encouragement and protection this could have changed, 'their attachment will soon vanish'. The 'Bulk of Mankind', he believed, wanted only peace and quiet

> nor concern themselves with the Rights and Titles of Princes who are but willing to protect them, nor with the Orthodoxy of the Establisht Religion, if they may peaceably enjoy their own.

An opportunity of binding English catholics more closely to their country and its institutions had been lost.

> I hear already some crying out.. *nos Patriam fugimus* and I with the rest am preparing to follow Plato, and call myself a Citizen of the world, so many brave Ancient Noble Familys must no more be stiled of this place or that place . . . Tho' its a Glorious Elegy to be a Lover of one's Country, yet I don't think it so great as to be a Lover of Mankind.[59]

Magdalene College
Cambridge

---

[58] Ushaw College, Eyre MSS 2, fol 807 *seq*. James Booth to Lord Langdale, 4 February 1763.
[59] UCM ii no 3, Edward Blount to William Pulteney 23 July 1723.

EIGHTEENTH-CENTURY GENEVA AND A CHANGING CALVINISM

by LINDA KIRK

CALVIN'S reformed Geneva had as its motto *post tenebras lux*; the city set on a hill found an identity not only in maintaining the precarious miracle of political independence but in the God-given task of preserving truth and shedding light. In the sixteenth century the republic bore witness to its salvation through a corporate life of ordered righteousness, by printed propaganda and through a stream of missionaries and martyrs. Sympathisers also poured into Geneva but while many sixteenth-century exiles from France and French-speaking territories had quickly assumed important office in the Genevan church and the economic and political life of the republic, those who arrived after 1685 found themselves for the most part trapped in second-class employment enjoying second-class civil rights. Briefly, the central change was that Calvin's city had depended for its survival on the commitment and capital of newcomers—like Calvin himself—while eighteenth-century Geneva had bred and trained its own clergy and men of affairs. In 1769 Jacob Vernet wrote of the hereditary right of the Genevan citizen to his rôle in the city's life.[1]

The heroic international phase of reform was over by the eighteenth century; Genevan pastors in 1705 explicitly disclaimed any interest in subverting the structure of the Church of England and were hurt to hear that the English still saw Geneva and Rome as twin sources of error. They explained away their own rites and institutions as necessary to their republican form of government.[2] What then did enlightened Geneva suppose to be its vocation? If the republic no longer nurtured dissidents to capture Christendom for the reformed faith, if it no longer had room or need for great numbers of refugees, what did God mean it to do? Jean-Alphonse

---

[1] [Jacob] Vernet, *Reflexions [sur les moeurs, sur la religion et sur le culte]* (Geneva 1769) p 11.

[2] *Several letters from the Pastors of the Church of Geneva to the Archbishop of Canterbury, the Bishop of London and the University of Oxford with their Answers to them* (London 1707) pp 5, 11.

Turrettini, preaching in 1719, took the view that God still meant to use Geneva to shed light, the light of the gospel, the light of the reformation; eighteenth-century opinion however would best be won by showing the world the many blessings enjoyed by Genevan citizens: their wise, moderate government, rational laws and abundance of material goods.[3] Such utilitarian criteria for assessing the community's well-being eventually proved incompatible with traditional Calvinism.

This paper will show how Geneva's national identity ceased to be bound up with the grim and punitive creed of the sixteenth century. That Geneva was a nation was clear to eighteenth-century minds; her dependent territories amounted only to a cluster of estates and the reformed cantons of Switzerland were mostly distrusted allies. As the eighteenth century proceeded the enlightenment blurred the strict division between the cultures of Geneva and France while by the revolutionary period politics had come to take the place of religion as the focus for Genevans' commitment and intransigence.

There is ample evidence for the growth of a softer theology in eighteenth-century Geneva. Perhaps the most important single change was the decision to discard the strait-jacket of the *Formula Consensus Ecclesiarum Helveticarum* (agreed in 1675 by the reformed cantons). Since 1679 anyone entering the Genevan ministry had been obliged to subscribe to this formula; in 1706 Jean-Alphonse Turrettini argued that the requirement be dropped. Even requiring only that intending pastors should teach nothing contrary to the formula's rigid doctrines of predestination and biblical inspiration amounted, Turrettini thought, to 'a very odious kind of inquisition' and it was folly to lay snares for men's consciences by making them consider even what they said in private on 'so many little questions that are of no importance'. He pointed out that in other reformed cantons as well as in Germany and England people in general had 'grown more moderate as to these affairs' and had benefited from doing so. He rejected the charge that this freedom would amount to a betrayal of the purity of faith it had cost their predecessors so much to establish and maintain, for if 'those pious persons . . . had lived now . . . they would have entered into our

[3] Jean-Alphonse Turrettini, 'Sermon on the Jubilee of the Reformation in Zurich preached 1 January 1719 at Geneva' in Samuel Werenfels, *Sermons sur des Vérités Importantes de la Religion* (Basel 1720) pp 529–30.

sentiments'. Turrettini won the argument, and in 1725 even the requirement that ministers would teach nothing in church or the academy contrary to the regulations of 1649 was abandoned. (The Council, however, begged the venerable company to give this relaxation no publicity and asked them particularly to avoid mentioning it to friends living abroad.)[4]

As the century proceeded the Genevan church set its face against fanaticism and was particularly embarrassed by French co-religionists who claimed to have seen visions, prophesied and worked miracles. Such claims, Samuel Turrettini explained in 1723, were contrary to common sense. Jacob Vernet admired the commitment of the martyrs but thought their devotion rather extreme. Before 1720 Ezechiel Gallatin not only preached a Christianity illuminated by reason as well as scripture but thought we should believe 'as much as could be proved'.[5] This view permeated Jean-Alphonse Turrettini's *Fundamental Articles*: here he argued that all protestants shared belief in those few articles of faith necessary to salvation and that through this common ground a way would be found to eventual reunion. This relaxed, unemphatic attitude towards the finer points of doctrine—'toleration is the greatest friend to truth' —was yoked to a total condemnation of Roman Catholicism. Yet Turrettini could condone doubts about predestination like those for which Bolsec had been banished in 1551.[6] The 1743 edition of the liturgy includes the assertion that God does not want one soul to perish. By 1756 Jacob Vernet could write confidently of free will and explain the force of such terms as 'chosen' and 'predestined' as bearing only on God's uncovenanted generosity in extending his grace beyond the Jews; an English translator of Charles Chais was happy to reassure his non-Calvinist readers that 'the Author's peculiar tenets are seldom introduced' while Antoine Jacques

---

[4] Jean-Alphonse Turrettini, 'Speech previous to the Abolition of all subscriptions' (trans S. Chandler); on Samuel Chandler, *The Case of Subscription to explanatory articles of faith as a Qualification for Admission into the Christian Ministry Calmly and Impartially Reviewed* (London 1848) pp 160–74; [Geneva] B[ibliothèque] P[ublique et] U[niversitaire] MS fr 469.

[5] Samuel Turretin (*sic*), *Preservatif contre le Fanatisme ou Refutation des pretendus inspirez des derniers siécles* (Geneva 1723) pp 228–9; Vernet, *Reflexions* p 54; Ezechiel Gallatin, *Sermons sur divers textes de l'Ecriture Sainte* (Geneva 1720) p 67. (In these notes eighteenth-century French accents and spelling have been left unmodernised.)

[6] Jean-Alphonse Turretin (*sic*), *A Discourse concerning Fundamental Articles in Religion in which a Method is laid down for the more effectual uniting of Protestants and promoting a more general Toleration among them* (London 1720) pp 17, 48, 74.

Roustan stated flatly that liberty constitutes the 'true nobility of man' and that if we were not free, God could not reward us.[7]

Most surviving sermons of eighteenth-century Genevan ministers contain arguments based on natural law and natural theology and analogies familiar to us from eighteenth-century English deists; the notion of God the clock-maker seems particularly apposite in a Genevan context. The new classical front to the church of saint Pierre gave architectural expression to the city's wish to bring its religion up-to-date. Observers noted the rapid dilution of Calvinism: François Bruys claimed that of some thirty-three fellow-students of theology in 1728 only five or six were orthodox Calvinists while amongst the remainder were some who had no religious convictions at all.[8] Montandon has shown how many of Geneva's great scientists in this century began by reading theology but allowed their other interests to win them away from it.[9] In 1762 du Pan wrote that since his youth both sin and the Trinity seemed to have disappeared from the catechism and the liturgy; indeed Jacob Vernet's much-used catechism answered its opening question 'what is the natural desire of all men or the chief end they propose in all their enterprises?' with the utilitarian formula 'to be happy'.[10] D'Alembert, of course, told the world in 1757 in the heart of his controversial *Encyclopédie* article how many Genevan pastors had adopted 'a perfect Socinianism'; 'Respect for Jesus Christ and for the scriptures,' he wrote, 'is perhaps all that distinguishes the Christianity of Geneva from pure deism'. Many ministers, he reported, speak of the utility rather than the necessity of revelation while 'the sermons are almost entirely concerned with morality'.[11] It is well known that this article represented what Voltaire had wanted to see in Geneva as much as what d'Alembert himself had

[7] *La Liturgie [ou La Manière de célébrer le Service Divin dans l'Eglise de Genève]* (Geneva 1743) p 12; [Jacob] Vernet, *Instruction Chretienne [divisée en 5 volumes. Seconde edition retouchée par l'auteur]* (The Hague 1756) 2 p 89; Stephen Freeman, 'Advertisement' to Charles Chais, *A Sermon on the Judgments of Mankind* (London 1790); A. J. Roustan, *A Catechism upon a new and Improved Plan* (Warrington 1793) pp 19–20.

[8] François Bruys, *Mémoires historiques, critiques et littéraires* (Paris 1751), *Voyageurs européens [à la découvert de Genève 1685–1792*, ed J-D Candaux] (Geneva 1966) p 42.

[9] Cleopatra Montandon, 'The Development of Science in Geneva in XVIIIth and XIXth Centuries: the Case of a Scientific Community', unpubl Columbia university PhD thesis (1973) p 112.

[10] BPU, Correspondance de du Pan-Cramer, 6 letter 29; Vernet, *Instruction Chrétienne* 1 p 1.

[11] J. d'Alembert 'Geneva' in *Encyclopedia Selections* ed N. S. Hoyt and J. Cassirer (New York 1965) pp 138–9.

managed to find out in less than three weeks,[12] nonetheless the pastors of Geneva were concerned not only to deny its charges in their collective response of February 1758, but to remedy those deteriorations in their city's faith and morals which had given rise to them.

Jean-Alphonse Turrettini's *Dissertations on Natural Theology* spelt out that utility was too weak a basis for righteousness. Pierre Mouchon saw no point in a God without goodness, justice or holiness and Rousseau (for once) voiced the convictions of the venerable company when he denounced the decadence intrinsic to theatres and theatricals as destructive of the true spirit of Geneva.[13] Vernet attacked d'Alembert both for his reply to Rousseau and for the original article; in 1768 Roustan blamed the growth of evil on the growth of unbelief while in 1769 Vernet attempted to stop the rot with his *Reflections on manner, religion and worship*. He thought the luxury of the last forty years had brought laxness and corruption into the city: Geneva had lost her earlier discipline, piety, industry and charity. Like Antoine Maurice and Charles Chais he explicitly disavowed the loose charms of deism. Men were reducing God to a speculative proposition or an axiom in physics with no bearing on morality, and staying away from sermons just because they found them dull. He dismissed Rousseau's *Profession of Faith* —which sceptics found fulsome in its unfocused piety—by saying that the odd circumstances of his upbringing had prevented Rousseau from knowing real Christianity.[14] Jean-Edme Romilly pointed out that natural religion as practised by the Greeks and Romans had not brought sanctity, let alone salvation. David Claparède wrote against Rousseau and Voltaire for attacking miracles.[15] For d'Alembert had been mistaken. The greater part of

---

[12] J-D Candaux, 'D'Alembert et les Genevois: quelques documents inédits', *Musées de Genève* 77–8 (Geneva 1967) pp 3–6 shows d'Alembert had already made Genevan contacts of his own.

[13] John Alphonso Turretine (*sic*), *Dissertations on Natural Theology*, trans W. Crawford (Belfast 1777) p 318; Pierre Mouchon, *Sermons* (Geneva 1798) p 6; Jean-Jacques Rousseau, *Lettre à d'Alembert sur les Spectacles* (Amsterdam 1758).

[14] *Les Lettres critiques d'un Voyageur Anglois sur l'Article Genève du Dictionnaire Encyclopédique, et sur la lettre de Mr. D'Alembert à Mr. Rousseau touchant les Spectacles* (Copenhagen 1766); Vernet, *Reflexions* p 25, 113, 112, 36, 95, 73; John Stephenson Spink, *Jean-Jacques Rousseau et Geneve* (Paris 1934) p 140.

[15] Jean Edme Romilly, *Sermons*, 3 vols (Geneva 1788) 1 p 218; D. Claparède, *Considerations upon the Miracles of the Gospel; in answer to the Difficulties raised by Mr. John-James Rousseau in his Letter from the Mountain* (London 1758).

the Genevan clergy were ministers of the gospel by calling and conviction and only tentative in their enlightenment; whatever the shifts in tone which may be remarked in the catechisms and the liturgy, what was taught remained worlds away from a cult of reason or a supreme being. The liturgy had after all only been tinkered with, not rewritten as if Calvin had never lived. Is there so very much difference between 'sinners conceived and born in iniquity and corruption' and those merely 'born in corruption'? There is not a great deal more optimism in seeing man as sinning 'every day in many ways' rather than sinning 'endlessly and ceaselessly'.[16]

So most of the pastors still believed and taught a form of Christianity recognisably like that of sixteenth-century Geneva. But how did people respond to this teaching? How did they see themselves in relation to their church and their city? Did they still flock to sermons and denounce adulterers? Observers of the period give mixed testimony. Certainly the strength of church discipline had dwindled and excommunication had ceased to be an important mechanism of social control. In the *Confessions*, however, Rousseau speaks of the upright piety of his father and his three aunts and assumes it is normal to go to church on Sundays. It was often difficult for those without their own seats to secure a place in one of the city's five churches but congregations on ordinary Sundays predictably fell below the peak levels of Christmas, Easter, Pentecost and the September fast.[17] Visiting the 1758 Pierre-Jean Grosley still found Genevans for the most part had very high standards of personal behaviour but he also thought that their faith had been turned into something metaphysical and arid which suited philosophers better than ordinary people: all the oversight and regulation in the world could not prevent such an industrious population from being more interested in prosperity than piety.[18] In 1773 Jacob Björnståhl thought that there remained an important

[16] [*La Forme des*] *Prières* [*et Chants Ecclesiastiques*] (Geneva 1542) not paginated, second page; *La Liturgie* pp 1–2.
[17] A[rchives d'] E[tat de] G[enève] Reg[istres du] Cons[istoire] for 1710, 1720, 1770 and 1780; [Charles] du Bois-Melly, *Les moeurs genevoises* [*de 1700 à 1760 d'après tous les documents officiels pour servir d'introduction à l'histoire de la Republique et Seigneurie à cette Epoque*] (Geneva 1875) pp 126, 283–5; Rousseau, *Confessions*, trans J. M. Cohen (Bungay 1971) p 66 p 49; Anne-Marie Piuz, 'Charité privée et mouvements des Affaires à Genève au XVIIIe siècle', *Colloque Franco-Suisse d'histoire Economique et Sociale 5–6 May 1967* (Geneva 1969) p 75; BPU MSS Ami Lullin 35–36.
[18] Pierre-Jean Grosley, *Nouveaux Mémoires, ou observations sur l'Italie et sur les Italiens,*

body of ministers who still clung to the old teaching, but Genevan church ceremonies struck him as oddly unceremonious: it was hard to hear sermons for the noise and people walked straight out of church after taking communion.[19] As late as 1790 a Russian visitor noted Genevan women moved to tears by a sermon but in 1785 William Beckford thought the old Genevan plainess had completely given way to free thinking and immorality, smuggled in—thanks to Voltaire—under a mask of liberalism.[20]

Calvin's college did not provide mass education in the eighteenth century, but from 1736 onwards, when Jean-Alphonse Turrettini instigated the foundation of the society of catechumens, almost all the city's children, boys and girls alike, received not only a basic primary schooling but a grounding in their catechism and scriptures. Genevans were not allowed to be ignorant of their faith, but many of the edicts promulgated in the eighteenth century, by what they forbid or condemn, point unmistakeably to the currency of undesirable conduct. In 1739 cafés and bars were ordered to close on Sundays, and parents and masters were to see that young people were sent to be catechised. In 1749 balls and dancing were banned; in 1772 dancing had to stop at ten in the evening; in 1785 it was positively forbidden after midnight; in 1786 dancing masters had to be licensed by the city authorities. The sumptuary ordinances banning extravagance at weddings and funerals, forbidding luxury in dress or furniture were issued eight times between 1700 and 1790 showing only minor changes as new fashions caused new alarms: in 1739 the circumference of skirts was to be limited in response to the new craze for paniers. At the beginning of the century playing with cards was forbidden, by the end it was obligatory for playing cards to bear a stamp showing tax had been paid.[21] In 1711 a troop of actors was banned from entering the city as their presence would be

---

par deux gentilhommes suédois—Traduit du suédois (London 1764), Voyageurs Européens, pp 71–2.
[19] Jacob Björnstahl, Resa til Frankrike, Italien, Sweitz, Tyskland, Holland, Ängland, Turkiet och Grekland (Stockholm 1780–4), Voyageurs Européens p 103 p 106.
[20] Nicolai Mikhailovitch Karamzine, Pissma rousskago poutéchestvennika (Moscow 1797–1800), Voyageurs Européens, p 169; [William] Beckford, [The Travel] Diaries [of William Beckford of Fonthill, ed G. Chapman,] 2 vols (Cambridge 1928) 1 p 320; for evidence of this in the 1760s see esp Charles Pictet to Rousseau 3 Feb 1764 in Correspondance [complète de Jean-Jacques] Rousseau, [ed R. A. Leigh], 19 (Banbury 1973) pp 108–9 and throughout this correspondence.
[21] BPU Edicts catalogued in date order.

LINDA KIRK

contrary to Genevan law and custom; in 1766 the French mediator
was able to insist that a theatre be built but in 1768 it burnt down,
perhaps by accident. In 1784 a stone theatre was built outside the
walls and the city gates had to be reopened to let late-night revellers
back to their beds.[22]

Some evidence of popular attitudes that does not depend on the
accident of the eighteenth-century travellers' observation can be
found by considering the chamber of proselytes, freemasonry and
the last flickers of alarm over witchcraft. The Genevan chamber of
proselytes was founded in 1708 in response, not to a wave of
prospective converts, but to a tied donation of 10,000 écus. It met
once a week at first but less than ten times a year in the second half
of the century. The chamber dealt with twelve hundred people in
its ninety years, not proselytising but checking the sincerity of
claims to conversion. It acted in part as a relief agency and in part
one for processing and passing on refugees; people who registered
with the consistory that they had changed their faith had not
necessarily come before this chamber. This was not an age of
missionaries and martyrs; proselytising was not a key function of
the Genevan church in the eighteenth century.[23]

Freemasonry in Geneva—as everywhere—has a history composed chiefly of conjecture and rumour. It is said to have been
introduced by the English in 1736; certainly it was banned by the
council in 1744. Fears centred on the political dangers posed by
cercles in general, whether masonic or not, and all private gatherings
of this type were banned in 1782. The unsuccessful application
made in 1786 for permission to restart such groups emphasised that
members were eager to fulfil all the duties of a citizen and a
Christian. Since it is reckoned that there were seventeen lodges in
1775 and still eleven in 1788 it is clear that at this stage Genevans
were not content with the measure of sociability and corporate
activity which the church provided.[24] They were not, however,
flying off to sabbaths. Geneva's record in the heyday of witchhunts

[22] *Fragments Biographiques et Historiques extraits des registres du Conseil d'Etat de la
République de Genèva dès 1535 à 1792* (Geneva 1815) p 256; Beckford, *Diaries* 1
p 320.
[23] Gustave Moeckli, *Conversions religieuses au XVIIIe siècle: La Chambre des Proselytes
1708–98* (Geneva 1950) pp 338–9, 352–3, 370.
[24] F. Ruchon, *Histoire de la Franc-Maçonnerie à Genève de 1736 à 1900* (Geneva 1935)
pp 7, 13, 24–5, 36, 44; see also Théodore Tronchin to Rousseau 13 Nov 1758,
Correspondance Rousseau 5 (Geneva 1967) pp 219–21.

and witchtrials had been relatively enlightened, but there had been periods of panic associated with outbreaks of plague during which almost half of those accused as witches had been condemned and burnt. No-one suffered this fate after 1652, indeed almost no-one after 1626. By the eighteenth century only a few casters of charms and hawkers of books purporting to contain magical formulae came to the notice of the authorities; in 1773 procureur-général Galiffe told one printer, 'Formerly those who meddled with sorcery were punished very severely, but today, now that the reign of superstition is over, they are only punished in relation to the actual wrong they have done to society and the harm they have caused individuals'.[25] It was, however, enlightenment rather than Calvinism which stopped people taking witchcraft seriously.

More light is shed on Genevan attitudes in this period by demographic evidence and by studies of wills and inventories. That Genevans of all classes were consciously controlling their fertility by the end of the century does not point to a rejection of their church's teaching; Calvinism had never insisted that procreation was the chief end of marriage. Indeed the sixteenth-century marriage service made no mention of children and it was the eighteenth-century revised version which urged that any children God sent be brought up in the true faith.[26] What remained forbidden was fornication, but it was evidently on the increase. Eleven per cent of three hundred and nineteen Genevan brides of the mid-1720s were pregnant when they married. By 1772 the percentage in a similar sample had risen to twenty-five.[27]

Divorce, again, was not unknown to sixteenth century Geneva and was reluctantly allowed for adultery and desertion. It was much easier for a man to divorce his wife than for a woman to divorce her husband: it took seven years of male desertion to justify divorce if there were no bad behaviour to take into account. Voluntary separation had always been frowned upon, but became a legal possibility in 1766. Various ideas for divorce reform proposed in the 1770s came to nothing, so figures showing a rise in

[25] E. W. Monter, *Witchcraft in France and Switzerland* (London 1976) p 61; W. Deonna, 'Superstitions à Genève aux XVIIe et XVIIIe siècles' *Archives Suisses des traditions populaires* 43 (Basel 1946) pp 344, 347–9, 367–8.

[26] A. Bieler, *L'homme et la femme dans la morale Calviniste* (Geneva 1963) p 89; *Prières*, not paginated, four pages just preceding last page; *La Liturgie*, p 87.

[27] Yves Brütsch, 'Population Genevoise du XVIIIe siècle', unpubl Master's thesis (Geneva 1973) p 91.

375

applications for divorce in the second half of the century must give some real indication of a rise in the number of marriages which broke down. Something between one and seven applications per year were normal from the beginning of the century until 1766, while the next three years saw a sudden surge to twelve, thirteen and fifteen. The 1770's saw a return to a lower level, but at the end of the decade applications rose again from thirteen in 1778 to a peak of twenty in 1781. From then on it was rare for there to be as few as eight applications in any year and new peaks were set with twenty-one in 1788 and twenty-six in 1791. The consistory had pleaded in vain in 1769 that this trend be resisted; they had prophesied then that more and more Genevans would see marriage as a revocable contract.[28]

Suicide also became more common in eighteenth-century Geneva. Expressed as a number per hundred thousand per year the rate for the first half of the century was 3.8 while that for the second half was 18.5—concealing 26.4 for the period 1781–98. In itself this increase marks a rejection of traditional Christian teaching, but it is perhaps even more significant that after 1732 no suicide was dragged through the streets on a hurdle nor were the suicide's goods often confiscated (as the law enjoined). After 1738 exclusion from normal places of burial was the only penalty visited upon suicides or their families while there is no record of a popular reaction against growing official liberalism. In 1735 procureur-général Jean du Pan said there was no point in treating suicide as a crime since all normal people preferred life to death; those likely to kill themselves were thus by definition incapable of being influenced by legislation or stern example. So far as motives for suicide were established at the time, either by confession or investigation, it is clear that leisured but troubled people committed suicide far more than those affected by want. Of final messages which survive, over a third were preoccupied with religion but over a half are more narrowly personal and addressed to intimates. Contemporaries took to using the term melancholic to denote someone sane enough to know what he was doing but unable to help himself. Here, then, there is no split between the orthodox and the liberal: while suicide remained a sin it became one which

---

[28] Bernard Sonnaillon, 'Etude des divorces à Genève dans la seconde moitié du XVIIIᵉ, unpubl Master's thesis (Geneva 1975) pp 9, 11, 31, 60–4; AEG Reg Cons, Remonstrances adressés . . . au magnifique Conseil 15 Aug 1769.

attracted popular sympathy rather than vengeance and which the authorities declined to treat as a matter of church or civic discipline.[29]

The declaration of faith made in Genevan wills of the eighteenth century show a shift, although not a steady one, away from clear Calvinist statements. After 1740 people stopped thanking God they were protestant; after 1765 it ceased to be normal to recommend one's soul to God; after 1762 people seldom spoke of being washed in the blood of the lamb. Wills with no religious clause were always rare, but grew more common up to 1762—when this trend was briefly reversed; the use of the rather offhand 'etc.' in religious clauses actually declined after 1760 but by the end of the century few people thanked God for material possessions.[30]

Increasingly secular attitudes must at least in part have been the consequence of what Genevans read—and by the end of the century a large majority of the city's inhabitants were literate.[31] Although the press was by no means as free as some outsiders supposed printing and publishing flourished and many works of the enlightenment were available in Geneva: Montesquieu's *L'Esprit des Lois* was first published there. Thanks to many local gifts and legacies the public library in Geneva was said to contain thirty thousand volumes by 1756, and it was meant to receive a copy of every book printed in the city.[32] Inventories of dead people's goods sometimes included lists of the books they owned; by the late 1770s a significant number of artisans had small libraries. Theological works predominated between 1700 and 1715 but by the end of the century Calvin and Beza had given way to Rousseau and Voltaire; indeed a mounting interest can be see in works bearing on Genevan political controversy. In the council of two hundred some supported and some resisted the revolution of 1781–2; libraries studied suggest that both groups acted on informed conviction, having

[29] Laurent Haeberli 'Le Suicide à Genève à 18e siècle' *Pour une histoire qualitative: études offertes à Sven Stelling-Michaud* (Geneva 1975) pp 118–20, 126–8.

[30] Peter Burch, 'Les Comportements devant la Mort au XVIIIe siècle à Genève', unpubl Master's thesis (Geneva 1974) pp 81–2. Ten per cent of wills made were studied.

[31] R. Girod, 'Le recul de l'analphabétisme dans la region de Genève', *Mélanges d'histoire economique et sociale en hommage au professeur A. Babel* (Geneva 1963) p 183. Up to 90% signed marriage registers.

[32] John R. Kleinschmidt, *Les Imprimeurs et libraires de la Republique de Genève 1700–1798* (Geneva 1948) pp 28–9, 46; BPU, Registre des Assemblées des Messrs. les Directeurs de la Bibliothèque 1702–33 pp 93–95.

read the arguments for and against the popular cause.[33]

Man can of course be both a religious and a political animal but in eighteenth-century Geneva the waning of rigid Calvinism ran parallel with the growth of serious and intermittently angry interest in the government of the city. In 1707, in the 1730s, in the 1760s, in 1771 and in 1781–2 trouble flared up, sometimes only with demonstrations, sometimes in actual street fighting. By ancien régime standards the Genevan patriciate governed efficiently and cheaply; the few great families who monopolised power were rich but none had obviously become so through confusing public and private monies. The issues changed as the century proceeded: could the governing group tax without consent; should citizens vote by secret ballot; should the laws be properly codified and published; were the city's troops to repel external enemies or to be turned on the local populace; was Rousseau justly condemned for *Social Contract* and *Emile*; was the general council sovereign or merely to be consulted; should long-term residents and their children be permanently excluded from full citizenship—but in the end a single theme had clearly emerged: where did sovereignty lie? On this Genevans split. By 1781 one important group would entrust it to all the republic's adult male householders while most of the traditional governing class dismissed this notion as anarchy. Karl Küttner, a Saxon, described the situation in 1781: everyone was obsessed with his rights; political arguments raged; women as well as men read books and insisted their views be heard. Too much prosperity had given people ideas above their station and the average Genevan was 'too educated'. The enlightenment, Küttner thought, had done Geneva a great deal of harm—and the clergy were caught up in it all.[34]

Pastors were not inevitable supporters of either side. A number had supported the radicals in the affair of the anonymous letters of 1718 and almost none of them, with their moderate incomes paid

[33] F. Grounauer, 'Livre et Société à Genève au XVIIIe siècle', unpubl Master's thesis (Geneva 1969) pp 7, 24, 27. Inventories from 1700 to 1715 and 1775 to 1790 were studied, and by the author those found for the Council of 200 1781–2: AEG, Jurisdictions civiles: Inventaires après décès 1781 onwards.

[34] [Patrick] O'Mara, ['Geneva in the Eighteenth Century: A Socio-Economic Study of the Bourgeois City-State during its] Golden Age', unpubl PhD thesis (California 1954) p 141; Karl Küttner, *Briefe eines Sachsen aus Schweiz an seinen Freund in Leipzig* (Leipzig 1785–6), *Voyageurs Européens* pp 123–4, 127–8; John Moore noted this trend in 1772. See his *A View of society and manners in France, Switzerland and Germany* 2 vols (London 1779) 1 pp 158–9.

by the state, could identify with Geneva's plutocrats.[35] Nonetheless Jean-Alphonse Turrettini who did so much to liberalise Genevan Calvinism was appalled by the presumption of the bourgeois claims of 1734. The liturgy and catechism continued to inculcate deference and gratitude towards the magistrates long after a more spirited and sceptical attitude became common. Vernet's *Reflections* mark an interesting moment of transition. Here he used Montesquieu's logic to promote piety and public order in Geneva: as a republic the city had to rest on the constitutive principle of virtue. Calvin had meant his city to be a model of piety but here the emphasis seems to have been reversed. Once Genevans had to lead godly lives to show they were saved; now it seemed that being saved only lent weight to the self-evident utilitarian case for cleanliness, decency and sobriety. Public worship, for instance, was a specific against street brawls.[36]

It is not the case that Genevans abandoned their Calvinism for politics, or took to politics to console themselves for the loss of belief; nor did the mellowing of Calvinist teaching in any direct sense stimulate political activism. But while religious commitment had provided the city republic with a single identity political commitment split it in two. In 1782 the patricians felt themselves forced to choose between bowing to popular insurrection and calling in foreign troops. The government subsequently installed under the black edict had shown that it felt more in common with the ruling classes of France than their fellow-protestants in Geneva. France, Berne and Zurich had intervened as guarantors in 1738 and 1766 but this was a new development: Geneva was no longer a single community with a shared system of belief and an overriding sense of religious purpose. To be a Genevan meant one thing to the traditional ruling group and their supporters but quite another to the radical leaders, many of whom were forced into exile. The miracle of Genevan independence, always in fact a result of the

---

[35] O'Mara, 'Golden Age' p 154; Patrick O'Mara, 'L'Affaire des Lettres Anonymes et l'Agitation Politique à St. Gervais en 1718', *Bulletin de la Société d'Histoire et d'Archaeologie de Geneva*, 10, 3 (Geneva 1954) pp 255–60.

[36] Jacob Vernet, 'Eloge Historique de Mr. Jean Turrettin, Pasteur et Professeur en Théologie et un Histoire Ecclesiastique à Genève', *Bibliothèque Raisonée des ouvrages des Savans de l'Europe*, 22, 1 (Amsterdam 1738) p 463; Vernet, *Reflexions* pp 9–10, p 104.

The author wishes to thank Anthony Fletcher for reading and commenting upon a draft of this paper.

refusal of Savoy and France to allow the other power to take over the city, proved more fragile than eighteenth-century Genevans had had to realise. In the event the French invasion of 1798 did not destroy the city's protestant tradition, and church and state were not formally separated until 1907, but the republic's Calvinist identity—so laboriously imposed—was destroyed by the events and intellectual developments of the eighteenth century.

University of Sheffield.

RELIGION AND THE DOCTRINE OF NATIONALISM IN ENGLAND AT THE TIME OF THE FRENCH REVOLUTION AND NAPOLEONIC WARS.

by WILLIAM STAFFORD

THE MAXIM my *country right or wrong* is unquestionably difficult and perhaps impossible to justify; certainly no Christian can easily regard the nation as the supreme object of loyalty. Yet during the revolutionary and Napoleonic wars intensive efforts were made in press and pulpit, through the courts and through informal social pressure, to enhance patriotism. Patriotism almost certainly became stronger and more widely diffused.[1] How did the denominations respond to this dilemma? My aim is to suggest some links between denominational affiliation and attitudes to nationalism. The topic is an important one; at this time religion usually set the terms of the debate about loyalty.

Disloyalty could be expected in 1789 from old dissenters, and especially from so-called rational dissent.[2] During the eighteenth century there had been in dissenting ranks a drift away from their position of support for the monarchy and constitution of 1689. Many with Priestley and Price had favoured the Americans during their war of independence, for ties with co-religionists in the new world were strong. Dissenters worked for parliamentary reform, and agitated for repeal of the Test and Corporation Acts.[3] Dissent therefore could not be expected to be patriotic without qualification. Patriotism is discussed by the distinguished unitarian minister, Dr Richard Price, in his *Discourse on the love of our country*:[4] this

[1] C. Emsley, *British Society and the French Wars 1793–1815* (London 1979) pp 67, 113, 115. But acute social and religious tensions prevented patriotic unanimity.
[2] Especially unitarians, but radically minded rationalists could be found in other branches of old dissent.
[3] A. H. Lincoln, *Some Political and Social Ideas of English Dissent* (Cambridge 1938) p 20. M. R. Watts, *The Dissenters: from the Reformation to the French Revolution* (Oxford 1978) p 479.
[4] [Richard] Price, [*A Discourse on the Love of our Country, delivered on November 4, 1789 at the meeting-house in the Old Jewry, to the Society for commemorating the Revolution in Great Britain*] (4 ed London 1790) pp 2–11.

sermon was immortalised by becoming the unfortunate target of Burke's *Reflections*. Price argues that love of country is a passion which, like other passions, must be regulated and directed. It must not degenerate into prejudice, blinding us to the merits of other countries and the faults of our own. Patriotism can be a form of collective selfishness:

> What was the love of their country among the old *Romans?* We have heard much of it; but I cannot hesitate in saying that, however great it appeared in some of its exertions, it was in general no better than a principle holding together a band of robbers in their attempts to crush all liberty but their own.[5]

Christianity rather advocates Universal Benevolence. Some patriotism is allowable; we can do most good to those near us, and God has therefore endowed us with partiality for kindred, neighbours and fellow-countrymen. But partial affections must be subordinate to universal benevolence. Price was not the main target for nationalists; his measured statement was eclipsed by Godwin's defence of cosmopolitanism in *Political Justice*. By 1793 Godwin had evolved through congregationalism, Sandemanianism and unitarianism to atheism; but his thought still owed much to Calvinist dissent.[6] Not only does he condemn patriotism utterly;[7] he also attacks lesser partialities for friends and family. If I could save Fenelon or my father from a fire, I should choose Fenelon, because he is pre-eminently virtuous and useful to mankind.[8] Godwin's remarks provoked many defences of domestic affections and patriotism. Three aspects of Price's and Godwin's anti-patriotic argument may be highlighted. First, they insist that loyalty to a nation should be proportioned to that nation's worth; Britain, though worthier than almost any other state, is not perfect:

> It is too evident that the state of this country is such as renders it an object of concern and anxiety. It wants (I have shewn you) the grand security of public liberty. Increasing luxury has multiplied abuses in it. A monstrous weight of debt is

---

[5] *Ibid* p 6.
[6] This is argued at length in my article, 'Dissenting religion translated into politics: Godwin's *Political Justice*', *History of Political Thought* 1 no 2 (1980) pp 279–99.
[7] William Godwin, *Enquiry Concerning Political Justice*, ed I. Kramnick (London 1976: reprint of 3 ed 1798) pp 508–9.
[8] *Ibid* pp 169–171.

crippling it. Vice and venality are bringing down upon it God's displeasure.[9]

Second, their hostility to patriotism stems from a suspicion of human emotion which has its roots in Calvinism.[10] Patriotism is a natural affection, and nature, the flesh, is corrupt. This attitude is widespread among contemporary Pauline dissenters and anglicans:[11]

A disposition to love the creature more that the Creator, is undoubtedly a part of a proof of our natural depravity. This evil principle, described by the apostle under the names of the Flesh, the Old Man, and Indwelling Sin, however weakened and mortified in a true believer, is not extirpated. The opposition between nature and grace, flesh and spirit, renders the Christian life a state of constant warfare.[12]

Third, the culture of educated old dissenters was dominated by a religious and philosophical individualism which impeded unmitigated nationalism. The dissenting academies of the eighteenth century reinforced protestant individualism with the philosophies of Locke and Hartley. Just as a sinner obtained grace on his own directly from God rather than mediated through a church, so human knowledge grew within the mind of the isolated individual, as he organised sense-data in accordance with the principles of association. In this epistemology, the ideas which an individual gets are prior to any language or categories developed in society. Lockean politics, in strict analogy, suppose individuals, pre-constituted outside of civil society, uniting in a social contract to establish a state which is merely a device to satisfy wants which those individuals already have. So in religion, epistemology and politics the individual is prior and fundamental, the community is posterior and instrumental. Hence there is no essential reason why any community should be privileged over others; no reason why an

---

[9] Price p 46.

[10] Price like Godwin abandoned the Calvinism of his youth but remained greatly influenced by it. D. O. Thomas, *The Honest Mind: The Thought and Work of Richard Price* (Oxford 1977) p 6.

[11] An influential statement was Jonathan Edwards, 'The Nature of True Virtue', *Two Dissertations, 1. Concerning the end for which God created the World 2. The Nature of True Virtue* (Boston 1765).

[12] [J.] Newton, 'On the comforts and snares of social and relative affections', [*The Works of the Rev. John Newton, late rector of the united parishes of St. Mary Woolnoth, and St. Mary Woolchurch Haw, London*], ed R. Cecil, 6 vols (3 ed London 1824) 6 p 481.

Englishman should prefer England to France, or his nation to mankind. There may be accidental or practical reasons for preference; England may be more free, or perhaps I can do more for the poor of London than for the natives of Borrioboola-Gha: but still a man is a man, a member of the human race, before he is an Englishman.

After the beginning of the terror in 1792 and the outbreak of war in 1793, reaction set in against the cause of reform with which the rational dissenters were associated. Especially after 1802, when there was a real threat of invasion, patriotism became the order of the day. In this changed climate, unitarianism declined. All branches of dissent fell under suspicion, and attempts were made to revoke or reduce toleration.[13] Loud protestations of loyalty were a common dissenting response to this crisis.[14] Was the anti-patriotism of Price and Godwin replaced by a philosophy of nationalism? Godwin's assault upon the domestic affections was criticised within old dissent by William Enfield,[15] a presbyterian minister, by Robert Hall,[16] a baptist, and by the young Coleridge[17] who in the 1790s was preaching unitarian sermons. All three employ an argument borrowed from Hartley, and so they refute Godwin from his own premises.[18] The same argument is used by Samuel Parr,[19] an anglican with reformist sympathies. Hartley had argued that benevolence was not natural but acquired. The promptings of pleasure and pain first teach us concern for self; but within the domestic circle we experience the pains and pleasures of others, associating them with our own and thus the first stirrings of sympathy arise. Later we learn to care for neighbours in the same way, then for fellow-countrymen; ultimately we generalise from our experience and develop the sentiment of benevolence to the whole human race. Benevolence is developed in easy stages, in

[13] W. R. Ward, *Religion and Society in England 1790–1850* (London 1972) pp 52, 56.
[14] *Ibid* p 25.
[15] [William] Enfield, ['Enquirer' *Monthly Magazine* (May 1796)] pp 274–277.
[16] [Robert] Hall, [*Modern infidelity considered with respect to its influence on society: in a sermon preached at the baptist meeting, Cambridge*] (2 ed Cambridge 1800) pp 51–7.
[17] [Samuel Taylor] Coleridge, *Lectures 1795* [*on Politics and Religion*], ed L. Patton and P. Mann (London 1971) pp 46, 162–5, 351–3.
[18] The debate between Godwin and his critics is discussed and the influence of Hartley demonstrated by Patton and Mann in Coleridge *Lectures 1795* pp lxix–lxxi.
[19] Samuel Parr, *A Spital sermon, preached at Christ Church upon Easter Tuesday, April 15, 1800* (London 1801) pp 2–12, 44n.

accordance with the principle of association. The constitution of the human mind therefore requires family affections and patriotism as necessary preconditions of general benevolence.

> In order to render men benevolent, they must first be made tender: for benevolent affections are not the offspring of reasoning; they result from that culture of the heart, from those early impressions of tenderness, gratitude, and sympathy, which the endearments of domestic life are sure to supply, and for the formation of which it is the best possible school.[20]

> Jesus knew our Nature—and that expands like the circles of a Lake—the love of our Friends, parents and neighbours leads us to the love of our Country to the love of all Mankind.[21]

This Hartleian argument marks a retreat from Calvinist hostility to natural emotions, but sustains only a qualified nationalism. Love of mankind remains the ideal; domestic and patriotic affections are merely the scaffolding with which, or at best the materials out of which[22] general benevolence is constructed. Partial affections and limited benevolence are necessary only because men are 'weak, shortsighted mortals'.[23] Futhermore, this argument does not break the individualist framework. It is a psychological theory, not a sociological one: the moral culture occurs within the individual, and is not embodied in social practices or customs: the social groups within which this moral culture occurs simply provide experiences of a certain kind and almost any social groups would do the same. Man grows to full stature in society, but particular forms of association, such as family or nation, are not essential. Old dissent, therefore, could be patriotic; but its culture contained elements which sat uneasily with unbridled nationalism. This ambiguity is revealed in a congregationalist sermon by Edward Parsons. Parsons is anxious to defend dissenters against the charge of disloyalty:

> And, although he may be most foully aspersed by infuriate politicians, and malignant bigots, as an incendiary in the state because of his dissent from the church, he is still a man of peace.[24]

---

[20] Hall p 51.
[21] Coleridge, *Lectures 1795* p 163.
[22] Enfield p 275.
[23] Hall p 55.
[24] Edward Parsons, *The true patriot. A sermon, preached at Salem-Chapel, Leeds, on the fast-day, Wednesday, February 8, 1809* (Leeds 1809) p 34; see also pp 36–7.

We should love our country because such love follows the example of Christ and accords with human nature. But patriotism is conditional; England is to be loved only if loveable. England is worthy of love because of her rational liberty, and above all because of her Reformation. In England conscience is free: 'the most zealous devotees of the blindest superstition, or the wildest fanaticism have no reason to complain of persecutions, or restraint'.[25] The true patriot is marked by his gratitude for national deliverances. Parsons mentions three: the overthrow of the Spanish armada, the discovery of the popish plot, and the revolution of 1688. Indeed no man can be a true patriot who does not love the memory of William of Orange: 'Away with such loyalists, such patriots, such Christians! Let them retire to some distant realm of absolute and unlimited prerogative . . .'[26] Parsons is patriotic; but freedom of conscience comes before love of country. What is more, he is not altogether proud of England. The true patriot is deeply affected by the vices of his country, and England suffers from a low state of morals which may bring disaster. Vice begins among princes and nobles: 'When was common moral decency ever more openly set at defiance, especially in *High life*?'[27]

A high degree of commitment to the nation might be expected among evangelical anglicans and methodists. For the equivalent revivalism and 'heart' religion in Germany, pietism, was a factor in the rise of German nationalism.[28] Leading evangelicals and the official spokesmen of methodism were generally conservative in politics and loyal to king and constitution.[29] Yet evangelical and methodist patriotism was often qualified. In a work of 1797 Wilberforce defends Christianity against Rousseau's charge that it is an enemy to patriotism: Christianity is the surest preservative of patriotism, enjoining service of others and subjugation of self. But Christianity encourages only *true* patriotism, which is peace-loving and subordinate to universal benevolence. Christian charity
   . . . resembles majestic rivers . . . they begin with dispensing

[25] *Ibid* pp 16–17.
[26] *Ibid* p 27.
[27] *Ibid* p 31.
[28] The argument of K. S. Pinson, *Pietism as a Factor in the Rise of German Nationalism* (New York 1934).
[29] A. Armstrong, *The Church of England, the Methodists and Society, 1700–1850* (London 1973) pp 87, 151–2. For evangelicalism in particular, see [V.G.] Kiernan, ['Evangelicalism and the French revolution' PP 1] pp 44–56.

beauty and comfort to every cottage by which they pass. In their further progress they fertilize provinces and enrich kingdoms. At length they pour themselves into the ocean; where, changing their names but not their natures, they visit distant nations and other hemispheres, and spread throughout the world the expansive tide of their beneficence.[30]

Wilberforce has a low view of the moral condition of the nation, especially of its upper classes:

> . . . my only solid hopes for the well-being of my country depend not so much on her fleets and armies, not so much on the wisdom of her rulers, or the spirit of her people, as on the persuasion that she still contains many, who, in a degenerate age, love and obey the Gospel of Christ. . . [31]

This is developed by another evangelical, John Newton, who describes himself as a methodist within the established church. Newton loves his king, glories in the constitution, and detests political radicals; but he regards the nation as degenerate and wicked,[32] perhaps the most sinful in Europe.[33] England's African slave trade causes more iniquity in one year than the French have perpetrated since the commencement of their revolution.[34] Newton takes no pride in naval victories:

> A proud boasting spirit, and a vain confidence in our own strength and resources, is a prominent part of our national character . . . we still boast in our fleets and armies.[35]

Victory should instead be attributed to the arm of the Lord. He identifies himself, not with his nation but with the minority of truly religious anglicans and dissenters *within* the nation.[36] Turning now to methodism, generalisations are dangerous, for after Wesley the movement was much divided. Protestations of political respec-

---

[30] William Wiberforce, *A practical view of the prevailing religious system of professed Christians in the higher and middle classes in this country, contrasted with real Christianity* (London 1797) p 398.

[31] *Ibid* p 489.

[32] ['Motives to] humiliation and praise. [A sermon preaced in the parish church of St. Mary Woolnoth, on December 9, 1797, the day of general thanksgiving to Almighty God for our late naval victories'), Newton 5 p 297.

[33] *Ibid* p 280.

[34] 'The imminent danger and the only sure resource of this nation. A sermon preached in the parish church of St. Mary Woolnoth on Friday February 28 1794, the day appointed for a general fast', Newton 5 p 263.

[35] Newton, 'Humiliation and praise' p 292.

[36] *Ibid* pp 297–8.

tability were common however. In his sermon *Fear God: Honour the King* Henry Moore praises the political quietism of the early Christians:

> And when they were persecuted by the civil government, the same mind was found in them which was also in Christ Jesus: for their Master's sake they were content to be killed all the day long, and counted as sheep for the slaughter.[37]

Thomas Wood argues the same: kings are divinely appointed, even such as Nero, hence revolution is always wrong.[38] Stable government is essential because of the desperate wickedness of the greater part of mankind.[39] Englishmen have special reason for obedience in their glorious constitution and liberty, especially in respect of conscience.[40] But Moore's text is *Render unto Caesar*, and he places equal weight on both parts of the text. Christians must be ready to offer passive resistance and even to die for conscience. His heroes are Shadrach, Meschach, Abednego and Daniel; he criticises not only the persecuting Stuarts but also Elizabeth, and attacks the Act of Uniformity.[41] Wood asserts the right of private judgement, and hence of resistance to intolerance: he is depressed by the rampant vices of the nation and he calls for reform.[42] Evangelicals and methodists therefore, even when conservative and loyalist, have divided loyalties; true religion and freedom of conscience matter as much as or more than the nation. Political loyalty is more likely to be directed towards king and constitution than towards the nation. Their strong sense of sin works for obedience but against nationalism: because of man's wickedness the state is essential; but characteristically their pride in their native land is reduced by their sense of its depravity.[43]

Some anglicans exhibit a more wholehearted national pride. Three who also develop interesting nationalist doctrines are Burke, John Bowles and Coleridge, though even their strong nationalism is challenged by other beliefs and allegiances. Both Burke and

[37] [Henry] Moore, [*Fear God: honour the King. A discourse on MATT. xxii. 21. preached in the methodist chapel, Bath, on Sunday January 19, 1794*] (London 1794) p 12.
[38] [Thomas] Wood, [*Essays on civil government and subjection and obedience to the higher powers*] (Wigan 1796) p 42.
[39] *Ibid* p 49.
[40] *Ibid* p 9.
[41] Moore pp 12, 19–21.
[42] Wood pp 17, 51–72.
[43] This is argued in Kiernan.

Bowles justify nationalism by emphasising emotion, giving it preference over reason.[44] Our feelings have been planted by God to direct our conduct;[45] they are *natural*, and 'Never, no never, did nature say one thing and Wisdom say another'.[46] To identify nature with feeling rather than reason is a romantic reversal of classicist attitudes; to regard nature, thus interpreted, as admirable is to move far from Calvinism; to trust the heart is to weight the scales towards nationalism. Burke frequently uses the Hartleian argument that benevolence builds up in easy stages from family and local attachments;[47] it can develop in no other way, therefore those who profess to prefer mankind to kin and country are selfish and corrupt.[48] Second, Burke answers the question, *why should I serve my country?* with the insistence that duties are not abstract, to men in general, but concrete, determined by the social relationships into which we are placed. Each man has several social relations: as child, husband, parent and citizen; each relation brings duties. This anticipates the extreme collectivist nationalism of F. H. Bradley:[49] but whereas Bradley's position is underpinned by a philosophy of cultural and moral relativism, Burke's doctrine has a religious foundation; our station and duties have been 'marshalled . . . by a divine tactic'.[50] Burke's political philosophy is centrally concerned with *practices*, to use Oakeshott's term.[51] Practices are formally or informally established ways of behaving, embodied in political and religious institutions, or existing as conventions, customs, habits and prejudices. Burke's emphasis on practices supports both nationalism and belief in an established church, and has two main theoretical justifications. One lies in his doctrine of social training and discipline. Burke, like Bowles, believes that man is wicked and

---

[44] [John] Bowles, [A] *view [of the moral state of society at the close of the eighteenth century. Much enlarged, and continued to the commencement on the year 1804]* (London 1804) pp 10, 44.

[45] [Edmund] Burke, 'Speeches on the impeachment of Warren Hastings', [*The Works of the Right Honourable Edmund Burke*], 8 vols (Bohn ed London 1854–8) 8 p 141.

[46] [Burke, *Letters on a*] *regicide peace*, 5 p 278.

[47] [Burke,] *Reflections [on the revolution in France]* (Everyman ed London 1910) pp 44, 193.

[48] Burke, 'A letter from Mr. Burke to a member of the National Assembly', *Reflections* pp 263–4.

[49] F. H. Bradley 'My station and its duties' *Ethical Studies* (2 ed Oxford 1927) pp 160–206.

[50] [Burke, *An appeal from the*] *new to [the] old Whigs*, 3 pp 79–80.

[51] M. Oakeshott, *On Human Conduct* (Oxford 1975) pp 55–60.

sinful—a belief which does not square easily with his romantic enthusiasm for natural feelings.[52] Seventeenth and eighteenth century dissenters often thought social discipline should be exercised by the community of believers in the locality, but this involved no departure from religious individualism. Burke's theory makes the community fundamental and the individual derivative; it looks not to the locality but to established church, state and nation. To tame and civilise the beast into a man is a long and arduous process which can only be achieved through the practices—the institutions and conventions—which have gradually developed. A nation is a web of practices which must not be disturbed; disturbance will disrupt the hard-won system of social training which keeps a Hobbesian state of nature at bay. An essential ingredient of this discipline is an established church, which is required 'in order to build up that wonderful structure, Man . . .'.[53] A substantial section of the *Reflections* defends church establishments, which consecrate the state and provide powerful incentives to obedience and order.[54] Burke is in substantial disagreement with dissent: man cannot find salvation, cannot grow to full humanity, on his own. Emphasis shifts from the individual to the corporate body. Likewise, the nation becomes important; it is the sum total of practices which educate the individual and secure civilisation. The individual is perfected, not by his own efforts, nor as part of mankind, but by his nation. This is a much more collectivist theory of personal development that that borrowed from Hartley by Hall, Enfield, Parr and the young Coleridge. It focusses on the social institutions and conventions which mould the individual, whereas the Hartleian theory describes the process of development by association within the individual mind. Burke's other justification of practices is a rejection of any final, universal or uncontroversial truth in religion and politics. He takes issue with protestant dissenters who think that the individual can, by reading the scriptures, discover religious truth for himself. The scriptures require interpretation, Burke answers; and before interpretation can begin, it must be decided which books of the bible are canonical. Such decisions and interpretations require church authority; truth is not discovered but *established*, embodied in

[52] *Reflections* p 91. Bowles, *View* p 13; Bowles, *The Retrospect* (London 1798) p 297.
[53] *Reflections* p 85.
[54] See also Bowles, *View* p 14.

institutions and practices. Similarly in politics there is no true or ideal system of society and government, based upon facts of human nature. For 'Art is man's nature . . .',[55] and man is 'in a great degree the creature of his own making . . .'.[56] There is no natural order for statesmen to establish; political systems are conventional.[57] Attention therefore shifts from truth which individuals might discover, to practices which are collective achievements. By implication, Burke has provided a powerful reply to cosmopolitans who object to nations as artificial and arbitrary; all human life is artificial and conventional, and each nation embodies a specific set of conventions. The nation as a system of practices is a distinctive mode of collective existence.[58] So Burke has a battery of arguments for nationalism, but his nationalism should not be exaggerated; specifically nationalist doctrines occupy little space in his writings, and significantly in his assault on Price's sermon he takes issue with the defence of popular sovereignty and support for the French revolution, but makes no mention of Prince's antipatriotism. Very often he speaks as a member of Christian Europe rather than of the English nation. Above all he is a fairly consistent supporter of religious toleration, which he regards not as a necessary evil but as an essential principle of Christianity.[59] He argued for the repeal or modification of the laws discriminating against both protestant dissenters and Roman catholics. After the French revolution he opposed toleration of unitarians, but on the ground that they were political subversives; he continued to support *religious* toleration.[60] Belief in toleration significantly qualifies nationalism, betokening a recognition that national unity need not be perfect, that individuality and diversity are at least as important.

Burke, though usually cited as the chief English nationalist thinker of the period, is less important than Coleridge. Coleridge's nationalism is fuller and subtler, and occupies a larger proportion of his writings. He is more interested than Burke in national character,

[55] *New to old Whigs* p 86.
[56] *Reflections* p 89.
[57] *New to old Whigs* pp 82–3.
[58] *Regicide peace* pp 219–20.
[59] Burke, 'Letter to William Burgh, Esq.', 8 pp 455–6; 'Speech on the second reading of a bill for the relief of protestant dissenters', *Ibid* 6 pp 104, 110; *Reflections* p 147.
[60] Burke, 'Speech on the petition of the unitarians' Burke 6 pp 118–9, 123.

which he considers the key to history.[61] He alone in England approaches the intensity and absolutism of Schleiermacher and Fichte. His early patriotism, drawing on Hartley, has been noted; later he rejected associationism, but continued to argue that benevolence develops in easy stages.[62] To this argument the mature Coleridge, now a supporter of the established church, added most of Burke's, and others partly derived from contemporary German philosophy. Much of his nationalism derives from religion. First, like Burke, he shifts emphasis from individual to national community by placing social discipline and training at the centre of his social theory. He abandoned the optimism of his pantisocratic days and returned to the doctrine of original sin;[63] in strict accord he rejected primitivism and any Wordsworthian idealisation of rustic simplicity.[64] Society must undertake the task of raising man from beast to angel. Coleridge is deeply interested in education which he conceives not as a free and spontaneous unfolding of the pupil's potential, but as discipline, in which form is imposed upon disorder.[65] This is the key to his distinction between *civilisation* and *cultivation*: an education which fills the head with information and imparts practical skills is *civilisation* and inadequate; *cultivation*, a higher form, gives moral and spiritual training.[66] His ideas on education are part of a philosophy of culture.[67] Without using the word he develops the concept of culture in two senses. Cultivation is moral *culture*, the training up of good men. But this training is inseparable from the *culture* in the anthropologist's sense; from the way of life of the society, resulting from the interaction of economic, social, political, philosophical and religious spheres.[68] The locus of this culture, the social whole which is a whole because

[61] [Coleridge,] *Essays on his times,* [ed D. V. Erdman], 3 vols (London 1978) 1 p 324, 2 p 94, 3 p 191.
[62] *Ibid* 2 p 330; [Coleridge,] *Table Talk* (Bohn ed London 1884) p 244.
[63] B. Willey, 'Coleridge and religion', [*S. T. Coleridge*, ed R. L.] Brett (London 1971) p 238; *Table Talk* p 129.
[64] Coleridge, *Biographia Literaria*, ed J. Shawcross, 2 vols (Oxford 1907) 2 p 129.
[65] *Table Talk* p 103.
[66] *Ibid* p 173; [Coleridge,] *The Friend*, [ed B. E. Rooke], 2 vols (London 1969) 1 p 500; [Coleridge, *On the Constitution of the*] *Church and* [*the*] *State*, [ed J. Colmer] (London 1976) pp 42–3.
[67] Coleridge's contribution to the *philosophy of culture* is discussed by J. S. Mill, 'Coleridge' *Mill on Bentham and Coleridge*, ed F. R. Leavis (London 1950) and by R. Williams, *Culture and Society 1780–1950* (London 1958).
[68] For a vivid and powerful expression of this conception, see *Church and State* pp 61–70.

of it, is the nation. Even more explicitly than Burke, Coleridge connects his conception of national culture which forms the citizens with his advocacy of church establishments. Just as the individual requires the discipline of society to become a man, so the Christian needs the guidance of the church. He rejects the view of many dissenters that the believer can discern religious truth on his own reading the bible without commentary.[69] The bible is not plain and easy throughout: 'there are shallows where the lamb may ford, and depths where the elephant must swim'.[70] Religious individualism is mistaken: truth is discovered and conveyed by the national church. He also argues that the national church or *clerisy* should be the main agent of cultivation, 'to form and train up the people of the country to obedient, free, useful, organizable subjects, citizens, and patriots, living to the benefit of the state, and prepared to die for its defence'.[71] National unity is secured by the church.[72] His theory of education as culture, his nationalism, and his defence of an established church are therefore intimately related. Second, patriotic enthusiasm itself can serve as a powerful cultural factor, elevating the state and its citizens. The French wars caused hardship, but had their golden side, making the nation more serious, moral and unified.[73] In 1834 he suggested that another threat of invasion might be good for morale.[74] Nationalist fervour turns ordinary men into athletes of virtue: 'even the common soldier dares force a passage for his comrades by gathering up the bayonets of the enemy into his own breast: because his country *"expected every man to do his duty"*'[75] Commendation of such moral heroism and forgetfulness of self in the service a greater whole is a nationalist adoption of the Christian ideal of self-sacrifice.[76] Finally, the leitmotiv of Coleridge's thought is the idea of *unity*. In philosophy, the faculty of Reason, and the Ideas it perceives; in aesthetics, the imagination; in

[69] [Coleridge,] *Lay Sermons*, [ed R. J. White] (London 1972) p 201. [C. R.] Sanders, [*Coleridge and the Broad Church Movement*] (Durham, North Carolina 1942) p 51. [J.R.] Barth, [*Coleridge and Christian doctrine*] (Cambridge, Massachusetts 1969) p 164.
[70] *Lay Sermons* p 179. See also p 191.
[71] *Church and State* p 54.
[72] *Table Talk* p 157.
[73] *Essays on his times* 2 pp 432–3.
[74] *Table Talk* p 274.
[75] *The Friend* 1 pp 292–3.
[76] Coleridge makes the yet stronger claim that the individual has no identity, no self, apart from his nation—he is a mere abstraction. [D.P.] Calleo, [*Coleridge and the Idea of the Modern State*] (New Haven 1966) pp 80–3.

science, the principle of life: these, his key ideas, are all concerned with the apprehension and creation of unity. So in politics, he explicitly likens the state to an organism,[77] and idealises national unity. This pervading concern is an extension to all spheres of thought of a religious vision possessed from his youth up, reinforced later with Spinoza, early and renaissance neoplatonism and postKantian idealism. It sees all things as emanations from a central spiritual source, into which man, when true to his higher nature, seeks to become immersed and reabsorbed:

> 'Tis the sublime of man,
> Our noontide majesty, to know ourselves
> Parts and proportions of one wondrous whole!
> This fraternizes man, this constitutes
> Our charities and bearing. But 'tis God
> Diffused through all, that doth make one whole.[78]

The temper of his mind is synthetic rather than analytic; his inclination is not to break things into their component parts but to see them as wholes: 'Depend upon it, whatever is grand, whatever is truly organic and living, the whole is prior to the parts'. This search for 'the feeling of the one, and the magnificent power in the one'[79] entails an abandonment of individualism in all spheres of thought. Coleridge therefore argues powerfully for the reality of the nation, and advocates national unity and patriotism. But he is not totally consistent in praise of unity, and as with Burke nationalism is not absolute. His state is not and should not be a perfect unity;[80] individuality must be preserved. This has its counterpart in and perhaps stems from the religious toleration he almost always defends, and sees as the crowning glory of the Church of England.[81] In spite of his belief in religious authority and ecclesiastical guidance, he does not abandon private judgement.[82]

> In two points of view I reverence man; first, as a citizen . . . and, secondly, as a Christian. If men are neither the one nor the other, but a mere aggregation of individual

[77] R. J. White, *The Political Thought of Samuel Taylor Coleridge* (London 1938) pp 139–41.
[78] Coleridge, 'Religious Musings', *Poetical Works*, ed E. H. Coleridge (London 1967) pp 113–14 lines 126–31.
[79] Coleridge, *The Philosophical Lectures,* ed K. Coburn (London 1949) p 196.
[80] *Table Talk* p 146.
[81] Sanders p 88.
[82] Barth pp 164–5.

bipeds, who acknowledge no national unity, nor believe with me in Christ, I have no more personal sympathy with them than with the dust beneath my feet.[83]

Finally his epistemological theories do not, with those of Herder, Fichte and Hegel, maintain that knowledge is shaped by concepts and categories peculiar to the national culture: indeed the cultural relativism of these German historicists poses problems for any thinker convinced of the pentecostal mission of Christianity and of the validity of its message to all nations. In epistemology therefore Coleridge is closer to the universalism of Kant: the Ideas of Reason are the same for all and hence there is but one truth.[84] Coleridge's Christianity therefore looks away from the nation in opposite directions: towards the individual conscience, and towards eternal and universal truth.

To conclude, Englishmen of this period could draw from religion ideas and arguments to justify the apparently unjustifiable —preference for one's country. It would be a mistake however to suggest that religious ideas were simply used to defend nationalist (or anti-nationalist) positions already adopted, that religion had no impact but was merely ideologically exploited. The evidence shows that most varieties of English religion could support a moderate nationalism, but had a tendency to qualify more extreme manifestations, to militate against the total submersion of individuality and to challenge the nation with other loyalties and higher concerns.[85]

Huddersfield Polytechnic

---

[83] *Table Talk* p 162.
[84] Coleridge's avoidance of relativism is linked to his Christianity by Calleo pp 129–34.
[85] This is the judgement also of S. W. Baron, *Modern Nationalism and Religion* (New York 1947) pp 88, 129, 161; though he does not examine English thought of this period in any detail.

THE FRENCH EXILED CLERGY IN ENGLAND AND NATIONAL IDENTITY, 1790–1815

by D. T. J. BELLENGER

R EVOLUTION confuses nationality. The French Revolution drove from France's shores many émigrés who carried the conviction that they, rather than the masters of the new order, enshrined the *true* France. This sentiment was encouraged by the experience of exile which produced an exaggerated consciousness of Frenchness, especially among the clergy.

This paper has two intentions. Firstly it wishes to show how internal and external influences worked on the exiles in England to create a mentality of deep separation. Secondly it wishes to hint at the implications of this separation especially in that highly developed sense of religio-national identity which became so clear a characteristic of the emigration.

At the heart of émigré society in England was the knowledge that, strictly speaking, most of its members were not emigrants but deportees. Somewhere between four and five thousand of the émigrés in England were 'non-juring' priests, that is priests who had chosen exile in preference to accepting the new constitutional church which they considered schismatical.[1] This commonly held great refusal combined with strong local and diocesan ties (mainly Norman and Breton by origin, in exile they tended to live in groups determined by diocese[2]) made their Frenchness peculiarly resilient and their corporate identity singularly cohesive. Their letters to their friends and relations in France indicate a deep nostalgia for 'the old country' which never had a chance to diminish into the sentimentality of the long-term exile.[3] When the chance came to return to their native soil few, beside the dead,

---

[1] 4008 clergy were receiving relief on 5 December 1793, BL Add MS 18592 fol 3.
[2] For example D. T. J. Bellenger, 'The French exiled clergy in the North East', *Northern Catholic History* 2 (Newcastle 1980) p 22.
[3] [E.] Robo, [*The story of*] *a catholic parish* [*St Joan's Farnham*] (Farnham 1938) pp 33–59.

remained behind. Only one of the surviving parish clergy expelled
from Angers failed to return as soon as possible as his native city.[4]
Most of the exiled clergy had little concourse with English
people. There were exceptions. The occasional fashionable emigrant like the abbé Delille, a minor poet, who was lionised by
London society,[5] or a distinguished academic like the abbé Gervais
de la Rue, a classical archaeologist, who became an honorary fellow
of the Society of Antiquaries,[6] were able to penetrate English social
life. More commonly, however, the exiles lived on the margin.
Many tended to seek employment as tutors in private households
and as 'professors' in small private schools. Here contact was
minimal. Using 'the direct method' they rarely spoke in their
pupils' tongue.[7] The emigrant school at Penn, in Buckinghamshire,
more or less administered by Edmund Burke and paid for out of
government funds, sought (and it was not alone in this) an
education which would continue, in full splendour, the cultural
integrity of Bourbonism.[8] Uniforms were worn, the monarchy and
the church decked with vocal tributes, the sabres rattled—if at a safe
distance—and all in Buckinghamshire seemed much as it had once
in the Ile de France. Even those who took jobs, as many clergy did,
as chaplains to remote English catholic strongholds showed a
marked obliviousness to their surroundings. Cosmopolitan despite
themselves, often old and set in their ways before arrival, men like
the abbé Fidèle of Pocklington, in Yorkshire, whose four broken
English sermons came forth with monotonous regularity one
Sunday every month for twenty years, and whose wig powdering
took on the aspect of an arcane ritual, seemed unprepared to make
any concession to changed circumstances.[9] Indeed, although William Cobbett's Tutor Anglais, first published in 1795, had reached
perhaps sixty editions by 1833,[10] indicating a certain interest in

[4] J. McManners, French ecclesiastical society under the ancien régime (Manchester 1960)
p 298.
[5] E. Holland, The journal of Elizabeth Lady Holland (1791–1811), ed the Earl of
Ilchester (London 1908) 2, pp 67–8.
[6] J. Evans, History of the Society of Antiquaries (London 1956) p 198.
[7] J. H. Newman, Apologia pro vita sua (London ed 1955) p 30.
[8] J. Prior, Memoir of the life and character of the Right Hon. Edmund Burke (London
1826) 2, pp 352–9.
[9] W. B. Ullathorne, From cabin-boy to archbishop, the autobiography of archbishop
Ullathorne (London 1941) p 4.
[10] M. L. Pearl, William Cobbett, a bibliographical account of his life and times (Oxford
1953) p 26.

learning English in some quarters, it is also evident that many of the emigrants themselves compiled dictionaries and word lists nearly all concerned with teaching French rather than with assimilating English. When, in 1800, the abbé Tardy, the most successful of the French lexicographers, published a guide to London he was able to describe a whole French sub-culture.[11] The majority of the exiles gravitated to the metropolis. The nobility and the bishops made their home there, and held court. There, too, the relief committee and its formidable agent, Jean François de la Marche, bishop of Saint-Pol-de-Léon, in Brittany, held its meetings and dispersed its monies. The relief committee had started as a voluntary subscription, under the aegis of John Wilmot, MP for Coventry, who had previously been charged with the distribution of monies to the American loyalists.[12] In 1793 the committee began to come under government control, with an annual grant of two hundred thousand pounds, and as time went on became more insistent on proof of loyalty to the immortal memory of Louis XVI as well as actual need as a prerequisite of aid.[13] As 'the principles' of those who received money were known to the committee, wrote Wilmot to Charles Long, joint secretary of the treasury, 'it would be a good idea if all were to appear before the French committee', and 'state their principles', and if 'those who do not appear, or who do not give a satisfactory account of themselves should be sent out of the kingdom, or otherwise disposed of, as the secretary of state should think proper, under the Alien Bill . . .'[14] The gradation of income by status, and the emphasis on loyalty to the ancien régime were fully in line with the character of the emigration which preserved the rigid class divisions of pre-revolutionary society.

The area of London an emigrant lived in was often, if not always, an indication of his social position, or rather his *ci-devant* social position.[15] The 'Faubourg Saint Germain' was translated, as it were, to somewhere between Baker Street and Oxford Circus; the lesser but still well-born nobles tended to settle in the vicinity of Marylebone, Somers Town and Bloomsbury; the provincial

[11] [J.] Tardy, [*Manuel du voyageur à Londres*] (London 1800).
[12] J. Eardley-Wilmot, *Historical view of the commission for enquiring into the losses, services and claims of the American loyalists* (London 1815).
[13] PRO MS T 93 I, 19 December 1793, unfoliated.
[14] PRO MS T 93 8, p 30.
[15] J. Vidalenc, *Les émigrés Français 1789–1825* (Caen 1963) pp 233–4.

emigrants sought accommodation in Southwark or on the fringes of London in places like Hampstead and Tottenham.[16] Some lived in greviously miserable poverty, too proud to accept charity and unable to obtain suitable employment.[17] Others lived, in reduced state, much as they had in France. The archbishop of Narbonne, Arthur de Dillon, was one whose scale of values was firmly set in 'the grand century', and whose way of life survived exile.[18] Some years before the revolution, in conversation with Louis XVI, he had revealed his attitude to life. 'It is said', remarked the king, 'that you, monsignor, have great debts from gambling'. 'I will direct my steward, your majesty, to enquire into the matter', replied the archbishop. 'But I am told also, monsignor, that you hunt a good deal. Is it not a bad example to your curés?' 'Well, sire, for them it would undoubtedly be a grave fault to go hunting', concluded Dillon, 'but for me it is only a taste I have inherited from my ancestors'.[19] This flavour of witty wordly wisdom stayed with the archbishop in London, where his life as *doyen* of the French episcopate in London appears to have been a long round of social functions, mounting debts and policy meetings which despite his advanced years (he died aged ninety-two in 1806[20]) and increasing deafness were a logical continuation of his previous life. It was, at one level, as if the revolution had never happened. Yet, in one sense, Dillon was exceptional. For many the revolution had been a chastening experience and in searching for a truer Frenchness many turned to the mothballed Gallican church in exile as the most perfect expression of corporate identity.

It was perhaps only in the French chapels which mushroomed in London that the class-conscious *ci-devant* ancien régime could truly be termed united.[21] The failure of the royalist attack at Quiberon,[22] the virtual dismissal of the Comte d'Artois to the gloomy splendours of Holyrood House,[23] and the growing duration of the exiles' stay drove them into a *recherché du temps perdu*, into liturgical ceremonies which endlessly calling up the ghosts of the terror and

[16] *Ibid* p 234.
[17] Duchesse de Gontaut, *Memoirs* (London 1894) p 51.
[18] A. Sabarthès, *Arthur-Richard Dillon, demier archevêque de Narbonne* (Narbonne 1943).
[19] *The Jerningham letters* ed E. Castle (London 1896) I, p xxxix
[20] *Memoirs of Madame de la Tour du Pin*, ed F. Harcourt (London 1969) p 5.
[21] M. Weiner, *The French exiles 1789–1815* (London 1960) p 124.
[22] J. Godechot, *The counter-revolution* (London 1972) pp 254–60.
[23] V. W. Beach, *Charles X of France* (Boulder, Colorado 1971) p 89.

'the martyrdom' of Louis XVI gave a melancholy and spiritual tone to the emigration.[24] The revolution was seen as the work of Antichrist[25], and the only salvation as a complete return to what there had been before.[26] In the formation of that belief the *ésprit de clocher* provided the central catalyst. Among the tattered flags in their small chapels the emigrants wept and conjured up the Zion of their longings.[27]

Two men, in particular, fed the introverted character of much of the emigration, one the Breton bishop de la Marche,[28] the other the abbé Guy Carron, another Breton, friend and confidant of the young Lamennais, writer and educator, philanthropist and polemicist, the 'Vincent de Paul' of the emigration.[29] The bishop of Saint-Pol-de-Léon had begun his career as a soldier, and he never lost the military touch.[30] Never flinching in his loyalty to the old ways he had established wide contacts in England and was soon relied upon not only by the other Frenchmen but also by the British government. In this capacity he was asked to advise on the suitability of candidates for various missions, including the ill-fated Quiberon adventure.[31] He demanded a high degree of loyalty from his subordinates, and although, legally speaking, he had no episcopal jurisdiction his word was law. In his printed *avis* to the clergy he laid down strict rules of obedience. 'You know, Gentlemen', he wrote, 'and it is fitting that the people of England should learn from your conduct, that our religion teaches that wherever we are settled, it is our duty to observe the laws, and to respect the constitutions established for the public good'.[32] Those who thought differently to the bishop soon found themselves leaving the country.[33] However wide a chain of authority restricted the clergy there

[24] G. F. de Grandmaison-y-Bruno, *La chapelle Français à Londres* (London/Paris 1862).
[25] A. Barruel, *Memoirs illustrating the history of Jacobinism* (London 1797) 1, p xxi.
[26] Lubersac, *Apologie de la religion et la monarchie Françoise réunies: grandeur, force et majesté de ces deux puissances spirituelle et temporelle* (London 1802).
[27] B. Ward, *Catholic London a century ago* (London 1905) p 46.
[28] [L.] Kerbirion, [*Jean-François de la Marche*] (Quimper 1924).
[29] D. T. J. Bellenger, 'The abbé Carron', *London Recusant* 6 (London 1976) pp 19–36; Dom Jausions, *Vie de l'abbé Carron* (Paris 1866).
[30] Kerbirion p 3.
[31] BL Add MS 37856 The bishop of Saint Pol-de-Léon to William Windham, June 1794, fols 74–6.
[32] J. F. de la Marche, *Pastoral letter and ordinance* (London 1891).
[33] A[rchives of the] A[rchbishop of] W[estminster], Bishop Douglass's Diary December 1798.

was a weak link in the desperate neediness of some. With the exception of the Middlesex Hospital, which graciously set a ward apart for the French,[34] and limited government aid, there was little provision for care until the abbé Carron opened up his 'cradle to grave' establishments in Somers Town. Schools, hospitals, baths, old people's homes, two chapels, a library and a seminary all sprang up under the watchful eye of the abbé who still found time to write a series of lives of 'the martyrs' of the revolution, and many devotional works[35] which became part of the staple reading of a generation of restoration emigrants.[36] Thus, in London, with body, soul and mind adequately catered for the exiles were able to continue living without paying much attention to what was going on in the country which surrounded them.

Outside London co-existence was the dominant motif of life. One striking example of this was the self-contained society of the King's House at Winchester where several hundred exiled priests lived as a disciplined community for several years.[37] Another example was the Cistercian monastery established at Lulworth in Dorest, an institution which is of interest, too, in the re-establishment of the monastic life in England.[38] Although the 'monk' as a figure of Gothick fiction was very popular in the 1790s, Matthew Lewis's novel of that name was perhaps the most sensational work of fiction of this generation; the very nature of the 'monk' generally depicted was so remote from reality that the religious seemed to be a man from another planet. Yet, when Thomas Weld of Lulworth Castle, the catholic landowner with the largest estates in England, presented a farm to a community of Trappist monks they carried on with their lives as if being a monk was much like being a miller or a cowherd. The monastic round was followed with complete obedience according to the observances of La Trappe. Although there were some defections the community grew and subsisted for

[34] Middlesex Hospital Archives, Fair Minute Book 1791–8, pp 115–16.
[35] P. Broutin, 'La pieté sacerdotale au début du XIXᵉ siècle', *Revue d'ascétique et de mystique* 20 (Toulouse 1939) pp 168–75.
[36] Carron's *L'ecclésiastique accompli ou plan d'une vie vraiment sacerdotale* (London 1799) was in its fifth edition at Paris in 1823.
[37] J. Milner, *The history civil and ecclesiastical and survey of the antiquities of Winchester* (Winchester 1799) 2, pp 167–9.
[38] D. T. J. Bellenger, 'The French Revolution and the religious orders. Three communities 1789–1815', D Rev 98 (1980) pp 26–34.

almost thirty years. The secret of their survival was their complete attachment to the past.[39]

It was not always easy for the exiles to survive in an England devoted for most of the emigration period to the destruction of the French nation, and the hostility of many helped to increase the life apart which was the norm for the exile. The ordinary people were reluctant to admit that any Frenchman could be a good thing. The clergy of the established church made constant appeals for the confessors of 'King and altar' from France but their words, as a collection of letters in Lambeth Palace suggests, were frequently met with sullen silence.[40] J. B. Burges, under secretary of state in 1793, reflected that 'the fools here are opening subscriptions for their relief and support, which I understand our own poor take amiss, and in my judgement, not without reason'.[41] And take it amiss they did. Priests and Frenchmen before Englishmen? What sort of system was this? 'No jews. No wooden shoes. No popery'.[42] These were basic verities, and throughout the period of the emigration there was trouble and misunderstanding. Emigrants were sometimes found murdered, clubbed,[43] or, in at least one case, poisoned.[44] The deep rooted distrust which in 1792 and 1794 had greeted the royalist refugees as, admittedly, the most unlikely of Jacobins and republicans[45] was as strong in 1804 when the militia at Dorchester in Dorset had to be called into the Lulworth estate to search out Jerome Bonaparte who, it was said, had landed on the English coast with fellow-plotters and arms, and was hiding among the brothers in the Trappist priory. Needless to say nothing was found but the *grand peur* of the countryside was only dispelled when a printed broadsheet, authenticated by officers of church and state, was circulated which said all was well.[46] But there was always something threatening about these dark, silent, strangely spoken foreigners, especially as they were catholics. It is surprising that more was not made by polemicists and popular opinion of the menace to protestant England inherent in the reception of so many

[39] *Ibid* p 33.
[40] Lambeth Palace Library Fulham Papers 150.
[41] Auckland, *Journal and correspondence* (London 1861) 2, p 442.
[42] M. D. George, *London life in the XVIIIth century* (London 1925) p 134.
[43] BL Add MS 18592 fol 101.
[44] M. J. Bailey, *Ashley*, Staffordshire catholic history 4 (Birmingham 1963/4) p 34.
[45] Robo, *A catholic parish* p 25.
[46] Dorset Record Office Weld Papers R 17, printed notice 14 August 1803.

catholics. But the self contained nature of the emigrants left little room for criticism on the grounds of prosletysing; where (and these were very few) efforts were made they were stamped out ruthlessly.[47] There was some anti-catholic feeling prompted by the emigrants including an attack on T. J. Mathias's influential satirical poem, 'The Pursuits of Literature'.[48] To some extent, at least, the people with their government, were beginning to find agreement that it was now the French revolution and not the Roman church which formed the main threat to national law and order.[49].

The government was at first officially neutral towards the events in France, but as time went on and the worst excesses of the revolution became more apparent neutrality was transformed into hostility. Yet, even so, the government was reluctant to waste too much money on redeeming Europe. It had its own interest to look to. The émigrés were to be used as part of a cut-price package. If at first men like Edmund Burke in his *Reflections* and in his appeal for the suffering clergy of France' were voices crying in the wilderness, their suggestion of using the victims of the revolution as living parables of loyalty soon caught on. The committee for emigrant relief was too important to be left to the do-gooders. 'In my opinion', wrote Burke to Lord Buckingham,[51] this charity is as politick as it is noble. We have at last put the war on its right footing, if not in practice, at least in open and avowed profession. It is a war to civilize France, in order to prevent the rest of Europe from being barbarized; the French clergy are the great instrument, by which this end is to be accomplished—and if we can make any serious impression upon France by arms in the beginning, this clergy will be of more effect in the progress of the Business, than a hundred thousand soldiers'. The extent to which the charity became associated with the war against France was shown in the way in which William Wilberforce regarded becoming a member of the relief committee in 1793 as sufficient proof that his sympathies were on the side of counter revolution.[52]

[47] AAW XLVI 1795–6 p 136, John Milner to bishop Douglass 10 January 1796.
[48] T. J. Mathias, *The pursuits of literature, third dialogue* (London 1796).
[49] E. Halevy, *England in 1815* (London 1949) p 476.
[50] First published in *The Evening Mail* (17–19 September 1792) and later distributed as a pamphlet, reprinted in *The Annual Register* (1792) and translated into French.
[51] P. J. Marshall and J. A. Woods, *The correspondence of Edmund Burke* 7 (Cambridge/Chicago 1968) p 498.
[52] R. I. and S. Wilberforce, *The life of William Wilberforce* (London 1838) 1, pp 368–9.

It is not clear, however, that the beneficiaries of the charity continued to exercise political pull. Although the bishops were frequently used as a channel of information for testing the temper of France, or a part of France, as the emigration grew longer the channels of communication became more bleared. In 1793 the exiled bishop of Bayeux had been able to receive some wine from his cellar, through a friend, when his former property had been auctioned.[53] By 1799 not only had many of the schemes of reconquest failed but Napoleon had appeared on the horizon, and the French church, or what was left of it, had become used to living without its bishops. It was the tragedy of Quiberon that had exposed the irrelevance of the émigrés. If in Urbain de Hercé bishop of Dol-en-Bretagne, *martyrisé* at Quiberon, the seers of the restoration could find yet another martyr what was really needed was success, not blood.[54] So, even as political tools, the appeals of the clergy in exile and their aristocratic backers to their flocks in France fell on deaf ears. The religious zeal of the royalist invasion collapsed into nothing. The chouanage itself, restricted to the dark woods and to sordid back streets, had become just another species of night bird.

In England the government still had to look after the emigrants it had built up as exemplars of what a good Frenchman was. They were really rather an embarrassment. The first thought of government was to shift them out of England, and resettle them as far away as possible. Canada, bleak and remote, and with a substantial French catholic population, seemed an ideal place. A mission was sent out as early as 1793 to explore the ground, and its report was favourable.[55] Lack of interest, and a reluctance to use large sums of money, ensured that nothing happened. Nothing, that is, except to give the emigrants themselves yet another reason for fear and insecurity. The administration, in the end, was forced to compromise. As far as possible those who could were accommodated in government-administered centres, where they could be kept out of harm's way, living or partly living, awaiting a restoration.[56]

[53] O. H. Hufton, *Bâyeux in the late eighteenth century* (Oxford 1967) p 177.
[54] C. Robert, *Urbain de Hercé* (Paris 1890).
[55] A. Bois, 'L'Angleterre et le clergé Français refugié pendant la révolution', *Proceedings of the Royal Society of Canada* 3 (1886) p 80.
[56] BL Add MS 18591 fol 3.

The clearest indication of the alienation of the émigrés from English life is perhaps the relationship between the English catholics and the French emigrant clergy. The vicars apostolic in England made little use of them. In London, for example, in 1795 there were over one thousand, seven hundred French Roman catholic priests.[56] None of them was serving as pastor to an English congregation. Some served French congregations (indeed in 1800 there were more French catholic chapels in London than English ones)[58] but there seemed to be little contact between the two groups. Temperamentally the English catholics were a 'martyr church', shunning the light of day. They had little to sympathise with in the triumphalism of the French who represented a church that may have been past its best but retained its pretensions. The divergence widened. As in the person of bishop John Milner[59] the English catholics continued to underline their curious blend of patriotism and papalism, the French clergy under the leadership of bishop de la Marche, with theologians like bishop Alexandre de Thémines, who advocated a Gallican separatism,[60] and the abbé Blanchard, who led a schismatical movement, preaching their gospel, the French exiled clergy came nearer and nearer to an open breach with Rome and the proclamation of an exalted role for the catholic French nation.

The exiled clergy thrown in upon themselves by many influences, self inflicted as well as external, tended to see France as a static entity and clothe it in an unreal nationalism which enshrined their hopes and fears and was part of a wider inability to come to terms with changed circumstances. An extreme viewpoint which articulated these feelings is the one presented by the exiled bishop of Blois, Alexandre de Thémines, in his *considérations sur l'état présent et sur la fin des choses*.

The bishop's *considerations* are partly autobiographical, partly a last will and testament, and partly (and most importantly) an

[57] BL Add MS 18592 fol 66.
[58] Tardy p 213.
[59] F. C. Husenbeth, *Life of the right rev. John Milner, DD* (Dublin 1862).
[60] D[ownside] A[bbey] A[rchives], papers of Alexandre de Thémines 717 'Considérations sur l'état présent et sur la fin des choses'.
[61] A. Dechêne, *Contre Pie VII et Bonaparte. Le Blanchardisme 1801–1829* (Paris 1932).

exposition and apologia of the exile. The enemy is identified as change in any form. On the verge of the apocalypse, as he saw it, he was not concerned with *temps* only with *éternité*. The thing to be defended at all costs was the integrity of a France whose national identity was encapsulated in the counterbalance of throne and altar. This was as immutable as the office of bishop which de Thémines saw as the cornerstone of the church.[63] The Napoleonic concordat had, by violating the sacred office of bishop in demanding the resignation of the surviving pre-revolutionary hierarchy, committed the sin of 'apostolicide' and had revealed the invalidity of the Pius VII's pontificate.[64] Indeed in the bishop's view the rot had spread to such an extent that even the restoration of the French monarchy was not in itself sufficient; only a complete return to the pre-revolutionary model would be satisfactory.[65]

The bishop's views were paralleled, sometimes in a less forthright way, by many writers of the emigration including the much imitated abbé Augustin Barruel whose belief that the revolution stemmed from a deep seated plot against the ancien régime,[66] strengthened the exiles' position, and, most tellingly in the life of the exiles which bore witness to de Thémines's ideal. Such views were an important element in the creation of what is called 'the two Frances'; the royalist, Gallican, inward-looking French church in exile fed a view of the nation quite contrary to the republican, free thinking, liberal view given life by the revolution. The royalist view would have had far less force if the French exiled clergy had not lived a lonely life in England as a chosen people, a nation set apart, living examples of a French national view which even the revolution could not destroy.

Downside School

[62] DAA 717, 'Considérations', 2 p 114.
[63] *Ibid* p 511
[64] DAA 717, 'Considérations', 3 p 131.
[65] DAA 715, Thémines's letter to the King 15 March 1815 p 40.
[66] J. M. Roberts, *The mythology of the secret societies* (London 1974) pp 199–219.

NATIONALITY AND LIBERTY, PROTESTANT AND CATHOLIC: ROBERT SOUTHEY'S BOOK OF THE CHURCH[1]

by SHERIDAN GILLEY

THE Victorian liberal Roman catholic historian lord Acton thought that the history of the world was one of the growth of liberty. By liberty, he meant national independence and freedom of speech and worship, the liberties of nineteenth-century liberalism: and in his conception of the past, he drew on the whig interpretation of English history[2] as a conflict between a progressive tradition and a reactionary one: between churches, parties and classes representing either freedom or authority. The classic statement of the idea is the whig lord Macaulay's in 1835:

> Each of those great and ever-memorable struggles, Saxon against Norman, Villein against Lord, Protestant against Papist, Roundhead against Cavalier, Dissenter against Churchman, Manchester against Old Sarum, was, in its own order and season, a struggle, on the result of which were staked the dearest interests of the human race; and every man who, in the contest which, in his time, divided our country distinguished himself on the right side, is entitled to our gratitude and respect.[3]

This whig progressivism in its crudity is epitomized in *1066 and All That's* distinction between the roundheads who were right but repulsive, and the cavaliers who were wrong but romantic: Saxons, villeins, protestants, roundheads, dissenters and Mancunian liberals were right, and Normans, lords, papists, cavaliers, churchmen and

[1] For help in the preparation of this paper, I would especially thank Dr [A. L.] Sanders, of Birkbeck College, London, whose thesis [*Some Aspects of the Use of Anglo-Saxon Material in Nineteenth Century Literature*] (Cambridge M. Litt. 1975) contains a discussion of Southey's *Book of the Church*.
[2] Herbert Butterfield, *The Whig Interpretation of History* (London 1931).
[3] *Critical and Historical Essays*, 2 vols (London 1946) I, p 293.

the rotten-borough jobbers of Old Sarum were wrong. This perspective may seem outdated, but is alive among socialist historians of the right if repulsive working classes, and the Marxist theologians for whom the holy ghost grows out of the barrel of a gun. For underlying whig and Marxist historiography is a secularized providence which declares that as some men are right and others wholly wrong, so God, or his substitute, the historical process, is with the big battalions, and will make the right side win. This is an inversion of the conservative conviction that the powers that be are of God, and are right because He ordains them; and it is open to similar criticism. Yet providentialist understandings of English history as a conflict of freedom and authority, point to an important fact: that the English idea of liberty is not simply the achievement of Macaulay's progressives, but has arisen from the clash of radicals and reactionaries, who have both thereby contributed towards it. The freedoms of Britain are by-products of controversies which neither side has quite lost or won. These conflicts have also spurred English historical study to produce the protestant and catholic, whig and tory, conservative and radical interpretations of the English past. They complement one another, with due allowance for prejudice, for when historians disagree, they are seldom merely disagreeing about history.

There is a similar explanation of the liberty of opinion which prevails in the church of England. As the creation by a number of traditions, she claims the glory of medieval Roman catholics and protestant reformers, of puritan and high church divines, and even of men like Wesley and Newman who have founded or seceded to other communions. The history of the church of England is like the history of England, a clash and conflict between rival traditions, Erastian and anti-Erastian, catholic and protestant, conservative and liberal, sectarian and latitudinarian: and her internal freedoms have emerged because of the losing sides in her history, none has quite lost the fight or been excluded from her. Despite expulsions and secessions of liberal, protestant, and popish-minded clergy, she retains the whole spectrum of English religious opinion, from the crypto-Roman catholic to the crypto-infidel. Thus the curious insularity of the church of England has been offset by the self-contradictory complexity of her theologies: despite the claims for Anglican theological method, the diversity of Anglican theologies defines Anglican theology, and the unity of the church of England is not susceptible of theological definition. The church's unity is of a different character: it arises from her self-understanding as a profoundly national institution, with a sense of continuity through fifteen hundred years, and with her own part played in every phase of English history.

This was the church of England's understanding of herself, as an equal partner of the English state, co-extensive with the English people: as the English state in its spiritual aspect, as the English people at prayer; or as Matthew Arnold described the church, as the 'most national and natural'[4] of institutions. At no time, however, was that status more sharply questioned than in the third decade of the nineteenth century as England entered on her imperial century as mistress of the seas and workshop of the world. The challenge induced a crisis of self-identity about the church's role as the church of the English. The industrial revolution had impaired her parochial system, by reducing villages with churches to hamlets, while no provision was made for new churches to accommodate the poor of the huge new factory towns. The agricultural and industrial revolutions had increased some ecclesiastical incomes, and made the church even more attractive than of yore as a featherbed and source of outdoor relief for aristocratic unemployables, by enhancing the inequalities in clerical wealth which had existed in the church since the middle ages, and which neither papists nor puritans had reformed.[5] As privileged persons, the high church parsons were identified with the unpopular monarchy of their fat Adonis, George IV, and with the tory administrations which had ruled England since the outbreak of the French revolution, and which had repressed political unrest since the end of the Napoleonic wars.

More than ever did the church of England then seem to be the tory party at prayer. The ramshackle medieval machinery staffed by plutocratic prelates and starving curates could do nothing to stem the mushroom growth of protestant nonconformity after 1790, nor despite the reverend Mr Malthus, the multiplication of Irish Roman catholics, nor the spread of a vicious republican anticlericalism rare in English history. Never it seemed did so many Englishmen wish to strangle their king with the entrails of the

[4] Cited Basil Willey, *Nineteenth Century Studies* (London 1964) p 82.
[5] A. D. Gilbert, *Religion and Society in Industrial England: Church, Chapel and Social Change, 1740–1914* (London 1976).

archbishop of Canterbury. By the late 1820s, an unholy alliance of nonconformists, Roman catholics and anticlerical whigs and radicals seemed poised to smash the Anglican monopoly of national and local government, to repeal the Test and Corporation acts which excluded catholics and dissenters from public office, to undermine the church's control of the universities, primary education and charity, to abolish the rates or tithes which every household paid the parish church, and to sweep away the laws and customs by which almost the entire population were christened, married and buried with the rites of the church of England.[6] The Test and Corporation acts were repealed in 1828 and catholic emancipation came in 1829, but the erosion of Anglican privilege took fifty years, and left the church an establishment, with a state connexion and residual rights which have preserved her national pretensions. Moreover from the 1830s, the church was to be in limited measure reformed for her most urgent tasks. By 1830, however, the whole rickety structure seemed about to collapse, as dissenters, papists and radicals insisted that the church of England had lost her role as the church of the English.

One curious byproduct of this alliance after 1820 between English radicals and Roman catholics has enjoyed a continuing readership among catholics: the protestant William Cobbett's *History of the Protestant Reformation* published from 1824 and typical of the polemic of the period in its appeal to history. Cobbett's denigration of the English reformers as plunderers of the church and poor was popular among catholic controversialists with their Tudor martyrology; and like Cobbett's work the catholic contribution to the controversy of the day had an immediate political relevance and long-term causes in the national character of English catholicism.

The English catholics had been granted freedom of worship by the relief act of 1791. As a small community led by lay noblemen and gentlemen, they hoped for a further measure of catholic

---

[6] For standard accounts, see S. C. Carpenter, *Church and People, 1789–1889* (London 1933) pp 49–67; Francis Warre Cornish, *The English Church in the Nineteenth Century*, 2 parts (London 1910) I pp 100–23; Owen Chadwick, *The Victorian Church*, 2 parts (London 1971) I pp 7–166; and the specialist accounts in W. L. Mathieson, *English Church Reform 1815–1840* (London 1923); Geoffrey Best, *Temporal Pillars. Queen Anne's Bounty, the Ecclesiastical Commissioners, and the Church of England* (Cambridge 1964); and, on the sequel, G. I. T. Machin, *Politics and the Church in Great Britain, 1832 to 1868* (Oxford 1977).

emancipation to give them access to the principal professions and to public office under the crown, and the social acceptability and political influence to which their rank and riches entitled them. As landowners, the English catholic gentry shared the outlook of their class. They loved England and her king, if not her church. In their own eyes they were patriots as stout as any, and were rightly part of the political nation, though unfairly excluded from it. The protestant charge of treason against them for acknowledging a foreign prince, the pope, struck at their fondest aspirations and cherished self-image as Englishmen.[7]

This was indeed a sensitive theme, for the conflicting loyalties to fatherland and faith had divided English catholics for centuries. The dilemma dated from Henry VIII's executions for denying his headship of the church: it was sharpened by the bull of Pius V deposing Elizabeth. The bull separated catholics into those who accepted the pope's deposing power, and rejected Elizabeth as heretic and usurper; and those who rejecting or ignoring the bull, saw Elizabeth as heretic but rightful queen. The outcome was that English catholics wasted much energy fighting one another. By 1790 the deposing power had fallen into disuse, but it haunted protestant memories, and in 1791, Roman catholics denied it on oath as a condition of their newly-won freedom. The form of the oath then bitterly divided them, and the deposing power remained an embarrassment to them, and a weapon in the hands of their foes.[8]

After 1791, the division among catholics survived through the activities of the lawyer Charles Butler and leading catholic laymen, who in return for emancipation were prepared to grant the government a veto on the appointment of their bishops, as security of their church's good behaviour. The proposal was opposed by the Irish bishops and their English representative, John Milner, an old foe of Butler and vicar apostolic of the midland district from 1803. For Milner, Butler's plan meant improper non-catholic interference

---

[7] See Eamon Duffy, 'Doctor Douglass and Mister Berington—an eighteenth century retraction', *DR* 88 (July 1970) pp 246–69; and 'Ecclesiastical Democracy Detected: I (1779–1787); II (1787–1796)' *Recusant History* 10 (January and October 1970) pp 193–209 and 309–31. John Bossy, *The English Catholic Community* (London 1975), is a sustained apology for the native English Roman catholic tradition.
[8] E. I. Watkin, *Roman Catholicism in England from the Reformation to 1950* (London 1957) pp 156 *seq.*

in the church, and lay interference with the clergy.

The theological difference between Butler and Milner was reflected in their attitudes to church-state relations. Butler was an Anglo-Gallican, in English parlance, a 'cisalpine,' believing in national catholic churches and a limited papacy; Milner was a 'pro-papal' ultramontane. Moreover where Butler was eirenical, Milner was a polemicist, the 'English Athanasius',[9] as Newman styled him, a writer, a biter and a fighter, who defended the exclusive claims of the Roman church in a warfare culminating in 1818 in the publication of *The End of Religious Controversy*. As controversialists, he and Butler had much in common. Like Butler, Milner represented shared Anglican and catholic doctrine as Anglican acknowledgement of catholic truth, while Butler admired Milner's polemical writing and cited it in his own.[10] Indeed no popery polemic was to unite them when Milner's *End of Religious Controversy* turned out to be its beginning.

Yet there were essential differences between Milner and Butler. Butler wished to be thought 'broad-minded and charitable'[11] to protestants if not to ultramontane catholics; Milner's polemic against protestants and 'cisalpine' catholics made no pretence to be impartial. Moreover Milner was an enthusiast for continental catholic miracles and hagiography, for the cult of the sacred heart,[12] and for the more spectacular kind of conventual sanctity, and claimed illumination from a Roman nun who was later disgraced as a fraud.[13] Butler underplayed these alien and exotic aspects of catholicism, by defining the essential minimum of what catholics must believe. This is not to deny his attachment to his church; his asceticism was distinctly Roman. But he shared with his uncle Alban Butler, author of the famous *Lives of the Saints*, a restrained English piety; and a similar note was struck by other writers— Lingard, Berington and Kirk—who in the first quarter of the

---

[9] Wilfrid Ward, *The Life of John Henry Cardinal Newman*, 2 vols (London 1913) 1, p 119.
[10] He is said to have sat up all night to read the *End of Religious Controversy* as soon as it appeared: [Bernard] Ward, [*The Eve of Catholic Emancipation*], 3 vols (London 1912) 2, p 287.
[11] See 'Charles Butler' in *DNB*.
[12] Ward, 2, pp 102–3.
[13] *Ibid* pp 113–15.

nineteenth century, effected a catholic literary renaissance in England.[14]

The bulk of their work was history and polemic reflecting their ambiguous relations to the English state and nation. On the one hand, they were loyal to their church; on the other, they sought to make catholicism attractive to the average Briton by criticizing past ecclesiastical corruptions, persecutions and excesses of papal power, especially the deposing power, while painting in glowing terms the church's services to the laws and liberties of England. This difficult reconciliation of catholic apologetic with a critical attitude was best achieved by a priest John Lingard, in his *History of England*.[15] Lingard wrote with polemical intent to justify Rome's ways to Englishmen, but he did so with scholarly accuracy, a novel passion for unearthing unpublished documents and a judicious moderation of tone calculated to win him a protestant audience as a dispassionate historian. This muted the providentialist insistence that God was always with the catholics. Certainly in Lingard's *History*, He was not always with the pope or the jesuits or Thomas à Becket, whom Lingard treated with an impartiality that Milner denounced as heretical. To some protestants this suavity showed an insidious cunning more frightening than Milner's intemperance, for more subtly than Cobbett, who used Lingard as a source,[16] Lingard queried the national claims and religious pretensions of the church of England.

The established church had many high church defenders; but they had to fight both catholics and the 'rational' radicals possessed by a different idea. Is the church of England useful, to make men happy? Her condition admitted but one answer: to defend her thus was to defend the indefensible. The conservative must of course defend reality, warts and all, unlike the radical who need only defend the purity of his own ideal. But what if the reality is a species of walking wart? A different reply was suggested by a new kind of romantic nationalism. Against radicals and catholics, Anglicans invoked an ideal of the church of England as she had been and ought to be: by painting her services in the past, as the

[14] *Ibid* I, pp 270–304: compare my 'John Lingard and the Catholic Revival' *SCH* 14 (1976) pp 313–27.
[15] [Martin] Haile and [Edwin] Bonney, [*Life and Letters of John Lingard 1771–1851*] (London 1911).
[16] James Sambrook, *William Cobbett* (London 1973) p 136.

embodiment of the nation's highest spiritual achievement, the guardian of its civilisation and culture, and thereby the guarantor of its freedom. It was in this belief that in the 1820s, two English poets turned to English history, for their defence of the established church. They were the poet laureate, Robert Southey, and his friend and successor as laureate, William Wordsworth. Like our present poet laureate, that arch-exponent of the Englishness of the English church, they articulated the homespun loyalties—and prejudice—of Englishmen without power to express them.

It is usually argued that their Anglicanism was simply political conservatism, as Wordsworth and Southey abandoned the revolutionary idealism of their youth in which they had planned a perfect new society, a pantisocracy, on the banks of the Susquehanna river. Thus their later romantic religiosity is deplored as the fruit of political reaction by lord Clark of *Civilisation*: that 'Few episodes in history are more depressing than . . . Wordsworth saying that he would give his life for the Church of England'.[17] Yet it is a saying which civilisation must record: and there is a continuity between the youthful radicalism of the lake poets and the religious nationalism in which they saw fulfilled their early ideals of nationality and liberty. Not that their religion was solely political, but politics entered into those primary loves of nature, family, country, and fellow countrymen through which they returned to the church of their fathers. Despite Wordsworth's early flirtation with the French revolution and the French lady who bore his child, his antecedents were impeccably Anglican. His brother Christopher Wordsworth was master of Trinity College, Cambridge, editor of a six volume *Ecclesiastical Biography* of the English reformers, who tried to prove against Lingard that Charles had written his alleged testament, *The Eikon Basilike*, a favourite manual of high church piety.[18] Of Wordsworth's nephews, one, his biographer and literary executor, became an immensely learned

[17] *Civilisation* (London 1971) pp 304–5. A possible source for the remark is the *Diary, Reminiscences and Correspondence of Henry Crabb Robinson*, ed Thomas Sadler 3 vols (London 1869) I, p 389 (31 May 1812): 'Wordsworth defended earnestly the Church Establishment. He even said he would shed his blood for it'. On the other hand he still thought 'All our ministers are so vile' and could not remember when he had last been in church.
[18] *Who wrote Eikon Basilike? considered and answered, in two letters addressed to his Grace the Archbishop of Canterbury* (London 1824); *Documentary Supplement* (London 1825). For the sequel, see footnote 66.

bishop of Lincoln; another was bishop of St Andrews. The Wordsworth family loyalty to the church implied a loyalty to the ancient civil and ecclesiastical polity of England; and the same was true of Robert Southey. Of his children, one son, his biographer, became a clergyman; a daughter married a cousin, another clergyman, and a third child was the wife of the reverend J. Wood Warter, editor of Southey's *Common Place Book*, and a distinguished antiquarian. Religious feeling also informed Southey and Wordsworth's idealisation of the poor, who they insisted, were materials for great poetry. Their own poems about them do not prove the point, but they extolled pedlars, paupers and peasants, at the cost of perpetrating their worst excesses of sentimentality and bathos. This compassion inspired Southey's early revolutionary poem *Wat Tyler,* published in 1817 by his radical foes to embarrass him, and his tory paternalist enthusiasm for laws to protect factory workers: with the difference that his later concern for the poor invoked Christian morals and religion.

The neanderthal conservatism of Wordsworth's worship of nature was closer still to the heart of Anglican nationalism. His earliest spiritual experience was his delight in the English landscape, and in the pantheist English God revealed in English sunsets and forests and waterfalls. The local particularity of his love of the hamlets and dales around his native lakes, like his love of its peasantry, was exactly mirrored in the local particularity of his love of the Anglican religion. Thus his idolatry of English institutions was an extension of his love of the land and people who had created them, and had been created by them; and they all had their virtue from the one divine source which had made English hearts and English fields, and the English church and state, so that family and friends, and the very pattern of the countryside and ancient constitution, were all bound up with the single loyalty to the lord who had given them life. This conviction that everything in Britain is if not the best of the worlds, better than anywhere else as the creator's special handiwork, might be called gut toryism. Wordsworth and Southey called it patriotism. It is difficult to define more closely than this their most intimate sense of good fortune and gratitude to the kindly providence which had made them Englishmen.

Thus even as conservatives they wrote about a uniquely English freedom fostered by English nationalism and religion. Wordsworth developed the theme in his *Ecclesiastical Sketches*, a collection of sonnets on Anglican church history published in 1822.[19] Independently, then in conscious parallelism, Southey wrote a prose history of the church of England, entitled *The Book of the Church*, published early in 1824. The theme of the work is summed up in its concluding paragraph for which Southey was nominated to parliament in the tory interest by lord Radnor. The church of England, wrote Southey,

> has rescued us, first from heathenism, then from papal idolatry and superstition; it has saved us from temporal as well as spiritual despotism. We owe to it our moral and intellectual character as a nation; much of our private happiness, much of our public strength. Whatever should weaken it, would in the same degree injure the common weal; whatever should overthrow it, would in sure and immediate consequence bring down the goodly fabric of that Constitution, whereof it is a constituent and necessary part. If the friends of the Constitution understand this as clearly as its enemies, and act upon it as consistently and as actively, then will the Church and State be safe, and with them the liberty and the prosperity of our country.[20]

Here was a dangerously providentialist theme: with the British constitution as the embodiment of the holy ghost, and God an English tory. Yet so Southey was convinced that the deity had preeminently blessed Great Britain with the gifts of British law and liberty, through his gift of the Anglican religion. Thus as with Wordsworth, Southey's nationalism was entwined with his toryism, as with his Anglicanism: a set of loyalties confirmed for him by the French revolutionary chaos across the channel. In 1795, Southey was in Portugal, and saw reason 'to thank God that I am an Englishman'.[21] He projected a history of Portugal which bore

---

[19] First called the *Ecclesiastical Sonnets* in the edition of 1837. Wordsworth noted (24 January 1822) that

> The Catholic Question, which was agitated in Parliament about that time, kept my thoughts in the same course; and it struck me that certain points in the Ecclesiastical History of our Country might advantageously be presented to view in verse . . . When this work was far advanced, I was agreeably surprised to find that my friend, Mr Southey, had been engaged with similar views in writing a concise History of the Church *in* England. If our Productions, thus unintentionally coinciding, shall be found to illustrate each other, it will prove a high gratification to me, which I am sure my friend will participate.

The Poetical Works of Wordsworth, ed Thomas Hutchinson (London 1956) p 721.
[20] [*The*] *Book* [*of the Church*,] 2 vols (London 1824) 2, p 528.
[21] [Geoffrey] Carnall, [*Robert Southey and his Age the Development of a Conservative*

fruit in a fragment, a curiously learned history of Portuguese Brazil, but the study stiffened his dislike of popery as the sire of superstition and thus of infidelity, as of despotism and revolution; and Portuguese popery deepened his loyalty to English religion as the mother of enlightenment and freedom. Thus in *The Book of the Church*, Southey linked English liberty and civilisation as twin children of English protestant Christianity. The Roman church had cleansed the church from the barbarous corruptions of late medieval Christianity, without, unlike the puritan Calvinists, losing the riches of the medieval tradition.

Thus England enjoyed a threefold deliverance from pagans, papists and puritans. The present reference was clear: the heathens were the radicals, the puritans had as their spiritual descendants the more aggressive nonconformists, and the papists were unchangeably the same. The church's new political foes all had old faces; and they were also enemies of England. Southey thought that *The Book of the Church* would 'strike both the catholics and the Puritans harder blows than they have of late years been accustomed to receive. The Emancipationists, therefore, [Roman catholics] and the Dissenters will not be pleased . . .'[22] These latter-day papists and puritans were birds of a feather: for Southey old priest was new presbyter, Rome and Geneva were different forms of ecclesiastical dictatorship, and English liberty had been defined in rejection of papal and presbyterian tyranny. England had uniquely kept a balance between church and state, in which neither tried to dominate the other. This nationalism implied a theology: though in private, Southey remained a unitarian,[23] he wrote publicly as a semi-Erastian protestant high churchman of the generation before the Oxford movement, which was to divorce high churchmanship from Erastianism and protestantism. But Southey's pantheon of heroes included both the protestant martyrs burnt by the papists, and the seventeenth-century high church victims of the puritans, Cranmer, Ridley and Latimer, Charles I and archbishop Laud. Southey drew his protestant martyrology from Fox's *Book of*

Mind] (Oxford 1960) p 38; Sanders p 183. On the importance of Portugal to Southey, see Adolfo Cabral, *Robert Southey Journals of a Residence in Portugal 1800–1801 and a visit to France 1838* (Oxford 1960) pp xxi–xxii.
[22] [Charles C.] Southey, [*The*] *Life* [*and Correspondence of Robert Southey*], 6 vols (London 1850) 5, p 112.
[23] Carnall pp 215–20.

Martyrs, his high church hagiography from divines like Peter Heylin, combining them in a national tradition in which Cranmer and Latimer, Laud and Charles I, were champions of England's church and freedoms.[24]

Thus Southey's book was a polemic, a brilliant but bigoted indulgence of his gift for controversy with intellects as acid as his own. His royalist poem on George III's reception into heaven had been parodied by the radical lord Byron; his pity for the plight of the pauper victims of the industrial revolution was to provoke lord Macaulay, who thought the poor better off in factories than in draughty cottages in the country. A radical like Byron, a utilitarian enthusiast for capitalism like Macaulay, were alike anathema to this romantic tory, who loved the monarchy and pitied the poor. But *The Book of the Church* gave Roman catholics most cause for offence, the more wounding because Southey claimed to be fair. Southey could praise the Roman church. Like Cobbett and other romantics he admired the social forms of the later middle ages.[25] He wanted religious sisterhoods in the church of England, and the first Anglican convent was established as his posthumous memorial. He expressed to Lingard an interest in the uses of hagiography for history.[26] But *The Book of the Church* was conceived as an answer to Lingard,[27] though he is not mentioned in it by name; and Southey held an even balance between the glories and ghastliness as he saw them of Roman catholic Christianity.

Thus on the one hand the dark age church was 'however defiled' 'the sole conservative principle by which Europe was saved from the lowest and most brutal barbarism',[28] while the Norse were converted 'by the steady system of the Popes, the admirable zeal of the Benedictines, and by the blessing of God, which crowned all . . .'[29] Yet this Christianity was 'as much a system of priestcraft as that which at this day prevails in Hindostan or Tibet';[30] indeed only priestcraft could advance truth among an unenlightened people;

[24] *Book*, 2, is entirely given over to the sixteenth and seventeenth centuries.
[25] This point that Southey's medievalism was qualified by his anti-catholicism, is neglected by Alfred Cobban in his *Edmund Burke and the Revolt against the Eighteenth Century* (London 1929) pp 198–9, 265–6. In his attitudes to the catholic church, Southey is Voltairian.
[26] Haile and Bonney p 177.
[27] At least so Lingard believed: *ibid* 204.
[28] *Book* I, p 98.
[29] *Ibid* pp 77–8.
[30] *Ibid* p 98.

and 'a system which admitted of pious fraud opened a way for the most impious abuses'.[31] Priestcraft had been an obsession with the eighteenth century rationalists, and with his unitarian convictions, and despite his romanticism, Southey had the rationalist temper which ascribed miracles to sacerdotal fraud. He had been fascinated and repelled by the miracles of hagiography, after his visit in the winter of 1795–6 to the Franciscan convent in Lisbon, where he saw murals depicting St Francis. 'I do not remember ever to have been so greatly astonished', he told his English readers. '"Do they believe all this, sir?" said I to my companion; "Yes, and a great deal more of the same kind", was the reply.'[32] In 1817, he bought a fifty-two volume Bollandist *Acta Sanctorum*, and thought of writing a history of the monastic orders. Thus by 1824, he had acquired a knowledge if not an understanding of hagiography, and in *The Book of the Church*, he reported that one old protestant bogeyman, St Dunstan, worked a miracle by ventriloquism, and pretended to have grabbed the devil's nose with red hot tongs.[33] The same defective rationalism informed the judgement that St Ignatius Loyola, 'like St Francis, was in a state of religious insanity when he began his career.'[34] Southey weighted his balance against Thomas à Becket, and in favour of the lollards, Henry VIII and Elizabeth. Even more tactlessly and trenchantly, he declared that the Roman catholic martyrs of Tudor England 'suffered for points of State, and not of Faith; not as Roman Catholics, but as Bull-papists; not for religion, but for treason.'[35] Southey thereby plunged into the Hibernian bog of a no popery controversy. *The Book of the Church* was extensively refuted by Charles Butler, in his *Book of the Roman Catholic Church*,[36] and in a short and sharp pamphlet, *Strictures on the . . . Book of the Church*,[37] by Milner. Southey replied to Butler and Milner in another book, the *Vindiciae Ecclesiae Anglicanae*, and

[31] *Ibid* p 38.
[32] Robert Southey, *Vindiciae Ecclesiae Anglicanae Letters to C. Butler, Esq. comprising Essays on the Romish religion and vindicating 'The Book of the Church'* (London 1826) p 8.
[33] *Book* I, p 94.
[34] *Ibid* 2, p 283.
[35] *Ibid* p 288.
[36] [*The Book of the*] *Roman-Catholic Church* [: *in a series of letters addressed to Robt Southey, Esq. LL.D on his 'Book of the Church'*] (London 1825). This whole controversy has been largely ignored, but is briefly surveyed in John Hunt, *Religious Thought in England in the Nineteenth Century* (London 1896) pp 80–1.
[37] [John Merlin (anagram for Milner),] *Strictures* [*on the Poet Laureate's Book of the Church*] (London 1824).

another twenty or so fiercely protestant books, tracts and review articles by Anglican divines were composed to sustain and support him. As Lingard said, *The Book of the Church* had 'plainly been written for a purpose, to please the high-church party',[38] and the high church party greeted it with paeans of praise. The bishops of London and Durham thanked Southey for his work.[39] So did the *British Quarterly*, the *British Critic*, and half a dozen more organs of the predominantly tory press in a wave of no popery enthusiasm,[40] as in the *Vindiciae* and its attendant abusive volumes, an interest in the virtues of the Church of England was eclipsed by a headier fascination with the vices of the church of Rome.

Some of this writing was not undistinguished: the *Quarterly* article was by Henry Hart Milman, destined to become a formidable ecclesiastical historian.[41] Nor was the high church position entirely unreasonable. Most Anglicans did not want to withdraw the freedom of worship granted catholics in 1791. But catholic emancipation threatened the time-hallowed union of church and state, and the church of England's central role in English life, as the church of the English nation, while admitting catholics to parliament posed problems for a church for whom parliament held an ultimate authority.[42] As Southey said with his usual clarity, the British constitution 'consists of Church and State, and it is an absurdity in politics to give those persons power in the *State*, whose duty it is to subvert the *Church*'.[43] From parliament, it might seem that catholics could assail the church of England from within, and disturb her fundamental protestantism. That made a political

[38] Lingard to his publisher Joseph Mawman, 14 February 1824; Haile and Bonney p 204.
[39] Southey, *Life*, 5, pp 165–6; [Kenneth] Curry, [*New Letters of Robert Southey*] 2 vols (New York 1965) 2, p 264.
[40] Butler declares 'that "The Book of the Roman Catholic Church", has been a subject of regular criticism in THE BRITISH CRITIC,—BRITISH REVIEW,—BLACKWOOD'S EDINBURGH MAGAZINE,—THE CHRISTIAN OBSERVER,—QUARTERLY REVIEW,—QUARTERLY THEOLOGICAL REVIEW,—WESTMINSTER REVIEW, and probably in some journals which I have not seen': these publications were mostly tory. Charles Butler, *Vindication of 'The Book of the Roman Catholic Church'* (London 1826) p lxxi.
[41] [H. H.] Milman, ['The Reformation in England',] *Quarterly Review* 33 (December 1825) pp 1–37. For identification of authorship, see *The Wellesley Index to Victorian Periodicals 1824–1900* 3 vols (Toronto 1966–1979) I, p 704.
[42] Geoffrey Best, 'The Protestant Constitution and its Supporters, 1800–1829', *TRHS* fifth series, 8 (1958) p 105.
[43] Southey, *Life*, 5, p 137.

question, catholic civil rights, a religious one, the integrity of Anglican protestantism, and brought the clergy into politics in support of their political champions. As bishop Blomfield of Chester said in 1825, 'Whatsoever measure threatens the Established Church with a diminution of its property, its privileges, and its securities, is justly regarded *by us* as hostile to the interests of religion itself . . .'[44] Thus there was a desperate political relevance to Southey's furious spilling of ink over medieval miracles, as *The Book of the Church* encouraged an outpouring of writings intended to preserve the civil disabilities of catholics and to deny them the freedoms of the constitution, because as exponents of civil and religious tyranny, the very notion of liberty was unknown to them. Hence the appeal to history, especially to the English history of the sixteenth and seventeenth centuries. All these learned treatises on Latimer and Laud were to demonstrate the tyrannical character of the Roman church, and to reinforce what church and state had always assumed, that only members of the national church were entitled to full rights as Englishmen.

Thus Southey's appeal was calculated to awaken an anti-catholic prejudice which was, in Charles Butler's words, not even 'wholly eradicated from all the liberal and informed'. Butler intended his reply, *The Book of the Roman Catholic Church* in the better spirit of St Francis of Sales 'that a good Christian is never outdone in good manners'.[45] In eirenic fashion he recalled the Benedictine Leander's report to Rome in 1634, that both in its outward forms and doctrinal teaching, the church of England had preserved much of its catholic inheritance, and with 'so near an approximation in religious creeds', wrote Butler, 'there certainly should be an equal approximation in christian and moral charity'.[46] He recalled past discussions between catholics and protestants, as between Leibniz and Bossuet, and archbishop Wake and the Gallicans. He collected Anglican and Lutheran texts acquitting catholics of idolatry, and arguing in favour of purgatory and confession, the real presence in the sacrament, even an Anglican form of commutation of sin corresponding to indulgences.[47] Butler was angry that Southey had

[44] C. J. Blomfield to Lyttelton, 22 June 1825, in Alfred Blomfield (ed) [*A Memoir of Charles James Blomfield, Bishop of London with selections from his correspondence*] 2 vols (London 1863) I, p 125.
[45] *Roman Catholic Church*, pp iv, vi.
[46] *Ibid* p 3.
[47] *Ibid* p 112.

attacked Roman catholics for doctrines and devotions which were no essential part of their religion. So Butler enunciated the Gallican and ultramontane definitions of papal authority, declaring his preference for the Gallican;[48] but he insisted, catholics were free to choose between them. It was a 'crying inustice', he wrote, 'to impute to our general body, what, in justice, is only chargeable on individuals; or to estimate the writings or actions of our ancestors in the dark ages, by the notions and manners of the present age . . . . '.[49] The rule of religious controversy should be 'THAT NO DOCTRINE SHOULD BE ASCRIBED TO THE ROMAN-CATHOLICS AS A BODY, EXCEPT SUCH AS IS AN ARTICLE OF THEIR FAITH'[50] in the creed of Pius IV and the Tridentine catechism. All other beliefs were private opinions; 'and a catholic may disbelieve them, without ceasing to be a catholic'.[51]

Butler's summaries of catholic doctrine on miracles,[52] and the veneration of saints, images and relics also insist on the letter of the Tridentine formula, even if the popular piety of catholic countries went beyond it. He defended Dunstan and Becket, deplored the reformers, and questioned the reliability of Fox's *Book of Martyrs*: a matter taken up with vehemence by Milner, who pursued the 'pretended martyrs' and 'notorious falsehoods' of the 'lying Fox' through thirty pages of invective.[53] Butler showed more reserve, but insisted that the Tudor catholic martyrs had died for their faith and not for treason, and he struck hard at Southey's inconsistency in condemning catholics for their persecutions, while defending the persecuting protestant laws under which catholics suffered still.

Butler's good manners were rewarded; his opponents complimented him on his courtesy, and distinguished him as an English gentleman from other catholics, especially Milner. Milner's pamphlet was published under the anagram John Merlin, that 'old Deceiver', as a protestant critic called the Celtic magician.[54] In

---

[48] *Ibid* pp 121–4.
[49] *Ibid* p iv.
[50] *Ibid* p 9.
[51] *Ibid* p 11: catholics are not required to believe in any miracles, save those in which protestants also believe, because they are recorded in scripture.
[52] *Ibid* pp 37–49.
[53] *Strictures*, pp 25 seq.
[54] [Rev Henry] Phillpotts, [*Letters to Charles Butler, Esq., on the Theological Parts of his 'Book of the Roman Catholic Church,' with remarks on certain works of Dr. Milner, and Dr. Lingard, and on some parts of the evidence of Dr. Doyle before the two Committees of the Houses of Parliament*] (London 1825) p 2.

Milner's onslaught, Southey got as good as he gave, and it sharpened the edge of his reply.

> Mr. Butler [he wrote] flattered as he has been by his fellow Catholics, and by the Whigs will not sleep on roses. I am glad that the Romanists have provoked the controversy, but sorry for his sake that he should have been the person to draw upon himself the exposure which must be made of so much sophistry and disingenuousness. He believes every thing which he finds in the writings of Milner and such people . . . Now Milner is a man who has shown almost as little regard to truth as Cobbett himself . . .[55]

Southey was in correspondence with Mortimer O'Sullivan, an Irish catholic converted to protestantism, who under the pseudonym 'A Munster Farmer',[56] had written against catholic emancipation, and now offered Southey proofs which Lingard might have given him, of Milner's inaccuracy in references and quotations. 'I shall treat this Titular Bishop', declared Southey 'as freely with the twigs of the birch as he would treat me . . . with the faggots'. This treatment went into the *Vindiciae*, and Southey was delighted with his handiwork, rejoicing that it was 'ready for publication just when parliament meets', to guide the counsels of the tory politicians. 'Mr Butler will call it a terrible task', he wrote, 'for it is many a long day since Mother Scarlet has been carted so properly . . . I have beat up the enemy(')s quarters, and exposed abuse after abuse as . . . that blackguard fellow Milner put them in my way . . . laying on like Talus, with an iron flail'.[57] Southey's new work was over five hundred pages long, and ranged over every aspect of Roman catholic life, thought and doctrine, to prove that as catholics were intolerant, superstitious and un-English, they must be excluded from the government of England.

Southey's supporters were legion. 'I believe not fewer than 17 answers to my book of the Roman Catholic Church have been published',[58] Butler wrote to Kirk, as Milner and Lingard were dragged into a fray, raising echoes of earlier controversies. Butler was now in his seventy-fifth year, but rallied creditably with a book of over two hundred and fifty pages. It might have been

---

[55] Curry 2, pp 278–9.
[56] 'A Munster Farmer', *Captain Rock Detected* (London 1824).
[57] Curry 2, pp 279, 291.
[58] Butler to Kirk, 6 August 1825, A[rchdiocesan] A[rchives of] W[estminster].

longer still. Butler thought of asking Milner to swell it with a further reply to one Richard Grier's defence of his earlier attack on the *The End of Religious Controversy*;[59] and Lingard supplied an addendum to Butler's work. Its massive title gives the comic character of the accumulated masses of Anglican polemical bile: *VINDICATION of "The Book of the Roman Catholic Church", against the Reverend George Townsend's "Accusations of History against the Church of Rome": with notice of some charges brought against "The Book of the Roman Catholic Church", in the publications of Doctor Phillpotts, the Rev. John Todd, M.A., F.S.A. the Rev. Stephen Isaacson, B.A. the Rev. Joseph Blanco White, M.A. B.D. and in some anonymous publications. With copies of Doctor Phillpotts's Fourth Letter to Mr. Butler containing a charge against Dr. Lingard; and of a letter of Dr. Lingard to Mr. Butler, in reply to the charge.*[60] The meat of the controversy was Tudor and Stuart history. The reverend Stephen Isaacson's complaints appeared in his introduction to his annotated translation of the Tudor bishop Jewel's *Apology for the Church of England* against the church of Rome.[61] The reverend Henry John Todd, archdeacon of Cleveland, a pluralist and monster of industry was ultimately author or editor of some two score publications, including the works of Spenser and Milton.[62] He now assailed Butler, Milner and Lingard for slighting archbishop Cranmer, in his introduction to Cranmer's *Defence of the True and Catholic Doctrine of the Sacrament*,[63] and his response to Butler's reply appeared in an expanded introduction to a new edition of the work in 1826.[64] There was no reason why the matter should ever end, as

---

[59] *Ibid.*

[60] (London 1826).

[61] *An Apology for the Church of England, by the Right Reverend John Jewel, D.D., Lord Bishop of Salisbury. Faithfully translated from the original Latin. To which is prefixed a memoir of his life and writings, and a preliminary discourse on the doctrine and discipline of the Church of Rome; in reply to some observations of C. Butler, Esq., addressed to Dr. Southey, on his 'Book of the Church'* (London 1825)

[62] See 'Henry John Todd' in *DNB*.

[63] *A Defence of the True and Catholike Doctrine of the Sacrament of the Body and Blood of our Saviour Christ . . . By the Most Reverend Thomas Cranmer, Lord Archbishop of Canterbury. To which is prefixed an introduction, historical and critical . . . in vindication of the character of the author, and therewith of the Reformation in England, against some of the allegations . . . recently made by the Reverend Doctor Lingard, the Reverend Doctor Milner, and Charles Butler, Esq.* (London 1825).

[64] Subtitled *The second edition, with notices of Dr. Lingard's and Mr. Butler's remarks on the first edition* (London 1826). Compare the survey of the controversy in *The British Critic*, 23 (May 1825) pp 449–62.

Todd battered Lingard through a further publication,[65] when both found themselves under attack from Christopher Wordsworth, for denying that the *Eikon Basilike* had been written by Charles the first.[66]

Butler introduced his *Vindication* with an epistle in which he dealt with Todd, Isaacson and five other writers. The rest of the volume was in the form of letters to the reverend George Townsend, also centred on Tudor and Stuart history. Townsend lives today as the hero of monsignor Knox's delightful essay on 'The man who tried to convert the Pope'[67] by a mission to Rome in 1850. He was rewarded for his assault on Butler with a prebendal stall in Durham cathedral, by the bishop of Durham, Shute Barrington, a doughty opponent of the catholic claims and old antagonist of Lingard's, now in his nineties a commanding symbol of the stern unbending tory protestantism of the church of England.[68]

Indeed Barrington's politics had enhanced the notoriety of the Durham cathedral clergy, who had a special place in whig and radical demonology for their indecent wealth as members of one of the richest corporations in England.[69] Among their defenders was Henry Phillpotts, the pluralist incumbent of the golden rectory of Stanhope in the diocese, promoted in 1828 to the deanery of Chester and to the bishopric of Exeter in 1830. Phillpotts had tangled with Lingard in the past, and reverted to this old controversy in his answer to Butler, which he dedicated to Barrington.[70] Nor was this the end of Durham's labours. Phillpotts and Townsend each wrote a supplementary *Letter* against the

---

[65] *A Reply to Dr. Lingard's Vindication of his History of England as far as respects Archbishop Cranmer* (London 1827).

[66] Christopher Wordsworth, *King Charles the First the author of Icôn* (sic) *Basilikè, further proved in a letter to his Grace the Archbishop of Canterbury, in reply to the objections of Dr. Lingard, Mr. Todd, Mr. Broughton, The Edinburgh Review, and Mr. Hallam* (Cambridge 1828); compare Todd's *Bishop Gauden the author of Icôn Basilikè, further shewn in answer to the recent remarks of the Rev. Dr. Wordsworth upon a publication of the present writer* . . . (London 1829). Compare footnote 18.

[67] Ronald Knox, *Literary Distractions* (London 1958) pp 114–33; 'George Townsend' in *DNB*.

[68] 'Shute Barrington' in *DNB*.

[69] See footnote 6.

[70] See footnote 54. On Phillpotts's part in the controversy, see [G.C.B.] Davies, [*Henry Phillpotts Bishop of Exeter 1778–1869*] (London 1954) pp 59–88.

Vindication.[71] As with Todd, the controversy waxed fat by feeding on itself, and the *odium theologicum* was fired by the passions of whig and tory politics.

Though a high church tory Phillpotts insisted that he was not attacking Rome just to defeat catholic emancipation; though he hoped that his writings might help prevent it.[72] But he also discerned the political intent of Butler's style of apologetic: 'there is another reason', Phillpotts wrote, 'more peculiarly belonging to the times in which we live for this eagerness to represent the creeds of the two Churches as similar as possible . . .' This was 'the great political object which engages all your hopes . . . no better expedient, than this, can be adopted, to reconcile the minds of Englishmen to the removal of the remaining political restrictions under which you labour . . .'[73] Phillpotts's own political interests were sufficiently apparent in his letter to whig earl Grey, on that peer's ecumenical misunderstandings of Roman theology, originally published in 1819, and now reprinted in the *Letters to Butler* as an appendix.[74] Philpotts's attack on the papal deposing power equally reflected the inextricable entanglement of religion and politics: a matter to which Butler and Phillpotts returned to 1828 in a clash over the coronation oath, by which the monarch abjured transubstantiation and swore allegiance to the church of England.[75]

As a theologian, Phillpotts insisted that Butler had blurred essential distinctions between protestant and catholic doctrine; as in understating the difference between the real spiritual presence in the eucharist taught by high Anglicans, and the corporeal presence of transubstantiation rejected in the 39 articles.[76] Phillpotts also offered evidence that Butler's presentation of Catholic doctrine on saints, images and relics fell short of Trent. Like Southey and Townsend, however, Phillpotts poured scorn on catholic practices and teaching

[71] Henry Phillpotts, *A Supplemental Letter to Charles Butler, Esq. on some parts of the evidence given by the Irish Roman-Catholic Bishops* (London 1826); George Townsend, *Supplementary Letter to Charles Butler, Esq.: in reply to his vindication of the Book of the Roman Catholic Church* (London 1826).
[72] Phillpotts p 7.
[73] *Ibid* pp 6–7.
[74] *Ibid* p 321.
[75] Charles Butler, *A Letter on the Coronation Oath* (London 1827); Henry Phillpotts, *A Letter to an English Layman, on the Coronation Oath . . . in which are considered the several opinions of Mr. Jeffrey . . . Mr. C. Butler, etc* (London 1828). Compare Davies p 73.
[76] Phillpotts pp 231–58. The relevant article is 28.

in no way binding on catholics as of faith, and invoked in proof of catholic idolatry some dubious canons of the second council of Nicaea,[77] which Lingard despatched in his addendum to Butler's reply. Nor did Phillpotts effectively refute Butler's sneer at the ideological chaos of Anglicanism. It was left to Blomfield to answer Butler's reiteration of Gibbon's famous phrase that many Anglican divines assented with 'a sigh or a smile' to the 39 articles.[78] Here Butler's legal abilities shone in a demonstration of the various senses in which Anglicans subscribed them.[79] Newman's reconciliation of the articles with Tridentine doctrine in *Tract 90* was to be the *reductio ad absurdum* of this sort of exercise; before Newman, it merely indicated the prevalence of latitudinarian opinion in the church of England, and her more fundamental claim on all Englishmen who could accept her national character. But no high churchman like Blomfield or Phillpotts could acknowledge the point, and it was easy for catholics to mock the divisions of the church of England.

But it was as easy for protestants to stress aspects of catholicism unacceptable to Butler, though acceptable to Milner. Phillpotts taunted the Gallican Butler with Milner's ultramontanism, while alleging the inconsistency in Butler's Gallicanism;[80] other Anglicans exploited the difference between catholics who believed in the pope's deposing power and catholics who denied it.[81] This was also the distinction between the faith of Irish peasants and Italian priests, and the religion of an English gentleman: as between the half-protestantized catholicism of the English catholics, and the fully developed superstition of latin Europe. This last was the theme of

[77] *Ibid* pp 76–91.

[78] C. J. Blomfield, *A Letter to Charles Butler, Esq. of Lincoln's Inn, in vindication of English Protestants from his attack on their sincerity in the 'Book of the Roman Catholic Church'* (London 1825). The third edition contains a postscript with a reply to Butler's reply. Compare Alfred Blomfield, I, pp 128 *seq.* Blomfield supported the repeal of the Test and Corporation acts, but not catholic emancipation.

[79] *A Letter to the Right Reverend C. J. Blomfield, D.D., Bishop of Chester; from Charles Butler, Esq. in vindication of a passage in his 'Book of the Roman Catholic Church' censured in a letter addressed to him by his Lordship* (London 1825).

[80] Phillpotts pp 271–307.

[81] 'From the accession of Elizabeth to the present moment, the Roman Catholics have been divided into two parties; the one who, with some sacrifice of their religious consistency . . . have possessed so much of English loyalty and patriotism as divested their divided allegiance of half its danger . . . the other, who have adhered to the old Popish doctrines in all their uncompromising bigotry . . . ' Milman p 36.

the most moving contribution to the controversy, by the reverend Joseph Blanco White,[82] an apostate priest of Irish parentage, who had held office in the church of Spain, fled to England, and after passing through a phase of unbelief had become an Anglican clergyman. 'There are few men whom I respect so highly', declared Southey[83] of White, who like Southey, wrote for the tory *Quarterly*. White has enjoyed a modest modern reputation through his connexion with Oriel College, then the centre the Oxford renaissance.[84] His book against Butler[85] was dedicated to Edward Copleston, provost of Oriel, and it was at Oriel that White introduced catholic ideas to the young John Henry Newman. White was a tragic figure, and in the stifling confines of Hispanic orthodoxy, had become a covert unbeliever. His later desertion of the church of England and relapse into unitarianism indicates a rationalist temper of a mind highly suspicious of revelation and miracle. His book against Butler, designed to prove that '*sincere* Roman Catholics cannot conscientiously be *tolerant*',[86] was largely autobiographical; and in his revelations of his past he agonized over the inner conflict which was always to torment him, between a spirit that craved, and a mind that rejected, the consolations of revealed religion.

White's hatred of Roman superstition was echoed by his clergyman friend the philologist Richard Garnett, who had written for the *Protestant Guardian* some 'extremely humourous and sarcastic exposures of the apochryphal miracles attributed to St. Francis Xavier'.[87] White and Southey urged Garnett to reply to Butler in similar vein.[88] Dread of superstition also haunted Southey's last

---

[82] [*The life of the Rev. Joseph Blanco White, written by himself*], [J. H.] Thom, 3 vols (London 1845) I pp 226, 410–30.

[83] Southey to the bishop of Limerick 22 October 1823; Southey, *Life* 5, p 147.

[84] David Newsome, *The Parting of Friends* (London 1976) pp 66–7, 86–90.

[85] *Practical and Internal Evidence against Catholicism, with occasional Strictures on Mr. Butler's Book of the Roman Catholic Church: in six letters, addressed to the impartial among the Roman Catholics of Great Britain and Ireland* (London 1825). Also *A Letter to Charles Butler, Esq. on his notice of the 'Practical and Internal Evidence against Catholicism'* (London 1826).

[86] *Ibid* p vi. White's rationalism prevailed over his anticatholicism in 1829 to support catholic emancipation, to the disgust of his former allies: Thom I, pp 453–65.

[87] 'Richard Garnett', in *DNB*.

[88] The work was all but completed, but never published: apparently because of the depression into which Garnett was plunged by the death of his wife and child. Compare *The Philological Essays of the late Rev. R. Garnett, of the British Museum. Edited with a memoir*, ed Richard Garnett (London 1859) pp iv–viii.

exchange with Butler over Southey's *Quarterly* article[89] on the *Revelations* of 'Soeur Nativité',[90] a Breton nun whose ferocious ascetism and naive mysticism had been approved by Milner. The indefatigable Butler responded with an incisive pamphlet[91] deprecating 'Soeur Nativité's' wilder fancies, while administering Southey a needed lesson in mystical theology. 'IS IT NOT HIGH TIME' Butler concluded, 'THAT ALL CHARGES AND RECRIMINATIONS OF THIS SORT SHOULD HAVE AN END? DO NOT ALL GENTLEMEN DESIRE IT?'[92]

Alas, the appeal to 'gentlemanliness' was out of sorts with the changing mood of nineteenth-century religion. Even Butler was not proof against it, as he reflected that 'all their Anti-Catholic Efforts are of no avail to them. Every day, the established Church of England, visibly declines'.[93] That sentiment sounded less like Butler than Milner, who died in 1826 still insisting that Butler must retract his Gallican opinions if he wanted to go to heaven.[94] No popery, however, meant the end of Anglo-Gallicanism, for it made even Butler's old friends regret that he did not write like Milner;[95] and that was proof that Southey's book signified a new heat in the relations between the churches,[96] and the reversal of the latitudinarian tendencies of eighteenth-century Christianity.[97] The religious peace of Augustan England had rested on an unchallenged establishment, and catholic and dissenting minorities which only asked to be left alone. In the nineteenth century, the Anglican church was convulsed from within, while assailed from without by a renascent nonconformity, and a catholicity which prayed for the conversion of England. The Roman church of the Victorian era reflected Milner's ultramontane aggressiveness, not Butler's

[89] 'The apocalypse of the Sister Nativité', *Quarterly Review*, 33 (March 1826) pp 375–410.
[90] Abbé Genet, *Vie et Révélations de la Soeur de la Nativité [Jeanne le Royer] Religieuse converse au couvent des Urbanistes de Fougeres . . .* (Paris 1817). Southey had met with it 'by mere chance' while in Flanders: Curry 2, p 294.
[91] Charles Butler, *Reply to the Article in the Quarterly Review, for March 1826, on the Revelations of La Soeur Nativité* (London 1826).
[92] *Ibid* p 23.
[93] Butler to Kirk 4 July 1826, AAW.
[94] Ward 3, pp 101–4.
[95] Berington to Butler 24 December 1824, Archdiocesan Archives of Birmingham.
[96] 'I know not what people mean in saying, that Merlin's reply to Southey is a complete failure . . . If he (Butler) succeed as well, I shall be satisfied . . .' Berington to Kirk 5 November 1824, AAW.
[97] W. R. Ward, *Religion and Society in England 1790–1850* (London 1972).

Gallican politeness; while a new extreme evangelicalism fired the passions of Anglican protestantism. This trend was observable in the exchange between Milner's biographer, Husenbeth, who had replied to Blanco White[98]; and George Stanley Faber, another Durham cleric,[99] and uncle of the father Faber who was to embody a supranational ultramontane catholicism. And so too, protestantism would find champions in Irish and latin converts like Blanco White, to fight the father Fabers of catholic England.

Thus the nineteenth century witnessed a revival of providentialist interpretations of history in the service of partisan positions. Southey's Book of the Church was to pass through eight editions by 1870, while it was Cobbett's work, so much more bitter than Butler's, which kept its readers among catholics. Phillpotts' two collections of letters to Butler and his letter to earl Grey, with, for good measure, an attack on Tract 90, proof of Anglican disunity, were to be republished as late as 1866. Townsend set to work on his eight volume edition of Fox's Acts and Monuments, with a biography of Fox and a defence of his historical accuracy against Milner,[100] and so he entered upon the road which led him to Rome in 1850. In this company, Butler spoke for a dying age; a heightened sectarian ecclesiology and rival catholic and protestant histories were to dominate British religion in the future.

University of Durham

[98] F. C. Husenbeth, Defence of the Creed and Discipline of the Catholic Church, against the Rev. J. Blanco White's 'Poor Man's Preservative against Popery': with notice of every thing important in the same writer's Practical and Internal Evidence against Catholicism (London 1826).

[99] G. S. Faber, The Difficulties of Romanism (London 1826); F. C. Husenbeth, A Reply to the Rev. G. S. Faber's Supplement to his Difficulties of Romanism (Norwich 1829); The difficulties of Faberism (London 1829); Faberism Exposed and Refuted: and the Apostolicity of Catholic Doctrine Vindicated (Norwich 1836)

[100] The Acts and Monuments of John Foxe, 8 vols (editions London 1841, 1843–9, 1853–70). The work spawned a further controversy with S. R. Maitland: Notes on the contributions of the Revd. George Townsend . . . to the new edition of Fox's Martyrology (London, 1841–42); and Townsend's Remarks on the errors of Mr. Maitland . . . (Durham 1842).

BISHOP GOSS OF LIVERPOOL (1856–1872) AND THE IMPORTANCE OF BEING ENGLISH.

by PETER DOYLE

The papal bull *Universalis Ecclesiae* of 1850 set up a hierarchy of bishops with ordinary power to replace the vicars apostolic who had ruled the catholic church in England since 1688.[1] It stated explicitly that the new bishops were to have all the necessary powers to rule their dioceses in the same way as titular bishops elsewhere, and it spoke clearly about the resumption of the 'common law of the church' in England. Yet the commitment of the Roman authorities to a fully independent hierarchy was not wholehearted. The church in England was to remain under the aegis of the Congregation of the Propagation of the Faith (Propaganda), whose normal brief was to look after missionary territories not stable enough to have properly constituted hierarchies. According to the bull, the English bishops were to send regular reports on the state of their dioceses to Rome, and were to be diligent in informing Propaganda 'of everything which they shall think profitable for the spiritual good of their flocks'.[2]

The main reason why Rome regarded England as being in need of continued surveillance was a fear of a gallican spirit in the English clergy and even in the new bishops.[3] As a result, Propaganda was eager to interfere in the acts and decisions of the English hierarchy to an extent unknown elsewhere. This fear of gallicanism resulted from a misunderstanding of the outlook of some of the English bishops, and was unfortunately fostered in Rome by

---

[1] Latin text in *Decreta* [*Quatuor Conciliorum Provincialium Westmonasteriensium 1852–1873*] (2 ed London nd) pp 75–83; English translation in [*The English Catholics 1850–1950*] ed [G. A.] Beck (London 1950) pp 107–15.
[2] Beck p 112.
[3] [R.] Schiefen, ['The Organisation and Administration of Roman Catholic Dioceses in England and Wales in the mid-nineteenth century'], PhD thesis (London 1970) pp 105–6; also his article, '"Anglo-Gallicanism" [in Nineteenth-Century England'], *CHR* (1977) pp 14–44.

Manning and his henchman Talbot.[4] It was shared even by cardinal Barnabo, the otherwise astute and able prefect of Propaganda, who, for example, regarded it as essential to support Wiseman against the bishops even when he thought the bishops were in the right, for Wiseman seemed to be 'the mainstay of Rome against universal gallicanism'.[5]

In another pontificate this interference might not have been so important, but at a time when there was a positive drive towards centralisation in Rome it could be dangerous. Pius IX's pontificate witnessed a tendency to interfere directly in diocesan affairs and to impose an all-embracing uniformity.[6] Many catholic bishops did not object to these developments, and were willing to refer more and more of their decisions to the Roman congregations, accepting in practice a diminution of their own authority and a corresponding increase in that of the curia. The congregations' consultative role changed to an authoritative one. Moreover, the pope deliberately used his charm and personal popularity to win over wavering bishops, calling them to Rome either as individuals or for great emotional gatherings, as in 1862 and 1867.[7] He revived the practice whereby bishops paid regular *ad limina* visits to report on the state of their dioceses, and regarded both the visits and reports as very important.[8] In 1854, for example, he wrote to the Irish bishops urging them to make the visits at the appointed times and to make clear the state of their churches, so that as much help as possible could be given them in carrying out their duties; similar letters were written to the Austrian bishops and those of the oriental rite.[9] There is a presumption in these letters that it is up to the pope to look after every diocese and to provide the means for the local bishops to do their work, and a strong suggestion that all problems should be taken to Rome for solution.

[4] On Talbot see [J. D.] Holmes, [*More Roman than Rome*] (London 1978) pp 73–4; Schiefen, 'Anglo-Gallicanism', p 24; [F.J.] Cwiekowski, [*The English Bishops and the First Vatican Council*] (Louvain 1971) pp 39–41.

[5] Bishop Goss to the bishop of Shrewsbury, 14 January 1862, L[ancashire] R[ecord] O[ffice], RCLv 5/4/246.

[6] [R.] Aubert, [*Le Pontificat de Pie IX (1846–1878)*], FM 21 (Paris 1952) pp 281–94.

[7] 1862: the canonisation of the Japanese martyrs; 1867: the eighteenth centenary of the martyrdom of Saints Peter and Paul.

[8] Aubert p 287.

[9] *Pii IX Pontificis Maximi Acta,* 6 vols (Graz, Austria, 1971) 1, p 585; 2, p 527; 3, p 431–2.

The importance of being English

Bishop Ullathorne of Birmingham was clear about what was happening; he complained to Manning in 1862 that 'Rome is always more and more limiting the original privileges of the bishops, and we are anxious to be limited as little as possible'.[10] Manning called this remark *purus fructus gallicanismi* and replied that the bishops owed any privileges which they had to delegation from the Holy See and not to any divine institution.

In addition to objecting to it as a lessening of their position, some of the English bishops disliked Roman interference because, despite their reports and visits, curial officials did not know enough about local circumstances for interference to be helpful. It is strange that, with so many opportunities for obtaining information, so much reliance should have been put on people like Talbot to redress this ignorance. Indeed, Propaganda's general lack of knowledge and understanding of the countries which it controlled led one French writer to remark that it was like the court of Louis XVI in France, except that it was more virtuous.[11]

Bishop Goss of Liverpool (1856–72) complained to a fellow bishop about Talbot's 'backstairs influence',[12] and generally had a low opinion of Propaganda's interference in English affairs and of Manning's influence there. After all, he argued, Rome had lost the temporal power 'by its own bad management', and if it were allowed to dictate policy to the English bishops they would soon 'be brought to nought'. For, he added, 'Rome is only Manning in Italian. It learns all from him and acts by his suggestion . . . Rome lives in an ideal world, in a cloud of incense offered by the nauseous Tablet, Universe (*sic*), Civilta and Osservatore. Who is Herbert Vaughan or Veuillot to dictate a catholic policy to the world?'[13]

Goss, however, in opposing what was happening at Rome, was concerned about something much deeper than the attention paid to Talbot and Manning. The first important occasion on which he voiced his opposition was in connection with the condemnation of

[10] Quoted in [C.] Butler, [*The Life and Times of Bishop Ullathorne*], 2 vols (London 1926), 1, p 237.
[11] Aubert p 281.
[12] Butler, 1, p 228.
[13] Archives of the English Benedictine Congregation, Ampleforth; Miscellaneous box, file 'Letters to Brown, various'; Goss to Brown of Newport, 19 December 1870. Vaughan was editor of *The Tablet*, Veuillot of *L'Univers*.

435

the liberal catholic review, *The Rambler*.[14] Cardinal Barnabo wrote to the English bishops ordering them to issue pastoral letters against the review. Goss was indignant and wrote to bishop Brown of Shrewsbury; his reactions were based on a mixture of expediency and principle: 'What next? I suppose you have received Cardinal Barnabo's instructions about pastoralising the Rambler, a sure plan to rekindle the gallican spirit among catholics, to alienate the Converts and to bring down the whole Protestant press upon us.'[15] Goss did not agree with the spirit of the review, but, he went on to ask, 'has it exceeded the freedom of discussion formerly exercised by the Schools on much more serious and holy subjects? Is it sinful to blame the administration of the Pontifical States?' He then asked why the periodical, if it had been so bad, had not been forbidden by cardinal Wiseman, as it had been published in his diocese. This led him on to his main complaint: 'If Rome has thought it necessary to censure it, why has it not done so in its own name? Why throw the odium and the responsibility upon us? Is it not unusual to prescribe the bishops to issue pastorals on particular subjects? Does it act so with France or Germany? If not, why are we treated so exceptionally?' Here we have two of the points which were at the bottom of much of Goss's suspicion of Rome for the rest of his episcopate. Firstly, when Rome interfered in English affairs it did so in such a way as to make it appear that it was the bishops who were making the unpopular decisions, and yet failed to consult the bishops fully beforehand. Secondly, Rome treated England in a special way, as though her bishops were not fully bishops and could not be trusted to defend the interests of the church.

Goss was now in full flow and brought up something which had been rankling for some time. Propaganda had refused to ratify the decree of the third provincial synod on the constitution of the English colleges, even though it had been carefully drafted and agreed to by nearly all the bishops; instead, each bishop had been ordered to send his ideas in separately to Barnabo.[16] Goss commented to Brown, 'Provincial Synods are never set aside unless

[14] J. L. Altholz, *The Liberal Catholic Movement in England* (London 1962), gives the full story of *The Rambler* and its condemnation.

[15] LRO, RCLv 5/4/355, 14 July 1862.

[16] [D.] Milburn, [*A History of Ushaw College*] (Ushaw, Durham 1964) has the fullest account of the disputes over the colleges; see also Schiefen, caps 5–7.

they contain enactments contrary to faith or morals . . . but ours have been set aside or squashed: . . . like a set of schoolboys we have been ordered to send up our themes to Propaganda: and now we are ordered to write pastorals on a given theme within a given time! Verily, are we anything better than VGs? Does Talbot or Manning or cardinal Barnabo govern our dioceses? We certainly do not.' Goss did not write a pastoral letter on *The Rambler*, the only English bishop not to do so.

What Goss basically wanted was to be left alone to get on with his main task, the advancement of religion in his diocese. Undue interference by others meant an unnecessary increase in business, long delays and decisions which did not take into account all the local circumstances. In some cases it could also lead to injustice, as he claimed had happened over the disputes about diocesan funds.[17] In June, 1863 he wrote to bishop Grant of Southwark to complain of 'the child's play' going on over the funds: the bishops were being bandied about from Propaganda to York Place (Wiseman's residence), and had to waste time arguing and defending the 'petty details' of their rule over and over again. Goss, who could always exaggerate to make a point, said that they were being treated like 'Our Lord . . . sent from Pilate to Herod, a way of proceeding which made . . . Saint Thomas of Canterbury declare that it was as hard for a bishop to obtain justice in the court of Rome, as Our Lord to meet with it in the courts of Pilate and Herod.'[18]

In part, Goss's attitude stemmed from his low estimate of the ability of the Roman curial officials.[19] He spoke of them as 'little men' who had hardly enough ability to run an English mission, and who covered up the weakness of their reasoning by constantly using the pope's name and appealing for loyalty: if there was a danger of gallicanism in England, said Goss, then such a cavalier action was a sure way of arousing it.[20] Moreover, Rome was full of what he called frightening gossip, and a bishop's good name was readily blackened if he did not say just what those 'fussy busy bodies chose to dictate'. Goss was always outspoken and honest, and he hated the intrigue of the curia; he wrote later to Newman,

---

[17] Many thousands of pounds were involved; Milburn, p 246, and numerous letters in LRO, RCLv 5/3.
[18] Archives of the diocese of Southwark, B.13, 1 June 1863.
[19] For a similar judgement see Aubert p 281.
[20] LRO, RCLv 5/5/147, Goss to canon Oakeley, 24 April 1867.

'Nothing ever wounded the simplicity of my faith so much as the trickery with which I became acquainted on my official intercourse with the curia.'[21]

In contrast to these 'little men' who had small regard for the truth stood, in Goss's eyes, Newman himself. There would appear to have been little in common between the scholarly Oxford convert and the blunt, practical, Lancastrian bishop, but Goss sincerely admired Newman and his Englishness, and on a number of occasions wrote to him for advice and treated him as something of a confidant. Newman, for his part, appreciated Goss's support, and there was more than mere courtesy in his reference to him as 'good bishop Goss'.[22] To Goss Newman was 'the great champion', too humble and retiring to defend himself; efforts to assail a name that was 'without stain' were 'lamentable'.[23]

In 1867 the bishop, in a reference to Propaganda's prohibition of Newman's plan to go to Oxford,[24] wrote that it was 'infamous'; what had he done to be 'cast aside in so contemptuous a manner'?[25] At the same time he commented on Propaganda's decision that the bishops should issue pastoral letters against catholics' attending the universities. His immediate reaction was similar to that in the case of The Rambler: here was further unnecessary interference, with the bishops' again being left to bear the responsibility. He was not in favour of catholics' going to the universities, but Propaganda had no right to order the bishops to prohibit something under pain of mortal sin.[26] He wrote, '. . . we should sustain our position by presenting a firm remonstrance, couched not in the flattering mode of the day, but in the more English style of Saint Thomas . . . if we publish [the brief] we should do so simply, leaving to Rome the responsibility of its own act. If Germans and Americans are allowed to attend mixed universities, how can we condemn of (sic) mortal sin those who do [so] in this country?'[27]

Goss also complained about the last sentence in the brief, which

[21] A[rchives of the] B[irmingham] O[ratory], Goss to Newman, 28 March 1870.
[22] The Letters and Diaries of John Henry Newman, ed C. S. Dessain, 21 vols (London 1961–77), 29, p 69, Newman to canon Fisher, 9 March 1879.
[23] Goss to Oakeley, n 20 above.
[24] Butler, 2, cap 13, deals with the question in full.
[25] ABO, Goss to Ullathorne, 10 September 1867.
[26] V. A. McClelland, English Roman Catholics and Higher Education 1830–1903 (Oxford 1973) pp 212–13 for Goss's views.
[27] Goss to Ullathorne, n 25 above.

had said that the archbishop of Westminster was to see that the pastorals issued by the bishops were uniform in content and written in a uniform way.[28] Goss's belief was that each bishop should be left to interpret Roman rulings (or decisions taken in common by the English bishops) as he thought best for his diocese.

On this occasion he did write a pastoral letter.[29] In it he quoted the two most important paragraphs of Propaganda's letter and added a little about the dangers which faced catholics at the universities; he also referred to the general teaching of the church about avoiding occasions of sin. Most of the pastoral, however, was about the dangers which faced catholic children who attended protestant schools: this was a far more pressing problem in Liverpool. The whole pastoral is a very good example of how a bishop could interpret a general ruling to suit the circumstances of his people.

It is not surprising that Goss was in the lists again in 1870. He did not attend the council because of bad health; had he done so he would have been another voice on the anti-infallibilist side.[30] In the course of an important letter to Newman about the council he explained what he thought the role of a bishop was in matters of doctrine.[31] A bishop should not judge according to his personal theological opinions, but should be a witness of the tradition and teaching of his church. Goss implied that the general belief in England was against a definition of infallibility; unfortunately, he went on, anyone who spoke against it was being branded a heretic by an 'aggressive and insolent faction' – Manning, *The Dublin Review* and *The Tablet*. What was being done by Manning's faction in Rome smacked of the intrigue which Goss hated, and he complained, 'Truth, simple English truth, seems to have departed from the whole faction. I generally believe any assertion which they are unanimous in contradicting.' He also feared that the council would result in a lessening of the bishops' rights, because they would be subordinated even more to Rome, and 'the patriarchal sceptre' would be changed into 'the dictator's truncheon'; the bishops, who had gone to the council to confer with the pope,

---

[28] *Decreta*, p 332.
[29] A[rchives of the] A[rchbishop of] L[iverpool], Pastorals[of bishop Goss], 2nd Sunday of Advent 1867.
[30] Cwiekowski pp 293, 322, 324.
[31] ABO, 28 March 1870; printed, with some misprints and minor omissions, in Cwiekowski, pp 169–72.

would, he felt, 'return like satraps despatched to their provinces, where they may find waiting them for obedience the very decrees which they had refused to sanction in Council.'[32]

Part of the trouble, Goss thought, was that the pope's judgement had been spoilt by flattery and the excesses of the pro-papalist party; for years no one had dared to contradict him, and his amiability had won a 'sort of hysterical affection from ladies and young priests', so much so that he felt that the bishops would succumb to the same fascination. Moreover, 'the Pope has been so much flattered by four great assemblages of the Bishops . . . that he has been led to think that he can rule them as a pedagogue rules his pupils. The dealings of Rome, at any time, with the Bishops have been of the ferula and bonbons type: they are not dealt with as grown-up men but as difficult children.'[33]

Goss tried to keep clear of the papal charm. He did not attend the great gathering in Rome in 1862 to celebrate the canonisation of the Japanese martyrs. As he wrote to Errington, he had a good excuse because his health would not stand a Roman summer, but there was another reason as well. He did not want to sign an address to the pope which he did not agree with; if he was in Rome he could hardly refuse to do so. The address would not contain what the bishops 'really thought best', but would be drawn up by the 'officious few' who hoped to gain increased influence as a reward.[34] This letter is additonally interesting in that it makes clear that pressure was put on the bishops to attend. Cardinal Rinaldini had written to Grant of Southwark to say that 'offence would be given in high quarters' if he and Goss did not go. Goss's letter of excuse was accepted by Barnabo, who wrote to say that the pope had been pleased with the bishop's expressions of love and veneration; clearly, Goss did not push his independence too far.[35]

What has been said so far is evidence that Goss was intent on maintaining his independence of Rome. This was partly a matter of principle, based on his view of the episcopal office, and partly a matter of practicalities, for outside interference could be harmful if it did not take into account the particular conditions which existed

[32] Ibid.
[33] Ibid.
[34] LRO, RCLv 5/4/340, 1 July 1862.
[35] Archives of the Propagation of the Faith, Scritture riferite nei Congressi, Anglia, 16, 1861–3, n 580 Goss to Barnabo 4 June 1862; Barnabo's reply of 24 July is in Lettere della SC Congregazione dall' anno 1862.

The importance of being English

in his diocese. This second consideration was one of the reasons why he refused to allow his clergy and people to have anything to do with an address and petition in favour of the pope which was circulated throughout England in 1870.[36] He was afraid that accompanying demonstrations or public meetings might cause an outbreak of anti-catholicism in a town marked by bitter antagonism between Orange protestantism and Roman catholicism. After all, a debate on the question, 'Is Garibaldi a patriot?', had started a serious riot some years before, and cardinal Wiseman had been stoned after a public meeting because he had been indiscreet and had 'put on the lion's skin', as Goss had put it.[37] The local ordinary was in the best position to judge the seriousness of such dangers, and Goss told Barnabo so when the latter reprimanded him for his action.[38]

There was, however, a more important reason why he had objected to the address and petition, and here we touch on something which was very basic in Goss's thinking and in his approach to the question of episcopal independence. Already we have had hints of it in his attitude to Newman and his contrasting of curial intrigue with 'simple English truth'. He had been intensely annoyed to find that the petition had argued that all catholics, whatever their nationality, were 'citizens of Rome', an idea which had been put forward by some extreme papalists.[39] For his part, the bishop was always concerned to stress that English catholics were citizens only of England, and that in no sense could the pope claim even the smallest degree of that obedience and respect which a civil ruler could demand from his subjects. As well as resurrecting old accusations of divided loyalty against catholics, such an argument would only strengthen in Englishmen's minds the prejudice that catholicism was something foreign and un-English.

The bishop frequently touched on these matters in his sermons, especially when there were protestants present. For example, when

---

[36] AAL, Ad clerum letters of bishop Goss, 31 October 1870; *The Tablet* (London) 12 and 19 November 1870; ABO, Goss to Newman, 24 January 1871.

[37] For the riot, see [T.] Burke, [*Catholic History of Liverpool*] (Liverpool 1910) pp 154–5; for Wiseman, *ibid* p 138 and LRO, RCLv 5/2/466 and 468, Goss to Errington and Briggs, 4 February 1859.

[38] Goss told Newman what he had written, ABO, 24 January 1871.

[39] See the discussion in F. Dupanloup, *De La Souveraineté Temporelle Du Pape* (Paris 1849) p 15.

he was laying the foundation stone of a new church near Preston, he urged his hearers not to regard the ceremonies as a 'foreign superstition' or to think of catholics as Italian in their ideas and feelings and not genuine Englishmen.[40] Catholics, he continued, did not have a divided allegiance, nor was their loyalty suspect; indeed, they had been loyal for three hundred years, and that was why they had supported the Stuarts against Cromwell, even though the Stuarts had frequently persecuted them. It was, he said, 'the very principle of their religion—they cannot, and they dare not, be otherwise—they must be loyal as they must be honest . . . Let no one say that we are traitors or foreigners.' On another occasion he wrote, 'To the Sovereign of these realms we own allegiance, and we give it . . . It would be as great a sin to give to the Pope what belongs to the Crown as to give to the Crown what belongs to the Pope.'[41] Goss, indeed, gloried in his Englishness and in his loyalty to the queen. More than once he said of himself and his fellow catholics, 'we are not Italians, but Englishmen'.[42] Wiseman apparently envied his ability to put himself forward in such a light, and wrote to Propaganda that Goss was always telling his people, 'I am English, I am a real John Bull, indeed I am a Lancashire man'.[43]

For Wiseman, however, there was also something suspect in all this. He accused Goss of boastfully maintaining an 'Anglican . . . unRoman spirit',[44] an accusation which Manning would have agreed with. The latter thought that Goss was among those who were too English ever to be truly Roman, and wrote to Talbot that those who supported Newman held 'low views' about the Holy See, were 'cold and silent', to say no more, about the temporal power and were 'national' and 'English'.[45] Such a statement only underlines the lack of subtlety in their judgements about men and ideas, for Goss, despite all that has been said, was not anti-papal.

He believed that the pope held the primacy over the whole

---

[40] The sermon was published in *The Preston Chronicle*, 3 September 1864; a revised edition was published as a pamphlet, *Sermon and Address on the laying of the Foundation Stone at Euxton*; copy in Downside Abbey Library, pamphlet collection, A151 F, 12mo pamphlets number 34.
[41] AAL, Pastorals 14 Febraruy 1871.
[42] See n 40 above.
[43] Schiefen, 'Anglo-Gallicanism', p 43, n 117.
[44] Cwiekowski p 44, n 1.
[45] Butler, 1, pp 358–9.

church, that his person was 'august and sacred' and that the
catholics of Liverpool, as his devoted children, owed him 'profound respect, veneration and dutiful obedience' and shared in his
sufferings.[46] The pope was the supreme visible head of the church in
matters of faith and morals.[47] In 1859 he arranged for a diocesan
collection to be taken and for an address to be circulated for signatures,
as proof of 'the deep interest which we feel' in the pope's welfare.[48] The
address was signed by over fifty-three thousand people, and the
collection raised a staggering sum in excess of £7,000. The bishop
presented the address and the money in person in Rome, and on his
return wrote to pass on to the people the pope's gratitude and blessing.
Privately, however, he had been very disappointed with the papal
response and wrote that he had hardly been thanked at all and had taken
nothing back to his diocese but his independence.[49]

Some years later he issued a strongly worded pastoral letter on
the pope's temporal power, including in it an encyclical of the pope
on the same subject.[50] His views were very straightforward:
Garibaldi was a pest to society, and governments which had failed
to stop him were unfaithful and untruthful. It was puerile, he
continued, to say that the pope would have more respect without
his temporal possesions, since they were a necessary guarantee of
his independence. Furthermore, it was hypocritical of Englishmen
to say that spiritual and temporal power were incompatible in one
person, or that Rome belonged geographically to Italy: what about
the queen, and what about Gibraltar? The letter ended with
arrangements for a triduum of prayers and special services for the
pope, and another collection. The latter raised almost £2,000.[51]

Finally, in 1871, at a time when he was very critical of what had
been happening in Rome and was himself being criticised in papal
circles, he wrote another pastoral letter on the same subject. Again
he defended the temporal power, and he called on the British
government to exert itself to uphold the rights of its catholic
citizens.[52] The letter is more balanced in tone than the previous one.
The bishop admitted that the temporal power was not in any sense

[46] AAL, Roman Documents, *Address to the Holy Father 1860* (Liverpool 1860).
[47] AAL, Pasotrals 14 February 1871.
[48] AAL, Ad clerum letters, 3 and 25 December 1859, and 13 March 1860.
[49] LRO, RCLv 5/4/311, Goss to bishop Grant, 16 April 1862.
[50] AAL, Pastorals 11 December 1867.
[51] AAL, Roman Documents, Barnabo to Goss, 6 March and 18 June 1868.
[52] Above n 47.

essential to the papacy but was in practice part of God's plan. Its importance lay in ensuring that no political barrier should exist between the pope and his spiritual subjects, who must have free access to him for succour from every part of the world.

Whether Goss's approach to this new criterion of orthodoxy was sound enough for the papalists we do not know;[53] perhaps, at least, it surprised some who thought that he was un-Roman in his views. He fully accepted the papal primacy as being one of jurisdiction and not just of honour, but he saw a danger in the expansion of curial business and of Roman interference that the primacy would be so extended in practice as to undermine the position of the diocesan bishops, who were, in his eyes, 'princes of the household' to be consulted and conferred with, not given orders.[54] Moreover, the contemporary heavy stress on papal infallibility meant that there was an added danger of its being so extended as to claim some sort of administrative inerrancy for the pope and the Roman congregations.[55] Goss feared that the church in England would be dominated by curial thinking, that Italian solutions would be found for English problems and that, in the process, the church would lose its Englishness and its ability to appeal to Englishmen.

At the same time, he would have been naive to suppose that his frequent assertions of loyalty and patriotism were welcomed by all who heard them. When he declared, for example, of his fellow religionists, 'We have been born on the soil and have all the feelings of Englishmen. And we are proud of the government under which we now live. We believe it to be the best, the most perfect government in the world . . . We belong to the nation; in heart we are English, in purpose we are loyal,'[56] what did he think it meant to his predominantly Irish audience? He knew well that they had little cause to look favourably on English rule for he had written that, after centuries of government of a kind which could hardly be parallelled even in Russia, England had failed to win the affections

[53] Holmes, p 116, summarises the thinking on this issue.
[54] Goss to Newman, see n 31 above.
[55] Nobody was clear what the papal primacy of jurisdiction meant in practice; see the excellent discussion in G. Sweeney, 'The Primacy: the small print of Vatican I', in *Bishops and Writers*, ed A. Hastings (Wheathampstead 1977), pp 179–206; the German bishops issued an important document on the topic in 1875 which was approved by the pope (and the English bishops), see H. Küng, *The Council and Reunion*, (London 1961) pp 283–95, and also 196–204, 234–6.
[56] Above n 40.

of the Irish or to reconcile them to her rule; he even admitted that the injustices which they had suffered had been so great as to justify rebellion.[57] What was the relationship between himself and the Irish catholics in his diocese?

While one noted Irish nationalist described him as 'an Englishman of the best sort',[58] others were critical and believed that he was not interested in their affairs. He angered them when he said publicly that the Liverpool Irish stood as much chance of preferment as their English counterparts if only they would 'abstain from drink and other vices',[59] and on a number of occasions he outspokenly condemned fenianism, which was strong in the diocese.[60] It is clear that he felt that only by playing down their nationality could they be accepted in society, and so gain the position which 'their natural ability and the fertility of their mental resources' deserved.[61] On one occasion he went so far as to claim that he had no Irish priests in his diocese, for it was an English diocese ruled by an English bishop, and the clergy who served it were English clergy, whatever their country of origin.[62]

He attempted to defend himself against Irish charges of indifference and even hostility by claiming the existence of some ultra-national citizenship in which they all shared. At a Saint Patrick's night banquet he said that he was aware that it was said 'in some quarters' that he was so English and so Lancastrian that he had no sympathy with any problems outside his diocese. He repeated that he was proud to be an English subject, and that he thought this country was one of the greatest in the world; he went on, 'when I say this country I mean England, Ireland and Scotland, because it is perfectly chimerical to attempt to separate them – it is an impossibility. The people are spread and intermixed amongst each other, and there is hardly any work done or great act achieved, which is

[57] AAL, Pastorals 5 Frebruary and 28 September 1866.
[58] J. Denvir, *The Life Story of an Old Rebel* (Dublin 1910, reprinted 1972), p 156. Denvir was a Fenian, editor of *The Catholic Times*, arms smuggler and secretary of the Home Rule Confederation of the 1870s.
[59] Burke p 185–6.
[60] AAL, Pastorals 5 February 1866; Sermon of 29 September 1867, reported in *The Weekly Register* (London) 5 October 1867, pp 212–3. On Fenianism in the area see W. J. Lowe, 'Lancashire Fenianism 1864–71', *Transactions of the Historic Society of Lancashire and Cheshire* (Liverpool) 126. (1977) pp 156–85.
[61] LRO, RCLv 5/1/141, Goss to James Whitty, Esq, 19 March 1856; 5/3/64, Goss to Rev. Lans, 15 April 1859.
[62] Sermon of 29 September 1867, see n 60 above.

not equally shared by natives of the three different parts of the country.'[63]

However laudable this was as an ideal, it was unlikely to impress those who harboured long-standing feelings of injustice and who felt that they had to fight against prejudice when they tried for jobs or preferment. It is interesting that a later writer of strong Irish sympathies tried to defend Goss's attitude by saying that he sincerely believed that everyone had equal opportunities in England, and that he found it difficult to accept that his own countrymen could be deeply prejudiced against the Irish.[64] It may be that the bishop was right in thinking that there was little anti-Irish prejudice as such, for the evidence seems to show that the opposition was to them as catholics and not as Irish, and that the 'no Irish need apply' signs were not much in evidence in the 1850s and 1860s.[65] But there was opposition, and the immigrant no doubt found it of little interest whether he met it wearing one hat or another.

One must conclude that the bishop was prepared to allow a large number of his subjects to feel let down by his attitude to them, because to speak otherwise would for him have been dishonest, and because he attached the greatest importance to convincing protestants that catholics could be fully English. Did he perhaps also hope that his constant repetition of how English he and his fellow religionists were would effect what it signified among his Irish hearers?

Nineteenth-century controversialists delighted in attaching labels to their opponents and supporters, but little is to be gained by trying to decide whether Goss, and others like him, should be called 'sober ultramontane', 'gallican', 'radical anti-Romanist' or 'anglo-gallican'.[66] For him, being suspicious of what the curia and even the pope were doing did not mean being anti-papal, and being intensely English did not mean being anti-Roman or unsympathetic to

[63] The speech was reported with acclaim in *The Porcupine*, an independent Liverpool weekly, issue number 26, 30 March 1861.

[64] Burke p 186.

[65] W. J. Lowe, 'The Irish in Lancashire 1846–1871, A Social History', 2 vols, PhD thesis, Trinity College, Dublin 1974, pp 386, 393, 467; and S. W. Gilley, 'Evangelical and Roman Catholic Missions to the Irish in London 1830–1870', PhD thesis, Cambridge 1971, pp 30–5 for the relatively minor part played by anti-Irish sentiments in anti-catholicism.

[66] Butler used 'sober ultramontane' of Ullathorne, 2 p 48, and 'gallican' of Goss, *The Vatican Council*, 2 vols (London 1930) 1 p 206. Talbot used 'radical anti-Romanist'

the Irish; he, his priests and his people were just English Roman catholics.

Bedford College of Higher Education.

and 'anglo-gallican' of the English bishops; Schiefen, 'Anglo-Gallicanism', pp 36, 41.

THE KNOW-NOTHING PARTY, THE PROTESTANT EVANGELICAL COMMUNITY AND AMERICAN NATIONAL IDENTITY

by RICHARD CARWARDINE

B Y THE mid-nineteenth century, two generations after the revolution and the creation of an independent state, Americans were still unsure of the ultimate limits and character of their nation. If there was too much evident optimism over the country's prospects to write of the nation's suffering a crisis of identity, it is equally clear that the major questions of the 1840s and 1850s—territorial expansion, the future of slavery, and massive immigration—provided issues the precise resolution of which would fundamentally affect the future direction of the Union. Over the first two of these the evangelical protestant community, the dominant and most influential opinion-forming religious group in American society, found itself seriously divided; indeed by the eve of the civil war the slavery question had split all the major evangelical denominations. In contrast, this same community appeared to show much more cohesion and unanimity in defending the nation's evangelicalism against the swollen tide of foreign immigrants, three million of whom poured into American ports between 1845 and 1854, the vast majority victims of Irish famine and refugees from the European revolutions of 1848. The immediate danger to American nationality, as evangelicals defined it, lay not in the immigrants' poverty and foreignness, but in their catholicism. The Lutheran minister, Frederick Anspach, likened the American nation to a virgin who should 'sacredly guard her honor' against catholic vampires who 'would convert her into a courtezan for the Pope.'[1] If others used more discreet similes they nonetheless agreed that the nation's religious identity and funda-

---

[1] [Frederick R.] Anspach [, *The Sons of the Sires: A History of the Rise, Progress and Destiny of the American party . . .*] (Philadelphia 1855) p 171.

mental values were under threat. It is that identity, and the argument over the means used to defend it, that form the subject of this paper. For it was to become clear that evangelicals, unanimous in their anti-catholicism, were far from united over the methods they should use in this crusade, and that many considered the most extreme manifestations of anti-popery, particularly the know-nothing party, to vitiate their highest national ideals and values.[2]

That God acts not just through individuals but through nations, that every nation has a particular role to play in God's scheme of things, and that the role assigned to America is something quite special and distinct from that assigned to other nations is a set of beliefs that has undergirded much American thinking throughout her history. The particular expression that it received in the hands of antebellum evangelicals was nicely represented in Charles Boynton's historical excursus before the Cincinnati Native Americans in 1847. In his plan for the spread of Christianity, God committed to individual nations 'a solemn trust of principles and territory; . . . and when false to the trust . . . He has swept them away and chosen Him other instrumentalities'. His first trustee, the Hebrew nation, proving false to his charge, God replaced it as steward with the Christian church, which was itself soon corrupted by an emergent papacy that for over a thousand years drove 'truth and liberty . . . out of society . . . into the recesses of the mountains'. During the reformation the system of apostolic Christianity·re-emerged, was given first to Germany, where it lost its purity and power, and then to England under Cromwell, where again it was cast out. Only when God had led out the puritans from England and planted them in North America, as he had the Jews in Palestine, and had taken the side of the revolutionaries in the struggle for independence, did the future integrity of the principles of apostolic Christianity, now renamed puritanism, seem secure.[3] For Boynton and other evangelicals these principles embraced not just religious freedom and the separation of church and state, but also the dominant political values and forms of mid-nineteenth-century society: civil liberty, democracy and republicanism. Pro-

---

[2] There is a considerable secondary literature on anti-catholicism and the know-nothing party which cannot, for reasons of space, be considered here. Strangely little of it considers tensions *within* the evangelical community and this is what in part this paper seeks to do.

[3] [Charles B. Boynton,] *Oration* [, *delivered on the Fifth of July, 1847, before the Native Americans of Cincinnati*] (Cincinnati 1847) pp 14–16.

testantism, with its declaration of 'individual worth and individual rights [as] embodied in the teachings of the Saviour', with its emphasis on freedom of will and freedom of thought, and with its appeal to reason and to common sense, was a synonym for 'American principles'. To be true to God and his solemn charge to them, Americans had simply to maintain 'a Christian, Protestant, Democratic State'. In no other nation was the power of free institutions linked to an unfettered Christianity; 'here, for the first time on a large scale, the untrammelled gospel is working in concert with republican laws'. This uniqueness confirmed her status as chosen nation and new Israel.[4]

Insofar as Americans already enjoyed civil and religious liberty they could claim at mid-century to have fulfilled their role as guardians of God's sacred charge: democracy, at least for adult white males, and republicanism were firmly established. In return God had smiled on them and, although they saw dangers in its prosperity, evangelicals reflected with satisfaction on the size, fertility and wealth of their country, 'the very garden of the Lord, a Goshen among the nations'.[5] But there was still much to be accomplished. As a new nation, 'an unfolded bud', she was still an 'enigma', 'a germ of boundless things', who would usher the world into a new age in which false religion and false doctrine would yield before the power of protestant Christianity. The extensive and detailed reporting of foreign religious news in the weekly denominational presses makes plain the evangelical vision of the world as a battlefield between Mohammedanism, catholicism and other forms of error on the one hand, and a protestantism whose ultimate world-wide triumph was assured on the other.[6]

Evangelicals saw popery as not only deficient in doctrine—in its failure to build its theological scaffolding on the firm ground of justification by faith alone; in ecclesiastical organisation—its hier-

[4] *Ibid* pp 7–10; [Charles B. Boynton,] *Our Country[, the Herald of a New Era. A lecture . . .]* (Cincinnati 1853) p 20; [J. P.] Stuart [, *America and the Americans versus the Papacy and the Catholics. A lecture . . .*] (Cincinnati 1853) pp 12–18. Particularly helpful in understanding the American sense of mission are Ernest L. Tuveson, *Redeemer Nation: The Idea of America's Millennial Role* (Chicago 1968) and Sacvan Bercovitch, *The American Jeremiad* (Madison, Wisconsin 1978).

[5] *C[hristian] W[atchman and] R[eflector]* (Boston) 26 November 1857; Laurens P. Hickok, *A Nation Saved from its Prosperity only by the Gospel. A Discourse . . .* (New York 1853) pp 8–9.

[6] *Our Country* p 4; Erskine Mason, *'Signs of the Times'. A sermon . . .* (New York 1850) pp 12–20.

archical, centralised and 'despotic' structure; in its practices—its 'mummery', rituals and observance of empty forms and ceremonies.[7] It also corroded the political and social fabric. 'Republicanism and Romanism [were] antagonistic in their elements and tendencies', the powers wielded by catholic priests over their laity imcompatible with democracy; moreover, the secular policies of the pope and what was regarded as an unchanging, monolithic papacy—whether in opposition to Italian unity or Magyar nationalism—indicated a readiness to crush liberty wherever 'the scarlet woman of Rome' had the power to strike.[8] The free institutions of the United States stood in danger from 'the insidious workings of perjured Jesuits' operating hand in hand with the 'pettifogging demagogues', 'wire-pulling pimps' and the 'unprincipled and corrupt political hacks', particularly of the Democratic party.[9] By exploiting the ballot-box, manipulating gullible catholic voters, and thereby overthrowing the principle of state neutrality in religion, the pope aimed to destroy the protestant American republic. At the same time the popular ignorance and superstition that catholics sought to sustain through their 'war against literature and knowledge' would destroy any hope of social progress; the attempts of the catholic hierarchy in America in the 1850s to keep the king James bible out of the public schools was seen as an attack on education and the fundamentals of American life, which if successful would only increase the incidence of crime, poverty, intemperance and Sabbath-breaking, the bed-fellows of ignorance and priestly instruction.[10] Romanism sought to revive 'the darkness and barbarism of the Middle Ages'; wherever it was the dominant religion, even in naturally rich countries like Brazil, it acted as 'a

---

[7] See, for example, CWR 8 May 1856. The most authoritative treatment of American anti-catholic arguments in this period is [Ray Allen] Billington [, The Protestant Crusade 1800–1860] (New York 1938 and Chicago 1964; citations are to the latter edition).

[8] Anspach p 35; CWR 10 April 1856; Charles B. Boynton, Address before the Citizens of Cincinnati delivered on the Fourth Day of July, 1855 (Cincinnati 1855) pp 5, 15–16; W[estern] C[hristian] A[dvocate] (Cincinnati) 12 and 19 June 1850, 30 April, 7 May 1851.

[9] C[hristian] A[dvocate and] J[ournal] (New York) 18 June 1857; [Charles R. Atwood, 'The American Movement', in Our Country (New York 1854), ed W. H.] Ryder, pp 53–61.

[10] Edmund H. Kendall, A Sermon on the Primitive State of the Christian Church, the Usurpations of the Bishop of Rome, and the Corruptions and Abuses of the Papal Hierarchy (Boston 1853) pp 21–2; Stuart pp 5, 13, 19–20; Anspach pp 26–7, 34; CAJ 8 January, 27 August, 5 November 1857.

clog to progress'. 'The Pope' concluded a baptist correspondent of the *Christian Watchman,* 'has a natural dread of railroads and the other great enterprises of modern civilization.'[11] In short, for the American evangelical community, catholicism functioned to throw into sharp relief the fundamental elements of American nationality. The United States was all that the catholic church was not: republican, democratic, forward-looking, prosperous, vigorous, and committed to education, civil liberty, religious toleration and the separation of church and state.

Evidence for a Romish conspiracy seemed to increase in the early 1850s. Archbishop John Hughes spoke menacingly of the imminent 'decline of Protestantism'. The papal nuncio Gaetano Bedini arrived in 1853 to settle the dispute over 'trusteeism', the control of property within the catholic church, and was swiftly identified as the advance guard of a papal invasion. The American catholic hierarchy now began to flex its muscles and to offer a more self-confident uncompromising aspect to the protestant world. Evangelicals rallied by refashioning a number of their institutions along more systematically anti-catholic lines, by making even greater use of pulpit and press, and by creating an entirely new organisation, the American and Foreign Christian Union, designed to sustain evangelical lecturers and missionaries at home and abroad.[12] But were the weapons of moral suasion enough? Already in the 1840s nativists had attempted independent political action in New England and the northeast, and, though the Jacksonian two-party system had survived, its break-up was confidently predicted and worked for by those who considered that neither major party offered a platform around which protestantism could rally politically: the Democrats, whose Jeffersonian traditions committed them to a policy of religious toleration, successfully wooed the vast majority of catholic voters, while the whigs, though the bearers of the puritan tradition in politics and disproportionately evangelical in their popular support, refused as a party to wave the anti-catholic flag.[13] The victory of the Democratic candidate Franklin Pierce in the presidential election of 1852, and his appointing the catholic

---

[11] *CWR* 17 April 1856, 3 September 1857.
[12] Billington pp 289–300.
[13] *Oration* p 24; Lee Benson, *The Concept of Jacksonian Democracy: New York as a Test Case* (Princeton 1961) pp 278–87; Ronald P. Formisano, *The Birth of Mass Political Parties: Michigan, 1827–1861* (Princeton 1971) pp 137–64; [The] *Know-Nothing Almanac[; or True Americans' Manual for 1855]* pp 52–6.

James Campbell to the office of postmaster-general, convinced many nativists that their doom had been sealed by the foreign vote, that the whigs could not be trusted, and that the time had come to create a new political alliance. They turned to the Order of the Star-Spangled Banner, a secret society founded in New York in 1849 with the aim of pursuing a policy of secret political lobbying and of supporting for office the anti-catholic candidates of the major parties. Helped by a new leadership and by the national political disarray triggered by the Kansas–Nebraska bill, the order in 1854 established a national organisation with its own political wing, the American party and demanded that its members renounce allegiance to all other political groupings and maintain secrecy by replying, when interrogated, 'I know nothing'.[14]

The secrecy of the new movement means that precise evidence about its membership is scant. But evangelicals of all denominations clearly flocked to its standard, and were well represented in its leadership. Joseph Wright estimated that at least two thirds of all methodist ministers in Indiana were by autumn 1854 connected with 'these Secret Political organisations, as well as many ministers of other Denominations'; John Forney regarded baptists and methodists as the backbone of the movement in Pennsylvania; in Maryland the leadership drew disproportionately from the presbyterian and methodist churches.[15] Such recruits not only served to strengthen the semi-religious organisation of the movement, with its ranks, creeds and ceremonies, but to ensure that, following the startling know-nothing political successes in a number of state elections in 1854 and 1855, the legislative programmes of the party reflected its protestant evangelical pedigree. In addition to keeping catholics out of office, the know-nothings sought to disfranchise recently arrived immigrants by limiting voting to naturalised and literate immigrants who had served a twenty-one-year probationary period before citizenship. They looked for legislation that would require a daily reading of the king James bible in the public schools, that would allow for the investigation of nunneries, and

[14] Billington pp 380–5; [John Raymond] Mulkern [, 'The Know Nothing Party in Massachusetts'], unpubl PhD thesis (Boston University 1963) pp 33–44.
[15] Joseph Wright to Matthew Simpson, 23 October 1854 [Library of Congress] M[atthew] S[impson] P[apers, transcripts kindly lent by Dr. W. E. Gienapp]; [John W.] Forney[, *Address on Religious Intolerance and Political Proscription, delivered at Lancaster, Pa . . .*] (Washington 1855) pp 27–8; [Jean H.] Baker [, *Ambivalent Americans: The Know-Nothing Party in Maryland*] (Baltimore 1977) p 69.

that would give the catholic laity, not the bishops, control of church property.[16] By such measures would know-nothings preserve the Christian character of the nation, maintain a sharp definition of its identity, and remain true to the party's statement of its purposes as set out in its *Almanac* for 1855: 'Anti-Romanism, Anti-Bedinism, Anti-Pope's Toeism, Anti-Nunneryism, Anti-Winking Virginism, Anti-Jesuitism, and Anti-the Whole Sacerdotal Hierarchism with all its humbugging nunneries. Know-Nothingism is for light, liberty, education, and absolute freedom of conscience, with a strong dash of devotion to one's native soil.'[17]

For a while during the political turmoil of the mid-1850s it seemed that the American party might become the major political force in the country. Moribund whigs and frightened Democrats looked in awe at its mushroom growth, particularly at the political revolution in Massachusetts, where the know-nothings had emerged overnight from obscurity to take control of executive and legislative branches, and feared that the party would sweep to power nationally in the 1856 presidential election. Yet despite the best efforts of clergy and party propagandists to turn that election into a struggle 'not . . . of parties, but of nationalities', Millard Fillmore and the Americans secured only twenty-one per cent of the total vote.[18] America was an overwhelmingly protestant country, essentially evangelical in its orientation, not in the sense that 'every individual is a pious Christian, but [in] that the spirit of the evangelical system is in sufficient power to give to religious opinion and sentiment the complete ascendant in society.'[19] As such it might have been expected to give far greater support than it did to a party that sought to protect its protestant identity. Yet know-nothings never controlled either house of the national legislature, they made very little impact in the north-west, where there was a substantial catholic population, even in those states where they won power they failed signally to pass their legislative programme, and by the late 1850s the American party was everywhere a spent force. Why was this?

To some extent know-nothings were having to fight political

---

[16] Billington pp 327, 416; *CWR* 15 May 1856; Mulkern pp 8–9.
[17] *Know-Nothing Almanac*; Anspach pp 75–7, 105, 175.
[18] Anspach p 175.
[19] James Dixon, *Personal Narrative of a Tour through a part of the United States and Canada* . . . (New York 1849) p 143.

inertia and party loyalty. William G. Brownlow, methodist lay preacher and combative nativist, castigated 'the hypocritical and profligate portion of the Methodist, Presbyterian, Baptist and Episcopalian membership in this country' for its continued loyalty to the Democratic party. His explanation for their political behaviour ('they are in love with the *loose moral code* of Romanism . . . Backslidden, unconverted, or unprincipled members of Protestant Churches, find in Popery a *sympathising irreligion*, adapted to their vicious lives')[20] may have been too simple-minded, but it well illustrates the frustration of American party leaders at their failure to loosen the cement binding the Jacksonian party together; the issues around which the Jacksonians had focused in the 1830s and 1840s—broadly speaking, economic, political and moral laisser-faire—were still sufficiently potent to keep many protestants in a party that embraced the catholic community. Nor was the know-nothing cause strengthened by its failure in practice to live up to its high political ideals. It was easy for their opponents to characterise them in office as incompetent and politically maladroit. Soon the charges of 'corruption', 'intrigue' and 'hypocrisy' that know-nothings had themselves used to wrest power from the political establishment were echoing in their own ears. Exposés of political chicanery, written by expelled know-nothings could perhaps be brushed aside;[21] but it was less easy for the party to defend itself against charges of the abuse of power when it was revealed, to cite the most notorious example, that the 'nunnery' or 'smelling' committee of the Massachusetts legislature had misspent public funds while investigating the state's catholic institutions, and that its chairman, Joseph Hiss, had used his position to frighten catholic girls, make sexual propositions to nuns and charge to the state hotel expenses incurred while enjoying the company of a woman of easy virtue.[22] Most seriously, the know-nothing movement was weakened by the return of the slavery question to the centre of the political stage with the repeal of the Missouri compromise and the unfolding of events in 'bleeding' Kansas. Not only were there

[20] William G. Brownlow, *Americanism Contrasted with Foreignism, Romanism, and Bogus Democracy, in the light of Reason, History and Scripture* . . . (Nashville, Tennessee 1856) p 6.
[21] See, for example, [*History of the*] *Rise, Progress and Downfall of Know-Nothingism* [*in Lancaster County. By Two Expelled Members*] (Lancaster, Pennsylvania 1856) p 10 and *passim.*
[22] Mulkern pp 162–95; *CWR* 8 May 1856.

many anti-slavery northerners who were suspicious of the party's commitment to Unionism on southern terms and who believed that nativism hurt abolitionism, but southerners, too, were equally (and legitimately) suspicious of the abolitionist sympathies of northern know-nothings.[23] Those who stifled such concerns and joined the new party were soon forced to recognise their errors. Antislavery men who enlisted on the grounds that popery and slavery shared a common paternity, and that the catholic church and the immigrant were the most committed defenders of the peculiar institution could not indefinitely remain in peaceful tandem with southerners whose membership derived from a belief that in the American party lay their best hope for preserving the Union and avoiding the poisonous question of the status of blacks.[24] In June 1855 the movement split in two; thereafter the breach was never properly healed. When the 'south Americans' nominated Millard Fillmore for the presidency in 1856, northern know-nothings—or 'know-somethings' as they had now become—found themselves manoeuvred into supporting the Republican candidate, John L. Fremont. That they were prepared to support a Republican platform that made no reference to nativism, and a candidate who was widely—but mistakenly —believed to be a catholic, suggested that by late 1856 slavery had absorbed nativism as the major political question at national level.[25]

But the explanation for the failure of the American party to win broader support must be deeper than this. The know-nothings' fundamental weakness was that while they paraded as the guardians of the nation's evangelical and republican identity, their methods and rhetoric seemed to undermine the very values they sought to defend. In the first place, the secrecy of the movement, its ceremonies, handshakes, grips, signs, passwords and pledges, served not only to create an excitement and mystery that helped

[23] Augustus B. Longstreet, *Letter from President Longstreet to the Know-Nothing Preachers of the Methodist Episcopal Church South* (New Orleans 1855) pp 6–7; *Corning Journal* 27 October 1854 (transcript kindly lent by Dr W. E. Gienapp).
[24] *CWR* 17 April 1856, 1 January 1857; James H. Broussard, 'Some Determinants of Know-Nothing Electoral Strength in the South, 1856', *Louisiana History* 7 (Lafayette, La., 1966) pp 5–20.
[25] *The Duty of Native Americans in the Present Crisis* (np 1856); *J. C. Fremont's Record. Proof of his Romanism. Proof of his Pro-slavery Acts* (np 1856). For an example of a northern Methodist who left Fillmore for Fremont in 1856, see George Law and Chauncey Shaffer, *Geo. Law and Chauncey Shaffer's reasons for repudiating Fillmore and Donelson* (New York 1856) pp 7–8.

attract members, but also to alienate many who argued passionately that secret societies were anti-Christian. The presbyterian
minister, Jonathan Blanchard, a life-long critic of secret organisations, considered them proscribed by Paul's injunction that the
Christian should 'have no fellowship with the unfruitful works of
darkness'. Secret ceremonies turned Christianity into 'popish
mummeries', 'a religion of forms without Christ' similar to the
popery they aimed to enfeeble; the pledge to remain silent was a
form of blasphemy.[26] True Christianity operated openly and
directly, and shrank 'instinctively from every scheme which pro-
poses to work underground like a mole'.[27] 'American principles'
and 'American taste' were equally threatened by the anti-democra-
tic and anti-republican tendencies of these organisations. It was
more than political partisanship that prompted a leading Indiana
Democrat to criticise his Methodist colleagues for turning their
backs on 'open and fair discussion': public debate and an appeal to
men's reason was essential to the democratic process.[28] A southern
evangelical voiced a related concern over the know-nothings' secret
pledge to support whatever man or measure the organisation
proposed: thereby they surely lost their status as freemen and
became 'the serfs of opinions and measures coined for them . . . by
a corporate body'. Secret societies were despotic institutions,
inegalitarian in their use of titles, ranks and degrees, which allowed
their leaders such power as no republic operating on the consent of
the governed could allow. Here was papal priestcraft in different
clothes.[29] Indeed here too was freemasonry under another guise; for
it seems clear that in some areas the secrecy and ritual of know-
nothingism attracted members of masonic and temperance lodges:
in Maryland thirty-one per cent of all nativists were freemasons.[30]
Conversely it is evident that opposition to know-nothingism drew
strongly on a vigorous anti-masonic tradition within evangelical
churches. When Jonathan Blanchard denounced the seemingly
innocuous Sons of Temperance for their attachment to secrecy he

[26] [Jonathan] Blanchard[, *Secret Societies, An Argument* . . .] (Chicago 1851) pp 5,
7, 9, 23–4.
[27] [P.] Godwin [, 'Secret Societies—The Know Nothings'], *Putnam's Monthly
Magazine* 5 (New York 1855) p 85.
[28] Joseph Wright to Matthew Simpson, 23 October 1854, MSP.
[29] ['A] Calm Discussion [of the Know-Nothing Question',] *Southern Literary
Messenger* 20 (Richmond, Va. 1854) p 542; Blanchard pp 6–7, 10–11, 16, 28;
'Know-Nothingism', *Democratic Review* 37 (Washington 1856) p 492.
[30] Baker pp 69–71.

was moved as much by fears of recrudescent freemasonry as by abstract principle. The frequent condemnation of secret societies in church minutes in the 1850s, even after the demise of know-nothingism, indicates that he was by no means alone.[31]

Know-nothings courted further criticism from within the evangelical community for encouraging, at least implicitly, a hatred of the foreigner. Their anti-catholicism did not necessarily have to spill over into a nativist fear of all newcomers: William H. Ryder strenuously denied the charge that the American movement was 'little less than a crusade against those who have sought a home in the country'; Alfred B. Ely agreed that every man 'should be measured by his intrinsic worth'; Charles Boynton insisted that '[g]enuine American principles . . . neither demand nor imply the slightest hatred or prejudice' against the European immigrant.[32] But even the most dedicated know-nothings had to admit that xenophobia and prejudice did exist in their ranks, and their evangelical opponents were quick to identify the apparent encouragement or at least tacit endorsement that the movement gave to rabble-rousing and mob action against the immigrant community.[33] More specifically, to exclude the foreign-born from the political process would 'establish in our midst an alien and finally a hostile population', 'an immense body of political lepers'; it would be wholly at odds with the vision of America as a tolerant, inclusive democracy and asylum for the poor and oppressed.[34] True Americanism, as a southern baptist saw it, was not the 'two-penny patriotism' and 'pride of race' of the American party but '[t]he sublime principle of human fraternity' and of democracy.[35] It was on this principle—that a man's American-ness derived from his commitment to democracy and protestantism, and not from his ethnic type—that evangelicals multiplied their missions to the foreign-born and foreign-language speaking communities, particularly the Germans and Scandinavians, in the 1840s and 1850s. This was the basis of the reassurance offered to his vigorously anti-

[31] Blanchard p 9 and *passim*; *WCA* 12 June, 23 October 1850, 28 May 1851; John R. McKivigan, 'Abolitionism and the American Churches 1830–1865: A Study in Attitudes and Tactics', unpubl PhD thesis (Ohio State University 1977) p 184.
[32] Ryder p vi; [Alfred B.] Ely [, *American Liberty: its sources, its dangers, and means of preservation. An oration . . .*] (New York 1850) p 17; *Oration* p 16.
[33] Ryder p vii; *WCA* 23 January 1850.
[34] Forney p 35; Godwin p 96.
[35] 'Know-Nothingism' pp 490–1.

catholic readers by the New York correspondent of the methodist *Western Christian Advocate* in 1851: 'I have little fear that Romanism will become properly neutralized in this country, by the agency of the Irish. They become Americans too readily, and sink their original nationality in the newly-adopted character with too much facility'. Encouraged too by the vigorous denunciations of nativism by evangelical immigrants, many protestants came to recognise the conflicting premises on which these missions and know-nothing activity were based.[36]

By the mid-nineteenth century it had become an article of faith of almost all Americans that the separation of church and state was to the best advantage of the religious community and in the true interests of republican freedom. The evangelical opponents of know-nothingism consequently directed their most severe criticisms at the movement's efforts to use the power of the state for sectarian religious purposes. Protestant ministers running for political office to promote legislation that discriminated on the basis of religious belief represented what George B. Russell described as a fanatical denial of religious freedom by those 'who once boasted that [in the United States] Politics and Religion were forever divorced.'[37] Know-nothings themselves argued that fire had to be fought with fire: ultramontane catholics in Europe and America sought political power to rule both church and state, and restricted the religious freedoms of non-catholics.[38] Why should Americans extend toleration to a church which, as well as using its political power to prevent the preaching of a protestant gospel by American missionaries in Rome, made no secret that through the ballot-box and immigration catholics would acquire enough power in America to end religious freedom there? To defend American principles of equality, toleration and separation of church and state all means were legitimate. It is significant that when the congregationalist know-nothing Alfred B. Ely explored the origins and character of Christian liberty in America he should have

[36] *WCA* 5 February 1851; Robert P. Swierenga, 'The Ethnic Voter and the First Lincoln Election', *Civil War History* II (Iowa City 1965) pp 27–43.
[37] George B. Russell, 'Unended Controversy', *Mercersburg Review* 7 (Lancaster, Pa., 1855) p 235. [Winthrop S.] Hudson[, *The Great Tradition of the American Churches*] (New York 1953) examines the voluntary system, without considering the know-nothing movement. Billington, too, is oddly silent on this issue.
[38] Anspach pp 28–32; Henry W. Davis, *The Origin, Principles and Purposes of the American Party* (np 1855) pp 26–37.

extolled Cromwell as one of the nation's greatest benefactors: 'If he was despotic, it was the despotism of Divinity, which compels men to do right because it is right, and to live under and enjoy the sanctions of equal privileges and duties whether they will or no.'[39] For Ely and many like him the removal of the last formal vestiges of the union of church and state—in Massachusetts in 1833—did not absolve the government from its responsibility to protect protestant freedoms and to remind men of their moral and religious obligations.

By no means all were persuaded by this line of argument. For instance, the know-nothing distinction between the catholics' religious rights, which would be left unscathed, and catholic political intrusions, which would be stubbornly resisted, appeared empty and unrealistic: 'is it not apparent, that if you deprive the adherents of a particular form of religious belief, from the enjoy- ment of public office, you are to that extent crippling the church, of which they are members, and thus hindering the free exercise of religious opinions?'[40] Moreover, even if such a distinction could be sustained, any attempted exclusion of catholics was inconsistent with the federal constitution's protection of religious freedom, and was more in keeping with the religious intolerance associated with the old world.[41] Matthew Simpson, editor of the largest Methodist newspaper in the west, noting the efforts of Pius IX to prevent services in the protestant chapel in Rome, and the more-or-less simultaneous introduction of the ecclesiastical titles bill into the British parliament, insisted that American protestants had far too much vigour and confidence to want similarly to infringe upon the rights of minority religious groups.[42] Indeed, to concede the principle that the majority could use its political power to legislate against the interests of a minority, left the way open for further crusades once catholicism had been proscribed: 'Next, we shall have a similar crusade against the High Church Episcopalians —some of whom it is even now affirmed, are but a step removed

[39] Ely pp 10–12.
[40] 'Calm Discussion' p 541.
[41] Article 6 of the constitution specified that no religious test should be required as a qualification for political office. That one and a half million American catholics were native-born made the attempts to exclude them from office seem particularly proscriptive. Forney pp 22, 32; *Buchanan and Breckinridge: The Democratic Handbook . . . recommended by the Democratic National Committee* (Washington 1856) compiled by Michael W. Cluskey, pp 33–4.
[42] *WCA* 29 January, 4 May, 20 August 1851.

from the Catholics—then the Low Church Episcopalians will share the same fate;—then the Presbyterians and so on until the country shall become the scene of a religious, civil and social war'.[43]

This argument seemed particularly plausible to those whose churches and denominations had historically suffered at the hands of the established churches. Persecution suffered by, as it might be, methodists and baptists at the hands of congregationalists and episcopalians in New England and the Old South, had served to drive many into the arms of a Jeffersonian democratic party opposed to what has been called the 'right-wing' puritan tradition.[44] Disestablishment did not end this political association. For these evangelicals were often happier staying in a party that did not look to the state for the regulation of morals. They saw first the whigs and then the know-nothings as bearers of the traditions of the right-wing puritanism that they mistrusted. A Virginian who was both a high Calvinist baptist and a democrat spoke for this group when he explained that, though he might despise the catholic system and its representatives, 'he certainly never felt severely frightened at them, or disposed to do that violence to the memory of Roger Williams or Lord Baltimore, to attempt the disfranchisement of an American citizen because he—the said citizen—fancied the well-served mass of Catholicism . . . instead of a plain hymn and sound sermon on faith or predestination'. Instead he would remain loyal to a party that adhered to a belief in the capacity of the people for self-government, in the need to limit the role of all government, and in the application of the voluntary principle in all things.[45] It was not through legal and political pressure but through moral suasion, through the preaching of the gospel, through revivals that catholicism would crumble. Romanism could not survive in a free environment fostering free enquiry: it grew in America not through conversions, but through immigration.[46] 'Frank and friendly discussion', wrote Laurens Hickok, 'the

[43] 'Calm Discussion' pp 541–2. See also, John L. Dawson, Speech . . . before the great Democratic mass meeting at Waynesburg, Greene County, Pennsylvania, August 21, 1856 (Washington 1867) p 34.

[44] For a discussion of 'right-wing' puritanism and its commitment to a 'Standing Order', and of 'left-wing' puritanism, which was sceptical about the reliance of the church on secular institutions, see Hudson pp 42–62.

[45] 'Know-Nothingism' pp 495–6. See also Oscar P. Fitzgerald, Judge Longstreet: a Life Sketch (Nashville, Tennessee 1891) pp 109–27.

[46] George Coles, My First Seven Years in America (New York 1852) p 37; CWR 10 April, 1 and 15 May 1856.

preaching of Protestant truth in its purity, and full permission to the Catholic to preach Romanism as he will, but to meet him in candor and love, in faithfulness and firmness, at all times and in all places of the land,—this will ultimately assimilate all on the right basis.'[47]

Instead, then, of rallying to the know-nothing party in the face of catholic intrusions, many evangelicals in the mid-1850s chose either to stay in the Democratic party or join the emergent Republican organisation. This they did not simply because of the slavery issue, though this must be the primary explanation of the electoral patterns of 1856, nor because they had weakened in their anti-catholic resolve, as the great revival of 1857–8, which represented a sort of sabre-rattling at the Pope and his troops, made clear.[48] They shunned know-nothingism because, despite its protestations to the contrary, it seemed to challenge the principle of voluntarism for which so many of them had fought; it seemed to favour a flawed, exclusive democracy. By having nothing to do with religious tests and by avoiding the rhetoric of nativism, both Republican and Democratic parties could present themselves as bearers of the best national traditions, as defenders of the nation's true identity, and hope to win the support of those whom the methods of the American party had offended so deeply.[49] The know-nothings' secrecy, their fanning of xenophobia, and their readiness to use the power of the state for proscriptive purposes was, as one disillusioned member of the movement explained, 'no way to rear a nationality and perpetuate freedom.'[50]

University of Sheffield.

---

[47] Hickok p 13.
[48] Richard Carwardine, 'The Religious Revival of 1857–8 in the United States', *SCH* 15 (1978) pp 404–5.
[49] *The Pope's Bull and the Words of Daniel O'Connell* (New York 1856) p 6.
[50] *Rise, Progress and Downfall of Know-Nothingism* p 29.

RELIGION AND IDENTITY IN MODERN BRITISH HISTORY

(PRESIDENTIAL ADDRESS)

by KEITH ROBBINS

'THE Church of England' declared a leading article in *The Times* on 8 July 1980 'is the British national church'. Such a novel declaration produced apoplexy at the presidential breakfast-table. My topic is an impossibly wide one, only tackled previously, in his distinctive fashion, by Dr Daniel Jenkins.[1] I cannot hope to cover every aspect of it. That apparently innocent sentence in the newspaper does, however, provide me with my text. Its context was an article concerning itself with the possibility that the Prince of Wales might marry a Roman Catholic. Not even a president of the Ecclesiastical History Society can offer comment as to probabilities in this matter and, like *The Times*, we are only concerned with principles. Concluding, perhaps not surprisingly, that it would seem intolerable to the 'broad public' that an excellent heir to the throne should be excluded because of his wife's religion it added that 'any sensible person' would hope that the matter would not be raised. There were still what it called 'anti-Catholic prejudices' among a relatively small minority in England and Wales, a rather larger minority in Scotland and a considerable proportion of the Protestant community in Northern Ireland. A constitutional issue 'which would bring all these birds flapping down out of the rafters' was not desirable.[2]

Whatever view we take of the leader and the language it employed, modern British history, perhaps more than the history of any other European state, discloses a complex inter-relationship betwen political attitudes, ecclesiastical allegiances and cultural traditions. The Christian religion in the British Isles, in its divided condition, has in turn been deeply involved in the cultural and political divisions of modern Britain and Ireland. Churches have been, in some instances and at some periods vehicles for the cultivation of a 'British' identity corresponding to the political

[1] D. T. Jenkins, *The British: their Identity and their Religion* (London 1975).
[2] *The Times*, 8 July 1980.

framework of Great Britain and Ireland. They have also been instrumental, in part at least, in perpetuating and recreating an English, Irish, Scottish or Welsh identity distinct from and perhaps in conflict with 'British' identity, both culturally and politically. Sometimes this role has been quite unconscious, but in other instances it has been explicit and deliberate.

We must, I suppose, linger a little on the term 'national identity'. To tackle it comprehensively would take a lecture in itself. Nations may be defined by a supposed common ethnic origin, by use of a particular language, by a shared literary inheritance, by reference to a well-defined geographical region—and so on—but few nations have all of these characteristics and some have none. Indeed, prolonged immersion in the literature written by nationalists and in the writings of scholars primarily concerned with nationalism speedily leads to the conclusion that the nation is a very subjective concept.[3] Some nations have had a long history of statehood, some a short, and some have never achieved it at all. To reverse the order, some states have, in time, become consolidated into nations, whereas others have continued to contain distinct nations, living in harmony or conflict as the case may be. Given the frequent pattern of conquest, migration or dynastic merger, national identity has rarely been fixed and constant through time.[4] Some historians would argue that we cannot helpfully talk about national identity until, say, the end of the eighteenth century; others find such a sharp break untenable. The churches have played an ambiguous and contradictory part in the preservation or stimulation of national consciousness. It would be premature to generalize at the beginning of this paper—just as it will be impossible to generalize at its conclusion!

In such a context, it is not a straightforward matter to characterize British national identity or, to put it another way, how many national identities there are in the British Isles. The United Kingdom of Great Britain and Ireland of 1800 had been achieved through a centuries-long process of coercion and consent. I do not need here to discuss it in detail or to assess the degree of coercion and the extent of consent as regards each component part. It could appear that a British state would emerge—North, West and South Britain—which would transcend and perhaps submerge, in time,

[3] For example, A. D. S. Smith, *Theories of Nationalism* (London 1971).
[4] H. Seton-Watson, *Nations and States* (London 1976).

the nations—if that is what they were—of England, Ireland, Scotland and Wales. In this arrangement, there was no disputing that the English were the strongest (by almost any indicator one chooses) and arguably the most coherent. The terms 'Britain' and 'England' could seem virtually synonymous, particularly given the tendency of Europeans to refer simply to England. It therefore seemed in the logic of events that the consolidation of Britain should entail some degree of 'Anglicization'. Not wishing to imply a systematic policy to this end, I deliberately use a vague expression. 'Anglicization', however, although frequently criticized by its opponents, is not an easy term to use. At its simplest, it means only that, by one means or another, knowledge of the English language should become universal in Ireland, Scotland and Wales. This was judged to be necessary not only for administrative convenience but also in the interests of 'improvement'. To become fluent in English was to enter the commercial, intellectual and industrial world of the nineteenth century. 'Anglicization', however, involved more than language; it meant a subtle process of assimilation and acculturation. English methods and mores would tend to become the norm beyond the boundaries of England. Not that the exchange was all in one direction; over the period under consideration, travel and migration was to bring about an increase in the non-English population of England on a scale never before achieved. Although in this sense England became Britain in microcosm it was an open question how far immigrants would seek to maintain any kind of separate identity.

My suggestion is that the churches of the British Isles were inescapably caught up in this process of linguistic and cultural adaptation. The central problem was this: the main confessional families—Roman Catholic, Episcopalian, Presbyterian, Methodist, Baptist/Congregationalist, not to mention smaller groups—had all, by the nineteenth century, spread to all parts of the United Kingdom. In this sense, the British Isles could be thought of as one entity from an ecclesiastical standpoint. However, although all denominations could be found in all countries they did not, of course, exist in the same proportions in all countries. And, throughout the nineteenth century and into the twentieth there were to be significant shifts in those proportions within England, Ireland and Scotland in particular. This concentration within diffusion ensured that during our period no British church—of any confessional family—emerged. The Roman Catholic Church was unique insofar as the seat of its authority existed beyond the boundaries of the state but within the state it too organized itself on a basis which accepted Ireland and Scotland as distinct units, though England and Wales were taken as one single unit.

At the beginning of the nineteenth century, constitutionally and formally, the United Kingdom could be characterized as a protestant state. By the close of the First World War, again in constitutional terms, this was only partially the case. The most striking changes were the disestablishment of the Church of England in Ireland and in Wales.[5] These two measures constituted a recognition of the fact that the ecclesiastical situation in these two countries was distinctive. The Church of England remained the established church in England and the Church of Scotland in Scotland. The United Kingdom therefore remains unique among unitary states in operating three different relationships with the churches in different parts of its territory. I say three deliberately, since the nature of the establishment in Scotland, both before and after 1929, is different from that in England and, of course, involves churches belonging to different confessional families. In the absence of devolved government, the churches have come to be perhaps the most significant institutional embodiments of regional or national identity.

In England, the Church of England rarely hesitated to claim that it embodied the Englishness of English Religion. Its spokesmen, clerical and lay, often referred to it with approval as 'Our National Church'.[6] That claim rested upon the intertwining of church and state at many levels, consolidated over centuries. Its ethos was the essence of the English ethos. It was comprehensive and dogmatically generous, with an apparently instinctive capacity for compromise and conciliation. The English church suited the English character and the English character had made the English church. It was the corporate expression of the Englishman's kind of Christianity. Anglican headmasters and bishops were not loathe to talk about 'the English people' and 'the English character'. At its best, of course, they embodied true Englishness themselves. A wide

[5] P. M. H. Bell, *Disestablishment in Wales and Ireland* (London 1969).
[6] Some other material on this theme can be found in R. H. Malden, *The English Church and Nation* (London 1952), and C. H. E. Smyth, *The Church and the Nation: six Studies in the Anglican Tradition* (London 1962).

variety of illustration would be possible and I only put forward a few examples. Thomas Arnold, not unexpectedly, declared that he could 'understand no perfect Church, or perfect State, without their blending into one in this ultimate form'. His conviction of the importance of the royal supremacy—'the assertion of the supremacy of the Church or Christian society over the clergy' made him 'equally opposed to popery, High Churchism, and the claims of the Scotch Presbyteries, on the one hand; and to all the Independents . . . on the other.'[7] To achieve the Christian England of his dreams he wished to make the Church of England even more comprehensive and draw in dissenters—although Roman Catholics, Unitarians and Quakers would be unlikely to join.[8] He noted in 1834 the 'tremendous influx of Irish labourers into Lancashire and the west of Scotland' which was 'tainting the whole population with a worse than barbarians element.' It was not surprising that 'the Roman Catholics are increasing fast amongst us'.[9] Believing that the thorough English gentleman—Christian, manly, and enlightened —was 'a finer specimen of human nature' than any other country could furnish, it was the duty of the Church of England to protect this paragon from the assaults of his enemies.[10] Whether the dissenters could really assist was doubtful because, for all their admirable qualities they also exhibited the characteristic faults of the English mind—narrowness of view, a want of learning and a sound critical spirit.

In the same decade, in *The Kingdom of Christ* F. D. Maurice wrestled with the problem of universality and national identity. 'We count it a great happiness', he wrote 'if we can discover forms of worship which have stood the test of ages; because the feelings that we most express in worship, are our deep, primary, human, universal feelings, not those which belong to our condition, as living in one period, or under one condition of circumstances. But though this be the case, here, too, the difference of language and manners must intrude itself. Our worship will not be true, will not really belong to us, if, starting from that deep and general

[7] A. P. Stanley, *The Life and Correspondence of Thomas Arnold*, 2 vols (London 1845) 2 pp 190–1.
[8] Thomas Arnold, *Principles of Church Reform*, ed M. J. Jackson and J. Rogan (London 1962).
[9] Stanley, *Arnold* 1, p 397.
[10] *Ibid* 1, p 391.

foundation, it does not adapt itself to our own peculiar position, and avail itself of our native forms of expression.'[11] A proper stress upon the national identity of the Church of England did not compromise its catholicity. The nation was the appropriate unit of ecclesiastical organization because the nation too embodied God's purpose. Although later in the century Charles Kingsley was to express his profound regret that Germans were not members of the Church of England, Maurice thought that even to talk of converting continental peoples to be members of the English church was 'a solecism in thought and language, of which I trust no reader can suspect me of being guilty'. The task of a patriot was 'to seize, confirm, and magnify all those principles and institutions of his Church, which belong not to one country but to all'. And, in the subordinate and ceremonial parts, to 'give effect and expression to that which is peculiar in the character and feeling of his own country'.[12] If asked why there should not be a Church of London or of Liverpool Maurice replied that 'we wish to adapt ourselves to God's methods, and not to man's. If he sees it good that the people of London should talk one language and the people of Liverpool another, that the people of London shall have one king and the people of Liverpool another, *then* must we also shape ourselves according to His designs, and submit to those differences which He has made necessary.'[13] Maurice does not seem to have considered the possibility that the people of London and Liverpool did talk different languages.

At the end of the century, Mandell Creighton as bishop of London was writing that 'the English Church must be the religious organ of the English people. The people need not agree about details, but the general trend of the Church must be regulated by their wishes. The Church cannot go too far from the main ideas of the people.' The nation, he argued 'exists by virtue of a particular type of character. Character is largely founded on religion. There is in some quarters an attempt to bring back religious observances of an exotic kind which do menace English character'. The function of the Church of England was to be the church of free men. The Church of Rome was 'the Church of decadent peoples: it lives only on its past, and has no future . . . The Church of England has

---

[11] F. D. Maurice, *The Kingdom of Christ*, 3 vols (London 1838) 3, pp 356–7.
[12] *Ibid* 3, pp 368–9.
[13] *Ibid* 3, p 358.

before it the conquest of the world . . . The question of the future of the world is the existence of Anglo-Saxon civilisation on a religious basis. The Church of England means a great and growing power in America and in the Colonies.'[14] J. N. Figgis in his *Hopes for English Religion* (1919) stressed 'the extraordinary power of the English character to stand by the old while assimilating the new, which has been her greatest political strength in the past, and is likely to be her greatest contribution to the future.'[15] So it was with the future of the English church. Nothing would be gained by members of the English church looking across the water and wishing that they were there. The path of what he called 'English Catholicism' was to be quite distinctive. Hensley Henson saw 'the best hope' for English Religion in the effective union of the evangelical and liberal elements. Such an union could not be restricted to the Church of England, but would draw together men of goodwill in all the Churches of English speech.'[16] To take the Church of England off in any other direction would be to forfeit its place in the consciousness of the nation. The love affair of bishops with the English people continued unabated. Luke Paget, for example, was described as seeing in them 'a patience and good-humour, a soundness of judgment and readiness to forgive, a fairness and tolerance and, above all, a strange, tenacious, inarticulate recognition of Almighty God'. He hoped that 'the reserve, freedom and balance of English Churchmanship had contributed to this desirable amalgam.'[17]

This constant harping upon English attributes and virtues seems largely to have been passed from generation to generation. A common core of Englishness was self-evident; to have attempted to define it would have been un-English. 'Those, who have never left their own country' wrote R. W. Jelf in 1835 in a preface to sermons he had preached in Berlin 'and who continue in the bosom of the Church, should learn to value their English blessings, and to thank God for their own exemption from danger'. He continued that 'the number of persons annually exposed to the immorality and unbelief of France, to the rationalism of Germany, to the *sensual* devotions of the Church of Rome, and to the religious neutrality

[14] L. Creighton, *Life and Letters of Mandell Creighton*, 2 vols in 1 (London 1913) 2, pp 301–2.
[15] J. N. Figgis, *Hopes for English Religion* (London 1919) p 101.
[16] H. Hensley Henson, *In Defence of the English Church* (London nd) p 43.
[17] E. K. Paget, *Henry Luke Paget* (London 1939) p 21.

engendered by a cursory view of many modes of worship in succession, cannot be contemplated without alarm . . .' English parents who were settling abroad for the purpose of educating their children should realise that 'foreign accomplishments can be too dearly bought at the experience of those homebred qualities, which, with all the faults of our nation, do still distinguish the genuine *English* character.[18]' Some Germans, as F. W. Robertson noted, wished to be delivered from 'the affliction of that horrid nation passing through our towns and besetting us like a plague of flies in our diligences, hotels, walks, with their stupid faces, their vulgarity, their everlasting inquisitiveness about hotels and sight-seeing, and utter inability to appreciate anything higher'. Robertson himself found that there was more scope for soul-searching of a high order in Heidelberg than in Cheltenham.[19]

This equation of the national ethos with the Church of England posed problems for dissenters both Protestant and Roman Catholic. Protestant dissenters pressed, with varying degrees of persistence and enthusiasm for the disestablishment of the Church of England. They sought no recognition from the state for themselves. They played no official part in the ceremonial ife of the state. Their role in the nineteenth-century armed services, for example, was slight.[20] Yet that expanded role in parliament and public life actively sought and in large measure gained necessarily weakened their own internal coherence and sense of being, to an extent, a 'nation within a nation'. Independents, for whom 'the Church' might be the church at Pembroke Place, Liverpool, were in process of forming and expanding the role of national unions—in both the Baptist and Congregational traditions. English noncon-formists, who were, for the most part, English did not disavow their national identity or cease to feel as Englishmen felt. English preachers, like Newman Hall, could be recognized even on the summit of Snowdon and be compelled to preach a sermon. Two years later, in the same region, a man driving a cart containing a live pig gave him a lift and told him that his words had resulted in the conversion of fifty people. He added that 'as they only spoke

[18] R. W. Jelf, *Sermons, Doctrinal and Practical, Preached Abroad* (London 1835) pp vii, xi-ii.
[19] S. A. Brooke, *Life and Letters of F. W. Robertson* (London 1868) p 99.
[20] H. J. Hanham, 'Religion and Nationality in the mid-Victorian Army', *War and Society*, ed M. R. D. Foot (London 1973).

Welsh they did not understand a word you said'. Hall reflected that he 'greatly admired the religious zeal of the Welsh, and their diligent attendance at public worship' but felt their denomination-alism to be 'excessive' and to result in 'too great multiplication of churches'.[21] His extensive preaching in Wales made him aware that he was English. It made him, and other dissenters of his generation vulnerable to appeals to English history like that in a letter from dean Farrar. Farrar wanted to see cordiality established between the national church and all branches of Christian nonconformists. Religion as a whole would suffer by 'the nation's disavowing all connexion with the creed which it has held for 1,500 years . . .' Nonconformists would suffer 'as heavily as we, the *nation*, would suffer. The gain would be to Romanism and to secularism; the loss would be to the cause of Christ.'[22] Archbishop Magee, too, knew that the Englishman was almost as susceptible as the Irishman to the appeal of the past as a reason for maintaining the establishment. There was, he argued, still in the heart of the nation 'some reverence for the past, some love of old ways and institutions, not merely because they are old but becase their very age proves their strength and worth . . .'[23] This desire not to be thought a race apart accelerated in the twentieth century. Comparable problems existed for Roman Catholics. The particular quality of English Roman Catholicism was threatened from two sources during our period. Large-scale Irish immigration naturally posed great personal and organizational problems. The small English catholic community, largely socially distant from the immigrants, struggled between a not inconsiderable dislike of the habits and outlook of the Irish and their obligation to assist their co-religionists. Should English catholics seek to assist the Irish in becoming English and thus give Roman Catholicism in England a thoroughly English face or should they accept and perpetuate the Irish dimension thus per-petuating the notion that Roman Catholicism was un-English? The short answer would be to say that the outcome lay beyond the capacity of the English community to control. It was a matter which gave rise to considerable difficulty and tension, particularly where Irish priests in England in many instances frequently believed that the only way of maintaining a high level of practice in

[21] Newman Hall, *An Autobiography* (London 1898) pp 158–60.
[22] *Ibid* pp 356–7.
[23] W. C. Magee, *Speeches and Addresses*, ed C. S. Magee (London 1893) p 56.

English conditions was to replicate, as far as possible, at the parochial level a pattern of activities comparable to life at home. This in turn by no means pleased their English parishioners and could result in a situation where some churches were de facto Irish. Their task was made easier by the fact that Irish immigration to England tended to be proportionately higher from the least anglicized parts of Ireland, both before and after independence. The second problem stemmed from the flow of English conversions to Roman Catholicism.[24] It was not infrequently the case that acceptance of the authority of Rome was accompanied by a glorying in practices, devotional and otherwise, most calculated to shock and startle their fellow-countrymen or former associates. It was all part of the complete sea-change required to purge away all elements of protestantism. To adapt a phrase, the Italianate Englishman became the epitome of sanctity. It may even be suspected that conversion allowed a small minority of Englishmen who have always wished they had been born Italian to become Italian relatively painlessly. Yet it was not necessary to become 'more Roman than the Romans'. An English attitude of mind and manner of worship was quite compatible with the acceptance of the claims of the Roman Church. To fashion such a spirituality required a degree of self-confidence not frequently found.

Creighton's conquest of the world by the Church of England had to suffer the no doubt temporary loss of Wales and Ireland. In both instances, the position of the Church of England was made untenable as the established church by its numerical strength and, ultimately, by its image on those sensitive issues of nationhood. In Wales, in the early nineteenth-century, prominent figures in the episcopate either came from outside the principality or were not Welsh-speaking. The attitude of a Copleston of Llandaff towards the relatively limited amount of Welsh used in his diocese was frankly contemptuous. There could be no higher calling than to extend the work of the Church of England in Wales through the English language. It was not difficult, in those areas of Wales where Welsh predominated to see the church as an anglicizing force.[25] Its opponents frequently referred to it as the 'English church' though visitors from England tended not to have a high opinion of it. John

[24] J. Derek Holmes, *More Roman than Rome: English Catholicism in the Nineteenth Century* (London 1978).
[25] *A History of the Church in Wales*, ed D. G. Walker (Cardiff 1976).

Keble, on a visit to Snowdonia in 1840, was appalled at the dirty and disrespectful condition of the parish church at Llanberis in which he sought to worship. Everything, from the tottering three-legged communion-table to the tumbled frill of the clerical surplice showed a consistent dislike of soap and ecclesiastical decency.[26] W. E. Gladstone, somewhat later, found the amount of noise and chatter which went on during a Welsh service somewhat below his exacting standards. Welsh clergy, particularly Welsh-speaking clergy, increasingly found themselves in a dilemma. The young generation of the 1840s felt a need to stress that the Church of England in Wales was a Welsh institution. Young Rowland Williams, oppidan of Eton and Fellow of King's, but Welsh-speaking son of a Welsh-speaking vicarage, attended the first St David's day dinner held in Cambridge in March 1839.[27] The following year, he was at the eisteddfod held in Liverpool and there spoke against objections to eisteddfodau as tending to separate nations united by one crown. Excellence in music and literature elevated character which in turn lessened national animosities. His lines, *The Tears of Cambria or The Ancient Church of West Britain against the Tyranny and Usurpation of the Ecclesiastical Commission* were composed in protest against the proposal to unite the sees of St Asaph and Bangor in the interests of Manchester. Looking across the Irish Sea in 1845 he commented that 'The mere Protestants in Ireland are not a national Church, but an overbearing sect of foreigners. My whole sympathies are with the Celts, who are both abstractedly the injured party, and are my kinsmen, rather than the mere English.[28]' He did not feel his own church to be composed of an overbearing sect of foreigners.

Even the foreigners were not invariably overbearing. The very English Connop Thirlwall, Bishop of St David's, soon developed a fluency in Welsh. Such gestures, however, could not alter the strength of Welsh dissent or the vehemence of its opposition to establishment. H. T. Edwards, dean of Bangor, claimed in a letter to Gladstone that the alienation of the church from the affection of the people was to be found 'in the violation of their national sympathies'. The influence of the higher classes would not avail and

---

[26] J. T. Coleridge, *A Memoir of the Rev. John Keble* (Oxford/London 1869) pp 348ᵛ.
[27] G. Williams, *Religion, Language and Nationality in Wales* (Cardiff 1979) pp 121–2.
[28] *Life and Letters of Rowland Williams*, ed his wife, 2 vols (London 1874) I pp 51, 101, 116.

the efforts of the church to regain the attachment of 'the religious Cymric masses' would depend upon the efforts of a 'native' clergy and episcopate.[29] As the campaign for disestablishment gathered momentum, apologists for the church increasingly stressed that it was not a mere English importation.[30] The Celtic Church became the subject of an intense scholarly scrutiny not unrelated to immediate concerns. One writer in 1912, for example, did not believe that there was any other institution in Wales which could compare 'in the prestige of its hoary antiquity, with the national Church of the Cymry'.[31] One figure, not without some disciples, expressed himself even more forcefully. 'Dominant alienism, the real mischief, must be removed once and for all' wrote Wade-Evans 'The Church of England in Wales must cease, and what is left in the Establishment of the national church, the Ecclesia Wallicana, must be given opportunity to recover.[32]' Disestablishment was not averted but the linguistic and cultural orientation of the Church in Wales (as it was significantly called) have remained. While some writers have taken the view that 'the Church of Christ attaches no importance to nationality or language' others have argued that the church in Wales does have a special responsibility to the Welsh language.[33] Although it cannot claim to be the national church it remains a church committed to a nation. Conspicuous efforts have been made to remove the taint of being the 'English church'. In recent decades prominent members of the Church in Wales, both clerical and lay, have identified themselves with political nationalism to some degree or other. During the recent campaign before the referendum on devolution in Wales, the present archbishop of Wales took a prominent part in favour of the proposals. The outcome may show how complex is the question of a Welsh nation.

Despite the controversial reorientation of the church in Wales, a reorientation by no means complete throughout Wales, recent studies have confirmed that in contemporary Wales there is a high correlation between regular attendance at a Welsh-speaking non-

[29] H. T. Edwards, *A Letter to W. E. Gladstone* (London 1870) p 49.
[30] K. O. Morgan, *Freedom or Sacrilege? A History of the Campaign for Welsh Disestablishment* (Penarth 1966).
[31] J. E. de Hirsch-Davies, *A Popular History of the Church in Wales* (London 1912) pp 334–5.
[32] A. W. Wade-Evans, *Papers for Thinking Welshmen* (London 1907) p 59.
[33] D. Ambrose Jones, *History of the Church in Wales* (Carmarthen 1926) p 269.

Church in Wales place of worship, membership of Welsh-medium cultural societies, self-definition as Welsh rather than British and intention to vote for Plaid Cymru.[34] It is a testimony to the enduring strength of the Free Churches in nineteenth-century Wales and the extent to which language, cultural and, to an extent, political identity became fused. All the important denominations— Baptists, Independents and the relatively small number of Wesleyans—operated virtually separately according to the use of Welsh or English. Immigration into industrial South Wales and the requirements of holiday makers and settlers in North Wales accelerated the building of new churches for English-language services. Throughout Wales, in the nineteenth century, small towns or villages went through the agony of trying to determine the language for worship. For example a correspondent writing to Jabez Bunting from Llanidloes in mid-Wales in 1836 reported that 'the circuit town prefers at present an equal division of Welsh and english. The english congregation here is the largest most respectable, and the most liberal; beside the english is the prevailing language in the town. Landinam, 6 miles east of Llanidloes where we have a Society of 50 members, and 2 other places contiguous to this give the decided preference to the english language . . . There are 9 other Small places connected with the Llanidloes end that decidedly prefer the welsh.'[35] Two years later, also speaking of Llanidloes, another correspondent reported that 'language is a perpetual subject of contention'. Nothing but a separate English cause seemed likely to settle the matter.[36] Similar problems attended the establishment of English-language Baptist churches along the North Wales coast from the 1860s onwards.[37] When a new Baptist chapel was opened in Bangor in 1865 the then minister of what was a Welsh-speaking congregation was prepared to introduce certain English services, though no English-speaking church was in contemplation. It was partly because the Welsh-speaking did not look with favour upon their minister's ventures into English-language services that a distinct English Baptist congregation emerged in 1872.[38] However,

[34] C. J. Thomas and C. H. Williams, 'Language and Nationalism in Wales: a Case Study', *Ethnic and Racial Studies*, 1 (2 April 1978).
[35] John Simon to Jabez Bunting 27 July 1836 Bunting MS. I owe this letter and the following one to the kindness of Professor W. R. Ward.
[36] W. Drewett to Jabez Bunting 9 April 1838.
[37] W. T. Whitley, *Baptists of North-West England, 1649–1913* (London/Preston 1913).
[38] G. Roberts, *History of the English Baptist Church, Bangor*, (Bangor 1905).

KEITH ROBBINS

the language issue caused most controversy amongst the Welsh
Calvinistic Methodists—considerably more numerous in Wales
than Wesleyan Methodists and, arguably the 'national' church of
Wales insofar as it had emerged in peculiarly Welsh circumstances.
Although it was to style itself the Presbyterian Church of Wales in
the twentieth century it was a somewhat distinctive addition to the
reformed family even so. Whether there were to be English-
speaking congregations and what degree of organization they were
to be permitted was a source of lengthy controversy in the late
nineteenth century.[39] The Union of Welsh Independents maintained
uneasy relations with the Congregational Union of England and
Wales. Inevitably, too, Welsh nonconformists joined in the general
pursuit of the Celtic church as a volume by the Rev. J. Johns, *The
Ancient British Church and the Welsh Baptists* testifies.[40] 'It is not by its
own strength that Nonconformity succeeds' one English writer
argued 'it is simply because it is the one means that enables the
Welsh to resist the revived sacerdotalism that eager ecclesiastics are
trying to force upon them. Nonconformity comes far nearer the
old tribal idea of Celtic Christianity than anything else.' It is not
surprising to find two of the most ardent nineteenth-century
exponents of a political nationalism—Michael D. Jones and 'Emrys
ap Iwan'—drawn from the ranks of the Independents and Presbyterians. Nor is it surprising to find contemporary political spokesmen in Wales drawn from the same denominations.[41]

However, between the two world wars, a new element entered
into the picture. The conversion of Saunders Lewis, foremost
Welsh critic and playwright of his generation, to Roman Catholicism introduced a fresh emphasis. Brought up among the Welsh
diaspora of the Wirral, he was the son, grandson and great-
grandson of Calvinistic Methodist ministers. He became the president of the Welsh Nationalist party and his views reverberate
through Wales to the present day. The return to Rome enabled a
certain coterie of intellectuals to by-pass oppressive English protestantism.[43] One convert stressed how 'deeply instinctive' was the
Welsh feeling for Rome and how, under Rome the Welsh first grew

[39] R. Buick Knox, *Voices from the past: a History of the English Conference of the
Presbyterian Church of Wales, 1889–1939* (Llandyssul 1969).
[40] J. Johns, *The Ancient British Church and the Welsh Baptists* (Carmarthen 1889).
[41] J. W. Willis Bund, *The Celtic Church of Wales* (London 1897) p 510.
[42] R. T. Jones, *The Desire of Nations* (Llandybie 1974).
[43] *Presenting Saunders Lewis*, ed A. R. Jones and G. Thomas (Cardiff 1973) pp 62–3.

to nationhood.[44] But, in 'returning to the generative source of their own national body' the same writer recognized that in practice to become a Roman Catholic could seem to nonconformists 'nothing less than an act of desertion in the thick of the battle.'[45] On the other side, to the urban catholics of the south, largely of Irish descent, such concern with providing a Roman pedigree for Welsh identity seemed of little interest. Recent surveys suggest that pupils of English-medium Roman Catholic schools in Wales have little inclination to involve themselves in Welsh cultural life.

The position of the Church of England in Ireland showed obvious parallels with its position in Wales. Whatever its actual membership and composition it too was easily labelled the English church. During the period of its establishment it suited not only Roman Catholics but also Presbyterians to so regard it. Neither Presbyterianism nor Roman Catholicism was strong in England. It could therefore serve to stress both that catholicism was indistinguishable from Irishness and that presbyterianism was the authentic voice of the North-East. Yet, although Mrs Alexander, hymn-writing wife of the archbishop of Armagh struck what seemed to her the right note in her lines on disestablishment

Dimly dawns the New Year on a churchless nation
Ammon and Amalek tread our borders down

others refused to accept that their church was doomed to be regarded as simply 'Made in England'.[46] Lord Plunket, who followed the two Englishmen, Whately and Chenevix Trench as archbishop of Dublin wished to banish the word 'Anglicanism'. It has been noted how in mid-century the improved character of early Irish ecclesiastical studies was very largely due to what, pace Lord Plunket, we must call 'Anglican' scholarship.[47] Leading scholars talked of setting aside all their spare time to learn the Irish language. Some of the leading figures in the renaissance of the 'New Ireland' were protestants, Douglas Hyde being the most conspicuous example. Yet they remained exceptions. Those who talked of the need to roll back the tide of Anglicization normally assumed that protestantism would be rolled back too. Not all the Irish-language

[44] Catherine Daniel, 'Wales: Catholic and Nonconformist', *Blackfriars* (March 1957).
[45] Catherine Daniel, 'Catholic Converts in Wales', *The Furrow* (April 1956) pp 212–13; D. Attwater, *The Catholic Church in Modern Wales* (London 1935).
[46] Cited in *Irish Anglicanism, 1869–1969*, ed M. Hurley (Dublin 1970).
[47] *Ibid* p 36.

plays written by the protestant sixth earl of Longford could diminish this impression and the Irish-language services in the protestant cathedrals in Dublin were not excessively well-patronized. Even so, there was a minority at the special synod of the Church of Ireland in 1912 which argued that just as, so it seemed, opposition to disestablishment could now appear mistaken it was unwise to oppose Home Rule. However, the northern bishops of the Church of Ireland signed the Ulster covenant.[48] Their drift in this direction was a corollary of the apparent consolidation of the language movement and catholicism into one concept of integral nationalism. Yet, insofar as opposition to Home Rule stiffened in the North it created greater difficulties for the Church of Ireland than for either Presbyterians or Methodists. The Church of Ireland had greater strength in the south, particularly in Leinster, than they did.[49] Insofar as emotion centred around 'Ulster', even though Sir Edward Carson was a Dublin protestant, the crisis in the north aroused ambiguous feelings amongst southern members of the Church of Ireland. The 'two-nation' theory of Ireland's identity had little appeal in the Church of Ireland, certainly not in the south. If 'West British' values could not prevail, then it might be better simply to settle for a minority status within a partitioned Ireland. It is possible, too, to argue that the Irish catholic hierarchy came steadily to accept the view that a partitioned Ireland would in fact permit the catholic nation to become, substantially, a reality.[50] 'Since the coming of St Patrick, fifteen hundred years ago' Mr de Valera declared in a St Patrick's Day broadcast to the United States in 1935 'Ireland has been a Christian and a Catholic nation. All the ruthless attempts made down the centuries to force her from this allegiance have not shaken her faith. She remains a Catholic nation.'[51] The corollary of this view, inevitably, was that, after partition, Northern Ireland, in the eyes of its political masters, if not constitutionally, was a 'protestant state'. Yet, in fact, before the First World War, opposition to Home Rule among Presbyterians and Methodists was by no means solid.

[48] *Ibid* pp 86–7.
[49] R. B. McDowell, *The Church of Ireland, 1869–1969* (London 1975): D. H. Akenson, *The Church of Ireland* (New Haven / London 1971).
[50] D. W. Miller, *Church, State and Nation in Ireland, 1898–1921* (Dublin 1973) and also E. Larkin, 'Church, State and Nation in modern Ireland', *AHR* 80 (1975) pp 1244–76.
[51] Cited in J. H. Whyte, *Church and State in Modern Ireland, 1923–1970* (Dublin 1971).

One Irish Methodist writer suggests that only some 2% of Irish Methodists actually desired Home Rule, but a number of methodist ministers and laymen felt that it could not be opposed with a policy of 'blank resistance' and he admits that 'For a time it seemed as if the Church might be rent asunder'.[52] At the Irish Methodist Conference of 1914 'a resolution pledging continued opposition to Home Rule had 188 votes in favour but as many as 61 votes were cast against'.[53] There were similar cross-currents among the numerically more significant Presbyterian community. After the establishment of the government of Northern Ireland these hesitations and doubts were substantially submerged. The paradox remained that notwithstanding the fact that it was the religious expression of a 'national' conflict that had produced partition all the major churches maintained ecclesiastical organizations and structures as though partition had never happened. Whether there was, and is, an Ulster identity which is not simply the wish to be British in an Irish way admits of many answers, particularly at a time when the multi-dimensional nature of Irish identity is being explored by Irish historians, but it cannot be properly considered without a consideration of the final element in the British puzzle: Scotland.[54]

'The reunited Kirk is a national symbol' wrote one author in 1960. 'One may even doubt whether there could be a Scotland without it. Certainly there could be no Church of Scotland without a living Scotland.'[55] Professor Donaldson, writing at the same time, stressed that the insistence on a national church stemmed from the feeling 'not entirely without justification' that the English subversion of Scottish nationality in the cultural sphere would also be willingly completed in the ecclesiastical.[56] Such an assessment needs to be completed by two further observations. In the first place, Scottish nationality is itself a complex phenomenon and as a national church the Church of Scotland has had to accommodate

[52] *Irish Methodism in the Twentieth Century*, ed A. McCrea (Belfast 1931) p 18. See also F. Jeffrey, *Irish Methodism: an historical account of its traditions, theology and influence* (Belfast 1964).

[53] Hurley, *Irish Anglicanism* pp 86–7.

[54] 'The descendants of Scottish settlers under the Stuarts and Cromwells, I have always considered as Englishmen born in Ireland, and the northern counties as a Scotch colony. And yet I am told that this is not the true state of things' wrote a bewildered Crabb Robinson in 1826 *Diary, Reminiscences and Correspondence of Henry Crabb Robinson*, ed T. Sadler 2 vols (London 1872) 2 p 38.

[55] J. M. Reid, *Kirk and Nation* (London 1960) p 173.

[56] G. Donaldson, *Scotland, Church and Nation through six centuries* (Edinburgh 1960).

Highlander and Lowlander, English-speaker and Gaelic-speaker and antipathy between these groups was not unknown. For example, when the duke of Argyll appointed a Highlander to the Lowland congregation in mid-eighteenth century Campbelltown the Lowlanders left the church in a body, collected a substantial sum and erected a building to seat 1600 worshippers in eighteen months.[57] The propagation of evangelical doctrine in the Highlands was also an assault on a whole way of life which many Lowlanders found repugnant. In 1790 one preacher described their object as 'The rescuing of the remoter parts of the Kingdom and its adjacent islands from barbarism, disaffection, and Popery, by infusing into the minds of the inhabitants . . . the excellence of our civil constitution and the principles of our Protestant Reformed religion, that in process of time, Britons from North and South may speak the same language, live united and loyal under the same sovereign, and worship, agreeably to Scripture and conscience, the same God.'[58] The historian of the movement comments that 'a further important by-product of the Evangelical message was the fostering of a British, rather than of a local or even Scottish loyalty.' Scotland too contained at least two civilizations, though the success of evangelical missions in the Highlands, using Gaelic, meant that there was to be no simple equation between Gaelic culture and Roman Catholicism on the one hand and Scots/English and Protestantism on the other. Nevertheless, the regional pattern of distribution of the major presbyterian churches was marked. The United Presbyterians were scarcely known in the Highlands, and Highland suspicion among members of the Free Church delayed the formation of the United Free Church of Scotland.[60]

The second observation is that the Scottish scene was transformed by the large immigration of Irish Roman Catholics into the Glasgow area, south-west Scotland and, to an extent, to Dundee.[61]

[57] J. MacInnes, The Evangelical Movement in the Highlands of Scotland, 1688 to 1800 (Aberdeen 1951) p 98: Cf D. Bowen, The Protestant Crusade in Ireland, 1800–1870 (Dublin 1978): Manx impressions are recorded in Hugh Stowell Brown, ed W. S. Caine (London 1887) pp 12–13.
[58] MacInnes, The Evangelical Movement pp 244–5.
[59] Ibid p 3.
[60] O. Blundell, The Catholic Highlands of Scotland (Edinburgh 1900). The small contemporary Free Presbyterian Church of Scotland is a highland church, apart from a few congregations in the major cities. See The Free Presbyterian Church of Scotland (Inverness 1965).
[61] J. E. Handley, The Irish in Scotland (Glasgow 1964).

This influx has meant that in the view of one Church of Scotland writer 'the Church of Rome in modern Scotland is met, technically as a "foreign church", and bears the character of an Irish intrusion into Scottish life and tradition'.[62] Mid-century journals like *The Scottish Protestant* naturally devoted themselves to criticizing the 'Irish Catholic'. A committee of the Church of Scotland considered Irish immigration just after the First World War and did not mince matters in its conclusions. The commissioners attempted to make clear that their criticisms did not apply to Scottish Roman Catholics who had 'a right to call Scotland their country' or to Orangemen who were 'of the same race as ourselves and of the same Faith, and are readily assimilable'. The advent of the Irish and the consequential expansion of the Roman Catholic Church was destroying 'the unity and homogeneity' of the Scottish people. Irish economic pressure was compelling the flower of Scottish youth to leave their country. It suggested that 'the great plain of Scotland stretching from Glasgow in the west to Dundee and Edinburgh in the east will soon be dominated by the Irish race.' The Scottish sabbath was already wilting under the impact. If such comment was thought unseemly, the report had no doubt that the Irish race and the Church of Rome would not welcome the incursion of half a million Scottish protestants into the counties around Dublin. There was no mention of a population which had, in previous centuries, moved the other way. 'God' the commissioners concluded 'placed the people of this world in families, and history which is the narrative of His providence, tells us that when kingdoms are divided against themselves they cannot stand. Those nations which were homogeneous in race were the most prosperous and were entrusted by the Almighty with the highest tasks.[63]' Such comments give an idea of the strength of feeling. Not that relations between the Irish and the small indigenous Scottish Roman Catholic community were at all straightforward. The 1978 issue of the *Innes Review*, recently published in book form, brings to light some bitter arguments which were directly related to the national issue.[64]

[62] R. S. Louden, *The True Face of the Kirk: An Examination of the Ethos and Tradition of the Church of Scotland* (London 1963) pp 98–9.
[63] Report of a Committee to consider Overtures from the Presbytery of Glasgow and from the Synod of Glasgow and Ayr on 'Irish Immigration' and the 'Education (Scotland) Act 1918' (Edinburgh 1923).
[64] *Modern Scottish Catholicism, 1878–1978*, ed David McRoberts (Glasgow 1979). See also P. F. Anson, *The Catholic Church in Modern Scotland* (London 1937).

Whether the thistle or the shamrock or both should be sculptured on a font or altar could give rise to the most spectacular quarrels. For some one hundred and fifty years, the Irish catholic community in Scotland was served by Irish-born secular priests, many of whom took a cultural political view of their pastoral work. They also identified themselves frequently with what their historian calls 'Irish causes'—the Gaelic League, the Irish language and games (the pioneers of hurling at Maynooth were active in Glasgow) and other specifically political organizations. To a certain Father Lynch, for instance, president of the Springburn (Glasgow) branch of the Gaelic League goes the honour of being one of the first priests to preach in Irish in Glasgow during the St. Patrick's Day celebrations. The lines of division were firmly drawn and neither side anticipated substantial conversion. It needs scarcely to be added that they have not disappeared.[65]

The Scottish Episcopal Church forms a third element which also touches the national nerve.[66] While its indigenous origins are indisputable it too became vulnerable to the charge during the nineteenth century that it was the 'English' church in Scotland. And as late as 1950, John Highet, in his first book on the Scottish churches felt obliged to pursue the extent to which the Scottish Episcopal Church recruited Scotsmen to its ministry—Scottish baptist ministerial names were also subjected to similar scrutiny.[67] However, what differentiates the Episcopal Church in Scotland last century is that the 'anglicizing' tendencies took place from within. On the episcopal level, Englishmen could only be invited to Scotland not imposed, as they could be in Ireland and Wales prior to disestablishment. The expansion of the Episcopal Church, outside its traditional position in the north-east lay chiefly among the middle classes (particularly of Edinburgh) who were themselves attracted to English ways. Thus, in the adoption of the Thirty-Nine Articles as the doctrinal standard in 1804, the use of the English term 'rector' and the depression of the Scottish communion office in favour of the English, it did seem bent on becoming English in ethos. These steps, together with the rapid

[65] B. J. Canning, *Irish-born Secular Priests in Scotland, 1829–1979* (np 1979) pp 394, 419.

[66] I. B. Cowan and S. Ervin, *The Scottish Episcopal Church* (Ambler, Pa., 1966); A. L. Drummond and J. Bulloch, *The Church in Victorian Scotland, 1843–1874* (Edinburgh 1975); W. Perry, *The Oxford Movement in Scotland* (Cambridge 1933).

[67] J. Highet, *The Churches in Scotland To-day* (Glasgow 1950) pp 65–6.

development of 'ritual' widened the gap between episcopalians and presbyterians. By statutes of 1840 and 1864 Scottish episcopalian orders received full recognition in England. At the end of the century, Englishman followed Englishman as bishop of St Andrews. 'I would *far* sooner have a good Englishman than a less good Scotchman' was the comment of a reputedly 'very extreme' Scotch bishop on the appointment of Wilkinson in 1892.[68] It was not easy for a former bishop in England (even one who had laboured among the Celtic Cornish heavily protected against an English bishop by methodism and male voice choirs) to accept the minor position in Scottish life occupied by the Episcopal Church.[69] In his first charge, Wilkinson expressed a yearning 'in our inmost heart to have a more living place in the national life of Scotland' though it would be wrong to seek that at the expense of quenching the hope of reunion with other branches of the Catholic Church.[70] It also rankled that members of the Church of England, accustomed to worshipping in the national church often joined the Church of Scotland on going north of the border. Episcopalian hopes of 'damming this avoidable and unnecessary leakage' remained constant.[71] The stance to be adopted towards the Church of Scotland by members of the Church of England had varied. In 1798, for example, Charles Simeon recorded of a tour in Scotland that except when he preached in episcopal chapels he had 'officiated precisely as they do in the Kirk of Scotland: and I did so upon this principle; Presbyterianism is as much the established religion in North Britain, as Episcopacy is in the South: there being no difference between them, except in church-government.[72]' Fifty years later, after visiting St Giles' in Edinburgh, H. P. Liddon came to a very different conclusion: 'I left the church feeling a deep and unutterable aversion for a system whose outward manifestations are so hatefully repulsive. I thank God the Church of England *is* very different from the Kirk of Scotland'.[73] In between these two

---

[68] A. J. Mason, *Memoir of George Howard Wilkinson* (London 1910) p 305.
[69] T. Shaw, *A History of Cornish Methodism* (Truro 1967): J. C. C. Probert, *The Sociology of Cornish Methodism, Cornish Methodist Historical Association, Occasional Publication,* 8 (Bodmin 1964).
[70] Mason, *Wilkinson* p 305.
[71] Cited in Highet, *The Churches in Scotland* p 30.
[72] *Memoirs of the Life of the Rev. Charles Simeon*, ed W. Carus (London/Cambridge 1847) p 113.
[73] J. O. Johnson, *Life and Letters of H. P. Liddon* (London 1904) p 15.

reactions stand a wide variety of opinions. The late Ian Henderson's, *Power without Glory* which suggested, with no great delicacy, that what passed as ecumenicity in English-speaking countries was very largely Anglican imperialism is the recent exposition of a view from the other side which does not lack nineteenth-century precedent.[74] James Cooper, in an earlier generation, took a very different approach. He had advocated *A United Church for the British Empire* in 1900 and in a sermon delivered in St Paul's cathedral in 1918 he argued strongly against the scandal of ecclesiastical disunity. The war itself was a preacher of the obligation that the two national churches should agree. It would 'seal and consecrate the union of the British Empire' and hold out an olive branch to the rest of Christendom.[75] The British Empire is no more but the trends in churchmanship which these writers represent and their attitudes to England and the Church of England have their contemporary successors. Kirk and nation do indeed remain in close relationship, but not without some difficulties since ecumenical involvement and a revived nationalism have sometimes pointed the leaders of the church in different directions.[76] In the immediate past, many moderators and statements of the kirk have favoured political devolution for Scotland. During its period of growth, evidence seemed to suggest that the Scottish National Party drew more strongly from voters who described themselves as Presbyterians than from any other religious body. The difficulties experienced by the Labour Party in Scotland and in making up its mind about devolution in part stemmed from the nature of its Irish-descended support in the west of Scotland. And devolution failed. Perhaps paradoxically, if it had succeeded it is arguable that, in time, an assembly in Scotland would have deprived the general assembly of the Kirk of that still significant place as a forum for the discussion of national issues which it possesses in its absence.

In the last decade or so, prompted in large measure by events in Northern Ireland, the relationship between churches and nations within the British Isles has been subjected to fresh and largely hostile scrutiny. However admirable the comments of theologians

[74] I. Henderson, *Power Without Glory* (London 1967) p 42.
[75] James Cooper, *A United Church for the British Empire* (1902); *The Church Catholic and National* (Glasgow 1898); *Reunion: a Voice from Scotland* (London 1918).
[76] M. Small, *Growing Together: Some Aspects of the Ecumenical Movement in Scotland, 1924–1964* (Edinburgh 1975).

and sociologists, pleas for the prising apart of religion and national identity will only be superficial so long as the full complexity of that relationship within the British Isles is ignored.[77] This paper has attempted to draw attention to some of them, though its focus has meant that the contribution made to the ecclesiastical life of England by Irishmen, Scotsmen and Welshmen has been insufficiently stressed. The partiality of Scotsmen, from Tait to Runcie, for the see of Canterbury is a subject in itself and there was a period when congregational thought in England seemed exclusively in Scottish hands. A critical scrutiny of the career of the Wesleyan Hugh Price Hughes which makes no mention of his Welshness neglects a complete dimension.[78] Lines addressed (in Welsh) by Saunders Lewis to the Rev. Dr. J. D. Jones, C.H. (late of Bournemouth) give some indication of the tensions involved:

> From your feathered pulpit your tallow sermon
> Dropped upon the gluttons,
> The lard-droppings of your greasy English
> Was a service for the guzzlers.
> Now your return to the land of the poor
> That's sore under the thumb of the blusterer,
> With your harsh ranting to a fragile nation
> To bend to the yoke and the cord.[79]

'The concept of united national and regional churches goes back' concludes a Scotsman at Oxford 'to the days of homogeneous societies geographically demarcated and, even so, represents a tradition that has proved itself hostile to freedom and openness.'[80]

University of Glasgow

[77] A. E. C. W. Spencer, 'Christian Proposals for the Irish Churches' *The Month* (January 1973); S. G. Mackie, *Ireland's Conflict diminishes me* (London 1974).

[78] J. H. S. Kent 'Hugh Price Hughes and the Nonconformist Conscience', *Essays in Modern English Church History*, ed G. V. Bennett and J. D. Walsh (London 1966). For a Welsh contemporary he was 'Un o Gymry enwocaf yr Oes' (one of the most celebrated Welshmen of his time), J. Price Roberts, *Hugh Price Hughes, Ei Fywyd a'i Lafur* (Bangor 1903). See H. Scott Holland, *A Bundle of Memories* (London nd) p 153.

[79] Translation by Gwyn Thomas in Jones and Thomas, *Saunders Lewis* p 181.

[80] J. Macquarrie, *Christian Unity and Christian Diversity* (London 1975) pp 12–13.

RELIGION AND NATIONAL FEELING IN NINETEENTH-CENTURY WALES AND SCOTLAND

by D. W. BEBBINGTON

WALES and Scotland were in the nineteenth century, as they have remained in the twentieth, nations within a multinational state. Where boundaries of nation and state did not coincide in nineteenth-century Europe there was commonly a surge of feeling in favour of achieving a remedy. This was equally true of nations like Italy and Germany that were divided internally by political frontiers and of nations like the Serbs and the Rumanians who were lumped together with other peoples under the rule of greater powers. There was an efflorescence of nationalism, that is, of the political assertion of nationhood. The British Isles were not immune, for Ireland was deeply affected by the new mood. Yet Wales and Scotland were largely untouched by the nationalist spirit. Only from the 1880s, with the example of the Irish Home Rulers to imitate, was there any significant stirring of aspirations after self-government, and then the vanguard in both nations gave no thought to the possibility of taking independence as its goal. Wales and Scotland were remarkably quiescent when viewed in a European context.[1]

This phenomenon has a number of explanations that call for no reference to religion. First and probably most important, the British state was not autocratic and seldom oppressive. Elsewhere, as in Russian, Austrian and Turkish territories, nationalism commonly emerged in harness with liberalism as a protest against unjust and despotic rule. The British state liberalised itself and with relative ease accommodated the rise of a liberal party that drew widespread support from the Welsh and Scots. Secondly, the rising economic interests of Wales and Scotland did not seem to diverge from those of England. Both possessed prosperous centres of

[1] The general state of nineteenth-century national feeling in Wales and Scotland has been most usefully analysed by [Sir Reginald] Coupland, Welsh and Scottish Nationalism]: a study] (London 1954) and by Michael Hechter, Internal Colonialism: the Celtic fringe in British national development, 1536–1966 (London 1975).

industrial manufacture that appreciated the wide market of England and the wider markets of the world that seemed to be secured by the leanings of British policy towards free trade. Thirdly, there was no threat to the indigenous population. Several of the towns of South Wales became Welsh-speaking for the first time with the influx of rural Welshmen in the earlier stages of industrialisation, and it was only in the 1890s that there was a large-scale immigration of English workers into Wales. South Wales and the west of Scotland had earlier received more than their share of Irish immigrants, but their presence tended to encourage a sense of being British among the natives rather than the reverse. Fourthly, there was little threat to distinctive Welsh or Scottish institutions. In Wales, this was chiefly because most of them had disappeared long before the nineteenth century, although there was a ripple of discontent at the abolition of the last separate Welsh courts in 1830. In Scotland there was some objection to the termination of the Scottish Court of Exchequer and the Scottish Board of Customs and Excise. But the security of the Scottish legal system was assured, and in neither nation was resentment sustained. Finally, it was possible for national feeling to find an outlet through cultural activities. In Scotland there was the cult of Burns and Scott; in Wales there were the *eisteddfodau* that had begun in 1789. National identity had sufficient expression for the taste of the people without assuming a political form. The weakness of nationalism need cause no surprise. Yet religion cannot be left out of the picture. Henry Richard, the parliamentary spokesman of Wales, once informed Gladstone that 'happily we have no unbelievers in Wales'.[2] A Scottish representative might have claimed little less, for religion played a central part in the life of each nation—a greater part, it was always said, than in England. This paper attempts to explore the ways in which religion affected national feeling in both.

Perhaps the most striking difference between Wales and England in the nineteenth century was the contrast in the strength of the Christian denominations. The two nations shared the same established church, but there the similarity ended. The established church in Wales suffered in the eighteenth century from particularly low stipends in a high proportion of its livings. The corollaries were pluralism and absenteeism. Its service, catering especially for

---

[2] Richard to Gladstone, 23 April 1870, BL Gladstone Papers Add MS 44426 fol 159ʳ.

the anglicised gentry, were normally in English and so uncongenial to the primarily Welsh-speaking population. Between 1714 and 1870, as is well known, no bishop could speak Welsh at the time of his appointment, though bishop Thirlwall made the effort to learn the language once settled in the see of St David's.[3] The church was specially slow in erecting places of worship in the industrialising areas of south Wales.[4] Consequently the growing population increasingly practised its religion outside the church of England. At Merthyr Tydvil in 1840, for instance, there was one parish church, but twelve chapels.[5] In the second half of the century there were vigorous efforts to revitalise the church of England. In 1848 the diocese of Llandaff was served by only fifty clergy, but in 1870 the figure had risen to 201.[6] Nonconformity nevertheless retained at the end of the century far more support in Wales than the established church. In 1891 it was estimated that there were 111,249 regular Anglican communicants. In the same year the combined membership of the nonconformist denominations was just over 400,000.[7] Nonconformity had become the religion of the people. Wales produced its own nonconformist denomination, the Calvinistic methodists, who shared the zeal and much of the organisation of Wesley but the theology and something of the sense of church order of the old dissent in England.[8] Welsh independents formed their own Welsh-speaking union in 1871 which rapidly generated an ethos of its own, while the Welsh baptists, unlike most in England, were staunch in their refusal to countenance admitting those not baptised as believers to the Lord's supper.[9] Only the methodists, who in Wales were chiefly Wesleyans, conformed closely to English practices, and that was because of their large measure of central organisation. Secular activities could not be immune to the fervour of Welsh nonconformity. When at the turn of the twentieth century football turned into a mass

---

[3] E. T. Davies, *Religion in the Industrial Revolution in South Wales* (Cardiff 1965) p 97.
[4] *Ibid* pp 25–30.
[5] [David] Williams, [*A History of*] *Modern Wales* (London 1977) p 249.
[6] W. D. Wills, 'The Clergy in Socety in Mid-Victorian South Wales', *JHSChW* 24 (1974) p 29.
[7] [Robert] Currie, [Alan] Gilbert and [Lee] Horsley, *Churches and Churchgoers[: patterns of church growth in the British Isles since 1700]* (Oxford 1977) pp 128, 145, 149.
[8] M. W. Williams, *Creative Fellowship: an outline of the history of Calvinistic Methodism in Wales* (Caernarvon 1935).
[9] Currie, Gilbert and Horsley, *Churches and Churchgoers* p 152. [*The*] C[*hristian*] W[*orld*] (London) 25 January 1900 p 6.

spectator sport the legacy of the chapels was obvious. Tom Richards, a mining MP for West Monmouth and a congregational deacon, urged Welsh supporters to 'find some less objectionable method of rejoicing over their victory than by singing filthy doggerel songs alternately with the sacred hymns that were associated with some of the most blessed experiences of their parents and friends'.[10] The more respectable miners' choirs also sang sacred music for preference and the poetry of the Welsh bards was charged with biblical imagery. Wales was marked off from England by being a land of chapels.

The progress of nonconformity owed much to its espousal of the Welsh language. John Wesley had spoken of 'the heavy curse of the confusion of tongues'[11] as a disadvantage to the advance of the gospel in Wales and in 1871 only 61% of Wesleyan membership belonged to Welsh-speaking circuits, the lowest proportion in a major nonconformist denomination.[12] The Calvinistic methodists were overwhelmingly Welsh-speaking and 86% of congregationalism remained so in 1900.[13] There was in the nineteenth century no threat of extinction hanging over the language—more than half the population could speak Welsh in 1891[14]—and so it was not a spur to nationalism in the sense that it has become one in the twentieth century. In the second half of the nineteenth century there was nevertheless a tendency for families to encourage the use of English, for it seemed the key to advancement in education, commerce and the professions. English-speaking chapels were set up in larger numbers, especially in the urban areas. A few Welshmen felt uneasy. Their fears were voiced most eloquently by Michael Jones, an independent minister who had served the Welsh community in Cincinnati, Ohio. He had been dismayed to witness the steady erosion of his people's Welshness—first their language, then their customs and finally their religion. Jones discerned a similar process beginning to operate in Wales itself. Provoked primarily by the ultimate threat to the faith of the Welsh people, he began to denounce the increase in English-speaking chapels in terms that smacked of cultural nationalism. 'I hold', he wrote in

[10] *CW* 10 January 1907 p 3.
[11] Williams, *Modern Wales* p 149.
[12] Currie, Gilbert and Horsley, *Churches and Churchgoers* p 145.
[13] *Ibid* p 152.
[14] Coupland, *Welsh and Scottish Nationalism* p 251.

1877, 'that the greater part of the demand among us for English chapels arises from the haughty pride of men made servile by adulation of the English . . . We have many families who are doing their best to bring up their children English-speaking, and in ignorance of Welsh . . . Why do so many of our ministers of religion support this attitude?'[15] Jones became the advocate of creating settlements of Welsh sheep-farmers in Patagonia, where, he believed, their language, customs and religion would be safe from Anglo-Saxon depredations. Absorption would be no risk among the lethargic Spaniards. His emigration scheme caught the imagination of many. The settlements grew to over 50,000 and the plains of Argentina were studded with nonconformist chapels.[16] Jones was to be proved wrong about the impotence of Latin American culture, for Welsh is hardly a memory in Patagonia now. But his project represents a fascinating, if isolated, attempt to preserve the way of life symbolised by the language. There can be no doubt that the defence of the faith was a motive that loomed large in the mind of this Christian minister. Insofar as language was a stimulus to enterprise on behalf of the Welsh people in the later nineteenth century, it was bound up with religion.

Language was also involved in a controversy surrounding education that probably generated more national feeling in Wales than any other issue during the century. The Welsh were sensitive about their education arrangements because they were the springboard for upward social mobility. There was therefore an outcry when there was published in 1847 a government report on the state of education in Wales that laid great stress on the ignorance of the people. The commissioners of inquiry, three young English lawyers, had taken evidence chiefly from the Anglican clergy and the anglicised gentry. They admitted that the Sunday schools, overwhelmingly nonconformist institutions, were 'the main instrument of civilization',[17] but criticised their education standards. Most Sunday scholars were said to know more of the geography of Palestine than of the geography of their own nation.[18] This seemed

---

[15] *Y Ddraig Goch* (June 1877) pp 65 *seq* quoted by [D. G.] Jones, 'National movements in Wales in the Nineteenth Century', [*The Historical Basis of*] *Welsh Nationalism* (Cardiff 1950) p 114.

[16] Jones, *Welsh Nationalism*, p 120.

[17] *Reports of the Commissioners of Inquiry into the State of Education in Wales* (London 1848) p 519.

[18] *Ibid* p 8.

an unnecessary slur on the religion of the people. Further, they attacked the language without restraint. 'The Welsh language is a vast drawback to Wales, and a manifold barrier to the moral progress and commercial prosperity of the people. It is not easy to over-estimate its evil effects . . . It dissevers the people from intercourse which would greatly advance their civilization, and bars the access of improving knowledge to their minds.'[19] The ignorance that was allegedly the fruit of using Welsh was held by some witnesses to be the root of the disturbances of the Chartist years. And perhaps the greatest defamation was the charge that sexual immorality was 'the peculiar vice of the Principality'.[20] Again this was a reproach to the moral teaching given in the chapels. The report was rebutted by a number of Welsh writers. Its publication went down in Welsh folklore as 'the treachery of the blue books' on the analogy of the incident when the Anglo-Saxons were said to have tricked and slain some Celtic leaders, 'the treachery of the long knives'.[21] Wales was far more conscious of being a separate nation than during recent years. It is hardly surprising that the next widely publicised official report on Welsh education, the Aberdare report on the secondary schools of 1880, was careful to begin by acknowledging the distinct nationality of Wales lest it should provoke a similar uproar.[22] Once more, though, it is clear that a cause of national feeling, resentment of educational calumny, was closely linked with a desire to defend the standing of the chapels.

This is equally true over the one economic issue that was the basis for something like a nationalist movement in nineteenth-century Wales. The farmers of the Welsh hills were hard hit by agricultural depression in the late 1880s and so commonly requested a reduction of the tithe charged on their land. When this was refused, as it usually was, they demanded a change in the land laws and sometimes refused to pay tithe at all. The ecclesiastical beneficiaries of tithe belonged to the church of England and were sometimes themselves in England. In the spring of 1887, for instance, at Meifod in Montgomery, Christ Church, Oxford, was the institution refusing a tithe abatement when more than forty of

[19] Ibid p 309.
[20] Ibid p 534.
[21] Glanmor Williams, Religion, Language and Nationality in Wales (Cardiff 1979) p 105.
[22] Coupland, Welsh and Scottish Nationalism p 200.

the fifty farmers on the estate refused payment and six had their goods distrained.²³ The 'tithe war' undoubtedly intensified national feeling. David Lloyd George, still at this time a country solicitor but secretary of the South Caernarvonshire Anti-Tithe League, requested Tom Ellis, the rising hope of militant Welshmen in the commons, to address one of its meetings on 'a national policy'.²⁴ By 1891 Lloyd George was himself in the commons and sharing in attempts to press forward a bill to modify tithes. The parliamentary battle, he assured Ellis, 'was such a glorious struggle for Wales'.²⁵ The campaign against tithes was deliberately designed to rouse a form of Welsh nationalism. 'Do you not think', Lloyd George wrote in the first letter, 'that this little business is an excellent lever wherewith to raise the spirit of the people?'²⁶ But it was also, and more obviously, a question of ecclesiastical rivalry. The farmers were overwhelmingly nonconformists who resented making payments for the benefit of Anglican clergy. Tithe refusal stood in the tradition of the denial of church rates that had marked the middle years of the century in England as well as Wales. At the sales of distrained goods the great theme of the speeches was the injustice of exactions imposed by the church of England on members of other denominations.²⁷ The religious issue intermingled with the economic issue. Out of the mixture Lloyd George and a few others tried to generate a genuine nationalism.

Religion also laid the foundation of the political campaign that formed the expression of Welsh national feeling in the second half of the century. In the 1860s the nonconformist pressure group aiming for the separation of church and state, the Liberation Society, decided to rally Wales to its cause. Previously it had drawn little strength from the principality, but now it organised lecture tours, engaged representatives and distributed literature on a wide scale. Welsh nonconformity proved responsive.²⁸ As it happened, the 1868 general election turned on the issue of disestablishment,

---

²³ *CW* 19 May 1887 p 387.
²⁴ Lloyd George to Ellis, 19 May 1887, Aberystwyth National Library of Wales Thomas Edward Ellis Collection MS 679.
²⁵ Lloyd George to Ellis, 11 April 1891, MS 683.
²⁶ Lloyd George to Ellis, 19 May 1887, MS 679.
²⁷ J. P. D. Dunbabin, *Rural Discontent in Nineteenth-Century Britain* (London 1974) pp 211–31, 282–96.
²⁸ I. G. Jones, 'The Liberation Society and Welsh Politics, 1844 to 1868', *WelHR* 1 (1961).

since Gladstone had declared in its favour for Ireland. The new eagerness to end the privileges of the established church was reflected in the election results. Whereas before there had been a majority of conservative MPs representing Wales, now twenty-three out of thirty-three were liberals.[29] The liberal predominance in Welsh politics that lasted until the rise of labour was in large measure the result of the desire of the nonconformists of Wales for disestablishment. They were delighted when, in 1883, Welsh disestablishment was first debated in the commons.[30] From the mid-1880s, however, there was an effort to transform the issue from a sectarian into a national question. Stuart Rendel, an Anglican landowner and MP for Montgomeryshire, wished to turn the disestablishment movement into a protest against 'all Anglicising influence in Wales'.[31] He succeeded in wresting the leadership of the Welsh campaign out of the hands of the London-based Liberation Society and angled for the support of Welsh conservatives. During the liberal administration of 1892-5, Rendel ensured that English nonconformists knew nothing of the strategy of the Welsh disestablishers. 'Cymru Fydd', the Young Wales organisation led by Tom Ellis, used the issue as a focus for their vision of a vigorous and united peope.[32] Disestablishment, in the words of one leading Welshman, was being taken up 'as a *National question*'.[33] But it had always been that, though to a lesser extent, since the 1860s. Religion threw up the issue that contributed most over the long term to the Welsh sense of identity. Bound up as it was with the other issues that gave rise to less sustained assertions of the Welsh identity—the language, education and agrarian discontent—religion must surely be accepted as the most important single factor in encouraging Welsh national feeling in the nineteenth century.

Scotland was less likely to feel threatened by an advancing tide of anglicising influence than Wales both because it was larger and because it was further from London. It was also more self-confident since it had entered into what was theoretically an equal

---

[29] [K. O.] Morgan, *Wales in British Politics [1868–1922]* (Cardiff 1970) p 25.
[30] *Ibid* pp 33 *seq*, 67.
[31] *The Personal Papers of Lord Rendel*, ed F. E. Hamer (London 1931) p 306.
[32] Morgan, *Wales in British Politics* pp 104–6.
[33] Thomas Gee to Stuart Rendel, 17 March 1887, Aberystwyth National Library of Wales Letters and Papers of Lord Rendel MS 19450C fol 127.

union with England rather than being assimilated by a greater power. Scotland retained its own law, different from English law in its principles as well as its details—orderly, rational, Roman-inspired. Scotland also possessed a national system of education long before England. Like the law, the schools, at least one for every parish, were a source of patriotic pride. The Reverend George Lewis, secretary of the Glasgow Educational Society, could comment in 1834 with an apparent forgetfulness of the law: 'In all but our parochial churches and parochial schools we have lost our nationality. In these alone we survive as a nation—stand apart from and superior to England'.[34] But, as Lewis observed, the churches of Scotland also made the nation distinct. Its established church was presbyterian and the episcopalians, the spiritual kin of the church of England, were relegated to the margins of the nation's religious life. Only rarely outside the north-east did episcopalianism dominate whole communities. In 1792, it was supposed, there were some 12,000 communicants in the episcopal church in Scotland; by 1855, despite the demographic explosion, the number of communicants had risen to only 14,234, although membership was held by 38,113. By contrast, it has been estimated that the church of Scotland had some 367,000 members in 1840.[35] Furthermore, the largest groups of protestant churchgoers outside the church of Scotland were also presbyterian. The chief bodies of protestant dissenters had combined by 1847 to form the united presbyterian church, which in 1856 possessed 142,956 communicants.[36] Presbyterianism was bound up with the myth of Scottish identity. John Knox was usually treated in the nineteenth century as a hero rather than a villain, and Jenny Geddes, who reputedly threw a stool at the head of bishop Lindsay in 1637 when Laud's service book was first used in St Giles' Cathedral, was firmly instated as a heroine despite doubts over her real name. After 1707 there had been no parliament in Scotland and so the state of the nation was most conveniently discussed in the general assembly of the church of Scotland. The established church was effectively the bearer of the nation's traditions, but its very security made it unlikely to provoke any political expression of nationhood.

[34] George Lewis, *Scotland a Half-educated Nation* (1834) p 75 quoted by Stewart Mechie, *The Church and Scottish Social Development, 1780–1870* (London 1960) p 145.
[35] Currie, Gilbert and Horsley, *Churches and Churchgoers* pp 131, 132.
[36] *Ibid* p 132.

The disruption of the church of Scotland did, however, help to foster nationalism as a political force. In 1843 about a third of its ministers left the church under the leadership of Thomas Chalmers to form the free church of Scotland. Coupland argues in his study of Welsh and Scottish nationalism that this was not a nationalist movement,[37] but in reality it did possess some of the marks of nationalism. First, it was directed against an upper class that was significantly anglicised. The evangelicals who set up the free church wanted to take away the right of landlords to appoint ministers against the wishes of the congregation, a process they labelled 'intrusion'. The primary concern of the 'non-intrusionists' was that landlords tended to appoint men of sophistication and educated taste like themselves, members of the moderate party in the church, rather than evangelicals who would appeal to the consciences of their hearers. This attack on patronage set the non-intrusionists against virtually the whole aristocracy and the great majority of the gentry. At the disruption only one aristocrat, the marquis of Breadalbane, seceded; and only 35% of elders who were either landowners or their associates, the lawyers, seceded, while 58% of the elders in other professions did so.[38] And the landowners, like their Welsh counterparts, had succumbed far more than the rest of the population to English ways. A large proportion of the aristocracy, as the non-intrusionists were scornfully aware, had even become episcopalians.[39] So to criticise the landowners was to launch an offensive against what seemed to be an alien class. Secondly, the non-intrusionist campaign sought redress from the parliament at Westminster, but received none. The whig administration before 1841 gave no heed to their calls for parliament to reverse court decisions in favour of lay patrons. In a letter lord Melbourne dismissed Chalmers with the characteristic comment that 'I think him a madman and all madmen are also rogues'.[40] After 1841 the tory government did no more for them. The parties organised on a British basis seemed uninterested in Scottish affairs. Thirdly, the

[37] Coupland, *Welsh and Scottish Nationalism* p 264.
[38] I. F. Maciver, 'The Evangelical Party and the Eldership in General Assemblies, 1820–1843', *Records of the Scottish Church History Society* (Edinburgh) 20 (1978) pp 11, 12.
[39] Hugh Miller, *My Schools and Schoolmasters* (Edinburgh 1881 edn) p 548.
[40] Melbourne to Maule, 28 October 1840, Edinburgh Scottish Record Office Dalhousie Papers GD 45/14 fol 640 quoted by G. I. T. Machin, *Politics and the Churches in Great Britain, 1832 to 1868* (Oxford 1977) p 125.

grievance was actually caused by the Westminster parliament in the first place. The act of union had prohibited patronage in the Scottish church, but in 1712 parliament had treacherously restored it. Non-intrusionist meetings sometimes concentrated on the theme of English perfidy. In 1840, for instance, the main speaker at Coupar Angus was D. M. Makgill Crichton of Rankeilours: 'as the proceedings advanced, and especially when the Crichton broke forth in his stirring national appeals, it was manifest that all were carried along with the same irresistible tide of Scottish feeling and enthusiasm'.[41] The degree of passion that went into the ten years' conflict that preceded the disruption has often seemed inexplicable. The theological conviction that the church should not be subordinate to the state was one powerful reason for it, but the strong infusion of national sentiment that has normally been overlooked was another. It was obvious to contemporary observers. Lord Shaftesbury noted in his diary for 26 August 1839 his sympathy 'with the Scottish people in their resistance to English aggressions'.[42] The disruption was partly fuelled by something very close to nationalism.

The free church of Scotland continued to foster national aspirations. In the 1850s there arose an Association for the Vindication of Scottish rights that is now commonly regarded as the first stirring of Scottish political nationalism.[43] It was directed against a number of minor symptoms of the administrative assimilation of Scotland to England such as the erroneous placing of the Scottish lion in the second rather than the first quarter on royal standards flown north of the border. Scotland, it argued, must have its own secretary of state in order to avoid 'sinking into the position of an English county'.[44] It was all-party and drew support from no single Christian denomination, but the spokesman who took the most extreme line was Dr James Begg, a leading free churchman. Remembering the unresponsiveness of the Westminster parliament before 1843, Begg thought it might be necessary to call for 'such a change in the existing system as would secure them some legislative body in their own country to dispose of purely Scottish

[41] *The Witness* (Edinburgh), 22 January 1840.
[42] G. F. A. Best, *Shaftesbury* (London 1964) p 74.
[43] H. J. Hanham, 'Mid-Century Scottish Nationalism: romantic and radical', *Ideas and Institutions of Victorian England*, ed Robert Robson (London 1967).
[44] *Address to the People of Scotland [and Statement of Grievances by the National Association for the Vindication of Scottish Rights]*, Edinburgh 1853) p 8.

questions'.[45] He was the first to propose Scottish devolution. Begg was not alone. *The Witness*, the free church journal, supported the association and John Fleming, professor of natural science at the free church college in Edinburgh, was one of the two ministers apart from Begg sitting on the general committee.[46] Furthermore, later in the century the free church took up a cause that evoked much more widespread enthusiasm for a national cause: disestablishment of the church of Scotland. It is often contended, by Coupland for instance, that the campaign for Scottish disestablishment had no nationalist flavour since it was directed against a purely domestic Scottish institution.[47] But that is not the whole of the story. The free church disestablishment campaign took its rise from what appeared to be an act of gross injustice by the Westminster parliament. In 1874 Disraeli's government carried a bill to abolish patronage in the church of Scotland. Those who set up the free church had demanded precisely this measure before 1843, but now it was being done artificially to bolster the popularity of the church of Scotland. The free church deeply resented that it should reap a reward from being established. The majority of the free church under principal Rainy became disestablishers because of a practical grievance against Westminster, not because of any commitment to the theory that state churches should never exist. Rainy saw disestablishment as a necessary preliminary to the unity of both church and nation in Scotland, a step on the path to national greatness.[48] Gladstone, who seriously considered undertaking Scottish disestablishment in 1877–8, treated it as a 'national' question.[49] It made the free church emphasise its own claims to represent the authentic national tradition of the reformation and the covenanters. And it compelled protagonists of the established church to do the same. The leader of the Scottish Church Defence Association also spoke of going back to the days of the covenanters and of meeting on the hillside 'the traducers of our mother church, foot to foot and hand to hand'.[50] There was a competition in trying

[45] Thomas Smith, *Memoirs of James Begg, D.D.*, 2 vols (Edinburgh 1888) 2 p 150.
[46] *Address to the People of Scotland*, 2nd edn, p 10.
[47] Coupland, *Welsh and Scottish Nationalism*, pp 264 *seq*.
[48] P. C. Simpson, *The Life of Principal Rainy*, 2 vols (London 1909) 1 pp 277–81, 2 p 3.
[49] A. T. Innes, *Chapters of Reminiscence* (London 1913) pp 124–33, 157.
[50] Dr R. H. Story in 1885 quoted by J. G. Kellas, 'The Liberal Party and the Scottish Church Disestablishment Crisis', *EHR* 79 (1964) p 34.

to annex the Scottish past. Thus it came about that the two main presbyterian denominations loudly protested their Scottishness in the course of a struggle that was central to Scottish politics from 1875 to 1895. Religion heightened a consciousness of Scottish identity and encouraged its assertion in the public arena.

If religion strengthened Welsh and Scottish national feeling, it also contributed to the countervailing current of a sense of British identity. Underlying it was an awareness of the religious unity of Britain that transcended national and denominational boundaries alike. The common element was normally evangelicalism, the popular religion of the century. Thus at the end of the 1820s the young Gladstone at Oxford used to forward the new evangelical Anglican journal *The Record* to a Miss Bethune, one of a group of 'God-fearing females' in the evangelical church of Scotland congregation at Dingwall; and in the 1870s the minister of the same Dingwall church used to correspond enthusiastically with C. H. Spurgeon of the baptist metropolitan tabernacle in London.[51] The great name of Chalmers brought Scotland's religion into high esteem in a wide cross-section of the English religious public, whether evangelicals, defenders of the established church or ecclesiastical political economists. The flow of books back and forth over the national boundaries was unceasing and the flow of men hardly less so. Many of the most prominent figures in the English churches hailed from Wales or Scotland. The leader of the advanced Wesleyans at the end of the century, Hugh Price Hughes, came from Carmarthen;[52] the greatest preacher in the north of England, the baptist Alexander Maclaren of Manchester, was originally a Glasgow man;[53] the first principal of the congregational Mansfield College, Oxford, was A. M. Fairbairn, brought up in Edinburgh;[54] and Edinburgh even supplied an archbishop of Canterbury, A. C. Tait.[55] Newer denominations straddled the Anglo-Scottish border as a matter of course: the Christian brethren and the

[51] Anne M. Gladstone to W. E. Gladstone, 31 October 1828, Hawarden St Deiniol's Library Glynne-Gladstone MSS. Alexander Auld, *Life of John Kennedy, D.D.* (London 1887) pp 48, 51 *seq*, 71

[52] D. P. Hughes, *The Life of Hugh Price Hughes* (London 1905) p 1.

[53] E. T. McLaren, *Dr McLaren of Manchester: a sketch* (London 1912) p 5.

[54] W. B. Selbie, *The Life of Andrew Martin Fairbairn, D.D., D.Litt., LL.D., F.B.A., ETC.* (London 1914) p 3.

[55] R. T. Davidson and William Benham, *Life of Archibald Campbell Tait, Archbishop of Canterbury*, 2 vols (London 1891) I p 5.

churches of Christ struck root both north and south;[56] and the Wesleyans failed to make much impact on Scotland not because of any inherent resistance to them in Scottish culture but because of financial mismanagement.[57] All these bonds could not fail to have an effect in diminishing the force of Celtic particularism.

Religion played a significant part in fanning the flames of an alternative to Welsh or Scottish nationalism. The primary factor here was the threat to the protestantism of Britain posed by the influx of Irish catholic immigrants from the late 1820s onwards. Anti-catholic attitudes in the 1830s, accentuated by suspicions of the Oxford movement, generated a potent protestant nationalism in England, Wales and Scotland.[58] Outside England popular protestantism was emphatically British in flavour rather than Welsh or Scottish, for Britain as a whole seemed a protestant bastion against Roman ambitions. Each disturbance by the catholics of Ireland, from O'Connell's campaigns of the 1840s to Parnell's in the 1880s, served to reinforce this stance. The protestant-catholic divided, so salient in nineteenth-century minds, made the Celtic-English divide pale into insignificance. As the century wore on a further dimension was added to the strengthening of British feeling in Wales and Scotland. Religion began to give its sanction to imperialism. Missionary supporters easily adopted a belief in the extension of British civilisation throughout the world. The empire was a joint enterprise by the nations of Britain. There could be a friendly rivalry, especially between the Scots and the English, but their purpose was one. Thus if New Zealand had its Christchurch, English and anglican, it must also have its Dunedin, Scottish and presbyterian. Scottish patriotism found a wider fulfilment in British imperialism. The Reverend John Ker, a united presbyterian minister writing on 'Scottish Nationality' in 1887, argued that the retention of Scotland's distinct identity 'has made England strong in the attachment of the old Northern kingdom, while it has made the British Empire richer by all the contributions of literature and social character which a separate history has enabled Scotland to

---

[56] F. R. Coad, *A History of the Brethren Movement* (Exeter 1968) pp 172 *seq.* D. M. Thompson, *Let Sects and Parties Fall: a short history of the Association of Churches of Christ in Great Britain and Ireland* (Birmingham 1980) p 34.

[57] W. R. Ward, 'Scottish Methodism in the Age of Jabez Bunting', *Records of the Scottish Church History Society* (Edinburgh) 20 (1978) pp 47–52.

[58] G. A. Cahill, 'Irish Catholicism and English Toryism, 1832–1848', *Review of Politics* (Notre Dame, Indiana) 19 (1957).

give'.[59] Imperialism was not felt to be an alternative to Scottish national feeling, but in practice it was. Similarly Gwynfor Evans, the president of Plaid Cymru, has argued that the 'Welsh National ideal waned as the new imperialism waxed'.[60] Religion, in underwriting the empire, helped inhibit the force of Scottish and Welsh nationalism until, in the 1960s, the eclipse of empire contributed to permitting a new surge of Celtic nationalism. British identity was reinforced by the churches of Scotland and Wales.

The conclusion must be that religion played its part both in encouraging Welsh and Scottish national feeling and in repressing it. The contribution of religion to Welsh national aspirations is normally given its due, for it was so clearly the driving force. It is less often realised that the Scottish case was parallel. Scotland, like Wales, generated a religious community that was suspicious of the parliament in England and the anglicised landowners within its own boundaries. In both nations the result was support for disestablishment, a cause that gave national feeling a political edge. The Scottish movement was weaker, not least because its grievances were slighter, and it failed to reach the goal of disestablishment that Wales achieved in 1920. But it remains true that in the absence of a nationalist party, religion gave rise to a form of surrogate nationalism in Scotland as well as Wales. On the other hand, one of the many reasons why Celtic nationalism did not emerge as a greater power in the nineteenth century is that religion bound Wales and Scotland to England through their common protestantism, its anti-Irish corollaries and the British imperialism they encouraged. The Welsh and Scottish churches were for the most part well content to live within a multinational state.

University of Stirling

---

[59] John Ker, *Scottish Nationality and Other Papers* (Edinburgh 1887) p 5.
[60] Gwynfor Evans, 'The Twentieth Century and Plaid Cymru', *Welsh Nationalism*, p 131.

THE SCOTTISH RELIGIOUS IDENTITY IN
THE ATLANTIC WORLD 1880–1914

by BERNARD ASPINWALL

IN THE generation before the first world war, Scottish national identity was found not in the church, established or free, but in the town hall; in an ethical Christian community faith rather than 'churchianity'.[1] For Scotland was a working model of the civic church of W. T. Stead.[2] In particular in Glasgow, that faith of the 'new' professional layman proved itself flexible, responsive to urban social problems and readily exportable.[3] Civic patriotism was at once national *and* international.

The Scots, thanks to the communications revolution and their widespread settlement throughout the world, were peculiarly well placed to play a role far beyond their numbers. Confident in their providential mission to bring about an ethical world community, they were less concerned with territorial boundaries and structures, more with an ethos. They united evangelical zeal with moderated reason in seeking to establish a universal consensus on individual morality and social concern. Combined these qualities would ascendingly regenerate the family, the city, the province, the nation and, ultimately, the world. But the city was the central problem: it had to be won for humanity in Christ and the nation. In the American urban crisis, Glasgow was an inspiration—though not

---

[1] Compare Henry Drummond, 'The City in many of its functions is a greater church than the church.' *The City Without a Church* (New York 1893) quoted in Paul Boyer, *Urban Masses and Moral Order in America, 1820–1920* (Cambridge, Mass., 1978) p 253. Also see Washington Gladden, *The Church and the Kingdom* (London 1894) pp 5–6, 14. Gladden was a great admirer of Glasgow see his *Social Facts and Forces* (London 1902). Rev. John Hunter, congregational minister of the influential Trinity Church, Glasgow spent part of a summer in Columbus, Ohio in 1910. He had also visited Jane Addams at Hull House, Chicago in 1907.

[2] W. T. Stead in *Review of Reviews* (September 1893) pp 316–19.

[3] Rev. Josiah Strong, author of *Our Country*, 1885, wrote to R. T. Ely, 22 February 1896, 'What we especially need now is a city well organised which will serve as a practical demonstration of the practicability and value of the work. Such a city would be of inestimable value'. Ely Papers, Wisconsin Historical Society, Madison, Wisconsin, U.S.A. Also see [B.] Aspinwall, 'Glasgow Trams and American Politics, 1894–1914' *ScHR*, 56 (1977) pp 64–84.

the only one—in the Atlantic world.[4] Influential elements in American society for ethnic, religious and intellectual reasons naturally looked upon the city as a working Christian model, whose civic patriotism would naturally ascend to national patriotism and ultimately to mankind. This progressive religious impulse, as Norman Angell saw, 'cut across state boundaries which are purely conventional and render the biological division of mankind into independent and warring states a scientific ineptitude.'[5] Idealism would act as an antidote to class consciousness, provide an interim shelter for those eager to generate civic and national patriotism and contribute to universal peace.[6]

Religion as practised with a Scottish accent would give roots in a fluid society, unite the various classes and ethnic groups and rekindle the folk memory at home and abroad.[7] Scotland and Scottish religion, as dynamic entities, seemed to contain the vital virtues for the English speaking world: a strong work ethnic, sobriety, probity, thrift and duty informed by a Christian democratic missionary sense. It was a means of capturing the commonwealth for protestantism, bringing the ministers closer to the masses and celebrating the triumph of bourgeois values.[8] In the United States, Scots and those of Scottish extraction found comfort and reassurance in this idea: their traditional standing was threatened by millions of non-protestant polyglot immigrants. A suppressed nation carrying the highest evolutionary qualities could make a decisive contribution to the 'ultimate' race.[9] The unique Scottish characteristics could vastly improve the prospects of the

[4] See above.

[5] N. Angell, *The Great Illusion* (London 1912 ed) px. Glasgow was the leading British supporter of his ideas. Also see *Peace and the Churches: Souvenir of the visit to England of the Representatives of the German Christian Churches, May 26 to June 3, 1908 including the visit to Scotland 3 June to 7 June 1908* (London 1909) pp 97, 233. One visitor said Glasgow was 'the Mecca to which municipal pilgrims from all countries came in order to learn and admire as we are doing today'.

[6] See J. T. Ely *The Labour Movement in America* (London 1890) p 332; R. A. Woods *Americans in Progress* (Boston 1903) p 370; J. B. Gilbert, *Work Without Salvation: AMerican Intellectuals and Industrial America, 1880–1910* (Baltimore 1977); D. T. Rodgers, *The Work Ethic in Industrial America, 1850–1920* (Chicago 1978).

[7] The Scottish 'kailyard' writers, invariably free churchmen enjoyed enormous vogue in America. Ian MacLaren, S. R. Crockett and others.

[8] J. A. Hobson, *The Social Problem* (London 1901) pp 14–15; W. R. Hutchinson, *The Modernist Impulse in Americam Protestantism* (Cambridge, Mass., 1976) pp 134–5, 140, 158–9.

[9] See E. A. Ross, *Changing America* (New York 1912) and *The Old World in the New* (New York 1914) E. R. L. Gould, an American episcopalian admirer of Glasgow

whole human race; that was a well recognised national trait: to a leading American reformer 'the old Scotch race were the most respected of any on this planet'.[10]

The Scottish religious identity, unlike many others, was less confined to a geographical area and more expressed the inner mind and soul of man. The tradition of an individual, internalised self-regulating moral mechanism, suitably 'modernised', was particularly appropriate to the raw, mobile population of industrial America.[11] The contemporary social democratic cult of Burns, admired both the Scot *and* the universal man. As the home of Adam Ferguson, one of the first sociologists, the racial ideas of Robert Knox, of Owenite experiment, as well as numerous merchants, missionaries and explorers, Scotland seemed to be invariably in the van of human progress. Unlike the scattered Irish, few Scots dreamed of a separate independent state: some wanted home rule but most took pride in the republic of the mind and blood. Scottish religious attitudes likewise travelled well. They were readily trans-

---

in his *The Social Condition of Labour* (Baltimore 1893) showed Scots invariably earned more than any other group at home and abroad, p 36.

[10] Joseph Lee, *Constructive and Preventive Philanthropy* (New York 1902, 1913 ed) p 205.

[11] For example Sir Samuel Chisholm, former lord provost of Glasgow, speech at *Alliance of the Reformed Churches holding the Presbyterian System, 9th General Council* (New York 1909) ed G. D. Mathers (London 1909) pp 34–35. The sixth meeting was held in Glasgow in 1896. R. M. Wenley, university of Michigan wrote in *Educational Review*, 1897: 'Were a constant stream of the select minds of America to be directed towards Scotland, the results could not fail to be of most fortunate augury. I say deliberately Scotland. For here more than in England, the American finds himself at home. Partly by temper, partly by force of circumstances the Scot is a citizen of the world. This is the main reason why he is so popular with Americans. Perhaps they regard him as a member of a nationality which has been downtrodden by the English. But I would remind them that Scotland has been subdued only twice. John Knox conquered her head and Robert Burns won her heart. Otherwise she stands still where Wallace and Bruce put her, and this is yet another reason why the free people of the great republic find it easier to come to terms with her sons. More cautious and for a little seemingly less approachable, the Scot has none of the Englishman's *morgue*; poor and less the pray of social conventions, he is, if not more pleasant, than a more suggestive companion. There is more 'to him' as the expressive phrase has it. These characteristics have passed from the nation into the university system. Nowhere has so much been accomplished on so little; the income of the four universities is but a bare half of that enjoyed by Oxford. And this has been done by individual effort. This must always be an attractive feature to the quick and independent American. Scotland is for him the best gateway to an understanding of the Scottish people' *Reviews of Reviews* (May 1897) p 459.

planted to any part of the globe, as flexible, adjustable, internalised and suitable to (American) national and international development. Scots took considerable pride in their providential mission as the social and technical engineers of the Anglo-Saxon race: church and nation were one and indivisible. If the nation, according to Stanton Coit, was 'the living church of her citizens; national idealism in the hearts of the citizens is in the nature worship, of religious praise and of the sum of spiritual communion and dependence which inform prayer'.[12] Scots richly contributed to that identity.

With 'Each lesser finding leading to the larger',[13] Scotland then offered fact and theory of nation building within a family of nations, a role for which she was well qualified by her experience within the British Empire. Glasgow, the second city of the empire had grown at an American pace through the nineteenth century. Between 1871–1880, it had grown, to American astonishment at a faster rate than Chicago.[14] Rapidly industialised, the city had assimilated tens of thousands of Irish and highland immigrants as well as considerable numbers of German, Italian and Jewish arrivals. This had been accomplished with minimum adjustment to the traditional religious ethos, a result of active involvement of Christian businessmen in moral pressure groups and municipal government. A caring Christian commonwealth had overcome the divisive religious, class and political issues and produced a cohesive city with a strong identity and a firm patriotic identity.

This sense of mission, the positions of leadership and influence held together with the difficulty of mounting a viable *independent* national identity, except as a proud form of self expression within a larger unit, whether the British Empire or the United States, gave Scottish relations with the state a unique character. The Scottish tradition of Christian voluntaryism in meeting social or ecclesiastical problems stood them in good stead in other lands. If the

---

[12] Stanton Coit, *The Soul of America* (New York 1914) p 89.
[13] John Bascom, *Education and Religion* (New York 1897) pp 167, 183.
[14] Samuel Lane Loomis, *Modern Cities and their Religious Problems* (New York 1887, 1970 edition) p 24. Adna Ferrin Weber, *The Growth of Cities in the Nineteenth Century: a study in statistics* (Ithaca 1963 edition). On the background to Scottish identity see Gladys Bryson, *Man and Society: the Scottish Inquiry of the Eighteenth century* (Princeton 1945); George Elder Davie, *The Democratic Intellect: Scotland and her Universities in the Nineteenth Century* (Edinburgh 1961; [E. L.] Tuveson, [*Millenium and Utopia: a study in the background of the Idea of Progress*] (Gloucester, Mass., 1972).

Christian nation, as Fremantle claimed, 'is in the fullest sense a church',[15] calling forth the gifts and capacities of individuals and classes within a decentralised body, then the strength and efficiency of local Christianity would be reflected in a truly Christian national life. Glasgow embodied that ideal in a practical and effective manner.

This peculiarly Scottish idea was partly subsumed in the general desire for the closer union of English speaking peoples.[16] With this union of liberal progressive internationalists, Scottish liberals and churchmen could happily identfy. In a way they were celebrating the triumph of their own principles. Shortly after his return from Chicago, W. T. Stead gave form to this idea. (Interestingly enough he spoke first in Glasgow where his brother, Herbert, was at university.) In his proposed civic church, Stead hoped to locate a 'moral caucus'.[17] In establishing a basic minimum social standard below which none should fall, the civic church would 'energise all the institutions which make for righteousness.'[18] Local insight and local initiative would contribute to national progress: 'As the Civic Church is in advance of the State, so the individual reformer is ever in advance of the Civic Church. The heretic always leads the van. What the Civic Church can do is to generalise for the benefit of all the advantages which hitherto have been confined to the few.'[19]

Robert A. Woods, following his visit to Glasgow and contributing to the Glasgow *Modern Church* was confirmed in his view that 'the state has its being in the village sense of the people who pass their days in spontaneous neighbourhood relationships which they have learned to direct to effective ends,'[20] Jane Addams aspired to a dynamic practical faith: 'the doctrine must be understood through the deed. It is the only possible way, not only to stir others to

[15] W. H. Fremantle, *The World as Subject of Redemption* (London 1885) p 349.
[16] F. H. Stead, 'Federation of the English Speaking Peoples', *International Congregational Council, London 1891, authorised record of proceedings with an introduction by R. W. Dale* (London 1891) pp 229–33. Nine Glasgow delegates attended. And his *The Story of Social Christianity* 1 (London 1924) pp 203–4.
[17] W. T. Stead, *Reviews of Reviews* (October 1893 and January 1893).
[18] *Review of Reviews* (September 1893) p 314.
[19] *Ibid* p 315 The full programme is in the September 1893 issue pp 316–19.
[20] Houghton Library, Harvard University, Robert A. Woods Papers, R. A. Woods to Rev. Mr. Wragge, 22 June 1891. Wood's articles appeared in the *Modern Church*, 9 April, 2 May, 16 July, 10 September, 19 November 1891 and 3 March 1892. Other regular contributors included R. M. Wenley. A reverend G. B. Stafford was a regular American contributor.

action but to give the message itself a sense of reality.'[21] There should be 'a cathedral of humanity' which was 'capacious enough to persuade men to hold fast to the vision of human solidarity.'[22] As Woods said many Scots had a lay Christian religion which did not need the aid of the church to get hold of hearts.

Glasgow's Christian enterprise drew together the various intellectual social movements into one harmonious whole.[23] In so far as they were protestantised by this culture, catholic and Jew alike could see social morality in action.[24] Ethical culturist could see Edward Caird's influence. Positivist and socialist could see an approximation to their ideal.[25] The upholders of traditional Christian morality against science and the ill disciplined masses found a strategic role in humanising the stratified and 'segregated' city. The temperance crusade was a classic case. Were cleanliness next to godliness, then Glasgow and her municipal socialism was godliness itself. If religion was on the defensive intellectually, it was on the offensive for social amelioration. If the old elite, or business Christianity, was on the defensive it could reassert its leadership in Christian social concern. All elements could unite in fostering a new healthy organic national unity.

To some contemporaries then the town council had to show the practical action of the church in the present; 'it ought really to present the theocratic idea – i.e. government by the highest good.[26] That Glasgow took that to heart can be seen in the careers of Sir Samuel Chisholm and Sir Daniel Macaulay Stevenson.[27] Both were

---

[21] Jane Addams, *Democracy and Social Ethics* (Cambridge, Mass., 1964 edition) pp xii, 7, 274.

[22] *The Social Thought of Jane Addams,* ed C. Lasch (Indianapolis 1964) p 24. Compare Walter Rauschenbusch, *Theology of the Social Gospel* p 13.

[23] James Bryce, *The Government of British Cities* (New York 1912) p 15 stressed the virtual absence of party politics in Scottish city government.

[24] Louise C. Wade, *Graham Taylor, Pioneer for Social Justice, 1851–1938* (Chicago 1964) p 126.

[25] See Sir Henry Jones and J. H. Muirhead, *The Life and Philosophy of Edward Caird* (Glasgow 1921) and Christopher Harvie, *The Lights of Liberalism: University Liberals and the Challenge of Democracy, 1860–1886* (London 1976).

[26] Elizabeth Blackwell, 'On the decay of municipal government', *Essays on Medical Sociology,* 2 vols (London 1902) pp 176–210, p 181, and *The Religion of Health* (Edinburgh 1888). Also [Mary P.] Follett, [*The New State*] (London 1918, 1934 ed) p 161.

[27] F. C. Howe, *The British City: the beginnnings of democracy* (London 1907) pp 145, 166. Sir Samuel Chisholm 1836–1923, city councillor, Lord Provost. JP, leading temperance advocate, whose second wife was the widow of the founder of the Anchor Line shipping company with considerable links with the USA; *Who Was*

lord provosts, businessmen, liberals and churchmen. But they differed considerably in their emphasis. Chisholm, a wholesale provision merchant, member of Kent Road UP Church, and staunch temperance campaigner, stressed the legal enforcement of the good life when he made all municipally owned properties dry. But Stevenson, a far wealthier, more intellectual character, stressed the innate goodness of man which could be liberated through art (his brother Macaulay was an artist), literature and music. Emphasising moral suasion, Stevenson was a phenomenal benefactor of Glasgow, Liverpool and London universities, the Glasgow School of Art and the Academy of Music. A wholesale coal exporter, he was described as 'one of the most distinguished private citizens of Britain.'[28] A member of the reverend John Hunter's Trinity Church, Stevenson was an advocate of free public libraries, Sunday opening of galleries, a founder of the Glasgow civic society and latterly a member of the Union for Democratic Control. Both men failed to secure election to parliament and both remained in the city, greatly admired by their American friends, as progressive Christian patriots.

Glasgow as a model Christian municipality was instrumental in converting American businessmen to reform. Philanthropy was not merely virtuous but paid a handsome social *and* financial dividend. In philosophical terms, it demonstrated Bergson's *élan vital*; positivist and evolutionary qualities. Above all Glasgow was the centre of British idealism under Edward Caird. For almost thirty years Caird exercised his influence over Glasgow students.[29] At the same time he was involved in practical civic reform; in

Who 1836–1923. Sir Daniel Macaulay Stevenson, 1851–1944. Coal exporter, city councillor 1892–1914, Lord Provost, chairman of the Glasgow Workman's Dwelling Company, a model housing body, founded the chairs of citizenship, Spanish and Italian at Glasgow University, International History, London University, the Directorship of the Institute of International Affairs, and endowed scholarships for Scottish students in Europe; *Who Was Who.*

[28] New York Public Library, Albert Shaw Papers, W. J. Ashley to A. Shaw, 11 January 1895.

[29] See James Mavor, *My Window on the Street of the World,* 2 vols (London 1923). J. H. Muirhead, 1855–1940, educated Glasgow University, MA. 1875, contemporary of Sir Henry Jones and John Maccunn; Professor at Birmingham 1896–1922; visited USA twice; very important in establishing Birmingham University; married to the sister of Graham Wallas. *DNB*; David Watson, *Chords of Memory* (Edinburgh 1936); *The Life of C. S. Horne, M.A., M.P.* ed W. B. Selbie (London 1920): R. M. Wenley, 1861–1929, graduated 1884, studied in Paris, Rome and Germany, and after a spell at Glasgow became professor at Michigan in 1896.

model housing, in education and woman suffrage. His students included many who were to beam his idealism through the Atlantic world: John Buchan; professor James Mavor of Toronto University, friend of American progessives and briefly a member of Hyndman's Social Democratic Federation: professor R. M. Wenley of Michigan, who did so much to establish extra-mural university education in Scotland; Herbert Stead, brother of W. T. Stead, warden of Browning Hall, London and advocate of the welfare state; Charles Sylvester Horne, MP for Ipswich and a congregationalist minister with American interests; professor John Maccunn of Liverpool, philosopher and practitioner of reform; professor William Smart, friend of R. T. Ely, the American economist, and like him an active social reformer; Sir John Mann Jr., who was a housing and health reformer in Glasgow with American links; the reverend David Watson, minister of St Clements, Glasgow, a reformer again with American interests.

The urban university seemed eminently practical and Scottish. Glasgow sent its message to Johns Hopkins University in its formative years: Lord Bryce and Lord Kelvin gave seminars on the civic and scientific ideal. Bryce about to become renowned as *the* critic of American civic failings conducted seminars for Herbert Baxter Adams students. Some like Albert Shaw, later American editor of W. T. Stead's *Review of Reviews*, were to become enthusiatic advocates of Glasgow gospel; E. R. L. Gould, special government investigator in Europe and dedicated episcopalian housing reformer in New York City, greatly admired the social gospel of Glasgow, as did F. C. Howe, the leading municipal expert.[30]

If we add the links between Scottish and American religious

Largely responsible for establishing the university extension movement in Scotland. Author of numerous religious and philosophical works. *Who was Who in America, 1897–1942;* R. M. Wenley, *The University Extension Movement in Scotland* (Glasgow 1895); William Smart 1853–1915, first professor of political economy in Glasgow, active in civic debates; F. H. Stead, 1857–1928, congregationalist minister, warden of Browning Hall, London, author of several books including *The Story of Social Christianity*, and a driving force in the movement for old age pensions.

[30] A. Shaw, *Municipal Government in Great Britain* (New York 1895); E. R. L. Gould, 1860–1915 published widely on housing, temperance and civic reform, see necrology in *The Johns Hopkins Alumni Magazine November 1915* pp 82–4. I am indebted to Dr T. J. Jacklin for this reference; [F.C.] Howe, [*European Cities at Work*] (London 1913).

leaders, knowledge of Glasgow was widespread. The various missions of Moody and Sankey; the visits of Henry Ward Beecher; of various temperance advocates; educational connections; as well as summer pulpit exchanges all contributed to wider influence. The university, press and pulpit could project an image of a working Christian commonwealth.

Numerous American visitors came to Glasgow.[31] It was frequently the port of entry. With a sense of duty they visited the social democratic land of Burns but became increasingly fascinated by Glasgow. It seemed so like an American city in its gridiron plan, its business enterprise and democratic friendliness. It was invariably compared to Chicago; less often with Pittsburgh, Philadelphia or New York. Impressed by its staunch religious culture and ancient urban university, which produced dedicated public servants, missionaries and high minded businessmen, they returned home to advertise the spiritual glories of the city. Robert A. Woods, F. C. Howe, Jane Addams and many others found Glasgow the ideal city of the social gospel, building individual and national identity. Civic patriotism begat national patriotism. To Washington Gladden nothing compared to Glasgow in the sense of social service.[32] Professional social workers and ministers were not the only Americans to discern the new Jerusalem in the city. Practising politicians like mayor Dunne of Chicago, Tom Johnson of Cleveland, William Jennings Bryan, Brand Whitlock and Samuel 'Golden Rule' Jones were enthusiastic admirers. To Jones Glasgow exemplified spiritual and national renewal through municipal ownership.[33]

F. C. Howe found a form of religious enthusiasm for the city just

[31] For example Albert Shaw, *Municipal Government in England* (Baltimore 1899) pp 3–8. 'I think the experience of Glasgow is full of lessons for our new communities that are springing up all over the United States'. There are numerous eulogies of Glasgow in the Albert Shaw Papers, New York Public Library, New York. Americans invariably felt at home in Scotland and with Scots. Alice Hamilton, *Exploring the Dangerous Trades* (Boston 1943) p 85 found English radicals intolerable snobs.

[32] Washington Gladden, *Social Facts and Forces*, (London 1966) pp 158, 172–4, 189.

[33] See B. Aspinwall, 'Scottish Trams and American Politics 1894–1914' *ScHR* 66 (1977) pp 64–84; W. J. Bryan, *The Old World and Its Ways: A Tour Around the World and Journeys through Europe* (St. Louis 1907); *The Letters and Journal of Brand Whitlock*, ed Allan Nevins (New York 1936) pp 157, 169; Typescript speeches of mayor Jones, 3 August 1898 and 26 July 1899 in Toledo Public Library, Toledo, Ohio, Jones Papers; municipal ownership would awaken the social conscience and 'arouse a pure and noble conception of patriotism'.

as earlier Bret Harte had found Glasgow had 'no gaiety, no brilliancy, no sense of enjoyment visible but a stern stupid respect on the part of business as if they were intoxicated from a sense of duty'.[34] A dynamic industrial city, inspired by basic Christianity, proved, flexible but stable, enterprising but humane: 'religion can habituate the ordinary citizen to live for unseen and distant ends'.[35] It was an attitude in keeping with the Scottish moral philosophers and with contemporary racial ideas as well as a recognition of the self-esteem of the individual: 'Particularism and universalism are not mutually exclusive. The best way to serve the universal interest is to be thoroughly the particular man you were destined to be by individual and racial endowment. Particularism has its place and value in the character of elect peoples, not less than in that of the elect man'.[36]

The American city posed massive problems. Religion and national unity seemed very much at risk. The rapid growth of American cities, fluctuating economic conditions of boom and slump; the permanent stratification into classes and the apparent fragmentation of the old civic communities by residential 'segregation' of the classes emphasised the gap between protestantism and the masses. The consolidation of the giant business corporation, the emergence of trade unions, labour unrest and the growth of political machines with their party professional challenged the Christian social conscience. If in intellectual life, it was time of short term leases, in many cities, the population was even more mobile.[37] Few stayed long enough to put down roots and identify with their neighbourhood. Even fewer had been born in a city and so lacked even that tradition. While centralisation and bureaucratisation of government and business eroded local control, character

[34] Howe, p 273. Quoted in George R. Stewart Jr., *Bret Harte: Argonaut and Exile* (Boston 1931) p 285.

[35] See also Brooks Adams, *The New Empire* (Cleveland 1967 ed 1902) p 196. G.Le Bon, *The Crowd* (London 1952 ed 1896) p 185; J. Maccunn, *The Ethics of Citizenship* (Glasgow 1894) p 84.

[36] A. B. Bruce, *The Providential Order of the World* (London 1897) p 293. Also see his *The Moral Order of the World* (London 1898). Bruce was a professor in the free church college in Glasgow. On the tradition and background see Tuveson.

[37] Among the now massive literature see for example Stephan Thernstrom, *The Other Bostonians, 1880–1970* (Cambridge, Mass., 1973) and Howard P. Chudacoff, *Mobile Americans: Residential and Social in Omaha, 1880–1920* (New York 1972). Recent writers have challenged these views. For example, John W. Briggs, *An Italian Passage: Immigrants in Three American Cities, 1890–1930* (New Haven 1978).

and leadership so the traditional role of the clergy diminished in the face of the new professional, the expert, the new graduate.[38] The discovery of poverty and the realisation of the gap between the masses and institutional Christianity forced a radical reappraisal of American Christian culture.

The pastoral crisis for Christian churches gave added impetus to the development of non-dogmatic, non-sectarian social Christianity. It gave an identity, a justification and a purpose. That would unite 'the broadly religious spirit which seems to activate Protestant, Roman Catholic, Jew and ethical culturalist alike,'[39] In this crisis it was foolish and impractical to exclude the constructive elements of any religious tradition: 'Any rational campaign based on the accepted principles and traditions of particular classes tend toward social disintegration. It is only the newer impulses and ideals which all have in common that serve as a basis of unity.'[40]

The assumption was that there was a readily established religious consensus. Education, publicity and moral preaching would bring it about. As the custodians of 'modernised' religion and efficient business methods these groups believed they were non partisan activities forging a national Christian democratic majority against sin: 'a private kingdom of self service . . . ready to thwart the progress of mankind toward justice and toward a fraternal organisation of economic life'.[41] That meant that they sought cheap efficient, incorruptible local government with increased public control over basic monopolies like gas, water, electricity, transportation, the eradication of intemperance and the availability of education in the broadest sense of libraries, galleries, lectures and recreational facilities. For 'the cheapest most effective way to protect . . . class against class within the state is to provide the conditions of growth'.[42]

National identity began at the local level. If the essence of religion was 'not to answer a question but to govern and unite men by giving them common beliefs and duties' the process had to

[38] Christopher Lasch, *The New Radicalism in America, 1889–1963: The Intellectual as a Social Type* (London 1966) and B. J. Bledstein, *The Culture of Professionalism: The Middle Class and the Development of Higher Education in America* (New York 1976).
[39] Quoted in Louise C. Wade, *Graham Taylor*, p 126.
[40] [Simon N.] Patten, *The Theory of Prosperity* (New York 1902) p 208. See also pp 206–23.
[41] [Walter] Rauschenbusch, [*Theology for the Social Gospel*] (New York 1917) p 52.
[42] John Bascom, *Sociology* (New York 1887) p 159

begin with the neighbourhood: 'a common environment and common desires create a united race and a rational basis of action.[43] A new community could not have a tradition: the traditions which migrants brought with them would merely serve to further divide the already fragmented city: 'A community of purpose . . . is more effective than tradition because it pervades the whole of man'.[44] Intellectually and socially that would appeal to the local influential groups. The dual threat of science and the masses could be contained. An evolutionary Christian approach as Henry Drummond of Glasgow saw, recognised the positive values of each church and sect in overcoming denominational barriers.[45] Men of good will were united in a common cause: 'a progressive group is always united because the beliefs of its members come from their acts and impulses: a stationary group falls apart through a tendency to emphasise a past in which other groups did not share. The objective was to construct an environment which would inspire emotional attachment, loyalty, to the community'.[46] As Simon N. Patten observed 'Race ideals are kept alive, not by reasoning but by the motor powers created by their perception. So long as these ideals have a social value and a possible verification in the history of the race, they will be perpetuated even if the metaphysical basis is insecure'.[47] Otherwise men would become wild sensualists over whom religion and morality had no hold.

Ideals had to be vivid, impressive and dramatic to influence the masses: 'to know the art of impressing the imagination of crowds is to know at the same time the art of governing them.[48] Jane Addams endorsed that view, 'ethics and political opinions come to the common people only through example—through a personality which seizes the imagination'.[49]

Man could only appreciate the immediate tangible quality of the ideal. That placed a decided onus on the well to do: to generate enthusiasm for the province:

[43] Frederic Harrison, The Philosophy of Common Sense (London 1907) pp 349–50 and Patten, Theory of Prosperity p 207.
[44] Hugo Munsterberg, The Americans (London 1905) p 5
[45] Henry Drummond, The Ascent of Man (London 1894).
[46] [Simon N.] Patten, The Development of English Thought, (New York 1899) p 388 and Theory of Prosperity p 206.
[47] The Development of English Thought p 363
[48] Gustave Le Bon, The Crowd (London 1952 edition) p 71
[49] Quoted in Margaret Tims, Jane Addams of Hull House, 1860–1935 (London 1961) p 61.

We need . . . a new and wiser provincialism . . . I mean by such provincialism which makes people want to idealise; to adorn, to enoble thier own province; to hold sacred its traditions, to honour its worthy dead, to support and to multiply its possessions, I mean the spirit which shows itself in the multiplying of public parks, in the work of local historical associations, in the enterprise of village improvement societies—yes, even in the genealogical societies and professional clubs. I mean also the present form of that spirit which has . . . endowed and fostered the colleges and universities of our Western towns, cities and states and which is so well shown throughout our country in our American pride in our local institutions of learning . . . The Scotsman's love for his own native province—these are the sort of loyalty upon which the British Empire has depended. We want to train national loyalty through provincial loyalty. We want the ideals of the various provinces of our own country enriched and made definite and then to be strongly represented in the government of the nation.[50]

The settlement house, private or municipal model dwelling houses, health visiting, the provision of moral recreational centres like the People's Palace in Glasgow, were part of American desire to import this moral drive into their cities. To curb drink, vice, police corruption and prevent the industrial exploitation of women and children was to safeguard the future of the nation and race. It was also, hopefully, to win loyal affection of the new democracy for the protective state. Religious concern and national self interest combined to further the hopes of mankind. Peace at home meant peace abroad, and vice versa. International interdependence and interchange would contribute to the evolutionary progress of mankind. To the churchman that meant the triumph of

---

[50] Josiah Royce in 'The Philósophy of Loyalty' in *The Basic Writings of Josiah Royce*, ed John J. McDermott, 2 vol (Chicago 1969) 2, pp 952–3. Also see his essay 'Provincialism' *ibid* pp 1067–88; Patten, *The Development of English Thought*, p 6, where 'a sharply defined' locality meant 'men reared in such an environment would have an overflow of energy and activity'; R. T. Ely, *Socialism* (London 1895) pp 328, 350–52. A. Cameron Corbett, MP and generous benefactor of Glasgow with parks and country estate in the west highlands as part of his temperance campaign gave an almost identical address on receiving the freedom of the city in 1908. A. Cameron Corbett collection, Glasgow University archives. I am indebted to Dr John McCaffrey for this reference.

God's providential plan. Only through the religion of democracy and a democratic religion could that dream be realised: 'Our universe is not a despotic monarchy with God above the starry canopy and ouselves down here; it is a spiritual commonwealth with God in the midst of us.'[51] As Henry Demarest Lloyd, an unrepentant admirer of Glasgow wrote; 'This love of man for man is fordestined to crown and consummate the apprenticeship in the family, the guild, the city, the nation, the Church, by widening into the love of all for all men—the love of Humanity.'[52] In short democracy would bring about the Theophany.[53]

In less rhetorical terms, Glasgow had contributed to the development of American national identity informed by religion. The city had shown itself as a working ethical entity which could achieve desirable social reforms under the directing influences of Christian businessmen. The city could generate local loyalty and national patriotism. Unfortunately the church militantly striving for social reform could too easily become militant, unquestioningly in support of war, with a few notable prophetic exceptions, but that is another story. The Scottish dimension was important and influential in sustaining a British identity and still more an American identity for the urban immigrant millions.

University of Glasgow.

[51] Rauschenbusch p 49.
[52] H. D. Lloyd, *Man, the Social Creator* (New York 1906) p 11.
[53] Follett p 161.

ENGLISH FREE CHURCHMEN AND A
NATIONAL STYLE

by CLYDE BINFIELD

W E ARE building a Church', wrote Ernest Barson, minister
of Penge congregational church in 1911, '. . to welcome
to worship and service men and women . . . of real faith,
such as we often meet in our homes, in business, in social service,
but for whom room and freedom have not always been found in
the Churches . .'[1] A year later he opened his church. A minister
from Purley spoke on the church and the businessman, and one
from Brixton spoke on worship: 'the church must be learned,
common and catholic'. This speaker delighted in paradox:

the minister incurred a grave responsibility who deprived any
one of the right to utter prayer and praise. [But] the overwhelming experience of Christianity was in favour of a
Liturgy . . . Then their Church must be Catholic. They
should forget that they were Nonconformists in their worship
. . . and never never forget that they worshipped not as
Nonconformists, but as members of the holy family of the
Church.[2]

For Penge this meant a capped and purple-gowned choir, like the
City Temple, and a service book called *Prayer and Praise* (1914).

What sort of building encouraged such attitudes? On 6 January
1911 the Penge building committee considered plans submitted in
competition for their new premises. There were eight. All save
three were eliminated, none received general assent, only one was
at all acceptable. Design number seven 'did not look good enough
for the money proposed to be spent,' and was dismissed as a
mixture of '[n]o style and bad style'. As for number six, Mr
Hopper, a nurseryman, liked the plan, disliked the 'circular choir
seats'; Mr Feaver, a Bermondsey tin box manufacturer, found the
interior excellent but the exterior 'no use'. In the opinion of Mr
Tarrant, who was a Wimbledon umpire, 'the Byzantine style [was]

[1] *Penge Congregational Church: Fourth Annual Report . . . for 1911* (Penge 1912) p 11.
[2] *Norwood News, Penge and Anerley News, Sydenham and Forest Hill News, and General
Advertiser for Selhurst, Woodside, Thornton Heath and Croydon*, 2 November 1912.

unsuited to the neighbourhood and [he] could not possibly vote for the design,' at which Mr Hodgson, who was a printer, protested that 'the design was not Byzantine but Lombardian Romanesque. [He] thought the style more suited to Congregational worship than Gothic and liked the whole scheme entirely'. The minister spoke last. He 'was enamoured with the ground plan . . . but dare not recommend the whole scheme as one likely to raise the enthusiasm of all our people'. Consequently the building committee commended design number two to the church council. This was in unexceptionable gothic and, as Feaver put it, the plans were 'fairly good on the whole'.

The church council was inclined to agree but then Feaver's brother Alfred, who had the president of the RIBA in mind, suggested outside assessment, so the council compromised by approaching the Architectural Association whose fees were cheaper (twenty guineas inclusive, as opposed to the RIBA's thirty guineas plus one fifth of one per cent of the building's cost) and whose president, Arthur Keen, was an experienced chapel architect who had already expressed interest in the project. Keen acted decisively. He passed over designs seven, six and two and selected number eight as the most meritorious of them all. 'An appointment was made on the telephone to meet [the architect] at his office on the next day'; it was intimated that 'the general feeling was in favour of a Gothic type' and the architect asked for time 'to develop a Gothic idea'.[3]

Whatever the merits of the eighth design, its creator's subsequent gothic idea still dominates Beckenham Road, Penge. Inside, the first impact is from the arcades of pointed arches on octagonal piers, their corbels massively carved with emblems of the evangelists, but then the attention is properly drawn to the communion table, where all lines converge, thence to the cross, thence to the window of Christ in majesty. The flavour is unmistakable:

[a]scending the chancel steps we see the simple outline of a Celtic Cross in the marble pavement; on each side the oak choir stalls are arranged facing each other as in an Anglican Church; small brass plates fixed to the backs indicate the

---

[3] *Building Committee Minutes*, I, 29 October, 20 December, 1910; 6 January, 13 February, 20 February, 21February, 28 February, 6 March 1911. Penge congregational church.

customary seat of deceased choirmembers who gave many
years of faithful service.

In the north transept, enclosed since 1933, there is a chapel of
youth. Two pictures from the studio of Frank Salisbury stand
behind its communion table. One of these, 'The Human Awaken-
ing', shows a youth who has just emerged armed for battle from an
archway symbolising parents, home, school and church. The
other, 'Duty's Call', shows the young warrior summoned by an
angelic trumpeter: 'when he answers that call, he will receive the
helmet which rests in the crook of the angel's arms'.[4]

As for the exterior, the *Congregational Year Book* was accurately
concise:

> [t]he new church may be described as a free treatment of the
> late traditional Gothic style tempered to Congregational uses.
> All churches appear to be classed indiscriminately under the
> generic terms, Classic and Gothic, and all modern buildings
> suggest some approximation to a period within these broad
> distinctions. To adhere rigidly to any definite style is imposs-
> ible and archaic. The beauty of all Gothic work is in its
> elevation, and in proportion to its size and cost, height has
> been aimed at. The shape of the tower is unusual but it arose
> out of a desire to give cumulative effect to the various roofs
> meeting at this point. The Church feels that the architect, Mr.
> P. Morley-Horder, F.R.I.B.A., has achieved their ideals of
> simplicity and worshipfulness which has been their aim from
> the beginning. The building has seating accommodation for
> 600 persons and has cost £10,000 with hall and caretaker's flat.[5]

Here indeed is the battle of the styles as fought by south London
businessmen out for their money's worth, with gothic as victor,
more free than dissenting no doubt, yet defined at every turn by
established values. Except that it was not quite like that. The action
taken by these businessmen was informed and popular. Their
church at Penge reflected decisions responsibly made, minister,
building committee and church council reacting on each other.
Their resort to Arthur Keen reflected assurance, not ignorance, and
their subsequent experience with their architect confirmed this.

That architect, Percy Morley Horder (1870–1944), is today best

[4] J. M. Young, *Some Notes on the History and Buildings of Penge Congregational Church*,
undated, unpaginated typescript, author's possession.
[5] *The Congregational Year Book, 1913* (London 1913) p 145

known for the range of buildings forming the major part of Sir Jesse Boot's benefactions to the university of Nottingham (1922–9), but in his earlier years he had a distinctive line in congregational chapels. Horder was dramatic, wayward, utterly charming. He was the very devil with chapel building committees, and his credentials were impeccable. His father, W. Garrett Horder (1841–1922), was a London minister whose hymn book, *Worship Song* (1905), was widely used by thoughtful congregations. Indeed, Garrett Horder had preached for the Penge congregationalists in their early days and *Worship Song* had been adopted by them. The Horders, like so many established ministerial families, afford a cross-section of the Victorian professional and commercial classes: Samuel Morley (1809–86), the Gladstonian hosier and congregational stonelayer par excellence, was Morley Horder's first cousin twice removed. Morley Horder knew and reflected the Chapel constituency and if his chapels were disconcertingly promiscuous when it came to style, he was unaccommodating where it concerned fittings, colour and material. Horder's generation was the one most affected by the arts and crafts ideals which had made English vernacular architecture internationally famous, and his first master, George Devey (1820–86), had been a particularly fashionable pioneer of the domestic revival, with Samuel Morley notable among his clients. The craftsman's ideals of harmony and integrity, translated for an industrial society and realised in a suburban one, were unusually pertinent for free churchmen whose buildings, reflecting the homely needs but other worldly aspirations of select local communities, were bound to be prominent incidents in any townscape.

At Penge Morley Horder produced an architect's church, 'churchy' beyond doubt, full of borrowings from architect's architects. In the tower and general massing there were echoes of Norman Shaw's nearby All Saints, Swanscombe (1894–5) and his famous All Saints, Leek (1885–7): can such mannerisms have influenced the assessment of Arthur Keen, who had been Shaw's pupil and venerated him? Penge's deeply recessed east window was strongly reminiscent of Henry Wilson's Saint Peter's, Ealing (1892), and the tower was yet more strongly reminiscent of E. S. Prior's Saint Andrew's, Roker (1904–7), 'the best English church of the early 20th century'.[6] Yet even Horder's eclecticism deferred to the

[6] C. Grillet, 'Edward Prior', *Edwardian Architecture and its Origins*, ed [A.] Service

associations of his constituency. Saint Peter's, Ealing, was the nearest notable new church to his father's own church, while Saint Andrew's, Roker, was an inescapable landmark for up-to-date visitors to Sunderland where Ernest Barson had energetically ministered from 1905 to 1908. Penge's tower, largely paid for by the Feaver brothers, was a masterly, flattering tribute to Penge's minister while Morley Horder's freely eclectic gothic was in fact a reasoned and harmonious tribute to the community whose wishes he realised. Manifestly ecclesiastical, it nonetheless reflected, with its meeting rooms, kitchens and caretaker's flat, that half-way point between the domestic and the public which was the mark of successful free church buildings. It was a monument to what might not unfancifully be called the free church battle for national style.

It has been urged that 'perhaps the most intense architectural achievements of the beginning of the century in England were the churches built by the Arts and Crafts architects', their manner suggesting a new style springing freely from gothic roots, but retaining the gothic principle of fitness for purpose.[7] Part of this principle was experienced in the integration of architecture, sculpture and painting and it has been further urged that the 'integration of sculpture into the exterior, and painting into the interior of buildings seems to have led steadily towards a free Baroque revival'.[8] In 1890 Henry Wilson's partner, the better known J. D. Sedding, told the Architectural Association:

[i]f you are to succeed in architectural design along modern lines it will only be by being enthusiastic about the handicrafts —by knowing how to design interesting stonework, wood-work, ironwork, embroidery and other of the sub-industries of architecture.[9]

Seen thus, and with Englishmen pre-eminent at last in architecture's many sub-industries there might appear to be less conflict between the styles and less cause for surprise at architects flitting from free gothic to free baroque. What needs to be recognised however, is the extent to which free church architecture was receptive to this flowering of national excellence. Where there was a battle between styles a more or less free gothic probably won; but

(London 1975) p 147.
[7] A. Service, *Edwardian Architecture* (London 1977) p 118.
[8] *Ibid* p 44.
[9] Quoted *ibid* p 79.

the free churches were more likely than the state church to experiment with other styles and to do so with sophistication and integrity. Whatever the style, theirs too was national architecture. Penge was not unique.

Nonetheless certain general distinctions may be made, and usefully applied to free church architecture. By the end of the century the classical, italianate and gothic in housing had been largely replaced by the domestic free style, intensely English, widely admired. In public buildings they had been replaced by forms of baroque frequently wrenaissance and therefore more truly English. In ecclesiastical buildings, where the field remained hotly contested, the many shades of early English matured into later and freer gothic, which historically minded protestants might approximate to the styles of Wyclif or Cranmer. Chapel architecture embraced all three types. Keeping up with the anglican Joneses was taken for granted but, in significant contrast, the old meeting house image was increasingly cherished, that of the public building was enhanced, and in each instance there was a national gloss. The meeting-house was Cromwellian, and the great man's tercentenary fell in 1899; the public hall was a partial consequence of the mayor's-nest chapels which some cities had harboured since 1835; even the gothic and cruciform had ceased to be dissenting gothic and become free church, the truly national alternative to a so-called national church.

Could the same be said of the chapel goers? Their needs dictated the building and the successful building reflected the interaction of chapel committee, architect, minister, congregation, and sometimes patron, not necessarily in that order. Did they reflect the generality of the religious public, or were they in any way distinctive?

Obviously they represented the generality in the sense that most of them belonged to the various gradations of the middle class. That is to say, they saw themselves as part of the major new political fact, the national class, indeed the imperial class, for their heroes were missionaries and their kinsmen were emigrants. Politically they tended to support the liberals, who were the natural party of government and they frequently, perhaps usually, enjoyed the prospect of municipal dominance. The waves of taste and culture washed over them too, and their architecture too was bound to express the tendencies of their age. But they were distinctive nonetheless. They were as inevitably moulded by the implications of generations of dissent as they were by the implications of their churchmanship. The former had social and political ramifications, the latter was immediately visible in the practicalities of pulpit, table and baptistery, of auditorium, schoolroom, lecture hall and lavatory. The constraints of their dissent were balanced by their freedom from parish boundaries, but if political circumstance had formally deprived them of national status it had forced them back to the localised and the autonomous as well as out to the foreign and unknown, for there was an increasing internationalism about dissent which strengthened their merely national aspirations. The church of England was a national church no doubt, but many dissenting leaders (and the extent to which the nonconformist ministry provided a formidable intelligentsia has been undervalued) came from Ulster, Scotland and Wales. They were British not English, a distinction powerfully echoed in the British Schools which dissenters preferred to National Schools, the British and Foreign Bible Society in which dissenters could share, *The British Quarterly Review* which mid-Victorian dissenters promoted to balance other quarterly reviews, *The British Weekly* in which political dissent later rejoiced, even *The British Banner* which a previous generation scurrilously waved. Earlier in the century *The Patriot* made a similar point, later *The Christian World* extended it. For to be British meant the South Seas and the white dominions, and to be British dissenters meant cousins in the States and kindred souls in reformed Europe. It was a vision bounded only by the tops of office desks and communion tables (or pulpits) and it defined attitudes which were not all mere caprices of taste.

There was, in short, a foundation for a dissenting architecture which transcended dissenting gothic, which was properly national because it was free.

The concept of a free church was helped enormously, indeed given general currency, by the Scottish disruption in 1843. The disruption's most notable English tremor occurred in London when Regent Square joined the seceders. Edward Irving's ministry (1822–32) had made Regent Square nationally notorious, but the flavour of the congregation's aspirations is better conveyed by Thomas Shepherd's engraving of their recently built church as it appeared in 1829. Above the legend 'New National Scotch Church' and with the words *Ecclesia Scotica* carved high on its façade, pure

street scenery scaled down to suit the eastern marches of Bloomsbury without revealing the preaching box which it was, is Sir
William Tite's version of York Minster. [10] Regent Square's fortunes
were restored by James Hamilton, minister from 1841 to 1867,
impeccably Scottish and an unwilling dissenter who justified his
London ministry by a special mission to a country whose pulpit
ministrations 'are in doctrine very meagre and very jejune'. [11] In
1839 assembly week in Edinburgh had convinced Hamilton that
'[t]he Church of Scotland is the only Establishment which neither
owns a secular jurisdiction in her things spiritual nor claims a
jurisdiction for herself in things temporal. I am thankful that I
belong to such a Church'. [12] The disruption proved otherwise, but
his London experience brought home the national need for rigorous churchmanship: 'I only repeat that it is a vitalized Presbyterianism, sound doctrine in warm English hearts, and from fluent
English lips, guided by Scottish sense, and systematically propagated by Presbyterian organization, which promises, in the hand
of the quickening Spirit, to retrieve the interests of Evangelical
piety in England.' [13] Such views were no more easily applied to the
established habits of English dissent than they were grateful to
uneasy anglicans, and presbyterian congregations were seldom free
from the atmosphere of an embassy—or at least a consular—church.
Yet the sympathies of outsiders could not fail to be braced by them.

In 1869 six congregationalists and baptists, three of them barris-
ters, two ministers, the sixth a physician, published a book of
essays. Inevitably they were defensive. They aimed to describe
their polity, 'the forms of character and opinion which it has
contributed to produce', and 'the basis of reason' on which it
rested; they claimed to represent the younger generation. [14] Inevitably they were dissident. Their title, *Religious Republics*, which had its
charms in 1869, did not speak of national harmony. They were also
topical, responding to *Culture and Anarchy*, to Irish disestablishment,
then almost in the bag, and to *Origin of Species*, which they were

[10] The foundation stone was laid on 1 July 1824 by Lord Breadalbane, taking the
place of the duke of Clarence. The church cost over £21,000 and was demolished
after major damage in the second world war.
[11] W. Arnot, *Life of James Hamilton DD, FLS* (London 1870) p 378.
[12] *Ibid* p 136.
[13] *Ibid* p 310.
[14] *Religious Republics*[: *Six Essays on Congregationalism*] (London 1869) preface.

entirely prepared to take on board. They were pragmatic, prone to celebrate their polity as spiritual expediency, emphasising its consequent individual and intellectual freedom, tying it to the spirit of the age with the assurance of men who took servants for granted. Perhaps that is the clue to them, for they were neither cringing nor shrill and harmony is a precondition of assurance. They took their epigraph from Bunsen:

> [m]y general impression is, that in the minds of the men of highest intellect a preparation is going forward for a new epoch; . . . a period of serious and yet free research after the reality of Christianity among the Catholics, and of advancement in the same direction among the learned Protestants, with a quick growth and spread of congregational life.

Their congregational wares too were conducive to ultimate harmony. Indeed, Philip Henry Pye-Smith, suspecting that the state church ('which in its merits as in its faults is emphatically English') was bound for disestablishment, anticipated that it might assume 'the flexible and light-armed organisation of [the congregational] branch of the great Christian army.'[15] For the Nottingham born barrister, Edward Gilbert Herbert, the spiritual reality of light-armed congregational fellowships reflected a no less harmoniously flexible mutuality of believers.[16]

It was left to a baptist minister from Newcastle, T. H. Pattison, to write on 'Congregationalism and Aesthetics'. Here too his entire theme was harmony: '[o]ur Nonconformity does effect materially our doctrine, our practice, our worship, our training, our modes of thinking, and indeed our whole life . . . Therefore, it must be a power telling on taste.' Yet our nonconformist 'is not a mere incarnation of system . . . he yearns, oftentimes passionately, for 'light and sweetness', . . . the harmony and perfection which go to make up the fulness of life are quite as essential to his constitution as to that of any other man' and, imagining a cultivated young dissenter, he found gospel comfort: 'from the New Testament we learn how possible it is, whilst cultivating taste, to dissent from established forms . . . Christ himself was a dissenter all his life. Yet . . . [n]o one can read the Great Biography without being

---

[15] P. H. Pye-Smith, 'Congregationalism and Science', *Religious Republics* pp 199–201.
[16] E. G. Herbert, 'The Congregationalist Character', *Religious Republics* pp 91–132.

conscious of a fine harmony . . . He came to bring light and sweetness to man.'[17]

So Pattison came to architecture, the visible, natural expression of principled, reasoned freedom. With crude sweeps he dismissed both gothic (congregationalists 'have been so enamoured of the national style, that they have sown the land over with miserable imitations of Gothic churches. But as our principles are understood, and acted out, this abuse will cease') and classical architecture ('[w]hat teaching is there for us in classic plans or classic details?'); but the determined reader might disregard such strokes as pulpit rhetoric. Pattison's real message lay in principled expediency disciplined by the proper mutuality of people, architect and minister. The need was buildings convenient for sight and sound: '[t]o these two essentials all questions of style and design ought to be subservient'. In this the dissenting client 'has peculiar advantages, inasmuch as he is generally obliged to build for himself' and the chapel architect 'is powerless on many points where the architect of the church is supreme. He cannot plead precedent'. As for the parson, he very often 'knows less than anyone else in the building about its comfort or beauty. He is too active to be much affected by them'.

From such interaction came harmony: 'a chapel carefully thought out in design and substantially executed in honest materials . . . lasting proof of the power of the Congregationalist system to clothe its principles decorously and in suitable garb'.[18] But Pattison's harmony was rather equipoise: '[o]f course there will be forbidden ground for us, which is a very Eden to the church architect. We cannot indulge in symbolism; no hidden language will be spoken to the initiated by carving or capital; no quaint fancy will lurk in boss or bracket. All that is will be seen and understood by all . . . But all the while it must be remembered that we are free to employ the ornamental as well as the useful. There is no reason why we should not devote the same taste which adorns the dwelling-house to making God's house a Palace Beautiful for all who enter it. We must preserve harmony in proportion; and in colour we may have frescoed walls and painted glass; we may call

---

[17] T. H. Pattison, 'Congregationalism and Aesthetics', *Religious Republics* pp 136–7, 143–6.
[18] *Ibid* pp 158–63.

in the art of the sculptor and the worker in metals'.[19] Honest materials, harmonious ornament, the balanced expression of need and personality, enshrining the ceaseless relevance of spiritual expediency: what could be more representative of Victorian England? More to the point, Pattison believed that the art of chapel building was keeping pace with its practice: 'I think it is a most remarkable testimony to the power of our principles, not only that the buildings have been raised, but that they are so pleasing to the eye and so satisfactory to the judgment'.[20] Pattison was not being entirely fanciful. It can be argued, at least from a reading of *Congregational Year Books* and *Baptist Handbooks*, not just that Victorian and Edwardian chapel building expressed the congregational harmonies but that in its range and flexibility it was more nationally representative than most other types of public building. Pattison notwithstanding, the search for fitness ended most frequently with gothic, but its happiest results are to be found in the vernacular style, its most interesting in the meeting house revival and its most revealing in the public hall.

No chapelgoer could deny that the most consistent English expression of Christianity had been in gothic. What is notable about dissenting gothic is less its increasing correctness, largely made possible by increasing resources, than its fitness. As to the former, W. H. Lever's trio of congregational churches, Blackburn Road Bolton, Saint George's Thornton Hough and Christ Church Port Sunlight, built between 1895 and 1907, by Jonathan Simpson, J. Lomax Simpson and William and Segar Owen may stand as type and *ne plus ultra*. Yet even Lever's stance was more complex than a mere annexation of the nicer parts of anglicanism. As to the latter, the work of George Baines and Son may bear witness.

George and Reginald Palmer Baines designed for several denominations but their distinctive work was baptist. It was also nationwide and it extended, widely copied, for nearly seventy years.[21] The Baineses aimed certainly at honest materials, sensible

---

[19] *Ibid* p 161.
[20] *Ibid* p 162.
[21] George Baines's early work was in Lancashire in the 1870s. By the mid 1880s he had offices in Accrington and Great Winchester Street, London. By the late 1890s, he was in Clement's Inn. By the 1920s George Baines and Son were at 121 Victoria Street, SW1. Between 1885 and 1914 over 60 Baines designs were described in the *Baptist Handbook*, their last church, Brighton Road, Newhaven, appearing in B[aptist] H[andbook] (1938) p 364.

ornament, and general efficiency in an arts and crafts setting. As expressed at Beverley Road, Hull, their trademark was a 'late period of Gothic freely treated in order to obtain a quaint and picturesque effect.'[22] At Wellingborough this meant a façade of whole white flints dressed with red bricks, a roof of brindled Broseley tiles, 'a square tower, with an open arched and traceried cupola, surmounted by a curved roof covered with oak shingles and wrought-iron weather vane', and internal constructive wood-work and joinery stained transparent green and varnished.[23] It also often meant an interior with seats radiating from the central pulpit, so that 'every hearer will directly face the minister', sometimes a horseshoe gallery on the same principle, a baptistery so designed that 'after baptism the candidates will be immediately out of sight', leaving for separate dressing rooms by a door beneath the pulpit, and an increasing use of electric light, 'wrought-iron fittings relieved by copper ornaments'.[24]

These were churches for towns and important suburbs. For the suburban village or the smaller seaside resort there was a delightful alternative, truly vernacular because at once protestant and English. J. Wallis Chapman (1842–1915), who was one of John Clifford's deacons at Westbourne Park, designed a small union chapel for Pembury near Tunbridge Wells. A melancholy significance attached to the scheme for it was the last in which that old chapel-building impresario, Sir Morton Peto, had any part. Externally it could have been a refugee from Bedford Park. 'A very plain type of "Queen Anne" has been adopted, with red-brick facings, red-brick dressings, and green-slated roof'.[25] Internally, however, the atmos-phere was more of the approaching puritan revolution than of the receding glorious revolution. With its stuccoed walls, plastered ceiling, deal ribs and trusses, it was a pre-Laudian chapel of ease.

Echoes of the seventeenth century turning into the eighteenth, meeting house style this time, were clearly to be heard in a quite different setting when a new congregational church was opened at Leyton in May 1900. *The Leyton Express* found it both foreign and modish:

[22] *B H* (1904) p 383.
[23] *B H* (1901) p 371. The green stain in such general favour among arts and craftsmen is said to have started with Ford Madox Brown. P. Henderson, *William Morris, His Life, Work and Friends* (London 1967) p 71.
[24] Thus the account of Ferme Park, Hornsey. *BH* (1898) p 340.
[25] *BH* (1890) p 364; (1888) p 342.

[t]he shape and style of the exterior is more common on the continent than in this country. It presents a square and somewhat severe aspect, with small leaded windows, and an outer coat of pale pebble plaster . . . The interior . . . affords an example of the modern aestheticism, which is an elaborated revival of an older School of artistic perception. The modern cult of aesthetics owes much to the enthusiasm of Mr. Walter Crane, the artist, who is one of the most ardent disciples of the science of the beautiful. The effect to some is extremely pleasing, but as one of the trustees remarked, it is curiously strange to the majority of Leyton folk . . . a triumph of colour over material.[26]

Beguiled by the hammered brass and iron gas standards, the deep restful green gallery seats, the chocolate brown pulpit and pillars and the cream washed walls, the Leyton journalist missed the real significance of the interior. Leyton's new church, bravely placed in an entirely artisan suburb, was in fact the historic Fetter Lane chapel whose congregation, thanks to Thomas Bradbury's presence of mind, had been the first to know that queen Anne was dead.[27] Its rooms were named after dissenting heroes and principal Fairbairn hammered the point home in his ordination charge to the minister:

[n]o longer can you enjoy the delights of the College common room, of the pursuit of the ball in the field, the intellectual exhilaration of the high debate. All you have learned is now to be turned into reality . . . Feel that you stand in an apostolic succession of the very noblest sort. The invisible hands of Thomas Goodwin, Thankful Owen, Stephen Lobb, Thomas Bradbury and George Burder are laid upon your head . . . Mark that they bid you preach, not be a priest; for they would say, 'The only priest of our confession is Christ Jesus; we dare not enter into competition with Him!'[28]

Such were the meeting house associations, liberating and mercantile, which had been recreated with rare sensitivity for east London to face the new century.

The architect was Morley Horder, whose different intentions for

---

[26] *Leyton Express*, cutting, undated [*c*7 May 1900], possession of Mrs Barbara Horder West.
[27] A. Pye-Smith, *Memorials of Fetter Lane Congregational Church, London* (London 1900) pp 16–17.
[28] *Ibid* pp 38–9.

the Penge congregationalists would so impress Arthur Keen; and Keen himself played with similar associations in his distinctive version of the fourth type of nonconformist building, the public hall.

In 1855 James Hamilton had delighted in a Liverpool experience: 'a lovely chapel, it is a vast amphitheatre, without galleries, and the seats, all lined with crimson cloth, rising tier above tier round the room. Nothing can be more comfortable and cozy'.[29] However seldom such efficient loveliness was achieved, other factors than large congregations continued to require it. The Nonconformist conscience's public-meeting dimension was one; the organisational complexity inherent in denominationalism was another.

At the turn of the century the baptists built their headquarters in Holborn, on a site which was to include the venerable Eagle Street meeting. The complex was designed by Arthur Keen (1861–1938). The frontage to Southampton Row was baptist baroque, a stone-faced variant of the grand manner, but the northern façade, facing Catton Street, was brick wrenaissance to match the rebuilt chapel which completed it. Here Keen had recreated Eagle Street as a Wren city church, with red brick and Portland stone dressed tower and porch leading to an octagon. Here the echoes were from a later period, perhaps the tabernacles of Whitefield's revival, with arts and crafts touches to the outside and a domed interior worked with plaster reliefs of biblical trees.[30] It was not a large church—it seated four hundred—and its retention was chiefly sentimental but its message was clear. Baptists were woven into the fabric of the world's greatest capital city. They were a national force in an international setting. A defiantly congregational denomination which refused to see itself as a church had built a Church House, facing Kingsway; Eagle Street meeting had become Kingsgate chapel. Such tribute to Caesar was ambiguous, for which king did baptists serve?

The last word, however, should rest with Philip Henry Pye-Smith, one of the 'religious republicans' of 1869 but later to become vice-chancellor of London university. What he applied to science was capable of wider application and it suggested the national attitude properly taken by liberated nonconformists, not least when it came to style:

[29] W. Arnot, *Life of James Hamilton DD, FLS* (London 1870) p 448.
[30] A. T. Ward, *Kingsgate Chapel* (London 1912) passim; *BH* (1940) p 351.

. . . the form of Christianity which has most chance of dealing effectually with oppositions of science, falsely so called, is that which is the most free, the most varied, the most elastic. Uniformity is always artificial, and here it becomes peculiarly detrimental. Comprehension is yet more dangerous, for it makes religious differences seem unimportant, while differences in science are admitted to be all-important. It fosters the growth of esoteric doctrines of enlightenment, different from those publicly and officially professed; and this is what all true disciples of science most detest in their own pursuits. It makes religion more or less the instrument of worldly policy for its own ends, and deprives Christianity of what to a lover of knowledge is its highest claim, as the doctrine of unbiassed truth. Lastly, it fosters that exclusive spirit of nationality which was once the besetting sin of Jews, and is now of Englishmen—a spirit of which science is in modern times the greatest opponent.[31]

Hence the nation's need for religious republics?

University of Sheffield

[31] P. H. Pye-Smith, 'Congregationalism and Science', *Religious Republics* pp 199–200.

ULSTER PRESBYTERIANS AND IRISH NATIONALISM

by R. F. G. HOLMES

THE stubborn resistance of the protestants of Ulster to the Irish national movement is a notorious fact of modern Anglo-Irish history. Though such resistance to national movements by a minority is by no means a unique phenomenon in the history of nationalism,[1] it may be, as Peter Gibbon claims, in his *Origins of Ulster Unionism*, that 'nowhere else has such a movement encountered a rival of comparable effectiveness, popular support and staying power'.[2] Much of that popular support and staying power came from the presbyterians of Ulster, for, as T. W. Moody has written:

> The stronghold of Ulster protestantism has always been the presbyterian church, rooted in the Scottish reformation and maintaining close and continuous contact with Scotland. Probably the most important social institution of protestant Ulster, it is the only church in Ulster whose members are concentrated in the province and whose structure and government are provincial.[3]

Significantly, until the formation of the general assembly of the presbyterian church in Ireland in 1840, the mainstream presbyterian body in Ireland was the synod of Ulster.

The existence of a substantial presbyterian community on Irish soil was, of course, the result of movements of population from Scotland to Ulster, chiefly in the seventeenth century. Of these, the official plantation of Ulster was only one and in fact the strongest concentration of presbyterians is to be found, not in any of the officially planted counties, but in the two eastern counties of Antrim and Down, which are closest to Scotland.

As early as 1605 an Irish lord deputy, Sir Arthur Chichester,

---

[1] L. B. Namier, *Vanished Supremacies. Essays in European History 1812–1914* (London 1962) pp 204–5.

[2] P. Gibbon, [*The Origins of*] *Ulster Unionism* (Manchester 1975) p 4.

[3] T. W. Moody, 'The Social history of Modern Ulster', *Ulster since 1800*, ed T. W. Moody and J. C. Beckett second series (London 1958) p 231.

recommended that English and Scottish settlers should be introduced to Ulster to strengthen royal control of that last stronghold of Irish Gaelic particularism and resistance to English rule.[4] From the beginning, then, the Scottish settlers who were encouraged to come to Ulster were cast in the role of supporters of the crown, which, significantly, was then being worn by the former James VI of Scotland.

The Scottish settlers did not come to Ulster as complete aliens, however, for the proximity of Scotland and the north of Ireland had meant that movements of population from one to the other had often occurred, and indeed in the mythology of some modern Ulster protestants the seventeenth-century immigrations are known as 'the great return'.[5] The manner of their coming, however, to supplant the native occupiers of the soil, and the fact that they were protestants and the natives catholic, in the main, in an age when reformation and counter-reformation were locked in conflict throughout Europe, envenomed relations from the beginning.

Not that those who came were all religious zealots—the description of them of Andrew Stewart, a contemporary presbyterian minister is scarcely flattering: 'And from Scotland came many, and from England not a few, yet all of them generally the scum of both nations, who, for debt, or breaking and fleeing from justice, or seeking shelter, came hither, hoping to be without fear of man's justice in a land where there was nothing, or but little, as yet, of the fear of God.'[6]

The fear of God came quickly, however, in the first of a series of religious revivals which have contributed to the special character of Irish presbyterianism.[7] There is significance also in the fact that the first presbytery in Ulster was constituted by the chaplains of a Scottish army which had come over in 1642 to protect the settlers from the fury of a native Irish rebellion.[8] There was little in their seventeenth century experience in Ireland, with their colony

[4] A. T. Q. Stewart, *The Narrow Ground, Aspects of Ulster 1609–1969* (London 1977) p 22.
[5] I. Adamson, *The Cruthin: a history of Ulster, land and people* (Belfast 1978) pp 65–7.
[6] A. Stewart, *History of the Church in Ireland . . . after the Scots were Naturalized*, ed W. D. Killen (Belfast 1866) p 313.
[7] W. D. Bailie, *The Six Mile Water Revival in 1625* (Newcastle, Co. Down 1976).
[8] J. M. Barkley, [*A Short History of the Presbyterian Church in Ireland*] (Belfast 1959) p 10.

threatened with extinction in 1641 and in 1688–9, to tempt them to forsake their predestined role as allies and supporters of the British interest. Indeed two centuries later a French observer of the Irish scene could describe them still as: 'the Scotland of Ireland' characterised by 'the ancient anti-catholic prejudice which they had brought with them as colonists of James I'.[9]

It might seem then, that the Ulster presbyterians were always an alien presence on Irish soil, but this would be a misleading oversimplification. If some aspects of their Irish experience encouraged the continuation of their relationship with the British crown—a relationship recognised by the provision from 1672 of *regium donum* for their ministers—other aspects contributed to an anti-English attitude of mind which was never altogether unnatural in Scotsmen and which led to their positive and prominent involvement in the birth of modern Irish nationalism at the end of the eighteenth century.

Their presbyterianism, which separated them from their catholic fellow-countrymen, separated them also from the anglican English, whose church became the established church of Ireland, and after a brief and inevitably temporary period of compromise in the early seventeenth century, when their ministers were allowed to take livings in the episcopal church which was struggling to establish its structures and discipline in Ulster, they found themselves, as dissenters, second class citizens. Although they played their full part in the stirring events of the late seventeenth century, at Derry, Aughrim, Enniskillen and the Boyne, they did not share in the full spoils of victory. The oppressive system of penal law, erected to keep the catholic Irish in subjection, affected them also. With their natural leaders shut out from office and influence, some of them, like their catholic compatriots, were tempted to become anglicans and join the establishment, Castlereagh, the British statesman being a good example. Their merchants, frustrated by Westminster's interference with Irish trade and industry, and the majority of them, tenant farmers, chafing under the injustices of landlordism, with falling prices and rising rents and ever increasing tithes and taxes, they became increasingly alienated from a regime which they could serve but in the rewards of which they could not

---

[9] G. de Beaumont, *L'Irlande, Sociale, Politique et Religieuse* (Paris 1839) quoted in N. Mansergh, *The Irish Question 1840–1921* (London 1975) pp 207–8.

share. Many emigrated to the American colonies where they became involved in the colonists' fight for independence and some who remained, inspired to some extent by events in America and also by the ideas which were influential in the American and French revolutions, began to plan and prepare for a revolution in Ireland.[10] The national and revolutionary movement in Ireland in the late eighteenth century began as a constitutional agitation for Irish free trade and the legislative independence of the Irish parliament but it spawned an extra-parliamentary and popular demand for radical change, ultimately the democratisation of the legislature and separation from Britain. Nowhere in Ireland were these ideas more enthusiastically propagated than in presbyterian Belfast where, in 1791, the society of United Irishmen originated, the aim of which was 'to unite the whole people of Ireland, to abolish the memory of all past dissensions and to substitute the common name of Irishman in place of the denominations of protestant, catholic and dissenter'.[11]

The name of the Dublin protestant barrister Wolfe Tone has been traditionally and rightly associated with this movement but it has been shown that its real founder and original ideologue was the Ulster presbyterian Dr William Drennan.[12] As early as the 1780s he was writing to his friend the reverend William Bruce, who had succeeded Drennan's father as minister of Belfast's 'first' presbyterian congregation, expressing his conviction that 'no reform in parliament and consequently no freedom will ever be attainable by this country but by a total separation from Britain. I think that this belief is making its way rapidly but as yet silently among both protestant and catholic . . . reform to be anything must be revolution.'[13]

Drennan's position was too radical for William Bruce and many presbyterians, who, like Bruce, were reformers rather than revolutionaries, drew back from a movement, which, in the words

[10] R. F. G. Holmes, 'Eighteenth century Irish presbyterian radicalism and its eclipse', *The Bulletin of the Presbyterian Historical Society of Ireland*, no 3 (Belfast January 1973) pp 7–14.

[11] *Life of Theobald Wolfe Tone . . . Written by Himself*, ed W. T. Wolfe Tone (Washington 1826) I pp 51–2.

[12] A. T. Q. Stewart, 'A stable unseen power. Dr William Drennan and the origins of the United Irishmen', *Essays Presented to Michael Roberts*, ed J. Bossy and P. Jupp (Belfast 1976) pp 80–92.

[13] Drennan to Bruce, undated, D 553/70 Public Record Office Northern Ireland *Ibid* p 87.

of one of them, the reverend Robert Black of Derry, 'wished to overturn the constitution' and would inevitably' expose its leaders to the punishment and infamy due to an act of such atrocious folly'.[14] In practice the union of dissenter and catholic against the British government involved for many Ulster presbyterians a leap which they could not contemplate. The Ulster presbyterians were being confronted with what a marxist historian of Anglo-Irish relations has called 'a momentous decision . . . the alternative of fighting the catholic peasants on the side of the landlords, or of fighting the landlords with the help of the catholic masses and the political future of Ireland depended on their choice.'[15]

The more ardent spirits like Henry Joy McCracken and the reverend William Steel Dickson did decide to fight against the landlords in 1798 but their action brought them the fate that Robert Black had threatened. Many other presbyterians, however, took the other decision. Brigadier general Knox, in command at Dungannon in the heart of Ulster, could report that he was able to 'rest the safety' of Fermanagh, Tyrone, Derry and Armagh on the 'fidelity and bravery' of the local yeomanry, most of whom were presbyterians.[16] Sir Richard Musgrave, the tory historian of the rebellion, who was no friend of dissenters, judged that 'though the presbyterians lay under a general imputation of being disloyal, it appears that a great portion of them were steadily attached to the constitution and ready to draw their swords in its defence' and 'though many dissenting ministers of the counties of Antrim and Down were disaffected, great numbers of them were distinguished for exalted piety and unimpeached loyalty'.[17]

In the pulpit of the Belfast's first presbyterian church the reverend William Bruce flayed the rebels so enthusiastically that one of his hearers, Martha McTier, William Drennan's sister, considered that he should have concluded the service with the singing of the Orange song, 'Croppies lie down'.[18]

In spite of such effusions of loyalty, the synod of Ulster, at its annual meeting in 1798, appealed 'to history to attest the Inviolable Attachment of the Presbyterians of Ireland to Monarchy, Counsel-

---

[14] B[elfast] N[ews] L[etter], 25 January 1793.
[15] E. Strauss, *Irish Nationalism and British Democracy* (London 1951) p 25.
[16] R. Musgrave, *Memoirs of the Different Rebellions in Ireland* (Dublin 1802) I, p 237.
[17] Ibid pp 237–8.
[18] Mrs McTier to Drennan, 30 November 1798, *The Drennan Letters*, [ed D. A. Chart] (Belfast 1931) p 283.

led by an Hereditary Nobility, and supported and limited by an Elective Representative of the Commons,' while viewing 'with grief and Indignation . . . crimes which we ourselves deem inexcusable',[19] the presbyterians of Ulster were now, as Castlereagh described them in a letter to the prime minister, Addington, 'an object much more of jealousy than of support to the government'.[20] He went on to outline his plans to restore them to their proper role as supporters of the British interest in Ireland which included a massive increase in the *regium donum* which would in future be given only to those ministers whose loyalty was attested by local magistrates and, in fact, Steel Dickson, though pardoned for his participation in the rebellion, was deprived of his share of the *regium donum* for the remainder of his ministry.[21]

Castlereagh's task was made easier by presbyterian disillusionment with revolutionary nationalism. One of his Ulster correspondents, Alexander Knox, informed him in July 1803,

this is perhaps a more favourable moment for forming a salutary connexion between the government and the presbyterian body of Ulster than may again arrive. The republicanism of that part of Ireland is checked and repressed by the cruelties of Roman catholics in the late rebellion and by the despotism of Bonaparte. They are therefore in a humour for acquiescing in the views of government beyond which they ever were or (should the opportunity be missed) may be hereafter.[22]

We have some access to the experience of a presbyterian rebel in the verses of James Orr, the bard of Ballycarry, a folk poet of the period. Orr had contributed political pieces to the radical presbyterian newspaper, the *Northern Star* and, with many of his neighbours in Ballycarry, had 'turned out' in 1798, after which he had to flee to America for a time, with a price of fifty pounds on his head. His disillusionment with rebellion and extreme nationalism resounds through his later verses.[23] Orr found that noble aspirations were

---

[19] R[ecords of the G[eneral S[ynod of] U[lster, 1691–1820], 3 vols (Belfast 1890–98) 3, pp 208–9.

[20] Castlereagh to Addington, 21 July 1802 [*Memoirs and correspondence of] Castlereagh*, [ed Marquess of Londonderry], 8 vols (London 1848–53) 4, p 224.

[21] W. D. Bailie, 'William Steel Dickson', *The Bulletin of the Presbyterian Historical Society of Ireland* no 6 (Belfast, May 1976) pp 3–31.

[22] Alexander Knox to Castlereagh, 13 July 1803, *Castlereagh* 4 p 288.

[23] D. H. Akenson and W. H. Crawford, *James Orr, bard of Ballycarry* (Belfast 1971) pp 10–17.

soon corrupted in the fear and cruelty of actual battle and his observation of events in France seemed to teach him that revolution led only to military dictatorship. In his 'Soliloquy of Bonaparte, spoken on the day of his coronation', he asked:

> Can shouts like these allay the widow's pain,
> Who tells her infant of its sire bereav'd,
> How many thousands fled, like him. in vain,
> To free the land that Bonaparte enslav'd?[24]

Orr, like many Ulster presbyterians, had come to believe that, as the synod of Ulster's loyal address to the lord lieutenant in 1793 had declared: those reforms 'necessary to the perfection of the constitution and the security and maintenance of public liberty' were to be attained only by 'constitutional means . . . rejecting with abhorrence every idea of popular tumult or foreign aid'.[25]

The final eclipse of the ideas of the United Irishmen among the Ulster presbyterians was completed under the impact of the forces which were forming the shape of Ulster and Ireland in the nineteenth and twentieth centuries. One of these was Evangelicalism. Ulster presbyterianism in its beginnings owed much, as we have seen, to an experience of religious revival, and it was that tradition, stimulated by repercussions from the Evangelical revival in Britain associated with Wesley and Whitefield, which became dominant in the nineteenth century in the wake of failure of political utopianism in 1798.[26] In general evangelicalism had the effect of narrowing the gap between presbyterian and episcopalian and widening that between presbyterian and catholic and of absorbing energies in religious activity which had gone into politics in the eighteenth century. Evangelicalism had its political implications, also, linking Irish evangelicals more closely with their brethren in Britain who became involved with them in the great task of converting the catholics of Ireland.[27]

There is some evidence of more precise political influence in the preaching of certain evangelists whom Drennan's sister, Mrs McTier, heard in the autumn of 1801. She found them 'extremely zealous and loyal, well fitted for drawing off the people to their

---

[24] *Ibid* p 12.
[25] *RGSU*, 3 pp 156–7.
[26] J. S. Reid, *The History of the Presbyterian Church in Ireland briefly Reviewed and Practcally Improved*, (Belfast 1828).
[27] D. Bowen, *The Protestant Crusade in Ireland 1800–70* (Dublin 1978).

apparent purpose, a zealous religion, very judiciously blended with loyalty'.[28] It was this combination which was to triumph in a bitter conflict which split the synod of Ulster in the 1820s, when the new evangelicalism, the outlook of nineteenth century Irish presbyterianism, defeated the liberalism and latitudinarianism of the eighteenth century, and Henry Cooke, the apostle of unionism and conservatism, defeated Henry Montgomery, the heir of the men in 1798.[29] Not that Cooke's toryism could be said to have become the politics of the Ulster presbyterians for after a lifetime of serving conservative political interests he had the chagrin in 1868 of seeing the electoral triumph of the liberal party in Ulster in spite of his deathbed appeal to the protestant electorate.[30]

Economic change reinforced, if it did not cause, religious change.[31] Certainly religious and political change were taking place against a background of economic and social change. The industrial revolution in the Lagan valley which had begun in the eighteenth century gradually turned east Ulster into what has been described as 'a province of the industrial empire of north-west England and south-west Scotland',[32] and began a process of separating Ulster's economic interests from the predominantly agricultural south.

One of the effects of this industrial revolution was to destroy the independent weavers, the class from whom men like James Orr came, and who were noted for their independence of thought which corresponded to their independent economic position. In his *Origins of Ulster Unionism*, Gibbon argues that it was these economic changes which destroyed the fragile basis of eighteenth-century Ulster presbyterian radicalism and created the conditions in which unionism flourished.[33] Certainly, as we shall see, the industrialisation of north-east Ireland did create a vested interest in union with Britain in that area.

[28] Mrs McTier to Drennan, 27 September 1801, *The Drennan Letters* p 313.

[29] J. M. Barkley, 'The Arian schism in Ireland, 1830', *SCH* 9, *Schism, Heresy and Religious Protest* (1972.

[30] *BNL* 26 October 1868; E. R. Norman, *The Catholic Church and Ireland in the Age of Rebellion 1859–1873*, (London 1965) p 351.

[31] P. Gibbon, *Ulster Unionism*, pp 1–65, argues that the religious changes in Ulster in the nineteenth century were the epiphenomena of economic change. See also D. W. Miller, *Queen's Rebels. Ulster Loyalism in Historical Perspective*, (Dublin/New York 1978) pp 80–6.

[32] M. W. Heslinga, [*The Irish border as a Cultural Divide* (Assen 1971)] pp 188–9; E. R. R. Green, *The Lagan Valley 1800–50. A local history of the Industrial Revolution* (London 1949) pp 96–8, 105–7.

[33] Gibbon, *Ulster Unionism* pp 22–65.

Equally important for the changes which were taking place in the political and social life of the Ulster presbyterians were developments in the rest of Ireland. It is often said that after 1798 Ulster left Ireland, but it could equally well be said that Ireland left Ulster, that the Irish nationalism which developed in the nineteenth century was no longer the non-sectarian nationalism of the United Irishmen. It may be that Irish nationalism was inevitably and intrinsically catholic because of the part the catholic church had played in Irish history, but certainly the national self-consciousness which developed in the nineteenth century was a catholic self-consciousness. It was largely created by Daniel O'Connell through his campaigns for catholic emancipation and the repeal of the union, although O'Connell himself was not an Irish nationalist in the later sense of the term. 'It was Daniel O'Connell's destiny', K. B. Nowlan has written, 'to become almost completely identified with the hopes and aspirations of a catholic Ireland slowly emerging from that inarticulateness which had characterised it for so long'.[34]

Ulster presbyterians had long given official support to the cause of catholic emancipation, in 1793 and in 1813 the synod of Ulster had expressed its approval of full civil rights for catholics[35] and although Cooke and his lieutenant, Robert Stewart of Broughshane had mounted a belated campaign to rouse a last ditch resistance to the measure of 1829, it was completely unsuccessful.[36]

The repeal issue was a different question, however. Significantly when O'Connell visited Belfast in 1841 to preach repeal Henry Cooke had the support of the *Northern Whig* in his challenge to O'Connell to debate the issue publicly.[37] The identification of majority Ulster presbyterian opinion with the cause of the union had begun. And at the subsequent conservative demonstration to celebrate O'Connell's failure in Belfast Cooke provided a characteristically rhetorical enunciation of the economic argument for union:

> Look at the town of Belfast. When I was myself a youth I remember it almost a village. But what a glorious sight does it now present—the masted grove within our harbour—our

[34] K. B. Nowlan, *The politics of Repeal* (London 1965) p 4.
[35] *RGSU* 3 pp 157, 397.
[36] [*The N[orthern] W[hig]* 26 March and 2 and 16 April 1829.
[37] *NW* 7 January 1841.

mighty warehouses teeming with the wealth of every climate—our giant manufactories lifting themselves on every side—our streets marching on, as it were, with such rapidity, that an absence of a few weeks makes us strangers in the outskirts of our town. And all this we owe to the union. In one word more I have done . . . Look at Belfast and be a repealer, if you can.[38]

The argument was not original. It had appeared in the *Northern Whig* a few weeks before,[39] and it was often repeated in years to come.

It was not merely that in the course of the nineteenth century Irish nationalism became virtually identified with Roman catholicism in spite of the efforts of the non-sectarian nationalists of the Young Ireland movement and significantly the eldest daughter of John Mitchel, the Ulster presbyterian Young Irelander, became a catholic, because, Mitchel wrote, of 'her very deep Irish feelings . . . a kind of sentiment that one cannot be thoroughly Irish without being catholic'.[40] What made matters worse from a protestant point of view was the fact that the liberal Gallican catholicism of men like Murray, Doyle and Crolly was superseded by the ultramontane triumphalism of Cullen and the determined nationalism of MacHale of Tuam or Croke of Cashel. Cullen was bitterly anti-protestant and he regarded the Ulster presbyterians as not Irish at all but invaders who occupied land unjustly confiscated from its true owners.[41] It is scarcely surprising that they, in turn, had little enthusiasm for the prospect of an Irish state in which ecclesiastics like Cullen would have a dominating influence.

Cullen died in 1878 and by then, Emmet Larkin claims, 'Irish and catholic were already as interchangeable as nationalist and catholic, and unionist and protestant, were to become by 1886'.[42] It must not be forgotten, however, that there were at least two nationalist movements or traditions in Ireland; the one constitutional and very largely catholic, the tradition of O'Connell and the parliamentary party, the other, the tradition of John Mitchel and the Fenians,

[38] *The Repealer Repulsed*, (Belfast 1841) pp 10–11.
[39] *NW* 2 January 1841.
[40] J. Mitchel, *Jail Journal* p 408, quoted M. Heslinga, p 186 note.
[41] E. D. Steele, 'Cardinal Cullen and Irish Nationality', *Irish Historical Studies*, 19 no 75 (March 1975) p 257.
[42] E. Larkin, *The Roman Catholic Church and the creation of the modern Irish State* (Dublin 1975) p 395.

revolutionary and republican, and opposed by Cullen and the Catholic church. Neither tradition was attractive to the majority of Ulster presbyterians who may not have distinguished sufficiently clearly the difference between them though, as Patrick Buckland suggests, the constitutional nationalists may have given insufficient attention to the task of communicating positively with their political opponents,[43] and, of course, under the leadership of Parnell, there was a temporary alliance between the two traditions.[44] It was to be the achievement of Pearse and De Valera to hold together the forces of revolution and catholicism in the twentieth century when the revolutionary tradition triumphed.[45]

The extent to which Ulster presbyterians were alienated from the Irish national movement was made clear when Gladstone introduced his first home rule bill for Ireland in the house of commons in 1886. It is sometimes suggested that opposition in Ulster to home rule was engineered from without by Randolph Churchill and the tory party for selfish political interest, and from within by the protestant ascendancy ruling class. Undoubtedly both played their part but there is no denying the popular strength and unanimity of the opposition to home rule among the presbyterians. A special meeting of the general assembly on 9 March expressed that opposition in a series of resolutions which were carried without a dissentient voice. Even the reverend J. B. Armour who was to champion the home rule cause in 1893 and 1912 was opposed to the 1886 bill because, as the assembly's resolution declared:

> . . . a separate parliament for Ireland, or an elective National Council, or any legislation tending to imperil the legislative union between Great Britain and Ireland, or to interfere with the unity and supremacy of the Imperial Parliament . . . would in our judgement, lead to the ascendancy of one class and creed in matters pertaining to religion, education and civil administration. We do not believe that any guarantees, moral or material, could be devised which would safeguard the rights and privileges of minorities scattered throughout

---

[43] P. Buckland, *Irish Unionism 1885–1922* (Historical Association 1973) p 11.
[44] T. W. Moody, 'The new Departure in Irish politics 1878–9', H. A. Cronne, T. W. Moody and D. B. Quinn ed, *Essays in British and Irish History in honour of James Eadie Todd* (London 1949) pp 303–33.
[45] P. O'Farrell, *Ireland's English Question* (London 1971) p 77.

Ireland against encroachment of a majority vested with legislative and executive functions.[46]

As J. M. Barkley has written: 'In other words, presbyterians, having escaped from the yoke of an anglican ascendancy in 1870 were unanimous in their opposition to the establishment of a Roman catholic ascendancy in 1886'.[47]

The general assembly made it quite clear, however, that they were not against change or reform. In particular they deprecated the association of legislation on the land problem, which they considered urgent and necessary, with the question of home rule.[48] The assembly resolutions were seconded by Thomas Sinclair who has been described by the historian of the first century of the general assembly as 'the leading ruling elder of the church for a generation'.[49] He emphasised that presbyterians were not insensitive to the 'rights of the Irish people and the wants of Ireland', for, in common with their Roman catholic fellow-countrymen they had been victims of penal laws, but, and here from a presbyterian businessman we have the economic argument again: the policy of protection which an Irish parliament would adopt 'would empty their mills, clear their rivers and shipyards, would stop their looms, would make the voice of their spindles silent and would cause a complete destruction of the industry that had made the province so prosperous.'[50]

Gladstone's 1886 bill did not pass the commons but his 1893 measure did and again vociferous opposition came from the Ulster presbyterians. The unanimity of 1886 had gone, however, and now a sturdy minority led by men like J. B. Armour and J. L. B. Dougherty, satisfied that the 1893 bill provided adequate safeguards for minority rights, opposed the anti-home rule majority. Armour and others have claimed that their opposition was only defeated by intimidation inside and outside the general assembly, that ministers and elders were afraid to resist the unionist juggernaut, but it seems certain that a majority in the church did oppose home rule.[51] Significantly, at the great Ulster unionist convention

[46] M[inutes of the] G[eneral] A[ssembly] 1886 p 104.
[47] [J. M.[Barkley, ['The Presbyterian Church in Ireland and the] Government of Ireland Act, [1920'], SCH 12 Church, Society and Politics (1975).
[48] [The] Witness 12 March 1886.
[49] [J. E.] Davey, [The Story of a Hundred Years] (Belfast 1940) p 50.
[50] Witness 12 March 1886.
[51] [W. S.] Armour, [Armour of Ballymoney] (London 1934) pp 96–117.

assembled in Belfast in 1892, to give notice of anti-home rule feeling on the eve of the general election which returned Gladstone to power, it was the presbytarian elder and former Gladstonian Liberal, Thomas Sinclair, who, to enthusiastic cheers, enunciated a policy of passive resistance towards a future home rule parliament. 'We will have nothing to do with a Dublin parliament', he declared, 'If it be ever set up we shall simply ignore its existence'.[52]

By 1911–12, when it became clear that home rule in some form would become a reality, presbyterian feelings had been intensified by controversy over the papal *ne temere* decree of 1908 and a particular case in Belfast in which a presbyterian woman's marriage to a Roman catholic by a presbyterian minister had been ruined.[53] These feelings are reflected in the resolutions of a so-called presbyterian convention held in Belfast on 1 February 1912—so-called because it was convened without the authority of the church though it was given a certain retrospective recognition in the official minutes of the general assembly held later that year.[54] One resolution stated: 'Under home rule . . . the parliament and executive alike are certain to be controlled by a majority subject to the direction of the author of the *ne temere* and *motu proprio* decrees against whose domination all safeguards designed for the protection of a protestant minority . . . would be wholly valueless.'[55] As J. M. Barkley has commented again: '. . . presbyterians, who had so recently escaped from an anglican denial of the validity of their marriages and the legitimacy of their children, were not going to risk finding themselves in a situation where it was possible for the church of Rome to place them in the same position, if it could possibly be avoided.'[56]

In 1913 the vote against home rule in the general assembly was overwhelming—nine hundred and twenty-one votes to forty-three. By then many presbyterians, who had been among the five hundred thousand who had signed the Ulster covenant on 28 September 1812, pledging their refusal to recognise the authority of a Dublin parliament, were quietly and resolutely preparing to

[52] *Witness* 24 June 1892.
[53] MGA (1911) pp 84 and 97–8; W. Corkey, *The McCann Case* (Edinburgh 1912).
[54] MGA (1912) p 351.
[55] *Witness* 2 February 1912.
[56] Barkley, 'Government of Ireland Act' p 395.
[57] MGA (1913) pp 635–6.

take up arms again as their forefathers had done in 1798, but this time to retain, and not to break, the British connection.[58]

The Ulster presbyterians had emphatically rejected constitutional Irish nationalism and in so doing they may have contributed to the ultimate victory, in the rest of Ireland, of the more extreme, separatist, revolutionary nationalism of Sinn Fein which made, and still makes, any reconciliation between them and the modern Irish nation still more difficult, for even those presyterians who, like J. B. Armour, were prepared to welcome home rule within the context of a sovereign British state, were utterly opposed to the separatist, Gaelic, anti-British ethos and ideals of Sinn Fein.[59] For if religious conviction, not to say prejudice, and economic self-interest were the staple ingredients in the Ulster presbyterian resistance to modern Irish nationalism, there was also the influence of a rival, and, in the nineteenth century, very attractive, nationalism, British nationalism.

At the jubilee general assembly of the Irish presbyterian church in 1890, the moderator, William Park, declared: 'Seldom, if ever, have any of us been ashamed to declare we are Britons . . . whatever quarrels with British policy members of the Assembly may have had from time to time, and whatever their views of the best solution of the Irish problem, the sentiment of loyalty towards and pride in the British inheritance and commonwealth of peoples has been common to us all.'[60] Significantly Park's statement was repeated and endorsed by J. E. Davey in his centenary history of the general assembly in 1940 and twenty years later by J. M. Barkley in his history of the presbyterian church in Ireland.[61] Today, after another twenty years and much suffering and soul-searching, and in spite of the emergence of a kind of Ulster nationalism, I believe that the majority of Ulster presbyterians regard themselves as, and wish to remain, British.

Union Theological College
Belfast

[58] A. T. Q. Stewart, The Ulster Crisis (London 1967) pp 58–68.
[59] Armour pp 75–95.
[60] Davey p 62.
[61] Barkley p 61.

THE CHURCH OF SCOTLAND AND
SCOTTISH NATIONHOOD

by HENRY R. SEFTON

'THE Church of Scotland has consistently upheld Scotland's historic nationhood and identity'.[1] The purpose of this paper is to consider the validity of this claim by examining the records of the general assembly of the church since 1946. The general asembly's pronouncements on this theme take the form of deliverances on the reports submitted by the committee on church and nation.

The general assembly of 1946 declared their conviction that Scottish interests were being increasingly jeopardised by disregard of Scottish sentiment and the claims of Scotland as a nation. The remedy proposed was 'a greater decentralising of authority and an increased measure of independence within the sphere of Scottish administration.'[2] The following year the call for decentralisation was placed with the context of 'schemes of nationalisation' and 'the possible invasion of human rights and local independence by large-scale collectivism.'[3]

In 1947 a remarkably representative gathering was called together to discuss reform of Scottish government. It was chaired by John MacCormick, leader of the Scottish convention, a moderate nationalist group,[4] but it was claimed that it was not a creature of the convention.[5] This 'Scottish National Assembly' consisted of about four hundred people, including Scottish representative peers,[6] the Scottish members of parliament of all parties and officially appointed representatives of many county councils, town councils, trade unions, commercial, industrial and political

---

[1] *Reports [to the General Assembly of the Church of Scotland]* (1968) p 112.
[2] *Minutes [of the Proceedings of the General Assembly of the Church of Scotland]* (1946) p 85.
[3] *Minutes* (1947) p 229.
[4] Founded in 1942 by dissidents from the Scottish National Party.
[5] [Keith] Webb, [*The Growth of Nationalism in Scotland*] (Glasgow 1977) p 63.
[6] Until 1963 the peers of Scotland elected sixteen of their number to represent them in Parliament. Since 1963 all Scottish peers have been summoned to Parliament: Sir James Fergusson, *The sixteen peers of Scotland* (Oxford 1960).

associations and various other public bodies. Several presbyteries of
the Church of Scotland appointed delegates and other churches were
also represented.[7] In its report to the general assembly of 1948 the
church and nation committee commented: 'Clearly in a matter
which so profoundly affects the life of the nation and has such far-
reaching implications, the Church has a real concern, and must
watch further developments with close attention, ready to give
sympathetic guidance as it may be required.'[8] The report was well
received and a motion stronger than the committee's own proposed
deliverance was unanimously passed. This recognised 'the necessity
for a greater measure of devolution by Parliament of legislative and
administrative power in Scottish affairs' and urged 'that an enquiry
into all the issues involved should be instituted'.[9]

Among individual churchmen who took a prominent part in the
preceedings of the Scottish national assembly was Dr Nevile
Davidson, one of the royal chaplains and minister at Glasgow
cathedral. He was one of the speakers at the third assembly which
met on 29 October 1949 to launch a covenant demanding a Scottish
parliament to deal with Scottish domestic affairs within the
framework of the United Kingdom and in loyalty to the crown.
Davidson contended that there was a spiritual dimension in the
national movement and indeed opened the fourth assembly in April
1950 with prayer. In one of his speeches he claimed: 'The Church is
perhaps the greatest remaining depository of our Scottish national
sentiment and self-consciousness and the true symbol of the
national character and temperament . . . only a rediscovery of our
Christian heritage, values and convictions will provide the necessary inspiration and dynamic for a revival of the Scottish nation in
the widest sense of the word'.[10]

The success of the covenant was quite remarkable. Within a
week of its launching it was signed by 50,000 people[11] and by May
1950 it had attracted over a million signatures. This was noted by
the Church of Scotland general assembly of 1950 which appealed
'to His Majesty's Government to appoint a Royal Commission to

[7] A. C. Turner, *Scottish Home Rule* (Oxford 1952) pp 20 *seq.*; Webb p 63; *Reports*
(1948) p 318 *seq.*
[8] *Reports* (1948) p 319.
[9] *Minutes* (1948) pp 386–8.
[10] [Nevile] Davidson, [*Beginnings but no Ending*] (Edinburgh 1978) pp 75–7; [J. M.]
MacCormick, [*The Flag in the Wind*] (London 1955) pp 129 *seq.*
[11] MacCormick p 131; Webb p 66.

investigate all the issues involved in the proposed measure of devolution'.[12] The exact number of signatories to the covenant seems to be unknown but is thought to be over two million.[13] Keith Webb has suggested that the strength of this document was that emotionally it could unite disparate groups. Its weakness was that it did not commit anyone to any specific action.[14] Indeed the leaders of the movement had no programme of action beyond presenting the covenant as a petition to London[15] and even this proved difficult as neither the prime minister nor the leader of the opposition would receive them.[16] Christopher Harvie points to John MacCormick's involvement in 'the Buchan-like adventure of stealing the Scottish Coronation Stone from Westminster Abbey on Christmas Day 1950' as another cause of the failure of the covenant movement. He describes it as 'popular but inappropriate: it enhanced emotional nationalism rather than the moderate consensus MacCormick was trying to promote'.[17]

The church and nation committee included a section on 'The Stone of Scone' in its 1951 report but the general assembly refused after a lengthy debate to receive it and deleted all references to the Stone of Destiny from the proposed deliverance which in its final form simply urged upon the government the appointment of a royal commission to investigate the issue of Scotland having a larger measure of control of her own affairs.[18]

A royal commission was appointed in 1952 but its terms of reference prevented any consideration of self-government for Scotland for it was instructed 'to review with reference to the financial, economic, administrative and other considerations involved, the arrangements for exercising the functions of Her Majesty's Government in relation to Scotland and to report'.[19] In evidence to the royal commission the Church of Scotland representatives suggested the creation of a strong council, which would include Scottish MP's of all parties and representatives of local authorities, to consider and to receive representations on matters affecting the

[12] Minutes (1950) p 709.
[13] Webb p 66; H. J. Hanham, *Scottish Nationalism* (London 1969) p 12.
[14] Webb pp 65 *seq*.
[15] J. M. Reid, *Scotland's Progress* (London 1971) p 185; Davidson, p 76.
[16] MacCormick p 135.
[17] Christopher Harvie, *Scotland and Nationalism* (London 1977) p 236.
[18] *Reports* (1951) pp 340 *seq*; *Minutes* 1951, pp 72 *seq*.
[19] *Report of the Royal Commission on Scottish Affairs 1952–1954*, (Cmd 9212) p 9.

well-being of the Scottish people. Recommendations would then be made to the secretary of state for Scotland for transmission to the government.[20] When the royal commission reported in 1954 the church and nation committee described it as a 'wee bit tinkering with one or two of the wheels in the machinery'[21] but the general assembly of 1955 did welcome the royal commission's declaration that 'in the absence of convincing evidence of advantage to the contrary the machinery of government should be designed to dispose of Scottish business in Scotland.'[22]

Nevile Davidson was convener of the church committee from 1955 to 1960 but there is comparatively little said on Scottish nationhood by the committee of the general assembly during that period. A deliverance passed in 1957 seems to accord with his approach to the question: 'The General Assembly remind all Scottish people of their great heritage as a nation and call for a maintenance of those qualities of independence, hard work, integrity of character and Christian Faith which are the foundations alike of success and happiness.'[23]

A petition asking for the support of the Church of Scotland in recalling the Estates of Scotland was presented by Miss Wendy Wood to the general assembly of 1960.[24] The petition was examined by the church and nation committee and on its report the general assembly of 1961 found the formal basis of the crave of the petition to be at best very uncertain but encouraged the committee to reconsider the question of Scottish self-government on its merits.[25] The spectacular growth in the number of votes cast in favour of Scottish national party candidates at the general elections of 1964 and 1966 gave greater urgency to the church and nation committee's deliberations and it is significant that the capture of a safe Labour seat by the Scottish national party at the Hamilton bye-election of 1967 was followed by a considerable report on 'Scottish Nationhood' to the general assembly of 1968.[26] The outcome of a lengthy debate was a much amended but still forceful deliverance: 'The General Assembly, convinced of the need for an effective

[20] *Reports* (1953) pp 693, 708; *Minutes* (1953) p 401.
[21] *Reports* (1955) p 364.
[22] *Minutes* (1955) p 722.
[23] *Ibid* (1957) p 259.
[24] *Ibid* (1960) pp 790 *seq*.
[25] *Ibid* (1961) p 103.
[26] *Reports* (1968) pp 112–5.

form of self-government in Scotland within the framework of the United Kingdom, ask Her Majesty's Government for the early appointment of a Royal Commission, consisting of Scots widely representative of Scottish interests to meet in Scotland with powers to call for evidence, to make recommendations which may enable the people of Scotland to choose the form and extent of self-government best suited to the nation's well-being, and to treat the matter with the utmost urgency.[27]

The royal commission on the constitution which was appointed under the chairmanship of Lord Crowther in 1969 was very different from the one requested by the general assembly for its remit included the whole of Great Britain, Northern Ireland, the Isle of Man and the Channel Islands. Its members however included a notable Scottish churchman, the very reverend J. B. Longmuir, and a Scottish judge, Lord Kilbrandon succeeded Lord Crowther as chairman. The royal commission's report was not published until 31 October 1973 and included no fewer than four models for devolution.[28] The response of the general assembly of 1974 was a deliverance which welcomed 'those proposals in the report of the Commission on the Constitution which provide for a legislative assembly for Scotland with appropriate devolved powers'. The general assembly went on to exhort the government to consider the report with the utmost urgency and to make their proposals for legislation at an early date.[29] Government white papers on devolution to Scotland and Wales were published in September 1974[30] and November 1975.[31] The general assembly of 1976 welcomed 'Her Majesty's Government's firm binding commitment . . . to establish a Scottish Assembly' but regretted that its proposed powers were inadequate to deal with Scottish problems. The general assembly also urged that the new legislative body be known not as 'The Scottish Assembly' but as 'The Scots Parliament' or by some other suitable name.[32]

The general assembly of 1974 had rejected a motion instructing the church and nation committee to consider the implications of the

---

[27] *Minutes* (1968) pp 416, 419 *seq.*
[28] Royal Commission on the Constitution 1969–73, *Report* (Cmnd 5460, 5460–1).
[29] Minutes (1974) p 102.
[30] *Democracy and Devolution* (Cmnd 5732).
[31] *Our Changing Democracy* (Cmnd 6348).
[32] *Minutes* (1976) pp 103*seq.*

idea of a referendum.[33] In 1977 however the general assembly were of different mind and they agreed without a vote to a deliverance expressing disappointment at the slow progress of the legislation on devolution and urging the government and parliament to conduct a referendum in Scotland 'in order to learn the wishes of the Scottish electorate and to give effect thereto as quickly as possible'.[34] After the date of the referendum was fixed for 1 March 1979 the church and nation committee prepared a memorandum which it sent to every parish minister with the suggestion that it be read from the pulpit either on Sunday 18 or 25 February 1979 or both. The commission of the previous general assembly met on 22 February and passed a deliverance recalling the statement and ordaining that it be not read from the pulpits on Sunday 25 February. The reasons given were that the statement appeared to favour one side in an issue in which there was 'no specific Christian principle at stake' and that it contained an assertion regarding the result of failure to vote in the referendum which was 'utterly false in fact and seriously misleading in effect'.[35]

Despite this rebuff the church and nation committee prepared a strong worded report on 'The Nationhood of Scotland and its Government within the United Kingdom' for submission to the general assembly of 1980. In a discussion of the result of the Scottish referendum of 1979 the committee contended that its inconclusive nature[36] did not mean the end of the question of devolution. The proposed deliverance was: 'The General Assembly, remaining convinced that the historic and essential nationhood of Scotland under the Crown requires for its proper recognition and satisfaction an appropriate measure of devolved self-government, yet again request Her Majesty's Government to take the steps necessary to bring this about.'[37] A young minister proposed the deletion of the deliverance on the grounds that opinion in the country was too divided for the church to pronounce on this issue. The vote was sufficiently close to require a count and the deliverance was passed by 380 to 365.[38] Thus a reversal of the general assembly's policy for over thirty years was narrowly averted.

[33] *Ibid* (1974) p 104.
[35] *Ibid* (1979) p 134. The assertion was 'Failure to vote will be treated as a No vote'.
[36] 33% voted yes; 31%, no; 36% did not vote.
[37] *Reports* (1980) pp 103, 90.
[38] *Minutes* (1980) p 90.

The Church of Scotland and Scottish Nationhood

The claim that the Church of Scotland has consistently upheld Scotland's historic nationhood and identity can be justified. Successive general assemblies have not questioned the value of nationhood but on the other hand have never supported nationalism in the sense understood by the Scottish national party. They have always called for Scottish self-government 'within the framework of the United Kingdom' a phrase taken from the Scottish covenant of 1949. They have refused to identify with the symbolic gestures of Wendy Wood or those who brought the Stone of Destiny back to Scotland. It is difficult to resist the conclusion of a recent commentator that the church has followed rather than led opinion on this issue.[39] The general assemblies have reacted to nationalism, the Scottish covenant, the Hamilton bye-election and the various royal commission reports and government white papers. The most recent votes on the issue suggest that the Church of Scotland is as divided as Scotland itself on the question of self-government.

University of Aberdeen

[39] Jack Brand, *The National Movement in Scotland* (London 1978) p 127.

'NO-ONE IS FREE FROM PARLIAMENT': THE WORSHIP AND DOCTRINE MEASURE IN PARLIAMENT, 1974.

by GAVIN WHITE

IN RETROSPECT, we may agree that the prayer book crisis of 1927 and 1928 was not as critical as it seemed at the time,[1] but it did leave unfinished business for a future generation. The draft prayer book of the Church of England had been rejected by parliament, and if any saner revision of that church's worship proved acceptable to the church it would still have to be approved by parliament.

Gregory Dix, who worried about these things more than was good for him, expressed a common opinion in 1945. He felt that any return to parliament would be fatal, since 'the debate would inevitably circle around' the real presence in the eucharist, and instead he suggested that the church should 'not directly challenge parliament at all' but quietly institute a new book backed by about seven bishops at 'a moment when parliament was pre-occupied'.[2] This was not done. By the time the Church of England had some idea of how it wanted to pray, the debate about real presence was almost irrelevant. Furthermore, bishops were no longer the natural people to put forward a new book, though some of them did not know it. What was actually done was to slip in alternative series of eucharistic rites by liturgical scholars whose work was in fact revised at a more popular level. Their series 1, giving what so many were supposed to have wanted in 1927, was almost totally ignored. It proved something of a surprise to everyone that an overwhelming majority of parishes preferred series 2 and then series 3, despite or because of their uninspired prose. If the 1662 book of common prayer was almost totally abandoned in many areas, this was neither intended nor expected. Even had it been expected, it is hard

---

[1] Gavin White, 'That Hectic Night: the Prayer Debate, 1927 and 1928', *Theology*, 77, no 654 (London December 1974) pp 639–46.
[2] Dom Gregory Dix, *The Shape of the Liturgy* (Westminster 1945) pp 725–6.

to see what anyone could have done to prevent it. Once the church began using the 1662 communion office as the main service on every Sunday, a situation entirely novel and probably derived from falling numbers and the near-disappearance of non-communicant adherents, the leisurely pace of the 1662 rite became a liability rather than an asset. There would probably have been a demand for a liturgy which did not spell everything out Sunday after Sunday even had there been no alternative services officially available.

But the Church of England found it time-consuming to keep returning to parliament for this or that booklet, and it seemed reasonable to request powers to make changes without parliament. General synod agreed to this in 1972 by a vote of 340 to 10, with the proviso that the 1662 services would always remain available to any congregation wanting to use them. Even this proviso was too much for some who wanted full freedom, but it was argued that this might 'provoke a showdown with parliament', and a member of parliament who also sat in general synod warned that MPs were receiving letters about 'plans to dispose of the 1662 prayer book', and some MPs 'would see a large group of people who did not seem to be represented' in synods.[3] Having made their concessions, churchmen seem to have supposed that approval by parliament would be largely automatic.

The Church of England worship and doctrine measure duly came before the house of lords on 14 November 1974. It was a lordly debate. Archbishop Ramsey, on the last day of his primacy, was very soothing indeed. He refuted the notion that the general synod only represented 36,000 people by saying these were elected by about two million, gave a brief history of the enabling act, said self-government was now possible since the laity were involved, asserted that series 2 had drawn high and low churchmen together, and felt sure that 'noble lords will not be misled by talk about the destruction of the prayer book'. Of course noble lords were. The earl Waldegrave set the tone of the debate by assuming that church folk looked to parliament for protection from synod, and several others followed him. Lord Hawke, a devout churchman, argued in a very clear speech that parliament was a dispassionate judge deciding whether there was a 'substantial body of opinion in this country which has been overruled by a majority, and that it can only learn from its constituencies and from its postbag.' This was,

[3] *Church Times*, 10 November 1972 p 11.

of course, a mild form of Austinism, but it did imply that parliament was a court of appeal in absolutely everything. At the end of the day the archbishop returned and said of the 1928 fiasco, 'The sad thing was that intemperate debates in parliament happened because they were a reflection of the conflict within the church itself'. This view is only partly borne out by the record, but the humble approach was probably wise. The measure passed without a division after over four hours of talk but at one point, admittedly tea-time, there was only one lord temporal with the nine bishops in the house, so there was no reason to expect much interest when the measure came before the commons.[4]

The commons debate began just before four o'clock on Wednesday, 4 December 1974, and continued for nearly seven hours with no less than one hundred and ninety-four members participating in the vote at the end, and that despite the fact that Wednesday evenings are usually devoted to committee work. Despite what has been said by some observers, it is difficult to read the account without concluding that the debate was astonishing not only for the large numbers of those participating but also for its high level of intelligence and fair-mindedness. Forty members spoke to the issue, apart from those who merely interrupted.

One view underlay the thinking both of those in favour and those opposed. This was the doctrine of Lord Hawke that parliament was the court of last resort and in this case should determine, by constituency chats and the postbag, what ordinary people wanted. Amongst those in favour, A. J. Beith of Berwick-on-Tweed was typical in outlook, if more articulate than most. He held that the church of England had a special position and 'therefore parliament must look carefully before surrendering its power to have some influence over those services'. Although a methodist, he had attended Anglican services and shared the feelings of 'concern, unfamiliarity, and confusion' felt by so many at the new rites. Nonetheless, he did approve of the 'democratic machinery' grafted onto the church, and from 'fairly extensive soundings' he held most of his constituents felt the same way. He could thus trust general synod, but he hoped that the church authorities would remember the occasional worshipper who 'may not be directly involved in the chain of bodies that leads ultimately to the general synod'. Other members had also made soundings or claimed to have done so;

[4] *House of Lords Parliamentary Debates (Hansard)*, 5 series, 354 pp 867–945.

Frank White of Bury and Radcliffe had asked twenty clergy and found nineteen in favour, but it was lay opinion which most members rightly felt to be crucial.[5]

Opposing speakers were both more interesting and more passionate, even if some of them were unable to express their very deep feelings. Their speeches fall into four groups. First were those of members who, while reminded that the quality of series 2 or 3 was not the subject of debate, believed that it should have been. Seven spoke primarily on the merits or shortcomings of the new rites, including a Roman Catholic who was more troubled by liturgical innovation in his own church than in the Church of England. Most were moderate in their condemnation. Nicholas Fairbairn, a Scottish episcopalian, was the only member to support the old prayer book because it came from an age 'when the capacity to express in language was a paramount capability, and that is not a characteristic of the present generation'.[6]

The second category was restricted to two speeches by Enoch Powell and Fairbairn who put forward the dubious proposition that the Anglican communion depended on the Church of England. Powell was the great disappointment of the debate. He had just returned to the house as an Ulster unionist and was speaking on a subject with which he had long been familiar, but apart from a vague exaltation of the secular power through history he had little to offer. And neither Fairbairn nor Powell ever established what it was that they wanted to say about the Anglican communion.[7]

The third group of seven speeches centred on the assertion that the general synod was unrepresentative. It was accurately observed that some churchmen would never think of writing to a synod delegate but would more naturally write to their MP, and of course an MP was the last person to know that other churchmen would equally naturally write to a synod delegate and not to an MP. There were some phrases which showed a rather capricious failure to understand how synods worked, but there was also a justifiable caution about a new body with an admittedly complex system of elections.[8]

[5] [House of] Commons [Parliamentary Debates (Hansard)] 5 series 882, pp 1567–698, 1685–7, 1588.
[6] Ibid pp 1593, 1604–5, 1612, 1651, 1658–60, 1681, 1683–4.
[7] Ibid pp 1667–77, 1683–4.
[8] Ibid pp 1578, 1590–4, 1624–8, 1649, 1658–60, 1662, 1677.

No-one is free from parliament

The fourth group of five speeches upheld a view put forth by other speakers as a subsidiary argument, and this was that control must always remain with parliament, and not just because synods were held to be unrepresentative. The most extreme speaker was Eldon Griffiths of Bury St Edmunds who argued that, 'Parliament has its limits, but it is the only source of lawful authority in this country, and the argument that the church wishes to be free of parliament is simply a non-argument. No-one is free from parliament. Indeed, in my view, parliament guarantees freedom'. This Austinite view was re-iterated later when he said, 'It can seldom be good for parliament to abandon responsibilities, to a great extent irrevocably, for any of the major institutions of this country', and, 'Either parliament is omnicompetent or it is not, and as presently constituted it had better remain that way.'[9] Powell seemed at times to be saying much the same thing, while Ivor Stanbrook of Orpington declaimed, 'Parliament, and parliament alone, represents the English people. Parliament, with the queen, is sovereign over the church. Let us therefore say to the professionals and to those who want to take over our church, "We are the people. It is our church. You shall not have it"'.[10] And John Wells of Maidstone complained that, 'month by month, year by year, we give away such rights as we have for governing this country. We set up milk marketing boards, water authorities, the British airport authority, every kind of body. These new bodies come into being day by day, month by month, outside parliamentary control. The Church of England is one of our oldest allies working with us. If we give up this vital matter we will show ourselves to the country as overpaid and useless people'.[11]

Despite all this oratory, the general tenor of the debate had made it clear that most of the members present were in favour of the measure, and when the vote finally came it passed by one hundred and forty-five to forty-five, with two tellers on each side. Of those who voted in favour there were slightly more conservative than labour members, seventy-five to sixty-eight, together with a few liberals and nationalists. This was roughly representative of the house as it then was, but of the negative voters four were Ulster unionist, one Democratic unionist, one labour, and all the rest were

[9] *Ibid* pp 1667–70, 1677–80, 1631.
[10] *Ibid* p 1628.
[11] *Ibid* p 1688.

conservative. That more conservative than labour members were present may be partly explained by this being an English matter and England having a conservative majority in the house, though a labour majority existed overall. By denomination not much may be learned about those voting in favour. Of those opposed, twenty-five were Church of England, four Church of Scotland, two Roman Catholic, two Church of Ireland, two Methodist, one United Reformed, one Episcopalian, and one Irish Free Presbyterian. The remaining nine gave no answer to a questionnaire, perhaps in some cases by inadvertence, but the inescapable conclusion is that a significant minority of those who voted negatively had no real religious affiliation but were sufficiently concerned by the issues to stand up and be counted in what was hardly a popular cause. Finally, for those who still hold to the legend that Scottish members wrecked the prayer book measure in 1927 and 1928, only four Scots and four Ulstermen voted against the 1974 measure, and they were offset by the same proportions of non-English members voting in favour.[12]

Neither the passing of the measure nor the debate received much attention from the press, and few church people can have been aware of the views presented. Nevertheless, there was an awareness in the higher echelons of the Church of England that the opposition had been stronger than expected, and that it was even more essential to tread warily than had been supposed. When general synod met on 4 February 1975 the draft amending canon made possible by parliament was passed almost unanimously, but there were suggestions that all should read Hansard, as if general synod could best know the mind of the church by taking into account what churchmen had written to their MPs.[13]

Relations between church and state were further illuminated, if that is the correct word, on 8 June 1976 when a commons question from Mrs Thatcher brought on elliptical reply from Mr Callaghan, the prime minister, on the subject of episcopal appointments. 'The sovereign must be able to look for advice on a matter of this kind and that means for a constitutional sovereign advice from ministers. The archbishops and some of the bishops sit by right in the house of lords, and their nomination must therefore remain a

[12] *Ibid* pp 1695–8; Malcolm Hulke, *Cassell's Parliamentary Directory* (London 1975).
[13] *General Synod February Group of Sessions 1975, Report of Proceedings* 6, no 1 (4 February 1975) pp 6, 37.

matter for the prime minister's concern'.[14] This statement assumed
that a constitutional sovereign could only take advice on church
matters from government ministers, which denied the *imperium in
imperio* theory of British society.[15] With regard to the house of
lords, the argument might equally well have given the prime
minister a veto on whom peers might marry since their sons would
sit in the lords. The incident is important, not because it illustrates
any carefully thought-out doctrine, but because it reveals basic
assumptions which in themselves never see the light of day.

Finally, there has been a more recent campaign marked by
articles in learned journals and by three petitions in general synod.
This differed in significant respects from the parliamentary opposition. In the first place the petitioners tended to be upper class, while
the opposing MPs were generally middle class. In the second place,
the articles accompanying the petitions had an aesthetic rather than
a constitutional basis. From such a collection of air vice-marshals
and masters of colleges one might expect the assertion that corporal
punishment never did them any harm and neither did Cranmer's
English, but there was more to their protest than that. In a church
of England which had successfully moved downmarket they may
well have felt out of place, but since they would naturally have
supposed that no group of people could do anything without
someone to give a lead, they in this instance supposed that changes
in worship must have been imposed from above, and they associated those changes with action by general synod. The petition of
five hundred is almost an accusation, referring to 'policies and
tendencies which decree the loss of both the authorised version of
the English bible and the book of common prayer',[16] but since it
was addressed to the general synod rather than to parliament or to
the editor of *The Times* it may have given that body a legitimacy it
had not previously enjoyed. Indeed, this may have been the most
significant aspect of the whole exercise.

Yet the aesthetic element is not without interest. If we except
Professor David Martin who would have been happy with good
modern English but complained that the new rites were 'just not

[14] *Commons* 5 series, 912, 00 612–14.
[15] Harold J. Laski, *Studies in the Problem of Sovereignty* (New Haven 1926) p 122; *Cases
decided in the Court of Session, Tiend Court etc., and House of Lords*, 3 series 5M
(Edinburgh 1867) Forbes v. Eden, pp 51–2.
[16] *PN Review 13*, 6 no 5 (London 1979).

memorable',[17] there was a general belief that 'this is not a period of great writers' and 'modern English is slack'.[18] Furthermore, this view was essentially political since it was also argued that 'the prayer book lies very close to the innermost political realities', or that 'the king's English was rightly named, it was created as a result of royal policy and was coterminous with the English nation', and the prayer book's compilation 'co-incided with the age when for beauty of rhythm and splendour of diction, our language was at its zenith.' On the other hand, that golden age cannot be compared with 'the present competing banners of confusion', and 'it might be wiser to acknowledge the maturer political wisdom contained in the 1662 book', and, 'nowadays, even more than at any other time, no single individual could compose a liturgy, anymore than Shakespeare could nowadays write plays' since there is a 'loss of public agreement and objective spiritual certainty'.[19] The reader of these articles in their entirety may feel surprise at the poor English in which the writers express their devotion to good English, but by their lights they were right to illustrate the impossibility of good English in such an age as ours, and exceptions such as W. H. Auden have let down the cause.

Two things must be said about the petitioners. First, their argument differed from that of the parliamentary opposition, if we except Nicholas Fairbairn, the MP for Kinross, whose social background was nearer to that of the petitioners than those of his fellow-opponents in parliament. Indeed, it is just because it did differ that it demands close scrutiny, in order to show what the members of parliament were not saying. Secondly, the petitioners were not representative of any large group, while the parliamentarians were. The petitioners deserve respect and sympathy as men and women of good will, but it is hard to see what general synod or anyone else could have done for those worshippers amongst them who valued the Church of England for its archaic face. The new volume might be called an 'Alternative Service Book' but except in a few places the church just did not have enough worshippers to divide them up according to their liturgical preferences, and minorities were bound to come off worst.

[17] *Ibid* p 2.
[18] K. Grayston, 'Confessions of a Biblical Translator', *New Universities Quarterly*, 33 no 3 (London Summer 1979) p 287.
[19] *PN Review* 13 pp 9, 27, 40, 47.

No-one is free from parliament

With regard to the parliamentary debates of 1974, they showed that a large number of members believed that the Church of England still deserved serious consideration, and the overwhelming majority from amongst them favoured giving that church authority to make its own rules. But the emphasis was on giving that authority, and not on acknowledging that the church had any inherent right to that authority. The minority saw a threat to the 'vital relationship' between church and state which the majority believed the new measure would 'underpin and support',[20] but both groups favoured that relationship. Furthermore, the minority, while moved by a variety of arguments, seemed most influenced by the old views of John Austin and John Hope to the effect that all authority must flow from parliament.[21] Those views may have been relevant and indeed necessary when the reform act of 1832 was freshly passed, and when parliament stood in danger from oligarchical reaction, but in 1974 no body, ecclesiastical or other, really threatened parliament. It may be argued that some conservative members who argued for parliamentary control of the Church of England in 1974 were subconsciously supporting parliament from a supposed threat from trade unions, but this is speculation. What emerged was a belief that the Church of England and the national identity were still inextricably bound together and for the dignity of parliament must so remain, and if this view was never fully examined it was because it was never really questioned and no-one felt that it needed to be questioned.

University of Glasgow

[20] *Commons* 5 series, 882, p 1648.
[21] John Austin, *The Province of Jurisprudence* (London 1832) pp 270–1; John Hope, *A Letter to the Lord Chancellor on the Claims of the Church of Scotland* (Edinburgh 1839) pp 67–8.

MODERN SPAIN: THE PROJECT OF A
NATIONAL CATHOLICISM

by FRANCES LANNON

THE inseparability of national identity and catholicism in modern Spain has never been more pugnaciously and confidently affirmed than in the provocative hyperbole of Marcelino Menéndez y Pelayo. 'Spain, evangeliser of half the globe; Spain, hammer of heretics, light of Trent, sword of Rome, cradle of Saint Ignatius . . .; that is our greatness and our unity: we have no other'.[1] This uncompromising statement undoubtedly owes some of its stridency to the age of the author when he wrote it—he was twenty-five—and something to his abiding convictions and temperament. But one does not have to search very assiduously this most famous defence of catholic orthodoxy as the source of Spanish grandeur in order to realise that Menéndez y Pelayo's fervour and language are both sharpened by nostalgia. Volumes six and seven of his history of Spanish heterodoxy which trace the history of the eighteenth and nineteenth centuries constitute one long lament for lost catholic unity, lost cultural homogeneity and, lost with them, an irretrievable simplicity and clarity of national self-definition. When he wrote his eloquent and audacious lament in the early 1880s he was well aware that the uniformity of religious belief which he had unhesitatingly discerned beneath minor, and usually imported, heterodoxy in earlier Spanish history already belonged irrecuperably to the past. Moreover, he found himself as many lesser followers were also to do in the uncomfortably Canute-like position of opposing the uncontrollable while asserting an ideal which had to be articulated as a series of negative and necessarily unsatisfactory defensive reactions. His sweeping condemnation of all that he regarded as neither catholic nor Spanish—the enlightenment, the French revolution, German idealism and romanticism, Strauss, Renan and positivist philosophers[2]

---

[1] M. Menéndez y Pelayo, *Historia de los Heterodoxos Españoles*, 8 vols (Buenos Aires 1945) 7 p 558; originally published 3 vols (1880–2).
[2] *Ibid* 6 p 17.

—offered no better suggestions for creative action on the part of Spanish catholics than did later versions of the list of anathemas which successors extended to include socialists and communists. It is not surprising that Menéndez y Pelayo referred to the great age of Spanish catholic unity in the past tense. Not only had French and German cultural influences contaminated the tradition he extolled, but two major political controversies over the place of catholicism in the Spanish state and society dominated ecclesiastical debate at the very time he was writing. In 1876 the constitution of the recently restored monarchy was promulgated, including the contentious article eleven which, while recognising Roman catholicism as the religion of state, explicitly permitted the discreet practice of other religions. This toleration did not harmonise easily with the first article of the concordat agreed between the Spanish state and the Vatican in 1851 which affirmed categorically that the only religion of the Spanish nation, to the exclusion of all others, was catholicism. Faced with this discrepancy and convinced that even limited religious toleration, by admitting the rights of 'falsehood' and 'error' was in itself a form of apostasy, many catholics found the constitution of the restored Bourbon manarchy unacceptable. Even under a catholic monarchy, then, religious unity seemed unattainable, while divisions within the church itself about how to react to this new situation made the ideal of a united catholic nation appear yet more distant.[3] The second contemporary controversy whose outcome Menéndez y Pelayo deplored turned, almost inevitably, on education and more specifically its religious character. Whereas in 1875 a famous ministerial circular had reaffirmed the catholic character of all university teaching and thereby provoked an exodus of university lecturers unwilling to conform, in 1881 this was abrogated, leaving confessional control of university education ruined beyond repair, again in contravention of the concordat.[4]

Nor were signs of the impossibility of national religious conformity restricted to the divergencies of intellectual and political trends: the nineteenth century had seen recurrent, violent manifestations of a bitter anti-clericalism that went far beyond the bounds

---

[3] See D. Benavides Gómez, *Democracia y Cristianismo en la España de la Restauración 1875–1931* (Madrid 1978) pt 1, for a full discussion.
[4] See Y. Turin, *Education et L'Ecole en Espagne 1874–1902* (Paris 1959) pp 348–56.

of any catholic dislike of the clerical order. Furthermore, the rapid industrialisation which was to be such a conspicuous feature of the 1870s onwards, particularly in the Basque provinces and Catalonia, made even more obvious the duplication by large numbers of urban workers of the already notorious pattern common among landless peasants in the south who lived their lives outside any ecclesiastical structure or traditional religious practice.[5] There is something artificial and self-conscious, then, in attempts to use the opportunities afforded by the catholic conservative monarchy of the period stretching from the 1870s to its downfall in 1931 to recreate a catholicism which would be coterminous with the nation. That such an enterprise remained the ultimate, avowed aim of the hierarchy cannot be doubted. Its improbability, however, was constantly betrayed by the rather laboured and highly emotive terminology in which it was advocated; in order to refashion catholic Spain there was to be a revival, a restoration, a reconquest, a campaign, a crusade.[6]

To express the matter in categories suggested by Weber and Troeltsch, the catholic church in Spain in the late nineteenth and early twentieth centuries continued to aspire after a pure church-type presence in a society in which that was becoming increasingly impossible. Troeltsch was correct, I think, when he observed in 1911 that the church-type as contrasted with the sect-type requires a 'unity of instinctive world-outlook of great masses of people' and that therefore 'the days of the pure church-type within our present civilisation are numbered'.[7] In a country in which cultural plural-ism, unbelief, sharp class conflict and, by no means least significant, new local nationalist movements in Catalonia and the Basque territories were all unmistakably present, the assertion of a distinc-tive national catholic unity could scarcely avoid becoming an exercise in obfuscation.

---

[5] For southern peasants, see the classic study by J. Díaz del Moral, *Historia de las Agitaciones Campesinas Andaluzas* (Madrid 1977) pp 200, 353–4, originally pub-lished 1928, and more recently T. Kaplan, *Anarchists of Andalusia 1868–1903* (Princeton 1977) pp 85–6.

[6] The most sustained exploitation of this terminology is probably in the proceedings of the Catholic Congresses, *Crónica del Congreso Católico* (Madrid 1889), (Zaragoza 1891), (Seville 1893), (Tarragona 1894), (Burgos 1899), (Santiago 1903).

[7] E. Troeltsch, *The Social Teaching of the Christian Churches*, trans O. Wyon, 2 vols (London 1956) 2 p 1008.

Those who deviated from the proposed norm were no longer, as in much earlier times, Moors and Jews who might be distinguished by ethnic as well as religious characteristics and forcibly expelled. They were now either Spaniards who refused or neglected to consider catholicism as an essential ingredient of their basic self-definition, as was the case for example of many of the free-thinking intellectuals associated with the Free Education Institute (Institución Libre de Enseñanza)[8] as much as of anarchist peasants, or catholics who began in this period to reject a primary Spanish definition in favour of Catalan or Basque alternatives. In such circumstances a Spanish national catholicism not only became a project to realise rather than an approximate description of what existed, but it showed itself to be, precisely because of that, what Angel Ganivet called in 1896 a jagged idea rather than a round one displaying the feature he found typical and typefying of that category, namely 'an irresistible tendency to transform ideas into instruments of warfare'.[9] Since being catholic and being Spanish were quite evidently not inseparable notions in these years, affirmations that they were so threatened to commit the church to working towards a projected national catholicism which would render inadmissible the political or intellectual, social or religious stances of whole groups within Spanish society. In an attempt to equate being Spanish with being catholic, to elaborate what Richard Niebuhr outlined as 'the Christ of culture' understanding between the church and contemporary society,[10] it in fact denied the experience of significant sections of both the church itself and the society whose values it was trying to incorporate and enunciate. In claiming for itself that authority in relation to the whole of society which is a central feature of Troeltsch's church-type, it paradoxically made itself available as a weapon to be wielded by some parts of that society in conflict with others.

The clearest and most notorious instance of such usage was, of course, in the Spanish civil war of 1936–9 in which the official position of the catholic church was unambiguous support for one side, ironically in the name of national catholic unity.[11] It is the

[8] For the aims and personnel of this pioneering institute see L. Luzuriaga, *La Institución Libre de Enseñanza y la Educación en España* (Buenos Aires 1957).
[9] A. Ganivet, *Idearium Español*, trans J. R. Carey (London 1946) p 130.
[10] H. R. Niebuhr, *Christ and Culture* (New York 1951) pt 3.
[11] The postition was stated in a collective pastoral letter of 1 July 1937; it is reprinted

purpose of this paper to show how the self-understanding of the catholic church in relation to Spanish society and the state helped decisively to make available to the victors in the civil war a crusading, national catholic terminology in which to justify their military rising, and secondly to discuss how that rhetoric served to obscure less admissible political and sociological definitions both of Spanish catholicism and of the forces which took up arms against the republic in 1936. Two important aspects of church policy and activity have been selected as particularly appropriate for this study; education because it was a constant preoccupation of the church in its struggle for identification with and control of Spanish society; and the response to Basque nationalism which emerged as the most embarrasing complication in ecclesiastical alignment with the Spanish state.

In Spain, as in France in the same period, education was the necessary focus of conflicting views on desirable developments in society in general. Common ground could usually be established in recognition of the need to combat illiteracy. At the turn of the century forty-six per cent of boys and fifty-seven per cent of girls between the ages of eleven and twenty could not read or write, while ten years later the minister of education admitted that an additional nine and a half thousand primary schools were needed merely to provide the basic primary instruction supposedly assured by legislation which had then already been fifty years on the statute book.[12] Agreement faded, however, as soon as the questions of who should educate, and toward what end, were raised. Whereas the church repeatedly appealed to the concordat of 1851 and its provision that 'instruction in universities, secondary schools, seminaries and all kinds of public and private schools must conform in every way to the doctrines of the . . . catholic religion', reforming intellectuals based their contrary case on article twelve of the 1876 constitution which stated that 'any Spanish citizen may found and maintain establishments of instruction or education in accordance with the laws', which in practice seemed not to include the

---

in *Documentos Colectivos* [*del Episcopado Español 1870–1974*], ed [J.] Iribarren (Madrid 1974) pp 219–42.
[12] Information from C. Silió y Cortés, *La Educación Nacional* (Madrid 1914) p 32.

concordat. José Ortega y Gasset voiced the conviction of all those associated with the tiny but innovatory and immensely influential Free Education Institute when he declared that the Spanish problem was in essence pedagogical.[13] On its side the church was equally convinced, as can be seen immediately by the dramatic rise in the number of church schools opened in the period, particularly by the burgeoning religious congregations.

Although some politicians shared this concern, as witnessed for instance by the initiative to create the ministry of public instruction in 1900, the state was unable to impose or even offer any adequate school system of its own because it lacked the financial resources to fund it, even at primary level. Teachers in the state schools sometimes remained unpaid or were paid late, and the penury of the treasury was loudly but uselessly lamented by successive ministers of education. Even liberal ministers who might have found a solution along French lines congenial, therefore, had no real option but to rely upon the church to complement the state schools.[14] The only alternative would have been a massive increase in state expenditure on education, either through a radical reduction in the inflated army budget or through the introduction of a serious system of direct taxation, both of which were quite impossible for political reasons.[15] It was not until the advent of the republic in 1931 that the scale of state funding was drastically reassessed.[16]

Because lack of resources undermined any attempt at a state monopoly or even state dominance of schooling before the 1930s, it was only at university level that the question of control was decided early. After 1881 there was no hope of enforcing confessional criteria for the selection of university teachers, as Menéndez y Pelayo had realised with dismay, and the two private catholic universities of Deusto and El Escorial, founded by the Jesuits and Augustinians respectively, were initiatives on too small a scale to

[13] Quoted in P. Laín Entralgo, *España Como Problema* (2 ed Madrid 1957) p 654 (originally published 1948), and in M. D. Gómez Molleda, *Los Reformadores de la España Contemporánea* (Madrid 1966) p 496.

[14] See for example the preamble to the major educational reform law promulgated in the *Real Decreto* of 17 August 1901, in which some of the financial problems are acknowledged.

[15] For a discussion of the impasse over the army see C. P. Boyd, *Praetorian Politics in Liberal Spain* (Chapel Hill 1979).

[16] See A. Molero Pintado, *La Reforma Educativa de la Segunda República Española. Primer Bienio* (Madrid 1977).

threaten the official establishments. But battle was joined over the secondary schools, especially after the turn of the century. In 1901 the liberal government made religion an optional instead of obligatory subject for the *bachillerato*. An unsuccessful attempt was made later that year to restrict the numbers and activities of the religious congregations, many of which were involved in secondary education, and a similar attempt in 1906 also failed while the more detailed plans of the Canalejas government in 1910 were put through over violent church opposition although they were then allowed to lapse.[17] In 1913 the children of parents who did not consider themselves Catholic were allowed exemption from religion classes in the state schools. While on the one hand, therefore, liberal opponents of church control of education deplored the fact that the majority of children in secondary schools attended establishments run by the religious congregations, that the teaching personnel in these was expanding at an alarming rate, and that even in state schools instruction in catholic doctrine and practice was the norm, on the other hand church spokesmen regarded any weakening of ecclesiastical dominance as entirely unsatisfactory.

From the church's point of view, the catholic unity of the whole nation remained the ideal, and educational pluriformity an evil to be resisted and feared as an integral part of a wider apostasy. Spain's catastrophic defeat by the United States in 1898 was readily interpreted, by bishops among others, as divine retribution for national infidelity,[18] while a Jesuit polemicist, Ramón Ruiz Amado, attributed the horrendous anti-clerical violence sparked off in Barcelona in 1909 after the drafting of troops to fight Morocco to a typical joint betrayal of true religion and patriotism.[19] In another article he judged that Spain had been deprived of the progress enjoyed by other nations in the nineteenth century because the real, catholic Spain had been occupied in fighting the imaginary new Spain of the liberals and their false, destructive patriotism.[20] A textbook history of the church in use in private schools made the same

---

[17] J. M. Castells, *Las Asociaciones Religiosas en la España Contemporánea* (Madrid 1973) cap 4 is the most detailed consideration of the legal position of the religious congregations and their opponents. For an exposition of the wider political conflicts see J. A. Gallego, *La Política Religiosa en España 1889–1913* (Madrid 1975).
[18] For example the bishop of Vitoria in a pastoral letter of 11 February 1899, in *Boletín Eclesiástico del Obispado de Vitoria*, 35 (1899) pp 45–68.
[19] R. Ruiz Amado, *Razón y Fe* 25 (Madrid 1909) pp 5 *seq*.
[20] *Ibid* pp 413 *seq*.

point in referring to 'the invasion of free-masonry and impiety, the source of all the evils which our country suffered in the nineteenth century'.[21]

Although extreme in his bellicosity of style, Ruiz Amado was by no means atypical in the claims he made for the church's role in education and, by extension, in society as a whole. His most constant defence of catholic education in the early years of this century was unashamedly on the grounds that any other was a dissolvent of the nation's identity. He wrote in 1903: 'This nation has catholicism inscribed in its heart with letters of fire. Even more, catholicism is so incorporated and conaturalised within its very being, that it cannot cease to be catholic without ceasing, first of all, to be a nation'. And a few years later: 'Those who love the catholic church love our country. Those who hate the church, hate Spain . . . Woe to those Spaniards who merit the praises of just those sectarians who hate Spain'.[22] Such convictions were not limited to the Jesuits. Although the hierarchy never approved the complete rejection of the restored monarchy by intransigent traditional groups within the church, it nevertheless often urged a more conciliatory line in terms which made it clear that this was regarded as an unfortunate but necessary concession to a faithless and misguided age. In 1899 for instance, the bishops drew up a programme containing the following statements:

> Once again we declare that our constant aspiration is the establishment of catholic unity, formerly the glory of our fatherland. Its rupture now is the source of many evils. We also declare that we repudiate all the errors condemned by the Vicar of Christ . . . especially those contained in the *Syllabus*. And we repudiate all those liberties of perdition, offspring of the so-called new rights, or liberalism, the application of which to the government of our fatherland is the source of so many sins, and which leads us to the brink of the abyss.[23]

Much later, in 1923, rumours of a further liberalisation of article eleven of the constitution in the direction of fuller religious liberty provoked the hierarchy into a formal protest to the government.[24]

[21] Hermanos de las Escuelas Christianas, *Historia de la Iglesia Católica* (Madrid, Barcelona, no date but *c*1922) pp 351–2.
[22] *Razón y Fe* 7 (1903) p 189, 23 (1909) p 330.
[23] *Boletín Eclesiástico del Obispado de Vitoria* 35 (1899) pp 315–16.
[24] In Iribarren, *Documentos Colectivos* pp 116–17.

The episcopate in Spain was not at all prepared to meet or understand the incomparably more radical and unsympathetic onslaught on the church's hegemonic aspirations by the new republic in 1931. Perhaps even more revealing of the deep-seated catholic identification of religion with national identity than the well-known, official reactions to the republic's anti-clerical initiatives,[25] is the following spontaneous criticism by a De La Salle brother writing in a school annual report in 1932. The particular source of his complaint was a crude effort by the republican government to rob of their religious significance the feasts of Our Lady of the rosary (7 October) and Our Lady of the pillar (12 October):

> By official government disposition, 7 October and 12 October are public holidays in which the exploits of our soldiers, sailors and explorers will be honoured. How little such holidays say to the Spanish Christian spirit, for they have no roots in the patriotic and religious tradition which was the motive force behind the enterprises of our ancestors . . . History has engraved the redemptive sign ineffaceably into our actions, and the pillar and the holy rosary will always be a formidable focus of our nationality.[26]

There is nothing remarkable about such views in a country in which catholicism had been so dramatically and undeniably part of national culture for so many centuries. On the contrary, it would be extremely surprising if similar assumptions about the inseparability of religion and national identity were uncommon. What is of interest, however, is not the continuity of assumption but the more specifically political values implied by those assumptions in the changing socio-political context. Unease at the liberal insistence on religious toleration extended naturally to unease also at those other liberal innovations of parliament, party politics, a free press and cultural pluralism. The bishops' repudiation of the 'liberties of perdition' expressed a longing for a simpler, more authoritarian regime in which the church would not have to compete with alternative purveyors of truth. Thus one finds in a school text-book a desperate call from the catholic right for a saviour of the nation 'who, in order to halt the gangrene will cauterise without compassion,

---

[25] For example the letter drawn up by cardinal Segura 25 July 1931, in *ibid* pp 135–50.
[26] *Colegio Santiago Apóstol. Memoria Escolar 1931–2* (Bilbao 1932) p 11.

and if necessary mutilate all that is not purely catholic and Spanish',[27] and when general Primo de Rivera seized power and abolished parliament and the parties in 1923, few catholic tears were shed.[28] The liberal monarchist education minister Romanones was not merely indulging in rhetorical exaggeration when in 1902 he expressed a fear that the church, through the agency of the religious congregations, would utilise the constitutional liberty to teach 'to form the national soul . . . in so definitive a way that afterwards all other freedoms will be rendered quite useless'.[29] The struggle for church control of education was also a bid to establish one interpretation of what it meant in the late nineteenth and twentieth centuries to be Spanish which, by its very assertion of comprehensiveness, inevitably rendered itself exclusive by disallowing the validity of alternative interpretations. The denial of pluralism in the name of national religious unity looked increasingly like an intolerant guarantee of division in a society in which the projected unity could be achieved only by coercion.

Just as the national religious uniformity advocated by, among other ecclesiastical organs, the private schools tended to adopt discernible political features, so the structures of catholic education contributed a recognisable sociological shape to the projected catholic nation. The most striking phenomenon in the church education system from the 1870s right through to the republic was the rapid and sustained growth in the religious congregations, and the corresponding proliferation of their schools. Anti-clericals quoted with horror the statistics of membership of the congregations, estimated at approximately 44,000 nuns and 13,000 male religious in 1900, as contrasted with 17,000 and 2,000 respectively only fifteen years previously.[30] The equivalent figures for 1923 were about 55,000 and 17,000, and on the eve of the republic 61,000 and 20,000.[31] According to a Jesuit analysis of the 1923 statistics, over one half of male religious communities and just under one half of

[27] *Manual de la Clase 2 para alumnas de los Colegios del Sagrado Corazón* (Madrid 1908) pp 205–6.
[28] For a typical justification of the coup, see L. Izaga S. J.'s article, *Razón y Fe* 81 (1927) pp 43 *seq*.
[29] Quoted in *ibid* 7 (1903) p 184 from a parliamentary debate.
[30] L. Morote, *Los Frailes en España* (Madrid 1904) reached similar totals of 40,000 nuns and 10,000 male religious from different sources from those given here in a speech by Romanones quoted in *ibid* p 180.
[31] J. M. Castells, *Las Asociaciones Religiosas en la España Contemporánea* p 376.
[32] *Razón y Fe* 76 (1926) pp 276 *seq*.

their female counterparts were involved in education.[32] The extent of this expansion can perhaps be registered more directly by considering the case of a few of the major teaching congregations. The Brothers of the Christian Schools (De La Salle) for example, had one community in Spain in 1878 with thirteen members and 286 pupils; for 1900 the corresponding figures were forty-five schools staffed by 346 brothers with 10,648 boys; by 1931 the totals had leapt to 149 schools, 1,484 brothers and 32,000 pupils. Unlike the De La Salle brothers, the Escolapios (Poor Clerks Regular of the Mother of God of the Religious Schools) had been a part of the Spanish educational scene for generations, but they also expanded in this period and by the 1930s were educating about 30,000 boys. One of the best known of the women's congregations, the Society of the Sacred Heart, displayed a similar pattern to the Brothers of the Christian Schools but on a smaller scale. There were three foundations, 142 sisters and 900 pupils in 1876; seventeen convents, 668 sisters and over 6,000 pupils in the 1930s.[33]

Recruitment patterns to the congregations are very revealing. Where two-tier membership existed, as with priests and brothers in the Jesuits, and choir nuns and lay sisters in the Society of the Sacred Heart, candidates inevitably came from clearly distinct social classes, with both organisations attracting members from wealthy and titled families as well as less markedly affluent ones to become priests or choir nuns, and from poor and usually peasant homes to become brothers and lay sisters.[34] Less predictable, perhaps, is the case of congregations which, while putting most of their resources into the towns, recruited almost exclusively from rural areas. The recruitment director of the northern province of the De La Salle brothers depended heavily upon the good offices of parish priests and school masters in the villages of rural Castile who helped him contact and visit young boys who might through such contacts enter the junior noviceship at the age of twelve or thirteen. In the northern province of the Marists (Little Brothers of Mary)

---

[33] Figures from, respectively, C. Gabriel, *La Obra Lasaliana en España* (Madrid, no date but *c*1953) Appendix 3, table 1; V. Caballero, *En Propia Defensa: La Obra de las Escuelas Pías de España* (Madrid 1931) (pamphlet); *Catalogue de la Société du Sacré Coeur de Jésus* (1876, 1931) and Religiosas del Sagrado Corazón, *Cien Años de Educación Christiana 1846–1946* (Zaragoza 1946) pp 91–2.

[34] For the background of the members of one particular Sacred Heart community, see F. Lannon, 'The Socio-political Role of the Spanish Church—a Case Study', *Journal of Contemporary History*, 14 (London 1979) pp 194–6.

the same applied. One of the brothers who taught in the Marist secondary school in Bilbao, for example, spent the summers of 1921–8 foot-slogging from village to village in Castile 'and he would return with six, seven, up to twelve boys for the juniorate'. The writer of the obituary from which this information is taken added, understandably, 'naturally, not all persevered'.[35] Groups like the Marists and the De La Salle brothers, then, drew mainly on areas of small peasant farming rather than on urban classes. Between 1903 and 1931 only one boy from Balbao persevered in the northern province of the Marists.[36] Much the same was true of candidates for the secular priesthood in the area,[37] whereas the more prestigious Jesuits were able to attract candidates of urban middle class and sometimes very wealthy background who were conspicuous by their absence both in the ranks of the diocesan clergy and in the more lowly teaching congregations. Not only did the various institutes reflect in their own social ranking the class divisions of the wider society, but their failure to draw novices from certain clearly distinguishable social groups was a faithful indicator of the church's wider failure with exactly those classes.

A comparable picture emerges from a study of the schools themselves. It was both acknowledged to be the case and bound to be the case that private secondary schools were concentrated in the major towns and were dedicated to the provision of education for the bourgeoisie. As a Jesuit commentator writing about the need for more schools for the poor in Madrid in 1925 observed, there was no equivalent shortage for the upper and middle classes who were well supplied with church secondary schools.[38] Since secondary education was much more costly to provide than rudimentary primary instruction, and since there were no state subsidies for private secondary schools, these necessarily charged fees, albeit often at a very modest level, and hence catered for those who could pay them. For similar reasons free elementary schools run by

[35] Information on the De La Salle from manuscript paper prepared for me by brother Josué in Bilbao, April 1974; on the Marists, obituary of brother Antonio Agustín in *Norte. (Revista Mensual de la Provincia Marista de Este Nombre)* 5 (Madrid 1957–60) p 29.

[36] 'Registro del Noviciado de la Provincia Marista Norte', manuscript in provincial archives of the congregation, Valmaseda.

[37] See F. Lannon, 'A Basque Challenge to the Pre-Civil War Spanish Church' *European Studies Review* 9 (London 1979) pp 30–1.

[38] *Razón y Fe* 71 (1925) pp 288 *seq.*

congregations which also staffed more academically ambitious secondary institutions concentrated on basic skills to prepare children for manual or semi-skilled or skilled work but certainly not for wider opportunities which required further education. Since this limited education was financed by the rich, either through the fees of schools run by the same congregation, or through private benefaction, or through a charitable organisation like the Society of Saint Vincent de Paul, it was difficult for the church to avoid the charge that its education system perpetuated social divisions and, by relying on and extolling ameliorative charity, obscured the need for a more radical pursuit of social justice.

Dozens of examples of this kind of elementary education could be given, but just one must serve. It is again taken from the north, where most of my research so far has been concentrated. In the 1880s the De La Salle brothers opened in Bilbao a centre of elementary technical education to prepare boys for work in local heavy industry and to offer adult night classes for workers. The project was sponsored by the local Saint Vincent de Paul association which channeled into it considerable sums from local capitalists, like the Ibarra family, one of whose members was the association's president at the time. By 1900 there were 310 day school pupils, 900 at night classes and no fewer than 1,200 working men connected with the centre through its recreational facilities, classes, mutual aid schemes and so forth. The lay sponsors viewed the whole enterprise as part of 'the glorious campaign for a catholic restoration', which meant, among other things, keeping working men out of socialist unions. Nothing could be more profoundly conservative of the social order that this circular pattern of catholic industrialists funding vocational education to provide competent and if possible anti-socialist workers for their own foundries and ship-yards.[39] It is not easy to see how, in the actual socio-economic conditions of Spain, and especially the pitiful inadequacy of the education budget, the religious congregations could have avoided this kind of reliance on the upper classes and the concomitant, often unwitting purveying of values and attitudes which were marked by obvious class characteristics. No amount of generosity and dedi-

[39] *Escuelas y Patronato de Orbreros de San Vicente de Paúl de Bilbao. Memoria 1895–6* (Bilbao 1897) especially p 14, and *Génesis e Historia de la Fundación Católica de Escuelas y Patronato de San Vicente de Paúl de Bilbao* (Bilbao 1952).

cation on the part of religious teachers could alter the fact that the actual structures of catholic education tended to delineate a sociological outline of catholic Spain as propertied or dominated by the propertied classes, and hostile to radical social change.

Catholic education was one of the agencies for the formation of a national consciousness that would be both Spanish and catholic. An examination of its implicit as contrasted with its overt and ovowed values indicates some of the political commitments and sociological contours of catholic Spain. Much more directly embarrassing and problematic for ecclesiastical leaders, however, than failure to evangelise free-thinking intellectuals and large sections of the urban and rural proletariat was the quite different challenge presented by devout catholics whose political views did not fit within the acceptable range. In the crucial early years of the 1930s these included a few eminent catholic republicans—most notably Niceto Alcalá-Zamora, president of the democratic republic for most of its existence—and the Catalan archbishop of Tarragona, cardinal Vidal i Barraquer who, exceptionally among the hierarchy, was reluctant either to damn the republic or to approve the military rising of 1936, and for whom there was no place in Franco's Spain. Most embarrassing of all, and over a longer period, were the irreproachably catholic Basques who, precisely in this period, embarked upon a militant national programme which threatened to capsise the Spanish catholic national ship.

It would not be unreasonable to see the catholic nationalism of the Basque Nationalist Party (*Partido Nacionalista Vasca*) founded by Sabino Arana y Goiri in Bilbao in 1893 as a mirror image of the national catholicism the Spanish church so longed to fashion or refashion in Spain. The first manifesto unhesitatingly called for the establishment of a new nation state, Euzkadi, which would be officially catholic and in which, moreover, the state would be subordinate to the church, and politics to religion.[40] Enthusiasm for the ideal of a catholic state underpinned by a society with social and cultural valves derived from traditional catholic morality was a powerful source of inspiration for pious nationalists. They resembled the integrist right wing of Spanish catholicism, to which in fact many of them had belonged, and would have had no difficulty in subscribing to parts of the famous manifesto of integrist

[40] Text in M. García Venero, *Historia del Nacionalismo Vasco* (Madrid 1968) pp 281–3.

journalists produced in 1888: 'Catholic unity is the reign of Jesus Christ in society. It is Jesus Christ ruling in laws and customs, in public and private institutions, in all education, in all spoken or written propaganda . . . In a word, it is the reign of Christ the King, absolute lord and master of all things'.[41] The conservation of traditional catholic culture, increasingly threatened by immigrant workers from other areas of Spain flooding into the iron and steel and ship-building industries, and often joining socialist organisations, remained a constant preoccupation. One Escolapio priest from the Basque province of Guipúzcoa, for instance, argued in 1935 that Basque culture was being undermined by an imported disregard for authority, and corrupted by cosmopolitan innovations, including the use of cosmetics, jazz, cabaret, and scandalous dances like the waltz and the tango. As an elderly, nationalist priest said to me some years ago, living in a Basque village in the first part of this century was like living in a convent.[42]

Until the gradual emergence of a more modern Christian democratic style among young nationalist leaders in the 1920s and 1930s, Basque catholicism differed from its Spanish counterpart for ethnic and cultural rather than theological or ecclesiastical reasons. This is immediately obvious in the greater strength of the nationalist movement in the provinces of Vizcaya and Guipúzcoa, where the incidence of Basque speakers was high, than in inland Alava and, even more markedly Navarre, which were just as renowned for catholic practice but where the Basque language was less widely used. Indeed, a major factor in the reluctance of the republican governments of 1931–3 to grant an autonomy statute to the Basques as they did to the Catalans was their mistrust of the conservative, catholic aspirations of the chief advocates of autonomy, and their fear that the Basque provinces would become an unmanageable 'Vaticanist Gibraltar'.

What neither friend nor foe could deny was that the Basque nationalists had every right to regard themselves as quite spectacularly catholic. When a group of nationalist leaders visited the Vatican in January 1936 in order to explain their aims, they went armed with a formidable statement of their catholic credentials, which they hoped to present to the secretary of state, cardinal

---

[41] Text in M. Tirado y Rojas, *León XIII y España* (Madrid, no date) p 91.
[42] 'Ibar' (in fact, Justo María Mocoroa), *Genio y Lengua* (Tolosa 1935) p 183, and Claudio Gallástegui in interview in Bilbao, March 1974.

Pacelli, although in the event he declined to receive them and sent a substitute instead. The preparatory documentation drawn up in the summer of 1935 pointed out that in addition to the flourishing state of vocations to the priesthood and religious life in the Basque country, there were no fewer than fourteen bishops and nearly five thousand priests and religious from Vizcaya, Guipúzcoa and Alava active in missionary areas, a ratio of six to every thousand inhabitants of the area. Furthermore, fourteen episcopal sees within Spain had Basque incumbents. It was a major grievance therefore that all bishops before the then incumbents of the sees of Pamplona and Vitoria, which served Navarre and the other three provinces respectively, had not themselves been Basques and had 'demonstrated a partisan opposition towards us which has sometimes been more violent that that of the [regional] civil governors'. Put even more bluntly, bishops of Vitoria had: 'behaved in their dealings with Basque nationalism less like bishops of the catholic church than like fervent functionaries of the Spanish government and like faithful servants—let us express it more gently—like unconditional friends of the capitalists in our country who have always aligned themselves with the Spanish state because of their particular material interests'. Earlier in the century one bishop had prohibited the use of Basque names in baptism, another had written a pastoral letter denouncing the nationalist programme as 'darkening the minds and perverting the hearts' of the young. No episcopal protest had greeted the prohibition by the dictator Primo de Rivera of catechism classes in the Basque language, even in villages where the children knew no other. On the contrary, when blessing a new railway line in his diocese in the presence of the king and the dictator, bishop Martínez had congratulated the latter on bringing peace to the fatherland, and prayed that the new lines would 'communicate good ideas of peace, work and *españolismo*, and that the criminal notions of separatism would never pass along them'.[43]

Nor was the episcopate the only scandal to Basque catholics. A number of priests and very many members and superiors of religious congregations active in the Basque provinces had adopted a virtually persecutory role; some of the secondary schools and part

[43] I. Moriones, *Euzkadi y el Vaticano 1935–6* (Rome 1976) collects all the relevent documentation and prints it in full. The information in these paragraphs is taken from documents 4 and 11, drafts of the exposition being prepared for Rome, pp 29–65, 82–102.

of the devotional press run by the congregations were particularly offensive.

There are many examples of the kind of activity to which the documents sent to Rome referred. One piece of anecdotal but revealing evidence concerns the experience of a boy from Tolosa in Guipúzcoa who entered the Escolapio teaching congregation in 1913 at the age of eleven. At thirteen, he left the junior seminary for the noviceship, in Huesca province, taking with him a few books in Basque. His novice master took one look at them and exclaimed:

'This is separatism.' It was the first time I had ever heard the word. In my naiveté I thought it must be the name of some heresy . . . He took the books away from me for the duration of the noviceship, and moreover he formally admonished me to do everything possible to forget my native language. At this I began to cry, pointing out to him that my mother knew no Spanish. 'It doesn't matter', he replied, 'you must forget the Basque tongue.' . . . Years later I told the master of novices that it was primarily his fault that I had sometimes felt rise within me a deaf cry of 'Down with Spain'.[44]

It is hardly surprising that Basque Escolapios committed themselves in the 1920s to forming a separate province within the congregation on the grounds that non-indigenous personnel and customs in Escolapio schools in the Basque area were counterproductive and scandalous. After a very painful controversy with charges of political rather than religious motivation on both sides, the new province was eventually established in 1933. But the enterprise was completely undermined once the outcome of the civil war became apparent, and the Basque provincial was forced to resign his post in 1938.[45] The whole episode, however, together with the recruitment of candidates from Castile to work in the Basque country by congregations like the Marists and the Brothers of the Christian Schools make entirely understandable the plea from nationalist leaders to the Vatican in 1935–6 that religious congregations should be positively encouraged to follow the example of the Capuchins and the Carmelites and form specifically

[44] Justo María Mocoroa's autobiographical account was prepared for me in Bilbao, April 1974.
[45] Information from duplicated account by P. Galdeano, 'Apuntes para la historia de la provincia de Vasconia' privately circulated in 1965. Fr Galdeano was the provincial concerned.

Basque provinces with Basque personnel rather than include the Basque area in a larger unit dominated by Spanish religious.

In the case of devotional literature, the nationalist spokesmen almost certainly had in mind the *Messenger of the Sacred Heart* which was published by the Jesuits in Bilbao from 1886. The main targets of the contributors and more especially of Remigio Vilariño, editor from 1902 to his death in the civil war, were the usual ones of liberals, socialists, freemasons and Jews. In 1898 for instance, Vilariño was appealing for 'a strong man to sweep clean our peninsula of all that is not truly catholic and in keeping with our traditions'. But the rhetoric embraced hostility to Basque nationalism as it became too powerful to be ignored. When, in 1922, Vilariño enthusiastically welcomed an initiative from the hierarchy in launching a 'great social campaign', he ended his article with the injunction, 'Catholics, be patriots! Patriots, be catholic, because God wills it and the fatherland requires it'. There was no room for Basque rather than Spanish patriotism in such a scheme. It was essential for the integrist line consistently argued in the *Messenger* that catholic Spain should be clearly opposed to one simple alternative, apostate Spain. In 1902 Vilariño predicted that: 'an epoch is approaching in which the political struggle will be no other than a religious conflict between two extreme parties, the atheistic politicians and the catholic politicians, Christians and anti-Christians.' By 1931 the scenario had not changed very much: 'Communism is forging ahead. As we have said many times, a time is coming when all ideologies and all social movements will be resolved into two. Communism or catholicism: Rome or Moscow'.[46] This neat dualism did not baulk the violent implications of the polarised options it was offering. Another Jesuit discussed in 1902 the vexed question of whether it was preferable to kill or be killed for one's faith and country. He concluded that it was better to be a martyr than a hero, but that those with no vocation for martyrdom must at least aspire to the honour of heroism.[47] There was apparently no problem over inflicting death in a just cause, nor in identifying both the just cause and the enemy. It was this convenient division of the Spanish catholic good from the apostate bad which catholic Basque nationalism unpardonably confused.

[46] *Mensajero del Sagrado Corazón de Jesús* (Bilbao 1898) p 526, (1922) p 301, (1902) p 103, (1931) p 578.
[47] *Ibid* (1902) p 165.

When civil war actually broke out in 1936 many Spanish catholics found it hard to believe and impossible to understand that the Basque nationalists preferred to side with socialists and communists pledged to the defence of a republic that permitted Basque autonomy, rather than with the insurgents who fought for a catholic but centralist Spain.

Dissatisfaction with the political claims of Spanish catholicism was not new in the 1930s. Already in 1919 a Basque writer had concluded: 'We would be better catholics and better patriots under a Muslim or Cossack sabre, under the draconian legislation of a Bismarck or the iron rod of a Cromwell than we are with this erastian regime which tries to assassinate us with sweetness'.[48] But the first response of Basque nationalism to the Spanish confessional state was a proposed Basque state which was virtually theocratic in orientation and likely to confront one form of catholic conservatism with another. This was only gradually modified by circumstances. First of all the foundation of the Basque catholic union (*Solidaridad de Obreros Vascos*) in 1911 marked the beginning of a more successful unionisation than was achieved by the church anywhere else in Spain, even though it never approached the strength of the socialist unions in the area. Secondly, the unchanging monarchist loyalty of the vast majority of Basque industrialists enabled the Basque Nationalist Party eventually to present itself as socially reforming as well as anti-socialist. Finally, the intransigent centralism of the right wing governments of 1934–5 left the nationalists little option but to articulate a middle of the road, Christian democrat position, clearly differentiated from the Spanish catholic right as well as the socialist left. By 1936 it could not find common cause with the political right, as was shown in the February elections which it entered separately from both left and right, and then more dramatically in its armed opposition to the military rebels who fought the battle of the propertied classes of catholic Spain.[49].

Notwithstanding this alignment of Basque catholics with the republic, the Spanish hierarchy with only a couple of exceptions gave official blessing and backing to the military rising, not discreetly and guardedly, but publicly and in a notorious collective

[48] *Hermes* 50 (Bilbao 1919) p 366.
[49] For this gradual change, see J. Tusell, *Historia de la Democracia Christiana en España* 2 vols (Madrid 1974) 2 cap 1.

pastoral letter addressed to the catholic bishops of the whole world. They justified their position, and the rising itself, in terms of the catholic national identity of Spain: 'We affirm that the civil-military rising has sprung from two roots in the consciousness of the people —a sense of patriotism which has recognised in the rising the only way to restore Spain and avoid its definitive ruin; and a religious sense which saw it as the force necessary to reduce to impotence the enemies of God and to guarantee the continuity of the faith and the practice of religion'.[50] In March 1939 Pacelli, now Pius XII, sent a congratulatory telegram to Franco which ran: 'Lifting up our heart to God we give thanks with Your Excellency for Spain's catholic victory'. The equation of Franco's victory with a victory for catholicism was to be expected, given the terrifying anti-clerical violence in republican territories in the early days and weeks of the rising, which had resulted in the massacre of thousands of priests and religious. It remains true, however, that the equation was made in spite of the fact that General Mola's troops executed fourteen Basque priests in Guipúzcoa in October 1936, that dozens more were imprisoned or exiled, and that yet more not actually exiled by the new regime were sent out of Spain by religious superiors to join the republican 'enemies of God' in France and Latin America.

Official ecclesiastical support for the rising did not find its origin either in horror at the murder of priests and nuns or, as the collective pastoral letter claimed, in the theory that the rising was a pre-emptive strike to forestall a communist revolution. It originated in persistent patterns of catholic thinking which upheld the ideal of a totally catholic society and state from which heterodox elements should be expunged. The letter of July 1937 explicitly defended the use of the term 'national' by the insurgents, while also insisting that there was no real option for the church in a war understood by the bishops as a conflict between alien, atheistic communism on the one hand and Spanish catholicism on the other. But this understanding was itself a natural consequence of the constant aims and aspirations of the Spanish church which this paper has tried to outline. The availability to the insurgents of national catholic, crusade rhetoric was due largely to the long-term, hegemonic claims of the church, in the context of which anarchists, communists, socialists and liberals, and in a rather

[50] Iribarren, *Documentos Colectivos* pp 230–1.

different category Basque nationalists, could be seen as a modern re-incarnation of the Moors and Jews which an earlier crusade had banished from Spanish soil. Recent studies have shown in exhaustive detail that the major apologists of the crusade and of the Franco regime in the 1930s and 1940s, from whatever starting point—fascist, catholic conservative or ecclesiastical—and with whatever reservations, all united in presenting the war and its outcome as a project for the restoration of national catholicism. To give just a few examples: Manuel García Morente asserted that 'Spain is essentially identical with the Christian religion' and 'Spain is constituted of Christian faith and Iberian blood. Therefore, between the Spanish nation and catholicism there exists a profound and essential identity'. José María Pemán echoed the same idea: 'The Spanish nation, it is exists at all, is catholic'; and cardinal Gomá, primate of Spain and the force behind the 1937 letter wrote later, 'if catholicism and the fatherland are as it were consubstantial in the Spain of former times, "to form its genius and its tradition", then it would be suicidal to declare a divorce between them'.[51]

What is of interest here is not so much to catalogue such statements, of which there are hundreds, but to notice the function and inner definitions of the rhetoric. The major function is easy to identify, since the various groups which took up arms against the republic in 1936 had no positive political aim in common. Carlist and Alfonsist monarchists, fascists and conservative generals agreed on the need to destroy the republic but on little more. Their traditions and objectives were different, and military victory left many of them dissatisfied. As early as April 1937 Franco arbitrarily ordered the immediate fusion of all political groups into the 'Movement', the typically anodyne shorthand for the unwieldy conglomerate title (*Falange Española Tradicionalista de las Juntas de Ofensiva Nacional-Sindicalista*) of the new organisation. From the beginning he imposed unity partly by negating, partly by co-opting and partly by absorbing the programmes and personnel of the various political groups fighting the republic. Even during the

[51] All quotations from a survey of the literature by F. Urbina in *Iglesia y Sociedad en España* (Madrid 1977) pp 85–120. See also A. Alvarez Bolado, *El Experimento del Nacional-Catolicismo (1939–75)* (Madrid 1976), and an earlier essay in demystification by H. R. Southworth, *El Mito de la Cruzada de Franco* (Paris 1963).

war the Carlist leader Fal Conde narrowly escaped execution for resisting the new, unified order of things, while a leader of the fascist left, Manuel Hedilla, was imprisoned for life for refusing to accept the role allocated to him in the Movement. Neither the Carlist nor the Alfonsist claimant was invited to inherit his kingdom. No political or ideological formulation survived unscathed, or even in easily recognisable form, except that of national catholicism. This received massive publicity in the late thirties and early forties because the crusade and the new regime had to make the most of being national and catholic in the absence of any other agreed description. The rhetoric of national catholicism clothed the ideological nakedness of the military rising. It was a rhetoric that the church's self-understanding over generations had made familiar and accessible, and which awkwardly dissident voices like those of the Basque nationalists were not allowed to modify.

The sociological definition or base of the much publicised catholic nation was evident from almost the beginning of the republic, and confirmed the shape already outlined by the church education system. Insofar as the anti-clerical offensive of the republican constitution of 1931 was associated by catholic observers with cautious but unprecedented reforming measures on urban and rural wages and, most contentious of all, land-ownership, so the protection of private property was claimed to be inextricably linked with rallying to the church. The first manifesto of the National Action group, the nucleus of the catholic conservative alliance which emerged in 1933 as the mass political organisation of the right (*Confederación Española de Derechas Autónomas*), declared within a month of the proclamation of the republic that it intended to defend religion, the fatherland, the family, order, work and property. These it saw imperilled by atheistic communism, local nationalisms, free love and a tyrannical socialisation of property. The programme elaborated later that year re-emphasised these commitments, seen as interdependent, and the programme of the united catholic right (CEDA) in 1933 championed the church as its avowed first priority while also calling for the implantation of a corporatist regime, the restraint of local nationalist movements, the rejection of socialism and the re-formulation of agrarian reform policies in order to limit the possibilities of expropriation of the land and to ensure full compensation to the owners whenever expropriation actually occurred.[52] The catholic nation was centralist and conservative or corporatist in politics, propertied in economic status.

The only puzzling enthusiasts for this catholic nation were the very poor peasant proprietors of the centre and north, whom recent studies suggest were blinded by CEDA propaganda on the religious issue and led by the large land-owners who dominated the CEDA into forming the mass base of a political movement which ignored their socio-economic plight and interests.[53] It is not necessary to go so far. Although it is true that the catholic right did notoriously little for these poor supporters in the parliament of 1934–5, it is also true that the republican-socialist coalitions of the previous two years had offered them nothing. Moreover, at local level catholic rural co-operatives and mutual aid schemes organised by Catholic Action groups that helped launch the CEDA had represented for some of them the difference between survival and disaster over a much longer period.[54] In addition, the doubts of sceptical historians at the interpretation that some poor peasant proprietors lined up with the right first and foremost, and freely, out of religious conviction, do not in themselves prove such an interpretation entirely invalid, although obviously incomplete. The real problem is not so much whether land-owning elites, the church and ultimately army leaders deliberately manipulated religious language for their own ends, but why catholic terminology formed the common vocabulary, and behind it catholicism in Spain the common feature of those groups in Spanish society which in 1936 opposed the republic.

I hope that this paper has suggested that one major explanation is not far to seek. To return to Troeltsch's categories, the pure church-type aspirations of the catholic church in Spain in the late nineteenth and twentieth centuries necessarily referred to a model derived from earlier historical experience in which the nation and catholicism were coterminous. Such a model could accommodate

---

[52] Texts in J. R. Montero, *La CEDA. El Catolicismo Social y Politico en la Segunda República*, 2 vols (Madrid 1977) 2 pp 593–5, 601–11, 621–37.
[53] J. J. Castillo, *Propietarios Muy Pobres* (Madrid 1979) pp 9–18; P. Preston, *The Coming of the Spanish Civil War* (London 1978) pp 30–2.
[54] As both Castillo and Preston point out in the passages cited.

neither cultural pluralism nor incompatible conflicts of socio-economic interest. National catholic rhetoric was intrinsically anti-pluralist and, in the widest sense, anti-modernising. In the actual socio-political circumstances of modern Spain it became available as legitimising vocabulary for the prosecution of clearly distinguishable sectional and class purposes. It is beyond the scope of this paper to analyse the sociological and ecclesiological, the theological, psychological and political factors which combined to make it so peculiarly difficult for the catholic church in Spain to modify its self-understanding in changing conditions. But the failure to engage in a gradual re-appraisal facilitated instead a continuing commitment to the re-creation of a national catholicism even though such a project was unrealisable other than through some form of coercion. The positive and active identification of the Spanish nation with catholicism could not but be an exercise, albeit unwitting, in obfuscation: the church itself has not been least among the casualties of that process and that project.

Lady Margaret Hall
University of Oxford.

RELIGION AND NATIONAL IDENTITY IN YUGOSLAVIA

by STELLA ALEXANDER

RELIGION in Yugoslavia is a divisive, not a unifying force. The country is a federation of republics inhabited by six different nationalities which are historically identified with three great religious confessions, catholicism, orthodoxy, and islam. The pattern is complex and dense, the assumptions and reflex actions of the human beings who make up these communities are deeply rooted in centuries of history, and nationalism and religion are proving tougher than ideology.¹ My paper therefore must start by describing this mixture, this *macédoine*, if one may borrow a culinary expression which itself derives from one of the component territories of these lands.

The Slovenes and Croats in the western part of the country are catholics, the Serbs, Montenegrins and Macedonians in the eastern half are orthodox; they live on either side of the historic line which divides the western from the eastern church, Latin Christianity from eastern orthodoxy, the Habsburgs from the Ottoman Turks. Lying astride the line, at the core of modern Yugoslavia is Bosnia Hercegovina, inhabited by a mixture of orthodox Serbs, catholic Croats and Slav Moslems, descendants of converts to Islam under the Turkish occupation. Some of these Moslems considered themselves Serbs and some Croats (not infrequently members of the same family) but they form a distinct cultural group and, for reasons which will be examined later, they have been recognised since 1968 as a separate, sixth nationality.

These are the principal broad divisions, but the situation is further complicated by the numerous minorities within Yugoslavia—Hungarians, Slovaks and Romanians in the north, Albanians, Turks and Vlachs in the south and gypsies everywhere (with their own language now officially recognised). Albanians are mostly Moslem by culture, if not today by religion, but they call themselves Albanian, not Moslems, and the same is true of the Turks. Furthermore the majority nationalities appear as minorities within other republics; there is an important group of Serbs living within Croatia, who suffered greatly under the war-time fascist *ustaša* state, and who today constitute an irritant factor in Croatia with its simmering nationalism; and there are also small groups of Croats living in various parts of Serbia and Macedonia.

Religion played an important part in the formation of the Serbian and Croation nations, and became closely identified in each case with the concept of nationhood; its effect on the formation of the recently established Moslem nation has worked rather differently.

I propose firstly to examine, nation by nation, how this happened in history, and secondly its effects on the state of Yugoslavia, and, since the war on an ideologically secular regime.

I

Serbia

A few years ago a Serbian orthodox priest living in London told me that he would have to have very compelling reasons indeed before he would baptise a non-Serb into the Serbian orthodox church. This total identification of the church with the nation is rooted in its history, its culture and its whole way of life.

The Slavs in the south-eastern part of the Balkan peninsula became Christian under the eastern church in the ninth century and adopted the Cyrillic alphabet; this was to prove an important factor in separating them from the western south Slavs, who used the Latin alphabet. From the twelfth to the thirteenth centuries Serbia developed into a powerful state under the Nemanja dynasty, which used the church to consolidate its power. One of them, the younger son of Stefan Nemanja, secured the autocephaly of the Serbian orthodox church and established a national ecclesiastical administration for Serbia. As St. Sava, he became the principal cult-figure of the Serbian orthodox church. The Nemanjids were great builders of churches and monasteries, many of which survive, and are monuments to their faith and their high artistic achievement.

The Ottomans advanced up the Balkan peninsula during the fourteenth century, and in 1389 met and conquered the Serbian army and its allies at Kosovo, the Field of the Blackbirds, an event which like Dunkirk for the British, became one of the central myths of Serbian history and inspired a great cycle of epic poems.

Under the Ottomans, who divided their conquered subjects according to their religion and granted considerable local autonomy, the Serbian orthodox church took over the functions of government, with its own administrations and law courts; priests became the mediators and the go-betweens between rulers and ruled.

Modern Serbian nationalism was stimulated by the decline of the Ottoman empire, and at the same time the wars between Turkey and Austria sharpened the conflict between the catholic Croats in the north and the orthodox Serbs in the south, as each of the major combatants used them as pawns in their larger power game. The catholic church accompanied the Austrian advances and proselytised vigorously among the orthodox, laying the foundations for the rooted distrust of the catholic church which still underlies Serbian orthodox attitudes. But the Habsburgs also invited groups of Serbs to settle on and defend the military frontier between Turkey and Austria, promising them religious freedom and their own church structure. It was in this period that a great migration of Serbs from the heartland of Old Serbia took place, led by patriarch Arsenije III; they settled north of the Danube at the invitation of emperor Leopold I. The territory vacated by the Serbs gradually filled with Albanian Moslems; this alienation of the land which gave birth to the Serbian legend is a continuing source of grief and bitterness to the Serbs.

The eighteenth century saw further religious pressures on the Serbs, from the Austrians who established a Uniate church (Greek catholic) in areas under their control, and from the Greek officials of the Ottoman empire, the so-called Phanariots, who combined with the hierarchy of the Greek orthodox church in an attempt to hellenise the other orthodox churches. They secured the abolition of the Serbian patriarchate of Peć in 1766, deposed Serbian bishops and clergy and replaced the old Slav liturgies with the Greek rite. Although the Serbs succeeded in expelling the Phanariots less than fifty years later, the experience left a scar.

One effect of these centuries of outside pressures has been to make the Serbian orthodox church deeply conservative and backward-looking, feeding on its past; this, combined with its status, after the sixteenth century, as part of the machinery of Ottoman government and thus in some senses a part of the ruling establishment, made it inevitably resistant to change. It opposed with obduracy, for example, the reforms introduced into Serbian national life by two remarkable men, Dositej Obradović in the eighteenth century, who laid the foundation of modern literary Serbian, and Vuk Karadžić in the nineteenth century, who reformed the grammar and orthography of the Serbian language. Together the two men broke the exclusive hold of the orthodox church over the Serbian mind and introduced concepts of rationalism and secular nationalism. But at the same time many priests identified themselves with the Serbian national struggle for freedom from the Turks during the latter part of the eighteenth and nineteenth centuries; they fought with and sometimes even led the bands of half-revolutionaries, half-outlaws who harassed the weakening and retreating Ottoman forces. All this reinforced the church's concept of itself as the guardian and protector of Serbian nationhood, and did in fact help to create a Serbian national identity. It was however Ottoman religious toleration which made this attitude possible, whereas when the last war brought about a confrontation with Croatian catholics, there was no toleration, only a savage mutual lust to destroy.

Montenegro

Montenegro was part of the medieval kingdom of Serbia until the fourteenth century, when it broke away: they still consider themselves closer to the Serbs than to any other south Slav nation. It is a small, mountainous, inhospitable land which during its long struggle against the Turks became fiercely tribal and vengeful; it was the price the Montenegrins paid for their successful resistance. In the sixteenth century the bishops of Cetinje, the capital, assumed political power and took over the rule of the country and at the end of the seventeenth century this became hereditary, usually passing from uncle to newphew. Ecclesiastical and temporal authority became completely merged. This curious arrangement lasted until the middle of the nineteenth century and gave continuity and stability to the state.

Macedonia

The geographical area known as Macedonia lies between Greece, Bulgaria and Serbia, all of which have claimed the area; it is economically and strategically important because of the port of Salonika and the fertile surrounding plains, and because the valley of the Vardar is a strategic corridor to central Europe. The inhabitants of the territory are partly Slav, that is Serbs and Bulgarians, and partly a mixture of Albanian and Turkish Moslems, orthodox Greek and Vlachs; the Slav dialects of the region can be understood by both Serbs and Bulgarians and both have claimed the Slav inhabitants as part of their respective nations. It has, in fact, all the problems of Yugoslavia itself in miniature, and here also religion has been divisive, but in a different way.

The development of nineteenth century nationalism in the Balkans resulted in pressures on the inhabitants of Macedonia to declare for one or other of the contending nations, Greece, Serbia and Bulgaria. The Bulgarians obtained an initial advantage. Determined to throw off the corrupt and over-weening influence of the Greek patriarchate in Constantinople, and with Russian backing, they persuaded the Ottomans to establish an independent Bulgarian exarchate, with an exarch resident in Constantinople. The patriarch immediately excommunicated the new exarch and his followers, and a long and frequently bloody struggle followed between the adherents of the exarch and those of the patriarch. Bulgarian bishops were appointed and Bulgarian schools established. The Serbs were at a disadvantage, since they had no ecclesiastical organization covering Macedonia. They, however, enlisted the support of Austria-Hungary and at the end of the century they had opened a number of schools and secured the bishopric of Skopje for a Serb. The Greeks also continued to maintain schools in the area, and great educational rivalry sprang up. One curious result, noted by a contemporary writer[1] was that boys from the same family might be placed in schools run by different nationalities, and since it was a point of honour for a boy to adopt the language and nationality of the school which had educated him, a Greek family might have a 'Bulgarian' and a 'Serbian' son. Since Bulgarian schools greatly outnumbered the others, census counts showed a large but basically fictitious Bulgarian majority in the territory.

Serbia finally acquired the greater part of the territory of Macedonia as a result of the Balkan wars of 1912–13 and set about a regime of assimilation which included the Serbianisation of the Macedonian dialects and the placing of Serbian bishops in Macedonian dioceses. Some of them were strong Serbian nationalists who

---

[1] H. N. Brailsford, *Macedonia: Its Races and Their Future* (London 1906) p 102.

in the end provoked resentment both among those of the clergy who felt themselves Bulgarian and those who shared the growing sense of Macedonian nationalism.

Croatia

The Croats first emerged as a national unit when Tomislav, one of tribal chieftains assumed the title of king in about 924. The Croats claim an even longer unbroken link with the papacy going back to 879 when one of the local princes, Branimir, received a letter from the pope acknowledging his rule. The boundaries of Croatia fluctuated considerably over the next two centuries of independence; at its greatest extent it appears to have stretched from the Drava to the Adriatic, at one time including most of the Dalmatian coast. It is this kingdom to which modern Croatian nationalism harks back.

At the beginning of the twelfth century Croatia passed by marriage to the ruling Hungarian dynasty, thus beginning the long association between Croatia and Hungary; at the same time Venice was disputing Croatia's attempts to extend its rule over Dalmatia. The sixteenth to the eighteenth centuries saw the incursions of the Ottoman Turks from the east and a period of fragmentation and unrest. In the eighteenth century the centralising policy of the Habsburgs succeeded in uniting Croatia firmly to the empire, with a special relationship to Hungary. Meanwhile the Ottomans had conquered Bosnia-Hercegovina and were a constant threat to Croatia and the Dalmatian coast.

There was at this time no unified Croat language and several different dialects were spoken; the language of the upper classes was German or Italian and priests were almost the only literate people who used the Slav language. The counter-reformation gave an impetus to education and spurred the religious orders to set up many schools, seminaries and colleges where the true faith could be preserved and taught. It was during the seventeenth century that the Jesuit Kašić (Cassio) wrote a grammar of the Croatian language and chose for its basis the *štokavski* dialect of Bosnia, widely spoken in the hinterland of the Adriatic coast by both Catholics and Orthodox. This dialect thus became the basis of the Croatian literary language, and when in the nineteenth century Vuk Karadžić chose the similar dialect of neighbouring

Hercegovina for his Serbian grammar, the basis of a common Serb-Croat language was established. The catholic church and the Vatican, as opposed to the local clergy, remained rather cautious; the unique Slav liturgy of the Croats, known as the glagolitic and written in a variant of the Cyrillic script, had been banned ever since the tenth century and its use was only sanctioned in a few places. It is worth noting that under the present regime, which during the first two decades of its existence was deeply suspicious of the Italianising influence of the Vatican, encouraged interest in glagolitic as part of the Slav inheritance of the Croatian nation.

In the eighteenth and nineteenth centuries two remarkable prelates made outstanding contributions to Croat national identity. Bishop Vrhovac of Zagreb (1751–1827) was a romantic nationalist of a kind familiar in the nineteenth century, and believed that the church should be the guardian and sponsor of Croatia's national culture; he gave moral and financial support to the few young writers who were beginning to use the vernacular language. But his appeal to the clergy of the diocese to collect folk sayings and proverbs, folk songs and old books and manuscripts seems to have met with little response and one must conclude that in this aspect of Croatian nationalism he was before his time.

Bishop Josip Juraj Strossmayer of Djakovo (1815–1905) who was an early exponent of the idea of the unity of the south Slavs, believed that the deepening of true nationalism, both Croatian and Serbian, and true Christianity, both orthodox and catholic, would best be achieved through education and culture. At the same time he was a champion of Croatian national rights, hoping to establish within the framework of the Habsburg empire an autonomous Croatia which would become the nucleus of a south Slav state. He made important contributions to the literary and cultural life of the Croats, and founded the Yugoslav Academy of Arts and Sciences (note the early and deliberate use of the word Yugoslav: Yug=south). In the atmosphere of nineteenth century Catholicism he was virtually alone in the gestures of friendship which he made to the Serbian orthodox church, and he opposed to the last moment the doctrine of papal infallibility at the first Vatican council, knowing the deep offence it would give to the orthodox. Strossmayer's vision carried him far beyond the parochialism of the average Croat prelate, and remains unfulfilled to this day.

STELLA ALEXANDER

Bosnia Hercegovina

Religion in Bosnia Hercegovina, as in Macedonia, has been a divisive factor. In medieval times the population, tyrannised over by an undisciplined nobility, and divided between catholics in the north and west and orthodox in the south and east, turned in great numbers to the Bogomil heresy. This was a dualistic system of belief, similar to that of the Cathars, and was so fiercely persecuted by both the catholics and the orthodox that its adherents welcomed the Turks, who promised them full religious toleration. (The evidence is not entirely conclusive, but this is currently accepted as the most likely theory). A majority of the population converted to Islam; the feudal lords thus retained their privileges and the serfs became free peasants. Those who remained Christian became serfs to the Slav Moslem overlords, who adopted the way of life and mode of dress of the Turks, and became more Moslem than the Ottomans, in many cases rising to the highest positions in the state. They later resisted fiercely all the islamic movements of reform. As the Ottoman empire weakened and was no longer able to control the feudal lords, peasants were ground down and dispossessed, and by the eighteenth century large numbers had returned to Christianity; the orthodox church became the largest religious body in this area.

In the thirteenth century the Franciscans had been invited by the ruling Hungarian duke to settle in the northern part of Bosnia; in the fifteenth century they received a charter from sultan Mohammed II allowing them the free exercise of their religion. They also obtained papal permission to act as parish priests; this privilege which they have never relinquished has been and still is today the cause of lasting friction with the secular clergy and the bishop.

The Turks for whom religion was inseparable from nationality divided their subjects administratively by religion; all the Christians in the territory were put under the jurisdiction of the Greek patriarch in Constantinople. When Austria-Hungary occupied the territory in 1878 there was an influx of catholic officials from all over the empire; in addition a belt of land in the north along the banks of the river Sava was colonised by catholics from other parts of the empire, including Germans, Poles and Czechs, thus adding to the confrontation between eastern and western Christianity. The Serbian inhabitants looked increasingly to Serbia for support, revolutionary and terrorist activities sprang up and culminated in the murder in Sarajevo of the archduke Francis Ferdinand in 1914.

Even this brief and much over-simplified outline makes it clear that the seeds of religious and national tensions were present from the beginning in this mosaic of orthodox and catholic Christians, Bogomil heretics and Moslem converts, with power and status divided among them in complex and unexpected ways

2

The nineteenth century dream of south Slav unity was finally fulfilled at the end of the first world war and the break-up of the Habsburg empire when Yugoslavia (known at first as the kingdom of the Serbs, Croats and Slovenes) was established under a Serbian dynasty. The catholic higher clergy of Croatia, led by archbishop Bauer of Zagreb, were enthusiastic supporters of the union, but it was overshadowed from the start by a fundamental misunderstanding: the Croats looked forward to a union of equal peoples and nations, while the Serbs looked on the new state simply as a further extension of the kingdom of Serbia. Although all religions enjoyed equal legal status, the dynasty was orthodox and advancement in many walks of life favoured the orthodox.

The political history of inter-war Yugoslavia is complex and has no place in this paper but during the 1930s an episode took place which sharpened the tension between the catholic and the orthodox churches and inflamed national feelings particularly among the orthodox. A concordat was negotiated between Yugoslavia and the Vatican to replace the concordats which had regulated relations with the various component parts of the new state. As soon as the terms became known patriarch Gavrilo protested vigorously at what the Serbian orthodox church considered were the special privileges given to the catholic church; he spoke in the name of the Serbian orthodox church as a national institution and accused the government of betraying the last bulwark of Serbianism. Although the government at once promised that the orthodox and all other religious denominations would be accorded the same privileges as the catholic church the pretext was immediately seized on by right-wing opposition Serbian political parties to make common cause with the church in an attempt to overthrow the government. The church excommunicated the orthodox members of the government and all the deputies who had voted in favour of the concordat; feelings ran high, a religious procession of protest was attacked by the police and bishops were manhandled. The uproar was so great that the government backed down and did not proceed to the ratification of the concordat. The catholic bishops in their turn protested that the government had preached the principle of the equality of all faiths but was treating the Serbian orthodox church as though it was in fact the state church. This episode inflamed the antagonism between the Serbs and the Croats which bedevilled the political life of Yugoslavia between the two world wars and left a residue of hatred among Croat extremists which culminated, under the Croatian war-time fascist regime in the brutal murder of two orthodox bishops, the death of a third in a concentration camp and the severe ill-treatment of a fourth.

Yugoslavia was drawn into the second world war in April 1941. Under great pressure the government had in March signed the tripartite pact with the Axis; it was immediately overthrown by a popular coup d'etat led by Serbian officers in the army and enthusiastically supported by the patriarch Gavrilo and his clergy. Hitler was enraged and early in April launched an all-out attack by land and air in which Hungarian and Bulgarian forces joined. The campaign lasted for only eleven days after which resistance disintegrated. Yugoslavia was parcelled out among the Axis powers and their allies Hungary and Bulgaria, and ceased overnight to be a state. The ustaša independent state of Croatia (which included Bosnia Hercegovina, but not the Dalmatian coast which was annexed by Italy, to the bitter disillusionment of the Croats) was set up under German and Italian protection and was welcomed enthusiastically by the catholic hierarchy in Croatia for national rather than ideological reasons; the higher clergy in Slovenia accepted with good grace the Italian occupation of the southern part of Slovenia and were then driven by circumstances into ever closer collaboration with the German forces after the fall of Italy. Serbia was reduced to a small rump state under a puppet government, and the patriarch was arrested by the Germans and spent the war in detention and eventually in German concentration camps.

Macedonia was annexed by the Bulgarians, who in many cases were welcomed with open arms by those who still secretly considered themselves Bulgarians and resented Serbian domination. The Serbian bishops and many of the clergy were expelled and fled to Belgrade, and Bulgarian bishops and priests were introduced into their place. But, as an acute and scholarly observer has written: 'the conduct of the Bulgarian occupiers was sufficiently unpleasant to disillusion most of the population about the advantages of belonging to Bulgaria, while leaving a large enough sediment of pro-Bulgarian and anti-Yugoslav feelings to make difficulties for Marshal Tito in post-war federal Yugoslavia.'[2]

The distrust and suspicion between the catholic and the Serbian orthodox churches of which echoes still persist cannot be understood without a knowledge of the past history, which I have sketched, but above all without realising the extraordinary savagery of the conflict between the catholic Croats and the orthodox Serbs during the war, a savagery which takes one back to the wars of religion in the sixteenth century.

The *ustaše*, who governed the independent state of Croatia, proclaimed their allegiance to the catholic church and were determined to eliminate the Serbs and their church from their territory, although they were prepared to accept the Moslems of Bosnia Hercegovina, since they claimed that the Moslems had originally been Croats. In an episode which shocked even the German general in command great numbers of orthodox Serbs were either massacred, forcibly converted to catholicism or were deported or fled eastward to what remained of Serbia; the structure of the Serbian orthodox church in the new state was destroyed and bishops and priests murdered. At least one catholic bishop in his enthusiasm for Croat independence turned a blind eye, others were appalled but felt themselves helpless, and archbishop Stepinac of Zagreb, leader of the catholic hierarchy, who had welcomed the *ustaše* with open arms, protested to the government with growing anger, but in private; later he attacked the crimes in a number of sermons. Serbian Četnik bands retaliated savagely wherever they could against both the catholic Croats and the Moslems of Bosnia Hercegovina.

The attitude of the catholic bishops is a reflection of the close identification of religion and nationality among the Croats and Serbs. In principle they of course welcomed the prospect of bringing thousands of schismatics freely back to their true mother, the catholic church. But over the centuries this theological concept had been coloured by national and cultural differences. The Croats

[2] E. Barker, *Macedonia and its place in Balkan power politics* (London 1950).

felt themselves to be entirely European, heirs in part of a great catholic empire, while the Serbs belonged to the Byzantine east with its ecclesiastical quarrels and schisms. Under the influence of a romantic Slav nationalism they had become united into one state, which Serbs, as we have seen, tended to look upon as simply an extension of Serbia while the Croats chafed furiously at what they regarded as outrageous Serbian hegemonism. Suddenly the power of Belgrade was removed and the bishops saw within their grasp the intoxicating prospect of a huge influx of converts to be led gently back into the fold, a precious gift for the Holy See (this phrase was actually used).

The reports which bishop Mišić of Mostar (in Hercegovina, where some of the worst atrocities took place) was sending to archbishop Stepinac illustrate this further; after describing in detail the reign of terror,—

> 'men are captured like animals, they are slaughtered . . . living men are thrown off cliffs . . . in a single day 700 schismatics were thrown into their graves . . . six carloads of mothers, together with their children were thrown alive off the precipices . . .' (what echoes of Milton and the slaughtered saints!—

he added:

> If the Lord had given the authorities more understanding to handle the conversions with skill and intelligence . . . the number of Catholics would have grown by at least 500,000/600,000
>
> . . . This can serve neither the Holy Catholic cause nor the Croatian cause . . . we might have emerged into a majority in Bosnia Hercegovina and instead of coveting favours from others be able to dispense them ourselves.[3]

The proselytizing activities of the Franciscans seem to have given a particular zeal to their attacks on the orthodox population. Certainly there was justification for the accusation after the war that many *ustaša* leaders and high officials were trained in the Franciscan seminaries of Bosnia Hercegovina.

Although archbishop Stepinac protested and made many interventions in individual cases, and some of the bishops attempted to discipline the parish priests who collaborated openly with the *ustaše*

[3] R. Patee, *The Case of Cardinal Stepinac* (Milwaukee 1953) pp 390–1, quoted in S. Alexander, *Church and State in Yugoslavia since 1945* (Cambridge 1979) p 32.

and in some cases even took part in the slaughter, the attitude of the church and his own attitude were sufficiently ambiguous to provide a handle after the war to the communist authorities which they used to good effect not only within the country but internationally. This was only the last event in the long history of catholic-orthodox conflict in this region which made any common Christian solidarity against the communists after the war inconceivable; all Serbs, and the Serbian orthodox church, thought that archbishop Stepinac had got his just deserts at his trial and were angered at what they described as his 'posthumous amnesty' when he was buried in 1960 with full honours in Zagreb cathedral.

When the communist partisans took over the government of Yugoslavia at the end of the war, the country, always a poor one, was devastated, the population decimated and torn by the passions of the civil war.

Aside from the economic plight of the country one of the most pressing problems facing the new government was to create a sense of unity in the country. The partisans had made their revolution under the banner of 'brotherhood and unity'—*bratsvo i jedinstvo*—and the unity was no empty slogan; it was essential if the country was to survive. It was communist party policy, adopted during the war, to give full equality to all the constituent nationalities and to their languages (there is simultaneous translation today in the federal parliament) and it was made an extremely serious offence to incite national, racial and religious hatred and intolerance. The new constitution guaranteed freedom of religious belief and practice. This provision was largely ignored in the early years and the churches, especially the catholic and orthodox churches experienced harsh persecution and repression during the decade after the war. The following decade, from the mid-fifties to the mid-sixties was a much quieter time for the catholic church in particular, and after the mid-sixties there was a sharp turn towards liberalisation.

But the question of nationalism which the communists thought would be solved by their enlightened policies refused to go away; as soon as the rigidities and intolerance of the early years lightened, nationalist sentiments reappeared and Croatian nationalism, in particular, went so much further than the authorities considered safe for the unity of the country that in 1972 there was a sudden reversal of the trend to liberalisation and pluralism and a tightening of party discipline through the whole system of 'self-management

socialism'. The unity of the country took on a paramount importance, given urgency by the realisation that Tito was growing old
and his charismatic leadership must soon disappear. The authorities
realised the importance of enlisting the loyalty and support of
believers, but were determined to keep the churches as institutions
in their place. Simultaneously the churches were gaining confidence; the position of the catholic church in particular had been
transformed by the papacy of John XXIII and the second Vatican
council, diplomatic relations had been restored between the Yugoslav government and the Vatican, and president Tito and his wife
were received by pope Paul VI during an official visit to Rome.

The danger which the government foresaw was that the churches
would set themselves up as the embodiment of the nation and its
soul, the guardians of its 'Serbianism' or 'Croatianism'. Attacks on
this subject in the secular press began as early as 1969 and during
the latter '70s became very frequent; they continue unabated today.

The case of Macedonia is different; here, the concept of a separate
Macedonian nationalism—for the moment at any rate—draws the
Macedonians closer to the Yugoslav federation. At the end of the
war a Macedonian republic was established as a constituent
member of the Yugoslav republic, accompanied by an upsurge of
joyful nationalist sentiment. A national language was formed by
adopting one of the main regional dialects (which already had a
literary tradition) and it became evident that the nationalist ground-
swell was accompanied by a longing for a national church, one of
the validating marks of a true nation. (It is difficult to establish how
far this was a widespread grass-roots feeling, or whether it was
largely confined to the clergy. Among them, it was certainly
genuine). The Serbian bishops had all been expelled in 1941 and the
new government had refused them permission to return. A long
struggle now began between the Serbian patriarchate in Belgrade,
fighting desperately to preserve what it regarded as Serbian unity as
much as the unity of the Serbian orthodox church, and the
Macedonian clergy, enthusiastically backed by the Macedonian
republican authorities who understood that a national church
would strengthen internal solidarity and would give Macedonia a
useful weapon to resist Bulgarian claims that the inhabitants of the
territory were Bulgarian. The Macedonian clergy finally won the
battle and after nine years of uneasy 'autonomy' to which the
Serbian patriarchate had reluctantly agreed, proclaimed their own

autocephaly in 1967. The Serbian orthodox church considers that the schism has weakened it and undermined its claim to represent the whole Serbian nation (since they continue to regard the Macedonians as Serbs) and it is convinced—overtly outside Yugoslavia and in Yugoslavia always implicitly,—that the Macedonian orthodox church is simply a creature of the regime. I do not believe that this conviction is justified; it seems to me a genuine and historically predictable expression of Macedonian nationalism. Its support by the federal government strengthens Macedonia's loyalty to the federation and in this sense only can one say that the church is hand in glove with the authorities.

Today the Macedonian orthodox church is a state church in all but name and its archbishop is a public personality; it receives substantial grants of money from the government. It has still not been recognised by the ecumenical patriarch or any other orthodox church, but it is content to wait, remembering that other local orthodox churches, the Bulgarian and the Greek, for example, had to wait many decades before their independence was recognised. Its greatest danger, a spiritual one, lies in the rather suffocating embrace of the republican authorities.

We come finally to the Slav Moslems of Bosnia Hercegovina, who as we have seen, form a distinct cultural group. In the interwar years they played an important political role in Yugoslavia and during the war their allegiance was divided. Some Moslems joined the partisans, rejecting the claim of the Croatian *ustaša* state to be a country of two religions, Catholic and Moslem, but many others, feeling themselves Croat rather than Serb gave their allegiance to the *ustaše*. After the war their ambiguous position continued to cause them uneasiness; many began to describe themselves as Yugoslav by nationality. But the Yugoslav authorities very early gave up the attempt to impose an over-all Yugoslav national sentiment, recognising that it was an artificial, intellectual concept without ethnic or religious basis, and for some years most Slav Moslems described themselves as either Serbs or Croats. Finally the solution was adopted of officially acknowledging the existence of a sixth, Moslem, nationality to add to the already existing five nations in the federation; the category Moslem had already appeared in the 1961 census and in 1968 their separate nationhood was confirmed by the government. This solution was eagerly grasped by a large number of the inhabitants of Bosnia Hercegovina and was reflected in the 1971 census, when the number of those describing themselves as 'Yugoslav' dropped almost to vanishing point, the numbers of Serbs and Croats also diminished and the number of Moslems rose dramatically.

The world-wide islamic revival, added to the resurgence of nationalism has given a strong impetus to Slav Moslem feelings of nationality. Religious and secular elements are closely entwined in these feelings and this poses a dilemma for the authorities. It is ideologically difficult for them to accept the inescapable religious element in Moslem nationhood and they have only partly succeeded in avoiding the problem by stressing the concept of a Moslem culture in which religion is only one element.[4] The upsurge of national feeling has been accompanied by a religious revival which has touched even Moslem intellectuals. Efforts are being made to raise the educational level of the *hodžas* and a higher theological school has been opened to give the equivalent of a university degree; a *medresa* for girls—a revolutionary step for these religiously conservative men—was also established; Saudi Arabia and other islamic states sent generous financial contributions. The Iranian revolution appears also to have caught the imagination of some of the more extreme elements and Khomeini's name has appeared in slogans scribbled on walls. Moslem religious and cultural institutions are accused of setting themselves up as the only legitimate representatives of the national identity of Moslems, precisely the same accusation which has been made against the catholic and orthodox churches in Croatia and Serbia.

It is too soon to do more than note this latest example of the interaction of religion and national identity in Yugoslavia; but it is already clear that the authorities intend to keep it under strict control.

And so, looking back over the complicated intertwining of nationalism and religion which I have tried to trace, one might come to a rather paradoxical conclusion. Religion which in the beginning nurtured a sense of national identity as one way of resisting assimilation by alien powers has been overtaken by the growth of nationalism and has itself been weakened by the secularisation of present-day society; today there can be no doubt

---

[4] G. Schöpflin, 'Nationalism as a disintegrative factor in Yugoslavia', paper delivered at the School of Slavonic and East European Studies, University of London, 11 June 1980.

which is the stronger force. It is nationalism which feeds religious feeling, while the churches cling desperately to their role as guardians of the soul of the nation. This has recently been vividly illustrated in Croatia where the Catholic church has been celebrating thirteen hundred years of catholicism (dating from the establishment of the first bishopric at Nin in the seventh century) and the eleven hundredth anniversary of Croatia's unbroken link with Rome, (dating from the pope's letter to Branimir in 879) with processions and pilgrimages. It is difficult to see how these two historical events are linked in any except a romantic sense to the more recent history of the Croats, but the church has attempted to transform them into a symbol of the identity of catholicism with the Croatian people.

Professor Bohdan Bociurkiew of Carlton University, Ontario, who is working on a comparative study of church-state relations in east European communist countries has recently suggested that scholars working in this field tend to give too much emphasis to Marxist-Leninist ideology when dealing with the persecution of churches under communist regimes and not enough to political cultural and social factors, in particular nationalism and nationality. He suggests that nationalism is in fact more important than ideology and that everywhere communist regimes fear the identification of national feelings with religion and the churches. I am convinced that this is particularly true of Yugoslavia. This is not to deny the strong anti-religious feelings of many Yugoslav communists, particularly among the older generation, some of them with little education, who came into the party through the war-time partisans. But this is a dying phenomenon. The present generation is secularised, like their contemporaries in the west, and those among them who are religious have often been caught up in the swell of charismatic renewal. The catholic church in particular seems to have perceived this and is beginning to shift its ground from nationalism to 'human rights'.

The Yugoslav communists have reason to fear the disintegrative force of unfettered nationalism, and as long as the churches are associated with this, the regime will continue to attack them. The churches' real challenge to Marxist ideology lies elsewhere.

London

ABBREVIATIONS

AASRP   *Associated Archaeological Societies Reports and Papers*
AAWG   *Abhandlungen der Akademie [Gesellschaft to 1942] der*
     Wissenschaften zu Göttingen, (Göttingen, (Göttingen 1843–)
AAWL   *Abhandlungen der Akademie der Wissenschaften und der Literatur*
     (Mainz 1950–)
ABAW   *Abhandlungen der Bayerischen Akademie der Wissenchaften*
     (Munich 1835–)
Abh   Abhundlung
Abt   Abteilung
ACO   *Acta Conciliorum Oecumenicorum,* ed E. Schwartz
     (Berlin/Leipzig 1914–40)
ACW   *Ancient Christian Writers,* ed J. Quasten and J. C. Plumpe
     (Westminster, Maryland/London 1946–)
ADAW   *Abhandlungen der Deutschen* [till 1944 *Preussischen*] *Akademie*
     der Wissenschaften zu Berlin (Berlin 1815–)
AF   *Analecta Franciscana,* 10 vols (Quaracchi 1885–1941)
AFH   *Archivum Franciscanum Historicum* (Quaracchi/Rome 1908–)
AFP   *Archivum Fratrum Praedicatorum* (Rome 1931–)
AHP   *Archivum historiae pontificae* (Rome 1963–)
AHR   *American Historical Review* (New York 1895–)
AKG   *Archiv für Kulturgeschichte* (Leipzig/Münster/Cologne 1903–)
AKZ   *Arbeiten zur kirchlichen Zeitgeschichte*
ALKG   H. Denifle and F. Ehrle, *Archiv für Literatur- und Kirchengeschichte*
     des Mittelalters, 7 vols (Berlin/Freiburg 1885–1900)
Altaner   B. Altaner, *Patrologie: Leben, Schriften und Lehre der Kirchenväter*
     (5 ed Freiburg 1958)
AM   L. Wadding, *Annales Minorum,* 8 vols (Rome 1625–54);
     2 ed, 25 vols (Rome 1731–1886); 3 ed, vol 1–, (Quaracchi
     1931–)
An Bol   *Analecta Bollandiana* (Brussels 1882–)
Annales   *Annales: Economies, Sociétés, Civilisations* (Paris 1946–)
Ant   *Antonianum* (Rome 1926–)
APC   *Proceedings and Ordinances of the Privy Council 1386–1542.*
     ed Sir Harris Nicolas, 7 vols (London 1834–7.
     —*Acts of the Privy Council of England 1542–1629,* 44 vols
     (London 1890–1958.
     —*Acts of the Privy Council of England, Colonial Series (1613–1783)*
     5 vols (London 1908–12)
AR   *Archivum Romanicum* (Geneva/Florence 1917–41.)
ARG   *Archiv für Reformationsgeschichte*
     (Berlin/Leipzig/Gütersloh 1903–)
ASAW   *Abhandhungen der Sächsischen Akademie* [*Gesellschaft* to 1920] *der*
     Wissenschaften zu Leipzig (Leipzig 1850–)
ASB   *Acta Sanctorum Bollandiana* (Brussels etc 1643–)
ASC   *Anglo Saxon Chronicle*
ASI   *Archivio storico Italiano* (Florence 1842–)
ASL   *Archivio storico Lombardo,* 1–62 (Milan 1874–1935);
     ns 1–10 (Milan 1936–47)
ASOC   *Analecta Sacri Ordinis Cisterciensis* [*Analecta Cisterciensia*
     since 1965] (Rome 1945–)

ASOSB   *Acta Sanctorum Ordinis Sancti Benedicti*, ed. L'D'Achery and
         J. Mabillon (Paris 1668–1701)
ASP   *Archivio della Società* [*Deputazione* from 1935]
         Romana di Storia Patria (Rome 1878–1934. 1935–   )
ASR   *Archives de Sociologie des Religions* (Paris 1956–   )
AV   Authorised Version
AV   *Archivio Veneto* (Venice 1871–   ): [1891–1921, *Nuovo Archivio
         Veneto*; 1922–6. *Archivio Veneto-Tridentino*]
B   *Byzantion* (Paris/Brussels 1924–   )
Bale, *Catalogus* John Bale, *Scriptorum Illustrium Maioris Brytanniae Catalogus*,
         2 parts (Basel 1557. 1559)
Bale, *Index* John Bale, *Index Britanniae Scriptorum*, ed R. L. Poole and
         M. Bateson (Oxford 1902) *Anecdota Oxeniensia*, medieval and
         modern series 9
Bale,   John Bale, *Illustrium Maioris Britanniae Scriptorum Summarium*
   Summarium (Ipswich 1548, reissued Wesel 1549.
BEC   *Bibliothèque de l'Ecole des Chartes* (Paris 1839–   )
Beck   H-G Beck, *Kirche und theologische Literatur im byzantinischen Reich*
         (Munich 1959)
BEFAR   *Bibliothèque des ècoles francaises d'Athènes
         et Rome* (Paris 1876–   )
BEHE   *Bibliothèque de l'Ecole des Hautes Etudes: Sciences Philologiques et
         Historiques* (Paris 1869–   )
Bernard E. Bernard, *Catalogi Librorum Manuscriptorum Angliae et Hiberniae*
         (Oxford 1697)
BF   *Byzantinische Forschungen* (Amsterdam 1966–   )
BHG   *Bibliotheca Hagiographica Graeca*, ed F. Halkin, 3 vols + 1 (3 ed.
         Brussels 1957, 1969)
BHI   *Bibliotheca historica Italica*, ed A. Ceruti, 4 vols
         (Milan 1876–85), 2 series, 3 vols (Milan 1901–33)
BHL   *Bibliotheca Hagiographica Latina*, 2 vols + 1 (Brussels 1898–1901. 1911)
BHR   *Bibliothèque d'Humanisme et Renaissance* (Paris/Geneva 1941–   )
Bibl Ref *Bibliography of the Reform 1450–1648, relating to the United Kingdom.
         and Ireland*, ed Derek Baker for 1955–70 (Oxford 1975)
BIHR   *Bulletin of the Institute of Historical Research* (London 1923–   )
BISIMEAM *Bullettino dell'istituto storico italiano per il medio eve a archivio
         muratoriano* (Rome 1886–   )
BJRL   *Bulletin of the John Rylands Library* (Manchester 1903–   )
BL   British Library, London
BM   British Museum, London
BN   Bibliothèque Nationale, Paris
Bouquet M. Bouquet, *Recueil des historiens des Gaules et de la France.
         Rerum gallicarum et francicarum scriptores*, 24 vols
         (Paris 1738–1904); new ed L. Delisle, 1–19 (Paris 1868–80)
BQR   *British Quarterly Review* (London 1845–86)
Broadmead *The Records of a Church of Christ, meeting in Broadmead,
   Records Bristol 1640–87*, HKS (London 1848)
BS   *Byzantinoslavica* (Prague 1929–   )
Bucer, *Deutsche* Martin Bucers *Deutsche Schriften*, ed R. Stupperich and others
   Schriften (Gütersloh/Paris 1960–   )
Bucer, *Opera* Martini Buceri *Opera Latina*, ed F. Wendel and others
   Latina (Paris/Gütersloh 1955–   )

Bull Franc	*Bullarium Franciscanum*, vols 1–4 ed J. H. Sbaralea (Rome 1759–68) vols 5–7 ed. C. Eubel (Rome 1898–1904), new series vols 1–3 ed U. Höntemann and J. M. Pou y Marti (Quaracchi 1929–49)
BZ	*Byzantinische Zeitschrift* (Leipzig 1892–)
CA	*Cahiers Archéologiques. Fin de L'Antiquité et Moyen-âge* (Paris 1945–)
CaF	*Cahiers de Fanjeaux* (Toulouse 1966–)
CAH	*Cambridge Ancient History* (Cambridge 1923–39)
CalRev	Calumy Revised, ed A. G. Mathews (Oxford 1934)
Ca/LP	*Calendar of the Letters and Papers (Foreign and Domestic) of the Reign of Henry VIII*, 21 vols in 35 parts (London 1864–1932)
CalSPD	*Calendar of State Papers: Domestic* (London 1856–)
CalSPF	*Calendar of State Papers: Foreign*, 28 vols (London 1861–1950)
Calvin, *Opera*	*Io annis Calvini Opera Quae Supersunt Omnia*, ed G. Baumand others *Corpus Reformatorum*, 59 vols (Brunswick/Berlin 1863–1900)
Canivez	J. M. Canivez, *Statuta capitulorum generalium ordinis cisterciensis ab anno 1116 ad annum 1768*, 8 vols (Louvain 1933–41)
Cardwell, *Documentary Annals*	*Documentary Annals of the Reformed Church of England*, ed E. Cardwell, 2 vols (Oxford 1839)
Cardwell, *Synodalia*	*Synodalia*, ed E. Cardwell, 2 vols (Oxford 1842)
CC	*Corpus Christianorum* (Turnhol 1952–)
CF	*Classical Folia*, [*Folia* 1946–59]. (New York 1960–)
CGOH	*Cartulaire Générale de l'Ordre des Hospitaliers de St.-Jean de Jerusalem (1100–1310)*, ed J. Delaville Le Roulx, 4 vols (Paris 1894–1906)
CH	*Church History* (New York/Chicago 1932–*
CHB	*Cambridge History of the Bible*
CHistS	*Church History Society* (London 1886–92)
CHJ	*Cambridge Historical Journal* (Cambridge 1925–57)
CIG	*Corpus Inscriptionum Graecarum*, ed A. Boeckh, J. Franz, E. Curtius, A. Kirchhoff, 4 vols (Berlin 1825–77)
CIL	*Corpus Inscriptionum Latinarum* (Berlin 1863–)
Cîteaux	*Cîteaux: Commentarii Cisterciensis* (Westmalle 1950–)
CMH	*Cambridge Medieval History*
CModH	*Cambridge Modern History*
COCR	*Collectanea Ordinis Cisterciensium Reformatorum* (Rome/Westmalle 1934–)
COD	*Conciliorum oecumenicorum decreta* (3 ed Bologna 1973)
Coll Franc	*Collectanea Franciscana* (Assisi/Rome 1931–)
CR	*Corpus Reformatorum*, ed C. G. Bretschneider and others (Halle etc. 1834–)
CS	*Cartularium Saxonicum*, ed W. de G. Birch, 3 vols (London 1885–93)
CSCO	*Corpus Scriptorum Christianorum Orientalium* (Paris 1903–)
CSEL	*Corpus Scriptorum Ecclesiasticorum Latinorum* (Vienna 1866–)
CSer	*Camden Series* (London 1838–)
CSHByz	*Corpus Scriptorum Historiae Byzantinae* (Bonn 1828–97)
CYS	*Canterbury and York Society* (London 1907–)
DA	*Deutsches Archiv für* [*Geschichte*, –.EIMAR 1937–43] *die Erforschung des Mittelalters* (Cologne/Graz 1950–)

DACL	*Dictionnaire d'Archéologie chrétienne et de Liturgie*, ed F. Cabrol and H. Leclercq (Paris 1924–)
DDC	*Dictionnaire de Droit Canonique*, ed R. Naz (Paris 1935–)
DHGE	*Dictionnaire d'Histoire et de Géographie ecclésiastiques*. ed A. Baudrillart and others (Paris 1912–)
DNB	*Dictionary of National Biography* (London 1885–)
DOP	*Dumbarton Oaks Papers* (Cambridge, Mass., 1941–)
DR	F. Dölger, *Regesten der Kaiserurkunden des oströmischen Reiches (Corpus der griechischen Urkunden des Mittelalters und der neuern Zeit*, Reihe A, Abt I), 5 vols: 1 (565–1025):2.1025–1204);3 (1204–1282); 4(1282–1341); 5(1341–1543) (Munich/Berlin 1924–65)
DRev	*Downside Review* (London 1880–)
DSAM	*Dictionnaire de Spiritualité, Ascétique et Mystique*, ed M. Viller (Paris 1932–)
DTC	*Dictionnaire de Théologie Catholique*, ed A. Vacant, E. Mangenot, E. Amann, 15 vols (Paris 1903–50)
EcHr	*Economic History Review* (London 1927–)
EEBS	(Athens 1924–)
EETS	*Early English Text Society*
EF	*Etudes Franciscaines* (Paris 1899–1938, ns 1950–)
EHD	*English Historical Documents* (London 1953–)
EHR	*English Historical Review* (London 1886–)
Ehrhard	A. Ehrhard, *Uberlieferung und Bestand der hagiographischen und homiletischen Literatur der griechischen Kirche von den Anfängen bis zum Ende des 16.Jh*, 3 vols in 4. *TU* 50–2 . (= 4 series 5–7) 11 parts (Leipzig 1936–52)
Emden (O)	A. B. Emden, *A Biographical Register of the University of Oxford to 1500*, 3 vols (London 1957–9); *1500–40* (1974)
Emden (C)	A. B. Emden, *A Biographical Register of the University of Cambridge to 1500* (London 1963)
EO	*Echos d'Orient* (Constantinople/Paris 1897–1942)
ET	English translation
EYC	*Early Yorkshire Charters*, ed W. Farrer and C. T. Clay, 12 vols (Edinburgh/Wakefield 1914–65.
FGH	*Die Fragmente der griechischen Historiker*, ed F. Jacoby (Berlin 1926–30)
FM	*Histoire de l'église depuis les origines jusqu'à nos jours*, ed A. Fliche and V. Martin (Paris 1935–)
Foedera	*Foedera, conventiones, litterae et cuiuscunque generis acta publica inter reges Angliae et alios quosvis imperatores, reges, pontifices, principes vel communitates*, ed T. Rymer and R. Sanderson, 20 vols (London 1704–35), 3 ed G. Holmes, 10 vols (The Hague 1739–45), re-ed 7 vols (London 1816–69)
Franc Stud	*Franciscan Studies* (St Bonaventure, New York 1924–, ns 1941–)
Fredericq	P. Fredericq. *Corpus documentorum inquisitionis haereticae pravitatis Neerlandicae*, 3 vols (Ghent 1889–93)
FStn	*Franzikanische Studien* (Münster/Werl 1914–)
GalC	*Gallia Christiana*, 16 vols (Paris 1715–1865)
Gangraena	T. Edwards, *Gangraena*, 3 parts (London 1646)
GCS	*Die griechischen christlichen Schriftsteller der erste drei Jahrhunderte* 1897–)
Gee and Hardy	*Documents illustrative of English Church History* ed H. Gee and W. J. Hardy (London 1896)

ABBREVIATIONS

GEEB	R. Janin, *La géographie ecclésiastique de l'empire byzantin*;
CEM	1, *Le siège de Constantinople et le patriarcat oecumenique*, pt 3 *Les églises et les monastères* (Paris 1953);
EMGCB	2, *Les églises et les monastères des grands centres byzantins* (Paris 1975) (series discontinued)
Golubovich	Girolamo Golubovich, *Biblioteca bio-bibliografica della Terra Santa e dell' oriente francescano:*
	series 1, *Annali*, 5 vols (Quaracchi 1906–23)
	series 2, *Documenti* 14 vols (Quaracchi 1921–33)
	series 3, *Documenti* (Quaracchi 1928–)
	series 4, *Studi*, ed M. Roncaglia (Cairo 1954–)
Grumel,	V. Grumel, *Les Regestes des Actes du Patriarcat de Constantinople,*
Regestes	1: *Les Actes des Patriarches*, I: 381–715; II: 715–1043; III: 1043–1206 (Socii Assumptionistae Chalcedonenses, 1931. 1936. 1947)
Grundmann	H. Grundmann, *Religiöse Bewegungen im Mittelalter* (Berlin 1935. 2 ed Darmstadt 1970)
Guignard	P. Guignard, *Les monuments primitifs de la règle cistercienne* (Dijon 1878)
HBS	*Henry Bradshaw Society* (London/Canterbury 1891–)
HE	*Historia Ecclesiastica*
HistSt	*Historical Studies* (Melbourne 1940–)
HJ	*Historical Journal* (Cambridge 1958–)
HJch	*Historisches Jarhbuch der Görres Gesellschaft* (Cologne 1880–, Munich 1950–)
JKS	*Hanserd Knollys Society* (London 1847–)
HL	C. J. Hefele and H. Leclercq, *Histore des Conciles*, 10 vols (Paris 1907–35)
HMC	*Historical Manuscripts Commission*
Holzapfel,	H. Holzapfel, *Handbuch der Geschichte des Franziskanerordens*
Handbuch	(Freiburg 1908)
Hooker, *Works*	*The Works of . . . Mr. Richard Hooker*, ed J. Keble, 7 ed rev R. W. Church and F. Paget, 3 vols (Oxford 1888)
Houedene	*Chronica Magistri Rogeri de Houedene*, ed W. Stubbs, 4 vols. *RS* 51 (London 1868–71)
HRH	*The Heads of Religious Houses, England and Wales, 943–1216* ed D. Knowles, C. N. L. Brooke, V. C. M. London (Cambridge 1972)
HS	*Hispania sacra* (Madrid 1948–)
HTR	*Harvard Theological Review* (New York/Cambridge, Mass., 1908–)
HZ	*Historische Zeitschrift* (Munich 1859–)
IER	*Irish Ecclesiastical Record* (Dublin 1864–)
IGLS	*Inscriptions greques et latines de la Syrie*, ed L. Jalabert, R. Mouterde and others, 7 vols (Paris 1929–70) in progress
IR	*Innes Review* (Glasgow 1950–)
JAC	*Jahrbuch für Antike und Christentum* (Münster-im-Westfalen 1958–)
Jaffé	*Regesta Pontificum Romanorum ab condita ecclesia ad a. 1198*, 2 ed S. Lowenfeld, F. Kaltenbrunner, P. Ewald, 2 vols (Berlin 1885–8, repr Graz 1958)
JBS	*Journal of British Studies* (Hartford, Conn., 1961–)
JEH	*Journal of Ecclesiastical History* (London 1950–)

ABBREVIATIONS

JFHS	*Journal of the Friends Historical Society* (London/Philadelphia 1903–)
JHI	*Journal of the History of Ideas* (London 1940–)
JHSChW	*Journal of the Historical Society of the Church In Wales* (Cardiff 1947–)
JIntH	*Journal of Interdisciplinary History* (Cambridge, Mass., 1970–)
JLW	*Jahrbuch für Liturgiewissenschaft* (Münster-im-Westfalen 1921–41)
JMH	*Journal of Modern History* (Chicago 1929–)
JMedH	*Journal of Medieval History* (Amsterdam 1975–)
JRA	*Journal of Religion in Africa* (Leiden 1967–)
JRH	*Journal of Religious History* (Sidney 1960–)
JRS	*Journal of Roman Studies* (London 1910–)
JRSAI	*Journal of the Royal Society of Antiquaries of Ireland* (Dublin 1871–)
JSArch	*Journal of the Society of Archivists* (London 1955–)
JTS	*Journal of Theological Studies* (London 1899–)
Kemble	*Codex Diplomaticus Aevi Saxonici*, ed J. M. Kemble (London 1839–48)
Knowles, *MO*	David Knowles, *The Monastic Order in England, 943–1216*, (2 ed Cambridge 1963)
Knowles, *RO*	, *The Religious Orders in England*, 3 vols (Cambridge 1948–59)
Knox, *Works*	*The Works of John Knox*, ed D. Laing, Bannatyne Club/Wodrow Society, 6 vols (Edinburgh 1846–64)
Laurent, *Regestes*	V. Laurent, *Les Registes des Actes du Patriarcat de Constantinople*, I: *Les Actes des Patriarches*, IV: *Les Regestes de 1208 à 1309* (Paris 1971)
Le Neve	John Le Neve, *Fasti Ecclesiae Anglicanae 1066–1300*, rev and exp Diana E. Greenway, 1, St Pauls (London 1968); 2, Monastic Cathedrals (1971) *Fasti Ecclesiae Anglicanae 1300–1541* rev and exp H. P. F. King, J. M. Horn. B. Jones, 12 vols (London 1962–7) *Fasti Ecclesiae Anglicanae 1541–1857* rev and exp. J. M. Horn, D. M. Smith, 1, St Pauls (1969); 2, Chichester (1972); 3, Canterbury, Rochester, Winchester (1974); 4, York (1975)
Lloyd, *Formularies of faith*	*Formularies of Faith Put Forth by Authority during the Reign of Henry VIII*, ed. C. Lloyd (Oxford 1825)
LRS	*Lincoln Record Society*
LQR	*Law Quarterly Review* (London 1885–)
LThK	*Lexon für Theologie und Kirche*, ed J. Höfer and K. Rahnes (2 ed Freiburg-im-Breisgau 1957–)
LW	*Luther's Works*, ed J. Pelikan and H. T. Lehman, American edition (St. Louis/Philadelphia, 1955–)
MA	*Monasticon Anglicanum*, ed R. Dodsworth and W. Dugdale, 3 vols (London 1655–73); new ed J. Caley, H. Ellis, B. Bandinel 6 vols in 8 (London 1817–30)
Mansi	J. D. Mansi, *Sacrorum conciliorum nova et amplissima collectio*, 31 vols (Florence/Venice 1757–98); new impression and continuation, ed L. Petit and J. B. Martin, 60 vols (Paris 1899–1927)
Martène and Durand	E. Martène and U. Durand, *Veterum Scriptorum et Monumentorum Historicorum, Dogmaticorum, Moralium Amplissima Collectio*,

Collectio	9 vols (Paris 1729)
Thesaurus	*Thesaurus Novus Anedotorum*, 5 vols (Paris 1717)
Voyage	*Voyage Litteraire de Deux Religieux Benedictins de la Congregation de Saint Maur*, 2 vols (Paris 1717. 1724)
MedA	*Medium Aevum* (Oxford 1932–)
Mendola	*Atti della Settimana di Studio*, 1959– (Milan 1962–)
MF	*Miscellanea Francescana* (Foligno/Rome 1886–)
MGH	*Monumenta Germaniae Historica inde ab a.c. 500 usque ad a. 1500*, ed G. H. Pertz and others (Berlin, Hanover 1826–)
AA	*Auctores Antiquissimi*
Ant	*Antiquitates*
Briefe	*Epistolae 2: Die Briefe de Deutschen Kaiserzeit*
Cap	*Leges 2: Leges in Quart 2: Captiularia regum Francorum*
CM	*Chronica Minora 1–3* (=*AA9. 11. 13*) ws Rh. Mommsen (1892 1894. 1898 repr 1961)
Conc	*Leges 2: Leges in Quart 3: Concilia*
Const	*4: Constitutiones et acta publica imperatorum et regum*
DC	*Deutsche Chroniken*
Dip	*Diplomata in folio*
Epp	*Epistolae 1 in Quart*
Epp Sel	*4: Epistolae Selectae*
FIG	*Leges 3: Fontes Iuris Germanici Antique*, new series
FIGUS	*4: , in usum scholarum*
Form	*2: Leges in Quart 5: Formulae Merovingici et Karolini Aevi*
GPR	*Gesta Pontificum Romanorum*
Leges	*Leges in folio*
Lib	*Libelli de lite*
LM	*Ant 3: Libri Memoriales*
LNG	*Leges 2: Leges in Quart 1: Leges nationum Germanicarum*
Necr	*Ant 2: Necrologia Germaniae*
Poet	*1: Poetae Latini Medii Aevi*
Quellen	*Quellen zur Geistesgeschichte des Mittelalters*
Schriften	*Schriften der Monumenta Germaniae Historica*
SRG	*Scriptores rerum germanicarum in usum scholarum*
SRG ns	*, new series*
SRL	*Scriptores rerum langobardicarum et italicarum*
SRM	*Scriptores rerum merovingicarum*
SS	*Scriptores*
SSM	*Staatschriften des späteren Mittelalters*
MIOG	*Mitteilungen des Instituts für österreichische Geschichtsforschung* (Graz/Cologne 1880–)
MM	F. Miklosich and J. Müller, *Acta et Diplomata Graeca medii aevi sacra et profana*, 6 vols (Vienna 1860–90)
Moorman, *History*	J. R. H. Moorman, *A History of the Franciscan Order from its origins to the year 1517* (Oxford 1968)
More, *Works*	*The Complete Works of St Thomas More*, ed R. S. Sylvester and others Yale edition (New Haven/London 1963–)
Moyen Age	*Le moyen âge. Revue d'histoire et de philologie* (Paris 1888–)
MRHEW	David Knowles and R. N. Hadcock, *Medieval Religious Houses, England and Wales* (2 ed London 1971)
MRHI	A. Gwynn and R. N. Hadcock, *Medieval Religious Houses, Ireland* (London 1970)

MRHS	Ian B. Cowan and David E. Easson, *Medieval Religious Houses, Scotland* (2 ed London 1976)
MS	Manuscript
MStn	*Mittelalterliche Studien* (Stuttgart 1966–)
Muratori	L. A. Muratori, *Rerum italicarum scriptores*, 25 vols (Milan 1723–51); new ed G. Carducci and V. Fiorini, 34 vols in 109 fasc (Città di Castello/Bologna 1900–)
NCE	*New Catholic Encyclopedia*, 15 vols (New York 1967)
NCModH	*New Cambridge Modern History*, 14 vols (Cambridge 1957–70)
nd	no date
NEB	*New English Bible*
NF	Neue Folge
NH	*Northern History* (Leeds 1966–)
ns	new series
NS	New Style
Numen	*Numen: International Review for the History of Religions* (Leiden 1954–)
OCP	*Orientalia Christiana Periodica* (Rome 1935–)
ODCC	*Oxford Dictionary of the Christian Church*, ed F. L. Cross (Oxford 1957), 2 ed with E. A. Livingstone (1974)
OED	*Oxford English Dictionary*
OMT	*Oxford Medieval Texts*
OS	Old Style
OHS	*Oxford Historical Society*
PBA	*Proceedings of the British Academy*
PG	*Patrologia Graeca*, ed J. P. Migne, 161 vols (Paris 1857–66)
PhK	Philosophisch-historisch Klasse
PL	*Patrologia Latina*, ed J. P. Migne, 217 +4 index vols (Paris 1841–64)
Plummer, Bede	*Venerabilis Baedae Opera Historica*, ed C. Plummer (Oxford 1896)
PO	*Patrologia Orientalis*, ed J. Graffin and F. Nau (Paris 1903–)
Potthast	*Regesta Pontificum Romanorum inde ab a. post Christum natum 1198 ad a. 304*, ed A. Potthast, 2 vols (1874–5 repr Graz 1957)
PP	*Past and Present* (London 1952–)
PPTS	*Palestine Pilgrims' Text Society*, 13 vols and index (London 1896–1907)
PRIA	*Proceedings of the Royal Irish Academy* (Dublin 1836–)
PRO	Public Record Office
PS	Parker Society (Cambridge 1841–55)
PW	*Paulys Realencyklopädie der klassischen Altertumswissenschaft*, new ed G. Wissowa and W. Kroll (Stuttgard 1893–)
QFIAB	*Quellen und Forschungen aus italienischen Archiven und Bibliotheken* (Rome 1897–)
RAC	*Reallexikon für Antike und Christentum*, ed T. Klauser (Stuttgart 1941)
RB	*Revue Bénédictine* (Maredsous 1884–)
RE	*Realencyclopädie für protestantische Theologie*, ed A. Hauck, 24 vols (3 ed Leipzig, 1896–1913)
REB	*Revue des Etudes Byzantines* (Bucharest/Paris 1946–)
RecS	Record Series
RGG	*Die Religion in Geschichte und Gegenwart*, 6 vols (Tübingen 1927–32)
RH	*Revue historique* (Paris 1876–)

RHC,   *Recueil des Historiens des Croisades*, ed Académie des Inscriptions et Belles-Lettres (Paris 1841–1906)

  Arm   *Historiens Arméniens*, 2 vols (1869–1906)
  Grecs   *Historiens Grecs*, 2 vols (1875–81)
  Lois   *Lois, Les Assises de Jérusalem*, 2 vols (1841–3)
  Occ   *Historiens Occidentaux*, 5 vols (1844–95)
  Or   *Historiens Orientaux*, 5 vols (1872–1906)

RHD   *Revue d'histoire du droit* (Haarlem, Gronigen 1923–)

RHDFE   *Revue historique du droit français et étranger* (Paris 1922–)

RHE   *Revue d'Histoire Ecclésiastique* (Louvain 1900–)

RHEF   *Revue d'Histoire de l'Englise de France* (Paris 1910–)

RHR   *Revue de l'Histoire des Religions* (Paris 1880–)

RR   *Regesta Regum Anglo-Normannorum*, ed H. W. C. Davis, H. A. Cronne, Charles Johnson, R. H. C. Davis, 4 vols (Oxford 1913–69)

RS   *Rerum Brittanicarum Medii Aevi Scriptores*, 99 vols (London 1858–1911). *Rolls Series*

RSCI   *Rivista di storia della chiesa in Italia* (Rome 1947–)

RSR   *Revue des sciences religieuses* (Strasbourg 1921–)

RStI   *Rivista storica italiana* (Naples 1884–)

RTAM   *Recherches de théologie ancienne et médiévale* (Louvain 1929–)

RV   Revised Version

Sitz   *Sitzungsberichte*

SA   *Studia Anselmiana* (Roma 1933–)

sa   *sub anno*

SBAW   *Sitzungsberichte der bayerischen Akademie der Wissenschaften*, PhK (Munich 1871–)

SCH   *Studies in Church History* (London 1964–)

ScHR   *Scottish Historical Review* (Edinburgh/Glasgow 1904–)

SCR   *Scources chrétiennes*, ed H. de Lubac and J. Daniélou (Paris 1941–)

SF   *Studi Francescani* (Florence 1914–)

SGra   *Studia Gratiana*, ed J. Forchielli and A. M. Stickler (Bologna 1953–)

SGre   *Studi Gregoriani*, ed G. Borino, 7 vols (Rome 1947–61)

SMon   *Studia Monastica* (Montserrat, Barcelona 1959–)

Speculum   *Speculum, A Journal of Medieval Studies* (Cambridge, Mass. 1926–)

SpicFr   *Spicilegium Friburgense* (Freiburg 1957–)

SS   *Surtees Society* (Durham 1835–)

SSpoleto   *Settimane di Studio sull'alto medioevo*, 1952– , Centro Italiano di studi sull'alto medioevo, Spoleto 1954–)

STC   *A Short-Title Catalogue of Books Printed in England, Scotland and Ireland and of English Books Printed Abroad 1475–1640*, ed A. W. Pollard and G. R. Redgrave (London 1926, repr 1946, 1950)

Strype, *Annals*   John Strype, *Annals of the Reformation and Establishment of Religion . . . during Queen Elizabeth's Happy Reign*, 4 vols in 7 (Oxford 1824)

Strype, *Cranmer*   John Strype, *Memorials of . . . Thomas Cranmer*, 2 vols (Oxford 1840)

Strype, *Grindal*   John Strype, *The History of the Life and Acts of . . . Edmund Grindal* (Oxford 1821)

Strype,   John Strype, *Ecclesiastical Memorials, Relating Chiefly to Religion,*
   Memorials   *and the Reformation of it* . . . *under King Henry VIII, King Edward VI
    and Queen Mary I,* 3 vols in 6 (Oxford 1822)

Strype, *Parker*   John Strype, *The Life and Acts of Matthew Parker,* 3 vols
    (Oxford 1821)

Strype,   John Strype, *The Life and Acts of John Whitgift,* 3 vols
   Whitgift   (Oxford 1822)

sub hag   *subsidia hagiographica*

sv   *sub voce*

SVRG   *Schriften des Vereins für Reformationsgeschichte*
    (Halle/Leipzig/Gütersloh 1883–   )

TCBiblS   *Transactions of the Cambridge Bibliographical Society*
    (Cambridge 1949–   )

Tchalenko   G. Tchalenko, *Villages antiques de la Syrie du Nord,*
    3 vols (Paris 1953–8)

THSCym   *Transactions of the Historical Society of Cymmrodorion*
    (London 1822–   )

TRHS   *Transactions of the Royal Historical Society* (London 1871–   )

TU   *Texte und Untersuchungen zur Geschichte der altchristlichen Literatur*
    (Leipzig/Berlin 1882–   )

VCH   *Victoria County History* (London 1900–   )

VHM   G. Tiraboschi, *Vetera Humiliatorum Monumenta,* 3 vols.
    (Milan 1766–8)

Vivarium   *Vivarium: An International Journal for the Philosophy and
    Intellectual Life of the Middle Ages and Renaissance* (Assen 1963–   )

VV   *Vizantijskij Vremennik* 1–25 (St Petersburg 1894–1927),
    ns 1 (26) (Leningrad 1947–   )

WA   D. *Martin Luthers Werke,* ed J. C. F. Knaake (Weimar 1883–   )
    [*Weimarer Ausgabe*]

  WA Br   *Briefwechsel*
  WA DB   *Deutsche Bibel*
  WA TR   *Tischreden*

WelHR   *Welsh History Review* (Cardiff 1960–   )

Wharton   H. Wharton, *Anglia Sacra,* 2 parts (London 1691)

Whitelock,   *Anglo-Saxon wills,* ed. D. Whitlock (Cambridge 1930)
   Wills

Wilkins   *Concilia Magnae Britanniae et Hiberniae A.D.* 446–1717, 4 vols,
    ed D. Wilkins (London 1737)

YAJ   *Yorkshire Archaeological Journal* (London/Leeds 1870–   )

Zanoni   L. Zanoni, *Gli Umiliati nei loro rapporti con l'eresia, l'industria della
    lana ed i communi nei secoli xii e xiii, Biblioteca Historica Italica,*
    2 series, 2 (Milan 1911)

ZKG   *Zeitschrift für Kirchengeschichte* (Gotha/Stuttgard 1878–   )

ZOG   *Zeitschrift für osteuropäische Geschichte* (Berlin 1911–35) = *Kyrios*
    (Berlin 1936–   )

ZRG   *Zeitschrift der Savigny-Stiftung für Rechtsgeschichte* (Weimar)
  GAbt   *Germanistische Abteilung* (1863–   )
  KAbt   *Kanonistische Abteilung* (1911–   )
  RAbt   *Romanistische Abteilung* (1880–   )

ZRGG   *Zeitschrift für Religions- und Geistesgeschichte* (Marburg 1948–   )

Zwingli,   *Huldreich Zwinglis Sämmtliche Werke,* ed E. Egli and others, *CR*
   Werke   (Berlin/Leipzig/Zurich 1905–   )